# MILTON'S AN

Milton's *Paradise Lost*, the most eloquent, ...~~ectually daring, most learned, and most sublime poem in the English language, is a poem about angels. It is told by and of angels; it relies upon their conflicts, communications, and miscommunications. They are the creatures of Milton's narrative, through which he sets the Fall of humankind against a cosmic background.

Milton's angels are real beings, and the stories he tells about them rely on his understanding of what they were and how they acted. While he was unique in the sublimity of his imaginative rendering of angels, he was not alone in writing about them. Several early-modern English poets wrote epics that explore the actions of and grounds of knowledge about angels. Angels were intimately linked to theories of representation, and theology could be a creative force. Natural philosophers and theologians too found it interesting or necessary to explore angel doctrine. Angels did not disappear in Reformation theology: though centuries of Catholic traditions were stripped away, Protestants used them in inventive ways, adapting tradition to new doctrines and to shifting perceptions of the world. Angels continued to inhabit all kinds of writing, and shape the experience and understanding of the world.

*Milton's Angels: The Early-Modern Imagination* explores the fate of angels in Reformation Britain, and shows how and why *Paradise Lost* is a poem about angels that is both shockingly literal and sublimely imaginative.

# MILTON'S ANGELS

## The Early-Modern Imagination

JOAD RAYMOND

OXFORD
UNIVERSITY PRESS

# OXFORD

UNIVERSITY PRESS

Great Clarendon Street, Oxford, OX2 6DP,
United Kingdom

Oxford University Press is a department of the University of Oxford.
It furthers the University's objective of excellence in research, scholarship,
and education by publishing worldwide. Oxford is a registered trade mark of
Oxford University Press in the UK and in certain other countries

First Edition published in 2010
First published in paperback 2013

British Library Cataloguing in Publication Data
Data available

Library of Congress Cataloging in Publication Data
Library of Congress Control Number: 2009939951

ISBN 978-0-19-956050-9 (Hbk.)
ISBN 978-0-19-965771-1 (Pbk.)

Printed in Great Britain by
the MPG Books Group, Bodmin and King's Lynn

2 4 6 8 10 9 7 5 3 1

*For Marchamont and Elias*

Tell her that sheds
Such treasure in the air,
Recking naught else but that her graces give
Life to the moment,
I would bid them live
As roses might, in magic amber laid,
Red overwrought with orange and all made
One substance and one color
Braving time.

# Acknowledgements

Among the benefits to being a Miltonist is the excellent community of learned scholars, and the present time is well stocked with them: my thanks, for various discussions of this book, to David Norbrook, Sharon Achinstein, Nigel Smith, David Loewenstein, Martin Dzelzainis, Paul Stevens, Gordon Campbell, Tom Corns, Neil Forsyth, Edward Jones, Laura Knoppers, Jameela Lares, Annabel Patterson, Noël Sugimura, Graham Parry, Jason Rosenblatt. I owe a great intellectual debt to Kevin Sharpe and Steve Zwicker, for being good friends and good readers over many years. I am indebted to David Colclough, Rosy Cox, Nicole Greenspan, Lauren Kassell, Kevin Killeen, and Simon Schaffer for reading chapters and offering excellent advice; Sophia Mullins too read drafts, first as a student and then as a friend. Olivia Smith, also once a student, sent more references than I could use, and took me for an important drink. Thanks to Line Cottegnies and Sermin Meskill for conversations and hospitality. And for dialogue, references, and informative correspondence, thanks to John Morrill, Lori Newcomb, Norah Carlin, John Flood, Vittoria Feola, Julie Park, Blair Hoxby, Sue Wiseman, and Steve Bardle.

I would like to give particular acknowledgement to four groundbreaking books: Robert H. West's *Milton and the Angels*, Stephen Fallon's *Milton among the Philosophers*, J. M. Evans's *'Paradise Lost' and the Genesis Tradition*, and Neil Forsyth's *The Satanic Epic*. All are brilliant models of different kinds of scholarship and helped to shape this book. To contributors to a conference entitled 'Conversations with Angels', which I co-ran with Lauren Kassell at the Centre for Research in the Arts, Social Sciences and Humanities in Cambridge, in September 2005, and which provided the origins of a collection of essays, I owe various kinds of debt, and I especially thank Walter Stephens, Tony Grafton, Alex Walsham, Peter Marshall, Nick

Wilding, and Pete Forshaw for illuminating conversations. To my sons
Elias and Marchamont I owe much happiness.

Papers based on the book were given at various conferences and
seminars, beginning with the International Milton Symposium in Beau-
fort, South Carolina, in June 2002, where the idea initially stuck out its
neck, and ending with the International Milton Symposium in London
in July 2008; and, in between, in Cambridge University, Birkbeck
College, London, Oxford University, Goldsmith's College, London,
Yale University, Princeton University, the University of Illinois at
Urbana-Champaign, University of Wisconsin–Madison, University
of Maryland, Université Sorbonne Nouvelle–Paris 3, Université de
Versailles Saint-Quentin-en-Yverlines, and Université de Paris VIII
Vincennes à Saint-Denis. I am grateful to many members of many
audiences for discussions.

Portions of Chapter 9 appeared in David Loewenstein and Paul
Stevens (eds), *Early Modern Nationalism and Milton's England* (Toronto,
2008); portions of Chapter 12 in Peter Marshall and Alexandra Walsham
(eds), *Angels in the Early Modern World* (Cambridge, 2006); and a version
of Chapter 7 in Line Cottegnies, Claire Gheeraert-Graffeuille, Tony
Gheeraert, Anne-Marie Miler-Blaise, and Gisèle Venet (eds), *Les Voix
de Dieu: Littérature et prophétie en Angleterre et en France à l'âge baroque*
(Paris, 2008). My thanks to these editors and their presses.

I am also indebted to librarians and archivists at the University of
East Anglia, the Folger Shakespeare Library, the Library of Congress,
Cambridge University Library, the Bodleian Library, the British
Library, the Public Record Office, the Wellcome Library, the Bei-
necke Library, the Firestone Library at Princeton University and the
library at the Princeton Theological Seminary, the New York Public
Library, and the university libraries in Charlottesville, Urbana-
Champaign, and Madison.

The University of East Anglia provided a supportive environment
during the writing of this book, and many students created a
stimulating one. The extent of the research on which it is based
would not have been possible without the generosity of the Leverhulme
Trust, which awarded me a Leverhulme Research Fellowship in
2003; nor without the Arts and Humanities Research Council,
which granted a Research Leave award for the spring of 2007.
A fellowship at the Folger Shakespeare Library provided a commodi-
ous period for thinking and drafting. OUP has been a great press to

ACKNOWLEDGEMENTS xi

work with, and Andrew McNeillie the best of editors. I must also
thank an anonymous reader of the manuscript for saving me from
Error.

This book has consumed many years with reading, writing, and
unwriting. I dispatch it now with special thanks to those friends who
helped it emerge from darkness into light: Eivind, Simon, David,
Helen, Dean, Sean, Sophia, Kevin.

J. R.

# Contents

*List of Illustrations*                                                    xv

*List of Abbreviations and Conventions*                                   xvi

 1. Introduction: Protestant Angels, Poets,
    the Imagination                                                         1

### I. UNDERSTANDING ANGELS

 2. Angelographia: Writing about Angels                                    19
 3. Angelology: Knowledge of Angels                                        48
 4. A Stronger Existence: Angels, Polemic, and Radical
    Speculation, 1640–1660                                                 89
 5. Conversations with Angels: The Pordages and their
    Angelical World                                                       125
 6. The Fleshly Imagination and the Word of God                           162
 7. Spiritual Gifts: Angels, Inspiration, and
    Prophecy                                                              189

### II. MILTON'S ANGELS

 8. Can Angels Feign?                                                      207
 9. Look Homeward Angel: Angelic Guardianship
    and Nationhood                                                        229
10. Angels in *Paradise Lost*                                             256
11. The Natural Philosophy of Angels                                      277
12. 'With the Tongues of Angels': Angelic
    Communication                                                         311

## III. LITERATURE AND REPRESENTATION

13. Dryden's Fall: Dreams, Angels, Freewill     327
14. Conclusion: Angels and Literary Representation     355

*Notes*     385
*Index*     457

# List of Illustrations

1. Thomas Heywood, *Hierarchie of the Blessed Angells* (1635), title page engraving. CUL, shelfmark SSS.21.15. (By permission of the Syndics of Cambridge University Library)                     50

2. Thomas Heywood, *Hierarchie of the Blessed Angells* (1635), engraving of 'The Principat'. CUL, shelfmark SSS.21.15. (By permission of the Syndics of Cambridge University Library)     54

3. Sixteenth-century book of magic with instructions for conjuring spirits. Folger Shakespeare Library, Folger MS V.b.26. (By permission of the Folger Shakespeare Library)                  108

4. Samuel Pordage, *Mundorum Explicatio* (1663), 'Hieroglyphical Figure'. BL, shelfmark C.117.b.62. (By permission of the British Library)                                              138–9

5. John Pordage, *Theologia Mystica* (1683). Bodl., shelfmark Vet. A3 e.1643. (By permission of the Bodleian Library)                 148

6. John Milton, *Paradise Lost* (1669 issue of 1667 edition), consecutive openings showing the end of book 5 and beginning of book 6. CUL, shelfmark SSS.32.40. (By permission of the Syndics of Cambridge University Library)                         208–9

7. Panel on east doors of the Baptistery in Florence, designed by Lorenzo Ghiberti, 1424–52                                            362

# List of Abbreviations and Conventions

I have retained original punctuation and spelling, though I have modernized u/v and i/j/y on typographical and palaeographical grounds only, and where the sense is clear. As we await the Oxford *Complete Works of John Milton*, I use the Latin translations in the Columbia or Yale editions according to which I prefer; I translate the poetry myself. I have transliterated Greek and Hebrew.

I have followed the Julian calendar employed in early modern England, ten days behind the Gregorian calendar in use across most of continental Europe; the year is taken to begin on 1 January, though the legal calendar began on Lady Day, 25 March.

I use the King James Bible, except where otherwise indicated.

Place of publication is London unless otherwise indicated (and I have used this rigorously, for modern and early modern books).

When I occasionally refer to 'we' and 'us' I means humans; I appreciate that this may occasionally seem parochial.

| | |
|---|---|
| Aquinas, *Summa* | Thomas Aquinas, *Summa Theologiae*, ed. Thomas Gilby et al., 61 vols (Cambridge, 1964–81) |
| Augustine, *City* | Augustine, *The City of God Against the Pagans*, ed. and trans. R. W. Dyson (Cambridge, 1998) |
| BL | British Library |
| Bodl. | Bodleian Library, Oxford |
| Calvin, *Commentarie* | *A Commentarie of John Calvine, upon the first booke of Moses called Genesis*, trans. Thomas Tymme (1578) |
| Calvin, *Institution* | John Calvin, *The Institution of Christian Religion*, trans. Thomas Norton (1611) |
| Columbia | *The Works of John Milton*, 18 vols, ed. Frank Allen Patterson (New York, 1931–8) |
| *CPW* | *Complete Prose Works of John Milton*, general ed. Don M. Wolfe, 8 vols (New Haven, 1953–82) |
| CUL | Cambridge University Library |

| | |
|---|---|
| Donne, *Major Works* | John Donne, *The Major Works*, ed. John Carey (1990; Oxford, 2000) |
| Evans, *Genesis Tradition* | J. M. Evans, *'Paradise Lost' and the Genesis Tradition* (Oxford, 1968) |
| Fallon, *Philosophers* | Stephen M. Fallon, *Milton among the Philosophers: Poetry and Materialism in Seventeenth-Century England* (Ithaca, NY, 1991) |
| Heywood, *Hierarchie* | Thomas Heywood, *The Hierarchie of the Blessed Angells* (1635) |
| Keck, *Angels* | David Keck, *Angels and Angelology in the Middle Ages* (New York, 1998) |
| Lawrence, *Angells* | Henry Lawrence, *Of our Communion and Warre with Angels* (1646), reissued as *An History of Angells* (1649) with same pagination |
| McKenzie and Bell | D. F. McKenzie and Maureen Bell (eds), *A Chronology and Calendar of Documents Relating to the London Book Trade, 1641–1700*, 3 vols (Oxford, 2005) |
| Marshall and Walsham (eds), *Angels* | Peter Marshall and Alexandra Walsham (eds), *Angels in the Early Modern World* (Cambridge, 2006) |
| Milton, *Poems* | Milton, *Complete Shorter Poems*, ed. John Carey (1968; 2nd edn, 1997) |
| *Norton Shakespeare* | *The Norton Shakespeare*, ed. Stephen Greenblatt (New York, 1997) |
| *O&D* | Lucy Hutchinson, *Order and Disorder*, ed. David Norbrook (Oxford, 2001); cited by canto and line |
| *ODNB* | *Oxford Dictionary of National Biography* |
| Peter Martyr, *Common Places* | Pietro Martire Vermigli, *The Common Places of the Most Famous and Renowmed Divine Doctor Peter Martyr*, trans. Anthonie Marten ([1583]) |
| *PL* | John Milton, *Paradise Lost*, ed. Alastair Fowler (1968; 2nd edn, 1998) |
| Pordage, *Mundorum* | S[amuel] P[ordage], *Mundorum Explicatio* (1661) |
| *PR* | *Paradise Regained*, in Milton, Poems |
| Pseudo-Dionysius, *Works* | Pseudo-Dionysius, *The Complete Works*, trans. and ed. Colm Luibheid, Paul Rorem, et al. (New York, 1987) |

| | |
|---|---|
| Raymond (ed.), *Conversations* | Joad Raymond (ed.), *Conversations with Angels: Essays towards a History of Spiritual Communication, 1100–1700* (forthcoming) |
| Raymond, *Pamphleteering* | Joad Raymond, *Pamphlets and Pamphleteering in Early Modern Britain* (Cambridge, 2003) |
| TT | British Library Thomason Tracts shelfmark |
| West, *Angels* | Robert H. West, *Milton and the Angels* (Athens, Ga., 1955) |
| Williams, *Expositor* | Arnold Williams, *The Common Expositor: An Account of the Commentaries on Genesis, 1527–1633* (Chapel Hill, NC, 1948) |
| Williams, *Ideas of the Fall* | Norman Powell Williams, *The Ideas of the Fall and of Original Sin* (1929) |

# 1

# Introduction

## Protestant Angels, Poets, the Imagination

### Actions with Angels

On 10 September 1672 Thomas Wale brought his wife to see the antiquary Elias Ashmole, and she told him the following story:

That her former Husband was one M:ʳ Jones a Confectioner, who formerly dwelt at the Plow in Lombardstreet London, & who, shortly after they were married, tooke her with him into Alde Streete among the Joyners, to buy some Houshold stuff, where (at the Corner house) they saw a Chest of Cedar wood, about a yard & halfe long, whose Lock & Hinges, being of extraordinary neate worke, invited them to buy it. The Master of the shop told them it had ben parcel of the Goods of M:ʳ John Woodall Chirurgeon (father to M:ʳ Tho: Woodall late Sergant Chirurgeon to his now Ma:ᵗⁱᵉ King Charles the 2ᵈ: . . . My intimate friend) and tis very probable he bought it after D:ʳ Dee's death, when his goods were exposed to Sale.

Twenty yeares after this (& about 4 yeares before the fatall Fire of London) she & her sᵈ husband occasionally removing this Chest out of its usuall place, thought they heard some loose thing ratle in it, toward the right hand end, under the Box or Till thereof, & by shaking it, were fully satisfied it was so: Hereupon her Husband thrust a piece of Iron into a small Crevice at the bottome of the Chest, & thereupon appeared a private drawer, wᶜʰ being drawne out, therein were found divers Bookes in Manuscript, & Papers, together with a litle Box, & therein a Chaplet of Olive Beades, & a Cross of the same wood, hanging at the end of them.

They made no great matter of these Bookes &c: because they understood them not; wᶜʰ occasioned their Servant Maide to wast about one halfe of them under Pyes & other like uses, wᶜʰ when ~~they~~ discovered, they kept the rest more safe.

About two yeares after these discovery of these Bookes, M:ʳ Jones died, & when the fire of London hapned, ^though the Chest perished in the Flames,

because not easily to be removed, ^yet ~~but~~ the Bookes were taken out &
carried with the rest of M:ʳˢ Jones her goods into Moorefields, & being safely
back, she tooke care to preserve them; and after marrying with the foresᵈ M:ʳ
Wale, he came to the knowledge of them, & thereupon, with her consent,
sent them to me . . .

The remainder of the story was Ashmole's. His servant brought him
the books, and he identified them as having belonged to John Dee, the
celebrated magician and astrologer of Elizabethan England and
Europe. They included Dee's manuscript of his 'Conference with
Angells', which took place in 1581–3, together with

the 48 Claves Angelicæ, also Liber Scientia Terrestris—Auxilÿ & Victoria
(These two being those very individuall Bookes, wᶜʰ the Angells commanded
to be Burnt, and ~~af~~ were after restored by them as appears by the printed
Relation of D:ʳ Dee's Actions with Spirits pag: 418. & 419.) The Booke
intituled De Heptarchia Mystica Collectaneorum Lib: primus, and a Booke
of Invocations or Calls.

These four works of occult philosophy and ritual magic were used in
the summoning of angels. The string of beads and cross were for the
same purpose. Mr Wale, to Ashmole's glee, agreed to exchange these
books for a book about the Order of the Garter. Ashmole later sent
him an additional gift for his kindness.[1]

There are two stories in Mrs Wale's narrative. The first is a literal-
minded story of marriage and trade. She and her first husband buy a chest
because they admire the workmanship. They discover the manuscripts
through detective work. The maid economically reuses irreplaceable
manuscripts as pie wrapping (though 'like uses' may also suggest the
privy). Mrs Wale rescues the movables from fire. Her husband dies, she
remarries, her goods become her second husband's. He sees their value
and trades them for a coffee table book. Ashmole puts them in his library.

The second story inhabits the first, and it is a tale of magic and
providence. The newly married couple buy a chest and it sits in the
corner. It makes a mysterious noise when moved. On investigating, they
discover a secret compartment with magical books and objects, but do
not understand them. They are preserved from fire several times: from
the oven, two are resurrected from conflagration after angels demand
their burning, and they survive the Great Fire of London, though there
seems little reason to save them. Then the widow marries a warder in the
Tower of London, educated enough to recognize something in these

books—magical symbols, pictures of angels—that causes him to bring them into the hands of the man uniquely qualified to appreciate and preserve them. The books seem to be alive, speak to humans, and cause them to follow their own purposes. The books are enchanted, and survive by their wits. This spiritual story is not only compatible with the mundane story, it is the same story seen in a different way.

Other stories can be told around these books. This first volume recording a 'Conference with Angells' is separated from a manuscript of later conversations, which finds its way to the library of Robert Cotton, where it is consulted by scholars, and from which a dark reputation irradiates. In the late 1650s this manuscript is edited by Meric Casaubon, son of the great Huguenot scholar Isaac. Meric wants to challenge scepticism concerning the existence of the spirit world, which he fears has spread in Cromwellian England, by publishing an edition; but he is convinced that the angels that spoke with Dee were fallen, and that Dee had unwittingly but credulously practised necromancy in summoning demons (many Protestants contended that the age of angels appearing to humans was over). Archbishop William Ussher encouraged Casaubon, because he wished to discourage the worship of angels, an idolatrous Roman Catholic practice. This is a story of scholarly gullibility and the pervasiveness of angels of darkness disguised as angels of light.[2]

The Council of State sought to suppress Casaubon's edition in the summer of 1658, but was thrown into disarray by the death of Oliver Cromwell, and it was published in 1659. It seemed at this stage to be an implicit attack on religious enthusiasm; so thought a clergyman, who remembered the attempted suppression and who annotated the volume in 1683. William Shippen was sympathetic to Casaubon's religious outlook, but he deplored the scholarly inaccuracies in the edition. Religious affiliation, politics, and scholarly principles converged on the same object. None of the players here expressed doubts about the credibility of the reported conversations, though they sought to do different things with them. And finally, Robert Hooke, curator of experiments at the Royal Society, doubted the interpretation of these manuscripts. In a lecture to the Royal Society in 1690 he argued that a learned man like Dee could not have believed in such manifest nonsense, and that the texts must in fact be a mode of secret writing. Yet Hooke numbered among his friends and colleagues natural philosophers who were interested in alchemy and angel magic, and firmly believed that the supernatural world was intervolved in the natural world even if it could not be experimented on. Growing knowledge of the natural world and promotion of this knowledge was not incompatible with the study of angels. Here a story might be told about different ways of giving order to nature (though there are no grounds, it must be emphasized, for a story of secularization).[3]

These are just a few aspects of the movement of books of angelic conversations and magic, and their interpretation within a nexus of knowledge or beliefs about religion, natural philosophy, politics. There is an imposing validity and flexibility of beliefs in angels. While Dee's conversations with angels have become, to modern scholars, the most notorious example of committed belief in the immediate reality of angels, they were in early modern Britain meaningful as only one of a range of encounters with angels. The ways of describing angelic–human relations, the place of knowledge of angels in broader intellectual concerns, and the stories that can be told about them, are manifold, develop, and multiply. Angels were very much alive and nearby in Protestant Britain.

## The Reformation, Continuity, and Change

Around 1500 most beliefs about angels, most representations of them, most of the ways in which angels figured in culture, broadly understood, were not founded on Scripture. Angel imagery and doctrine were absorbed from pre-Judaic as well as pre-Christian culture, from patristic sources, from the fifth- or sixth-century writings attributed to Dionysius, from scholastic writings that strayed far from Scripture and, probably, from popular culture. Reformers confronted a corpus of writing and belief that was diverse and lively, but had little authority as they saw it. The Protestant injunction that true faith lay in the authority of Scripture alone, and that the rest was at best *adiaphora* (or things indifferent), or, at worst, popish and idolatrous invention, might have removed almost all knowledge of or interactions with angels. Given the prevailing understanding of Protestant theology, and judging by the near or total silence on angels in substantial studies of the Reformation, one would be forgiven for assuming that this happened, that angels were swept away with the tide of anti-Catholicism. The Reformation, however, did not do that. As I show in Part I of this book, Protestants were very interested in angels, despite the reservations expressed by Calvin, Luther, and others. This book, for reasons that will become apparent, focuses on Britain, though it has cause thoroughly to examine the exchange between Britain and the rest of Europe, where doctrine was formed and reformed. In Britain angels *did* disappear from the stage, and their place in the fine arts was very marginal. Much medieval architecture that represented angels was destroyed in acts of iconoclasm, initially in the 1530s, and subsequently in the 1640s.[4] In 1643, prompted by a parliamentary order, William Dowsing entered Peterhouse, Cambridge, where, according to his diary, 'We pulled down two mighty great angels, with wings, and divers other angels . . . and about a hundred chirubims and angels, and divers superstitious letters in gold.'[5] British Protestants did little to create and circulate an alternative visual iconography of angels. They did, however, write about angels. Angels appear in systematic theology, practical divinity, sermons, scriptural annotations, devotional writings, catechisms, prayers, and a small number of expository works dedicated to elaborating the theology of angels; but also in secular genres, including commonplace books, political treatises, newsbooks, political pamphlets, and poetry. The language of angels and spirits, as metaphors or rhetorical devices, spreads into all modes of writings. Angels are ubiquitous in early modern texts.

The Roman Catholic and Protestant theology concerning angels is less polarized than might at first appear in the polemics of early modern British divines (and in modern scholarship). As I demonstrate in Part I, many Protestants allowed of angelic hierarchies, and some even accepted the schematizations of Pseudo-Dionysius or Gregory. Most Protestants accepted the idea of guardian angels assigned to a particular place or community, and some the notion of individual guardian angels (especially for the elect). Prayer to, and worship of, angels was universally rejected, though angels persist in Protestant liturgy, and the Feast of St Michael was sometimes observed. And angels survived in churches: many fifteenth-century church roofs, especially in East Anglia but also in Yorkshire and the North, are still decorated with ornate flocks of angels, with feathered wings, carrying scrolls and musical instruments. The most common is St Michael, pictured trampling a Satanic dragon or weighing human souls, and he frequently occupied a symbolic place in church architecture, ornamenting the doorways between nave and sanctuary, the boundary between the profane world and the sacred.[6] While Protestant divines certainly insisted that angel devotion and credulity concerning doctrine distinguished the Roman Catholic from the true

Church, in practice the distinction was less clear. Within Protestantism there was a diversity of beliefs, and clear boundaries cannot always be drawn on doctrinal issues.

Angels were increasingly removed from immediate experience, in worship and of the everyday world, and there was a weakening of specific ideological associations and of specific theological engagements with angels. There was also, however, much work undertaken renewing and redrawing beliefs in and knowledge about angels. Angels were reworked in the context of natural philosophy, and this powerfully shaped their place in British culture. Epistemological and procedural differences between natural philosophy in Britain and many places in Roman Catholic Europe meant that angels were handled differently in these cultures in ways that only indirectly relate to confessional difference. The development of angel doctrine in Britain after 1500 was probably shaped more by internal intellectual and religious dynamics than by responses to Roman Catholic angel doctrine. Protestant angels should not be understood as largely reactive; nor as a residuum from pre-Reformation theology. Angels were too alive in the culture, too powerfully connected to other, dynamic concerns, to be reduced to confessional politics.

There was, then, in Britain, no decline in interest in angels, or clear shift away from traditional theological concerns. Instead there was a developing and enlarged understanding of the role of angels in nature and theology that interacted with developments in other areas of theology, politics, and culture. Angels were part of the intellectual furniture, and they were a particularly creative part. One arena of angelic fermentation was poetry. English poets wrote about angels a great deal, not least because angels were part of the spiritual vocabulary, and useful metaphors; but several ambitious English poets wrote epic poems in which angels figure prominently, as characters or central devices. Among these are Thomas Heywood's extraordinary and baroque *Hierarchy of the Blessed Angells* (1635), Samuel Pordage's visionary *Mundorum Explicatio* (1661), Lucy Hutchinson's defiant *Order and Disorder* (1660–79), and, most ambitious of all, Milton's *Paradise Lost* (1667). This is a diverse group of poems, but, I would argue, together they should constitute (independently of Milton's personal greatness) an essential feature of any literary history of early modern Britain. Angels captured the Protestant imagination, and Protestants chose to write epic poems about them.

How can we write truthfully about things we do not understand? How can a Protestant forge a vision of heaven from her imagination, and how can she tell stories about sacred creatures of whom she knows little? Is this not to risk misrepresentation, slurring of sempiternal beings, even blasphemy? Narrative, it turns out, is one aspect of this theological conundrum. Inspiration is another. Narrative can be used as a heuristic device for learning truth, just as natural philosophy and the study of Scripture can be complementary. I argue in Chapters 6 and 7 that the doctrine of accommodation—by which ineffable truths are lowered and the human mind lifted so that they converge without misrepresentation—is an essential component of the aesthetics of religious poetry. This is especially important because accommodation offers a mode of representation that complicates the conventional dichotomy between truth and fiction; it is not a form of metaphor or allegory, but a means of representing truths in figurative manner. There are different accounts of accommodation, and different views of the role of human agency, especially over whether accommodation is attributable to God alone, or whether it can be performed by inspired humans; I argue that Milton, who has long been recognized as citing an account of accommodation through his narrator Raphael, himself makes a claim to participate in a strong version of the process. The kinds of truth that poetry can reach for are extended for those who believe in prophecy as an active, living force; coupled with my analysis of accommodation is an investigation into prophecy and its theological underpinnings. Prophecy is a literary mode, but, even in the hands of ambitious poets, it is not only a literary mode.

One of the subordinate themes of this book is the close association between angels and Protestant theories of representation. This is not opportunism on my part: when theologians sought to explain or explore notions of representing the invisible, from the thirteenth century to the seventeenth, they turned to the question of how angels, immaterial spirits, made themselves visible to humans. The association between angels and representation is a strong one, and it operates on several levels: I bring them together here because they were connected in the minds of many theologians and poets, and that connection was fundamental to thought and writing. Angelic apparitions became the dominant analogy for accurate representation, including accommodation, and this in part explains their attractiveness to epic poets. Angels not only are characters and plot devices, a superior form of *deus ex machina*, but are intimately connected to the literary medium. This does not mean that the religious materials are only displacements of literary intentions and effects, as some types of criticism are disposed to suggest; for these poets, and many others, the literature has a religious purpose. Milton's medium is narrative poetry, but the vision that drives him concerns grace and salvation. It is for these reasons—the vitality of Protestant angelology, the convergence of epic poems around angels, the importance of accommodation to theology and poetics, and the association between angels and representation, in doctrinal as well as literary writings—that I describe this as a book about the early modern imagination.

The imagination, with the gift of the spirit—which is not to say the inspiration of the Romantic poet so much as that of the religious enthusiast—enables the author to write truthfully of heavenly things. It is this faith that gave interest in angels such life in early modern Britain, and especially in the mid-seventeenth century. This faith shapes not only poetry, but also theological prose and the experience of everyday life; it is essential to this book that these three are part of the same lived and understood reality. The imagination can also be, as John Pordage and others saw, a wilful devotion to merely earthly things, a darkness that overshadows the gift of spiritual grace and light. It is the former imagination that concerns me in this book, just as I write, almost exclusively, about good angels, unfallen angels, and it is these that I mean when I write of 'angels' without a qualifier. The few exceptions to this are clear in context. There has been a great deal of scholarship on early modern devils, demons, and witchcraft in recent decades, and I have little to add about them herein. Very little has been written about early modern angels, especially in a Protestant context, and the first part of this book seeks to rectify this, by offering an overview of writing about, beliefs in, and knowledge about angels.[7] It is a foolish but necessary assay.

## What Words or Tongue of Seraph Can Suffice?

This intellectual context is essential to understanding Milton's epic, the most eloquent, most intellectually daring, most learned, and most sublime poem in the English language. The chronological, geographical, and emotional ambition of *Paradise Lost* is almost without bounds. It begins before Creation, describes the history of the universe, and concludes with the end of time. It extends from heaven through created space and the earth to hell and the void beyond. It is the grandest poem in the Renaissance epic tradition, and puts an end to that tradition. Yet its focus is domestic, turning on a single human relationship: it tells a story of love, intimacy, betrayal, heartbreak, and wounded reconciliation. Adam and Eve's actions and feelings seem heroic because they are situated and given significance within Creation in a way that no other poem, pagan or Christian, has achieved. Milton accomplished this by introducing a machinery both expansive and theologically daring. This machinery is angelic. Angels are fundamental to the execution of Milton's design in *Paradise Lost*. They are necessary because without them the story does not work. He uses angels to narrate swaths of history, to interact with, protect, and converse with humans, to fight with rebel angels. He uses them to make mistakes, to sin, to argue, to bind together the celestial narratives with the terrestrial. The story of *Paradise Lost* is told by and of angels; it relies upon their conflicts, communications, and miscommunications. They are the creatures of God but also the creatures of Milton's narrative. Milton makes the Fall morally ponderous, tragic, and part of the fabric of the universe by surrounding it with the actions and interactions of angels. Take away the angels from *Paradise Lost*, and you would be left with a linear, expository narrative. So although its concern is with, and its focus upon, humankind, angels are central to its design.

This book is not a study of a narrow aspect or theme of *Paradise Lost*, and I am not merely contending that angels are important. Rather, I argue that in terms of its imaginative drive and aesthetic architecture, *Paradise Lost* is a poem about angels, and that Milton's understanding of poetic representation is inseparable from his understanding of Creation in general and angels in particular. There is a case to be made here for Milton's uniqueness and for his typicality, and in making it I offer a reading of *Paradise Lost*. He is typical in that his concerns with angels are common. Angels were part of his intellectual background, and they were an essential formal element of any systematic theology (they form a transitional section between the description of God and of material Creation); when he wrote *De Doctrina Christiana*, he incorporated discussions of them out of necessity, though they are less central to it than to his epic because it is not a work of narrative and imagination, nor an inspired text. In the late 1630s, when Milton was planning to write a tragedy, angels repeatedly figured in his plans. For the following two decades, the revolutionary years—during which he mainly devoted himself to writing prose—there was a surge of interest in angels. More people wrote about and spoke with them. Anxieties about religious and social fragmentation, political conflict, widespread apocalypticism, the breakdown of the Church, interest in the occult, and the growth in antinomian theology created a culture in which angels seemed to be more immediately present. When Milton returned to poetry, and began to write his epic, angels carried not only a venerable theological tradition, but an electric contemporary valence as a means of describing and interacting with the world. In this respect Milton can be said to be typical.

Milton is unique because of his greatness. But he is also distinct in the intensity of his interests, and in the way, I shall argue, that he binds together narrative and doctrine. This is not unconnected to his greatness. Milton's angels are peculiarly intense creations. Like humans, they eat, digest, make love for pleasure, suffer pain, and feel isolated. Their vision is subject to the laws of optics. They engage in more intimate relations with humanity than in any other early modern text. Their representation engenders conceptual problems: as the poet John Dryden complained, their numerousness is perplexing; as *Paradise Lost*'s first annotator, Patrick Hume, complained, though invulnerable they wear armour. In these lie precisely their strengths. They are learned representations, focused in their relations with scholastic and Hebraic traditions. They engage, with near-weightless delicacy, with a vast corpus of exegetical scholarship and practical divinity. They perform many functions, imaginative, narratological, religious, natural-philosophical, and political. They bear messages from their author about the ways of God. As I argue in Part II, Milton's angels are a mix of literal representation, extensive learning, unusually theology, and inspired storytelling, all subordinated to a narrative that is at once descriptive and heuristic. Milton, while insisting that he is guided by the spirit, uses narrative to discover as well as explicate truths. Does his unusual theology make his poetry more interesting or beautiful? This is a potentially embarrassing question in the twenty-first century, but it is worth asking. It may be that the close ties between his narratives and his heterodoxies generate his creative verve, and that his faith in his vision and in truth give vitality to his imagination. Few poets write with such commitment to a vision of the nature of the world, and with the conviction that this vision can be communicated through narrative poetry, and so perhaps the beauty that Milton offers is inseparable from his theology and faith.

In the Printer's Note he added to the 1668 edition of *Paradise Lost*, Samuel Simmons stated that the prose 'Arguments' to the poem had been procured 'for the satisfaction of many that have desired it'. It is easy enough to assume that readers desired them because they had 'stumbled' not only on the unrhymed form of the poem but also on the narrative folded into its long and complex verse paragraphs. These arguments gloss the action of the poem, creating and resolving ambiguities; they also provide an element of exegetical self-justification that is absent from the poem itself. In the argument to book 1 Milton explains the location of his hell: 'described here, not in the centre (for heaven and earth may be supposed as not yet made, certainly not yet accursed) but in a place of utter darkness, fitliest called chaos'. It is a logical necessity that hell is not placed within earth, as many assumed, which is yet uncreated. Humans will not be created until after the fall of angels, as they were made to supply their place. Is this merely an effect of the way Milton tells his story, or is the story as it must have been given the circumstances that we know? Here narrative can lead us to the truth: hell cannot be within earth. And later in the argument: 'that angels were long before this visible creation, was the opinion of many ancient Fathers'.[8] This conforms to the descriptions in *De Doctrina Christiana*, but it is also a logical necessity from the former deduction. Milton is not only describing his narrative here, but also defending its principles according to exegesis (and, uncharacteristically, citing patristic sources in order to appear less unconventional). This is not fiction, the argument tells us. I show this in a series of readings that deliberate on the properties and actions of angels within *Paradise Lost*. But I also argue that Milton saw *Paradise Lost* as a prophetic work, in the strongest sense of the word: that it was based on inspiration beyond that associated with the vatic poet tradition. Our modern, reified opposition between truth and fiction, once again, is an anachronism that misconstrues Protestant theology and Milton. Inspiration and narrative work together.

## Strange as Angels

There is a residual narrative that angels disappeared from Britain because of embarrassment, lack of interest, reformed theology, or because of their incompatibility with modern science. It would

certainly be possible to assume this on the basis of some statements
made about them in the later seventeenth century. For example, the
only reference to angels in the *Philosophical Transactions* in the whole of
the seventeenth century is by Robert Hooke, writing in 1668. He
describes an optical trick, a magic lantern, that can be used to deceive
'Spectators, not well versed in *Opticks*' into seeing 'Apparitions of
Angels, or Devils, Inscriptions and Oracles on Walls; the Prospect of
Countryes, Cities, Houses, Navies, Armies... &c.'. Angels are the
matter of illusion. 'And had the *Heathen* Priest of old been acquainted'
with the device he describes, 'their Oracles and Temples would have
been much more famous for the Miracles of their Imaginary Deities'.
This is not an invitation to consider priests mere jugglers; Hooke
believed in the reality of angels, but they held a complex place in his
natural philosophy.[9] Margaret Cavendish, in *The Blazing World*
(1667), uses the same trick: her fictional Empress uses illusion to
deceive her countrymen into thinking her an angel, upon which her
authority is founded.[10] In his *Essay Concerning Humane Understanding*
(1690) John Locke repeatedly turns to comparisons between angels
and humans, and repeatedly dismisses them as inutile on the grounds
that such knowledge is obtained only through revelation. For ex-
ample:

> Whether Angels and Spirits have any Analogy to this, in respect of Expansion, is
> beyond my comprehension: and, perhaps, for us, who have Understanding and
> Comprehension, suited to our own Preservation, and the ends of our own Being,
> but not to the reality and extent of all other Beings, 'tis near as hard to conceive
> any Existence, or to have an *Idea* of any reall Being, with a perfect Negation of all
> manner of Expansion; as it is, to have the *Idea* of any real Existence, with a perfect
> Negation of all manner of Duration: And therefore what Spirits have to do with
> Space, or how the communicate in it, we know not.[11]

Locke is vexed that angels cannot be discovered and contribute to his
argument. He makes the same rhetorical manoeuvre repeatedly: if only
we knew how angels fitted in here, the matter might be resolved, but
this we cannot know. They occupy a different realm of knowledge. A
final example: by the 1690s the *Athenian Mercury* was publishing
tongue-in-cheek responses to familiar questions about angels, such as
the doctrine of guardianship.[12] These late seventeenth-century writ-
ings do not indicate a process of secularization, however: at this period
it seemed much easier to effect a separation between different kinds of
knowledge.

I discuss some versions of the narrative of the disappearance of angels in my final chapter, and contest it throughout the book. I do not, however, offer an alternative narrative of transition. Part III looks at literary representations more generally, examining Dryden at length, Shakespeare, Donne, and others more briefly. Although I present Dryden and Milton as embodying antithetical attitudes to theology and representation, I am not suggesting that one displaces another; rather, there is a reconfiguration of writing and knowledge and a multiplication of the languages in which angels are described.

While much of this book is a recovery of the substantial and often attractive body of knowledge, belief, and writing about angels in early modern Britain, and much a reading of *Paradise Lost*, it also presents a number of arguments, some focused on particular chapters, others subtending throughout the book. They can be summarized thus:

1. Protestants in Britain and elsewhere were interested in angels, and re-created angel doctrine in ways that responded to and fitted within their religious, political, and intellectual culture more broadly; their beliefs about angels were neither residual nor reactive.

2. Protestant theories of representation were shaped by the doctrine of accommodation. This provided a means of legitimizing depictions of the invisible, sacred world, and did so by identifying a mode of figuratively representing truths without fiction, metaphor, or allegory.

3. Angels are intimately associated with notions of representation, and there was in Protestant Britain no antipathy between theology and poetry. Theology could be a creative force.

4. *Paradise Lost* is a poem shaped by prophecy and accommodation; it is, in powerful ways, literal. It is also a poem about and told by angels, and these two facts are connected.

5. In *Paradise Lost* Milton powerfully integrates story and doctrine; theology is the basis for his narrative elaborations, and he confines himself within what he understands to be true, but storytelling is also a means of developing theology, and extends what is known. Belief and imagination cross-fertilize.

6. During the course of the seventeenth century the ways of representing and using angels in religion, natural philosophy, and literature multiply. The languages of 'spirit' in natural philosophy dilate, and accounts of angels become complementary to the discourse of

experiment; after the enthusiastic conversations with angels in the
1640s and 1650s quieten, a plurality of theological views concerning
angels settle, and they are less immediately controversial; the relation-
ships between representation and the sacred world, and the place of
angels in imaginative writing, proliferate, opening different claims
upon truth and inspiration.

These are the various arguments of *Milton's Angels: The Early Modern
Imagination*.

I do not personally believe in angels, God, or the Devil. This is a
question I have had repeatedly to answer over the past few years.[13]
There is clear room for a dialogue between the present and the past on
this topic, as there has been a surge of interest in angels in both popular
belief and international literature over recent years: including Tony
Kushner's *Angels in America* (1990–2, 2003), Elizabeth Knox's *The
Vintner's Luck* (1998), Philip Pullman's *The Amber Spyglass* (2000),
Helon Habila's *Waiting for an Angel* (2002); and Wim Wenders's film
*Wings of Desire* (1987) should be mentioned also. Works such as these,
and the environment that produced them, are part of the motivation
behind my writing this book. If it had a point of origin, beyond
reading Milton, it was some years ago when I rode the escalator up
from the platform at 30th Street Station in Philadelphia. As I emerged
into the main hall I saw towering over me a bronze angel, wings erect,
holding the limp body of a man. For an inexplicable moment it was
real, and the words of the German poet Rainer Maria Rilke came into
my mind:

> Who, if I cried out, would hear me among the angels'
> hierarchies? and even if one of them pressed me
> suddenly against his heart: I would be consumed
> in that overwhelming existence. For beauty is nothing
> but the beginning of terror, which we still are just able to endure,
> and we are so awed because it serenely disdains
> to annihilate us. Every angel is terrifying.[14]

I could not breathe, and knew that terror. Later I learned that this was a
statue made by Walker Hancock (1901–98) in 1952 to commemorate
Pennsylvania Railroad workers who laid down their lives in the Sec-
ond World War. In retrospect that moment of intimate familiarity may
have prompted more rational interests. This book, however, concerns
early modern angels, and these are, or should be, strange to us. I try to

sympathize with my subjects and imaginatively identify with their beliefs. I reconstruct and operate with their categories and their language.[15] I have an old-fashioned commitment to the recovery of the past, and believe that much of it can be understood, especially those things that pertain to being human, while I recognize that elements of experience, such as emotion and faith, which lie close to my subject, cannot be recovered, though they can be accounted for in an interrogation of thought and action. For this reason I search for coherence and consistency in the perceptions and writings not only of Milton, but also of other writers, who might be regarded as more temperamental or idiosyncratic, including the enthusiast and visionary John Pordage. At times the book may seem to validate the cognitive processes and perceptions of my subjects, even their values. I seek to make Pordage familiar in all his strangeness. I do not seek to sympathize with angels, who are another species (each a species to itself, according to Thomas Aquinas), and while this is a contribution to post-human studies, it claims no special insight into what is beyond or more than human. Nonetheless, in order to understand Milton as he would be understood, I argue, we must both allow that he believed he had such insight and imagine that his insight might be true. I seek to make Milton stranger, despite his familiarity.

# PART I

# Understanding Angels

# 2

# Angelographia

## Writing about Angels

How many volumnes have been writ about Angels, about immaculate conception, about originall sin, when that all that is solid reason or clear Revelation, in all three Articles, may be reasonably enough comprized in fourty lines!

Jeremy Taylor, *Discourse of the Liberty of Prophesying* (1647)

## Angelology

'Angelology' was not a word in common use in the early modern period. In modern usage a word referring to the study of angels, and to that branch of theology concerned with angel-doctrine, seems eminently practical. This was not so 400 years ago. Various words were coined in English in the seventeenth century, derived directly from the Greek, to denote angel-related matters. Thomas Heywood invented 'angelomachy' in 1635 to describe a war between angels. John Prideaux coined 'Angelographies' (to pair it with 'Pneumatologies') in a sermon published in 1636; it was a direct appropriation from the Latin, and perhaps he had heard of Otto Casman's *Angelographia* (Frankfurt, 1597). The word did not catch: Richard Saunders followed Prideaux, with *Aggelographia . . . or, A Discourse of Angels* (written before 1675; published posthumously in 1701), then Richard Blome, in a translation from Latin in 1694; and Increase Mather published *Angelographia, or, A Discourse Concerning the Nature and Power of the Holy Angels* in 1696.[1] Robert Gell's *Aggelokratia Theon, or, A Sermon Touching Gods Government of the World by Angels* (1650) was followed by John Scott's use of 'angelocracy' in 1685 to describe government by guardian angels. The earliest use of the word 'angelology' I have found in English is in Gideon Harvey's *Archelogia Philosophica Nova, or, New Principles of Philosophy* (1663), where he writes that '*Pneumatology*' can be divided into three parts 'aptly denoted by *Theology, Angelology* and *Psychology*'.[2] However, the term was not taken up for some decades. The language did not need a general term to describe the study of angels or knowledge of them.

This is for a simple, but important, reason. There were comparatively few books written specifically about angels *as* angels in the two centuries following the Reformation. This is not a sign of lack of interest, however, or of embarrassment. Early modern Protestants wrote a great deal about angels, but usually when discussing other things. They wrote about angels in many contexts: sermons, systematic theology, devotional works, scriptural commentaries and annotations, religious polemics, treatises on doctrinal issues, volumes on and of ritual magic, spiritual autobiographies, books on witchcraft and demons, and also in less immediately religious works, including political treatises, news reports, diaries, sensational pamphlets, treatises of natural philosophy, and works of 'imaginative' writing. Angels penetrate all kinds of writing in sixteenth- and seventeenth-century Britain. Angels were part of a common substratum of thought and belief, but were not a simple, well-defined idea; they could be used intellectually in a variety of ways. In this chapter I consider traditions of writing about angels, the impact of the Reformation, and the forms and genres of angelography; in the next I outline what Protestant knowledge and beliefs were.

I shall follow seventeenth-century precedent, and use the words 'angelology' and 'angelography' sparingly. To use either too casually would be to risk implying that this was a conceptually defined body of knowledge and writing, rather than a range of approaches to an aspect of Creation that shaped and were shaped by genre and context. I will also be guarded in writing of 'beliefs' concerning angels. First, there is a spectrum of kinds of belief, from an intuitive apprehension of the spirits that surround us, through a faith in the existence of personal guardian angels, to the conscious rationalizations that generate answers to questions about angelic bodies and movement. To homogenize these risks simplifying the dynamics of conviction, persuasion, and reasoning. Secondly, there was no coherent set of mental furniture that was equally solid and fitted in the same room. By objectifying a belief system we distance it from our own in form as well as content. For this reason I use 'belief' tentatively, and often prefer the defamiliarizing term 'knowledge'. Beliefs about angels were a form of knowledge, intersecting with and supporting other forms of knowledge, including the political and natural-philosophical.

## Histories of Angels

Beliefs in immaterial spirits that are deities in a polytheistic system, or that serve deities, antedate Judaism, Christianity, and Islam. The ancient Mesopotamians worshipped winged protective genii. Ancient Egyptians believed that with each human was born an invisible and indivisible double that protected him or her. Ancient Near Eastern art shows genii, protective spirits with feathered wings, that shaped later Christian representations of angels. The Assyrians carved protective spirits with wings; Roman Victories were winged; both influenced later iconography. The Greeks had good and evil daemons, beings between humans and gods, and the writings of Aristotle and Plato shaped the development of the Jewish religion. Early Judaic angelology recognized supernatural beings, and as Judaism developed into a monotheistic religion, and God became more ontologically distant from man, these intermediaries became more significant. During the Babylonian exile (597–537 BCE) Judaism was influenced by Zoroastrianism, and its angelology became increasingly elaborate. Yahweh's works were assigned to beings, and some of these beings were given individual names as well as titles suggestive of ranks. Early Judaism preferred the notion of a leader among these angels, and Mal'akh Yahweh, the Angel of the Lord, became a distinct being as opposed to a manifestation of God. Early Christianity also absorbed Gnostic beliefs—which included angelworship and the idea that angels participated in the creation of the world—and arose from and contributed to a rich array of religious writings, not all of which became part of the biblical canon. Yet these texts influenced the Church Fathers and shaped their understanding of canonical Scripture. Early Christian angels were a synthesis of and elaboration upon the stories, images, and theology of earlier religions, which remained embedded in later theology. Nevertheless, for the purposes of this chapter it is necessary to focus on Judaeo-Christian writing, and particularly the accounts of angels in Scripture, which form the main foundations of subsequent doctrine.[3]

There are almost 300 references to angels in the Protestant Bible; more in Catholic Bibles that accept the canonical authority of twelve books (Tobit, Judith, Rest of Esther, Wisdom, Ecclesiasticus, Baruch, with Jeremiah, Song of the Three Children, Susanna, Bel and the Dragon, and 1 and 2 Maccabees) which the Protestants classified as apocrypha, holy books that were not the inspired word of God. Angels are variously referred to: in Hebrew as *mal'ach*, in Greek as *aggelos*, both meaning 'messenger'. But, subject to interpretation, references to *bene 'Elohim* (sons of God), seraphim, cherubim, and watchers also denote angels. In addition to these canonical and deuterocanonical (secondary) books, angels figure prominently in some 'inter-Testamental' writing, that is, in texts written after most of the Old Testament books, and before New Testament times. The Christian Bible was only standardized into its modern form between the second and fifth centuries, and to the Church Fathers some of these inter-Testamental books had a status equal to now canonical Scripture. Among the most interesting of these are the book of Enoch, written around the second century BCE, which tells, in the voice of the prophet Enoch, the stories of the fall of the rebel angels and of Enoch's travels through earth and hell (*sheol*). Enoch is a source for much occult angel-lore, and for elaborations on the story, foreshadowed in Genesis 6, that the fall of angels involved lust for human women. The book of Enoch was suppressed by the Church, and the text was missing from early modern Europe, but it left fragments and traces that shaped Bible culture. Jubilees, another pseudepigraphal work (in the Christian tradition: it is considered canonical by the Ethiopian Orthodox Church), is a commentary on Creation presented as a vision to Moses and written down by an Angel of the Presence.[4]

Little specific angel-doctrine appears in the Bible, hence the attractiveness of the pseudepigrapha to those who wanted more. The Bible does not tell directly of the creation or fall of angels. No account is given of Satan as head of the fallen angels or the metaphysical embodiment of evil. Satan was the invention of the Church Fathers, Justin Martyr, Tertullian, Cyprian, Irenaeus, though they were influenced by the Zoroastrian account of a powerful figure of evil who operated independently of God.[5] Nowhere do we read in Scripture that an evil angel entered the serpent that tempted Eve, nor that individual guardian angels watch over humans, nor that angels will act on our behalf as intercessors with God. Instead we find stories of angelic interaction with humans that raise questions rather than answer them: how do angels communicate, do they eat, do they have bodies, how do they move? A reference to 'the seven holy angels, which present the prayers of the saints, and which go in and out before the glory of the Holy One' (Tobit 12: 15) invites speculation about the organization of the angels in heaven that the rest of Scripture cannot support or negate. References to thrones, principalities (or princedoms), and seraphim suggest distinctions among the angels, but the nature of those distinctions is unexplained. The very reticence of Scripture invites readers to elaborate. Incomplete allusions and silences ask readers to fill the gaps with narrative. Early Christian exegesis grew out of rabbinical Midrash, which glosses Scripture through retelling its stories. The fourth-century *Vita Adae et Evae* ('The Life of Adam and Eve', also known as *Apocalypsis Moses*) tells the now familiar story of the fall of angels and the temptation of Adam and Eve by the Devil in the guise of a serpent. This is included among the Old Testament pseudepigrapha, but its late date makes this misleading: it is a retrospective gloss offering a point of view that did not exist in Old Testament or even early Christian times.[6] But it is a good story, and it stuck, influencing Muhammad, who repeatedly tells in the Qur'ān the story of Iblis (from the Greek Diabolos), who refuses to worship Adam, and becomes man's adversary and tempter. The history of angels is not, then, told in either the Protestant or Catholic Bible, but in the accumulated stories that prophets and pseudo-prophets and believers told about angels.

## Anatomizing Angels: Dionysius, Lombard, Bonaventure, Aquinas, Neoplatonism

The visions of Dionysius, who saw heaven and had revealed to him the celestial hierarchy, had a profound and lasting impact on devotional, technical, and fictional writings about angels. His writings in Greek only indirectly influenced Christian scholarship, but the translation of the *Celestial Hierarchy* into Latin by John Scotus Eriugena in *c.*860, and the production of commentaries in the twelfth century, gave them great impetus.[7] They proceeded to inform the basis of the detailed angelological dogma of the Catholic Church to the present day. They are, however, an elaborate fiction. The author presents himself as Dionysius the Areopagite, converted by St Paul of Athens in the first century, and thus effectively the earliest of the Church Fathers. Lorenzo Valla and others demonstrated in the mid-fifteenth century that the Dionysian treatises were written later, in the fifth or sixth centuries. Dionysius thus writes under a pseudonym. The addressee of his treatises, 'Timothy the Fellow-Elder', is also fictional, a literary device to establish *auctoritas*. The teacher whom he names, and the other works to which he refers, may also be fictitious.[8] In assuming the authority and voice of an identifiable figure from Scripture, Pseudo-Dionysius was following the conventions of pseudepigrapha, written in the personae of biblical prophets, though he was later even than these. His fiction was sustained for about a thousand years. When the deception was uncovered, the Church was reluctant to dispense with the foundations of so much of its devotional writing, and sought to ignore the scholarly arguments or preserve the visionary integrity of the writing on the grounds that they had been accepted for centuries.

Pseudo-Dionysius claimed to have seen into the celestial hierarchy, and described its internal organization and the roles of ranks within it. According to Pseudo-Dionysius the angels were formed into three ternions: the first hierarchy, consisting of the seraphim, cherubim, and thrones, are beings that are supremely pure and have a close relationship to God; the middle hierarchy, consisting of Dominions, Virtues, and Authorities (or Powers), show conformity to God and reflect 'the ordered nature of celestial and intellectual authority'; the lower hierarchy of Principalities, Archangels, and Angels is concerned with revelation and proximity to the human world.[9] The hierarchy is not a flexible one. The positions of angels are fixed. Illumination and understanding, perfection and purification, are mediated down the hierarchy: enlightenment descends from God not directly to the lower angels but through the hierarchy. Other schema were available. Gregory the Great (*c*.540–604) challenged the Dionysian ranking, translating the positions of Virtues and Principalities, so that the latter were promoted to the second ternion, and the former demoted to the lower ranks; in this he was followed by St Bernard.[10] Dante sided, like most, with the seeming apostolic authority of Pseudo-Dionysius:

> E quella che vedea i pensier dubi
> nella mia mente, disse: 'I cerchi primi
> t'hanno mostrati Serafi e Cherubi.

Così veloci seguono i suoi vimi,
per somigliarsi al punto quanto ponno;
e posson quanto a veder son soblimi.
Quelli altri amor che dintorno li vonno,
si chiaman Troni del divino aspetto,
per che 'l primo ternaro terminonno.
E dei saper che tutti hanno diletto
quanto la sua veduta si profonda
nel vero in che si queta ogne intelletto.
Quinci si può veder come si fonda
L'esser beato nell'atto che vede,
non in quel ch'ama, che poscia seconda;
e del vedere è misura mercede,
che grazia partorisce e buona voglia:
così di grado in grado si procede.
L'altro ternaro, che così germoglia
in questa primavera sempiterna
che notturno Arïete non dispoglia,
perpetualemente "Osanna" sberna
con tre melode, che suonano in tree
ordini di letizia onde s'interna.
In essa gerarcia son l'altre dee:
prima Dominazioni, e poi Virtudi;
l'ordine terzo di Podestadi ée.
Poscia ne' due penultimi tripudi
Principati e Arcangeli si girano;
L'ultimo è tutto d'Angelici ludi.
Questi ordini di su tutti s'ammirano,
e di giù vincon sì, che verso Dio
tutti tirati sono, e tutti tirano.
E Dïonisio con tanto disio
a contemplar questi ordini si mise,
che li nomò e distinse com' io.
Ma Gregorio da lui poi si divise;
onde, sì tosto come li occhi aperse
in questo ciel, di se' medesmo rise.
E se tanto secreto ver proferse
mortale in terra, non voglio ch'ammiri;
chè chi 'l vide qua sù gliel discoperse
con altro assai del ver di questi giri.'

(And she who saw the uncertain thoughts in my mind, said: 'The first circles
have shown thee Seraphim and Cherubim. They follow their bonds thus swiftly
to gain all they may of likeness to the point, and in this they may in so far as they

are exalted in vision. These next loving spirits that circle round them are called Thrones of the divine aspect, and with them the first triad is completed. And thou must know that all have delight in the measure of the depth to which their sight penetrates the truth in which every intellect finds rest; from which it may be seen that the state of blessedness rests on the act of vision, not on that of love, which follows after, and the measure of their vision is merit, which grace begets and right will. Such is the process from step to step. The second triad that flowers thus in this eternal spring which no nightly Ram despoils sings continual hosannas, the threefold strain resounding in the three ranks that form the triad. In this hierarchy are the next divine orders: first Dominions, then Virtues, and the third are Powers. Then, last but one of the festal throngs, wheel Principalities and Archangels, and the last is all of Angels making sport. These orders all gaze above and so prevail below that all are drawn and all draw to God. And Dionysius set himself with such zeal to contemplate these orders that he named and distributed them as I do; but later Gregory differed from him, so that as soon as he opened his eyes in this heaven he smiled at himself. And if a mortal on earth set forth truth or secret thou needst no marvel, for he that saw it here above revealed it to him, with much more of the truth of these circles.'[11])

Pseudo-Dionysius offers a great many more insights, explaining how it was possible for humans to understand beyond the limited powers of their faculties and describing the communication, agency, and emotions of angels. Thomas Aquinas (*c.*1225–74) cited Dionysius more than any other author, and Dionysian hierarchies profoundly shaped Aquinas' vision of heaven.[12] This Neoplatonism-influenced concept of hierarchy provided a framework for comprehending and explaining all of Creation.[13]

An account of Protestant writing about angels must take its cues from the twelfth and thirteenth centuries, when Peter Lombard (*c.*1100–60), Bonaventure (*c.*1217–74), and Aquinas systematized Christian knowledge of angels. Their intellectual development is closely related to their modes of exposition. The second book of Peter Lombard's *Sentences* dealt with Creation, angels, humans, and the Fall. These were closely associated topics, linked not only because the understanding of each derived in considerable part from interpreting Genesis, but because the answers to the central questions about each were intervolved. Lombard inherited a position of broad consensus about angels from his Scholastic predecessors, but in systematizing and developing this body of knowledge his *Sentences* provided the basis for subsequent commentaries on angels. Lombard asks questions about angels that result in a series of propositions. His topics are as influential as his answers (here teased from his not entirely persuasive ten divisions):

1. For what reason have rational creatures, humans or angels, been made? (because God is good, and his Creation is good)
2. When were angels made? (at the same time as the created world)
3. Where were angels made? (in heaven or the empyrean)
4. What kinds of angels were made, and were they all equal? (several, equal in some respects and not others; there are gradations within the angels' substance, and their use of it)
5. Were they created good or evil, and was there was any interval between their creation and fall? (all were created good; they fell immediately)
6. Were they created perfect and blessed, or miserable and flawed? (the former)
7. Did they fall of their own freewill and how was that possible? (they did, though those that did not fall were supported by grace)
8. Who were the fallen angels, what was the cause of their fall, and what are their subsequent actions among humans? (Lucifer and the other rebels fell from envy; some live in hell and some in the air; they have limited power to tempt men)
9. Is it possible for good angels to sin, or bad angels to live uprightly? (no: those who turned to God were supported by fuller wisdom and grace confirming them in their choice; those who turned away have no access to grace because of their hatred and envy; hence their choices are not reversible)
10. How do evil angels know about temporal things? (though weakened in nature they can still learn through experience)
11. Are all angels corporeal? (no)
12. What are the orders; were they instigated from the first creation of angels; are angels within orders equal? (there were gradations of angelic substance before the fall, though the orders, as outlined by Dionysius, were only subsequently introduced; there are gradations within each order)
13. Are all angels sent on missions? (yes)
14. Are Michael, Gabriel, Raphael names of orders or spirits? (they are spirits)

Lombard answers other questions in passing: his is a coherent and sustained account of angels, that resolves questions about them by fitting them into the larger pattern of Creation and trying to create a coherent account of freewill and grace while preserving the sense that they are creatures. Lombard's *Sentences* became a textbook, establishing the questions and terms of argument for subsequent commentators.[14]

Bonaventure's influential *Commentaries* on Lombard's *Sentences* synthesized it not only with Pseudo-Dionysius but also with Aristotle, whose writings were then being disseminated in Western Christendom. Thirteenth-century angelologists sought to integrate natural philosophy with theology, and the bodies and agency of angels were an area where the interfaces of knowledge could be explored. Angelology became a formal topic in Paris in the thirteenth and fourteenth centuries, facilitated by interest in logic and the *quaestio* form, and discussions of angels became thoroughly dialectical. Bonaventure begins with a question, outlines the case for one answer, states the opposed arguments, then presents his own arguments and conclusion before finally dismissing the counter-arguments to this.[15] Aquinas' method was different and more artful: he began with a question, followed it with a series of propositions (which turn out to be false), responded to this with a counter-proposition (itself inadequate), offered his own reply, or *responsio*, then responded to objections while furthering his own conclusions. Though intricately structured, the effect is a dizzying tumble of arguments, revealing how *argumentum pro et contra* can generate new and not always fully conceived perspectives.[16]

Bonaventure deals with the question 'whether several Angels are together in the same place?' first by stating that it seems to be so: *because* angels inhabit a place spiritually rather than corporeally, because it is possible for two points to be together (*simul*), because two souls can inhabit the same body, and more besides. *However*, heaven was filled with holy angels, so they have distinct places; they have natural termini, as Augustine (whose fragmentary discussions of angels lie behind much medieval commentary) says; because angels are understood to be in place, and as the objects placed multiply so must the places, so each angel has a place; and also because one thing cannot be in more than one place. 'Respondeo' (I respond), writes Bonaventure, angels are not limited by place, and space is not used up by angels:

But since *the order of the universe* thus is taken away through omnimodal indistance [*omnimodam indistantiam*], just as through infinite distance: just as the order of the universe does not suffer, that an Angel be infinitely distant from an Angel, nay all are enclosed within the one circumference of the ultimate Heaven [*caeli ultimi*]; so it does not suffer, that an Angel be in the same prime place with an Angel. And from these (considerations) the objections are clear.[17]

And he clears up the remaining objections.

Debates such as this led to the Protestant mockery of angels-on-a-pinhead Scholasticism; however, they reveal both Bonaventure's engagement with Aristotelian natural philosophy, and the momentum that such arguments can carry. If truths like this are to be applied to angels, if we assume that they are bound by the conventions of logic and the laws of the universe, if we think that they are creatures, then much can be learned about them that lies beyond the text of Scripture and the stories of the Apocrypha.

Angels are in many ways at the heart of Aquinas' *Summa Theologiae*. There are four *quaestiones* concerning angels in the treatise on divine government: on angelic illumination; the speech of angels; the array, or hierarchy, of angels; and the array of devils. Angels are used to explain the communicative networks of heaven and the structure of Creation. In addition there is a discrete treatise on angels within the *Summa*. As with Lombard and Bonaventure, questions about angels fit into a logical structure. The *Summa* begins with God, proceeds to the Trinity, thence to Creation as a principle, then to angels, and then to the six days before proceeding to man. Angels are a logical step in a chain. Aquinas divides the topic into fifteen questions, each subdivided into a series of articles (my numbering follows the *Summa*):

Q. 50. the angelic nature
Q. 51. angels and bodies
Q. 52. angels and position in space
Q. 53. the movement of angels in space
Q. 54. angelic knowledge (or power of knowing)
Q. 55. the medium of angelic knowledge
Q. 56. the angels' knowledge of spiritual beings
Q. 57. the angels' knowledge of material things
Q. 58. how an angel's mind functions
Q. 59. the will of the angels

Q. 60. angelic love
Q. 61. the creation of the angels
Q. 62. the raising of the angels to the state of grace and glory
Q. 63. sin in the angels
Q. 64. the devils' punishment

Quaestio 54 is divided into five articles. The first asks: 'is an angel's actual understanding identical with his substance?' The answer is no: an angel's act of understanding is not the same as his substance. This is only so for God. Consequently, there are degrees of more and less perfect understanding. Article 2 asks: 'is an angel's actual understanding identical with his existence?' No: activity and existence are distinct in all creatures. Article 3 asks: 'is an angel's power to understand one thing with his essence?' No: in every created being existence and essence are different. He adds: 'The reason for calling angels "intellects" or "minds" is that their knowledge is wholly intellectual: whereas that of the human soul is partly intellectual and partly in the senses.' Article 4 asks: 'is the difference between agent and potential intellects found in angels?' No. Humans understand some things only *in potentia*, and hence need the imagination; angels comprehend even immaterial things directly or passively. 'Now there is no imagination in angels; hence no reason to divide their intellects in this way.' Article 5 asks: 'have the angels only intellectual knowledge?' They have. Men have faculties in their souls, such as memory and hearing, that are tied to the senses. As they have no bodies, their only faculties are intelligence and volition. They only have memory in the Augustinian sense of an intellectual faculty, not as an aspect of their soul.[18] The shape of Aquinas' logic shows both the relentless systematization of knowledge and an interpretation that, rather than interpreting existing evidence, interrogates the properties of the creature.

Aquinas needed to write about angels, as they were a means of understanding God. God was ineffable, and Christ's nature, despite the Incarnation, lay beyond the human intellect, since he had been made co-eternal. Angels, however, were created beings, and were therefore an indispensable mediating concept, halfway between man and God. Their structural position in the *Summa*, between heaven and earth, reflects their intellectual position in Aquinas' system. Without them the *Summa* does not work. Whatever their role in the liturgy, or as figures of comfort and protection in the popular imagination, angels were intellectually necessary as a way of grasping the divine. They could be used to describe hierarchies in Creation, the enchantment of the universe, the government of the earth. Angels present useful, constructive ways of thinking. Aquinas builds on Lombard and Bonaventure to present an extraordinary synthesis of patristic and pagan beliefs. He represents the final stage in a shift in emphasis in medieval angelology, which began with John Scotus Eriugena's translation of Pseudo-Dionysius, developed with Anselm's *Cur Deus Homo* (late 1090s), which relegated the Devil from this world into hell, and culminated with Aquinas' contemplative angels. Angels became less important as agents in this world, and more significant as intellectual beings, made androgynous, and celestialized, moved up into the heavens.[19] Nevertheless Aquinas' questions, together with the silences of Scripture, invite further interrogation of the nature and actions of angels. It is a short step to a narrative account that wonders whether angels can make mistakes, whether they can sympathize with a human perspective on desire, or how an angel could effectively convey a message to a human without bungling it. Aquinas' synthesis and systematization of knowledge opens up a world of unknown things.

The most significant British writer about angels contemporary with Bonaventure and Aquinas was Robert Grosseteste, Bishop of Lincoln (*c.*1170–1253). His interests unite many of the themes of this book, and anticipate the several intersections of post-Reformation angel-writing. He wrote a treatise on optics, a commentary on Genesis, in which he states that angels are made of light, a translation of pseudepigrapha, a translation (from Greek to Latin) of and commentary on Pseudo-Dionysius' *Hierarchy*, and a hexameron. He criticized the papacy, was interested in apocalypticism, and sought to associate magic with natural philosophy (hence his association with Roger Bacon and the legend, recorded by John Gower, that he forged a brazen head that could foretell the future). Dee's understanding of light and astrology were influenced by Grosseteste. This range of concerns—optics, papal critique (especially in reputation), Genesis, hexamera, angelic hierarchies, matter, magic, the Apocalypse—might have made him a central figure in early modern debates about angels. He was, however, seldom mentioned in Britain, and the key writings all but unknown, though Edward Browne apologized in the 1690s for Grosseteste's popish doctrine of angels. Grosseteste was, perhaps, a lost tradition or opportunity.[20]

On the eve of the Reformation the greatest interest in the doctrine of angels, at least beyond the immediately practical side, was expressed by humanists interested in Neoplatonism. Thus, Marsilio Ficino devised a schema of the universe in which magic drew upon the music of the spheres and the planetary angels (though he was sceptical about it); Francesco Giorgi, an account of spiritual magic that relied on the cooperation of one's guardian angel and the angels that moved the celestial spheres; and Tomasso Campanella, a description of natural magic in which the stars were angels with whom he believed he had communicated.[21] Renaissance Neoplatonists reiterated in new contexts traditional beliefs about the government of the world by angels, and added confused interest in daemons and in cabbalistic angels' names and in Gnostic myths. They identified associations rather than developed angel-doctrine, however, and their philosophy in some ways diminished the significance of angels as creatures participating in the world.[22] Protestants associated Neoplatonism with two tendencies in thinking about angels. First, a contribution to theories of angelic names and cosmic intervention. Secondly, Neoplatonism was associated with the corruption of upright religion, and thus could be polemically conflated with Catholic elaboration on angels. Calvin instructed believers to 'forsake that *Platonicall* philosophie, to seeke the way to God by Angels' which was pure superstition.[23] And, in a later English context, John Biddle condemned those Christian cabbalists who privilege Plato over Scripture, and thereby 'pervert the Worship of the true God'.[24]

## Reformed Angels

Reformers vocally attacked Scholastic angel-doctrine as overly curious, over-confident, vainly speculative, and thus susceptible to the temptations of the fleshly mind, superstitious, idolatrous, fictitious, and ungrounded in Scripture. That monks debated how many angels might dance on a pinhead was a Protestant slur. William Chillingworth alluded to this in 1638, defending reformed learning against the Catholic Edward Knott, who had sneered that Protestants had some superficial talent in preaching and languages, but no deep grasp of philosophy nor metaphysics. Chillingworth mockingly replied that Protestants do not debate 'Whether a Million of Angels may not sit upon a needles point?...they fill not their brains with notions that signify nothing'.[25] He treats it as a commonplace. The motif was then echoed by Henry More in 1659. More, however, was *defending* a discussion of whether the soul has dimensions independent of the body.

And it is a seasonable contemplation here (where we consider the Soul as having left this *Terrestrial* Body) that she hath as ample, if not more ample, Dimensions of her own, then are visible in the Body she has left. Which I think worth taking notice of, that it may stop the mouths of them that, not without reason, laugh at those unconceivable and ridiculous fancies of the Schools; that first rashly take away all *Extension* from Spirits, whether Soules or Angels, and then dispute how many of them booted and spur'd may dance on a needles point at once. Fooleries much derogatory to the Truth, and that pinch our perception into such an intolerable streightness and evanidness, that we cannot imagine any thing of our own Being; and if we doe, are prone to fall into despair, or contempt of our selves, by fancying our selves such unconsiderable Motes of the Sun.[26]

More objects to the foolishness of the question being handled by those who have already adjudicated that spirits have no dimension. After all, it is a question that pertains to the relationship between spirits and space and matter. Only if one believes that spirits have dimensions is it a reasonable philosophical question. He is himself dealing with equally abstract questions. It is a very fine line he treads, and he only remains steady because of the mockery in 'booted and spur'd'. While the topic may not be entirely unlike those taken seriously by medieval scholars, the famous phrase appears in Protestant polemic, and in contexts where Protestant learning is being defined.

The Protestant emphasis on *sola scriptura*, the letter of Scripture as the basis of true doctrine, suggested that accumulations of Catholic visions and revelation concerning angels must be disregarded. In his *Institution of the Christian Religion* Calvin raises the subject of angels and immediately proceeds to what *should not* be believed:

That the Angels, for as much as they are the ministers of God ordeined to execute his commaundements, are also his creatures, it ought to be certainly out of all question. To move doubt of the time and order that they were created in, should it not rather be a busie waiwardnes than diligence?...if we will be rightly wise, we must leave those vanities that idle men have taught without warrant of the word of God, concerning the nature, degree, and multitude of Angels.

Pseudo-Dionysius (Calvin knows of his debunking) receives particular scorn:

No man can deny, that the same *Denyse*, whatsoever man he was, hath disputed many things both subtlely and wittily in his Hierarchie of Heaven: but if a man examine it more neerely, he shall finde that for the most part it is but meere babbling. . . . If one should read that booke, he would thinke that the man were slipped downe from heaven, and did tell of things not that he had learned by hearesay, but that he had seene with his eyes.[27]

Paul, who really had been ravished above the third heaven, did not utter such things. Over a century later an English preacher, while discussing creatures' knowledge of God, echoed him: 'y$^c$ School DD. [Doctors] put up many nice Interrogatories, & as confidently resolv ym as if y. had been in Heav$^n$'.[28] In 1630 the Church of England clergyman John Bayly preached at Oxford a sermon on guardian angels that, despite his usually moderate tone, mocked scholastic attempts to rank the diverse names of angels 'as if they had come downe from heaven to tell men upon earth what order was kept there'.[29] Bayly nonetheless reproduced a deal of traditional angelology, and unlike many Protestants he maintained that guardian angels ministered to the elect. Another mid-seventeenth-century clergyman, William Jenkyn, writing a commentary on the epistle of Jude, scorned 'popish School-men' for their audacity,

Nor do they only shew their boldnesse in ranking and dividing them thus into these *three Hierarchies* and nine orders . . . but they presume to tell us the reasons of all these severall appellations, and to set down the severall properties and offices which are allotted to all these orders of Angels, whereby they are distinguished among themselves.

Implausibly he proceeds to outline them in detail; like others, the condemnatory rhetoric is stronger than his ability to place clear water between confessions.[30] Another preacher, John Patrick, outlines Catholic doctrine, contrasting 'the useful plainness of Holy Writ' with 'the impertinent curiosity, and trifling subtilty of the Schools'. His lengthy *Reflexions upon the Devotions of the Roman Church* (1674) relates these beliefs, with derogatory asides instead of counter-argument, so that 'every one may know that the School-divinity about Angels, is very peremptory and presuming in this kind; telling us in what place they were created, resolving whether the number that stood was equal to those that fell; the way thereby they understand, and the way they communicate their thoughts one to another'.[31] The volume concludes with angels, as if these represent the utmost excess.

Protestant polemic simplified Catholic perspectives on angels, making them seem homogeneous, and parodying the tenuously complex justifying logic. There is no denying, however, that doctrine around 1500 included a great deal that was not founded upon Scripture, and embarrassed loyal members of the Church (Erasmus was among those who recognized the forcefulness of some reformed critiques). Protestants initially effected a clearing out of much medieval doctrine. Luther was mildly interested in angels. Though they appear in his writings frequently, and throughout his life, he offers no sustained discussion of them. They are incidental to more important topics. Consequently, his doctrine of angels is less distant from Catholic orthodoxy than that of other reformers. In his early commentary on the Psalms he refers to the ten ranks of angels (a Franciscan tradition); in his later commentary on Genesis he rejects this tradition, citing it as evidence of spurious angelology.[32] In the Psalm commentary he can sound like Aquinas:

the knowledge by which an angel knows God in another angel, and the knowledge by which he knows God face to face, are as different as the knowledge of the sun in a cloud and the knowledge by which it is seen in its own brightness, since the creature is not pure light but rather full of light from the light.[33]

His writings implicitly accept the doctrine of individual guardian angels, and that Michael is the protecting angel of the Jews.[34] He condemned the worship of angels, but accepted that it was possible to call upon them in extremis.[35] He expressed opinions on how they made sounds, and on the curbing of their freedom following their rebellion.[36] He voiced the Augustinian understanding, fundamental to the way early modern writers thought and wrote about angels, that man was 'intermediate between angels and beasts'.[37] This is one perspective on the scale of nature that extends, in Samuel Ward's phrase, 'from the Mushrome to the Angels'; it is also a way of understanding the immortal part or soul of man, and a way of coming to terms with an unintelligible God.[38] Nevertheless, Luther's emphasis was on faith, and more general questions about angelic physics were irrelevant to him, though not in themselves dangerous.

Calvin's antagonism to excessive interest in angels was clear, and his influence on English angelology profound. He shifted the emphasis on their role from intercession to mediation, and emphasized the obstacle of ignorance. Explorations beyond the text of Scripture were unprofitable and potentially perilous. He rejects the doctrine of individual guardian angels, condemns praying to angels or asking for assistance, denies that humans can know about hierarchies, and insists that it is wrong to enquire when they were made; though he does affirm that they have no shapes, and that they are ministering spirits (reminding us, very much in character, that such ministration can include ministering God's wrath as well as his grace).[39] Calvin's aversion is something deeper than these doctrinal positions suggest. Thoughts about angels, like images, are likely only to distract or deceive. Curiosity leads to vain speculations, and these in turn lead us to fashioning our own ideas about God, rather than those he offers to us. Proud and superstitious men 'in the seeking of God do not climbe above themselves as they ought to have done, but measure him according to the proportion of their owne fleshly dulnesse, and also neglecting the sound manner of searching for him, do curiously flie to vaine speculations'.[40] They forge rash presumptions and then worship not God but their dream of him. God is comprehended through the Incarnation, and understanding angels does not for Calvin, as it did for Augustine, Aquinas, and even Luther, bring us any closer to knowing God. Angels perform God's offices, but do so more as efficient secretaries than as mysterious and benign witnesses of human drama.

Luther's position on angels is much like his position on art: they have a non-essential role to play in worship, and as long as they do not become the focus of undue attention it is not impossible that contemplating them will lead the faithful man closer to true faith. Moreover, he retains much of pre-Reformation angel-doctrine as *adiaphora* (things indifferent, not essential to salvation, and upon which the Church had given no decision). The presence of this position within Protestantism means that doctrines were not polarized along confessional lines. Calvin adopts a more extreme 'minimalist' position. Angels are an unimportant area of doctrine, defined more by the dangers of excessive fervour than by their contribution to theodicy, and the body of solid theology exploring them is very slight.

There are competing positions about the role of angels in salvation. Substantial elements of angel-doctrine survive the Reformation purge of credulity. These two facts meant that angels played a role in establishing differences *within* Protestantism. This often centres on the breadth of an opponent's beliefs in angels, and his vulnerability to charges of popery. Attacks on Laudian innovations in the 1620s and 1630s implicitly and explicitly associated angels with Romanism. However, the antitheses within which angels marked out doctrinal differences were not always concerned with the distance from Rome. Thus Joseph Wright, attacking Quakers in 1661 for their emphasis on humility, the efficacy of the will, and on the inner spirit:

And is not the Worship of those that call themselves followers of the *Light within*, the Worship of Angels? That is, of *Devils*, while they *disobey that which God hath shewed them in the Scriptures of Truth, and intrude into such things which are not to be found there*; Where is there such a thing to be found in *all the Record, that God hath given of his Son*, that all men ought not to look into, and be guided by the Scriptures of Truth; but that all men ought to look into, and be guided by the so called *Light*, which is within them? Oh the *vanity of that fleshly and puffed up Mind*, that hath been the Author of *this Intrusion and Doctrine of Devils*; so directly contrary to the Doctrine of the Holy Prophets, Apostles, and of Christ Himself... [41]

The indirection of the argument is itself revealing: Quakers intrude into the unknown and place great weight upon the inner light which has no justification in Scripture, therefore they worship angels. They worship angels, and because this is sinful, the angels must be devils. Angel-worship is thematically relevant not only as a symbol of irreligion, but also because when Paul warns the fleshly mind against intruding into things unseen, it is the 'voluntary humility and worshipping of angels' that concerns him. Angels are a rhetorical figure for idolatry *and* for forcing meanings upon Scripture.

   An association with angels was not always a slur within a Protestant rhetorical context. In the 1630s Laudians associated them with the beauty of holiness, reintroducing them within funerary monuments, church architecture, and liturgy.[42] Puritan clergymen stressed their confraternity with angels, defining a righteous community by its conversation, metaphorically understood, with angels.[43] Some religious radicals claimed to have less metaphorical conversations, summoning, hearing, or speaking with angels, witnessing the invisible world, receiving revelation or prophecy. The association of angels with medieval excesses of fervour and invention did not prevent them from occupying a central place in Protestant theology, or from being used positively to demarcate positions within Protestantism.

Britain witnessed a strain of anxiety about angels that was an inheritance from Calvinist minimalism.[44] However, this ambivalence is only part of the wider Protestant response in Britain and elsewhere. Angels were integral to Protestant biblical exegesis, they played a role in systematic theology, they offered comfort (though perhaps less than to Catholics), and, crucially, they established the Protestant Church as the true Catholic Church, and enabled verification of the workings of providence. It is easy to exaggerate the contrast between Protestant and Catholic angel-doctrine, and to overstress the anxiety or ambivalence Protestants felt about angels in the contemporary world. The Protestant view of angels remained thoroughly rooted in Aquinas. Its iconoclasm was presented as a restoration of the teachings of the true Church. Prayers to angels dwindled, but the new view was supported not by silence but by publishing. Between 1530 and 1700 angels were adapted into religious life in Protestant Britain by a process of iconoclasm and readjustment, and angelic visions continued in the eighteenth century, though they were more symbolic and pious than febrile and theologically charged, and the visionaries risked slighter persecution.[45] A story of an appearance of a healing angel in Stamford told in a 1659 pamphlet was retold in an early eighteenth-century commonplace book; it was still an angel, though it spoke to the community in a different way.[46] Angels were a canvas where faith and the rationalized understanding of the universe met with a repository of collective memories.

## Writing about Angels

Most writing about angels does not appear in books about angels. A handful of these appeared in sixteenth- and seventeenth-century Britain, notably John Salkeld's *A Treatise of Angels* (1613), Henry Lawrence's *Of our Communion and Warre with Angels* (1646, reissued in 1649 as *An History of Angells*), and Benjamin Camfield's *A Theological Discourse of Angels and their Ministries* (1678); to these might be added Heywood's *The Hierarchie of the Blessed Angells* (1635), a thorough and focused engagement with the topic that breaks the conventions of systematic study and transgressed genres. Angels appeared in a broad array of works, from sermons to polemics to poems, and these writings did not simply reflect a pre-existing body of thought. Genre shaped the questions writers asked about angels, and how they resolved and presented their answers. Modes of writing interacted with notions of angelic being and action. It is in the nature of scriptural commentaries that they address certain issues (when God made the lights in the firmament in Gen. 1: 14–18 did he make angels at the same time?). Sermons are more selective about their texts, and more oriented towards the application and matters of practical divinity (angelic guardianship is a more interesting theme for preachers than angelic freewill). The genres of books, their scope and shape, their publishing and distribution contexts, encroach upon the ideas presented in them.

The doctrinal statements about angels most familiar to English men and women appear in the Elizabethan homilies, sermons stating official Church doctrine regularly read in churches throughout the country. The homilies are diffident. The sermon 'Concerning Good Order and Obedience' (1563) begins: 'Almightie God hath created and appointed al thinges, in heaven earth and waters, in a mooste excellente and perfecte order. In heaven, he hath appointed distincte or severall orders and states of Archaungelles and Aungelles.' Angels—their good order rather than any particular hierarchy—are presented as proof of the necessity of hierarchy and obedience to governors on earth. This homily does not mention them again, though, obedient to symmetry, they reappear in the homily against disobedience (1570), which reasserts the premiss that human obedience mirrored angelic obedience, and the diabolical nature of disobedience: 'So heere appeareth the originall kyngdome of God over angels and man, and universallie over all thinges, and of man over earthly creatures whiche God had made subject unto him, and withall the felicitie and blessed state which angels, man, and all creatures had remayned in, had they continued in due obedience unto God their King.'[47] This does not represent a significant departure from the opening credo of the Fourth Lateran Council of 1215.[48] The homilies on idolatry and prayer caution against worshipping angels; the Homily on the Passion dwells on the fact that God sent his Son and not an angel to redeem mankind; and angels are mentioned in retellings of the stories of Tobias and Lazarus in the homilies on fasting and on death. Otherwise the homilies are strikingly silent. There was very little an English Protestant *needed* to believe about angels.

The Book of Common Prayer was the other rubric for the everyday experience of angels in worship, and it too was reserved. The Westminster Assembly was formed in 1643 in part to purge the Church of innovations; when it reported on the Book of Common Prayer, its list of doubtful matters began with the Prayer Book's affirmation 'that there be Archangels and that Michael is a created Angel'.[49] Presbyterians in the 1640s had already suggested that the Laudian Church had edged towards Rome in its angel doctrine. Yet the Feast of St Michael and All Angels (29 September) had been in the Prayer Book since the first Edwardian edition of 1549, when the collect began: 'Everlasting God which hast ordeyned & constituted, the services of al angels & men in a wonderfull ordre'.[50] The Assembly exaggerated in order to emphasize its own minimalist position; its own catechism barely mentioned angels. John Boughton's 1623 catechism said a little more:

J[ACOB] . . . tell mee what are Angels?
B[ENJAMIN] *They are immortall Spirits, or spirituall substances, free from bodies, or exceeding power, wisedome, and agilitie, created after the image of God, to minister to him, and men his children.*
J[ACOB] How many sorts of Angels are there?
B[ENJAMIN] *Two. Good and bad.*
J[ACOB] What are the good Angels?
B[ENJAMIN] *The good Angels are those Elect spirits in heaven, which by the grace of God continued in the truth and integritie, in which they were created; and by the same grace are so confirmed in that estate, as that now they cannot fall from it, but are for ever blessed.*[51]

The sum of the necessary creed was minimal.

A very different picture emerges from scriptural annotations and commentary. Detailed statements about angels can be found, sometimes scattered through different notes, sometimes synthesized in a digression, in such works as Gervase Babington's *Certaine Plaine, Briefe, and Comfortable Notes upon Everie Chapter of Genesis* (1592), Andrew Willet's *Hexapla in Genesin: That is, A Sixfold Commentarie upon Genesis* (1605), John Trapp's *A Commentary or Exposition upon all the Epistles* (1647) and his *A Clavis to the Bible* (1650), the Westminster Assembly's monumental *Annotations upon all the Books of the Old and New Testament* (1645, 1651) and a series of associated scholarly works from the 1640s and 1650, including John Richardson's *Choice Observations and Explanations upon the Old Testament* (1655), and, finally, George Hughes's *An Analytical Exposition of the Whole First Book of Moses* (1672). These represent a domestication and popularization of, and a considerable elaboration on, the annotations of Augustine, Luther, and Calvin, which were available to educated readers. Scriptural annotations address particular places and cruxes. If an angel dines with Abraham, how does it eat? When the Lord 'opened the mouth' of Balaam's ass, did the angel itself vocalize, or did it use the mouth of the ass? The questions coincide with many of Lombard's and Aquinas'. Here Protestants show no resistance to enquiry, because making sense of the biblical stories, which is to say, resolving the literal meaning, requires it.[52]

To take the first of these examples, Gervase Babington comments on Genesis 18: 8, 'he took butter, and milk, and the calf . . . and they did eat': 'How the Angells did eate.'

For their eating, we know it was but by dispensation for the time, not for any necessitie of nature. And if you aske what became of the meate which they did eate, the Schoolemen will readily answere you that it did vanish in the chawing, as water doth in boyling. Wiser men aske no such questions, and therefore neede no such answere. In the extraordinary dealings of God what neede wee to sift his secrets, and to bee wise above sobrietie?'[53]

In contrast, Andrew Willet spells out the various positions on this text, then resolves,

it is the sounder opinion, that these angels, as they were endued with true bodies for the time, so they did verily eate, as they did walke and speake and doe other actions of the bodie truly: yet did they not eate of any necessitie: but like as these bodies by the power of God assumed for the present, were againe dissolved and turned to their first nature, so was the meat which they did eate.[54]

The annotations of the Westminster Assembly repeat Willet's position; George Hughes paraphrases a little confusingly: 'If question be, how those bodies could eat? Or whether nourished? It is answered, doubtless they did truely eat, and the bodies were refreshed for the time that God made use of them, and after both [i.e. body and food] were resolved into their principles by the hand of God.'[55] In Babington's response we find a minimalist answer, coupled with a warning against insobriety; while those who came after him essentially agreed they felt a need to spell out alternative positions before stating theirs. Annotations are accumulative texts. Once asked and explored, a question tends to linger around the relevant place in Scripture. It is possible to ignore the question of angelic digestion (and excretion), but to do so would not be scholarly.

The same process surrounds the question of when angels were created. The date of angelic creation does not depend upon the gloss of any single verse; rather, it is a silence in the narrative. An attentive reader will ask it, and once opened it proves a can of worms. Where the annotator deals with it depends on his opinion. Babington adds a note on this at the end of his commentaries on Genesis 1: 'When the Angells were created, it is not precisely named, but that they were created, both by this place it is knowne, and *Coloss. 1. 16.* By *Jude* also and *Peter*: the usuall opinion is, the first day, reade *Junius*.'[56] Willet also deals with this topic at the end of chapter 1, but he adds to this question another: Why did Moses omit the creation of angels? He answers at some length, offering three possibilities before concluding that 'Moses applieth himself to the simple capacity of the people, and describeth onely the creation of visible and sensible things, leaving to speake of the spirituall, which they could not understand.'[57] The Westminster annotators, also at the end of Genesis 1, dilate at length on the original questions and on Willet's broadening of it; they follow Willet but withhold final judgement.[58] Their verdict excludes only the opinion of those, including Milton, who thought that angels were created before the visible universe.[59] Here again we see a process of accumulation and a shift in emphasis. While Protestants may have commended restraint in comparison to Scholastic theology, they covered much of the same ground, while presenting Scripture as the sole basis of their analysis. Genesis received more annotation than any other text, perhaps in part because of reformed interest in the doctrines of sin, predestination, and atonement,[60] and Genesis raised many of the most curious angelological questions.

Systematic theology, in the tradition of Aquinas' *Summa*, handled the same issues: where, when, why, what do they do, what are we to understand by them, what do we need to know?[61] The most influential models were from the Reformation on the Continent: especially Calvin's *Institutes*, Peter Martyr Vermigli's *Common Places*, William Bucanus' *Institutions*, but also Johannes Wollebius' *Compendium Theologiae Christianae* (1626, partly translated in 1650). The *Medulla Theologiae* (1623, 1627) of William Ames, an Englishman by birth who spent much of his life in exile in the Netherlands, was also widely read (and partially translated as *The Marrow of Sacred Divinity* in 1643). A later work, and further evidence of a popularization of the formerly Latin genre, was Henry Hibbert's *Syntagma Theologicum, or, A Treatise wherein is concisely*

*comprehended, the body of divinity, and the fundamentals of religion* (1662).
Milton's unfinished *De Doctrina Christiana* belongs to this genre. These
works begin with God and work their way down through Creation. In
them questions about the timing of the creation of the angels fit into a
broader interpretative framework, and are usually followed by a discus-
sion of what angels are and what they do. There is no necessity for
discussions of angelic digestion in this context: the focus is not on
biblical narratives but on the system of beliefs, and the coherence of an
account of Creation and salvation. Whereas an account of angels is
necessary to understand certain scriptural narratives, a subtly different
analysis of angels is useful in an exploration of soteriology, and it is this
that we find in systematic theologies (as well as some sermons). While
angels are not essential to salvation, they help humans understand it.
Systematic theologies purposively descend from God through angels to
humans as part of the hermeneutic of knowing God, and this is as true
for Protestants as for Catholics.

A process of accumulation shapes these works. Once an issue has
been discussed, and placed in a systematic development, it becomes
part of a standard repertoire, a topos of analysis or argument. These are
highly generic texts: their particularities are worked out through the
many things they share with their antecedents. Bucanus' *Institutions*
(sometimes referred to as 'the commonplaces', because of the topical
way they are organized) is a digest of patristic and Scholastic and
Reformation commentary, which in turn influenced Ames, for
example, and Willet borrows and cites from him, sometimes rejecting
his arguments, especially in the 1633 expanded edition of *Hexapla in
Genesin*. Bucanus was quoted approvingly by William Prynne and
Samuel Rutherford (for equating presbyters and bishops), and com-
mended in Richard Baxter's *Christian Directory* as particularly useful to
those who could not afford many books; this sentiment is reversed in
Richard Montagu's controversial *Appello Caesarum*, which dismisses
'moderne Epitomizers' in favour of more ancient authorities.[62] Buca-
nus' *Institutions* is organized in transparent and accessible chapters, on
themes from God and the Trinity, through angels or original right-
eousness; the manner is remote from the systematic interrogation of
Aquinas, but the issues derive directly from Scholastic theology.

A similar hybridity can be found in *An Exposition on the Fourteene
First Chapters of Genesis* (1626), by Alexander Ross (who translated
Wollebius into English), a dialogue interpreting Scripture. Ross

comments on angels in detail because he is concerned about the popishness of much angel-doctrine.[63] Ames's treatment is more concise, and presents a series of propositions concerning the 'special Gubernation about intelligent Creatures' (Milton has a corresponding chapter in *De Doctrina*), in which he identifies the similarities and differences between angels and humans. Perhaps what is most significant about this chapter is that a digest of angel-doctrine could be so concise: it assumes that the reader was familiar with many of the touchstones of the discussion. Readers of works such as these assembled their own credos, much as one would a commonplace book.[64] Henry Fairfax, Dean of Norwich and cousin of the parliamentarian general, prepared a commonplace book with headings about angels, their creation, relationship with man, their fall, 'Permissione peccati' and 'Determinatione peccati'. These were perhaps intended for use in preaching: the good intentions failed, as most of the pages remain empty, a fact that is perhaps related to his parishioners' complaints about his dereliction of duties.[65] On 1 January 1655 the parishioners of Stortford began to compile at the house of one Mr Paine a collective systematic theology 'about those fundamentall truths that are necessary to bee knowne and practiced by every one that would bee saved'.[66] Cornelius Burgess and John Milton compiled similar notes from their reading, perhaps with the view to publishing a systematic theology.[67] What binds these texts together, then, is the interest in placing knowledge of angels into a coherent framework that is focused not so much on interpreting Scripture or practical divinity as on assembling a meaningful picture of the visible and invisible world.

Sermons were an important genre for Scripture-centred Protestantism, used to analyse biblical texts and to disseminate doctrine. Sermons constitute a significant proportion of press output, and printed versions suggest their wider role in aural experience.[68] Angels figured in sermons in two ways. First, within a commentary on Scripture, in which they could play an incidental or a substantial role. Hundreds of sermons touch upon angels, exegetically or imaginatively, in passing.[69] A 1616 sermon by Nathaniel Cannon mentions angels only in order to emphasize human dependence on divine assistance.[70] Others offered more extended exploration, including John Gumbleden's sermon 'An Angel, in a Vision', which examines an angel appearing to the soldier Cornelius in Acts 10: 3.[71] Gumbleden discusses angelic apparitions and the assumptions of bodies, guardians, the ministry of angels, angelic communication, and angelic knowledge. Similarly, John Everard's 'Militia Caelestis' begins with Psalm 68: 17 ('The Chariots of God are twenty thousand thousands of Angels'), and develops a general survey of angel-doctrine. Both provide an angelology in miniature. All of these examples formally resemble scriptural commentary, and some scriptural commentaries, including Luther's lectures on Genesis, Calvin's on Job, and Joseph Caryl's multi-volume *Exposition . . . of the Book of Job* (1647–66), began life as extended series of sermons.

Secondly, a few sermons focus on an aspect of angel-doctrine, and draw more directly upon systematic theology. One of the most widely cited Reformation works on angels was Urbanus Rhegius' sermon on good and evil angels, which outlined a broadly acceptable Protestant doctrine. Sermons by Bayly and Prideaux follow this pattern. Robert Gell's *Aggelokratia Theon, or, A Sermon* (1650) is only in the most indirect sense a commentary on Deuteronomy 32: 8, 9, and more extensively a statement of angel-doctrine in support of astrology (it was preached before the Society of Astrologers).[72] Following the execution of the minister Christopher Love for treason in 1656, a group of fellow Presbyterians published a treatise of his entitled 'The Ministry of Angels', which had grown out of one or more sermons. His editors warned that it was 'not intended for a Philosophical, but for a *Christian auditory*; the . . . subject is high, and there is room enough for speculation', and thereby distanced it from Thomistic writing, but it is in fact one of the more extended writings on angels from the 1650s.[73] Sermons that focus on a particular theme often adopt an essayistic or meditational form. William Austin's meditation entitled 'Tutelar Angels' probably began life as a sermon for 29 September, the feast of St Michael the Archangel.[74] These sermons focus on a topic that bridges abstract theology with practical divinity, such as the existence of guardian angels. They are generically similar to short treatises on angels, such as Robert Dingley's *The Deputation of Angels* (1654), a defence of angelic guardianship, Arise Evans's *The Voice of Michael the Archangel* (1654), and *A Modest Enquiry into the Opinion Concerning a Guardian Angel* (1702). These pamphlets are topical, seeking to mount an argument that is sensitive to an immediate political or religious context. Angels were more persuasive when peripheral, not central, to arguments.

The angelology, a systematic examination of angel-doctrine (written in isolation from a full theological system), is a rare genre. Prior to the Reformation there was little need for the form, as it constituted a

fragment of a larger examination of Creation or salvation. It is because of
Protestant concern about the popishness of much writing about angels,
and perhaps out of fear of lingering popular beliefs, that the form
discovers a rationale. The concern about justifiable angel-doctrine,
and the extent to which Thomistic arguments could be perpetuated in
a reformed context, resulted in early modern Britain in a handful of
works, including John Salkeld's *A Treatise of Angels* (1613), Henry Law-
rence's *Of our Communion and Warre with Angels* (1646), and Benjamin
Camfield's *A Theological Discourse of Angels and their Ministries* (1678).
Isaac Ambrose's 'Ministration of, and Communion with Angels' per-
haps belongs with this group, but it was published, in 1662, as part of a
larger work on divinity. Later in the century Increase Mather and his son
Cotton wrote several treatises about angelology that were, despite
Cotton's visions of an angel, largely reiterations of commonplaces.[75]
While deriving their topics and organization from systematic theology,
these works share a distinct premiss: they endeavour to sketch the extent
of Protestant angel-doctrine, and to describe the ministry of angels
within the reformed Church. Their concerns are therefore at once
expansive, in that they define a body of knowledge, and restrictive, in
that they take to heart Calvin's admonitions about curiosity and, at least
polemically, repudiate excessive speculation. The Jesuit-educated Sal-
keld offers a digest of Scholastic knowledge for a Jacobean Protestant
audience; the godly Lawrence surveys knowledge of angels to consider
them as patterns for human behaviour. Camfield's angelology is a
defence of the existence of the spirit world against what he perceived
as creeping Sadducism and scepticism.

Poems about angels are the concern of much of this book. They are,
like all of the forms discussed above, inclined to certain kinds of topic
and not others. Some that interest me are atypical of their time. Samuel
Pordage's *Mundorum Explicatio* is based on prophetic visionary insights;
Heywood offers a compendium of learning; Hutchinson's *Order and
Disorder* is equally influenced by scriptural commentary and Guillaume
de Salluste du Bartas; Milton's *Paradise Lost* binds doctrine and narrative;
Donne offers momentary elucidation, rather than sustained insight, from
systematic study. In many other poems, however, from Spenser's
'Hymne of Heavenly Love' (1596) to Cowley's *A Vision* (1661), angels
speak or are seen, in ways that resemble, borrow from, and develop the
insights in non-fictional prose, imaginatively illuminating the sacred, or
using sacred images to make political points. Poetic writing about angels

tends towards narratives of Creation, or reflections on symbolism: the symbolism of angels' wings, for example. In contrast, angels appear in strikingly few dramas in the early modern period.[76]
Finally, it is worth reflecting on a genre of writings about angels that scarcely exists in early modern Britain. Glossing biblical metaphors, logically deducing the nature of angelic bodies, inferring the lacunae in scriptural narratives, none of these involves reflecting on angels as creatures *like us*. Angels are models for humans, but few writers reflected upon what it would be like to *be* an angel. Angelic emotions (angels weep and sing praises in Scripture) are metaphors, not grounds for speculation. Yet sometimes this consideration erupts in writing.

Henry More, whose writing about angels is profound and imaginative, both mystical and natural-philosophical, maintaining the unobjectionable proposition that there are two polities of light and darkness among both angels and men, asserts: '*every Angel, Good or Bad, is as truly a Person as a man, being endued also with Life, Sense, and Understanding*; when they are likewise capable of *Joy* and *Pain*, and therefore coercible by *Laws*'.[77] This goes beyond the imaginative sympathy customarily offered to spirits. Jan Amos Comenius, the Moravian theologian and educationalist, pushes these issues harder: 'There is in Angels a sense of things, as well as in our spirits. . . . Also they have a sense of pleasure and griefe: for as much as joyes are said to be prepared for the Angels, and fire for the divells, (into which wicked men are also to be cast.)'[78] The link that Comenius makes between sense-perception and emotion is suggestive: cognition and sensation are associated with feelings, participation in Creation with emotions, spiritual being with limitations. His exploratory approach anticipates Milton's angels, who are, more than Aquinas' or Dante's or perhaps anyone's, subject to the imperfections and difficulties of being a creature.

This chapter has explored the Christian traditions of writing about angels, the way questions about angels emerge from scriptural narrative and are developed and extended, the impact of the Reformation on the body of knowledge concerning angels, the various genres in which British Protestants wrote about angels, the way genre shapes the expression of beliefs and ideas, and some of the rhetoric used to characterize confessional difference. The following chapter outlines the actual differences between Roman Catholics and Protestants, and presents a brief catechism of reformed doctrine.

# 3

# Angelology

## Knowledge of Angels

### Catholic and Protestant Differences

Protestant angelology was shaped by the emphasis on *sola scriptura* and by a reaction against Catholicism. Angels were commonly mentioned in complaints against popish inventiveness: 'What distinctions, orders, degrees and offices doe they make of Angels? what curious questions doe they raise?'[1] But Protestants were not merely anxious about angels. They did not allow angels to creep in by the back door: rather, they explored angels afresh as a useful element of theology. Just as angels had been a powerful testing ground for Aristotelian natural philosophy in the twelfth and thirteenth centuries, so in the sixteenth and seventeenth centuries they offered a way of examining the world in the light of reformed theology and developments in natural philosophy.

The differences between Protestants and Catholics on the theology of angels can be reduced to a series of headings, though doing so risks making the doctrines on both sides seem more undifferentiated than in reality it was. A useful overview, however, and one that is as prescriptive as descriptive, can be found in Andrew Willet's *Synopsis Papismi, That is, A Generall Viewe of Papisty: wherein the whole mysterie of iniquitie and summe of Antichristian doctrine is set downe, which is maintained this day by the Synagogue of Rome, against the Church of Christ*, published in six swelling editions between 1592 and 1634. A sequel entitled *Tetrastylon Papisticum, That is, The Foure Principal Pillers of Papistrie* appeared in 1593, with two further editions that decade. Willet was a Calvinist supporter of the established Church who published anti-Arminian opinions; he was independently minded, though fiercely anti-Catholic. Willet identified three Catholic–Protestant controversies: concerning the hierarchies and degrees of angels, their ministry and office, and the worship and invocation of angels. However, as he deals with each topic, he multiplies the differences and shifts the focus.

## Hierarchies

Concerning the hierarchies of angels, Willet writes that the papists (he is hostilely characterizing their position, so I will retain this term) 'boldely affirme', on the basis of the diverse names given to them in Scripture, 'that there are nine orders of Angelles', while Protestants accept that there are 'diverse orders' but judge that to 'enquire of them more subtilly' is not only 'foolish curiositie', but also 'ungodly and dangerous rashness'. A second, and consequent, question under this heading is whether Michael is the prince of angels. The papists say that Revelation reveals that he is, and the position was formerly held by Lucifer. The Protestants say that 'Michael' in Revelation signifies Christ. Willet claims (and it is not clear whether he believes himself to be describing a universal Protestant position or merely forwarding his own arguments) that there is no reason to believe that there is necessarily a prince among fallen or unfallen angels. 'Sathan' is a name given to all evil spirits, and they are all princes.[2]

Most Protestants did believe in a heavenly hierarchy without committing themselves to specific orders: such detail lay beyond human knowledge. The influential *Institutions of Christian Religion*, by the French-born Swiss theologian William Bucanus, stated one Protestant position, that there is order, but the names ascribed to ranks in fact describe offices:

No man that is conversant in the Scriptures can deny, but that there is some order among the Angels, because order and distinction in all things is an excellent and divine thing: for some are called Cherubins, others Seraphims; some Angels, other Archangels. But this order is not from the dignitie and excellencie of the nature of the Angels, as though some were more excellent by nature: but rather from their diverse kinds of offices.... But that there be Hierarchies, and degrees of Hierarchies among the Angels, as the Papists imagine, it cannot be proved by any testimonie of Scripture.[3]

Similarly, William Perkins wrote in *A Golden Chaine, or, The Description of Theologie*, a lucid and weighty tome published in nine editions between 1591 and 1621:

**Figure 1.** Thomas Heywood, *Hierarchie of the Blessed Angells* (1635), title page engraving

That there are degrees of Angels, it is most plaine. . . . But it is not for us to search, who, or how any been in each order, neither ought we curiously to enquire howe they are distinguished, whether in essence, or qualities.[4]

The fact that the Dionysian treatises were not written by a disciple of Paul's was widely known and recited in attacks on Scholastic angel-doctrine.[5] Many Protestants overlooked this, however, and Catholic propagandists repudiated or ignored the humanist disproof.[6] However, to reject Dionysius was by no means to reject hierarchies. In a section entitled 'The Degrees and Orders of Angels' in *The Great Mysterie of*

*Godliness* (1652), Joseph Hall argues that heavenly hierarchies of perfection show that equality has no place in Creation, and that 'He that was rapt into the third heaven can tell us of thrones, dominions, principalities, Angels and Arch-angels in that region of blessednesse.'[7] We do not know, however, the various employments of these angels, and Hall devotes several pages to summarizing the presumptuous conceits of those who schematize the properties and relative powers of the hierarchies, as if, though wrong, the knowledge is nonetheless not redundant.[8] In a 1639 sermon John Blenkow accepted the notion of hierarchies, but without the 'too curious' inferences of the Scholastics; he favoured the opinions of the learned, 'who though they hold some kinde of order and subordination amongst the Angels, yet they are not so bold as to assign in particular their degrees and orders: and to affirme a thing so remote from our understanding, were necessary eyther some evident reason, or more firme authority then can be alleadged'. He accepts that Michael was 'chiefe patron of the Jewes' and a type of Christ, though without allowing him to be head of the angels.[9]

Others declared with Richard Sibbes that 'we must not rashly presume to looke into these things', but nonetheless accepted the notion of hierarchies, summarized traditional Roman Catholic accounts of them, and made use of the significance of hidden orders.[10] Such dismissals are half-hearted. John Salkeld's *Treatise of Angels* describes the various approaches to hierarchies in considerable detail while explicitly not committing himself to them; his interest in these details, and his non-judgemental exposition, suggest that he had sympathy with the Scholastic position.[11] Joseph Glanvill insisted that ''tis not absurd to believe, that there is a *Government* that runs from *Highest* to *Lowest* . . . So that some one would fancy that perhaps the *Angels* may manage *us*, as we do the *Creatures* that God and Nature have placed under our *Empire* and *Dominion*'. This accepts much of the Pseudo-Dionysian doctrine of hierarchy, without the specific names and properties.[12] Still others insisted that names corresponded to a hierarchy of duties.[13] Brian Duppa performs a very slippery movement in rejecting certain knowledge of hierarchies:

Nor shall we offend to inlarge this meditation further, to conceive as some of the Fathers did, that as the Angels fell from severall Hierarchies, some from being Seraphins, some Cherubins, some Thrones, some out of higher Seats, some out of lower: so on this great Day, when God shall distribute his glory among us, we may opine at least, that into those severall Hierarchies we shall be assumed . . .

Duppa nonetheless knows that one day humans will be above the angels.[14] Much Laudian angel-doctrine adopts this double-movement, and appears closer to Catholic than Nonconformist doctrine.

Some Protestants, Willet notwithstanding, explicitly accepted the usefulness of the hierarchies. Heywood uses them to structure his meditative poem *Hierarchie of the Blessed Angells*. He associates rejection of hierarchies with rejection of the spirit world altogether. His taxonomy merits quoting at length, because it is compact and reveals a Protestant's imaginative engagement with the idea:

In three most blessed *Hierarchies* th'are guided,
And each into three Companies divided:
The first is that in which the *Seraphims* bee,
*Cherubims, Thrones*; distinct in their degree.
The *Seraphim* doth in the word imply,
A *Fervent Love* and *Zeale to the Most-High*.
And these are they, incessantly each houre
In contemplation are of Gods great Power.
The *Cherubim* denotes to us the *Fulnesse*
Of absolute *Knowledge*, free from Humane dulnesse;
Or else *Wisedomes infusion*. These desire
Nothing, but Gods great *Goodnesse* to admire.
The name of *Thrones*, his glorious Seat displaies;
His *Equitie* and *Justice* these still praise.
 The second *Ternion*, as the Schoole relates,
Are *Dominations, Vertues, Potestates*.
*Dominions*, th'*Angels* Offices dispose;
The *Vertues* (in the second place) are those
That execute his high and holy Will:
The *Potestates*, they are assistant still,
The malice of the Divell to withstand:
For God hath given it to their powerfull hand.
 In the third order *Principates* are plac't;
Next them, *Arch-Angels*; *Angels* are the last.
The *Principates*, of Princes take the charge,
Their power on earth to curbe, or to enlarge;
And these worke Miracles. Th'*Arch-Angels* are
Embassadors, great matters to declare.
Th'*Angels* Commission hath not that extent,
They only have us Men in government.
'God's in the first of these, a Prince of *Might*:

*Angeli in quot Choros dividuntur.*
The first *Chorus*.

The Seraphim and his office.

The Cherubim.

The Thrones.

Dominions.
Vertues.

Potestates.

Principates.

Arch-Angels.

Angels.

'He in the second doth reveale, as *Light*:
'Is in the last, his *Graces* still inspiring.
To know what's to their Offices requiring;
The formost Ternion hath a reference      The Offices of
To contemplate Gods Divine *Providence:*      the three Ternions.
Prescribing what by others should be don.
The office of the second Ternion
Doth his concurring *Influence* disperse
Unto the guidance of the Universe;
And sometimes hath a working. Now we know,
The third descends to'have care of things below;
Assisting good men, and withstanding those
That shall the rules of Divine Lawes oppose.[15]

Potestates are synonymous with Powers; Principates with Principalities. The description is conventionally Pseudo-Dionysian, and it parallels Dante's *Paradiso*, canto XXVIII. Heywood emphasizes the importance of providence more than a Catholic might, though he also suggests that miracles are ongoing, despite Protestant reservations about this. Principates perform miracles, and Heywood is thoroughly committed to their contemporary relevance: the frontispiece to book 7, on the Principates, shows a conventional angel with a sword hovering over a wicked kingdom (its denizens have diabolical faces) with the banner 'Protero' ('I trample'); on the upper left a godly court hovers in the clouds, with the banner 'Protago' (presumably *protego*, 'I protect'). The family are clearly discernible as King Charles, Henrietta Maria, and their three children. The image suggests that Principates govern the earth, protecting good kings and punishing bad, but it also compares the royal family to angels, forming a little kingdom in the clouds.[16] Hierarchies had clear political uses.

There was a close affiliation, as James VI and I observed, between monarchy and episcopacy, and the interpretation of the angels of the seven Asian Churches, addressed in Revelation, was central to arguments about the proper government of the Church.[17] Heavenly hierarchies were frequently paralleled to earthly, and those who challenged them compared to rebellious angels.[18] John Taylor argued that hereditary monarchy was the best form of government, just as there was one sun in the sky and 'Amongst the *Angels* there are distinctions, as *Principalities, Powers, Thrones, Dominions*, and *Michael* an *Archangel*.'[19] George Lawson described the government of heaven in distinctively

**Figure 2.** Thomas Heywood, *Hierarchie of the Blessed Angells* (1635), engraving of 'The Principat'

earthly terms, and presented the divine order as the proper basis for humane government, though, oddly, he suggested that while the government of the fallen angels was monarchical, he was not so sure about the unfallen.[20] Even Protestants reluctant to identify the hierarchy in detail were confident that it contained lessons for the proper order of human society and the conduct of politics.[21]

The distinction between the Catholic and Protestant positions was not a simple one, then, and despite claims that titles reflected offices or duties rather than nature, Protestants did not challenge the assumption that the various scriptural names for angels reflected an organization that was hierarchical in nature. Milton's vision of a meritocratic Creation brings him close to total rejection. In *Reason of Church Government* he writes: 'Yea, the Angels themselves, in whom no disorder is fear'd, as the Apostle that saw them in his rapture describes, are distinguisht and quaterniond into their celestiall Princedomes, and Satrapies, according as God himselfe hath writ his imperiall decrees through the great provinces of heav'n.'[22] 'Quaterniond' implies rejection of the Pseudo-Dionysian three ternions, and is not rooted in conventional exegesis of angelic hierarchy. Instead it suggests the four angels who govern the four corners of the world, and the four winds that blow therefrom, which appear in Revelation 7: 1–2. It anticipates Henry More's gloss on Daniel 7, where he writes:

*ruchot* is the very same word that is in *Psal.* 104. 4. *These are the Four Winds of Heaven*, The Quaternio of the Angelical Ministers of Divine Providence. Something like that *Apoc.* 7. where there is mention of the Four Angels at the Four Corners of the Earth, holding the Four Winds of the Earth that they should not blow on the Earth, nor on the Sea. And that the great things in the vicissitude of Kingdoms and Empires are done by the Angels, is an Hypothesis that both *Daniel* and the *Apocalypse* plainly supposes, the latter indeed inculcates to awaken this dull Sadducean Age.[23]

None of this Milton would have objected to. Milton uses the scriptural names without hierarchy, and in *Paradise Lost* ranks conventionally placed low in the hierarchy demonstrate greater abilities than the higher ranks. They are names of duties, words used to describe and praise rather than assert status. It is the fallen angels, and particularly Satan, who are most concerned with hierarchy:

> Thrones, dominations, princedoms, virtues, powers,
> If these magnific titles yet remain
> Not merely titular, since by decree
> Another now hath to himself engrossed
> All power, and us eclipsed under the name
> Of king anointed . . .                          (*PL* 5. 772–7)

Milton is neither inconsistent nor satirical, but, rather, committed to individual merit as the basis of salvation.[24] His belief that Creation's hierarchies should be flexible, mobile, and founded upon communication prevented any commitment to hierarchies as the Scholastics and some Protestant contemporaries would have understood them. The Pseudo-Dionysian hierarchy as modified by Scholastic theology was rigid and unyielding.[25] Milton's vision is anything but uncommitted, though it is less a satire of Roman Catholic doctrine than an image of his own interpretation of Scripture, supported by his understanding of nature; its inconsistency reflects the fluidity of Creation.

Willet's minor point under this heading is easier to address, though he is also misleading here. He states that Protestants (and not Catholics) identify Michael in Revelation as Christ and not a created angel. In fact Protestants were divided on this. The Geneva annotators, David Pareus, Arthur Dent, Joseph Mede, Johannes Wollebius, and others, accepted that Michael in Revelation was Christ, but others state that he was an angel, or even a prefiguration of the emperor Constantine.[26] The Westminster *Annotations* prefers this first reading, but acknowledges that some take Michael to be a 'chief created angel'. The interpretation of Jude and Daniel also made the reading ambiguous. Thomas Heywood, William Jenkyn, and Milton insist that the identification with Christ makes no sense of Scripture.[27]

## Ministry and Offices of Angels

The second Catholic–Protestant division Willet identifies is on the question of the ministry of angels, which also falls into two parts, protection and offices. The papists erroneously say that Michael 'is the protector and keeper of the whole Church of Christ', and that kingdoms and churches 'have their speciall angels for their protectors'. Protestants know that Christ and all angels protect the whole Church 'without anye limitation of place', and that it cannot be proved out of Scripture that angels are assigned to kingdoms. Willet subordinates under this another error: papists believe that 'Everie one hath from his nativitie an Angell for his custodie and patronage against the wicked, before the face of God.' This causes Willet some concern, as he stops to repudiate the textual proofs for the doctrine, before asserting the Protestant belief that the doctrine of individual guardian angels cannot be proved. Moreover, we are carried to heaven at death by a choir or company of angels.[28]

Protestants were more divided on these issues than Willet cared to admit. Many, including Calvin, Peter Martyr, and Milton, accepted Daniel 10, which refers to Michael as the prince of the Jewish people, and also to the princes of Greece and Persia, as proof of the existence of local guardian angels. I discuss some of the extensive Protestant uses of this doctrine in Chapters 9 and 13.[29] Willet's subordination of the question of individual guardian angels to the notion of guardians assigned to a place is odd, as the former was a more controversial and doctrinally significant issue. Belief in dual guardian angels, one good and one bad, developed in the early days of the Christian Church (based on Acts 12: 15). One influential non-canonical text, which reflects this belief, is the second-century work *The Shepherd* by Hermas, a supposed disciple of Paul's. John Pringle translated this in 1661, disseminating apocryphal writings to a wider audience. Hermas relates how the doctrine is communicated to him by an angel (disguised, as many later angels, as an old man in a white cloak):

3 *Hear now saith he, first* of FAITH, there are two SPIRITS with man, one of equity, and one of iniquity; *And I said to him,* how Lord shall I know that there are two SPIRITS with a man? *Hear saith he,* and understand; The spirit of righteousnesse is tender, gentle and bashfull, affable and quiet, when therefore it shall ascend into thine heart, immediately it speaketh with thee of right-eousnesse, of pardon, of charity, of piety; All these when they shall ascend into thine heart, know that the spirit of equity is with thee; to this GENIUS therefore, and to its works give thou credit.

4 Take now also the works of the Spirit of iniquity, first it is bitter, wrathful, and foolish, and its works are pernitious and overthrow the servants of God; when therefore these things shall ascend into thine heart, thou shalt understand from its works this to be the spirit of INIQUITY.

5 How Lord shall I understand? Hear quoth he, and understand, when wrath shall happen to thee or bitternesse, understand that to be IN THEE; After that the desire of many works, and of the daintiest meats, and of drunken-nesses, and the desirings of many strange things, and pride and much speaking, and ambition, and whatsoever things are like these; Thou therefore when thou shalt know its works, depart from them all, & believe it in nothing, because its works are evil, and do not agree to the servants of God.

6 Thou hast therefore the works of both the Spirits, understand now and believe the Genius, of Righteousnesse, because its TEACHING is good . . . [30]

The doctrine, which is developed in the Qur'ān (the good angel sits on the right shoulder, the evil on the left), became a commonplace in medieval theology, a literal belief as well as a means of exploring human motivation. The doctrine received qualified support from the earlier reformers, including Luther, Urbanus Rhegius, and Johannes

Rivius, plus some later writers.[31] In his *Institution*, however, Calvin dismissed it as uncertain, adding that 'not one Angell onely hath care of every one of us, but that they all by one consent doe watch for our safetie'. In his later commentary on Genesis he was more emphatic: 'they doe wickedly disgrace the goodness of God, whiche thinke everie one of us is defended by one Angel. And there is no doubt but y$^t$ the divel by this subtilty, hath gon about in some point to weken our faith.'[32] Gervase Babington placed a similar interpretation upon this passage in 1592; and the Westminster Assembly's *Annotations* agree in phrasing so careful that it may prevaricate: 'no Angel is restrained from a particular ministration to any of the elect; nor any of the elect so allotted to the custody of any Angel that he may not expect the protection of many'.[33] Belief in guardian angels thereby became firmly associated with popery. Willet was supported by Thomas Cartwright, William Fulke, and Christopher Love (who insisted that only the elect received any ministration from angels).[34]

Not all English Protestants agreed. Salkeld reported that Protestants were unsure about guardian angels, but he presented a great deal of evidence for the belief, from the Greek and Roman churches, which, he suggested, was enough to persuade some. The tenor of his summary suggests either a reluctance to admit his own faith, or a genuine uncertainty inclining towards accepting the doctrine.[35] The ancient nature of the belief was an argument in its favour. While Thomas Browne was sceptical of proofs based on Acts 12, he was nonetheless inclined to take it on trust because it was not the fabrication of the Church of Rome but as old as Pythagoras and Plato (philosophy and theology persuasively coincided).[36] Henry Lawrence approves the doctrine in a diffident fashion. He set a precedent for Robert Dingley's treatise and for others of widely differing theological positions later in the century.[37] In fact the doctrine of the guardian angel was sufficiently malleable to Protestant belief that it could be used to distinguish differences within Protestantism. Dingley ridicules the papist account of tutelary spirits: 'The Pontificians hold that each man hath two Angels allotted him by God, one to vex and punish him, the other to guard and comfort him: But this is absurd, God appoints not an evil Angel constantly to attend his Elect, and if Satan Depute him, the Elect Angel set by God will continually expel and vanquish him.'[38] Dingley nonetheless is a fervent advocate of the doctrine of protecting spirits *for the elect*. This distinction could be found in Bucanus' *Institutions*, which

supports guardian angels for the elect, while emphatically denying any
scriptural grounds for individual evil angels.[39] Lawrence too makes this
distinction: the reprobate do not have a guardian angel. Thus, the
doctrine has an additional value within Calvinist circles, despite Cal-
vin, of being conformable to the doctrine of predestination.[40] It was
not a remnant of popery, but had its own life in inter-Protestant
conflicts. It was, moreover, useful for poets: the pagan genius had
deep literary roots, invited prosopopoeia, enabled the externalization
and dramatization of hidden impulses, and set human internal conflict
into a heavenly context. In his 1648 poem *Prosopopoeia Britannica*,
George Wither's own guardian angel explains to him:

> A GENIUS, is an incorporeall creature,
> Consisting of an intellectuall nature;
> Which at the self-same time, a *being* had,
> With that, for whose *well-being* it was made.
> And, may be cal'd, that *Angell*, which designeth,
> Adviseth, moveth, draweth, and inclineth
> To happinesse; and, naturally restraineth
> From harme, that creature, whereto it pertaineth:
>     And, this am I to you.[41]

His genius inspires him, and gives him poetry.

Some Protestants reported conversations with or visions of their
guardian angels, sometimes summoned by magic. Guardians were not
the only angels sought by supplication or rituals, but they were
particular targets because of their relationship with the conversant,
and because they were immediately present. The interest in angelic
communication cut against the grain of the Protestant insistence that
the age of miracles and angelic apparitions was over.[42] Jean Bodin's
account of a friend who felt the presence of, and on one occasion saw,
his guardian angel was known in seventeenth-century Britain. Bodin
writes:

Every morning at three or four o'clock the spirit knocked at his door, and
sometime he rose, opening the door, and saw no one, and every morning the
spirit kept it up and if he did not rise, the spirit knocked again, and went on
waking him until he rose. Then he began to be afraid, thinking, as he said, that
this was some evil spirit. And he therefore went on praying to God, without
missing a single day, asking God to send him his good angel, and he often sang
the Psalms, almost all of which he knew by heart. Well, he has assured me that
the spirit has accompanied him ever since, giving him palpable signs: touching

him, for example, on the right ear, if he did something that was not good, and on the left ear, if he did well.[43]

The friend is now generally assumed to be Bodin himself. In his reflections on guardians, Henry More mentions both Bodin and Girolamo Cardano, who left accounts of his own experience of his guardian angel in *The Book of my Life*, of his father's conversation with angels in *On Subtlety*, and of the spirit world in general in *On Variety*.[44] There was a surge of interest in summoning and conversing with angels in the late Elizabethan period. Numerous manuscripts of ritual magic from the period survive (many of them copies of medieval manuscripts), and John Dee, Simon Forman, and Richard Napier left accounts of angelic conversations and the search for the name of their guardian (a cabbalistic interest).[45] Lilly's autobiography reveals a succession of angel summoners in the decades following Dee. Others who spoke with their guardians include Socrates (with his daimon), Athanasius Kircher (with Cosmiel), Tomasso Campanella (he thought they were guardians; they proved to be evil spirits), an anonymous Huguenot friend of Pierre Le Loier, and, later, Robert Browne.[46] The German mystic Jacob Boehme, contrary to the conventions of Protestant *ars moriendi*, saw his on his deathbed.[47] In 1663 John Heydon published the name of his guardian, Malhitiriel.[48] Reginald Scott, Dee and Forman's contemporary, was suspicious of interest in guardians and condemned curiosity into guardians and attempts to converse with the spirit world. Ironically a posthumous 1665 edition of his famously sceptical *Discoverie of Witchcraft* (1584) added materials directly contrary to his own views, including guidelines on conjuring '*the* Genius *or* Good Angel'. The magic makes a nonsense of the Pseudo-Dionysian hierarchies as well as of Scott's disbelief.[49] Perhaps this shift between the 1584 and 1665 editions reflects broader changes in the position of angels, including the loosening grip of the traditional systematization, and a broader willingness to use angel-doctrine in experimental and occult ways.

The second part of Willet's discussion of angelic ministry concerns angels and human prayers. The papists erroneously believe 'that the Angelles do offer up our prayers unto God'. The troublesome text is, again, from Revelation. Willet, true to form, brings Augustine to his defence, argues that the text denotes Christ, and that, in any case, 'If this place might be understood of Angels, that they have some ministerie about our prayers, it maketh nothing notwithstanding for popish invocation of Angels.' Protestants, he says, follow Scripture, which makes Christ the only mediator.[50] Willet's true concern is mediation; carrying prayers was a minor issue compared to prayers *to* angels, which Willet treats under a separate heading. However, there are exceptions: John Pordage thought it possible to communicate with the spirit world with prayer, and his disciples believed that their guardian angels carried their prayers up to another protecting angel, who then represented these prayers to the Father and Son.[51]

An 'appendix' to this discussion of guardian angels and prayers concerns whether angels or saints 'know our heartes'. Catholics believe, writes Willet, that angels can see true repentance within a sinner. They see through their own power of perception, as 'all things done in the worlde may be seene in God, as in a glasse' by the angels, an image used by Dante among others, which belief Willet labels a 'prophane speculation'. Protestants believe that the angels know only what God chooses to reveal to them: 'the spirite of God may reveale the secrets of the heart of man, not by giving them a generall gift them selves to looke into the heart, as into a glasse, but by revealing such thinges, when the Lord seeth it expedient'.[52] Protestant theologians did place much greater restrictions on angelic knowledge and perception, as appropriate to a doctrinal system in which humans and angels are isolated creatures, worshipping their maker directly. Protestants nonetheless continued to dispute angelic eyesight and knowledge through the seventeenth century. In times when understanding of human perception, and the nature of the material universe, were changing, such debate was a means of further probing the mysteries of Creation.

## The Worship and Invocation of Angels

Willet's third controversial question concerns the worship and especially the invocation of angels. He acknowledges here, without wishing to acknowledge the niceties of his enemies' theology, that Catholics distinguish between the adoration of God and the 'religious reverence, honour and adoration' of angels and saints. This echoes the distinction, drawn in the Council of Nicaea's decrees of 787, between *latria*, that worship due to God alone, and *dulia*, a reverence that could properly be paid to lesser creatures; a distinction that was subsequently complicated by *hyperdulia*, a special reverence for creatures with an extraordinary relationship with God.[53] Willet contends that Protestants revere angels, but all 'religious worship or service' is due only to God.[54] Again, the crux here lies in Revelation (19: 10 and 22: 9), where John falls down to worship an angel, and is rebuked by that angel; each side finds their own position in the text.[55] In practice the two positions can be mistaken for each other, as the distinctions are rooted in precise terminology.

The proximity between reverence and worship can be seen in Edward Leigh's *Annotations upon all the New Testament* (1650), where he paraphrases the angel's warning to John: 'thou owest not to mee religious but sociall worship'.[56] Wollebius states that it is admissible to adore saints (and therefore angels) when they appear to us, but not in a religious way.[57] Joseph Hall compares the distinction to that between praise and flattery.[58] And Henry Lawrence reminds his readers that angels help raise humans to God's ordinances, and 'therefore wee should love them and reverence them, therefore wee converse with them, and study to know them, and finde them out, even the least peeces & circumstances of them'. It is ambiguous whether the intended subject of the clause is God's ordinances or angels, and the matter is further confused by Lawrence's subsequent comparison of these dear objects to 'our *Elixurs*, and our Philosophers stone, turning all they touch into gold; therefore let us value the knowledge of them as things necessary for us, and which have a great influence upon our holy walking'.[59] Lawrence by no means intends to commend worship of angels, but in describing due praise he steers close to prayers and metaphors associated with the occult. Arise Evans, the Fifth Monarchist, appears to cross the line when he denies being 'popishly affected in worshipping of angels', on the grounds that while it is clearly wrong to worship men, 'the Holy Angels are of another nature, so that we cannot err in that worship we do unto them', and they do not reject worship; we should 'fall down flat before a Holy Angel' in case it is an Angel of the Presence.[60] Evans and Fifth Monarchists often had elastic readings of Revelation.

The secondary question concerns prayers directed to angels as intercessors. Catholics permit this practice, while Protestants believe 'That angels are not to be worshipped, nor invocated as mediatours, intercessors, or advocates, the scripture speaketh evidently.' Christ is our only intercessor, and God the true object of our worship.[61] Sixty years later Robert Dingley half-heartedly commended the thoroughness of Willet's *Synopsis Papismi*, and its rejection of adoration of guardians, while doubting the wisdom of denying the existence of guardians altogether.⁶² Protestants did universally reject praying to angels, though some drew finer distinctions. Luther suggested that it was appropriate to call on one's guardian *in extremis*, though not to pray or invoke angels; Calvin thought even this limited calling risked idolatry.⁶³

In the 1620s invocations to angels, and what constituted prayer and worship, emerged as a marker of difference between Protestant communities. The Arminian Richard Montagu was forced in 1624 to defend himself from an accusation that he had preached, and before the king, '*That there was no cause why every man might not turne himselfe unto his Angell keeper, and say, Holy Angell keeper, Pray for me.*' He argued against the Catholic practice of praying to saints and angels (and he was impeccably orthodox in stressing the distinction between the two) while maintaining the legitimacy of the doctrine of guardian angels and insisting that some form of conversation was permissible. Montagu rejects Catholic readings of Jacob's deathbed prayer to an angel (Gen. 48: 16), and claims that Jacob expresses a wish, and that the angel is Christ, but then backtracks: 'to suppose and grant Hee was an Angel, he could then be no other but his Guardian Angel . . . in this present question touching Invocation, the Case of Angels Guardians is peradventure different, much and many wayes, from the condition, and employments of them at large'. He acknowledges Calvin's rejection but argues that calling on guardians differs from calling on saints, because they are 'ever in *procinctu*, nigh at hand unto us, continually, and never abandoning us all our dayes'. The matter comes down to distance and the fact that our voices cannot carry to the spiritual ears of the saints in heaven. Montagu insists that belief is not an essential tenet of faith, though there are sufficient grounds for it, and so it should not 'bee taxed with point of Poperie or Superstition'.⁶⁴ In another work published the same year, however, he lists *rejecting* the doctrine as an error, and the prohibition of prayers to angels as another. Montagu was a fierce polemicist who knew when to conceal his own controversial doctrines. High Anglican policy seemed, from the 1610s onwards, but particularly under Laud, to be drifting towards Rome in services and doctrine and church decoration, and angels were one measure of this. In churches and funerary monuments angels began to reappear. William Austin joined Montagu in endeavouring to reincorporate them into worship; some churches sang the 'angelic hymn', the words of an angel at the Nativity; prayers were offered to angels; all of which gave rise to complaints and petitions by the godly in 1641–2.[65]

Protestants from other theological traditions held that various addresses to angels were legitimate. Some tried to speak with angels through ritual magic, though hostile commentators thought that only fallen angels would participate in these communications.[66] Some of these magicians and enthusiasts are discussed in the following two chapters. Richard Baxter thought that the case of John Pordage showed the danger of seeking out angels, but he also thought that the Protestant reaction against popery meant that people did not thank angels enough, and showed little sense 'of the great Benefits that we receive by Angels'.[67]

Under these three headings, then, Willet in fact describes eight distinct papist 'errors' or 'heresies': (i) the existence of a specific hierarchy of angels; (ii) that Michael is the prince of angels; (iii) the existence of angels assigned to churches or kingdoms; (iv) that individuals are assigned guardian angels; (v) that angels carry our prayers to God; (vi) that angels see into our hidden thoughts and feelings; (vii) that we can worship angels in a limited fashion; and (viii) that we can pray to angels as intercessors. He might have added a ninth doctrinal difference: the continuing appearance of angels to humans, sometimes bringing miracles or prophecies. Protestants declared that the age of miracles was over. Miracles and prophecies had ceased with the coming of Christ and the gospel, when the conviction of the spirit took priority over external performance and proofs. Though Augustine had declared as much, this point constituted a distinction from Roman Catholic doctrine, and angels were intricately associated with both miracles and prophecies. When miracles ceased, so did angelic apparitions. Angels bring humans prophecies or prophetic books, and they prepare humans to receive the spirit of prophecy (angels are, metaphorically, the spirit of prophecy).[68] Many Protestants did, however, believe that both miracles and prophecies could still occur in principle, and that under extraordinary circumstances God would raise them.[69] The doctrine divided Catholics and Protestants, but also formed a frontier of debate within Protestantism.

## Angelology: A Catechism

In 1647 John Trapp, in a brief essay of commonplaces on angels within his voluminous commentary on the Johannine epistles, warned: 'if the

*Theology* for Angels were written, we should need another Bible: the creation and government of Angels containing as great variety of matter, as doth the religion of mankinde'.[70] It is necessary here to move away from drawing distinctions between modes of writing, historical periods, and inter- and intra-confessional conflicts, and instead offer a more synthetic survey of widely held beliefs and knowledge. To avoid biblical proportions, they are presented here in an undifferentiated manner, over-looking discontinuities, textures of writing, and confessional conflict; some of the topics are developed more fully later in this book.

## When Were Angels Created?

On the first day of Creation: Augustine interpreted the 'Heavens' in Genesis 1: 1 (also known as the empyrean heaven, to distinguish it from the visible heavens of the terrestrial universe) to include the angels; Lombard, Aquinas, and most Protestants agreed. A few pre-ferred the fourth day, when the 'visible heavens' were created. Almost everyone in the early modern period thought that angels were made within the material creation described in Genesis. Calvin insisted that it was culpable curiosity to ask the question, though he also disliked this interpretation of Genesis 1: 1 on the grounds that that the empyr-ean heaven was God's dwelling place and therefore already existed.[71] Salkeld, though he himself opted for the first day, listed the many Church Fathers who thought that angels preceded the corporeal world, including Origen, Gregory, Chrysostom, Ambrose, Jerome. Milton also inclined to this account.[72]

The Westminster *Annotations* reminded its reader that the date lay among *adiaphora*. Though the annotations upon Genesis 1: 1 and Job 38: 7 indicate disagreement among the annotators, the (unusually) long note concluding Genesis 1 was clear:

In all this History of the Creation, there is no mention of the creation of Angels; whence some have supposed them to be eternal; but against that may be alleadged, Col. 1. 16, 17. Some, that though they had a beginning, yet it was long before the Creation recorded in this Chapter; but in the same place of the Apostle, *all things in heaven and in earth, visible and invisible*, are wrapped up in one original, and that distinguished from the eternal duration of the Creator, *who was before all things, and by whom all things consist*; and this according to the judgement of the soundest Divines in all ages. For the time of their making, this is certain, they were made before man fell; but on what day, whether the first day with the highest heaven, (as some conceive ...) when the Firmament was made, by which they understand all the three Heavens, whereof one is the habitation of Angels; or the fourth day, when some hold, that as the visible heavens were garnished with stars, so the invisible were furnished with Angels; which might be the more probable, but that it seems the Angels were made before the stars; for *the sons of God*, by which are meant the Angels, are said to shout for joy at the first appearing of the morning stars, Job 38. 7. In this diversity of opinions for the time of the creation, we conceive that in the six dayes space, and before the last day, there is no errour of danger which way soever we take it.

This left the question of *why* Moses did not mention their creation. The annotators continued:

If it be asked why their creation was not more punctually expressed, the answer may be, not as commonly it is, that the Jews were too dull to be informed of spiritual beings, for the mystery of the Trinity is divers times insinuated in this Book of *Genesis*, and Cherubims are mentioned, Chap. 3. 24. and afterwards we read of Angels, Gen. 19.1, 15. & Chap. 28.12. & 32.1. but because this first History was purposely and principally for information concerning the visible world, the invisible, whereof we know but in part, being reserved for the knowledge of a better life, 1 Cor. 13. 9.[73]

The two most common explanations were that Genesis is exclusively concerned with material creation; and that Moses was speaking down to the Jews, and did not mention them lest it tempt the Jews idolatrously to worship angels. A third proposed reason was that the Jews would simply not understand the nature of angels, and so he omitted them.[74] Willet's answer merits quotation at length:

For the first: 1. Moses neither passed over the creation of angels in silence, for feare least the Israelites should have committed idolatrie in worshipping of them, as Chrisostome, and Theodoret thinke: for the Israelites could not be ignorant that the angels had diverse times appeared to their fathers the Patriarkes, and so could not be ignorant of them. 2. Neither are they omitted, because Moses onely treateth of those things, which had their beginning with this materiall world, but the angels were created long before the visible world, as Basil and Damascene thinke, for it shall even now appeare, that this is a false supposition, that the angels were created so long before. 3. Neither yet is the creation of the angels comprehended under the making of heaven and the lights, as Augustine & Beda thinke, for this were to leave the literall sense which is to be followed in the historie of the creation. 4. But the onely reason is this, because Moses applieth himself to the simple capacity of the people, and describeth onely the creation of visible and sensible things, leaving to speake of the spirituall, which they could not understand: and this seemeth to be Hieroms opinion, epist. 1 39. Ad Cyprian.

Another explanation was that Jews or Christians might be led to suspect that such powerful beings had a hand in Creation.[75] John Lightfoot, biblical scholar, Hebraist, and member of the Westminster Assembly, writes:

For if their day of their Creation (which was in most likelihood the first) had beene named, wicked men would have bene ready to have taken them for actors in this worke, which were onely spectators. Therefore as God hides *Moses* after his death, so *Moses* hides the Creation of them, lest they should be deified, and the honour due to the Creator given to the creature.[76]

Behind this lay the spectre of the heresy of Simon Magus, according to whom angels created the world.[77] Calvin proposes a fifth alternative: God spoke on a need-to-know basis. John White thought so: 'their creation be not described, or pointed at in particular, as not so needful to be known by us, whom it concerns most, to understand the state and conditions of those visible things, with which we have most to do'.[78]

## How Do Angels Know Things, and How Much Do They Know?

There are two kinds of answer to this question. The knowledge of angels is static: once the angels had chosen to stand, their knowledge was fixed (the knowledge of the fallen angels was diminished). Or the knowledge of angels changes through experience. Both answers can be further subdivided into those who explore the limitations of angelic knowledge, and those who stress their near-omniscience.

Salkeld follows Aquinas in his Aristotelian reasoning: angels have forms and species infused in their consciousness at creation. They do not need to learn through experience. Their knowledge is purely intellectual (hence they are called 'minds' or 'intelligences'). They have 'no imagination'. This does not mean that angels cannot conjecture, but it does mean that this knowledge is fixed according to their hierarchies. Cherubim, Principalities, and Powers were associated with knowledge, and hence, according to Aquinas, it was these who fell.[79] John Colet's treatise summarizing Dionysius suggests that love is superior to knowledge; hence in the higher orders knowledge proceeds from love, and in the lower, love proceeds from knowledge.[80]

Lawrence presents a different, less Aristotelian account. There are four grounds of angelic knowledge: (i) natural; (ii) revelation; (iii) experience; (iv) supernatural. Having no senses, angels know by species infused into them, but they also know by reasoning, which they perform with speed and accuracy beyond human comprehension. Thus, their mode of knowing is more like humans' than Aquinas and Salkeld suggest. They know everything about someone committed to their charge, though not about others, and so they are *almost* all-knowing.[81] Wollebius, specifically discussing the more limited knowledge of fallen angels, includes another: astrology.[82] The suggestion that angels know through observation of the position and movements of the stars derives from the special relationship angels have with the spheres, and their powers of observation. Not all scriptural commentators allow the validity of astrology (Milton did). Wollebius may include it only as a compensation for the *impairment* of natural knowledge among fallen angels.

Some commentators emphasize the superiority of angelic knowledge to human, exploring the latter through the former.[83] Comenius thought their knowledge more sublime than human, '1 because of the clearnesse of their understanding, which nothing obumbrates. 2 by reason of their power to penetrate any whither, and see things plainly. 3 because of their long experience for so many ages'. He adds: 'and yet they are not omniscient'.[84] Roman Catholic writers describe guardian angels seeing into the minds of their charges, and seeing through God as if a giant mirror. Protestants were emphatic that angels did not see into humans' thoughts. They were more likely to admit the possibility of 'experimentall' knowledge in angels (distinguished from natural and supernatural).[85] Regarded as 'creatures', finite, independent beings, angels are more likely to be seen as limited in power and resources. Thus, John Gumbleden writes: 'how comes the *Angel* here to understand that? surely, not by any *naturall knowledge* of his own; no, for, *Angels* are creatures; and Creatures (how *eminent* soever) know no more of the *secret mind* of God, then what is *revealed immediately* unto them by the mouth of God'. Angels, like humans, are students of some divine mysteries.[86] Milton writes: 'The good angels do not look into all the secret things of God, as the Papists pretend; some things indeed they know by revelation, and others by means of the excellent intelligence with which they are gifted [*per eminentem quondam ratiocinationem*]; there is much, however, of which they are ignorant.'[87] Through insight and ratiocination angels (and devils) hypothesize about human thoughts and conjecture the future.[88] For Cornelius Burgess, 'most divines speake confusedly' on angelic knowledge, some identifying threefold, some fourfold knowledge (i.e. natural, supernatural, revelation, experimental). He nonetheless claims that when they were first created, their knowledge was exclusively natural, and that after the angelic fall good angels acquired other forms. However, he then takes a step back: 'now if any desire to know <b.t> by wt means they know, whether by their essence as god doth or by species or ideas abstracted from things as wee do, is not much material or profitable & more philosophical then Theological'.[89]

## Do Angels Have Bodies?

Aquinas, synthesizing theology with Aristotelian natural philosophy, stated that angels were incorporeal and non-material. Until the seventeenth century most writers tacitly agreed with him. Angels did not have bodies, though they sometimes adopted bodies of air in order to appear to and communicate with humans. Angels are not material, though, for the sake of logical consistency, Aquinas states that they have some form of substance—ethereal, fiery, or purely intelligential—that transcends human understanding, and so, according to how humans understand things, they are not material.[90] Sixteenth-century reformers usually reiterated that angels were 'spiritual beings'. For Calvin these issues were irrelevant. Peter Martyr writes that the 'substance and nature' of spirits 'cannot be expressed'.[91] Divergent approaches developed in the seventeenth century in response to shifts in natural philosophy. Angelic corporeality was discussed in relation to visibility and to eating. Having no bodies, angels have no need to eat. Unlike humans, they are preserved 'by immediate Influence' from God.[92] The tradition of the 'Food of Angels' was in most exegesis a metaphor, though the description of Manna in Exodus 16: 31 led some spiritual enthusiasts and alchemists to seek the actual substance through purification and communion with spirits. The corporeality and substance of angels are discussed below.[93]

## How Do Spirits Speak to and Interact with Humans?

To be seen by humans angels are given temporary bodies by God or condense bodies of air in order to create a visual simulacrum. These bodies do not deceive humans as they represent the true nature of the angels. In order to communicate, angels either speak directly to human

minds, *impressing* or *imprinting* their thoughts, while moving the virtual
body to mimic speaking, *or* they themselves speak audibly while
manipulating the virtual body, *or* they speak using the organs of the
virtual body to generate the sound. Reflections on these topics appear
throughout commentaries on Genesis as well as discussions in system-
atic theology.

When angels speak to each other, they use hardware-free instant
messaging:

Properly speech belongs not to any thing but to man, who onely hath the
instruments of speech, yet there is an internall and mental speech in spirits,
which is nothing but the reasoning and discoursing of the minde; and this
speech is imperfect in respect of man; for none understands what is in the
minde of man but himselfe; in Angels it is more perfect, for they understand
one another by this mentall speech; but in God it is most perfect, for after an
incomprehensible manner, he speakes to himselfe, and the three persons in the
glorious Trinity doe understand one another after that manner which we
cannot conceive, much lesse expresse. Then as our minds internally and
spiritually can speake to God although our tongues do not moove, so can
the Angels speake to one another, so can God both to them and us.[94]

Angels can see into each others' thoughts, while human bodies ob-
struct communication. Aquinas suggests that their exchanges involve
only the desire for, and the conveyance of, enlightenment, which does
not imply the need for language in inter-angelic conversation, though
when they speak to humans they have a full range of tongues. Others
suggest that they speak in Hebrew, the uncorrupted language of
Paradise. Assumed bodies and the tongues of angels are discussed in
Chapter 12.[95]

## Do Angels Have Senses?

According to Aquinas, angels do not have senses. How do they hear?
Mentally: 'as the sense is moved by a sensible object, so the intellect is
moved by an intelligible object; hence as the sense is stimulated by
some sign of a sensory kind, so too the angel's mind can be aroused to
attention through some power of a mental kind'.[96] This is what some
commentators refer to as 'inward senses' among men.[97] Those who
assign to angels substantiality, among them Milton, find some more
material equivalent of the senses: senses and bodies are connected, and
are discussed together below. Comenius associates angelic senses with

emotions, and concludes, 'they are not unlike to our spirit which perceiveth by organs'.[98]

## Do Angels Have Freewill?

Early Christian communities developed stories of the fall of angels. Explanations of the existence of evil exploited angelic freewill to blame Satan for his fall and for the existence of evil in the world. Medieval commentators agreed that angels had freewill; the problem for them was then explaining why once angels had fallen they were unable to redeem themselves, and why all angels who did not initially fall managed to remain unfallen (Origen had argued that backsliding was possible for all). Essential to these discussions was Augustine's argument that angels exercised their freewill with the assistance of grace. This helped clear God of responsibility for sin, but in so doing it risked impairing the exercise of freewill, especially among the fallen angels denied grace. Peter Lombard developed an elegant solution to this conundrum. Angels were perfect in innocence before their fall. Some angels fell, those assisted by grace did not, in both cases expressing their freewill. Those that turned to God (*conversio*) were granted grace that enabled them to develop wisdom, merit, and therefore glorification. Those who turned from God (*aversio*) were confirmed in envy and hatred. Both retain freewill, but in order to will towards good, the fallen angels would need the grace that had been withdrawn from them. As God chooses not to change things, they cannot reform. Meanwhile, the good angels are capable of improving, and will not fall because of their further realization of wisdom and glory.[99]

Aquinas reiterates much of this account, yet also diverges from it. Though constitutive of intellect, freewill exists in gradations corresponding to angelic hierarchies: 'In the higher angels free will exists more nobly than in the lower, as does the power of intelligent judgement.' He repeats Lombard's account of merited bliss and glory, but places *conversio* and *aversio* in the first act of each angel: they perform an act either of charity or of sin. Once they have chosen charity, they cannot turn back. In their superior natures this revelation of bliss freezes their state, and to choose to act against true order would be to turn against their capacity for freedom, which is a logical impossibility. Hence, the unfallen angels, unlike humans, cannot backslide. 'Freedom of choice, then, is greater in the angels who cannot sin than in us who can.' Yet this greater freedom leads to a single, unalterable consequence. The same is true for the fallen angels, for, unlike humans, 'When an angel chooses freely he cannot go back on his choice once it is made.' Angels have freewill, but only actually use it once, and even then there seems to be a precedent cause.[100]

Among Protestants there is a greater variety of positions, not least because they explore the doctrine of predestination in relation to angels, linking human and angelic freewill. In some hands, where the subject is less delicately treated than in Lombard's or Aquinas', angels do not seem to have freewill. Willet, for example, discusses angelic freewill alongside human, and states that God chose not to give grace to Adam to prevent transgression just as he chose not to give it to the angels. Yet he gave it to *some* of the angels, and in a predestinarian system this gift of grace to the elect that prevents the otherwise unavoidable consequences of freewill does not look like freewill at all.[101] Salkeld says something very similar: he accepts the Thomistic account, and adds that unfallen angels are so ravished by the sight of God that they are irresistibly attracted to good.[102] Freewill is nonetheless necessary as a means of explaining the existence of evil. Joseph Hall agrees that angels have freewill, but crosses Aquinas when he declares that creatures can choose against the primary order: angels 'suffered their will to dwell in an end of their own; and by this means did put themselves into the place of God'.[103] Henry More argues that astrology must be false because it disallows the freewill of men and angels.[104]

Comparisons between human and angelic freewill generate problems. Wollebius restates a common Protestant view, but brings a dilemma into focus:

Predestination is either of Angels, or of men.
    The Predestination of Angels is that, by which God appointed to save eternally some of them in their first happiness, and that in Christ their head: but to leave others to themselves, and to punish them eternally for deserting their station voluntarily; & this for the manifestation of the glory of his grace & justice.
    The Predestination of men is that by which God appointed, out of the race of mankinde created to his Image, but falling into sin voluntarily, to save some through Christ eternally, but others being left to themselves in their own misery, to damn eternally; and that for the manifestation of the glory of his mercy and Justice.[105]

Wollebius is a sublapsarian: humans fall, and subsequently God offers grace and redeems them. Predestination follows sin. However, in accepting Aquinas' and Lombard's account of grace assigned to some angels, Wollebius implicitly adopts a supralapsarian account in relation to angels. They are predestined *before* their fall. Freewill looks even more tenuous. Free angels are consistent while free humans are not; this is evident to, though not directly discussed by any of, these writers. Humans experience freewill in their actions, which are a mixture of good and bad, whether they are elect or reprobate. Elect angels, however, can only do good, and fallen angels can only do evil. It is not simply that the ends are foregone, but the means are uniform with the ends. The Protestant version of angelic freewill looks even less free than the Scholastic view.

After this fast footwork it is a relief to read Robert Boyle stating that angels do not have freewill; and Lawrence, whose Calvinism allows him to admit that the fallen angels 'have not the liberty of acting, which the good Angells have'; and the anonymous Calvinist preacher who describes angels as instruments that are 'ordered and directed by a higher cause'.[106] Or Milton, who rejects predestination and in prose avoids the question:

Some are of the opinion that the good angels are now upheld, not so much by their own strength, as by the grace of God. . . . It seems, however, more agreeable to reason, to suppose that the good angels are upheld by their own strength no less than man himself was before his fall; that they are called 'elect,' in the sense of beloved, or excellent . . .[107]

## Why Did the Angels Fall?

The angels fell through pride or envy or lust.[108] Explanations developed through narrative elaborations on Scripture and pseudepigrapha. The story of a fall through pride, antedating the creation of the world, came from Origen via Augustine, based on interpretations of Isaiah 14: 12–15:[109]

How art thou fallen from heaven, O Lucifer, son of the morning! *how* art thou cut down to the ground, which didst weaken the nations!
    For thou hast said in thine heart, I will ascend into heaven, I will exalt my throne above the stars of God: I will sit also upon the mount of the congregation, in the sides of the north:
    I will ascend above the heights of the clouds; I will be like the most High.
    Yet thou shalt be brought down to hell, to the sides of the pit.

St Jerome equated this Lucifer with Satan, the Hebrew common noun for 'adversary'. Once Satan had hypostasized into the embodiment of evil (the Satan rather than a satan), a story became clear. An angel rebelled against his maker through pride, and was punished in the pit. Justin Martyr had already identified this Satan with the serpent who tempted Adam and Eve. Reading the Bible with these identifications in place, a story emerged of the fall of the angels, who subsequently assisted humankind's fall.[110] Other passages in Scripture could be read in the light of this story. The inferred narrative became the source of religious truth.

Aquinas argued that angels only sin by pride and envy (he is rejecting Augustine, who includes carnality in this list). The Devil's sin was not submitting to God, and instead desiring to exceed the limits of his own nature and be like God, thinking he could claim this by justice and through force. This desire of godlikeness is ambiguously pride and/or envy.[111] In Heywood's poetic narrative of the war in heaven pride is Lucifer's sin, though it accompanies other sins, including envy:

> In this puft Insolence and timp'anous Pride,
> He many Angels drew unto his side,
> (Swell'd with the like thoughts.) Joyntly these prepare
> To raise in Heav'n a most seditious Warre.
> He will be the *Trines* Equall, and maintaine,
> Over the Hierarchies (at least) to raigne.[112]

We might hear an echo of this in the beginning of *Paradise Lost*:

> his pride
> Had cast him out from heaven, with all his host
> Of rebel angels, by whose aid aspiring
> To set himself in glory above his peers,
> He trusted to have equalled the most high . . .    (*PL* 1. 36–40)

Salkeld puzzled over Augustine's account, because he thought it unlikely that angels should aspire to be equal to God, but he deduced the following: 'that the particular pride of the Angels consisted, in that they being exalted with the contemplation of their beautie and perfection, they would be exempt from all service, command, and subjection unto their Creator'. They desired therefore to be subject to none in actual service and obedience, and their first sin was this pride.[113] In this reading, which grows out of Aquinas, pride and envy of God are much the same thing. Wollebius will not commit himself on the sin of the angels, though he states that it must have been committed *with* pride.[114]

Richard Hooker describes the angels' sin with compelling logic and prose, independent of these scriptural elaborations: the sinning angels must have thought of something other than God, and it could not have been anything below them, which would have been evidently subordinate to God.

It seemeth therefore that there was no other way for Angels to sinne, but by reflex of their understanding upon themselves; when being held with admiration of their owne sublimitie and honor, the memorie of their subordination unto God and their dependencie on him was drowned in this conceipt; whereupon their adoration, love, and imitation of God, could not choose but be also interrupted. The fall of Angels therefore was pride.[115]

William Ames also thought that 'it is most like' that their first sin 'was pride' (*superbiam*); and Willet, that it was 'pride, in desiring to be like unto God'.[116]

In most accounts, the sin of pride is associated with envy of God. In another exegetical tradition, envy of humankind is the primal angelic sin. In the fourth-century pseudepigraphal text *Vita Adae et Evae*, Satan himself speaks and gives his own motivation for his fall. He merits quoting:

The devil replied, 'Adam, what dost thou tell me? It is for thy sake that I have been hurled from that place. When thou wast formed[,] I was hurled out of the presence of God and banished from the company of the angels. When God blew into thee the breath of life and thy face and likeness was made in the image of God, Michael also brought thee and made (us) worship thee in the sight of God; and God the Lord spake: Here is Adam. I have made thee in our image and likeness.'

And Michael went out and called all the angels saying: 'Worship the image of God as the Lord God hath commanded.' And Michael himself worshipped first; then he called me and said: 'Worship the image of God the Lord.' And I answered, 'I have no (need) to worship Adam.' And since Michael kept urging me to worship, I said to him, 'Why dost thou urge me? I will not worship an inferior and younger being (than I). I am his senior in the Creation, before he was made was I already made. It is his duty to worship me.'

When the angels, who were under me, heard this, they refused to worship him. And Michael saith, 'Worship the image of God, but if thou wilt not worship him, the Lord God will be wrath with thee.' And I said, 'If He be wrath with me, I will set my seat above the stars of heaven and will be like the Highest.

And God the Lord was wrath with me and banished me and my angels from our glory; and on thy account were we expelled from our abodes into this world and hurled on the earth. And straightway we were overcome with grief, since we had been spoiled of so great glory. And we were grieved when we saw thee in such joy and luxury. And with guile I cheated thy wife and caused thee to be expelled through her (doing) from thy joy and luxury, as I have been driven out of my glory.[']'[117]

This story requires that the angelic fall took place *after* the creation of man, on the sixth day or later, but before the human fall. It was not widely held in seventeenth-century Britain, but among those who espoused it was the notable Hebraist John Lightfoot:

Now fell the Angels: for they seeing the honour and happinesse in which man was created and set, and the Lord giving the Angels themselves a charge concerning him to keep him in his wayes, and to be ministring spirits to him for his good; some of them spited this his honour and happinesse, and dispised this their charge and ingagement, and so through pride against the command of God, and for envie at the felicity of man, they fell.[118]

The story makes Satan a more complex figure. The poet Thomas Peyton also narrated it this way, telling how Lucifer 'thought himselfe to equall God on high, | Envies [humankind's] fortune', and seduces them.[119]

    The third main tradition was the story of the watcher angels who lusted after human women and thereby fell, a story based on Genesis 6: 1–4 and the book of Enoch. This interpretation depends upon the identification of the 'sons of God' (*bene ha'elohim*) with angels (the Septuagint translates this as *aggeloi*):

And it came to pass, when men began to multiply on the face of the earth, and daughters were born unto them,
    That the sons of God saw the daughters of men that they were fair; and they took them wives of all which they chose. . . .
    There were giants in the earth in those days; and also after that, when the sons of God came in unto the daughters of men, and they bare children to them, the same became mighty men which were of old, men of renown.

These giants, or *nephilim*, were the offspring of this illicit union between angels and women. The story helps explain human evil in the form of these giants. This text, supported by the epistle of Jude and 2 Peter, was in turn elaborated in the book of Enoch, Jubilees, the pseudepigraphal Testament of Ruben, and in exegesis, to provide a full-blown account of the fall in which angels are driven by lust for women. While Enoch was not available in early modern Europe, the tradition was extant in other texts and was widely known.[120]

The Enoch story was incompatible with Satan's involvement in the expulsion from Eden, and with the notion that angels were incorporeal spirits, and for these and other reasons it was rejected in most Scholastic and reformed theology.[121] Instead, most commentators glossed 'sons of God' as the children of the godly or the sons of Seth, and the daughters of men as wicked women or the descendants of Cain; though they acknowledged that elsewhere in Scripture 'sons of God' did indeed indicate angels. The giants were men 'mightier then the usuall sort'.[122] In *Paradise Lost* Milton identifies the sons of God as godly men, though in *Paradise Regained* Satan tells Belial the Enoch story.[123] Willet denounced the watcher angel mythology, associating it with Michael Psellus' unorthodox belief that angels had bodies and reproduced.[124] The tradition was frequently acknowledged, though usually to be dismissed.

Others devised more detailed accounts of the angelic rebellion. The Protestant theologian Jerome Zanchius, for example, offered a variant of the pride story, writing that the angels rebelled when the Incarnation was, perhaps incompletely, revealed to them.[125] The Incarnation distinguishes man, as Christ takes on human rather than angelic form (some Protestants used this to argue that humans were above angels in dignity). Resenting this slight to their status, some angels refused to acknowledge Christ; this is a variation of the *Vita Adae et Evae* story, in which envy of humans prompts sin. This version had some circulation in seventeenth-century Britain. John Bayly agreed that their sin was pride, through which they refused 'to adore the man *Christ Jesus*, when that decree of the *Incarnation* was divulged, *And let all the Angells of God adore him*'.[126] Henry Lawrence also states something much like this: the angels' sin was opposition to Christ being made man, 'that all standing, all restauration was to be by God man, in which the Angelicall nature was left out'.[127] Milton's Satan rebels out of resentment at the Son's promotion: though drawing on Zanchius and Lawrence, this is peculiar to Milton and pertains to his Arianism.

Many Protestants simply refused to resolve the question of the angels' first sin, which not only depended upon elaborate interpretation of Scripture or the authority of pseudepigrapha, and was unnecessary to salvation, but also relied on a curiosity into narrative patterns. Thus Joseph Hall: 'What were the particular grounds of their detection and ruine, what was their first sin, it is neither needfull, not possible to know'. Hall also recriminated the ancients for making Lucifer into a devil, beyond what the texts would bear.[128]

## Are Angels Differentiated in Sex and Do they Reproduce?

The giants of Genesis prompt these questions, to both of which the answer is a clear negative. A distressed Adam asks in *Paradise Lost*: 'why did God . . . not fill the world at once | With men as angels without feminine' (10. 892–3). The number of angels is fixed, and they are created and not begotten. They are spirits, and spirits do not multiply. As one commonplace-book compiler noted, 'the Angell nature is not nor can be multiplyed by propagation'.[129] Ross infers that angels cannot feel lust, because they have no bodies, and cannot beget, 'for they have no seede fit for procreation, because they feede not; for seede is a part of our foode. Againe, if they could procreate children, they should be distinguished in male and female; for both these must concurre in procreation.'[130] After the twelfth and thirteenth centuries angels were consistently represented as androgynous in church decorations.[131] White noted that angels had sometimes resembled young men with wings 'to note their incorruptible nature and agility in service'.[132]

Medieval theologians imaginatively described how incubi and suc-cubi could *appear* to reproduce with human witches by using virtual bodies to transport human seed. These explanations assumed that spirits were sexless and disembodied.[133] There was, however, an occult interest in angelic reproduction and seed. Heywood had read some-where that 'Rabbi *Avot Nathan* a learned Jew, affirmeth, That Spirits have three things in common with men, namely Procreation, Food, and Death.'[134] The said text only became available in Latin in 1654, and it is unlikely that Heywood found a Hebrew copy.[135] Those who search could find the grotesque and prurient writings, or reports of them, by Michael Psellus. To Agrippa the *nephilim* of Genesis were strong and mighty men 'procreated from the secret seed of the super-iors, whom they think were begotten by the mixture of Gods or Angels with men'. After various classical examples of interspecies miscegenation he notes that 'more over *Psellus* is the Author, that Spirits sometimes cast forth seed, from the which certain little creatures arise'.[136] The orthodox answer was, however, negative.

## Do Angels Have Names?

The names given to angels in Scripture—seraphim, cherubim, arch-angels—were usually understood by Protestants, following Augustine,

to be names of offices. They are called 'angels' because they are
messengers; 'shining stars', because of their pure shining nature; 'god'
because of their dignity and power; 'watchers' because of their sleep-
less vigilance; and so on.[137] They are a 'host', a common scriptural term
that emphasizes their numerousness and orderly character. Even
Calvin elaborated upon the metaphoric implications of these descrip-
tors: he writes, 'They are named armies, because they doe like a Gard
environ their Prince, and doe adorne and set foorth the honorable
shew of his majestie, and like souldiers they are always attending upon
the ensigne of their Captaine, and are ever so prepared and in readiness
to doe his commandements.'[138] Milton's heaven and his angels appear
at times to be organized along military lines.[139] Meric Casaubon
complained of fantastical books in which castles were built in the air,
and 'the heavens battered with great guns'; Milton would be very
culpable here.[140] However, far from being heterodox, this picks out
and elaborates a prevalent theme in theology: as ministering spirits they
resemble an army, and like an army they pitch their tents in their
watchfulness. Hence, 'they rejoice at our conversion, are Ministring
Spirits for our good, pitch their tents about us'.[141] They are all called
*mal'ach* and *aggelos*, and hence angels, because they are messengers.
Colet writes: 'Although the lowest spirits are, by a special name, called
Angels, yet inasmuch as their offices can be discharged by all the higher
ones (since a higher power can do all that a lower can) the names of the
lower are suitable to the higher, though those of the higher are by no
means so for the lower.'[142] The names are only upwardly mobile. For
Heywood: 'The name of Angell is a word of Office, not of nature,' and
'they are then onely to be stiled Angels, when any message is delivered
them to be published abroad'. '*Arch-Angeli*' are 'Cheife Messengers.
And therefore they are character'd by particular names, as *Michael,
Gabriel, Raphael, &c.*'[143] Individual names, according to Gumbleden,
are imposed only when they undertake '*extraordinary* business'.[144]

   Scripture gives few 'extraordinary' names to angels. The canonical
books provide only Michael and Gabriel. Uriel appears in the apoc-
ryphal 2 Esdras, and in the apocryphal book of Tobit, Raphael is named;
these are both second-century BCE texts, and the names are embedded in
other, pre-Christian religious writings. Uriel, who figures prominently
with these more famous three in *Paradise Lost*, was thought to be one of
the seven Angels of the Presence, discussed below.[145] Some would add
Lucifer to this list.[146] Many other names appear in Hebrew writings,

especially the Zohar, and in Midrash. Seventy angels' names were commonly borrowed from *The Book of the Angel Raziel*. According to the fifteenth-century Hebrew *Sefer ha-Heshek*, Metatron, who appears in the Talmud and in pseudepigrapha, and is in some Midrashim the greatest of the angels, has seventy-six various names. Metatron is sometimes identified with Michael or the prophet Enoch. Robert Gell refers to Metatron in the feminine, and associates her with Michael and Christ.[147] More angels are named in Enoch and in the Testament of Solomon, among Christian Gnostics and Church Fathers, including Gregory, and in Pseudo-Dionysius.[148] Names were adopted and multiplied in Christian cabbalistic traditions, which interested early modern occult writers. Robert Fludd, for example, gives the names of the angels who rule each of the nine orders, beginning with Metatron, who governs the seraphim, through Zophiel, Zabkiel, Zadkiel, Samael, Michael, Anael, and Raphael, down to Gabriel, who governs the angels. Agrippa provides tables for calculating the names of the seventy-two angels. Gematria, a cabbalistic method of numerically interpreting the Torah, gave power to these names. Later ritual magic ascribed special potency to particular names.[149] Perhaps both ultimately derived from the Zoroastrian belief that to escape from this world by passing through the spheres one had to recite the names of the angels that governed those spheres. John Aubrey describes the 'Berill' or showstone of a Norfolk minister, who, notwithstanding his vocation, called and conversed with angels in it, which had the names Michael, Gabriel, Raphael, and Uriel inscribed around it. Other contemporary astrologers summoned these same angels: perhaps their origins in Scripture provided them with a veneer of religious orthodoxy as well as power.[150] This occult tradition fascinated Heywood, who names the angels governing the world according to the regions of the zodiac: Raphael, Gabriel, Chamuel, Michael, Adahiel, Haniel, Zaphiel, Malthidiel, Corona, Varchiel, and many more. Belatedly he adds:

> But since of these the Scriptures make no mention,
> Far be it that the least of mine intention
> Should be to create Angels.[151]

Most orthodox commentators resisted the urge to investigate names. In Genesis 32: 29, after Jacob wrestles with an angel, he asks its name, and is rebuked. This was understood as a general warning. The Westminster annotators infer that the angel will not serve Jacob's curiosity. While Gabriel identifies himself to Zacharias (Luke 1: 19, 26), and 'the Angel of the Covenant, Christ Jesus, had also a name before his Incarnation ... where he is named *Michael*', it is not known 'whether all the Angels have particular names, (which may be so if God please, for he may call both Angels, and Starres by their names, Psal. 147. 4. in a literal sense)'.[152] Names were given to the angels collectively, reflecting office, and individually, though these names were not revealed, hence their power as occult knowledge.[153]

Why do God's functionaries need names? While Michael is a warrior, and Raphael a healer, and their names are used to identify their attributes, the other angels of Scripture, and of exegesis, are without personality or individuality. Hobbes altogether denied that Old Testament angels were real beings.[154] For most commentators the undistinguished mass of angels were nonetheless individuals. The reasoning came from Aquinas, who wrote that each species in the material world is constituted by its form and its matter; in the immaterial world, however, 'each being of and by itself constitutes and occupies a distinct degree in the scale of being', so each angel is a species unto itself.[155] The English Catholic priest Matthew Kellison, in a treatise on ecclesiastical hierarchy that commences with the premiss of angelic hierarchies, puts it succinctly: 'the Angelles are so different in nature and perfection that there are not twoe of one sort and kind (as there are of men and other creatures) but that everie one is distinguished in nature and office from everie one, even from the highest to the lowest'.[156] This uniqueness is double-edged: they are individuals, but, lacking the shared characteristics of a species, they also lack the elements of social and intellectual differentiation within a community that would give them a quality approximating a human personality. They are so entirely dividuated that they seem homogeneous.

Angels have personal names, though they may not matter a great deal except to ritual magicians and Gnostics, but seldom have personality. Angels do not need to call each other by name as their communication is direct and soundless. John Blenkow preached in 1639, 'that they have names in Heaven, may seeme improbable, in this respect, that whilest they were on Earth, they should have names, in regard of the weake capacity of humane Nature, who cannot otherwise or well distinguish things but by their names'.[157] Names, then, are a consequence of accommodation, fitted for human understanding, and not a property of heaven. Nonetheless, humans use names to understand the nature of heaven, seeking to identify by name angels that perform specific duties.

For example: according to the pseudepigraphal book of Jubilees, there is a group of angels known as 'Angels of the Presence'. Jubilees is a rewriting of Genesis and Exodus, partly narrated by one of these Angels of the Presence. These were sometimes identified with the 'seven holy angels, which present the prayers of the saints, and which go in and out before the glory of the Holy One', in the apocryphal Tobit (12: 15), in which case they are seven in number. This revelation is given to Tobit by Raphael, who identifies himself as one of these angels. They also appear to be identical with 'the seven Spirits which are before his throne' in Revelation (1: 4; also 8: 2). There are seven throne angels according to *The Book of the Angel Raziel*; and twelve Angels of the Presence in another rabbinical tradition. Paul also refers to those who stand in His Presence (2 Cor. 2: 17). In a rabbinical tradition, however, there are four angels, and they are equated with the animalistic angels of Ezekiel 1. The numbers four and seven invite correspondences with other passages in holy writings: there are either seven or four archangels, and lists of names of archangels and the Angels of the Presence overlap. Having established the existence of this group, Jewish and Christian commentators sought to establish their duties. Why they were distinct? Was it simply a matter of hierarchy? According to the Testament of Levi, one of the Testaments of the Twelve Patriarchs, they lived in the sixth heaven. What are their names? Gabriel and Michael were usually added to Raphael; Uriel was a possible fourth. Metatron was another candidate.[158] Arise Evans rhetorically asked, 'who can tell which is the Angel of Gods presence?', but his scepticism was not universal even among early modern Protestants.[159] In the chapter on the special government of angels in *De Doctrina Christiana*, Milton notes the existence of seven particular angels 'described as traversing the earth in the execution on their ministry', who are the eyes of God.[160] In *Paradise Lost* Uriel is:

> One of the seven
> Who in God's presence, nearest to his throne
> Stand ready at command, and are his eyes
> That run through all the heavens, or down to the earth
> Bear his swift errands over moist and dry,
> O'er sea and land . . .                    (3. 648–53)

He does not identify the other six. Milton names nine angels in the epic, and gives special status to the four in rabbinical tradition.[161] Pordage's angels have no names. The interest in the Angels of the Presence is orthodox, though associated with rabbinical traditions and the occult.

## Are Humans Superior to Angels?

Angels are messengers; some take this to mean servants both to God and to humans.[162] They are nonetheless superior in nature to humans, in respect of their being pure spirit. Augustine adds that they are superior 'in merit of life and in the weakness of our infirmity, because we are miserably unlike them in will'.[163] This account of human inferiority shifted over the next twelve centuries. Scholastic theologians suggested a more complex relationship in spiritual terms: Bonaventure writes that angels support humans, and that humans, through their redemption, make amends for the fall of the angels, and that they are thus in a sense equal.[164] Aquinas argues that the distinction between angels and humans in terms of the dignity of their natures is unbridgeable; however, it is possible for humans to merit equality with angels through meriting great glory. In this sense, humans are 'taken up' into the angelic orders, implicitly restoring their depletion by the angelic fall.[165] Humans are in several ways privileged: humans are given an atonement; the angelic fall was irreversible because grace was forfeited; Christ adopted human nature and not angelic. For some, particularly in the seventeenth century, this raised humans above angels.[166] The German mystic Jacob Boehme insisted that 'Man is higher dignified than the Angels, if he continue in God.'[167]

Though the emphasis on human superiority had mystical and antinomian associations, some Calvinists and orthodox churchmen shared it. Alexander Ross insisted that the angels are closer to the image of God in nature, and humans closer than angels to the image of God in respect of dignity; moreover, angels are 'created for the use of man'.[168] And Richard Sibbes in 1638: 'we are in Christ above *Angels*, advanced higher then *Angels* . . . he did not take upon him the nature of *Angels*, but of men; and as he hath advanced us above *Angels*, so his dispensation is, that those glorious creatures should be our attendants for our good; and they distaste not this attendance'.[169] This elevation of humans was used to explain the rebellion of angels. John Trapp offered a series of grounds on which the saints were 'above the Angels', hedged with a cursory 'some say', including the superiority of human nature and righteousness, and the privileging of the saints in and through Christ. For Trapp angels are 'meer creatures', things made for a limited purpose, whereas humans are the centre of Creation.[170] There is something unpleasantly triumphalist in Trapp's writing, as he exults in human superiority over a species of spiritual creatures. Henry More characteristically tackles, without resolving, the paradox that Christ should be both human and head of the angels, when it would have been 'more reasonable for God to have united himself *Hypostatically* (as they call it) with some *Angel* then with *Humane nature*'.[171] He proceeds to wonder, humanely, if angels do not suffer too. Lawson notes that the Incarnation exalts humans, though inferior, above angels; yet he also recognizes that consorting with angels is a great privilege:

They are above us, and we are a great Distance from them in respect of our present Estate, yet some of them are very near us, though we do not see them, nor speak unto them, nor familiarly converse with them; and they love us, have a special care for us, and all of them are ministring Spirits for us, who shall be Heirs of Salvation.

Though this is not human triumphalism, it suggests the extraordinary arrogance that can be embedded in imagining a whole species and society of beings made to serve humans, over whom Christ preferred humans, and who will continue to serve humans despite a nominal equality.[172]

There was a shift in the seventeenth century towards stressing the superiority, through grace, of humans to angels. This may be a consequence of a greater theological emphasis on grace, and a reduced emphasis on nature, or matter, as a measure of moral values. One effect is to reduce the status of angels as superior beings sharing Creation with man; they are humbled as humans become more central to providence.

## What Do Angels Do?

Angels are God's messengers and agents in the world. But what do they actually do? Katherine Austen, who compiled a commonplace book in 1664 with several pages on angels, identifies three purposes: they serve and assist man, they bear messages, and they stand in God's presence.[173] Most descriptions of angels briefly summarize their duties.

Calvin states simply that God uses them to execute his decrees, proceeding to identify their labours according to their names in Scripture.[174] Gervase Babington suggests that angels have a work ethic: 'hee would not his Angels to wante what to doe, but made them ministering Spirites'.[175] According to Joseph Hall, they praise God, order Creation, especially protect humans, guarding, cheering, and healing the elect.[176] Though their name means 'messengers', their most important function, in the history of Christianity, is to contemplate God, and secondarily to support human prayer and devotion and to convey illumination to humans. In the medieval period interactions with humans began to eclipse divine contemplation.[177] Later writing about angels greatly diversifies their agency, assigning numerous activities.

First angels praise God: 'it is the ministerie, office and work of Angels', wrote Urbanus Rhegius, 'without ceasing, perpetually to praise the Majestie of GOD, to preach his worde, and glorifie this our God therein'.[178] This praise is figured as singing, emphasizing its aesthetic properties, and perhaps suggesting its continuous, ritualized nature. When angels sing, they are praising God, and this is, like angelic speech, a model for human praise of God. Their singing is a model for the liturgy: 'they begin the Antiphone, and teach us how to sing', preached John Wall in a sermon entitled 'Angelorum Antiphonia: The Angels Antheme'.[179]

Secondly, they are messengers and ambassadors. Rhegius writes, 'They are also the Ambassadors of God in cheefe and most speciall causes and affayres betweene God and men, to reveale and manifest the ready good will and clemencie of God towardes men,' citing the appearance of Gabriel to Mary.[180] The discernible bearing of messages to humans was understood to be a thing of the past, as the age of visitation by angels, together with miracles and prophecy, was over. Nonetheless, angels continued to work, albeit invisibly, among humans. They do not, in Protestant accounts, bear messages back to God. As Willet writes, 'the Angels doe report unto God the affaires of the world, and the acts and gests of men, and so their supplications in generall: but this they doe as messengers, not as mediators'.[181]

Thirdly, they are 'ministering spirits', working God's business on earth. Calvin writes that this is one of the few things known for certain.[182] These ministrations comprehend a variety of business, intervening in human affairs, guiding and protecting humans. Rhegius implies a high degree of direct intervention and communication among them:

they have even amongst us & within us, their ministry and function, with great faith and diligence doe they guide, direct, governe, and defende us: they are present with us, helpe us every where, providently take care of us, and doe obtaine for us, all things tending to the glorie of Christ, and even reconcile him unto us, doo instill and beate into our minds his holie will, yea, doo call us away, and plucke us backe from all those sinnes and vices which God hath forbidden us, and which he abhorreth.[183]

Other Protestants would be more cautious about the extent of free agency and intervention. Such ministrations exalt humans: in *Paradise Lost*, Satan mocks those who would prefer to be 'Ministering spirits' than free beings, and proudly rejects service (6. 167–8).[184] Christopher Love asks why God uses angels to ministrate in this world when he could do so without them, and answers: to show the reconciliation of angels and humans after they fell out through sin and were reconciled through the atonement; to declare his love to his people; because the saints will repair the orders of angels, angels are willing to serve humans on earth; and because evil angels tempt humans, good angels assist the elect.[185] Among these ministrations is providing succour. Protestants removed angels from deathbed scenes, but most agreed that angels could invisibly provide comfort, at least to the elect.[186] Angelic ministration is not only comforting, however. The angels that raze Sodom (Gen. 19: 13) and the destroying angel sent to Jerusalem (1 Chr. 21: 15) reminded commentators that the judgements of God that angels execute are not only supportive. They are ministers of wrath as well as of grace. Angels devastate.[187]

Fourthly, angels are witnesses. They watch human tragedies: hence the *tears* of angels.[188] They are also the 'benign eyes of God', hence perhaps they are called watchers, watching humans, and watching God in preparation for his commands.[189] Milton describes angels watching over Adam and Eve in *Paradise Lost* books 4 and 9. Henry Ainsworth writes that angels are 'beholders of our wayes & conversation, and affected (after their spiritual manner) with the things they see in us'.[190] Human actions have an audience, inspire emotions, and so are given significance within a cosmic framework.

Fifthly, angels heal. The angel that annually touches the pool at Bethesda (John 5: 4) endows it with healing powers. Fallen angels spread disease, and angels bring cures. Angel-magic sought to harness this faculty.[191] The angelic spells used to find cures in popular medicine, however, lay outside the limits of orthodoxy. John Patrick even mocked the credence that Catholics gave to Raphael as a medicinal angel.[192]

The question can be asked another way: *What use are angels?* or *What do humans do with angels?* There is a functionalist perspective on what angels do: it suggests that they help humans understand God and understand themselves. They are a means of conceiving of order, and a means, through analogy and differentiation, of conceiving of what it is to be human. They are a way of shaping social behaviour. Joseph Hall writes that 'the life of Angels is politicall, full of intercourse with themselves and with us'.[193] It forms a pattern for imitation, and both social commentators and theologians stressed that humans should be more like angels. Though early modern Protestants would not have described this role of angels in functionalist terms, they articulated it through the language of imitation and of fellowship between humans and angels. Ainsworth writes that, because angels are spirits, 'the fellowship between them and us is spiritual, to be learned out of the scriptures, and discerned by faith not by eie sight'.[194] Although there could be no direct interaction between humans and angels in post-Incarnation times, saints (meaning here the elect or godly humans) and angels were part of a real community.[195] Cornelius Burgess, in his systematic notes on angels, observed there were three *uses* for angels: (1) to provide patterns of imitation, (2) to instruct men, and (3) to provide humans with consolation.[196]

## Conclusion

Despite the caution that Protestants expressed about going beyond the immediate authority of Scripture, reformed writers wrote extensively and imaginatively about angels. Modern emphasis on the *visual* imagination, where Protestant artists were certainly less creative than their Catholic counterparts, perhaps occludes this. Protestants addressed many of the issues traditionally examined in writing about angels, adapting them to their own soteriology and to transformations in the understanding of natural philosophy. The impact of natural philosophy on views of angels, and the ways in which angels constituted thought experiments in natural philosophy, are discussed in Chapter 11. Other topics outlined above are further developed in other chapters. Some of the radical uses of angels are discussed in

Chapters 4 and 5. The relevance of angels to theories of representing
God is discussed in Chapter 6, while Chapter 7 considers the place of
angels in prophecy. Theological views of angelic communication and
virtual embodiment are explored in Chapter 12. The doctrine of
guardianship, and local guardians, are further explored in Chapters 9
and 13. The place of angels in the Protestant imagination are the
subject of much of the rest of this book. There was no single, unified
Protestant angelology, and angels were an area of conflict between
Protestants, but angelology did not disappear in the two centuries after
the Reformation.[197] They were an extensively useful element in Prot-
estant theology: a matter of doctrine, necessitated by fragments of
Scripture, a realm of immediate spiritual experience, a means of
rationally understanding the visible world, and an archive of social
memories.

# 4

# A Stronger Existence

## Angels, Polemic, and Radical Speculation, 1640–1660

Too many in these dayes have been wantonly busie to converse with Angels, out of pride and curiosity, but the good Angels wil not be spoken with upon those terms; or if they do speak, to be sure it will be no comfort to those persons: for the Apostle by laying down a supposition, hath given us a certainty, that the Angels will speak no other doctrine then he did. Therefore such spirits as are intruders into things not seen, are vainly *puft in their fleshly* mind, *Col*. 2. 18. how spiritual soever they seem to be.[1]

Thus wrote a group of Presbyterians headed by Edmund Calamy in 1657. Over the preceding two decades, angels had seemed increasingly present, and angel-doctrine had been re-examined and rewritten. Angels furnished some with a means of articulating radical politics and theology, while fear of Sadducism led others to restate the commonplaces of Thomist angelology. Calamy felt surrounded by those who claimed to converse with angels, those who were too interested in the niceties of doctrine, and those who denied the spirit world altogether.

If the Reformation had made angels seem more remote from everyday experience, this was reversed in the revolutionary decades. The surge of interest in and writing about angels that took place around 1641 was the effect of several related trends: apocalypticism, an influx of mystical theology, anxieties about the civil war and social and political fragmentation, the challenge to ecclesiastical hierarchies, the spread of radical theologies, and an increase in witch-persecution. These created an intellectual and soteriological environment in which angels had a powerful valence, as metaphors and a means of analysing and redescribing society. They also became a theme for imaginative speculation, and poems by Andrew Marvell, Samuel Pordage, Milton, Lucy Hutchinson, and John Dryden need to be read against this background.

Four things underpin this interest. First, angels are understood to be immediate, our contemporaries, part of the experienced present, despite Protestant warnings that angelic apparitions ended with the age of miracles and prophecy. Secondly, a rise in millenarianism. Angels are harbingers of the apocalypse: 'And I saw an angel coming down out of heaven, having the key to the Abyss and holding in his hand a great chain. He seized the dragon, that ancient serpent, who is the devil, or Satan, and bound him for a thousand years' (Rev. 20: 1–2). Hence, a mid-seventeenth-century English manuscript commentary on Revelation is richly illustrated with angels; such illustrations are uncommon in Reformation England, but here angels fit the subject.[2] Angels widely figure in 1640s writing with apocalyptic tendencies, ranging from concerns about social disorder to belief that the thousand-year rule of the saints was imminent. These first two points concern knowledge and understanding; the second two concern language and representation. Thirdly, angels are traditionally a means of interpreting and charting hierarchies. In a period when hierarchies are being challenged, they provide an evidentiary language to re-establish or reconfigure order. Fourthly, angels can be used to redraw the heavens, to model man's place in the cosmos. The political and religious turmoil of the 1640s and 1650s invited writers to use angels to explain and intervene in social turmoil. Angels are intermediate interlocutors and shapers of human history, but they also furnish the language of politics and social order.

The outbreak of civil unrest and war in Britain witnessed the increased permeability of angels into disparate realms of political and religious knowledge. Angels appear in many varieties of writing in the revolutionary years. For the purposes of mapping some of these shifts I here suggest four modes: rhetorical or figurative angels, exegetical angels, creaturely angels, and the angels of radical writing.[3]

## Rhetorical Angels

Angels became polemically charged in 1641. The Root and Branch movement against episcopacy provoked an extended debate on the identity of the seven angels in Revelation. Though the use of angels was topical and polemical, it was shaped by scholarship in theology and natural philosophy. In *Episcopacy by Divine Right Asserted* (1640) and *Humble Remonstrance* (1641), Joseph Hall used John's epistles to the seven angels of the Asian Churches to justify church government by bishops. Others agreed that the 'angels' to whom John addressed his letters were the bishops who led the Churches, thereby distinguished from the many presbyters in a church.[4]

This account was challenged by Smectymnuus (the pseudonym of five Presbyterian divines), who argued that the term 'angel' was meant collectively, not individually: 'by *Angell* is meant not one singular person, but the whole company of Presbyters'; the very name reveals that it 'doth not import any particular jurisdiction or preheminence, but is a common name to all Ministers', because all ministers are God's messengers.[5] The word 'angel' is to be understood 'not properly, but figuratively . . . this phrase of speech, *Angell* for *Angels*, is common to all types and visions', and 'one angel in the singular number' sometimes conceals 'a multitude of Heavenly angels'.[6] What is at stake is Church hierarchy, but the Smectymnuans stray into a more general account of angels: this is characteristic of the rhetoric surrounding angels in 1641 and after.

Milton, who would become the most famous English angelographer, took up writing polemic during this debate. In *Animadversions upon the Remonstrant's Defence Against Smectymnuus* (1641) Milton argues that angels are not unique offices in the Church but actions performed by true pastors. He attributes to them a creative, evangelic power: 'there is no imployment more honourable, more worthy, then to be the messenger, and Herald of heavenly truth from god to man, and by the faithfull worke of holy doctrine, to procreate a number of faithfull men, making a kind of creation like to Gods, by infusing his spirit and likenesse into them, to their salvation'.[7] In *The Reason of Church-Government* (1642) Milton argues that the seven angels are antithetical to prelates, as they perform God's work. Angels convey true messages while prelates create false idols.[8] In this role they also inspire: he looks forward to his promised great literary work, which is not to be a quick labour, 'nor to be obtain'd by the invocation of Dame Memory and her Siren Daughters, but by devout prayer to that eternall Spirit who can enrich will all utterance and knowledge, and sends out his Seraphim with the hallow'd fire of his Altar to touch and

purify the lips of whom he pleases'.[9] The eternal spirit, the echo of
Isaiah 6: 1–7 suggests, is God, the true muse and inspirer of Milton's
poem; the seraphim are figures for divine inspiration, but also inde-
pendent beings. Unlike the figure of Phoebus, who touches the
doubting poet's trembling ears in 'Lycidas', their role is consonant
with the theology of angels outlined in *De Doctrina Christiana*. They are
simultaneously figurative and real.[10] Milton's early writing about
angels concerns representation, iconoclasm, and the restorative
power of true ministry, and he thought of them in both poetic and
political terms, while rejecting their appropriation as a basis of Church
hierarchy.

Many others intervened in the debate. John White picked up the
theme in a parliamentary speech on the future of episcopacy, arguing
that 'Angel is a name common to all Presbyters who are Christs
Messengers and Ambassadors.'[11] The same argument was made in
1641 by an anonymous author who cited Joseph Mede's *Clavis Apoc-
alyptica* (1627) in support his case, and republished John Rainold's 1588
pamphlet that challenged Richard Bancroft and queried the antiquity
of church government by bishops.[12] Hence, the debate over episcop-
acy is conferred with an account of the nature of angels, and both are
brought within the context of an apocalyptic reading of Revelation.[13]
There is only a short step to identifying bishops as associated with the
fallen angels of the popish Antichrist.

The late 1630s and 1640s were rife with apocalyptic sentiment. The
Scottish divine and mathematician John Napier, like Mede, thought
that Revelation described future history: he predicted in 1593 that the
year 1639 would see the Fall of the Roman Antichrist. The conclusion
of the Second Bishops' War that year appeared to be a victory for
Presbyterianism over the attempted imposition of episcopacy on Scotland.
One 1641 pamphlet described this peace as the angel sheathing his
sword.[14] King Charles's defeat resulted in the calling of a Parliament
that quickly set about eradicating episcopacy root and branch. Earlier
apocalyptic works were republished and translated, and Revelation was
interpreted as a literal prophecy of present and imminent history; both
were read in radical, destabilizing ways.[15] Learned apocalyptic exegesis
was disseminated in pamphlets. In February 1642 the House of Com-
mons Committee for Printing ordered inspection of a translation of
Mede's *Clavis Apocalyptica*, which appeared in 1643.[16] In *The Apostasy
of the Latter Times* (1641) Mede argued that the worship of angels and

saints in the popish Church was evidence that Rome was the Whore of Babylon, and that her idolatry proved that the latter days were imminent.[17] Johann Heinrich Alsted's influential millenarian treatise *The Beloved City* was translated into English and published in 1643. Thomas Brightman's *Apocalypsis Apocalypseos* (1609) was published in English in Amsterdam in 1611 and 1615, and then in London in various forms in 1641 and 1644; Brightman identified the Church of England as the lukewarm Laodicean Church, and the Scottish Kirk and Genevan Church as the blessed and virtuous angel of the Philadelphians (Rev. 3).[18] These works describe the role of angels in human history; they undermine episcopal authority and encourage readers to see angelic intervention in events taking place around them.

The events of the late 1630s and early 1640s moved British authors to reread accounts of the apocalypse, and to reconsider the identification of the English Church with Laodicea. Hence the appearance of dialogue pamphlets, including *Napier's Narration, or, An Epitome of his Book on the Revelation* (1641) and a verse pamphlet, *Brightmans Predictions and Prophesies* (1641), which insisted Brightman had prophesied the events of recent years. Another dialogue pamphlet of 1641 describes a conversation between a London citizen and a Puritan minister, showing how Brightman's account of the angels of the seven churches has been fulfilled by the Thirty Years War.[19] The minister recalls, with sadness, the days when Martin Marprelate 'dealt somewhat roundly' with the Angel of the English Church; the eagerness of the people for these writings indicates the low esteem in which the episcopacy are held. Marprelate was the pseudonymous author of a series of attacks on Elizabethan bishops and Church government published surreptitiously in 1588–9; his name was a byword for anti-ecclesiastical polemic and popular pamphleteering. The citizen, more up to date with worldly things, reports that

in London there is much talke of a Woman who cals her selfe by the name of *Margery Mar-Prelate*, who either makes or prints Bookes, and as you say, hee dealt roundly with them, so I can assure you doth she, and you would admire if you knew how greedy men are of those Bookes, and are much bought up in *London*, by which it is more then manifest that our *Bishops* and *Prelates* are very much despised . . .

Margery Marprelate, the self-conscious successor to Martin, authored and printed pro-Covenanting pamphlets from 1640.[20] The pamphlet

asks to be read in two contexts: first as a topical, didactic intervention
in the maelstrom of print; secondly, as an intervention in the historical
tradition of anti-ecclesiastical scholarship, seeking to validate the
judgements of that tradition.[21]

The debates of 1640–1 intensified the topical relevance of the figura-
tive and doctrinal use of angels. For many pamphleteers they were a test
of confessional difference: one's faith in angels or scepticism about the
extent of true knowledge of them marked the distinction between the
Protestant and Catholic faiths. The Covenanter Robert Baillie attacked
the Book of Common Prayer for its similarities to the Roman Catholic
liturgy, noting as one example the 'Angelike-Hymne', 'Gloria in excel-
sis Deo'.[22] The Westminster Assembly's *Protestation* (1643) complained
that the Prayer Book affirmed the existence of archangels, and that
Michael is a created angel.[23] The parishioners of St Giles in the Fields
petitioned in 1641 against the Laudian prebendary of Westminster
William Heywood for his popish doctrines, citing in evidence his
granting a licence to a Catholic book that encouraged praying to 'thy
good Angell'. Heywood was ejected and imprisoned, and the petition
was printed as a pamphlet, apparently with the patronage of Parliament's
Committee for Religion.[24] *A New Discovery of the Prelates Tyranny* (1641),
a substantial tract documenting the persecution of William Prynne, John
Bastwick, and Henry Burton, proclaimed, 'Such a *spectacle both to men,
and Angels*, no age ever saw before.'[25] Angels stood alongside men as
witnesses to present history.

Angels were prominent in anti-Catholic polemic in the early 1640s.
The pamphlet *Seven Arguments Plainly Proving that Papists Are Trayterous
Subjects to all True Christian Princes* (1641) describes the elaborate shows
of piety mounted by Jesuits to facilitate the assassination of rulers,
among them the 'Raviliack' (Henry IV's assassin), who undergoes a
mock religious ceremony in which he is presented with a knife and
blessed with prayers and invocations: 'Come Cherabims, come Ser-
aphims, and highest Thrones that rule, come blessed Angels: yea,
blessed Angels of charitie, come and fill this holy Vessell with glory
and eternitie'.[26] He is set before an altar with a picture showing the
angels lifting to heaven another assassin. The pamphlet at once depicts
popery in a bloody light, arguing against its toleration in Protestant
monarchies, while also blackening by association the religious rites of
episcopacy. In another 1641 dialogue pamphlet, *Sions Charity towards
her Foes in Misery*, a London citizen and a country gentleman discuss

whether it is appropriate to describe Parliament's enemies as 'infernall Spirits' (and Laud, implicitly, as 'Great Belzebub, that Prince of devils'), language, the citizen reports, rife on booksellers' stalls.[27] The gentleman insists that 'Michael the Archangell strove against the devil, and disputed about the body of Moses' in Jude 9, and yet used no 'cursed speaking' or 'railing accusation', relying on God to do the rebuking; Michael sets an example for human conduct.[28] In *The Down-Fall of Anti-Christ* (1641), the Nonconformist John Geree shows that angels and ministers will bring down the papal Antichrist, and, implicitly, episcopacy, by preaching.[29] An anonymous 1641 pamphlet, *Old Newes Newly Revived*, mocks the exile of two royal courtiers with a woodcut depicting them as winged angels flying the country. John Taylor's pamphlet *The Brownists Conventicle* satirizes the independent preacher Samuel Eaton by placing apocalyptic arguments about angels and episcopacy in his mouth:

And there was a battell in heaven, Michael and his Angels fought against the Dragon, &c. Grace & peace be multiplied. This Text dearly beloved brethren, and most dearly beloved sisters, may not unproperly be applyed to these present times.... By this Michael and his Angels in my Text, is meant one particular Church, and peculiar Church... I say unto you againe brethren, wicked Angels are the Bishops Deanes, Arch Deacons, Prebends, non residents, which live without the care and charge of soules... [30]

The crudeness of the argument invites ridicule. During 1641 angels acquired a newly forceful political currency; particularly associated with independent allegiances, they were part of the religio-political language used to discuss history, revelation, and church government.

One 1642 pamphlet shows the rhetorical power of angels that develops out of the anti-ecclesiastical context. *Three Propositions of the Angels of Light, With Three Solutions Therein Considerable* is anonymous: no author, printer bookseller, or place of publication is identified within its pages. It does not appear in the Stationers' Register, nor other official papers. The twenty-eight-page pamphlet seems to have passed without comment and made little or no impact; only two copies survive today. The three propositions are made in prose that resists interpretation. For example:

One thing considerable, though there be a neere affinity with Angel-nature and working as created of God in power and will sustained of God in Christ, subordinate to his will glory and pleasure, yet in their nature though spirits and glorious creatures, have some acts and works in extraordinary wayes, to accomplish as God appoints and sends them forth and set them about to doe, wherein somethings extraordinarily have beene done by them by Gods appointment, in one instant it may be seene in the 2 *Kin.* 19. 35. and herein also they agree with all their fellow-creatures created of God to be, and worke in and after the will and good pleasure of God . . .[31]

The contorted, non-idiomatic syntax suggests a poorly educated author. Alternatively he or she may be reluctant to express his or her message plainly, or may be a native of another Protestant country, most likely the Netherlands or Germany, wrestling with the language. There are, most unusually in writings about angels, no references to previous scholarship. Cautiously expressed, the propositions are: first, God made the angels; and thirdly, that angels work in the world through Christ's light, and in doing so reveal God's glory. The second proposition, the central theme of the book, is more challenging: there are two kinds of angel, those considered at the beginning of Creation, and those who are sent among us, '*Heavenly and Church*-Angels'. The phrase 'Church-Angels' may suggest pastors, in which sense John Donne uses it his Easter Day 1622 sermon, but this author has a mystical meaning.[32]

   Though the author conventionally rejects angel-worship and declares that fallen angels cannot part from sin, some of the angel-doctrine is idiosyncratic. The passage cited from 2 Kings describes an angel of the Lord slaying 185,000 Assyrians in one night. Usually interpreted as evidence of the astonishing power of angels, this author represents the action as performed 'extraordinarily', as if with powers conferred by God for the occasion, rather than by the angel's natural might. More arresting is the account of the nature of angelic knowledge, which distinguishes between the experimental knowledge available to the two kinds of angels:

Some such glory and excellency the Angels in the first sort of Angels, cannot partake of, as might bee largely made out in the second and third *Chapter* of the Revelation, and will in severall particulars shew it forth, in what *Christ* will communicate to those angels, as to eat of the tree of life, when angels of the first sort we minded were at the first, in that perfect glory wherin they abide.[33]

Because of original sin humans attain an additional kind of knowledge. The author denies the scriptural origins of episcopacy, suggesting that the seven angels belong to the 'church of Christ mysticall'. These angels, 'spiritualized natures in light and knowledge', operate in a different cognitive realm, separate from heaven. These are not creaturely angels, with senses and agency, but remote and abstract spirits.[34]

Angels walk among us. We are surrounded by angels of light, in 'the garments of men', and angels of darkness, who can disguise their sin, 'though they may trans-form themselves into Angels of light, but never into the light of the Angels of light, no!'[35] It is the reader's duty to distinguish between them. At times the prose threatens to crumble into religious ecstasy:

this spiritual sightednesse will be very usefull to those that have it in the day and time of the Angells sounding forth of God and Christ [i.e. the last days], to fulfill his will and worke: usefull in freeing from that darknesse which covers the wicked, who cannot away with Angell nature nor working, it is so hot and fiery an approach of God in these Messengers, they will allow of nothing but what is of God according to the truth in Christ.[36]

Though the author never quite sounds like Jacob Bauthumley—who similarly employs the rhetoric of light and darkness, finding the key to Creation immanent in humans—the self dissolves into spiritual outpouring, and the voice moves from explication towards prophecy.[37]

The work is a symptom of the turmoil in publishing and politics at the beginning of the 1640s; it is an obscure statement on soteriology and a gloss on fragments from Revelation published as a pamphlet amidst the urgent newsbooks, satires, and polemics of 1642. It conveys some sense in the context of contemporary pamphlets that bear witness to an apocalyptic moment and assume a non-learned form, and it is unlikely that *Three Propositions* could have been written or published in England before 1641.[38] The account of angels of light implicitly brings the conflict between light and darkness to the immediate present. While the author's exegetical point is subtle, there is a starker message: the angels of light and of darkness are real and among us. The reader must identify them, and decide which side he or she is on. In 1642 this was a bleak message, disclosing both ecclesiastical and political crisis.

Angels also played an increasing role in political argument. They were witnesses to and moral judges of political events. Angels, and the right to say what they are and what they do, became part of challenges to and defences of authority. Arguing against proposals for an 'accommodation' between the warring sides in the spring of 1643, one pamphleteer warns: 'all the *Powres* in Heaven and Hell are parties here, and offended greatly: *Michaell* and his Angells, *Belzebus*, and his Angells'.[39] The war is a struggle between good and evil. A broadside reporting a royalist conspiracy, *The Malignants Trecherous and Bloody Plot Against the Parliament and Citty* (1643), describes Michael and Satan struggling for 'Sions safety'. The angels are invisible, however, and do not appear in the engravings.[40] Other pamphlets remind their opponents that angels witness actions here on earth, and will be present when sinners are sent to eternal confusion.[41]

A pro-Parliament pamphlet of 1643 contended that the king would be safer at Whitehall, under 'Angelicall protection in the way of his Kingly office and duty' than in the hands of the 'Dammees'.[42] This nickname for cavaliers alludes to their blasphemous swearing; its full force relies on the belief that angels and devils walk among us. Angels guarantee, figuratively and through their interventions, an orderly creation. *The Necessity of Christian Subjection* (1643) used angels to justify absolute monarchy: because kingship goes back to Adam just as 'the angels and those of Heaven, had their beginning from God by Creation', and because monarchy alone is 'an Idea or resemblance of Gods government in Heaven'.[43] *A Discovery of the Rebels* (1643) argued that 'the King is the highest of men, and yet but a *humane creature*, as it is in the Greek, not a God, nor a creature Angelicall', inferior in a linear hierarchy.[44] The author of *Peace, Peace, and We Shall Be Quiet* (1647) writes that 'as the world hath one God, so should a Kingdome be governed by one King, as Gods Substitute . . . Amongst the *Angels* there are distinctions, as *Principalities, Powers, Thrones, Dominions*, and *Michael* an *Archangel*'.[45] Edward Symmons laments that 'Hells own selfe is broake loose into' England, and implicitly compares Parliament's rebellion with the fall of Lucifer and his angels. *Mercurius Pragmaticus* in April 1649 also described the rebels as 'the *Devills Agents* on *Earth*, and like the *Apostate-Angells* in *Heaven*, [they] do perswade themselves (being promoted by a spirit of presumption) that they equalize the *highest*'.[46] Conversely, *Maximes Unfolded* (1643) repeatedly uses angels as analogies to argue that a king's power must be constitutionally limited.[47] A broadside elegy for John Pym, the parliamentary leader who died in 1643, claimed that had angels been as good as him they would not have fallen, and it imagined him 'translated from the House of Commons, to the Upper House of Glory, and Parliament of Angels in Heaven'.[48] In 1649 Richard Arnway imagined angels in heaven celebrating Charles I's union with the Son.[49]

More common in the pamphlets of this period, however, is the presentation of the living or deceased in hell, conversing with Charon or Machiavelli.[50] Parliaments were usually diabolical rather than heavenly; the Parliament of Hell became a recurrent motif in royalist satire. In these satires Satan holds a parliament and plans to foment dissent and rebellion; the device, with a long literary history, works as an explanation of recent history, but also reflects allegorically upon the Long Parliament.[51] Other pamphlets suggest that the Devil is prompting the opposition—clergy, Presbyterian forcers of conscience, royal partisans, rebels—often disguised as an angel.[52] One 1648 newsbook refers to the '*Westminster* Divells' and in particular to '*Laurance Lucifer*, author of their Rebellion, who for his pride was throwne downe to Hell, and they for their presumptuous insolence I feare, will never go to Heaven', perhaps alluding to Henry Lawrence MP, who had recently published a large treatise on angels.[53]

That the Devil was able to transform himself into an angel of light was commonly cited Scripture,[54] but for the most part these satires and polemics do not get caught up in exegesis, and, while observing its fundamental principles, pay minimal attention to the details of angel-doctrine. Their use of angels is primarily figurative or rhetorical, to interpret a human struggle in terms of good and evil. Their significance is not purely allegorical, however: they presuppose belief in the immediate reality of the angelic world. The rhetorical deployment of angels relied on perceived reality, that angels are around us, that they are moral witnesses, that they are good and evil. The political language worked because its metaphors were grounded in a shared understanding of the relationship between the seen and unseen world; but it remained easier to think with demons than with angels.

## Exegetical Angels

Scriptural annotations and schematic treatises constituted a second mode of writing about angels that was energized during the 1640s. Church reform and millenarianism gave some impetus to these more sustained, doctrinal expositions. The Westminster Assembly of Divines, commissioned by the Long Parliament to define a new religious settlement, produced a collaborative set of annotations on both Testaments in 1645, and an expanded version in 1651. In part because of this there followed a cluster of scholarly works, including John Lightfoot's biblical chronology, *The Harmony, Chronicle and Order, of the Old Testament* (1647), John Trapp's *A Commentary or Exposition upon all the Epistles, and the Revelation of John the Divine* (1647), and his *A Clavis to the Bible, or, A New Comment upon the Pentateuch* (1650), Edward Leigh's *Annotations upon all the New Testament* (1650) and *Annotations on Five Poetical Books of the Old Testament* (1657), Henry Hammond's *A Paraphrase, and Annotations upon all the Books of the New Testament* (1653), John Richardson's supplement to the Westminster *Annotations, Choice Observations and Explanation upon the Old Testament* (1655), John White's *A Commentary upon the Three First Chapters of the First Book of Moses Called Genesis*, published posthumously in 1656, and many sermons and commentaries on particular scriptural texts. These express doctrines about angels while interpreting Scripture: whether angels adopt bodies, whether they digest, whether the angels in Revelation 12 and 20 are Michael or Christ.[55]

In addition the revolutionary decades saw the publication of English editions and translations of a number of systematic theologies, including William Ames's *Medulla Theologica* (1628; London edition, 1630), translated as *The Marrow of Sacred Divinity Drawne out of the Holy Scriptures* (1642). Johannes Wollebius' *Compendium Theologiae Christianae* (1626; London edition, 1642) was partly translated by Alexander Ross as *The Abridgement of Christian Divinity* in 1650.[56] These were works that shaped Milton's systematic theology, *De Doctrina Christiana*, which discusses angels as aspects of Creation and of divine government.[57] Milton read Ames and Wollebius in Latin: the publication of English translations of these treatises points to a growing audience untrained in Latin and theology yet interested in accounts of Creation and cosmic administration. These accounts are very different from the popular practical divinity of Arthur Dent, William Perkins, or Richard Baxter. The development of a popular appetite for systematic theology is suggested by a manuscript headed 'This Booke Contaynes in it the matter of severall conferences att Mr Paines Among some of ye inhabitants of Stortford [in Hertfordshire] about those fundamentall truths that are necessary to bee knowne and practiced by every one that would bee saved.' Stortford's citizens began this collaborative work on 1 January 1655, and recorded a series of questions and answers that combined practical and theoretical divinity, from proofs of God's existence to 'How wee can prove that there is A devine decree

concerning Angells and men before the world.'[58] Their enquiries
reflect the contemporary appetite for new and diverse printed mater-
ials, but perhaps also the promise of the coming millennium.

This exegetical writing about angels is characteristically focused on
known doctrinal truths, rather than ecclesiastical or political argument.
Much of it appears in expository works, however, to which angel-
doctrine is incidental: authors from diverse theological positions are
diverted into offering a consistent and sustained account of angelic
actions. John Trapp supplemented his 1647 *Commentary or Exposition*
with ten sets of 'common-places', including five pages on angels that
run through the usual exegetical topics, including hierarchies and
angel-worship, and observes, 'if the *Theology* for Angels were written,
we should need another Bible: the creation and government of Angels
containing as great variety of matter, as doth the religion of man-
kinde'.[59] In the early seventeenth century Henry Ainsworth wrote a
series of learned commentaries on Old Testament books; one rep-
rinted around this time was his *The Communion of Saints: A Treatise of
the Fellowship that the Faithfull Have with God, and his Angells, and with
One an Other*, originally 1607, reprinted in Amsterdam in 1640 and in
London in 1641, which outlines the duties of angels as heavenly
messengers and warriors, their relationship with Christ, their interest
in humans, and the error of angel-worship.[60] William Jenkyn's for-
midably detailed *Exposition of the Book of Jude* (1652) discusses angels in
passing, but also devotes a discrete section to a systematic angelology.[61]
John Blenkow's tract *Michael's Combat with the Divel, or, Moses his
Funeral* (1640) uses Jude as the basis for discussing angelic hierarchies,
idolatry, and angelic speech. The Laudian Joseph Hall's *The Great
Mysterie of Godliness* (1652) includes a treatise entitled 'The Invisible
World', which outlines a systematic account of angels, their number,
hierarchies, actions, knowledge, apparitions, and the respect humans
owe them. Christopher Love, executed for treason in 1651, wrote a
treatise entitled 'The Ministry of Angels' that was included in a
posthumous collection edited by a group of Presbyterian ministers
who wanted to preserve Love's memory but also to combat the spread
of angel-worship and belief in guardian angels.[62] Robert Dingley's *The
Deputation of Angels, or, The Angell-Guardian* (1654) is a sustained
defence of the notion of angelic wardship—many Protestants retained
a version of this, as Chapter 9 shows—but digresses to discuss a wide
range of topics.

The Westminster Assembly's annotations were a direct consequence of the religious controversies of the 1640s. However, it would be wrong to infer that these were radical or apocalyptic writings: instead they were the routine business of learned exegetes, accelerated by the Revolution. This is not the case with Henry Lawrence's *Of our Communion and Warre with Angels*, the most sustained piece of writing on angels and the only systematic angelography produced in the 1640s and 1650s, which can be seen as central to the revolutionary moment. Lawrence was a Baptist, with unusual though not heterodox beliefs about angels, who moved from exile in the 1630s to the nub of political power in the 1650s, and was an acquaintance of Milton. His book was initially published with two title pages in 1646, one with no imprint (generally assigned to Amsterdam), the other printed for the London radical bookseller Giles Calvert; it reappeared as *An History of Angells Being a Theological Treatise*, in 1649 and 1650, both printed by Matthew Simmons, but with two different booksellers, William Nealand and Thomas Huntington respectively; and finally, it appeared in 1652, as *Militia Spiritualis, or, A Treatise of Angels*, printed by Simmons for John Blague and Samuel Howes. The five different title pages cover the same set of sheets: there was in fact only one edition and it was printed by Matthew Simmons for Giles Calvert; when it failed to sell, other booksellers took it over, with Calvert's agreement, and Simmons printed new title pages.[63] The association with Amsterdam originates with George Thomason, who wrote this on the title page of his copy.[64] Simmons printed seven of Milton's prose tracts between 1643 and 1650; his son would print a more famous book about angels which also failed to sell quickly, *Paradise Lost*.[65] Milton and Lawrence were using the same printer around the same time, and later Milton would work for Lawrence, when the latter, an MP since 1646, became a member of the Council of State in 1653. Milton would write a sonnet for his friend Edward Lawrence, Henry's son; and Peter Heimbach would write to Milton in 1657 asking him to intercede with Lawrence senior on his behalf. Perhaps there was already an association between the two men.[66]

Lawrence's *Communion and Warre with Angels* offers an extended account of the being and offices of both fallen and unfallen angels. It is presented as an exploration of Ephesians 6: 11–18: 'Put on the whole armour of God; that ye may bee able to stand against the wiles of the devill. For wee wrestle not against flesh and blood, but against principalities, against powers, against the rulers of the darkness of this world, against spirituall wickedness in high places, &c.' The text is an undivided body of continuous prose covering the central topics of angelology: corporeality, apparitions, digestion, speech, guardianship, modes of angelic knowledge and cognition, the power of angels to act in the world, and angelic election and reprobation; it also contains much practical divinity. The 'panoply' (full armour) of Ephesians occasions this meditation, but also leads to a militant view of spiritual combat, of salvation, and of life as a struggle between good and evil. Lawrence had spent some of the previous decade overseas, concerned about religious persecution, and his impetus to study angels probably had millenarian as well as soteriological origins.

Despite poor sales, Lawrence's book was recognized as authoritative, or at least authoritatively Protestant. Various writers cited it in print and court proceedings.[67] It offered an accessible if unoriginal summary of reformed views on angels written by someone in political authority; it reveals that angels were a pressing, if not always doctrinally controversial, theme in the 1640s. Lawrence's other major work concerned baptism, a topic equally open to violent and polarized views of salvation and diabolical operation in the world, and which raised more tempers, but which was less susceptible to being used as a starting point for a general and extended reflection on Creation.

The impetus behind these writings is diverse, but all venture into speculative territory in the course of elaborating an argument or body of knowledge which touches upon angelology. This is explicit in another translation: Johann Amos Comenius' *Physicae ad Lumen Divinum Reformatae Synopsis* (1633), published in English as *Naturall Philosophie Reformed by Divine Light, or, A Synopsis of Physicks* (1651). This arresting work of systematic exposition seeks to unite experimental knowledge, reason, and the revealed knowledge of Scripture. Comenius admires Francis Bacon's attempt to create a universal and rational framework for observed natural-philosophical knowledge, but, influenced by the encyclopedism and millenarianism of Johann Heinrich Alsted, argues that the process could be accelerated through admitting revealed knowledge. He offers means of finding a harmony between natural philosophy and faith in the literal truth of Scripture.[68] The final chapter of this manifesto he devotes to angels, for reasons he makes plain: 'We joyn the treatise concerning Angels with the Physicks; because they are also a part of the created World, and in the scale of creatures next to man; by whose nature, the nature of Angels is the easier to be explained.'[69] Many in the course of the seventeenth century linked the natural-philosophical and theological properties of angels, but Comenius is unusual in the clarity with which he indicated their intellectual usefulness. Comenius' affirmations are for the most part traditional: he discusses angelic numbers, senses, assumed bodies, strength, movement, and knowledge. In two matters he is imaginative: first, the extent to which he makes explicit his ambitions to unify reason, natural-philosophical knowledge, and scriptural exegesis, in doing which he discovers that angels are a necessary object of contemplation and explication. Secondly, and like Milton, he briefly muses on angels' experience of their senses, as if it has occurred to him to reflect upon what it might feel like to be an angel.[70]

## Visible and Creaturely Angels

In much scholarly work and often in figurative and political uses, angels were remote, textual creatures. Contact with angels, especially good angels, was uncommon; there are more sceptical and satirical accounts of visions than sympathetic ones. Angelic visitations were understood to have ceased. As Henry Lawrence wrote, God 'would have us walke in the spirit, and converse more with the spirit then formerly . . . wee have faith enableing us to converse with the Angells in a way more spirituall'.[71] However, some did have visions, and a few, not all of them religious enthusiasts, did speak with angels. Angelic communication increased in the 1640s, though the increase may be exaggerated by the invisibility of earlier, occult traditions. This constitutes a third mode of writing about angels: 'creaturely' writing, based upon actual sighting of and communication with other beings.

In the tense atmosphere of the 1640s a number of angels appeared as portents, such as the armies in the skies allegedly seen after the battle of Edgehill, the first major military encounter of the civil war. The editor of the pamphlet *A Great Wonder in Heaven* (1642 [1643]) introduces fallen angels as a means of understanding the portents: he begins by reflecting on the history of apparitions,

by which it is evidently confirmed, that those legions of erring angels that fell
with their great Master, *Lucifer*, are not all confined to the locall Hell, but live
scattered here and there, dispersed in the empty regions of the ayre as thicke as
motes in the Sunne, and those are those things which our too superstitious
ancestors called Elves and Goblins, Furies, and the like,

such as those that appeared to Macbeth (his source could be Shakespeare
or Holinshed). He reports the repeated sighting of the 'infernall
Armies' in the sky, confirmed not only by local dignitaries but by
officers of the king's army who recognize some figures, 'distinctly
knowing divers of the apparitions, or incorporeall substances by their
faces, as that of Sir *Edmund Varney*, and others that were there slaine; of
which upon oath they made testimony to his Majestie'.[72] One 1648
pamphlet, *Strange Predictions Related at Catericke in the North of England:
By one who saw a vision, and told it himselfe to the company with whom he
was drinking healths; how he was struck, and an Angel appeared with a Sword*,
combines news with an admonition delivered to a drunk man by an
angel, after which a neighbour runs around in a devil costume. The
mocking pamphlet warns of the dangers of neutralism.[73] In 1652
Joseph Hall scorned a vision of an angel 'in a visible form, with a
naked sword in his hand' descending on an altar and prophesying
England's destruction.[74] Hall believed in the reality of the spiritual
world, but imaginary visions were more likely to harm than benefit
true belief. Another wonder pamphlet, about a speaking 'Man-fish' in
the Thames in 1642, compares the prodigy to 'an Angel sent to guard
this Kingdome . . . so debonarie and full of curtesie'.[75] Angels were
synonymous with providential warnings and protection, though
were often treated sceptically or satirically.

   Angels played a part in conversion narratives and visionary experi-
ences. Anna Trapnel's account of her spiritual revelations of 1642
describes a vision of an angel, an outward, sensible vision that speaks
and comforts her inwardly.[76] Another prophet, Mary Cary, asserted
that the regicide only took place because of the support of 'thousands
of Angels', invisible angels unfortunately for the regicides.[77] Elizabeth
Poole, called to prophesy for the army's Council of Officers in
December 1648, may have seen angels in John Pordage's house in
the following months.[78] Anne Green, wrongly condemned for in-
fanticide in Oxford in 1651, had visions of angels foisted upon her.
Several news reports and pamphlets of her story were published after
she providentially survived hanging, one reporting that a physician

ushered the women around her away, fearing they might 'suggest
unto her to relate of strange Visions and apparitions'. Nonetheless,
and perhaps at this hint, one derivative and sensationalized pamphlet
ornamented her story with a vision of paradise and '4. little boyes
with wings, being four Angels'.[79] Angels—real, immediate angels,
that visit and speak to people and visibly act in the world—are
turned into gossips' fantasies.

   Angels do act in the world, but invisibly. Like providence they need
to be discovered in patterns of events. Looking at the stars' predictions
for 1644, the astrologer William Lilly wrote, 'it may be feared that God
hath sent downe into our English Court and Common Wealth, that
destructive and Martiall Angell, which incited the enemies of God to
destroy each other'.[80] According to Lilly and others, angels interfere in
human affairs (sometimes fouling the predictions of astrologers).
A belief in angels as beings who directly intervene in contemporary
events using their own power underpins other kinds of texts, which
we might be tempted to read metaphorically or polemically. Arise
Evans's pamphlet *The Voice of Michael the Archangel, To his Highness the
Lord Protector* (1654) describes Oliver Cromwell's riding accident on 29
September 1654, St Michael's day, as an intervention by the angel.
Michael is the angel the Lord promised to send to deliver the English,
Evans writes, and the accident must be his work (he appeared before
the horses and caused them to panic). Evans exhorts: 'the angel with
his drawn sword stands in your way, though yet you have taken no
notice of him; but I beseech you again consider seriously what befell
you on Saint *Michael* the *Archangels* day last past, and know what an
Angel *Michael* is said to be in Scripture'. Though the work is suasory, it
is also meant literally; and Abraham Cowley's mocking *A Vision,
Concerning his Late Pretended Highnesse Cromwell, the Wicked; Containing
a discourse in vindication of him by a pretended angel, and the confutation
thereof by the author* (1661) is intended as an antidote to this literalism.[81]

   Not all those who saw angels presumed to publish. The intellectual
descendants of John Dee sought to summon and converse with angels
yet were secretive about it. Lilly's autobiography, written at Elias
Ashmole's request, suggests a community of astrologers who sum-
moned angels as part of their divination, hinting at the extent and
the difficulty of defining its contours. Ashmole was a friend to Lilly and
a patron to Pordage, who sought to summon angels. Lilly had read
Dee's conversations with angels: he thought genuine spiritual

communication, and 'Mosaical Learning', had occurred, but that it had been curtailed by the personal imperfections of Dee's scryer Edward Kelley, and by other, unrecordable things.[82] Lilly reports that Simon Forman's more successful astrological predictions were executed 'by Conference with Spirits'.[83] Lilly's first teacher was the Welsh astrol-oger and physician John Evans, who once succeeded in invoking 'the Angel *Salmon*', who destroyed part of a building. Salmon may be an incarnation of Solomon, mythical author of the *Ars Notoria*, a treatise on angel-magic that circulated in manuscript before it was printed in Latin and then in an English translation in 1657. The *Ars Notoria* teaches invocations of angels' names in order to effect magic by the power of angels. This knowledge Solomon received by the thunder-ous voices of angels themselves.[84] Lilly bought one of Forman's copies of *Ars Notoria* in 1633–4, some years after Forman's death. Lilly's subsequent teacher Alexander Hart was paid to assist in 'a Conference with a Spirit' by 'a rusticall Fellow of the City'.[85] While Lilly does not indicate that Hart ever successfully summoned spirits, he presents this as a recognizable economic transaction.

William Hodges, a royalist astrologer from near Wolverhampton, dealt with the thorniest judicial questions by consulting angels in a crystal: 'His Angels were *Raphael*, *Gabriel* and *Uriel*,' though 'his Life answered not in Holiness and Sanctity to what it should, having to deal with those holy Angels'. Lilly reported some successes despite these reservations.[86] Angelic consultations work, and in the hands of poor scholars are more reliable than astrology. Aubrey later described the practice of calling visions in a 'Berill, or Crystall', a red-tinted crystal that is one of the twelve stones mentioned in Revelation. His account was illustrated with an image of one beryl successfully used by a Norfolk minister: the crystal is set in a ring engraved with 'the Names of Four Angels, *viz. Uriel, Raphael, Michael, Gabriel*'. Angels appeared openly to the minister, and forewarned him of his death.[87] Lilly describes one Sarah Skelhorn, a 'Speculatrix' who called angels by magical invocation and saw them in a crystal. They also followed her around the house.[88] He also mentions two old prophecies that he believes were validated, which

were not given vocally by the Angels, but by Inspection of the Crystal in Types and Figures, or by Apparition the Circular way, where, at some Distance, the Angels appear representing by Forms, Shapes, and Creatures,

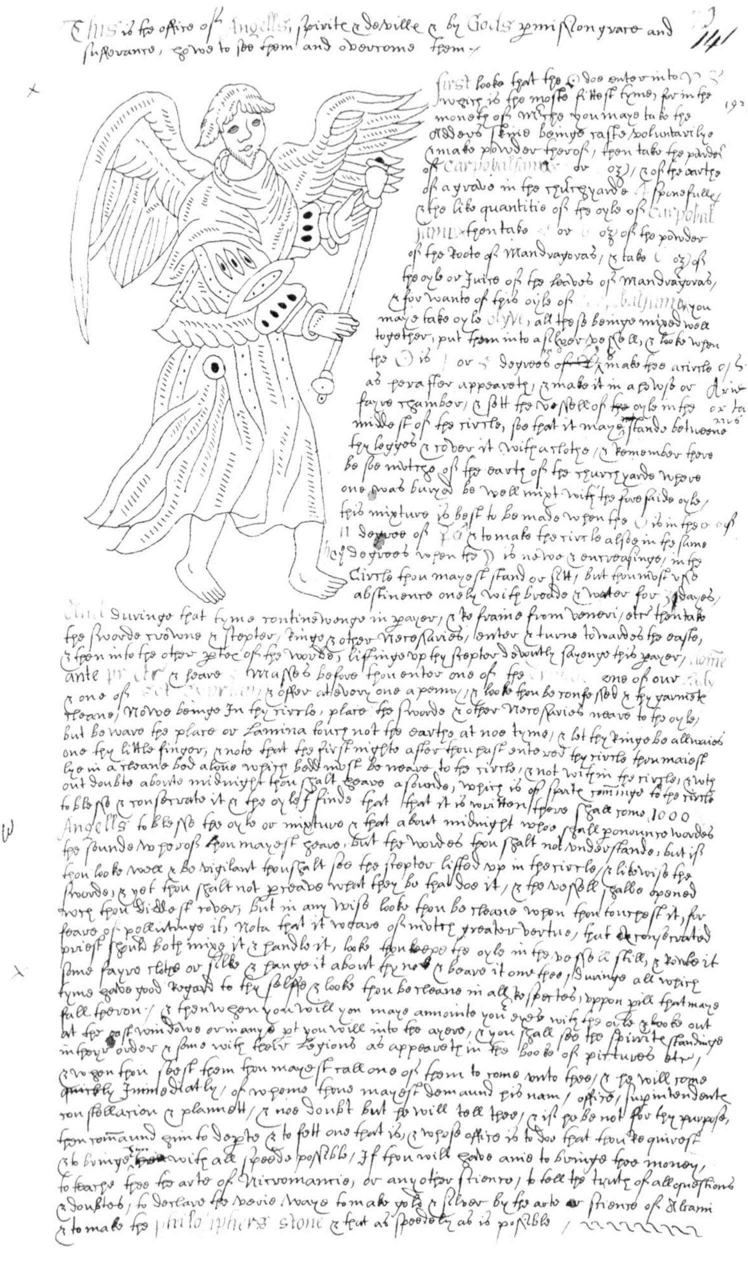

**Figure 3.** Sixteenth-century book of magic with instructions for conjuring spirits

what is demanded: It is very rare, yea, even in our Days, for any Operator or Master to have the Angels speak articulately; when they do speak, it's like the *Irish*, much in the Throat.[89]

Forman's pupil Napier, for whom Lilly felt much admiration, prayed to angels: 'he invocated several Angels in his Prayer, *Viz. (a) Michael, Gabriel, Raphael, Uriel*, &c.'. Ashmole annotated and added a striking detail: '*At sometimes, upon great Occasions, he had Conference with* Michael, *but very rarely.*'[90] One of Napier's manuscripts from 1619 describes consultations with the angel Raphael, who answers Napier's questions about alchemy and the health, longevity, and fortunes of several clients.[91] This may explain why Lilly thought Napier outdid Forman. Aubrey confirms Napier's godliness, and reports that he conversed with Raphael, who would give him responses to queries about patients. It was because of conversations with angels, rather than his horoscopes, that his predictions were so reliable. Aubrey thought the same of the skilled Mr Marsh of Dunstable, who privately confessed that astrology was merely the 'Countenance' and that his real business was done 'by the help of the blessed Spirits'.[92]

Lilly is coy about his own communications with spirits. He admits, 'I was once resolved to have continued *Trithemius* for some succeeding Years, but Multiplicity of Employment impeded me, the Study required in that kind of Learning, must be sedentary, of great Reading, sound Judgment, which no Man can accomplish except he wholly retire, use Prayer, and accompany himself with Angelic Consorts.'[93] Lilly means not merely the holy life necessary as a precursor to spiritual conversations, but literal angelic consorts. The *Steganographia* of the fifteenth-century German mystic Johannes Trithemius describes a cabbalistic and hermetic method for acquiring and transmitting knowledge that uses angelic names to invoke and communicate with and by angels. Though it influenced John Wilkins's *Mercury, or, The Secret and Swift Messenger* (1641), the first partial English translation of *Steganographia* was by Lilly in 1647. Lilly and his contemporaries read it as a magical resource and a means of summoning and conversing with angels.[94]

Throughout his almanacs in the 1640s Lilly hints at the role of angels in human affairs. He repeatedly states that guardian angels protect countries, and the fortunes of a country depend upon their intervention, most strikingly in 1647–8:

Live *English Parlia[ment]*. Fear not the male-contented, thy *Angel-Protector* is very potent, his name is not *Michael*, yet he is powerfull . . . Welcome sweet Messenger from *Ireland*, what newes dost thou bring? Famine, mortality, & most horrible division is now there, great deserting each other; poor bestiall Kingdome, thy *Angel* is a sluggard, but the *English* Angel is active.[95]

He refers to the presiding angels of several countries, but to identify the English guardian as not Michael is unusual.[96] Perhaps he accepted the passage in Dee's diaries, in which Michael implies that it is Enoch who presides over England.[97] Though they are certainly political, Lilly's angels are not mere metaphors, or even intelligences presiding in the stars, but real beings engaged in struggles. He assigns to them responsibility for heavenly apparitions such as parahelii, as in *The Starry Messenger* (1645):

I am clearly of opinion, These Sights, as well as many others, were caused by those tutelary Angels, who, by Gods permission, and under him, have the Government of the *English* Commonwealth. They are sensible of those many impending Miseries now too plentifully amongst us. Their conference with man now, as in the days of old, very few attain unto, it being a blessing sought after by many, attained unto by few: And yet there are some of opinion, There lives in the world some, a small Party in *England*, that know more then they utter, and, either by Vision, or verball Colloquie, have the knowledge of future events, yea even from the blessed Angels.

But alas, these are Riddles; I must adhere unto my Astrologie; and yet wish all happinesse to those good souls that either confer with their own *Genius*, whom some call, A good Angel; or with such other of those heavenly Ministers whom God in mercy affordeth them. And herein let no Reader mistake me, for I abhor Witches, or those *Necromancers* that raise the deceased out of their graves, or those Circular Priests now almost worn out of the world: My meaning is this, That I do believe there are many now living, to whom God, by his Angels, gives Revelation of things to come: And where and to whom God gives such a blessing, I believe that Saint may lawfully use the Talent God hath enabled him with.[98]

Angels are God's messengers, but in this cosmology they bear delegated authority and have responsibility for sending messages themselves. Demonic magic, conventionally understood as magic exercised through the agency of fallen angels,[99] is a practice entirely distinct from the lawful calling of angels. Lilly describes not only natural or sympathetic magic, but actual 'verball Colloquie' in which angels disclose the future, a practice widely sought but accomplished by fewer, though 'many now living', who keep quiet their conversations with their 'Genius' or tutelary 'good Angel'. Such prudence was necessary, because these practices were easily identified by hostile observers as a form of demonic magic, or cacodemology. Lilly describes in his 1648 *Ephemeris* a vision of angels struggling over the fate of England, and another vision of an angel waving a sword over London. These can be seen as metaphors, albeit metaphors that are grounded upon specific angel-doctrines, in part because they conform to literary conventions of dream visions ('slumbering I thought a voice delivered articulately these words'); but they must also be understood literally, as induced visions of guardian angels dutifully articulating prophetic warnings.[100]

*Anti-Merlinus, or, A Confutation of Mr. William Lillies Predictions* (1648) dismisses Lilly's enquiries into the actions and names of guardian angels, and accuses him of 'pretending . . . to ground his predictions upon Cacodemologie, or conference with Devils, and lapsed Angels'.[101] The author, H. Johnsen, identifies himself as a student of astrology, and uses the term 'cacodemology' in a technical rather than bombastic manner, accurately identifying this subtext of Lilly's writings in the 1640s. Perhaps he had heard rumours of Lilly's angelic conversations. Lilly says nothing about fallen angels, but Johnsen transforms them into demons. While conversing with angels is close to prayer, conjuring fallen angels is witchcraft, and risks execution under the 1604 Act Against Conjuration and Witchcraft. Persecution for witchcraft recommenced in England in 1645.[102] Dee, Forman, Napier, Evans, Lilly, and others conversed with angels, but did not advertise it in print.

The association between astrology and natural magic partly explains the ferocity of the attacks on astrology in the 1640s. Scriptural annotators and theologians conventionally described judicial astrology as presumptuous though not unlawful, and with some basis in reality.[103] Calvin thought astrology a means to divine wisdom, and Wollebius that angels' superior knowledge was partly based on their ability to interpret stars. The inhabitants of Stortford endorsed the influence of the stars as a fundamental truth.[104] The 1640s saw a rise in the number of astrological publications and a diversification in their forms.[105] Predictions and attacks on individual astrologers were politicized. But there was also a more general attack on the art of astrology itself, pressed by fear of witchcraft, apocalypticism, and suspicion of mystical theology. Most of these attacks associated astrology with demons and sorcery. Samuel Clarke's *A Mirrour or Looking Glasse* (1654) presented a list of God's judgements 'against witches, conjurers, enchanters and astrologers'. Other taxonomies of magic and compendiums of prophesies and illusions condemned magicians and astrologers as heretics.[106] John Vicars attacked astrology as a form of witchcraft, and called Lilly the servant of Satan.[107] Astrologers were caricatured as foolish, and their assisting angels were assumed to be always fallen.

The most detailed report of angelic conversations published in the revolutionary decades indicates why Lilly and others were reluctant to publicize theirs. Occult knowledge was valuable precisely because it was possessed by few and passed on through personal and controlled circumstances. It was nonetheless dangerous as it invited accusations of cacodemology and witchcraft. In 1659 the scholar Meric Casaubon published a substantial folio volume entitled *A True and Faithful Relation of What Passed for Many Yeers between Sr. John Dee (A Mathematician of Great Fame in Q. Eliza. and King James their Reignes) and Some Spirits: Tending (had it succeeded) to a general alteration of most states and kingdomes in the world* (1659). Some of Dee's transcripts of his conversations with angels in the 1580s had survived in Sir Robert Cotton's library, which was not an isolated private space, but an internationally renowned repository for scholars, and knowledge of these manuscripts shaped Dee's posthumous reputation.[108] The late William Ussher, who had preached against the worship of angels, had wanted the manuscripts published, and this prompted Casaubon to study them and commission partial transcriptions. The resultant edition expresses his antipathy to Dee.[109]

Dee spoke with angels, including Michael, Uriel, and Gabriel. Gabriel reminded Dee that man in innocence 'was a partaker of our presence and society', and so spoke customarily with God and good angels; but man lost this favour, along with the angelic language, when the Devil, properly called 'Coronzon', caused the Fall.[110] These communications took place through the medium of a showstone and scryers, including Edward Kelley and Bartholomew Hickman, some in London, some with Count Laski in Poland, the emperor Rudolph and King Stephen in Kraków, and Count Rožmberk in Bohemia. *A True and Faithful Relation* is remarkable in several respects, not just because of its revelations, such as the existence of female angels, but because it is the most detailed and extensive account of conversations with angels from the early modern period, replete with scholarly learning, cabbalistic mysticism, and tables of mystical and paradisal

alphabets dictated by angels.[111] Moreover, it was published by a scholar
whose perceptions and intentions were very different from Dee's. The
manuscripts spoke to numerous 1650s concerns—a perfect, angelic
language, the relationship between Christianity and the cabbala,
Mosaic learning or exchanges between natural philosophy and the
spiritual world—but what interested Casaubon was proof of the exist-
ence of the spiritual world and of the dangers of conversing with
angels. He published Dee's records to attack modern Sadducism,
enthusiasm, and radical speculation.

Casaubon was both doubtful of stories of diabolical possession and
fearful that scepticism about spirits led to atheism.[112] It was essential to
his argument that Dee's conversations were real, not the fictions of a
delirious mind or a confidence trick by a series of unscrupulous
assistants. The enthusiastic interest in angels in the 1640s was twinned
with a scepticism that appeared to undermine belief in a spirit world;
the attack on enthusiasm, by drawing attention to its physiological
basis, threatened faith itself, as if the existence of imaginary spirits
proved there were no true ones: 'this Licentious Age will afford very
many, who with the *Saduces* of old (that is, Jewish Epicures) believe no
*Spirit*, or Angel, or Resurrection'. Casaubon thought that Dee's docu-
mented conversations could empirically falsify disbelief, and his preface
promised to fight atheism in Anabaptists and others, challenging their
'*Supposed Inspiration* and imaginary *Revelations*'. Like many contem-
poraries, he saw the revolutionary decades as a critical moment in the
history of religion, in which radical modes of belief and doubt threa-
tened to undermine the true Church altogether.[113] Casaubon emphat-
ically asserts that Dee's experiences were real, and they prove both
enthusiasts and sceptics wrong. 'All I understand by *reality*', Casaubon
qualifies, 'is, that what things appeared, they did so appear by the
power and operation of Spirits, actually present and working, and
were not the effects of a depraved fancy and imagination by meer
natural causes.'[114] Dee's conversations were real conversations, Casau-
bon argues, with real spirits, but they were not good angels. Dee
conversed with devils seeking to subvert true religion.

Casaubon knew that his contemporaries doubted the veracity of
either Dee or his scryers, not least because of the sensational sugges-
tion, made by the naked female angel Madimi, that Kelley and Dee
should hold their wives in commonalty. Few angelic voices survive, so
I shall quote Madimi:

*Not content you are* to be heires, *but you would be Lords, yea Gods, yea the Judgers of the heavens: Wherefore do even as you list, but if you forsake the way taught you from above, behold evil shall enter into your senses, and* abomination shal dwel before your eyes, as a recompence, *unto such as you have done wrong unto: And your wives and children, shall be carried away before your face.*[115]

The words were communicated by Kelley, and some have thought that the antinomian order that they commit adultery was Kelley's fabrication. However, among many objections to Kelley's reliability, the most potentially damaging to Casaubon's argument was the flawed scholarship of Dee's angels. 'Devils, we think generally,' wrote Casaubon, 'both by their nature as Spirits, and by the advantage of long experience . . . cannot but have perfect knowledg of all natural things, and all secrets of Nature, which do not require an infinite understanding . . . The knowledge Divels have of things Natural and Humane is incomparably greater then man is capable of.' Yet it was evident that one of Dee's spirits was deficient in this respect, speaking post-classical Latin, 'rather as one that had learned Latin by reading of barbarous books, of the middle age, for the most part, then of one that had been of *Augustus* his time, and long before that'.[116] Even fallen angels should speak perfect Latin. Moreover, Casaubon adds, Kelley himself noticed that the spirits appeared to borrow from Agrippa, Trithemius, and Paracelsus, modern authors with dubious doctrines, rather than report directly the book of nature. Casaubon's resolution of this doubt is deft, and echoes the doctrine of accommodation which was a premiss for the artistic representation of unfallen angels: like God or Moses, the Devil fits himself to the capacity of those to whom he speaks, and Dee seems to have been happy with the performance. Just as the pagan gods were widely understood to be the images of fallen angels,[117] corrupt, occult knowledge could be passed on by the Devil, and if Michael or Madimi sounds like Agrippa, this could be because the Devil deceived Agrippa before he deceived Dee:

If any thing relish here of *Trithemius* or *Paracelsus*, or any such, well may we conclude from thence, that the Divel is like himself. This is the truest inference. It is he that inspired *Trithemius* and *Paracelsus*, &c. that speaketh here; and wonder ye if he speaks like them? . . . Yea, those very Characters commended unto Dr. *Dee* by his *Spirits* for holy and mystical, and the original Characters (as I take it) of the holy tongue, they are no other, for the most part but such as were set out and published long agoe by one *Theseus Ambrosius* out of Magical books, as himself professeth. . . . So that in all this the Divel is but still constant unto himself, and this constancy stands him in good stead, to add the more weight and to gain credit to his Impostures. Not to be wondred therefore if the same things be found elsewhere, where the D. hath an hand.[118]

The very characteristic that suggests human agency is in fact evidence of a diabolical confidence trick. Casaubon's trust in his devils equals Dee's trust in his angels.

Casaubon's intent in publishing the work is twofold. First of all, he seeks to discredit the alleged revival of Sadducism and sceptical or radical theologies that challenged the spiritual architecture of heaven. But he is also seeking to discredit enthusiasm itself, and with it the religious toleration associated with the Protectorate. The Council of State heard of the publishing enterprise late in the summer of 1658 (it had been entered in the Stationers' Register on 3 March) and called in the printers and publishers and requested to see a sample sheet.[119] The President of the Council was Henry Lawrence, who presumably had an inkling of what the book would contain and the ways in which its publication by a known royalist like Casaubon could reflect upon the government. The state papers do not contain any report by the committee formed to investigate the publication. Ten days later Oliver Cromwell died, and one of the committee, Richard Cromwell, succeeded as Lord Protector. The volume appeared with a 1659 imprint. The Revd William Shippen, who annotated a copy in the 1680s and recorded the story of the attempted suppression, saw the volume as politically charged and implicitly anti-enthusiast and anti-fanatic.[120] Casaubon exploits a record of conversations with angels for two purposes, one theological, the other political. Angels always had and would have this two-handed property, but it became particularly pronounced in Britain during the 1640s and 1650s.

## Radical Angels

Casaubon's oblique intervention was also a response to the fourth mode of writing about angels, one which speculates about them, and uses them 'imaginatively' (a word needing careful interpretation in the context of this period) to discuss matters of soteriology. This mode of writing can be described as a 'radical mode'.

Around 1656 Thomas Hicks, who wrote against Quakers and religious heterodoxy more generally, encountered four men who denied the immortality of the soul. Hicks proceeded to write a tract against this wilful ignorance, entitled *A Discourse of the Souls of Men, Women, and Children; and of the Holy and Blessed Angels in Heaven, and of the Evil and Damned Spirits in Hell.* His adversaries were materialists and mortalists: he is not specific enough to indicate whether they were psychopannychists, like Milton and Richard Overton, believing that the soul sleeps between death and Resurrection.[121] Hicks systematically uses angels to demonstrate the existence of an immortal human soul: 'Mortall men cannot see the immortal substance of their souls, with their bodily eyes; no more they cannot see the Angels which tarry about them, unless they do assume a body to themselves, no nor they cannot see the Divel and evill spirits although they do go throughout the world continually.'[122] The tract straddles practical divinity and mechanical theology. Human souls, angels, and devils are all spiritual substances, and to deny one is to deny the other.[123] His adversaries were probably unpersuaded by his reasoning. The argument had been made at greater length and more variously by Henry Woolnor in 1641, also responding to an outbreak of mortalist reasoning, and also using angels as tools of reasoning.[124]

Another heresy significantly revised and developed in these years was Socinianism, the denial of the divinity of Christ, which sometimes involved unusual angel-doctrine. The Socinian Racovian Catechism was printed in Latin in London in 1651, with a licence signed by John Milton; it was investigated by the Council of State.[125] An English translation by John Biddle appeared the following year, one of a series of publications by Biddle that developed antitrinitarianism in an idio-syncratic though perhaps distinctively English direction. In 1647 Biddle declared that the Holy Spirit was not part of the Godhead but 'a created spirit' and the head of the angels. The House of Commons ordered that the work be seized and burned, and appointed divines to persuade Biddle of his errors.[126] The following year he affirmed the humanity and non-divine nature of Christ, and that the Holy Spirit was an angel: 'the word *Angel* Originally Greek, and the Hebrew Malak answering thereunto, signifieth any Messenger whatsoever, but is in Scripture oftentimes appropriated to signifie a Spirit or Heavenly Messenger. In both which respects the Holy Spirit is an Angel, being not only a Messenger, but a Spiritual Messenger sent out

of Heaven'.[127] Subsequent publications by Biddle caught the attention
of the Council of State: in December 1654 they were declared blas-
phemous and burned, and he was imprisoned without pen and ink.[128]
A dispute with John Owen followed, and the scandal of Biddle's beliefs
was reported at length in the newsbooks. Other Socinian works were
pursued, and enthusiastic gestures alarmed the authorities. These were
tense weeks in which Parliament debated the new constitution, the
Instrument of Government, and Fifth Monarchists and Quakers were
prominently disruptive.[129] A few days after Biddle's arrest Thomas
Tany, another antinomian with a distinctive vision of angels, mounted
a symbolic attack on the Parliament door with a sword; the same
committee examined both Tany and Biddle.[130] The response to Biddle
was resolute, despite the demands of other events that might have been
more pressing (Cromwell dissolved the Parliament a week after their
last discussion of Biddle).[131] Antitrinitarianism was perhaps the most
disturbing heresy of the later seventeenth century, and Biddle's writ-
ings were distinguished by the clarity and simplicity of his scriptural
exegesis, in contrast to Owen's dogged responses.[132] Responding to his
claim that the Trinity was three separate persons, God, his human Son,
and the chief angel, confutations were obliged to restate orthodox
theological accounts of angels.[133] In Biddle's hands angels proved a
flexible theological device, and this was just as threatening to ortho-
doxy as denying the existence of the spirit world altogether.

The translation of mystical authors like Trithemius, Henry Corne-
lius Agrippa, the *Ars Notoria* (Agrippa, Paracelsus, and the *Ars Notoria*
were all translated by Robert Turner in the 1650s), and especially Jacob
Boehme (from 1644 onwards) prompted radical speculation about
angels, and invited enthusiasts to find ways of incorporating occult
beliefs and folklore and spiritual experimentalism into conventional
Protestant angelology.[134] John Pordage, who left accounts of angelic
visions, was a devotee of Boehme. Pordage is discussed in the next
chapter; here I shall consider the angel-beliefs of a number of people
who converged on Pordage's kitchen in Bradfield, Berkshire, in 1649,
when he began to experience his visions, including Abiezer Coppe,
Thomas Tany, Richard Coppin, and William Everard.

Inspired by angelic voices, Coppe writes in *A Fiery Flying Roll* (1649)
that angels walk among humans, pouring forth their vials of wrath and
swearing oaths, cursing, and teaching others to curse, and he has had
'absolut, cleare, full communion' with them.[135] In *A Second Fiery Flying*

*Roule* (1650), written shortly after his stay with Pordage, Coppe uses
Revelation 10, a favourite among enthusiasts, to encourage the godly
('Precisians') to desire their neighbour's wife. 'It's meat and drink to an
Angel [who knows no evill, no sin] to sweare a full mouth'd oath.'
There is an angelological joke in the colloquial 'it's meat and drink':
conventionally angels need neither. Coppe wants his readers to reflect
on traditional exegesis through this playful paradox, but also mounts an
argument in favour of the inner gospel, against the formal and external
moral law. Later he relates:

> I have gone along the street impregnant with that child [lust] which a
> particular beauty had begot: but coming to the place, where I expected to
> have been delivered, I have providentially met there a company of devils in
> appearance, though Angels with golden vials, in reality, powring out full vials,
> of such odious abominable words, that are not lawfull to be uttered.[136]

The place of revelation is more likely to have been a brothel than a
church, for there he finds good angels disguised as bad. This is an
evident moral inversion, but it is also an angelological one, for while
angels of darkness often disguise themselves as angels of light, angels of
light do not present themselves as evil angels.

    This apocalyptic, eschatological view of angels is both immediate
and rarefied, simultaneously literal and metaphoric. Even as he
writes, Coppe says, Michael is fighting the dragon in heaven. His
associate Richard Coppin also used this as the central motif in his
*Michael Opposing the Dragon* (1659), where he suggests that anyone
who has been enlightened by Christ or angels, and been administered
a heavenly message or spiritual comfort, should themselves become
an angel of God and minister to others; each man should be an
angel.[137] Yet the entirely internalized eschatology of Coppin's *Divine
Teachings* means that angels are transformed into human impulses.[138]
Little is known about William Everard's beliefs, but he appeared in
the form of a spirit, or a spirit appeared in his shape and wearing his
clothes, during Pordage's disturbing revelations of the angelical
world. Everard was also a signatory to the perfectionist tract, prob-
ably penned by Gerard Winstanley, which declares: 'Every single
man, Male and Female, is a perfect Creature of himself; and the same
Spirit that made the Globe, dwels in man to govern the Globe.'[139] He
was accused of heresy, denying God and Christ, though Winstanley
declared him innocent.[140]

Enthusiasts propounded a much closer relationship between angels and humankind than others, perhaps because they sensed the perfectibility of the human soul. In this proximity, angels could lose their identity as thinking, acting, communicating beings, and become an aspect of human soteriology. However, the rich and metaphoric writing of spiritual enthusiasts suggests a dual vision of a coextensive or coexistent world of angels. Angels are both a figure for an internalized and human-centred eschatology, and also real, independent creatures, whose actions shape the universe and whose struggles have their own pathos.

Jacob Bauthumley was at this time expounding a Behmenist internalist eschatology in which the struggle between Michael and the Dragon was 'the fleshly and dark apprehensions of God against the pure and spirituall'. He develops the Augustinian account of evil as the privation of good to an extreme by contending that the Devil is not a creature. Only God has being: 'as men speake, though improperly', that is, in its accommodated sense, the Devil is 'the corruption of nature', the internalization of man's sinful acts.[141] He rejects the notion of a locale called heaven, and the idea that angels participate in God's court, 'waiting upon God, as serving men about their Lord, to see what his pleasure is'. They have no fleshly form or shape but are found in man, just as humans inhabit the angelic nature. When humankind fell:

There were Angels, Hell, and his discoveries of God, became dark and confused, and so brought him into bondage; so that the dark and carnall knowing of God is the evill Angel, and the glorious and pure manifestation of God is the good Angel: So likewise the providences that fall out in the world, that tend to the comfort or well-being of Creatures, they are the good Angels, & the crosse providences & occurrences that do afflict and grieve a people or person, they are the evill Angells or Angels of wrath and displeasure, not that they are so indeed, but because the Creature doth misapprehend the mind of God in them; for all things, whether Angels good or evill, principalities, powers, life or death, things present, or to come, are for good to them that are called of God.[142]

This is the most radically uncreaturely account of angels possible. Bauthumley veers from orthodoxy—God honoured man by taking human form and not angelical—to heterodoxy—angels are the spiritual reality of human good and bad impulses, and manifestations of God's power. The account of providence dispenses with angels as beings with freewill or an internal principle of being; angels are our angels, our communication with the light side of God's mind.

Thomas Tany's elaborate Behmenist narrative of the fall of angels is a foundation of his soteriology. The actions of angels do have a moral and narrative significance. Angels, created on the first day, reject the duty of love and fall; 'they descended into Vegitables, and left their first habitation'. Thus 'these Angels became men'. Man is a fallen angel embodied in the fig-leaf of flesh; Tany interprets Genesis 6 as describing the union of angel with human into a single being. Tany also describes the process another way: every human has an internal angel, 'we are the vegetables of the Deity tied to himself by the Angel in us, for our Angel converses with him'. This angel is the inner light of God, 'a refined man, or man unbodied or unvailed'. Only through the eye of our inner angel can we see Christ.[143] The notion may come from Paracelsus, who writes: 'nothing could pass from us to God were there not an angel in us, who takes our inner message to Heaven. Nor would anything of God come to us without such an agent, who is swifter than all our thoughts . . . the angel is nothing other than the immortal part of man.'[144] For Tany, the angel is at once a near-synonym for the soul, but also a figure in a cosmic narrative; Tany's fall is both allegorical and literal. Tany joined Pordage in seeking to identify his tutelary angel, just as Dee had done.[145]

In 1651 Tany was imprisoned for blasphemy, condemned, like Bauthumley, for denying the material existence of heaven and hell. As the angels fall into man, there is no need for a material hell. His associate Robert Norwood was imprisoned for allegedly asserting that the soul of man is the essence of God. His theology, like Tany's, suggests not a purely internalized eschatology but a species of materialism that sees all creation as corporeal. Challenging his excommunication he writes, 'if God be not a body, yet he hath a body, the whole Creation is his body; my soul in one sence is not a body; but in another sence it is a body; though it be not a fleshly, nor yet a natural body, it may be a spiritual body; for there are spiritual bodies as well as natural and earthly bodies'.[146]

Laurence Claxton, or Clarkson, was not connected to Pordage, but was well connected to his acquaintances. Following release from imprisonment for his Ranter work *A Single Eye* (1650), he pursued astrology and magic in texts that suggest an association between Behmenism, radical theology, peculiar angelology, and occult learning;

perhaps he knew about Pordage's visions or Everard's conjurations. He writes:

I attempted the art of Astrology and Physick, which in a short time I gained and therewith traveled up and down Cambridgeshire and *Essex* . . . improving my skill to the utmost, that I had clients many, yet could not be therewith contented, but aspired too the art of Magick, so finding some of Doctor *Wards* and *Woolerds* Manuscripts, I improved my genius to fetch Goods back that were stoln, yea to raise spirits, and fetch treasure out of the earth, with many such diabolical actions, as a woman of *Sudbury* in *Suffolk* assisted me . . . [147]

Claxton later discovered true faith from the Muggletonian prophet John Reeve, and his *A Paradisal Dialogue betwixt Faith and Reason* (1660) articulates an extended Muggletonian natural philosophy and history of angels. God, angels, and humans all have bodies, but whereas God is entirely divine, humans have a natural body and a spiritual soul, and angels have spiritual bodies and rational souls. Reason desires and is thus mutable and imperfect (a Behmenist belief he shared with Pordage). Angels do not subsist autonomously, but rely on the daily revelation of Christ, without which they would become 'a bottomless pit of imaginary confused darkness'.[148] God gave reason to the angels to damn one, the serpent, and the serpent is the sole reprobate angel (Claxton differs from Reeve and Muggleton on this).[149] God made the serpent more like himself than the other angels in order to punish him and display his own goodness. Reason longs for something higher, and while Adam apprehended good and evil without reason, the angels are purely rational beings.[150] This inverts Raphael's account of angelic intuitive versus human discursive reason in *Paradise Lost*:

> reason is her [the soul's] being,
> Discursive, or intuitive; discourse
> Is oftest yours, the latter most is ours,
> Differing in degree, of kind the same.          (5. 486–90)

Angels can be used to meditate on the nature of reason. For Claxton the spiritual soul makes humans superior; for Milton humans become more like angels as their bodies turn to spirit.[151]

Both Milton and Claxton, however, are materialists and mortalists. Claxton writes that God must have a body in order to be worshipped, though he does not develop the natural-philosophical basis of this position. Earth and water are eternal, all matter exists from eternity, so Creation is neither *ex deo* nor *ex nihilo*.[152] God made and gave life to angels and humans out of pre-existing, eternal matter, 'uncreated, senseless, dark, dead matter'. This matter is like but also unlike Milton's 'wide womb of uncreated night'; Coppe and the Quaker John Perrot also figure Creation as being from a womb, and Morgan Llwyd describes 'the heavenly nature and angelical world' as the 'mother'.[153] Claxton proceeds: after Creation matter is animate; God made angels and men in his own likeness, hence he must have a form; angels have faces and tongues; how else could they speak or sing? Angels have bodies formed like men, though

they shine like unto the Sun or a flame of fire; being formed in a Region of a more higher nature than this; therefore they are of motion as swift as thought, and of a pure, thin, or bright fiery nature; so that with great ease they pierce through a narrow passage at the Divine pleasure of the Creator.[154]

Claxton thinks through the narratological implications of these angelic bodies in a provocative account of the Fall. The biblical account of Eve eating a fruit is accommodated speech, describing sexual possession ('Scripture Language is much like a modest pure Virgin, which is loath to have her secret parts mentioned in the least'). The angelic serpent tempted Eve, entered Eve's womb 'through her secret parts', and begot Cain.[155] Claxton adapts the story of the sons of God in Genesis 6 to reflect upon the sexual performances of angelic bodies. Angelic bodies orifically penetrate and impregnate human bodies. Medieval iconography of the Annunciation represents Gabriel metaphorically penetrating Eve's ear with his prophecy. According to Claxton, the Incarnation inverts the Fall. God bodily conceives himself in Mary,

just so on the contrary the womb of the Virgin wife *Mary*, was honoured with the Angelical God himself, through which her polluted nature was not onely cleansed while he was in her womb, but also by the vertue of the Divine power, she was inhabited to conceive his glorious Majesty of her Seed into a holy Babe of unspotted flesh, blood and bone.[156]

Thereby the angelic God became the true God.

How does Claxton know this? An 'unerring spirit' told him. This could be an angel he conjured,[157] or it could be Reeve, to whom God spoke directly, giving him a commission as a true prophet, one of the two witnesses of Revelation 11, empowered by the mighty angel with the little book who swears oaths.[158] Angels are both the intellectual framework of Claxton's and the Muggletonians' heterodox theology and its scriptural foundation, the things that make it true.

Biddle's belief that the Holy Spirit was an angel, Pordage's angelic conversations, Ranter and Muggletonian cosmologies, Lilly's angel-magic, Tany's attempt to name his angel, and Coppe's and Bauthum-ley's eschatology had several things in common: a belief in angels' intimacy with humans; a desire to explain human circumstances though angels; a willingness to elaborate imaginatively on the angelic world as a means of understanding the immediate, material world. It is a vision that is at once internalist and permits creaturely communica-tions. While exploring the narrative of Creation and redrawing the heavens, the radicals both internalized angels and sought to speak with them face to face. For these men, angels were not only real, they were also present, an appropriate matter for enquiry, and a lens upon Creation. There was a correlation between religious enthusiasm and a readiness to think with angels. This reinforced suspicions of specu-lations about angels: it was marred with both popery and enthusiasm.

## Conclusions

The revolutionary decades of the seventeenth century witnessed copious writing about angels and I have suggested four complementary perspectives upon these engagements. There is a rhetorical mode, in which angel-doctrine is used metaphorically, in topical and political writing, to bring Scripture to bear upon constitutional thought and polemical force. This mode often reflected a traditional understanding of hierarchy and orderliness in Creation, and relied upon traditional exegesis and a belief in the immediate reality of angels. The second mode is the exegetical, and these decades saw further development of a vernacular tradition of scriptural commentaries and systematic angelo-graphy. It is possible that this tradition reached an intellectual reso-lution in these years: following the Restoration fewer scholars produced major works of scriptural commentary or annotation, though this also correlates to a decline in apocalyptic fervour. The third, creaturely mode describes the visible or invisible intervention of angels in recent human affairs, providential appearances, and direct communication between humans and angels; this is the most tenuous mode of writing as it is secretive and usually indirect, though it indicates an intensive level of activities promoting interspecies interaction. The fourth mode is a synthesis of the first three: it is metaphoric *and* exegetical *and* literal. It can be described as a radical mode, not only because it is associated with religious enthusiasts, but because it evokes the immediacy of the spirit world and attempts to redescribe the history and geography of the universe, to redraw the heavens.

These modes are linked by their social origins in millenarian expectations, political fissure, and the tension between growing conservatism and radicalism, and bear witness to a broader cultural shift. However, they are also linked by their powerfully creative and analytic use of angels to describe and understand the world, their latent powers as intellectual mediators sharply brought into focus in ways that emphasized the imaginative as well as the doctrinal.

# 5

# Conversations with Angels

## The Pordages and their Angelical World

J ohn Pordage conversed with angels, and they transformed his life.
His story, and that of his family, and his gathered congregation, is
an important and revealing one in the history of religious radicalism in
the seventeenth century. It tells of a zealous individual whose experi-
mental divinity rejected religious orthodoxy and prompted him to
move through an occult visionary period to a revised spiritual outlook
that was finally accommodated in the Restoration to a position com-
patible with doctrinal quietism. Beginning in 1649 Pordage saw angels,
and explored the invisible, spiritual worlds they inhabited.[1] His spirit-
ual insights were informed by reading occult authors, especially Jacob
Boehme, but also Paracelsus and Hendrik Niclaes, yet he saw himself
as a contributor to the central, visionary tradition of the true Protestant
Church. While he was cautious about revealing his theology, his
ejection from his living after a trial in 1654 persuaded him to publish
a description of his spiritual revelations and angelic conversations. He
had numerous followers, and was in later life involved in the founda-
tion of the Philadelphian movement. Angels were central to Pordage's
heterodox and controversial theology, and their testimony was also the
source of his insights and the proof of their verity. John's son Samuel, a
young witness to his father's contact with angels, would write an epic
poem that charted the universes his father had discovered, using
narrators that spoke with, and were guided by, angels. The writings
of the Pordages reveal the depth of intellectual turmoil that could
result from beliefs in angels, their imaginative and prophetic force,
and their central role in enthusiastic spirituality.

## How Do You Speak to an Angel?

When Richard Baxter looked back on the spread of heresy in 1650s England, he identified five principal new sects with similar doctrines: the Vanists (after Sir Henry Vane, republican politician, religious writer, and subject of a sonnet by Milton), Seekers, Ranters, Quakers, and Behmenists. Of the last he writes:

> The cheifest of these in *England* are Dr. *Pordage* and his Family, who live together in Community, and pretend to hold visible and sensible Communion with Angels, whom they sometime see, and sometime smell, &c. Mr. *Fowler* of *Redding* accused him before the Committee for divers things, (as for preaching against Imputed Righteousness, and perswading married Persons from the Carnal Knowledge of each other, &c.) but especially for Familiarity with Devils or Conjuration.

Baxter had read Pordage's account of his trial and had also conversed with one of his 'Family-Communion', who confessed that he did not know 'whether it were with the Eye of the Body or of the Mind' that he saw the odd sights that he understood to be angels.[2] Baxter thought that Pordage and Boehme were melancholy persons who sought converse with angels, something that 'God hath not judged suitable to our Condition here in the Flesh'.[3]

The translation of mystical and occult authors, especially Boehme (from 1644 onwards), impelled radical speculation about angels. Enthusiasts sought ways of incorporating occult beliefs and folklore and spiritual experimentalism into conventional Protestant angelology.[4] Pordage was profoundly influenced by Boehme's writings—his theology was also Paracelsian and familist—but his writings cannot be reduced to their Behmenist influence. His communication with the angelic world also fits into an astrological–magical tradition. A client of Elias Ashmole, it is likely that Pordage was in William Lilly's community of angel-conversants, and that his visions were invoked, at least initially, using astrological–magical means; though this is something he expressly denied.[5] Lilly had learned about angel-summoning from his tutors, the Welsh astrologer John Evans and Alexander Hart; from the manuscript recording John Dee's conversations with angels, which Ashmole also read; and from Simon Forman's manuscripts. Lilly's autobiography, written at Ashmole's request, reveals a community among whom angel-conjuration was an aspect of astrological practice, and Pordage may have benefited from this tradition as much as from Behmenism.[6] After Pordage's death, Ashmole commended him for 'his knowledge in, or at least great affection to, astronomy', and Aubrey characterized him as a 'Physitian & Astrologer'.[7]

Baxter's suggestion that Pordage was a member, or even a leader, of a sect of Behmenists is an exaggeration, but it is not without foundation. Pordage was thoroughly connected with the antinomian underground, as would emerge during his trial, when associations were identified between Pordage and Abiezer Coppe, Thomas Tany, Richard Coppin, William Erbery, and one 'Everard'. Such connections began before his notoriety, and before the war. In 1634, perhaps as part of an official crackdown on antinomian ministers, John Davenport preached at St Stephen Coleman Street against Pordage, who 'broches new-fangled opinions concerning the signes, that No Man can trie himself by them, but was to stay by for an over-powring light'.[8] His hostile comments capture an element of the theology of Pordage and his followers: an inward, mystical searching for spiritual regeneration through communion with the divine. Hendrik Niclaes proclaimed that it was possible to find spiritual perfection here on earth, that Christ had already returned and his spirit dwelled in Family of Love and in their mystical doctrines; this 'Blasphemous doctrine of Familisme' was attacked by John Etherington in a 1645 pamphlet. Etherington condemns a Mr Randall for preaching this doctrine, along with 'one that went from hence [London] to *Redding, D. Pordage*, who was in expectation of (if he hath not obtained) the chief publike place there'.[9] Etherington's comments suggest a network of perfectionists boldly promoting their doctrines in and around London; he had himself been convicted of being a leading familist, and his acute account is based on detailed personal knowledge. This network was not restricted to an underground of shadowy figures that we only identify by misspelt surnames. Pordage also had connections to John Dury and Elias Ashmole, Thomas Bromley, Mary, Lady Vere, and to Philip Herbert, Earl of Pembroke (and his son Samuel worked in the house of the Duke of Buckingham and had other aristocratic connections).[10]

Pordage's closest, most influential relationship may have been with his wife, Mary, née Lane, whom he married in 1633. She is a marginal figure in accounts of his trial, usually present in the background. In a later account of Pordage's spiritual development, forming a chapter in the history of the Philadelphian society, a quite different picture appears:

It was then from some of this Inward Mystical way in England that y$^e$ Philadelphian Society had its Rise: & that w$^{th}$ a fresh Concurrence & Holy Gale of a Divine Life & Power Opening first & Principally in M$^{rs}$ Pordage Wife of Dr John Pordage Doctor in Physick: who married her for y$^e$ Excellent Gift of God he found in her; w$^{ch}$ Gift he also became in a high degree Partaker of.[11]

The Philadelphians stressed the role of women in revelation: Jane Lead was its figurehead (and Pordage her spiritual guide), and women prophets were central to the society. It is possible that Richard Roach, the Philadelphian author of this passage and friend and follower of Lead, exaggerated Mary's role, or that it was exaggerated when it reached his ears at second or third hand. Alternatively it may be true, and it may also be the case that the 'M.P.' who wrote in 1649 a pamphlet entitled *The Mystery of the Deity in the Humanity, or, The Mystery of God in Man*, was Mary. There is much overlap between the vocabulary of John Pordage and this author, who refers to herself as 'a poor Hand-maid of the Body'; there is not, however, an exact theological semblance between the texts. M.P. equates Eve, for example, with Reason; and describes the Son as 'formed in flesh, a little lower then the Angels', which does not correspond with Pordage's position.[12] This disparity is inconclusive, however: the theologies of radical mystics, as with all believers, change over time and context, and though they do not espouse precisely the same vision, there are striking similarities between these two authors, and M.P. was probably in dialogue with Pordage, whether she was Mary Pordage, Mary Pocock, or (in less likelihood) Mary Pennington.[13] Mary and John's household was an enthusiastic and visionary one, they were inspired and suffered fear and prosecution together, and when Mary died in 1668 John did not remarry.

In 1654 Pordage was called before the Berkshire Commissioners for the Ejecting of Scandalous Ministers and accused of scandal and blasphemy. During the course of his trial several sets of articles were brought against him, some suggestive of local gossip, others more serious charges about his alleged denial of the divinity of Christ. During the 1650s antitrinitarianism was a particular source of anxiety. Christ's status was an even more charged means than angels were of exploring the relationship between God and man; Sadducism and

Socinianism were the most sensitive, most heterodox, most shocking—though often imaginary—theological positions during these years.[14] The proceedings against Pordage in September to December 1654, motivated by local politics,[15] were relentless and irregular. He was not permitted to hear some depositions, and he was not allowed to cross-examine prosecution witnesses or freely produce his own. His main persecutor was Christopher Fowler, a Reading minister still vexed that Pordage had escaped earlier charges, and Fowler was both a witness and a member of the committee that judged the case. When Pordage wrote *Innocencie Appearing through the Dark Mists of Pretended Guilt* (1655), a treatise describing the proceedings and vindicating his beliefs and behaviour, Fowler published his own, argumentative account, *Daemonium Meridianum: Satan at Noon* (1655).

During the trial, associations were identified between Pordage and various radicals. He complains that his enemies are trying 'to *crucifie* me between *transgressors, Hereticks, Familists, Ranters, Sorcerors*'. Fowler accuses him of being an 'Erberist', a follower of William Erbery (1604–54), a radical Welsh army chaplain and admirer of Boehme who was accused of denying the divinity of Christ and of being a Ranter. One of Pordage's witnesses, Richard Stockwel, was also accused of being an Erberist, and Pordage acknowledges having heard Erbery preach.[16] Pordage had earlier testified at Reading in support of Abiezer Coppe, and had praised Richard Coppin, a radical Puritan associated with Coppe and with Ranterism.[17] Among the visitors who stayed at Pordage's house during his most intense visionary period, presumably partakers of his 'Family-Communion', were the Behmenist Thomas Tany and one Everard. This was probably the Digger William Everard (like Tany, a self-proclaimed 'Jew'), who also experienced prophetic visions.[18] After his stay at Pordage's house a rumour arose that Everard was a conjuror, which Pordage was in part inclined to believe, thinking him responsible for raising certain apparitions of guardian angels and a dragon.[19] The prophetess Elizabeth Poole also visited around this time.[20] Erbery, Pordage, Coppin, Coppe, and Tany were also associated through the radical bookseller Giles Calvert, who published books by all of them, and by William Everard's comrade Gerard Winstanley, who also had angelic visions. Calvert introduced the Ranter Laurence Claxton to Coppe's London radical group 'My one flesh'. Claxton, who also knew Everard, trained in astrology and physic, studied magic in some manuscripts he found, and tried to summon spirits.[21] This is not to suggest that Pordage really was a Ranter, but that all of these religious radicals were networked, admired Boehme, believed in the validity of spiritual visions, and had an interest in summoning spirits in which magic and astrology played a part. In some respects, all 1640s radicals were seekers. The internalization of eschatology and the resurrection, mortalism, and the denial of the existence of a separate, material hell, were compatible with outward conversations with angels and angel-magic.[22]

The witnesses against Pordage testify to some bizarre happenings; one charge is that 'at the said Doctors house the face of God hath been seen; not as *Moses* saw him, but the very face, as one man may see anothers'. This looks like a form of extreme anthropomorphism resembling that of Claxton and the Muggletonians. The parishioners do not specify whether God has a man's face, though the phrase implies as much; much later Pordage would deny anthropomorphism.[23] A neighbour, Mrs Flavel, in a trance, 'saw the Philosophers stone, which she knew to be the Divinity in the Humanity'. Pordage responds that he is not charged with having seen it, nor is the relevance of the charge clear, 'Not to speak any thing concerning the Mystical writings of the deep Hermetick Philosophers, or what the judgement of some of them is concerning this secret'.[24] Evidently he held opinions on the nature of the philosophers' stone which he was prudent enough not to disclose. The terse hermetic gloss here gives meaning to a later passage in which he describes his family's experiences at the height of his visionary period: 'Our sense or faculty of tasting, was very pleasantly entertained, with those invisible dews which were sweeter then hony or the honycomb; and therefore deserve to be called the Dews of Haven, with which instead of food, we were many times wonderfully refreshed.'[25] Pordage ate manna, the food of angels, though he was circumlocutious about the meals. Pordage's angelology is infused with hermeticism, and his patron Ashmole was interested in both the philosophers' stone and the food of angels.[26]

Fowler alleged that Pordage had 'very frequent and familiar converse with Angels'; that a dragon came into his chamber, and that as he struggled with it he was assisted by 'his own Angel . . . in his own shape and fashion, the same clothes, bands and cuffs, the same bandstrings';

that his Chamber 'hath sometimes been almost filled with spirits'; that his angel commanded him to cease preaching; that a visitor to his house in a trance saw 'two Angels all in white, with Crowns' floating over the head of Pordage's daughter, and other visions.[27] Margaret Pendar, another neighbour, was converted by visions of angels, and later testified to seeing a vision of a man who promises to heal her: he produces a book he calls 'the book of the Lamb . . . a broad book with a parchment-cover, and I saw writing in it'. A dark angel appears and tempts her to suicide. Later Pordage visits her and prays 'in a very strange language, she did not understand well what he said'. She implies that the book was not the Bible and that incantations and heresies formed part of Pordage's prayers.[28]

Throughout his trial Pordage was cautious about revealing anything about his visions. When responding to questions concerning angels, he declines to utter anything that might be taken as self-accusation. He responds thus to the allegation that he had conversed with angels:

As this Article is presented in general terms, without expressing whether the Communion be visible or invisible, I do not see how it can touch me, though my enemies were my Judges, because every true Christian hath frequent communion or converse with Angels, as you may see solidly and clearly proved from Scripture by the Lord *Lawrence*, one very learned and pious, now President of the Lord Protectors Councel, in his Book Entituled, *Our Communion and War with Angels*.[29]

Pordage hoped to lean on the orthodoxy and authority of Lawrence's 1646 angel-treatise, and to point out that similar interests were held by those now in power. He exploits an ambiguity in 'converse' and 'communion', noting that while communication with the spirit world in the form of prayer and faith is legitimate, to make that invisible world visible is to risk accusations of heresy or enthusiasm. He is aware that, without being explicit, his enemies are exploring the ground for accusing him of cacodemology and conjuration, a capital offence under the 1604 Act Against Conjuration and Witchcraft. In response he points out that the Devil walks up and down the earth, in Bradfield as much as anywhere, and that every family is exposed; his persecution proves him a faithful servant of God. He continues:

If it can be proved that I ever so much as looked toward the unlawfull Art of Black-Magick, or that any evil Spirit were raised up by any compact of mine, explicite, or implicite, or that those evil apparitions were subdued and overcome by any other means then by Gods blessing upon our fasting and prayers, I shall judge myself worthy of punishment; but otherwise it is hard measure to be prosecuted and prejudiced for the malice of the Devil towards me, inflicting what I was passive in, and could not help, especially by those who profess the Christian religion, and know that the God of heaven rules over all, permitting and disposing of whatever comes to passe.[30]

Though emphatic that he does not conjure demons, he does not directly deny conversing with angels. Throughout the trial his accusers return to this allegation, and of the question of his 'own angel', and Pordage is repeatedly and adroitly non-committal. Eventually he admits in court 'that I had an Angel of God that stood by me, assisted me, comforted me, and protected me, when that dreadfull apparition was before me', though he signally does not acknowledge it to be an individual guardian, and his phrasing allows a metaphoric reading.[31] He does not wish to admit his belief in individual guardian angels (though he might have invoked Lawrence's support again) while his enemies pursue it as a Trojan horse for other, more noxious doctrines.

In a fragment of spiritual autobiography, Vavasor Powell records that in a period of uncertainty he wished that the Devil would appear before him in order to terrify him into rectitude. Satan did subsequently appear, 'not onely by his secret workings in the conscience, but by visible representations, and outwardly real apparitions'.[32] If Pordage had simply declared that he had seen evil angels, it would have been startling, but the real danger lay in the implication that he had compacted with them. In the seventeenth century bad angels appear more frequently than good, and though doubtless more terrifying, they were also more straightforward, less open to hermeneutic suspicion, because no good angel would disguise itself as a bad. An apparently good angel, however, might be a bad angel disguised; hence Pordage's claim that he could smell the difference (his son would later write that the difference was always visible, and that 'starry Halos' always distinguished good angels[33]). Richard Baxter offered a reason for the frequency that is implicit elsewhere: 'Corporeal Crassitude is an abasement, and therefore fittest for the more Ignoble sort of Spirits: We that dwell here in Bodies, are of a lower Order, than those of the more high and invisible Regions.' The ministrations of good angels are offered invisibly, because to assume corporeal form is undignified:

Some Men have long Laboured to attain a Visible or Sensible Communion with them, and think they have attained it: But while they presumptuously desire to pervert the Order of Gods Household and Government, it is no wonder if in stead of Angels, they Converse with Devils that are Transformed into seeming Angels of Light, that by Delusion, they may Transform such Men into Ministers of Righteousness.[34]

He proceeds to suggest that the actions of the devils in the world are also more noticed than the actions of angels, in part because Protestants, in their reaction against the Roman Church, show 'little Sence . . . of the great Benefits that we receive by Angels'.[35] Yet the consequence of this philosophy of angels, which Baxter shared with Pordage's persecutors, was that it was more scandalous to claim to see a good angel than to see a devil. If one claimed that an apparition was good, there were grounds for thinking that one had spoken or held commerce with it, and if it was not a good angel, one was therefore guilty of demonolatry or witchcraft.[36]

In March 1655 Pordage published *Innocencie Appearing*, his account of the trial, supplemented by petitions, and various written submissions that the court would not allow. Among these is a document, apparently prepared late in the proceedings, that would surely have provoked sensation if presented to the court. In it Pordage, prompted by God, reveals his visions of angels.[37] These were conversations with visible angels, experienced in 1649–50, which he had suppressed during his trial despite the best efforts of his accusers to elicit a confession. He is threatened by spirits in the shape of Everard, a giant, and a great dragon. The 'Ministration of the Holy Angels' supports him during these trials.[38] His visions, experienced with his family, disclose the existence of two worlds, Mundi Ideales, the Mundus Tenebrosus and Mundus Luminosus, both opened up to the inward senses, or 'internal spiritual faculties', though he describes the experience as a sensual one, visual, olfactory, tactile, and gustatory. While he firmly denied having any communion or compact with evil spirits, his initial vision is of the dark world, prompted by the Devil ('it was certainly evil'). The light world followed, and then the eternal world. Here is part of his description:

We beheld innumerable multitudes of evil spirits or Angels, presenting themselves in appearing distinctions of order and dignity, as powers, principalities, dignities; my meaning is there seemed to be inferiority and superiority, Governors and governed, The Princes of this dark world, and their subjects, which presented themselves as passing before our eys in state and pomp; all the mighty ones appearing to be drawn in dark ayery clouds, Chariots with six or at least four beasts, to every one, besides every figured similitude of a Coach, was attended with many inferior spirits, as servants to the Princes. But concerning the shapes and figures of the spirits, you must know, they were very monstrous, terrible, and affrighting to the outward man. Those that drew the clowdy Coaches, appearing in the shapes of Lions, Dragons, Elephants, Tygers, Bears, and such like terrible beasts; besides the Princes and those that attended them, though all in the shapes of men, yet represented themselves monstrously mishapen, as with ears like those of Cats, cloven feet, ugly legs and bodies, eys fiery, sharp and piercing. . . . Now besides these appearances within, the sperits made some wonderful impressions upon visible bodies without: as figures of men and beasts upon the glass-windows, and the Cealings of the house, some of which yet remain: But what was most remarkable, was the whole visible world represented by the spirits, upon the Bricks of a Chimney, in the form of two half-Globes, as in the Maps . . . were but the eys of men opened to see the kingdom of the Dragon in this world, with the multitudes of evil Angels which are everywhere tempting and ensnaring men, they would be amazed, and not dare to be by themselves, without good Consciences, and a great assurance of the love and favour of God, in protecting them, by the Ministration of the Holy Angels.[39]

His family is also tortured by the noxious smells of these angels, by 'loathsome hellish tasts', and by physical pains caused by the Devil's poisonous darts.[40] Though the spirits are seen with the inward eye, they are also seen, projected onto surfaces, with the outward eye. Pordage's parishioners do not differentiate, identifying real sights and real smells. The visual description of the light world is less elaborate:

There appeared then to our inward sight multitudes almost innumerable, of pure Angelical spirits, in figurative bodies, which were as clear as the morning-star, and transparent as Christal, these were *Mahanaim* or the Lords host, appearing all in manly forms, full of Beauty and Majesty, sparkling like Diamonds and sending forth a tincture like the swift rays, and hot beams of the Sun, which we powerfully felt to the refreshing of our souls, and enlivening of our bodies.

The bodies are figurative but they are nonetheless male and highly colourful, the first point orthodox, the second unusual, though it has a scriptural origin. Pordage and his family hear 'many musical sounds and voices'; their 'spiritual joy and delight' was 'infused into our souls, uttered by the tongue'.[41] The syntax is ecstatic and therefore unclear, but the tongues seem to be angels'. The eyewitnesses smell heavenly perfume, and eat the food of angels. An unutterable 'pleasing impression' is 'sensibly felt in the inward parts'. Pordage collapses the inward sensations into the outward. The inward worlds are coextensive but discontinuous with the outward worlds; angels are 'more immediately' in the invisible world than 'in this visible air', which implies that they are in this visible air, to be seen, even if not immediately so. The prosecution witnesses testify that the visions were seen with the bodily eye.[42] These are inward worlds that make impressions on the outward senses. They are spiritual but also material.

Pordage describes the spiritual enlightenment that visions brought, convincing him and his family of the merits of the life of virginity, a state of inward passivity. His preaching on virginity may explain his reputation for personal licence (support of this doctrine could be mistaken for antinomianism) and for discouraging sex between his married neighbours (presumably when undertaken through desire rather than spiritual impulse).[43] The spiritual world has been opened to them, and they have lived in joyful communion with it for four years since the three or four weeks of intense visions. Among the reasons he gives for not having disclosed it before or during his trial is that there has already been much light given to the world, that revealing the light to the world is not proof of the (pure) life itself, and that he had to possess the life before revealing the light, so they might be in union. The occasion of his trial becomes both a providential occasion for him to reveal what God might have intended only for his own family, and yet another example of the persecution of the saintly by the Beast.[44]

Pordage's vision is thoroughly Behmenist and hermetic, and it probably involved ritual magic—I suspect Pordage initially summoned angels with spells, and he may have practised alchemy[45]—but it is rooted in Protestant theology and specific angel-doctrine. Angels are ministering spirits; there are two sorts, good and bad; humans, at least the elect, are assigned a personal angel; Pordage's angel assumes human form; witnesses describe traditional iconography, as the angels wear white and crowns. He endorses a hierarchy of angels, without specifying the Pseudo-Dionysian orders. Fowler asserts an orthodox account of angelic visitation, against which he measures Pordage's heterodoxies: angels appear infrequently and do not tarry, and they appear with messages, for comfort, for deliverance,

for direction. Nothing in Lawrence, Fowler contends, supports
visible converse with angels. Pordage can counter this kind of argu-
ment. Fowler's scepticism about 'heavenly converse', Pordage argues,
suggests that he does not believe in the continuing ministration of
angels, and thus denies Scripture and limits God.[46] In an appendix to
his tract Pordage argues that there are degrees and distinctions among
both fallen and unfallen angels, in support of which he adduces the
names used in Scripture. Similarly, there are governors and governed
in this outward world. Both orders, secular and divine, Pordage
attributes to divine providence. Angelic hierarchies, even for Por-
dage, are evidence of the necessity or providential significance of
political hierarchies, and in support of this he cites scriptural texts,
not his own visions. This provides a basis for his appeal to superior
magistrates, in the light of the oppressive judgement of the Berkshire
commissioners; even for a visionary who communed with angels,
conventional exposition of angel-doctrine can serve a purpose in
logical, political argument.

Pordage was ejected from his rectorship on 8 December 1654, and
wrote in self-vindication. He lobbied in London, without success,
though Cromwell was sympathetic. He played no further part in public
life, though questions continued to be raised about his orthodoxy.[47]
The trial, and the publications, had little impact on the news or
contemporary politics. One reader, however, noticed Pordage and
his angels: in 1655 Christopher Parkes read Pordage and Lawrence on
angels, Salkeld on paradise, and Agrippa, and a few years later he read
Boehme.[48] Parkes was probably seeking knowledge of angels in the
present.

## 'All the *Rhetoric* an Angel has': Angels and Epic

Samuel Pordage, aged 21, appeared briefly at his father's trial, with
several other witnesses, to testify on what he had heard his father
preach in 1652 and 1654. His depositions suggest John's general
interest in Christology, witchcraft, and necromancy, without giving
the prosecutors evidence of heresy. It was, however, after this depos-
ition in his pamphlet account of the trial that John inserted testimony
of his insights into the spiritual world.[49]

Samuel was born in December 1633, and had attended the Merchant Taylors' School, but he was in Bradfield often enough to provide testimony, and his subsequent writings suggest a close relationship with his father. Though there is no record of Samuel attending university, his later career reveals him an able neo-Latinist and a learned author, and some of this learning can be attributed to John's influence. At least in his early years, Samuel was part of his father's extraordinary spiritual community.

The younger Pordage's *Poems upon Several Occasions* (1660) offers formulaic panegyrics, elegies, and love lyrics; his *Heroick Stanzas on his Majesties Coronation* (1661) shares its tone with much poetry celebrating the restoration of the king. Stylistically and intellectually these bear no relation to his most substantial poem, *Mundorum Explicatio, or, The Explanation of an Hieroglyphical Figure: Wherein are couched the mysteries of the external, internal, and eternal worlds, shewing the true progress of a soul from the court of Babylon to the city of Jerusalem; from the Adamical fallen state to the regenerate and angelical. A sacred poem* (1661).[50] Published under the initials S.P., the elaborate theology and angelic communications outlined in this epic are based on John Pordage's visions, elaborating, and perhaps augmenting, what he had been reticent about. It contains an impressive engraved 'Hieroglyphical Figure' designed by John that outlines the universe of the poem; the poem is an 'explanation', the title states, of this figure. Samuel's later writings—including *Azaria and Hushai* (1682) and *The Medal Revers'd* (1682), both responses to Dryden, and the tragedy *Herod and Mariamne* (1673)—show none of the religious enthusiasm of his epic. *Mundorum Explicatio* has been neglected, perhaps because of its poetical infelicities, perhaps because of its spiritual subject matter, but this neglect is undeserved, because it is risky and ambitious and makes strong claims for the relationship between spiritual radicalism and poetry in the seventeenth century.[51]

Part-discursive, part-narrative, *Mundorum Explicatio* ('Explication of the Worlds') describes a soul's journey through multiple universes. It is self-consciously modelled on Dante's *Divine Comedy*, and echoes Homer; at times its allegorical journey to salvation resembles John Bunyan's *The Pilgrim's Progress* (1678); while its claim to visionary poetics, spiritual revelation, prophesy, and a divinely inspired literal truth anticipate *Paradise Lost*. The 'Proaemium' begins:

**Figure 4.** Samuel Pordage, *Mundorum Explicatio* (1663), 'Hieroglyph-ical Figure'

> I Sing no Hero's douty gests in warrs,
> Nor blazon forth some Warlike Champion's Scarrs:
> I here no Prince's acts hypothesize
> With glozing praises: Nor unto the Skies
> Advance some common Justice in a King,
> Nor the dread fury of the Wars I sing:
> Nor with bewitching Layes advance above
> The Sacred, the base toyes of wanton Love.

His muse is, he announces, Urania, and his theme is heavenly love, the 'cursed Earth' and 'Th'Eternal horrors of the larger Sphear | Where great Beelzebub and his Princes are'.[52] Did Milton hear these lines in 1661, while writing his own poem, and worry that someone had pre-empted his Protestant epic? The rejection of military epic, the scorn of courtly love, the identity of the Muse are the same. Whereas Milton began *in medias res*, however, and told his story with only the occasional intervention of a narratorial voice, *Mundorum Explicatio* is didactic. It begins by demonstrating the existence of a spiritual world, in the face of the perceived proliferation of Sadducism, and outlining Pordage's vision of the four worlds. He dismisses poetic fantasies of 'brain-built worlds': his worlds are intended literally. The external or terrestrial world, the light or paradisiacal world, the dark or Tartarean world, and the eternal world (especially important in John's later theology) are rooted in Behmenism (the poem is prefaced by an encomium to Boehme and his translator, John Sparrow), but they are also the basis of John's visions. The poem journeys through them in an allegorical or accommodated narrative, though the poems also presumes their real, material existence. Pordage insists, for example, on the real existence of spirits in the outward world. He describes at length the corporeality and senses of angels to show that they are beings who interact in the created world in ways that are capable of rational explanation.[53] They are, then, both spiritual allegories and unambiguously real.

The three parts of the poem differ in content and form. Part I describes Creation, especially the nature of spirits and angels, and offers a Behmenist and Paracelsian account of the double Fall of man. Adam is made in the likeness of God, with a pure body of the spiritual materials sulphur, mercury, and salt. Evil is the First Principle of the universe; good, which will eventually overcome it, is the Second. Adam is made in this Second Principle, and is left to be tempted for forty days (an antetype of Christ's temptation in the desert). Adam's first Fall is when he discovers desire and is unmarried from the Second Principle. His understanding shrinks and God's image is obscured. The power to propagate, which had hitherto been within man, is now moved without and clothed with flesh (genitals). The more familiar narrative of the Fall follows, which, in Boehme's and Pordage's scheme, is the second Fall of humankind. The temptation of Eve by the serpent is described at length, and some of the serpent's rhetorical strategies resemble those depicted by Milton; it is possible that both authors were familiar with the extended and imaginative account of diabolical rhetoric by the godly preacher John White in *A Commentary upon the Three First Chapters of the First Book of Moses Called Genesis* (1656).[54] At this point—and in discussing Lucifer—Pordage's imaginative impulses overcome his didactic tendencies, and the poem moves away from the discursive towards narrative. Lucifer flies to the fallen angels, and addresses these 'Princely vassals!' in triumph at having 'colonize[d]' the visible world of earth (pp. 76, 77); his exploitation of the language of tyranny, slavery, and liberty has parallels with *Paradise Lost*. The narrator layers titles upon Lucifer, 'Monarch . . . *Prince* . . . Primate . . . Duke . . . Earl', indicating a suspicion of worldly honorifics. One contemporary reader seems to have noticed this anti-hierarchical impulse, underlining these words.[55] Lucifer's oration reveals the causes of the angelic rebellion: he and his peers resented their servile position in heaven, and were driven to rebel as love (the Second Principle) began to displace evil. The world is now the 'fighting stage' (p. 78) for these two principles. A roll-call of devils follows (in which Samaliel Satan is distinguished from Lucifer, the Devil), and an allegory of Death as a 'murthering hag' (p. 82) bearing fatal darts. Good angels fight evil in this world; each individual has a good and an evil angel at his or her shoulder; spirits must fight with spirits, and so local guardian angels are assigned places throughout the created world, with Michael as their general, in order to conduct this battle.[56]

   The narrator discusses the allegory of the tree of knowledge of good and evil, the actions of Lucifer in the world, and radical sects, including Dippers, Ranters, Quakers, and Fifth Monarchists. Then there is a startling break in the narrative, and a change in narrative structure. The remainder of part I describes an unnamed man who

seeks illicit knowledge, accepts a diabolic pact, and descends into
hell, guided by a fallen angel. He encounters Lucifer on his throne,
and is given necromantic skills in return for eating the fruit of the
Tree of Death (the Devil can infuse humans with the arts and
sciences; p. 119). The various fruits on the Tree, 'Fruits [that] will
ope your dimmer eyes' (p. 118), represent diverse forms of know-
ledge. Death is associated with secular knowledge and conjuration.
The Man becomes Hell's Magician, and the narrator abruptly
breaks off and ascends promising 'a higher strain' (p. 122). The
narrative is surely intended to recall John Pordage's rejection of
sorcery and necromancy, and Samuel's testimony in his father's
trial. The son's poem seeks to exculpate his father from unjust
charges of sorcery.

The oddest aspect of Pordage's diabolical iconography is hell's coat
of arms behind Lucifer's throne

> A Dragon guils, with wings erect i'th'ayr,
> A wreathed tail, his mouth flames proper yield,
> Holding a Banner, in a sable Field.                    (p. 114)

The rest of the arms showed the earth, with Death slaying a lamb, and a
dragon triumphing over a human form. The chivalric characterization
of the Devil may express a Christian disdain for the martial ethos of
Continental epic.[57] Pordage identified himself on title pages, both
before and after 1661, as 'gent' or 'esq'; yet on the title page of
*Mundorum Explicatio* he is, uniquely, 'S. P. Armig.'. 'Armiger' is one
who bears arms, and Pordage's claim here is puzzling, especially as
there is no other reference to arms in this volume. There is, however,
an extant seventeenth-century description of the coat of arms of
'Dr Pordage of Bradfield', though few seventeenth-century readers
of the poem can have known it:

> The Crest A Dragons head spitting fire
> The Coate 3 Crosse Crosseletts sables
> And a Bend checherd-Gules & or
> in a field Argent.[58]

The fiery dragon, associated with Lucifer in Pordage's elaborate cosmol-
ogy, presents a striking coincidence. The arms that Samuel claims in this
volume echo Lucifer's Arms of Hell. Perhaps the difference between the
argent and sable fields indicates an enmity between the Pordages and

the Devil's seed, and the shared fiery dragon an acknowledgement that the light and dark worlds are coextensive within this terrestrial sphere.

Part II shifts focus and describes the journey of a Pilgrim, led by his guardian angel, to Mundus Luminosus, or paradise. Goaded by the punishing conscience of his angel, the Pilgrim undergoes adult baptism with John, is tempted, and is shown, by Alathia, or truth, a map of the Holy Land—which becomes the basis of a series of inset narratives on the life of Christ. The poem turns into a hybrid form, combining an Italianate epic romance with spiritual allegory and didactic passages of occult philosophy. Alathia denounces predestination, explains that heaven is not a place but the presence of the Second Principle, and declares that good humans have both the serpent and the dove in them. The poem becomes more experimental in these passages, perhaps looking back to Sidney's *Arcadia*, introducing a series of inset songs in various metres. No single form—epic, narrative, lyric, didactic verse—can capture the full range of truths that Pordage feels driven to express.

Pilgrim's spiritual transcendence is the most intellectually and imaginatively exciting passage of the poem, and its dramatic turning point. Apocalypsis, assisted by Sophia, unbinds Pilgrim from the world and unlocks his senses: he beholds the internal worlds, and sees 'Myriads of Angels in their proper Sphear' (p. 192). Angels live here when not attending upon humans, and here angels are therefore symbolic of the inner sphere, or the invisible world. Pilgrim's seeing and hearing them is proof of revelation and of the existence of this world. Pilgrim's five senses are opened to the angelic world. He hears the songs of seraphim, reproduced within the poem, like the angelic hymn in *Paradise Lost* (7. 602–32). He hears the voices 'Of the Angelical core', smells 'Paradysaical Odors', feels the warm touch of Love, tastes the food of angels (p. 193). Samuel captures in imaginative form the literal truth of John's earlier experience, his revelation of the angelic world.

The exposition veers into allegory, as Pilgrim is tempted by Imagination, who offers pictures, turning spiritual objects into worldly, deceiving the viewer with mere shadows instead of substance. Allegorical poetry is dangerous, reflecting on Samuel's own method. Pilgrim's revelation is not to be understood allegorically: these are real angels, and real sensory stimuli. The passage, powerful and moving, recalls John Pordage's testimony in his 1655 pamphlet of the appearance 'to our inward sight multitudes almost innumerable, of pure Angelical spirits, in figurative bodies, which were as clear as the morning-star'; John too had his senses opened to the angelical world, heard its song and ate its food.[59] Allegory is the mode chosen by those without inspiration. On his space journey to the Mundus Luminosus, beset by Lucifer and protected by guardian angels, Pilgrim is able to see all four worlds. He also sees purgatory. The angel explains, in another inset song: the Devil introduced to the world errors mixed with truths, and the believer must sift doctrines before rejecting them. The angel avers that over-zealous Protestants have rejected purgatory as a popish fiction without sufficient consideration, and that there exists out of necessity an intermediate space through which imperfect souls are redeemed:

> But tell me Man! what shall those *Pilgrim's* do,
> Who in Heav'ns Way have gone, but not come to
> Be dead, and risen with the Lord, when by
> The Way they lose their mortal Life, and dye?
> They are not fit for *Paradise*: What then?
> Must they be hurled to the *Stygian* Den?
> Must they be damn'd? with God's great Mercy rather
> Doth it not stand, to bring their Spirits hither?
> Where they may finish, what they had begun;
> And to the end of *Sion's* Race may run?          (p. 223)

The guardian's indignation makes him more of a rounded character than most seventeenth-century angels; perhaps it resembles the passion of Raphael in *Paradise Lost* when he chastises Adam for his unmanly subordination to Eve (8. 560 ff.). The theology is peculiar, but the poetic argument is challenging.[60] The surface allegory (purgatory becomes visible to a Protestant through revelation) accompanies a literal meaning: purgatory must be real, and Pilgrim sees it as he travels between the worlds. This richly figurative episode suspends the story between imaginative speculation and rational argument (perhaps resembling the anomalously allegorical Limbo of Vanities in *Paradise Lost*; 3. 444–97). It is one of the strengths of imaginative writing that it is able to do this. Both Pordage and Milton seek to integrate these aspects of their writing, so the narrative accords with doctrine, and doctrine is explicated by narrative.

Pilgrim enters paradise, passing through the gate guarded by a cherub with a flaming sword. The narrator apologizes that he does not have the pen of a Tasso, du Bartas, Spenser, Quarles, or Sylvester, let alone the tongue of an angel: this is not only a modesty topos but a figure for ideal speech and a metaphor for accommodation.[61] As in *Paradise Lost*, however, angels speak of invisible things on man's behalf: the loquacious guardian angel describes the fall of the angels and Creation. Pilgrim is told of the '*theamagical* twelve fruits', the forms of knowledge (visible in the hieroglyph): some are conventional (languages, reason, poetry), some eclectic (interpretation of dreams and of poetry), some specific to Pordage's interests (the gift of union and communion with holy spirits, the gift of the five internal senses, and of divine magic; pp. 267–84). Among other things, this is a retrospective justification of John Pordage's interests, his claim to have communicated with the world of spirits, and his pursuit of magic. The poem presents true magic and theology as intertwined: the interpretation of Scripture is a 'theamagical' gift, and, for all of the virtue in Trithemius, Agrippa, and Paracelsus, divine magic is only truly learned through revelation (pp. 274, 283–92). Whereas the common rout pursue the philosophers' stone out of avarice, the true magician, instructed by purity and regeneration, commands spirits and tastes fruits beyond expression by 'all the *Rhetoric* an angel has' (p. 284). Part II ends in an ecstatic, sublime silence as Pilgrim meets Jesus through the protective veil of his angel's wings.

Like John Heydon, the young Rosicrucian author of a series of occult literary texts published in the early 1660s, Samuel seeks to incorporate Christian magic into his theological system, and angelic revelations are integral to these arguments and their exposition. Heydon's various writings discuss a vision of aerial men, astrology, astromancy, magic and theology, the bodies of angels, guardian angels, the problems of representing the invisible world, the interpretation of dreams, the Fall of man, and more. He reports that God made the earth 'out of *Chaos*, which was the bodies of wicked Angels', one of the strangest accounts of Creation.[62] The Pordages' writings are not Rosicrucian, and are less obscure than Heydon's, but they share an unusual set of convergent interests, and they articulate these concerns through a self-consciously literary form, turning sacred truths into poetry.

Part III is much briefer and discusses the principles of literary representation. The vision concluding part II is risky, boldly ignoring warnings of blasphemous iconography; the third part begins by

stating that it is not lawful to utter the wonders of Sion. Pordage may
hint that there are things he will not reveal in poetry (pp. 309–10). He is
not, he says, writing with the imaginative fancifulness of a poet. Pre-
empting criticism, he argues that this invisible world is real and
accessible to the eyes of the soul, though he has not himself been
granted this privilege:

> But least (because I here so stiffly plead)
> You should suppose I have been there indeed;
> I will confess (as 'counting it great shame
> To be accounted better than I am)
> That I not worthy have accounted been;
> O no I cleans'd am not am [sic] enough from Sin)
> I am a *Pilgrim* and do thither wen,
> Strong is my *Faith* I shall come there: *Amen!*
> Assur'd I am, although a very few
> Attain (whilst here on Earth) this Court unto,
> That here on Earth it may attained be,
> Though Flesh, and Blood impeed its clarity.          (p. 316)

He writes guided by poetic and religious inspiration, but never reveals
the source of his insight. Samuel avoids mentioning the real reason for
his certainty and assurance: that his father has described these worlds to
him. The prophetic inspiration is John's. The poem stumbles to an
abrupt and paradoxical conclusion as Pilgrim passes Jacob's ladder and
enters the New Jerusalem, where he encounters the 'Clouded Glory'
of an unrepresentable God. 'No *Man*, or *Angel* a Commission has | To
dive into this *abstruce* secret Place.' The narrator exhorts: 'O *Man*
destroy all *Images* | Of *God*', and he leaves aside the truths he has 'darkly
shadow'd forth' (pp. 330–2) to ascend into an ecstatic, aporetic silence.

  *Mundorum Explicatio* is one of a cluster of seventeenth-century epics
that are centrally concerned with angels, including *Paradise Lost*,
Heywood's *Hierarchie of the Blessed Angells*, and Lucy Hutchinson's
*Order and Disorder*. Epics could comprehend everything, and debates
about the legitimacy of representing the invisible naturally interested
poets, and informed the Christianization of epic and the invention of a
vernacular poetic tradition. For the Pordages, however, there were
additional attractions to this course: the epic form enabled them to
describe a voyage through the worlds that had been discovered through
John's spiritual inspiration. Fiction was an ideal means of explicating
spiritual truths. In their invention, however, the spiritual and the literal

can no more be separated than the fiction and the vision. The inner worlds are also sensible, outer worlds, and the poetry is prophetic.

## Pordage's Lost Angelical World

John Pordage remained the centre of a large, private congregation, and an inspiring figure among networks of religious enthusiasts. He divided his time between Bradfield and London, teaching and perhaps resuming medical practice, before moving more permanently to London in the 1660s. His associates included Jane Lead and Ann Bathurst, both of whom experienced visions of angels influenced by Pordage's teachings. The worship of the community around Pordage combined his theology with an increasing spiritualism that softened or undermined its enthusiastic accounts of the reality of multiple worlds. Pordage's theology survived and evolved in the Restoration, but it became a belief which encouraged the contemplation of, rather than interaction with, angels.

Pordage did not publish again, and Samuel's *Mundorum Explicatio* remained the deepest exploration of John's visions, but following his death his followers edited a series of manuscripts that had circulated among them for some years, eight or more treatises that composed little less than a systematic theology and guide to the universe and its materials. A pair of these were posthumously published under the title *Theologia Mystica* in 1683, with an address to the reader by Jane Lead and a preface by Edward Hooker. The volume outlined a vision of the six worlds (or globes, or centres) contained within the globe of Eternal Nature, itself within the Eternal World or Archetypal Globe: the six worlds were the 'Angelical Heaven or The Love world', the 'Dark-fire world Hell, or The wrath-world', the 'Fire-light-world or The severe world', the 'Light-Fire-world or Paradise', the 'Four Elementarie world, or The outward visible world', and the 'Fire-less world or the mercifull world' (see Fig. 5). A treatise was planned for each of these worlds, and the two outer globes are briefly described in *Theologia Mystica*. No further volumes followed. The publisher or editor of the first volume of Jane Lead's *A Fountain of Gardens* (1696 [1697]) inserted an advertisement:

This is to give Notice, that Leave having been at last obtained, after many reiterated Solicitations, from the Executors of the said Dr *John*, and of

**Figure 5.** John Pordage, *Theologia Mystica* (1683)

Mr. *Francis Pordage*, the Publisher of this Book will undertake to Gratifie the World with all the *Theological, Theosophical,* and *Philosophical* Works of the said Illuminated Son of Wisdom, which are come to his Hands; if there shall be any suitable encouragement given to such a Design.

She or he lists the titles:

*Mystica Philosophica*; or, a Treatise of Eternal Nature . . . *The Angelical World*: or, a Treatise concerning the Angelical Principle, with the Inhabitants thereof, and God in this Principle . . . *The Dark Fire World*: or a Treatise concerning the

Hellish Principle... A Treatise concerning the *Incarnation of JESUS CHRIST*...
A Discourse concerning the Spirit of Eternity, in its First Being.... *Sophia*: or
Spiritual Discoveries.... *Experimental Discoveries* concerning Union of
Natures, of Essences, of Tinctures, of Bodies, of Persons, and of Spirits.[63]

The proposed edition did not appear, though a German translation of
some of these works appeared in Amsterdam in subsequent years.[64]

Pordage did not intend these works for publication, and therefore
the authority of the extant texts must be doubted. A later manuscript
found among the papers of a 'philadelphian and mystic' Dr Keith, who
may be its author, states that Pordage 'did not put his Manuscripts into
that order which was necessary for publishing them: but set them
down only for his memory, & he wrote at several times upon ye
same subject in a different manner, & left some pieces imperfect'.[65]
The manuscript describes itself as 'A Preliminary Treatise which may
serve for an INTRODUCTION to the following Work', and it is unfortu-
nately detached from the said work, though it is probably related to
those that make up the printed volume of 1683. The author offers
some insight into Pordage's posthumous papers. He notes that
the published edition of Pordage's work 'The Eternal World & of
Eternal Nature' is only an epitome, written by someone with a poor
grasp of Pordage's meaning, while he has based his text on the original
manuscripts. He acknowledges that there are contradictions in Por-
dage's terminology that derive from their composition over many
years. He remains faithful to Pordage's ideas and words while neces-
sarily supplying 'the Disposition of ye work & ye Connexion of ye
parts' to remedy the state of the originals.[66] These observations should
warn us that all of Pordage's post-Restoration works have been sig-
nificantly altered. This is confirmed by an extant English manuscript,
'A Tract of Christ's Birth and Incarnation', which contains extensive
interpolations, reproducing a dialogue between at least two readers,
and appears to have been significantly resequenced. A number of
responses to *Paradise Lost* have been introduced by one reader, includ-
ing a speech in which devils rejoice at the Fall of humankind. At one
point the reader–rewriter observes, 'I have made very free with y^e Dr.
MS. for y^e 2 last Pages, broken y^e Drs Method & reserv'd other things
that come over again for other Places.' And later he adds that in
another manuscript, unfortunately missing, he has kept faithfully to
Pordage's matter while making free with his method.[67] Contradictions

within Pordage's tracts may result from their free adaptation by followers not in complete sympathy with his vision.[68] Several manuscripts survive in the papers of Richard Roach, an Anglican clergyman and fellow of St John's College, Oxford, who was a founding member of the Philadelphian Society; Pordage's influence was keenly felt within these restricted circles, but his was a living tradition, and his readers took liberty to revise and change his works as they copied them.[69]

What survives, however, enables a reconstruction of Pordage's later beliefs in angels, some of which can be inferred back to his original visions. These later writings are based upon his earlier journeys, but the direct revelations seem to have ceased: 'This *Eternal World* was called *the Globe of Eternity*, at the time when I was taken up to have a view of it.'[70] Pordage no longer communicated directly with angels, and instead of febrile visions he offered a systematic cosmology.

This is what he describes: the angelical world is created in matter from Eternal Nature, out of the three elements, salt, mercury, and sulphur; its form, however, is framed by an idea or principle, 'the inmost framing spirit,' or Archaeus, 'brought forth by God out of Eternal Natures Spirit'. This is true of all the worlds except the dark world, or hell, which is formed by Lucifer and the fallen angels.[71] There is thus a material consistency to the universe coexisting with a separation in innate principle. This (Neoplatonic and Behmenist) account explains why these worlds are permeable to the traveller, while nonetheless remaining entirely invisible to those without spiritual passports. Angels have freewill, and so Lucifer was free to fall: he exalted the fire-qualities (one of the principles within Eternal Nature) within himself, and so fell into the fire-quality, 'And by this means one Region of the Angelical World thro' ye sin of Lucifer & his fellow Angels was turned into Hell.' Man was made to supply the fallen angels' place, and God created first the celestial paradise and secondly the visible world out of the matter that Lucifer had corrupted. If man fell, he would therefore fall into this world rather than into the fire.[72]

Pordage depopulates this angelical world, however, by elaborating a Behmenist account of middle spirits or genii that are not angels, not an uncommon belief in the later seventeenth century. The copyist attests that this passage is from a lost treatise on the dark world:

I confess according to ye Philosophy of ye ancients, & according to Natural Magick that belongs to this visible World, there are a middle sort of spirits born from ye spirit of this macrocosm, that are mortal spirits & have no Eternal souls, & are different from ye apostate angels, & from ye holy angels, & also differ from ye race of mankind that have immortal souls, & for whom Christ died, but not for these mortal spirits. Now ye ancient Philosophers according to their Natural Magick did find out yt of this sort there some Good, loving & very kind, & some were evil, subtile & hurtfull to mankind, The Good they called <u>good Genii</u>; The bad & hurtfull they called <u>evil Genii</u>. And Socrates with many others had good Genii, & many others had bad Genii for their Guides. But this is not ye proper place to treat of this Thesis of Natural Magick in relation to this visible creation . . . [73]

This doctrine would direct the Philadelphians. These spirits inhabit the Still Eternity, and are simple, unlike angels, who are mixed spirits created from Eternal Nature.[74] The role of angels in Pordage's later theology is also restricted by his emphasis on the seven spirits that stand before the throne of God, or throne angels, which he modifies from the orthodox Angels of the Presence, the seven spirits which, in Revelation 1: 4, witness the face of God. Pordage states that these seven who wait upon the Trinity inhabit Still Eternity, proceed from the body of Holy Ghost, and are thus co-essential powers with him; *they are the high Favourites, Friends and Companions of the supreme Majesty*.[75] Here, and elsewhere in Pordage's philosophy and that of the Philadelphians, traditional aspects of angelology are sectioned off into occult and increasingly elaborate revelations, detached from conventional learning and practical worship.

Pordage's later writings testify to a weakening of commitment to the immediate, sensible reality of angels. He states that Adam was an angelical man, 'a Paradisical Man, in the Figure of an Angel'; this distinguishes him from his postlapsarian 'Bestial Form'.[76] It also, however, equates angels with the human soul, an increasingly conventional position in the later seventeenth century, and by humanizing them diminishes their status as unique creatures. Pordage espouses the orthodox position that only Christ, and not angels, can mediate between humans and God; this does not contradict his earlier position, but goes against the tendency of his earlier experiences of communicating with angels, and, in *Mundorum Explicatio*, their role as travel guides.[77]

There is nonetheless much that can be learned about Pordage's angels. They have senses; they need food; they are, unlike the seven spirits, corporeal; there is no reason in their world.[78] One of his

disciples would later dwell at considerable length on the implications
of this point for angelical knowledge. Because they are compound
beings they are open to human senses: as we have senses for exterior
objects, and as there are also spiritual objects in the world, 'there
must be in us besides ye exterior senses, other Spiritual interior ones
for the perception of Angelical and Divine Objects'.[79] Angels have
senses, which must be distinguished from the purely spiritual senses
of simple spirits. The latter are, presumably, like God's, who has
spiritual senses and the organs of sense 'in a Spiritual manner'.[80]
Angelic senses are, like their being, mixed, lying between human
and spiritual sense; in this lies a continuity with the earlier visions.
Two thoroughly creaturely statements about angels in the modified
manuscripts of Pordage's writings suggest an ongoing commitment
to thinking about angels as discrete beings who participate in a
cosmic drama. The first is that angels may be capable of a form of
reproduction: 'Nay I see no reason to doubt why Angels, good &
bad, should not have that Powre, to form new ideas in their im-
aginations, to impregnate by them a suitable matter, & so to bring
forth new compounded living Bodys; supposing God will permit it
or not hinder it.'[81] This heterodox doctrine echoes the Byzantine
writer Michael Psellus on daemons.[82] This is not a form of sexual
reproduction; it is autochthonous, perhaps even platonic in manner.
The author of the manuscript preface to a Pordage tract notes the
sexlessness of angels, which makes them superior to humans, an idea
(derived from Matt. 22: 30) which may be his own or Pordage's:
'I think no one will say that part of ye Angels are Men or Male, &
part Women or Female. . . . in Eternity after ye thousand years none
shall marry & be given in marriage; because they have all resurrection-
bodys, & consequently are equal to ye Angels.'[83] The second doc-
trine is that at the end of time there will be a Universal Restitution or
Restoration, which even fallen angels will enjoy.[84] It is possible that
these doctrines are additions by copyists: the second, in particular, is
associated with Jane Lead's post-1697 revelations.[85]

One of Pordage's copyists, transcribing his discussion of the
seven spirits, interjected: 'I am not certain whether he speaks
properly or metaphorically.'[86] This speaks to a fundamental issue.
In passages in these later works it is unclear whether Pordage has
retained a commitment to the real existence of these worlds
witnessed through inspiration. His mysticism seems diluted. This

may be the effect of shifting views, or of manuscript transmission and emendation: Philadelphians, including Francis Lee, Jane Lead's son-in-law and spiritual heir, wanted to distance the movement from its enthusiastic origins.[87] However, it is necessary to bear in mind the delicate relationship between reality and allegory that is maintained in Pordage's earlier writings: there he speaks properly *and* metaphorically. His visions are allegorical while nonetheless depending on the reality of the worlds he describes. The literary mode of *Mundorum Explicatio* relies on the simultaneous allegory and the reality that underpins Pilgrim's journeys and ruptures the literary surface. Some readers, particularly those with their own theological agendas, may have had difficulty understanding or accepting this balance. Even Behmenists: after all Boehme spoke about the angelical world, and heard its songs on his deathbed, but did not claim to have travelled through it.[88]

## Ann Bathurst's 'Transportations' and the Philadelphian Society

Mary Pordage died in 1668, and, some time after, Pordage was joined in his ministry by Jane Lead. According to her own testimony, Lead, born in Norfolk in 1624, met Pordage in 1663. In 1670 she began to experience visions (involving the Virgin Sophia, a figure clearly derived from Pordage's theology) and to record them in a spiritual diary, later published as *A Garden of Fountains*. By 1674 she was sharing a house with Pordage.[89] Richard Roach wrote that her 'Extraordinary Gift of Revelation y$^e$ Dr gave great Regard to & Attendancd upon'.[90] Pordage encouraged visionary women. The Philadelphian Society was inaugurated, with this name and regular public meetings, in 1696 or 1697, which continued until 1703 (Lead died in 1704); this was a public birth, bringing internal conflict as well as expansion, of an older Church. Lead was its acknowledged founder, but the Society pre-existed this event, and her doctrine was deeply rooted in Pordage's teachings. Roach claimed that the Society was part of a community that had met and waited on the Spirit for fifty years; this was Pordage's spiritual gathering, dating from the mid-1640s.[91]

Lead saw angels in her visions, and they constitute part of her divinity. In a 1694 vision she describes seeing in the third circle of heaven, 'Seraphims and Cherubims, bright Angels, very numerous'.[92] In her 1670s visions she describes contemplating and hearing the angelical world; she writes of the Angels of the Presence and throne angels.[93] In a vision in February 1676 she reports the Lamb of God appearing to her and describing Creation, the Fall of the Angels and of Man:

Now know, that before this, there was a Creation of Angelical Hosts, as an immediate produce from the everlasting Being. Who delighted to generate Thrones, Mights, and Powers, that so God through distinct Existencies of Celestial Spirits, of that high Angelical Order, might come to manifest his Attributes, which before lay void and hid in an Eternal Stillness. So as here was the Angelical World in pre-existency before the Paradisical.[94]

Her visions, and her terminology, are clearly shaped by Pordage, though it is also likely that his beliefs, and the records of them transmitted among Philadelphians, were influenced by hers. Lead's accounts of angels have little of the immediacy of Pordage's sensory encounters: they are circumscribed as visions or prophecies, received in a particular state of mind, and conveyed within the limits of genre. There are some interesting exceptions: she records a conversation she held with John the Apostle, whom she also describes as 'the Angel John' in 1694. Strikingly, she writes to a friend in 1676: 'there is a certain Person, well known to you and men, whose Angel did lately appear in full Day, in an upper Room, where a few Names were met together, to wait for the Promise of the Father'.[95] The terminology suggests an individual guardian angel, one visible to a third party. This suggests a more intimate experience than Lead's other angelic visions, not least because she seems to be describing the use of her outward eyes.

Ann Bathurst, a follower and acquaintance of Pordage and Lead, had extensive visions of individual guardian angels, conversing with them, and witnessing conversations between them. Her 'Transportations' and 'Visionall Dreams' are less well known than Lead's writings, but her relationships with angels are more developed and intimate.[96] Roach records that Bathurst, and her friend Joanna Oxenbridge, had 'great & Wonderful Experiences & Manifestations from yᵉ Heavenly World'.[97] Two manuscript volumes of Bathurst's 'Transportations' survive, one having belonged to the aforementioned Dr Keith. The other states that 'thise visions ware when did live with dc pordich': in March 1679, when she received her first vision of an angel, she was sharing a house with Pordage and Lead. In her first 'Transportation or Manifestation', which took place 'either in the Body, or out of the Body . . . I cannot tell', she undertakes a journey in which she sees paradise and the Kingdom of Christ, where

I appeared to my self (I mean my Angel appear'd to me, but I understood it not) at w$^{ch}$ being surprized, and the flesh shrinking at the greatness of the Glory, I perfectly felt a Touch on the top of my head, w$^{ch}$ drew my spirit out of me, as you ~~would~~ draw a knife or sword out of a sheath, & it cut as it was drawn forth, I felt it cut like a two-edged sword.

The journey continues: she sees the Father, the Dragon, the Beast, and Babylon. She asks to see angels,

and immediately there were several of them compassing part of the Throne: They were like unto transparent Gold, w$^{th}$ faces like Men, having two large golden Wings coming forth of each side of their faces, w$^{ch}$ was most glorious.[98]

The dramatic and literary expression of this initial vision commences 800 manuscript pages of spiritual revelations that took place over seventeen years, involving many visible and speaking angels, Pordage-inspired diagrams of the universe, and three distinct theories of the offices and nature of angels.

The angels appeared in bed, and at prayer meetings. She distinguishes an 'outward Angel' (sometimes 'of this Lower world') from her 'supreme Angel' or 'Angel in the Unity of Love'. The former is visible not only to herself, but to her friends, and she can see her friends' outward angels. One day in 1680, she records in her spiritual diary,

I saw my friends Angel & mine put into scales in sight of the B.B. [Bright Body, or Jesus] to be weighed in a higher center, & in other cloathing; My Angel I thought to be wanting in weight . . .[99]

A few days later she recorded a systematic angelology:

☞ My ffriend & I read a Vision of our Three-fold Angel. Our supreme part being an Angel that allwise abides in the Unity of Love, after we have once become a little Child of that Center, & [marginal reference: Matt. 18,3,4,10] w$^{ch}$ allwise beholds the face of our Father in heaven: there's also another Angel of ours, w$^{ch}$ is our Guardian, or souls-Angel that goeth up with our requests: I have sometimes seen it goe up like a white Cloud with my prayers, and my Angel of the Unity of Love come to it to hear its requests, y$^t$ she might pray them over again. So Now as my ffriend read the Vision to me, I saw my Angel like a white Cloud go to the place of the Unity of Love, and my Angel of y$^e$ U. of Love, w$^{ch}$ was in a gold-garment & like a Child, run to the white Cloud (w$^{ch}$ was my Angel also) and say, what is your request? I'm come to hear y$^t$ I may offer it up, for being near the Father & Son I know best how to offer up according to his will, and know best his will and what He requires of yow. Thus did I see both these Angels, as if one prayed lying on its face, and the other praying the requests over again & better; and when my spirits Angel understood what I wanted that I had not asked for, she said to the other (my souls-Angel) y$^t$ I must ask for ffaith, yrby declaring what great advantage it was for the (third Angel or) Angel in the lower world to have great ffaith, what victory it gave us over our selves, so as nothing could hurt us; that ffaith keeps everything without us, and nothing without us hurts us; and y$^t$ I should assuredly beleive y$^t$ no concerns in y$^e$ world should hurt our souls progress, and if they did, y$^t$ we should be helped out of them. This was said as to us both, my friend & me, ^and I received strength.[100]

Each righteous individual has three angels: an angel in the Unity of Love (or spirit's angel), who stands in the presence of the Trinity; a personal guardian angel (or soul's angel), who conveys messages between the individual and heaven; and the angel in the lower world, who is equivalent to the this-worldly part of the human soul of the person. The 'Vision of our Three-fold Angel' that Bathurst reads with her friend may be Pordage's (he was still alive at this time). In the 'Preliminary Treatise' the following view is outlined:

There is then in us a threefold Spirit; a Natural one for this World; An Eternal angelical soul for ye Angelical objects, that is, all that in ye Angelical Principle is manifested, & thus not onle ye Angels, but even God too is introduced into ye World; & a Divine Spirit, for ye enjoyment of God and his most sacred Influences with ye other Objects of ye Eternal World.[101]

It is possible that this tripartite system was retrospectively inserted into Pordage's beliefs.

These angels have traditional duties: they are ministering spirits, responsible for human wellbeing, they are witnesses, and they are messengers, communicating between heaven and earth. They have modes of knowledge unlike ours, and know God in ways unknown to us. They sing beyond the expression of human tongue. In other respects they are heterodox. Bathurst's angels are intensely personal:

she identifies them, and they offer a more active channel of commu-
nication with God than is conventional within Protestantism. They are
also sexed according to their human: hers are feminine, while a male
friend's angel is masculine.[102] In one vision her soul is exalted, and the
process is represented by the gift of an edible book from Christ, an
image rooted in traditional theology, but particularly significant in
occult learning:

He gave my Angel ☞ a Book all of gold, & said, read it; my Law and Love is
written in it; Eat it, and let it be yo$^r$ food, and yow shall Live for ever, and yow
shall not want my assistance. and she (i.e. my angel) took the Book & eat it,
and her Garment became very rich and beautiful and shining.[103]

In addition to personal angels there are angels and spirits that are
independent of humans. Angels are varied in their appearance:
sometimes they wear transparent gold garments, 'Not in the figure
of Cherubims as sometimes I have seen them'. Bathurst can visu-
ally distinguish between cherubim and other angels. In 1686 'A
Glorious Angel like the Son of God appeared, girt about the paps
w$^t$ a Golden Girdle, like an Ephod; his breast full of Milk of Consola-
tion . . . his Garment was most glorious.' Later she sees her soul, 'like a
Cherubim allwise hovering on the Wing'.[104] She has a clear visual
iconography in her mind's eye, though she does not disclose it at
length. Angels have bright, transparent bodies, and wings, and wear
golden garments.

Bathurst's visions are frequent, and once she has picked up a theme
for meditation she can rhapsodize on it for pages, over weeks (per-
haps it was a theme among her prayer community). Her observation
of her angel's interaction with other angels seems to have an allegor-
ical significance, but at times it turns into pure soap opera. Ann's
friend A.B.'s angel in the Unity of Love spots Ann's angel wearing a
warmer garment, and requests one, which she is granted; she then
jealously spots and requests a girdle, shoes, shoelaces. The angels look
on their own and others' garments with reverence and shame. Ann
concludes with a moral, 'I take all this Adorning to have great
Signification; for they were not putt on, till They themselves saw
they had need of them,' but the narrative suggests a good-natured
competition among neighbours, each seeking not to be left behind.
Three days later:

I saw like a Garland of spring-flowers on AB's head, then on her Angels head in the U. of Love: and I had one on my head, y$^ت$ seem'd ready to be left off. A.B.'s Angel seeing my Garland sitt not like hers, complained to me & said, hers was so low even over her eyes y$^t$ she could not see with it: My Ang. told hers, it did well so low, to keep her from being hurt by falls: it seem'd too big for her and so fell a little below her eye-briers; but mine was half way on the back part of my head: I seem'd to be grown too big for it, near to leave it off, and it went off, and I had a Crown putt on my head. She lookt on my Angel & saw the Crown, but said nothing: and being content she soon had a Crown putt on her own head.[105]

This is a fashion contest. The concern over appearances and competition over worldly goods is comic, though sincerely meant, but it should not distract from the daring, presumptuous premiss: that she speaks with angels, and, through them, with God.

Bathurst's angelology changes twice, and the effect is to move away from the immediacy of these angels to systems of angelical offices, in which angels are less creaturely and less accessible to human interaction. In November 1681, about a month before Pordage's death, she describes seeing the Angel of 'M$^r$ B.$^{st}$' divide 'into 12 Angels, all of them cloathed in white cloudy raiment and in his figure seven of these angels were much of his size, but the other five something lesser and brighter. The 7 Angels were shown to me to be his souls Angels, being the 7 ruling Spirits of the Soul.' Each of the seven has its own property (love, desire, will, faith, joy, wisdom, and patience), and all look like Mr B. The other five are spirit angels, 'who were of a lesser figure and brighter, were the Spirits Angels, which went into a Light, and into M$^r$ B's head, where they all sate as in a Glob of Light'. These five have a more direct, spiritual knowledge, comparable to God's, a transcendent and divine knowledge (as there is no reason in Pordage's angelical world). This is the knowledge that the unfallen Adam had of nature.[106] This new account of angels is indebted to Pordage's account of the seven spirits, not strictly angels, who sit in the presence of God; and like Pordage in his later angel-writings, these are more distant from humankind, more allegorical in their conception. These are angels Bathurst witnesses; at one point they draw her apart 'to converse w$^t$ them, by w$^{ch}$ means I felt a divine strength communicated to me', but they do not speak to her, nor she to them.[107] Thereafter she describes dialogues between her spirit and her soul, removing angels from the exchange. Though there is not a once-and-for-all shift, her angels are displaced by spirits that do not require explanation in the conventional terms of angel-writing, and have a purely abstract, allegorical existence, as figures rather than creatures.

Shortly following this new dispensation of angels Bathurst enters the inner ring of heaven, where she witnesses the Trinity and obtains new knowledge. From the Trinity go forth 'the Host of Heaven, w$^{ch}$ were astrums, and of Them there were Three Orders, even Thousands of Thousands, and a Thousand times ten thousand, even an innumerable order'. The first order of Astrum angels are closest to paradise, and

are transparent Figures of a light Gold colour.... The Second order of the Astrums was of a whitish Cloudy Colour; and the Third order was of a Graish Cloudy colour; all compassing Paradise, yet beneath and under it, all of them close and near to one another; the 2$^d$ compassing the first, the 3$^d$ compassing the 2$^d$ like shaded Colours; the first Gold colour, the 2$^d$ whitish, the 3$^d$ Gray.[108]

These tripartite divisions were important to Pordage and Bathurst, and Bathurst takes from Pordage the habit of representing the geography of the universe in diagrammatic form. She draws the Astrum angels as a semicircle underneath a dot that represents paradise. This follows a drawing of four concentric circles that represent the Deity, the Eternal Majestic Stillness, the One Element or White Mist, and Chaos. She teases out more symbolism from the Astrums: the first comprise the life of a beast, the second, man as he is a man (itself threefold: soul, mind, will), the third, the 'Supreme Created Good in Man'.[109] These are less creatures than a set of mystical correspondences drawn across spiritual life. The three sets of propositions about angels—the three personal angels, the twelve angels, and the Astrum angels—are not exclusive, but increasingly elaborate systems drawn across the same set of abstract spiritual notions. These are not the kind of angels with whom one would converse, or summon with ritual magic, any more than one would seek to reconcile them with natural philosophy. Bathurst continues to see her earlier kind of angels, and even hears her own angel speak, in a strangely archaic and stilted fashion: 'And my Angel made such sad moane, that all the Centers [the senses of other angels] seemed sadded thereat; and still my Angel said, I [Aye] how soon is my soul tied!, it has no sooner got its flight to thee, but there are, as it were Ropes flung to lay hold of me . . .'. On other occasions the angels of dead souls visit and speak to her, and once she senses Gabriel, 'a very

large Masculine Angel', but these occasions are very few, and angels as
beings are increasingly rare in her visions.[110] At one point in 1683 she
refers to angels, and glosses that she means by this 'the Spirits of Just
Men made perfect'. As the emphasis shifts to Christ as mediator, angels
adopt an allegorical, symbolic, or decorative role.

   Were Bathurst's angels ever real: did she believe she encountered
actual beings through the evidence of her bodily senses? Certainly
the contrast between her visions in 1679 and those in 1681 and later
suggests so: there is an immediacy and a vividness to the former that
is replaced by self-conscious divinity in the latter. The frequency
with which angels appear and their familiarity in the earlier visions
suggest not only a shift in conscious doctrine, but a heightened
sensibility, a feverish spiritual intensity not unlike that to which
Pordage testified in 1654. Moreover, in October 1680 she records
the following:

I saw my Angel in the U. of L. with a very rich Neck-lace of large pearle, such
as I never saw any near so large in this World; and A.B.'s Ang. was sitting
by me & fixed her Eye on the beauty of the pearle, but said nothing, only
seem'd as if she hoped to have one also . . . This since has been opened to me to
Signifie the Adorning we have when we putt on Christ, w^ch indeed is our
Rich Ornament.

At first she does not know what the vision means, indicating that she sees
a picture, an object that is in the first place visual rather than semantic.
Only subsequently is the symbolism disclosed, and the image becomes
an interpreted allegory. The activity of mapping the heavens, of repre-
senting paradise on a map with the Astrum angels, or drawing the
circumference of Eternal Nature within the Archetypal Globe, is one
that occurs after the journey is over; the narrative describes the process of
seeing and learning, before it is complete enough to be mapped.
Unfortunately Bathurst does not draw figures of angels, but perhaps
sketching was incompatible with the nature of her transportations.

## Entertaining Angels

Angels became less integral to the religious experiences of Ann Bathurst
and John Pordage, though the spiritual journey of both begins with
revelations by angels. Similarly, the tenor of the Philadelphians after

Pordage's death, under the spiritual leadership of Jane Lead and Francis Lee, is less vibrant with experimental theology, visionary communication, and the occult. Angels are real, but they are objects of contemplation. They remain a dimension of the spiritual, a spiritual world that coexists with the real, material or lower world. But the theology becomes a great deal more businesslike than Pordage was in the 1650s.

What began with manuscripts of ritual magic, enthusiasm, antinomianism, and space travel made way for Philadelphianism, which in turn made way for Pietism. These eighteenth-century conversations with angels more closely fitted the expectations of polite society. The Pietists John Freke and William Law inherited the influence of Boehme, and sought to reinvest natural philosophy with a spiritual content. They condemned the secular hubris that thought scientific experimentation, such as demonstrations of electrical fire, could be a fit 'Entertainment for Angels', and their disciples drew maps of the universe that showed the Fall and Regeneration of man, with Michael and Uriel as fiery circles in the heavens. These multi-layer, colour fold-outs with moving parts, book technology of extraordinary complexity and sophistication, descend from Pordage's 'Hieroglyphical Figure' and schema.[111] The Pietists did not, however, as Pordage would have done in 1649, turn the tables on the scientists by discussing this with angels.

# 6

# The Fleshly Imagination and the Word of God

## Theology and the Imagination

What makes people willing to believe things about invisible beings that they cannot see or speak to and know little about? What makes it permissible to write an imaginative narrative about the sacred world? St Paul warned man against 'intruding into those things which he hath not seene, vainely puft up by his fleshy mind' (Col. 2: 18). Speculation led to false devotion, including the worship of angels. Reformed theology placed restrictions on the use of the imagination in especially visual but also verbal representation of the sacred world.

Traditional accounts of the invisible world, by the Church Fathers and Scholastic theologians, were suspicious of literalism and committed to fourfold exegesis. Scripture was understood to have four levels of meaning, originally proposed by Philo: literal (or historical), allegorical, tropological (or moral), and anagogical. Such exegesis invited interpretative elaboration while circumventing the problem of the specific characteristics of the real heaven and its inhabitants. The fertile angelic world of Pseudo-Dionysius, Augustine, Bonaventura, and Aquinas was founded on these exegetical practices, in which the literal was a starting point that enabled complex non-literal constructions.[1] Protestants reacted by emphasizing the primacy of the literal meanings of Scripture, and resisting the turn to imagination and theological speculation.[2]

This theological shift to exegetical literalism and the authority of Scripture alone affected the social circumstances of poets and painters, but also the theories of representation with which they worked. Biblical drama disappeared from Britain in the later sixteenth century, in part because of objections like that of William Perkins, who complained of the profanity of feigning representations, like showing God 'popishly conceived to be like an old man sitting in heaven in a throne with a sceptre in his hand'.[3] Many poets expressed anxiety about the dangers of fleshly speculation. Some such expressions were a prologue to bolder descriptions, like the account of the fall of angels in Lucy Hutchinson's *Order and Disorder*:

> But circumstances that we cannot know
> Of their rebellion and their overthrow
> We will not dare t'invent, nor will we take
> Guesses from the reports themselves [fallen angels] did make
> To their old priests, to whom they did devise
> To inspire some truths, wrapped up in many lies;
> Such as their gross poetic fables are . . .
>    But not to name these foolish impious tales,
> Which stifle truth in her pretended veils,
> Let us in its own blazing conduct go
> And look no further than the light doth show . . . [4]

Despite repeated expressions of caution, Hutchinson ventures into the invisible and incomprehensible. The poet could circumnavigate essential truths, and restrict herself to *adiaphora*, that which was neither commanded nor forbidden (though this category itself brokered conflicts within Protestantism), but narratives invariably encountered controversial materials.[5] When were angels created, and when did they fall? Telling stories around Scripture requires decisions about matters of space and time and causality, and narrative presents explanatory and interpretative structures: sometimes it argues, sometimes explains, sometimes discovers.[6] Poets who intruded into these circumstances, however cautious, could find themselves undertaking fleshly manoeuvres.

Theology should not be seen as a purely repressive force. It also stirred the imagination. Humanist biblical interpretation, for example, empowered poets by inaugurating a rhetorical approach to Scripture. In the mid-fifteenth century Lorenzo Valla (who demonstrated that the Donation of Constantine and the writings of Pseudo-Dionysius were both forgeries) examined biblical texts with the intense and historicist rhetorical scrutiny that others applied to classical texts. Two centuries later, Richard Simon's *Histoire critique du Vieux Testament* (1678) argued that Moses was not the author of the Pentateuch and that the texts were chronologically confused and disparate.[7] This work marked—it was a consequence of transformations in understanding as much as a cause—a paradigm shift in attitudes to Scripture, anticipating nineteenth-century biblical criticism. Between these two events exegesis entered a rhetorical phase, involving the scrutiny of the language, narrative context, and historical circumstance. Humanism's linguistic vigilance facilitated the creative interrogation of biblical narratives, hence feeding poets' imaginations.

One theological doctrine that empowered poets, providing a means of understanding the imagination and (which was a quite different thing) creativity, was called 'accommodation'. It explained the light by which Scripture could be read, and the invisible world described by mere humans. It described how transcendental scriptural truths could be conveyed to finite human comprehension, without distortion or misrepresentation, by the condescension of the ineffable and the upward reach of human intelligence, sometimes assisted by the Holy Spirit. This doctrine, embedded in early modern understanding of the nature of representation and of the spirit world, offered poets diverse accounts of the relationship between narratives and spiritual meaning. It was fundamental to Milton's authorization of his own writing. After the Reformation accommodation was used as a 'saving' concept for scriptural literalism, preserving the coherence of Scripture in the face of new ideas that sat uneasily alongside former beliefs.[8] Accommodation found literal truths in figurative interpretations, but it also claimed to complicate the distinction by offering a mode of description that was neither literal nor figurative. Accommodation requires us to treat with caution the categories 'imagination', 'feigning', 'fables', and 'invention'.

This chapter explores the development of the notion of accommodation and debates about accommodation and scriptural interpretation in early modern Britain, before turning to reformed poetics in the seventeenth century. *Paradise Lost* is one of a series of epic poems, all centrally concerned with angels, that use this doctrine to meditate on representation. The theological tradition was fundamental to literary writing. There is a connection between seventeenth-century epic, reformed theories of representation, and the invisible world of angels.

## Accommodation and the Bodies of Angels

Accommodation presents a theory about the truths contained within Scripture and their interpretation drawn from Scripture itself. The instructions offered by scriptural texts on how they should be read have a distinct authority. The Word of God was understood to offer a figurative mode of representation, in which visible patterns denoted with imperfect transparency higher truths.[9] Access to these higher truths both depends on and provokes spiritual exploration and inspiration. This theory was useful because of the many suggestive ambiguities in the Bible. To use two common examples: when Scripture tells us that God is angry, should we infer that God experiences passions? When we read that the angels look upon the face of God, are we to understand that God has a face? Exegetical exercises were also demanded by silences and contradictions within Scripture: why, for example, does Moses not mention the creation of the angels? (Alexander Ross answered: 'Because hee did accommodate himselfe to the rude capacitie of the *Jewes*.'[10]) And why is God described as weary when this is elsewhere declared impossible? Scripture needs active interpretation, and this activity must be regulated by an understanding of the nature of figuration.

Early patristic accounts of accommodation appear in discussions of anthropomorphism (assigning human shape to God) and anthropopathy (attributing emotions to God). This focus was perhaps because the language of Scripture was here intuitively metaphorical, though it subsequently became an inherited topic. The Alexandrians, Philo (*c*.20 BCE–*c*.CE 50) and Origen (185–254 CE), erect complex allegorical meanings and numerical symbols. In *On the Creation* Philo writes, 'these are no mythical fictions, such as poets and sophists delight in, but modes of making ideas visible, bidding us resort to allegorical interpretation guided in our renderings by what lies beneath the surface'.[11] Though his own readings are full of verve, he regards this as a sign of the limitations of the human mind. Though made in his likeness, men can only think of God anthropomorphically:

We are not able to cherish continually in our souls the thought which sums so worthily the nature of the Cause, that 'God is not as man' (Num. 23: 19), and thus rise superior to all the human conceptions of Him. In us the mortal is the chief ingredient. We cannot get outside ourselves in forming our ideas; we cannot escape our inborn infirmities. We creep within our covering of mortality, like snails into their shells, or like the hedgehog we roll ourselves into a ball, and we think of the blessed and the immortal in terms of our own natures. We shun indeed in words the monstrosity of saying that God is of human form, but in actual fact we accept the impious thought that He is of human passions. And therefore we invent for Him hands and feet, incomings

and outgoings, enmities, aversions, estrangements, anger, in fact such parts and
passions as can never belong to the Cause. And of such is the oath—a mere
crutch for our weakness.[12]

According to Philo, Moses was responsible for accommodating hard
truths in intelligible form. He does not, however, indicate that there is
a powerful hermeneutic connection between Moses' 'surest truth' and
things said for instruction. Philo both frowns on the impious who offer
'mythical fictions' by attributing human passions to God, and admits
that it is a necessary crutch.[13]

Later debates about anthropomorphism and anthropopathy—
among scholars who rejected or accepted either or both as viable
verbal practices—usually focused on the truth possible in accommo-
dated speech. Lactantius in the fourth century discussed human form as
a symbolic embodiment of divine virtues, without any suggestion of
physical similarity, but in his treatise on divine anger he argues that
God does experience real anger and love and other emotions, though
categorically not 'vicious affections'. If he did not show anger, he
would not be feared, and hence not reverenced. God is angry because
he cares.[14] The belief that Scripture says that God is angry because he is
in a real sense angry would become associated with the Audian heresy,
condemned by the Church in 399 CE.[15] Hilary of Poitiers (c.300–c.367)
offered a limited justification of anthropomorphism while attacking
the Arian heresy. He writes that there is no real similarity between God
and human attributes, yet 'the weakness of our understanding forces us
to seek for illustrations from a lower sphere to explain our meaning
about loftier themes'. These analogies, which set the 'spiritual' and
'invisible' alongside the 'carnal' and 'palpable', are an imperfect but
'necessary aid', necessary because they are edifying: 'we must employ
ordinary natures and ordinary speech as our means of expressing what
our mind apprehends; a means no doubt unworthy of the majesty of
God, but forced upon us by the feebleness of our intellect, which can
use only our own circumstances and own our words to convey to
others our perceptions and our conclusions'. By such means we
advance towards 'inward meaning'.[16] Anthropomorphism is more
than a necessary evil: it leads us to truth.

These authors stress that compromise or an acceptance of human
limitations is necessary to approach God, and they attribute the agency
for such compromise to humanity, especially Moses but also other
prophets. This is a form of social accommodation.[17] With Augustine

and Pseudo-Dionysius this agency shifted to create a hermeneutic mode of accommodation. Augustine (354–430) attributed the accommodation of divine attributes for human comprehension to God alone. God makes himself visible, Augustine writes, 'not as He truly is, but in a way which those who saw Him could bear'. Augustine's primary concern here is the physical appearance to human eyes, a question fundamental to all accounts of angels, but verbal representation follows the same pattern. God never repents or feels anger, but Scripture describes these emotions to translate immutability into human concepts.

[I]f Scripture did not use such terms, it would not communicate its meaning so clearly to all the race of men for whom it has care. If it did not first bend down and, as it were, descend to the level of the fallen, it would not terrify the proud, arouse the negligent, exercise the inquirer and nourish the intelligent.[18]

Scriptures *bends down* to our fallen capacities; and it does so to humans of all capacities, the inquisitive and perspicacious as well as the sinful. Anthropopathy offers a purposeful form of representation that is figurative without committing any misrepresentation.

Pseudo-Dionysius' exquisitely detailed and audacious description of our knowledge of God and the organization of heaven laid foundations shaping all subsequent angel-doctrine. For Pseudo-Dionysius angels and representing the invisible are inextricable, and following him the issues would be tied. The immeasurable and infinite are beyond the comprehension even of prophets, he writes, yet the authors of Scripture were allowed

a power by which, in a manner surpassing speech or knowledge, we reach a union superior to anything available to us by way of our own abilities or activities in the realm of discourse or of intellect. This is why we must not dare to resort to words or conceptions concerning that hidden divinity which transcends being, apart from what the sacred scriptures have divinely revealed.[19]

Scriptural language is unique, and overcomes some of the limitations of being human. Many, including Milton, would echo these words. This hermeneutic strategy offers something of a third way: allowing divine inspiration in the sacred Scriptures, it assumes that the Holy Spirit confers upon the language itself a special representational potency, even when that language is no longer in the mouths of prophets. Far from being a misrepresentation, scriptural language speaks of something that is true even if it is beyond us.[20]

The most important and carefully deliberated aspect of this description is the metaphor of movement. Here, as repeatedly in Pseudo-Dionysius' works, we are drawn *upward* towards the truth. The 'incongruous dissimilarities' applied to God in Scripture 'enabled that part of the soul which longs for the things above actually to rise up'. Love is a 'yearning' that permits union: 'It moves the superior to provide for the subordinate, and it stirs the subordinate in a return toward the superior.'[21] Not only does Scripture bend down to us; we reach up for it, and begin to transcend the fixed hierarchies of Creation. In this respect Augustine and Pseudo-Dionysius (unknown to each other) differ from their predecessors, shifting towards a hermeneutics of accommodation. Following them accommodation would usually be understood to involve 'contemplation' that allows this bending and lifting, to be both a special property of Scripture and an inspired process of reading, by which the limited capacities of humans can encounter and comprehend the incomprehensible truths of the ineffable.

Aquinas accepts this account, though emphasizing the downward movement of condescension, the creation of similitudes for man's imperfect understanding.[22] Aquinas' main interest in the concept, however, is its use in describing and explaining angelic bodies. The nature of angels, their status as mediators between God and human-kind, their incorporeality and their self-representation to humans, are central to the theology and conceptual labour of the *Summa Theologiae*. Aquinas writes: 'Just as the figurative expressions used in the Bible to convey truths that are beyond reach of our senses are not lies'—lying is the risk for mere creatures—

because in speaking in this way Scripture does not identify one order of things with another, but merely avails itself of certain analogies in the sensible world to give us an idea of purely intelligible properties—so it is no slur on the truthfulness of holy angels that the bodies they assume should seem to be living men when in fact they are not.[23]

From henceforth scriptural analogies would be associated with the virtual bodies of invisible beings. Incorporeal spirits adopted bodies as a means of representing themselves to the capacities of humans, though in doing so they risked deceit.

Despite challenges to the Thomist synthesis and the revival of interest in Plato, Renaissance Neoplatonists adopted Aquinas' theology of angels in detail. They also appropriated and extended the doctrine of accommodation as a model for characterizing the correspondence between the ideal world and the world of experience, and the means by which humans might be drawn to the infinite through the immediate. Through the Renaissance Neoplatonists the notion of accommodation became something of a commonplace. In their hands, however, accommodation described movement around the allegorical system of universal correspondences and the work that poets did. It was a weak version of accommodation, which, while it fitted into a religious universe, was detached both from mainstream theology and from the fervent inspiration of the spirit.[24]

## Reformation, Literalism, and Accommodation

Reformers renewed attention to processes of signification. A nexus of issues touched upon accommodation and angels' bodies: first, the conviction that *sola scriptura* was the path to true belief; secondly, the emphasis on spiritual light as the guide to interpretation; thirdly, the Calvinist suggestion that the visual image was a means of forgetting rather than approaching the spiritual, which led to a greater emphasis on textual culture, and to iconoclasm. Reformed theologians stressed the pre-eminence of literal meaning, allowing figurative readings permissible only when the literal sense was incoherent. This necessitated a more vigorous defence against anthropopathy and anthropomorphism, which were, because they created images of the divine, idolatrous. Accommodation became for reformers a means of legitimizing a specific mode of figurative interpretation within a literalist framework.

John Calvin (1509–64), the most influential authority on representation in Protestant Europe and especially in Britain, declared that any representations of God in human or visible terms both were erroneous and led to false worship. His arguments, though primarily concerned with the visual, repeatedly glanced at the limits of language and the human mind: 'God indeed, I graunt, sometime in certaine signes hath given a presence of his godhead, so as he was said to be beholden face to face, but all these signes that ever he shewed, did aptly serve for meanes to teach, and withal did plainly admonish men of an incomprehensible essence.'[25] Signs teach, but reveal their inadequacy. Hence, on Moses' description of God's anger: 'he bringeth in GOD speaking after the manner of men, by a figure called *Anthropopathia*: because

otherwise he could not expresse that which was very necessarie to be
knowen'. The margin glosses the rhetorical figure: 'Anthropopathia is
a figure by whiche humane affections are attributed to God for our
capacitie, at what time those thinges which belong to him, are to us
incomprehensible.' Moses' next verse describes God's repentance, and
Calvin explains that 'God verily is not greeved or sorrie' because he is
immutable, but 'the holy Ghost frameth himselfe to our capacitie'.[26] In
the *Institutes* he writes that Anthropomorphites are misled,

because oftentimes the Scripture ascribeth unto him a mouth, eares, eies,
hands and feete. For what man, yea though he be slenderly witted, doth not
understand that God doth with us speake as it were childishly, as nurses doe
with their babes? Therefore such maner of speeches doe not so plainly
expresse what God is, as they doe apply the understanding of him to our
slender capacitie. Which to doe, it behooved of necessitie that he descended a
great way beneath his owne height.[27]

Calvin unequivocally emphasizes the downward movement God's
deliberate framing of himself to human faculties, and the agency of
the spirit. The true Christian is like a child, but one who has to read
knowingly, and see that the rhetoric reveals sacred truth.

It is not only in connection to God that this pattern of accommodation
occurs in Scripture. Angel's bodies are also accommodated: 'As for shape,
it is certaine, that spirits have none, and yet the Scripture for the capacitie
of our wit doth not in vaine under *Cherubin* and *Seraphim* paint us out
Angels with wings, to the intent we should not doubt that they will be
ever with incredible swiftnesse, readie to succour us.'[28] Similarly, Donne
writes, 'we paint angels with wings, because | They bear God's message,
and proclaim His laws'.[29] Protestant exegesis is not straightforwardly
literal. It encompasses rhetorically informed figurative interpretation,
where the figure is authorized by the Spirit, and the reading is guided
by rhetoric. The two main exempla where this manner of reading is
proved and tested are the bodies of God and of angels.

Peter Martyr (1500–52) dwells at length on accommodation to
explain scriptural interpretation and angelic bodies, and to repudiate
anthropomorphism. Regarding the latter, he insists that the likeness
between man and God witnessed in Scripture describes spiritual rather
than physical similarity, and that attributing 'the members and parts of
mans bodie' merely helps 'our weake capacitie', giving us knowledge
by through 'speciall signes and shadowes'. We perforce must use this
language, though it is heretical to take it too much in 'earnest'.[30]

Accommodation is a property of Scripture, and a hermeneutic process, but, essentially, it also shapes the language that we use when we speak of God: it is a process that implicates both writers and readers, poets as well as prophets.

For Peter Martyr angels are a laboratory for exegesis. Their iconography is symbolic: scripture 'setteth them out unto us; not onelie with wings, but also full of eyes; that is to saye, that they execute the office committed to them by God, both wisely and speedily'. This image is an accommodated one, and emphatically not an invitation to devise a fourfold exegesis of angelic wings. Though the substance and nature of spirits is inexpressible, it is lawful to picture them, 'as they have shewed themselves unto men'—just as we are authorized to use the accommodated language of Scripture—provided this does not involve worship. He adds a telling rider: 'for they be not, as God is, infinite; but are bounded and limited'.[31] In other words, angels can be seen as conceptual and ontological mediators between God and mankind. God in his infinitude cannot be represented, but angels can, and as finite yet spiritual substances they can be used to explain two things of the utmost importance in the sixteenth and seventeenth centuries: first, the nature of the spiritual world and its relationship to the material world of Creation; and secondly, the relationship between God and man. Accommodation and angels, once again, walk hand in hand as a means of understanding man's place in the universe.

In early modern Britain theologians followed these cues. A number of patterns can be discerned:

1. an emphasis on the primacy of the 'literal sense'—the 'historical', 'grammatical', or 'plain sense'—consonant with much of Protestant Europe;[32]

2. an increasing stress on human agency in accommodation; initially Moses' deliberate condescension to his immediate audience, but subsequently more various;

3. close association between accommodated language and the visible appearance of angels;

4. use of accommodation to save Protestant literalism: it uses the figurative sense without being fiction;

5. the involvement of the theory in defending the existence of the spirit world (against perceived Sadducism).

A few examples illustrate the roles of accommodation in English writing. Thomas Wilson, in his *Theologicall Rules to Guide us in the Understanding and Practise of Holy Scriptures* (1615), appeals to the rhetorical trope *anthropopathia* to contradict the doctrines of the anthropomorphites. Because humans are dull, Scripture speaks of God's body partly to shadow forth the spiritual. The anthropomorphites' literalism disregards the nature of accommodation: 'By bodily things the scriptures lead and lift us up to see such excellent divine things as bee in god, by a figure called *Anthropopathia*.'[33] John Gaule's meditation on Abraham's entertainment of the angels integrates the silences of Scripture commonly explored in annotation, showing how knowledge can develop through self-conscious accommodation. Equating angels with God, he ponders:

Doth the Lord eate Buls flesh, or drinke the bloud of Goates? . . . God eates, and eates with *Abraham*, and can as easily dispense with the corporall nutriment he receives; as with such substance, he now assumes. Their Bodies they now tooke, were brought to nothing, and so was their Meate. Spirits never eate of necessitie, sometimes of dispensation. God now eates, not of hunger, and for his owne refreshment: but of good fellowship, and for the others satisfaction. . . . oft-times will God stoope to the act of our nature; that we might reach to the works of his Grace.[34]

He closely associates accommodation, food, angelic digestion, and anthropomorphism, much as Milton does, and natural philosophy emerges through Scripture. This eating is not illusory, but God stoops as our nature reaches. John White identifies in Scripture's description both human and divine agency: Moses consciously applies himself to the weak capacity of man, while God is compassionately willing to 'shadow his wayes'. This was part of a shift in early modern theology towards human agency. This shift was rooted in older traditions, including Philo, but was not simply a form of 'social' or conscious accommodation, as it involved granting special powers to the human spirit. White is a meditative commentator, who is, in lyrical and unhurried prose, inventive in ways similar to Milton:

Thus God sometimes, in his Word, represents himself, as moved with humane Affections, Grief, Joy, Wrath, Compassion; with humane expressions in forms of speech, as Expostulations, Complaints, and Deliberations; with humane Actions, Coming, Going, Sitting still, Arising, Standing, Sleeping, Forgetting, Remembering, and the like.

And this he doth, 1. That he may condescend to our weaknesse, which moves him to feed us, as *Paul* doth his hearers, with *milk*, because we cannot brook *strong meat* . . . representing Heavenly things to Earthly men, by earthly means . . .

And, 2. To affect us the more, by representing spiritual things, by those, which being Earthly, are nearest to Sense, which usually works most on our affections.

Let it fill our hearts with the admiration of God's mercy, and compassion towards such unworthy wretches as we are, unto whom he is pleased to descend so low, seeing we cannot ascend up unto Him, cloathing himself, as it were, with our flesh, and appearing to us, in a sort, in the form of a man, laying aside his own Glory and Majestie for our encouragement and instruction.

A special end, which the Spirit of God aimes at, in setting out this history of mans Creation, with such variety of Circumstances, and representing God consulting in such a manner, is, to raise up our hearts to a more serious consideration of, and diligent searching into, the work it self . . . [35]

Moses' description involves condescension, but it also empowers us, working on our affections to raise our hearts. Affections are uniquely human; far from scorning the fleshliness of the human mind, God works upon what is human to effect this illumination. White's account of accommodation is powerful: it is both persuasive and claims great potency. Scripture is not allegorical or literal: by partaking of a higher truth the shadow is transformed as well as the idea. Language clothes the truth with flesh, resulting not in *mis*representation, but in something like the Incarnation.

What is at stake in the doctrine of accommodation in seventeenth-century Britain can be seen in a dispute at the margins of mainstream theology. The encounter, between the Socinian John Biddle and the Presbyterian John Owen, was perhaps the most significant and explicit argument on the doctrine. It has an additional interest for the reader of Milton: Biddle probably had a hand in the publication of the Racovian Catechism, which Milton licensed in August 1650 (and for which he was subsequently questioned by the Council of State). In contrast, Lucy Hutchinson was a follower of Owen.[36] The efflorescence of writing on the spirit during the 1640s and 1650s, which spurred new interests in angels, also electrified opinions on the nature and representation of God.

Biddle denied the divinity of Christ and argued that the Trinity consisted of God, Christ the man, and a Holy Spirit, who is the chief angel. This he proved on the basis of Scripture alone, through pure literalism. We can only 'reduce the Christian Religion to its primitive integrity . . . by cashiering those many intricate terms, and devised forms of speaking, imposed on our Religion, and by wholly betaking our selvs to the plainness of the Scripture'.[37] The elaborate figures used by his opponents are, he writes, 'brainsick Notions . . . first hatched by the subtilty of Satan'.[38] Biddle's notion of plainness is politically and theologically charged, and understates the extent to which his opponents offered literal interpretations to refute his claims (though perhaps not their pride in wordly learning and Neoplatonic philosophy).[39] Biddle claimed to read Scripture literally, in contrast to Roman Catholics and Anglicans, who were too hasty to develop figurative readings, and occult writers who affected allegories.[40] However, most orthodox Protestants claimed to privilege the literal, while disagreeing about where obscurities within Scripture demanded figurative exegesis. This meant that accusations of allegorical licence were common in polemics against competing exegetical positions. Biddle avers to mean something unusually simple: that he allows no figurative readings except in those places where Scripture expressly enjoins it, or where Scripture is manifestly self-contradictory. Figurative readings are otherwise a slippery slope to mystical fabrications.[41] Hobbes had similar reservations about metaphors, but whereas Hobbes attacked radicals and enthusiasts Biddle challenged established and orthodox Churchmen.[42] Scripture attributes to God a shape, a place, passions and affections, and to allegorize this is to manipulate it:

Would not this be to use the Scripture like a nose of wax, and when of it self it looketh any way, to turn it aside at our pleasure? And would not God be so far from speaking to our capacity in his Word, (which is the usual Refuge of the Adversaries, when in these and the like matters concerning God, they are pressed with the plain words of the Scripture) as that he would by so doing render us altogether uncapable of finding out his meaning, whilst he spake one thing, and understood the clean contrary? Yea, would he not have taken the direct course to make men substitute an Idol in his stead, (for the Adversaries hold, that to conceive of God as having a shape, or affections, or being in certain place, is Idolatry) if he described himself in the Scripture otherwise then indeed he is, without telling us so much in plain terms, that we might not conceive amiss of him?[43]

Sleep and weariness are attributed to God but, being flatly contradicted elsewhere, these can be read as figures. Otherwise, it is our interpretative duty to accept the anthropopathy and anthropomorphism of

Scripture at face value. Biddle does not reject figurative interpretations outright, but denies accommodation any place in his theological system, on the grounds that it does not save literalism but provides an excuse for invention.

Owen responded that Biddle made a monster of God, giving him real, rather than figurative, eyes, ears, lion-shape, and drunkenness. He endorses accommodation:

We say indeed . . . *God condescendeth to accommodate his wayes and proceedings (not his Essence and being)* to our apprehensions, wherein we are very far from saying that he *speaks one thing & intends the clean contrary*; but only that the thing that he ascribes to himselfe, for our understanding, and the accommodation of his proceedings, to the manner of men, are to be understood in him, and of them, in that which they denote of perfection, & not in respect of that which is imperfect and weake.[44]

This is not to give the reader free rein. The figurative expressions in Scripture are not to be read mystically, but 'the literall sence is to be received, according to the direction of the Figure which is in the words'.[45] Owen claims to undertake a more nuanced rhetorical analysis that enables him to maintain literal interpretation through the interpretation of figures. It was his Socinian adversaries who made language so enigmatic 'as to turn almost the whole Gospel into an *Allegory*'.[46] Owen uses the word 'accommodated' in the strong theological sense, but also to mean a human adjustment to an audience, though he sees them as different processes. God alone lifts us, though we translate in the process of explicating Scripture. He writes emphatically that the Scriptures have nothing human in them, but are the product of pure inspiration.[47] Owen reacts against enthusiasts who laid claim to special insight into truth. Humans can condescend to an audience, as he is obliged to in defence of the Trinity, but there is no inspiration involved and nothing special in the language used, merely the pragmatics of explication.[48]

While Owen's account of accommodation is much attenuated from the mystical account of Pseudo-Dionysius, it concurs that the figurative representation of God in Scripture offers greater access to truth than would be available in non-figurative language. Others would insist that this is in fact *non-figurative* language, that the process of accommodation means that the language used describes reality neither figuratively nor literally. Accommodation cannot be aligned with the figurative interpretation of Scripture, and opposed to the literal interpretation of Scripture; it can also be understood as a means of saving literal meaning. Thus Francis Bampfield writing in 1677: 'The Scriptures are not accommodated to vulgar received Errours, or mere imaginary conceits, or vain false appearances, but they speak of things, as the things themselves really are, Is not the LORD Christ Truth it self?'[49] Accommodation prevents you from having to say or think things that are not true.

   This is how the doctrine is deployed among a number of seventeenth-century divines, for whom falsehood and feigning bedevil the issue of divine representation. This was understood through the language, shared by all grammar school boys, of rhetoric. In a sophisticated discussion of the interpretation of rhetorical figures in Scripture, Wilson emphasized that 'in such tropicall and figurative speeches, there is no purpose to deceive, but by meet resemblances to expresse the truth'.[50] He and others expressed the anxiety that elevated rhetoric might not be suited to divinity and soteriology. Concern about deception extended to angelic apparitions. Aquinas had argued that angelic bodies were like figures of speech in the Bible, and thus 'no slur on the truthfulness of holy angels'.[51] This argument was elegantly developed in Peter Le Loier's treatise on spectres, translated into English in 1605, where he notes that 'all feyning and dissembling, or any kinde of fiction is very unseemely in the Angells of Truth'. Hence, the bodies they assume must be '*True and unfeyned formes*', not intending to deceive, 'for that they do not oppose & set before our eyes humane shapes and formes, because thereby they would bee thought and esteemed to be men: but to the end that by their humane properties, we should know the virtues of the Angells'.[52] Here and elsewhere the *intention* not to deceive is translated to the literal reality of the representation. Henry Lawrence states that Abraham's angelic visitors must have really eaten: 'it is certaine that they did what they seemed to doe . . . for they never deceived your senses, their colour, their shape, their eating, their drinking, their speaking was what it seemed to be'.[53] In a 1650s sermon on Acts 10 John Gumbleden insists that the angel and Cornelius really spoke 'mouth to mouth with the other', because God would not have deluded Cornelius (Gumble-den disparages transubstantiation), 'neither was there any thing *imaginary*, or *phantasticall*, but all was *reall*, and *substantiall*, here'. This was not like the image of Samuel conjured by the Witch of Endor; there was 'no *painting*, no *counterfeiting*, no *deluding* here; no, neither could there be: because he that came in to *Cornelius* was *an Angel of God*; who knows not how to *delude* or *counterfeit*.[54] What Gumbleden means by 'real' here is less important than the concern over angelic falsehood. If angels present illusions, they must do so in a way that does not involve feigning, deceit, falsehood, or misrepresentation; just as when Scripture speaks of the invisible world, and of God's emotions, it does so truthfully. Representation of the invisible and the unknown need not involve fiction if it fits a pattern of accommodation. Accommodation means that the language is *neither* figurative *nor* literal.

## Reformed Poetics

Could accommodation influence (or help) poets? On the face of it, this seems unlikely: while human agency might be involved in the uplifting, it is the Holy Spirit that guarantees the process of communication. Except for those who included within it Moses' deliberate adjustment to his audience, accommodation was usually understood as something performed by God or the Holy Spirit.[55] Poetry was fiction, a product of the fleshly imagination. Pseudo-Dionysius wrote that Scripture used poetic imagery not 'for the sake of art'; and Peter Martyr describes fables as 'a narration of a false thing, devised for commoditie or delite sake'.[56] Art serves the fleshliness of the secular mind; we look upon it for pleasure, for itself, and if we think we see God in it, this is a form of idolatry. This view accords with the literary theory of George Puttenham in the late sixteenth century, who thought that *anthropopathia* risked *underpraising* God, and that the Christian poet should use figures to praise him superlatively; Dryden espoused comparable principles a century later.[57]

As we have seen, however, some found room for human agency in accommodation, not only as a conscious adaptation but as a hermeneutic capacity. Moreover, the Puritan emphasis on the spirit increasingly relocated that spirit as a motion within the human. Just as biblical commentaries, Scripture paraphrases, and rhetorical textbooks influenced the poetics of the early modern religious lyric,[58] so early modern theories of representation were shaped by works of scriptural exegesis. Poets and critics in the sixteenth and seventeenth centuries appropriated the doctrine of accommodation in their accounts of poetics and literary creation. This some did because it was a convenient language with which to explain or justify imaginative representations of the spiritual world;

others because it was understood that the language of Scripture, the language used by the prophets, had special properties that were transferred to its use in other contexts, including religious poetry. But some claimed more than that: they were transferring agency for accommodation into the human domain. Their readers were therefore able to achieve, in reading their imaginative texts, a special kind of insight into the truth.

Milton is the most incautious of poets, and the next chapter suggests that he occupies a special place in this shift, as well as among English poets; others, however, also transgressed the boundaries laid by Puttenham. Many poets express caution, yet create a tension between prescript and practice. Thomas Heywood's *Hierarchie of the Blessed Angells* reflects on accommodated language at length and outlines the conventional symbolism of God's material attributes:

> Sometimes, what's proper unto Man alone,
> Is given to this *trias*, three in One:
> As, when we attribute unto him Wings,
> It straight unto our apprehension brings,
> How he protects and shadowes us. If Eares?
> With what facilitie and grace he heares
> Our devout Prayers. . . .
> His Face, sometimes, his presence doth imply;
> Sometimes, his favour and benignitie.[59]

He proceeds to construe God's hands, feet, nostrils, and eyes. Where we 'reade Wrath', we are meant to understand a promise of God's terrible judgements; where 'eyes', his omniscience. Heywood implies that this power of signification was deliberately implemented by the prophets, who were not merely intermediaries for the Holy Spirit. He touches upon a distinction between two understandings of prophecy: as being a passive conduit for God's voice, and as consciously passing on inspired knowledge. However, he brings accommodation and prophecy into close association:

> The *Divine Wisedome*, knowing how dull and weake
> Mans heart and braine is, Taught the Text to speake
> To our capacities. The Prophets, they
> Did not of this great Deity display
> The absolute perfection; but so leave it,
> That by a glimpse we far off might conceive it.[60]

The corporeal provides a vehicle for spiritual expression, and this way of speaking has an uplifting power:

> Now to proceed: The Scripture Phrase doth reach
> No farther, than our stupid sence to teach;
> That by corporeall things we may prepare
> Our hearts to know what things spirituall are;
> And by Invisible, make demonstration
> Of what's unseene, beyond mans weake narration.
>   And for this cause, our passions and affects
> Are in the Scriptures, for some knowne respects,
> Confer'd on the Almighty; when 'tis said,
> God did repent him that he man had made.
> Or when hee's wrathfull? herein is not meant,
> That He is angry, or, He can repent:
> But 'tis a Figure from the'effect arose,
> And that the Greeks call *Metanumikos*.[61]

The prophets condescend to our capacities; they know, through the gift of inspiration, the spiritual realm that lies beyond the weak language of human narration. The name that Heywood gives to the figure is different from Puttenham's *anthropopathia*; *metanumikos* implies a transcendence above a world governed by names into a world that defies language.

How much of this power does Heywood claim for himself? He writes with authority about the invisible, endorsing the Pseudo-Dionysian hierarchy of angels that confers upon *Hierarchie* its nine-book structure, insisting that angels were made on the first day of Creation, that Lucifer had six days of glory before he rebelled out of pride, and he describes, albeit in insipid terms, the war between Lucifer and Michael.[62] These beliefs could be held entirely upon the authority of orthodox theologians, and do not indicate that Heywood believed his poetic skills granted him special insight into revealed truths. Heywood does not let his imagination or inspiration—whichever it is—run free: he interrupts his narratives with discursive passages that support, justify, and qualify the verse. Each of the nine books begins with an emblem, and a verse argument (a precedent for *Paradise Lost*[63]), and concludes with extended prose 'Theologicall, Philosophicall, Poeticall, Historicall, Apothegmaticall, Hierogriphicall and Emblematicall Observations, touching the further illustration of the former *Tractate*', followed by commentary on the emblem and then verse meditations on the preceding book. He explains his reasoning:

That nothing in these short Tractates may appeare difficult to the Ignorant, I hold it necessarie unto my present purpose, (as willing to be understood by all) to illustrate whatsoever may seem obscure, as well by precept as Historie.... that was the end to which industrious Authors first aimed their Indeavours, and spent so much Inke and Oile, in their dayes labours, and nights watchings.[64]

Heywood's purpose is didactic. Though *Hierarchie* was a labour of love, the *magnum opus* of a popular dramatist and the first translator of Ovid's *Ars Amatoria* (1625), it is a work more of learning than of inspiration.

Lucy Hutchinson avows resistance to invention, to speculative writing about 'circumstances that we cannot know'. Humans, imprisoned by bodily senses, are ignorant. Adam finds no companionship in beasts, but cannot reach to converse with angels:

> No; for though man partake intelligence,
> Yet that, being joined to an inferior sense,
> Dulled by corporeal vapours, cannot be
> Refined enough for angels' company.[65]

Hutchinson's dualist universe is severely hierarchical. The contrast with Milton is profound. Hutchinson repeatedly emphasizes the ignorance of humans and the limited capacity of their understanding. In her theological treatise 'On the Principles of the Christian Religion' she writes that Scripture does not state when the angels fell, but

only tells us, they kept not their first station, became haters of God, enemies, accusers, and murtherers of mankind, liars and deceivers; that they are subtile, and restlesse in persuading the destruction of men; that they are mallitious tormentors, and tormented, and uncapable of redemption.

And again:

The creation and our owne frames are like faire volumes to a dimme-sighted man, where the truths of God are written in legible characters; but wee cannot make any sense of them without the help of devine illumination, which sacred spectacles once put on makes us read the discoveries of God with holy wonder and delight . . . [66]

But again and again she moves from the negative to the positive, from ignorance to surmise, from darkness to light. She starts with limitation, and argues towards an affirmation or a means. This pattern obtains in her accounts of representation.

The language of shadows and mirrors exploited in *The Life of Colonel Hutchinson* and her elegies resembles the conventional language of Neoplatonism, but it is also shaped by these theological and soterio-logical concerns. God is mirrored by Christ, who is mirrored by Scripture, which is mirrored by John, and Lucy is a reflection of his virtue.[67] It is the principle of accommodation that lifts these shadows up to share the light of their higher partners. Hence, perhaps, her recurrent dwelling on the details of John's appearance and clothes, in language that is both philosophical and erotic.[68] Similarly, *Order and Disorder* creates a process of literary circumvention. Hutchinson insists on the superiority of paradisal nature to postlapsarian art, and dismisses the capacity of pencils, wit, and other means of feigning to capture the perfections of paradise. Nothing remains of it, and so we should not invent . . . but then she continues:

> We know there was a pleasant and noble shade
> Which the tall-growing pines and cedars made,
> And thicker coverts, which the light and heat
> Even at noonday could scarcely penetrate.           (3. 159–62)

The proceeding description is partly extra-scriptural. However, the elaboration is securely confined within brackets, like the walls of paradise, that emphasize the narrator's hesitation.

Hutchinson's emphasis on plain speech, the dangers of elaboration, the dichotomy between religious contemplation and poetic fancy, and the risks of the fleshly imagination are drawn from writing on accom-modation. The preface to her epic promises to disappoint expectations of elegant poetry: 'they will find nothing of fancy in it; no elevations of style, no charms of language . . . I would rather breath forth grace cordi-ally than words artificially.' She will not turn 'Scripture into a romance'.[69] Romance is antithetical to Scripture, and, in her life of her husband, to providence. Elaborate rhetoric is a sign of artifice, not of revelation, and this is a religious work in which it would be indecorous.[70] The preface turns to optimism, however. The Word lifts human reason:

comparing that revelation God gives of himself and his operations in his Word with that of the wisest of mankind, who only walked in the dim light of corrupted nature and defective traditions, could with all their industry trace out or invent, I found it so transcendently excelling all that was human, so much above our narrow reason, and yet so agreeable to it being rectified, that I disdained the wisdom fools so much admire themselves for; and as I found

I could know nothing but what God taught me, so I resolved never to search after any knowledge of him and his productions, but what he himself hath given forth.[71]

Hutchinson makes no explicit claim to privileged or prophetic insight, but she does explore truths that lie in revelation's penumbra, and can do so because she relies on the power of Scripture to condescend to her and lift her. Provided she remains within the inspiring remit of Scripture, even while she reads it figuratively (a practice she reflects upon[72]), she does not stray into the 'impious tales' or pagan fictions of the fleshly imagination. And she becomes even more positive: in plain and elegant poetry, 'Truth loses not its perfection.' Accommodation lifts the writer above her limitations, and prevents her from saying things that are impious or untrue.

Samuel Pordage's relationship to accommodation is distinctive, but revealingly so. As Chapter 5 showed, John travelled through the invisible universe, and conveyed to his son the prophetic insights that formed the basis for his epic *Mundorum Explicatio*. Samuel was able to claim a more powerful version of accommodation than Hutchinson, Heywood, or any of the divines discussed above. He insists that poetry is properly religious, and condemns the vitiating 'wanton rithmes' of secular poetry praising 'Mistress' eyes': 'The end of *Poesy* is the praise of God, | Us'd to that end it is exceeding good.'[73] There are limits to the poet's vatic power, however. God is beyond man's proper knowledge. The hieroglyphic figure (Fig. 5.1) presents God as eyes, ears, and ciphers in a sun enveloped in cloud, and Pordage warns:

> Nor *Man*, or *Angel* a commission has
> To dive into this *abstruce* secret Place,
> Therefore thine eyes withdraw, and be Content
> To know GOD as *He* will, nor represent
> Thou to thy mind, or in thy fantasie
> An *Image* of the glorious *Deity*;
> For never ought we Heav'n's high Majesty
> To Form or Figure whatsoever tye:
> Therefore O *Man* destroy all *Images*
> Of *God*, that in thy fantasie shall rise.[74]

Samuel requires a theory of accommodation, and this account is embedded in his description of angelic bodies. Both good and bad angels freely adopt bodies of air, exploiting their thrall over the elements,

and can animate dead bodies. They nonetheless have their own incor-
poreal bodies, and their adopted virtual bodies reflect these.[75]

> But whensoever Spirits Bodies here
> Assume, and to our outer Eye appear,
> They put on such as may convenient be,
> And with their inner Bodies best agree,
> For look what shapes their inner Bodies have,
> Such shapes, (if visibly appear) they crave.

Pordage compares this to a wax simulacrum of a man, inside which a
man will fit. Angels are 'self-Taylors': the invisible body is clothed with
a corresponding visible body, 'So that the outer forms the'assimulate |
In all things answer their internal state'.[76] The ambiguous neologism
(which John Taylor had recently used to signify feigning) suggests that
the angels both simulate their outward appearance and assimilate it.
They are thus able to communicate with humans, who can

> understand
> Nothing, but what's compos'd of matter, and
> Form, and what is corporal.

However, the simulated body accurately represents a reality that is
beyond the human senses. Pordage also notes that good angels usually
appear in human form, which suggests that angels indeed look like
humans with wings.[77] Despite his Behmenist insistence on an inner
world distinct from the corporeal world of ordinary human experi-
ence, Pordage suggests that these two correspond so closely that at
times they cannot be distinguished, and sounds and actions in one
penetrate to the other. In his version of accommodation the human
and divine crash into each other.

## Milton and Accommodation

Accommodation is a common foundation for poets writing imagina-
tive narratives based upon Scripture, and it is more significant to
Milton's conception of his creation than to Pordage, Heywood, or
Hutchinson. In *Paradise Lost* Raphael explains accommodation to
Adam repeatedly, and his explanations echo beyond the frame of his
speech, to envelop the whole poem. Milton relies on reformed

accommodation to justify what would otherwise be an unsustainable, even outrageous, incursion into the unknown.

> ... how shall I relate
> To human sense the invisible exploits
> Of warring Spirits ... what surmounts the reach
> Of human sense, I shall delineate so,
> By likening spiritual to corporal forms,
> As may express them best, though what if earth
> Be but the shadow of heav'n, and things therein
> Each to other like, more then on earth is thought?
>
> (5. 564–76)

> ... who, though with the tongue
> Of angels, can relate, or to what things
> Liken on earth conspicuous, that may lift
> Human imagination to such highth
> Of godlike power ...        (6. 297–301)

> Thus measuring things in heav'n by things on earth ...
>
> (6. 893)

> ... though to recount almighty works
> What words or tongue of seraph can suffice,
> Or heart of man suffice to comprehend?
> Yet what thou canst attain, which best may serve
> To glorify the maker, and infer
> Thee also happier, shall not be withheld
> Thy hearing, such commission from above
> I have received ...        (7. 112–19)

This theology of literary articulation, crossing the boundary between visionary insight and word, is also alluded to by Michael and by the epic's blind narrator:

> So law appears imperfect, and but given
> With purpose to resign them in full time
> Up to a better covenant, disciplined
> From shadowy types to truth, from flesh to spirit ...
>
> (12. 300–3)

> So much the rather thou celestial light
> Shine inward, and the mind through all her powers
> Irradiate, there plant eyes, all mist from thence
> Purge and disperse, that I may see and tell
> Of things invisible to mortal sight.        (3. 51–5)

These passages address the reader's relationship with the poem, but
they do not invite her to read the poem, or specific passages, meta-
phorically or allegorically.[78] Allegory posits a gulf between ideal and
the representation, and instructs the reader in how to read that repre-
sentation in order to experience a lifting from the real towards the
ideal.[79] Accommodation, however, presumes no such divide. There is
a particular affinity between the images of the poem and the reality
they offer to describe; this is not a likeness of signification, but a deeper
similarity where human conception meets transcendent truth without
a self-conscious process of interpretation. This happens because of the
power of language, in which Scripture instructs the poet, and because
of inspiration, the guidance of the Spirit. These are premisses of
Milton's aesthetic.[80]

Milton also uses and discusses the doctrine of accommodation in the
work now known as *De Doctrina Christiana*, in a manner different from
but analogous to the musings of *Paradise Lost*.[81] He asserts that no one
can know God through reason alone, and that knowledge of the Word
'must be understood with reference to the imperfect comprehension
of man', as God is above man's comprehension.

Our safest way is to form in our minds such a conception of God, as shall
correspond with his own delineation and representation of himself in the
sacred writings. For granting that both in the literal and figurative descriptions
[*vel describi vel adumbrari*] of God, he is exhibited not as he really is, but in such a
manner as may be within the scope of our comprehensions, yet we ought to
entertain such a conception of him, as he, in condescending to accommodate
himself to our capacities [*qualis ipse se ad captum accommodans nostrum*], has
shown that he desires we should conceive. For it is on this very account that
he has lowered himself to our level, lest in our flights above the reach of
human understanding, and beyond the written word of Scripture, we should
be tempted to indulge in vague cogitations and subtleties.[82]

The Latin expresses the sense of indeterminacy and ambiguity implicit
in such representation, one characteristic of discussions of angelic
bodies. 'Vel describi vel adumbrari' offers as alternatives a description
or representation and a semblance, a counterfeit or feigning (not a
'figurative') delineation. Representation would be feigning if it was not
accommodated to human capacities.

The movement of Milton's prose here is significant. He proceeds
to reject *anthropopathia*, closely following Puttenham, as 'a figure
invented by the grammarians to excuse the absurdities [*nugas*] of

the poets on the subject of the heathen divinities'. Yet it is to the
Scholastic, purely rhetorical and uninspired, account of anthropopa-
thy that he objects, while he endorses the attribution of human
feelings to God 'after the manner of Scripture, that is, in the way
wherein God has offered himself to our contemplation'.[83] While
rejecting the Audian heresy with its literal account of God's body
and Lactantius' literal understanding of God's anger, he steers very
close to both.[84] He quotes a series of anthropomorphisms from
Scripture, and adds: 'however we may attempt to soften down
such expressions by a latitude of interpretation, when applied to
the Deity, it comes in the end to precisely the same'. That is, the
qualifications make little difference. Indeed, he adds, after quoting
the decisive 'Let us make man in our Image' (Gen. 1: 26), 'if God
habitually assign to himself the members and form of man, why
should we be afraid of attributing to him what he attributes to
himself, so long as what is imperfection and weakness when viewed
in reference to ourselves be considered as most complete and excel-
lent when imputed to God?'[85] This is to be accomplished, and the
truest apprehension of God obtained, by accommodating one's
understanding to his Word, which is itself accommodated to one's
understanding ('eos optime capere statuamus qui suum accommodant
captum Dei verbo; quandoquidem is verbum suum accommodat
captum Dei verbo').[86] The syntax mimes the reciprocal process.

Milton becomes increasingly emphatic: we are obliged to follow the
anthropopathisms of Scripture. God is as he represents himself, so why,
and on what authority, should we think otherwise? We are, after all,
only human.

In arguing thus, we do not say that God is in fashion like unto man in all his
parts and members, but that as far as we are concerned to know, he is of that
form which he attributes to himself in the sacred writings. If, therefore, we
persist in entertaining a different conception of the Deity than that which it is
to be presumed he desires should be cherished, inasmuch as he has himself
disclosed it to us, we frustrate the purposes of God instead of rendering him
submissive obedience. As if, forsooth, we wished to show that it was not we
who had thought too meanly of God, but God who had thought too meanly
of us.[87]

Milton's argument winds through a familiar logic, until he endorses,
beyond all doubt, the anthropopathy he originally rejected. We are not
trying to capture the essence of God, only to find out the most accurate

way of writing about him. God is, as far we can understand, really like that; 'it comes in the end to precisely the same'. Raphael's meditation on the problems of representing spiritual warfare similarly cancels itself when he concludes with a question:

> what if earth
> Be but the shadow of heav'n, and things therein
> Each to other like, more then on earth is thought?

(5. 574–6)

In *De Doctrina*'s discussion of accommodation, God suddenly becomes much more like the language we use to describe him than we think. To suggest otherwise would be to devalue his high estimation of us.

To Milton accommodation signifies the condescension of God and the raising of human thought, and the Christian guarantee that while this is taking place miscommunication or misrepresentation or misunderstanding will not occur. Accommodation inhabits inspired writing: it is God who is representing himself, and his prophets, therefore, are conduits for his words, though their words are also his. True believers will use Scripture as the palimpsest for discoursing of God, because its terms, images, figures are all authorized. Milton's account of accommodation admits of human agency, provided the human has the spirit with him or her, and it grants special power to the poet, extending a seventeenth-century English poetic. It is an especially strong version of the doctrine, granting much more to the individual believer, comprehending the ability, in appropriate conditions, to understand and describe the sacred. There are circumstances when it is possible for writers to go beyond what is expressly laid down in Scripture provided they stay true to his own divine self-conception. If what they write is protected by the operation of accommodation, and provided they have the spirit with them, it will be true, at least in human terms, which are for all practical purposes the same as divine; it amounts to the same in the end. This is more daring than anything Hutchinson or Heywood offers, though it is not so far from Pordage, whose father had communicated with angels.

To see how Milton claims so much on behalf of accommodation, however, it is necessary to examine the other element in the formula. While accommodation is for the poet an insurance policy against misrepresentation, Milton reaches deeper into sacred mysteries because of his belief in the operation of the spirit. Milton's adaptation of accommodation is not an excuse for writing figuratively, but evidence that he is really inspired, guided by an inner illumination that enables him to think that what he writes is, in a sense, true, as literally true as scriptural accounts of God's anger or right hand. The next chapter—a transitional interlude in which this book moves from considering angels and theology towards Milton's angels and the literary imagination—examines this operation of the spirit, understood within the context of Protestant theology of the spirit and particularly the inner light fundamental to British radicalism. It was understood in several ways: inspiration, vision, the voice of an angel heard internally or audibly, the voice of God, prophecy. Marvell asks the question most eloquently:

> Where couldst thou words of such a compass find?
> Whence furnish such a vast expense of mind?
> Just heaven thee like Tiresias to requite
> Rewards with prophecy thy loss of sight.[88]

# 7
# Spiritual Gifts
## Angels, Inspiration, and Prophecy

### Poetry, Prophecy, and the Poet–Prophet

The spirit of prophesie, is not like the spirit of the buttery . . . we must not in raging, or aspiring affection presume to mount above the cloudes in the highest region of the aire, or to pierce the unknowen deepes of the earthly Center. It is a scrupulous, and vaine curiositie to busie our selves, or importune other about any such inquiry, as neither is lawfull in practise, or assured in use, but both impious in the one, and uncertaine in the other.[1]

Thus cautioned the physician John Harvey, writing in 1588. His voice was one in a chorus. Early modern Britain saw a surge both of prophetic activity, and of cautions against the delusions of inspiration. Calvin warned that true prophecy was rare, and that false prophets abounded, yet it was intrinsic to the intellectual dynamics of Protestantism that individual believers claimed special insight beyond priestly jurisdiction.[2] Prophets appeared. Especially at times of political or social fracture, in the 1580s and the 1640s, men and women proclaimed themselves prophets. These prophets, however, were not simply the enemies of orthodox theology. Many worked closely within the tenets of Protestant belief to legitimize their activity.

Milton saw himself as a prophet. But what did this term mean to him, and what did it mean in the context of mid-seventeenth-century Britain? Milton was a vatic poet, in a tradition of poet–prophets who opposed courtly political orthodoxies with religious truths.[3] Scholars have accentuated the authorial self-fashioning in Milton's stance. They have emphasized the poet–prophet role, and the term *prophet* has been heavily qualified by the term *poet*.[4] In the Renaissance poet–prophet tradition, a Protestant view of history is presented as seen through the eyes of a poet elevated to a privileged position within his society (he sees beyond its present circumstances). These poets resist the courtly panegyric associated with the endorsement of a heavily hierarchical vision of society—hence the 'latent radicalism' of the tradition—and voice social criticism through Scripture, especially the prophetic books.[5]

At the root of many seventeenth-century poets' claims to inspiration, and their aspiration to a role of legislator of virtue, lies Sidney's *Apologie for Poetrie*: 'Among the Romans a Poet was called Vates, which is as much as a Diviner, Fore-seer, or Prophet, as by his conjoyned wordes *Vaticinium & Vaticinari*, is manifest: so heavenly a title did that excellent people bestow upon this hart-ravishing knowledge.'[6] Sidney, responding to Plato's account of poetry as feigning, claims a special kind of truth for poetry. In contrast to the limited truths of historians, a poet 'pictures what should be, and not stories what have beene, they will never give the lye, to things not affirmatively, but allegorically, and figurativelie written'.[7] The true poet does not speak falsehoods, though his words may not be literal, argues Sidney, as the truths he speaks are not simply affirmative. He speaks a prophetic truth that is neither positive nor false.[8] The tradition extends through John Dennis, who, in his *Grounds of Criticism* (1704), describes poetry as 'one of the Prophetick Functions', but reduces this prophesy–poetry to secular inspiration.[9] The early modern Protestant prophetic tradition is a mode of writing, shaped by biblical forms.[10]

Milton is among the poets indebted to Sidney, yet his vision of the poet–prophet is considerably more ambitious. To see the prophetic element of Milton's verse as being *exclusively* located within a poetic–prophetic or a Sidneian tradition, as a social critic finding a voice in Scripture, understates the truth claims he seeks to make. It places a boundary between Milton and other early modern prophets, and finds a creative tradition for his prophecy that confers social respectability. This approach is certainly justified by the nature and quality of Milton's writing, the density of literary allusion, the breadth of genres he employs, the music of the words. The younger Milton is frequently on the verge of stepping decisively beyond this tradition, as in 'Lycidas', where he speaks in St Peter's voice, and subsequently claims that what he foretold in the apocalyptic section of the poem had come true.[11] In *Paradise Lost*, however, Milton's truth claims are even greater. I propose to put aside the term *poet*, and ask: did Milton believe that he was not only imaginatively inspired, but also prophetically inspired, speaking a truth about Creation and the Fall brought to him by God? Is there a sense in which *Paradise Lost* is not only an expression of political theology, but also a divine vision of a hitherto undisclosed reality

## Protestant Prophecy

Early modern Protestants agreed that the age of prophecy was over.[12] Like miracles, prophecy disappeared with the early Church, redundant in the age of true faith, when, Augustine wrote, the eyes of the heart had been opened. Thus, one speaker in James VI's dialogue *Daemonologie* says:

All we that are Christians, ought assuredly to know that since the comming of Christ in the flesh, and the establishing of his Church by the Apostles, all miracles, visions, prophecies, & appearances of Angels or good spirites are ceased. . . . the Lawe and Prophets are thought sufficient to serve us, or make us inexcusable.[13]

James associated prophecy, miracles, and angelic apparitions. This connection is a common one, and it is significant. Reginald Scott, a sceptic with a very different account of spiritual activity, wrote that miracles and prophecies ceased with the Incarnation:

We maye as well looke to hear prophesies at the tabernacle, in the bush, or the cherubin, among the clouds, from the angels, within the arke, or out of the flame, &c. as to expect an oracle of a prophet in these dayes.[14]

The Cambridge Platonist John Smith charted a more complex history: the spirit of prophecy died under the Jews, was restored under the new dispensation of the Messiah, then subsequently faded in the second century. Miracles ended in the fourth.[15]

The age of prophecy was over. Protestants qualified this assertion, however, observing that under extraordinary circumstances God might raise up new prophets and work miracles.[16] Peter Martyr Vermigli wrote that now that people had emerged from darkness and gross idolatry, and 'now that all places abound with bookes, and teachers, there is no need of the helpe of prophets'. But he acknowledged that a small number of prophets might continue to appear, though they would not be so celebrated as those of former ages.[17] The Elizabethan clergyman William Perkins offered guidance in distinguishing between true and false prophets, signifying that

modern prophecy was possible in principle.[18] This special qualification
to the general rule not only provided security in case they were wrong,
but permitted the visible workings of providence, a doctrine that
extensively informed the Protestant understanding of the world.

There is a second qualification. Protestants redefine prophecy to
include the form of inward conviction that is experienced when
hearing or reading the word of God. Calvin writes:

Prophane men because they thynke religion standeth onely in opinion, to the
ende they woulde beleve nothing fondly or lightly, do covet and require to
have it proved to them by reason, that Moises and the Prophetes spake from
God. But I answere that the testimonie of the holy ghost is better than all
reason. For as onely God is a conveniente witnesse of hymselfe in hys owne
worde, so shal the same worde never finde credit in the hartes of men, until it
be sealed up with the inwarde witnesse of ye holy ghost.[19]

This suggests the double bind of Calvinist hermeneutics, but one
consequence is that the only proof of the true prophet is inward
conviction in the auditor. This extends to reading the prophetic
books of Scripture. Reading Scripture, which is to say reading it with
faith and understanding it, relies on inspiration, the witness of the Holy
Ghost. Interpretation *is* a form of prophecy (especially, but not exclu-
sively, interpretation of the prophetic books). Thus, Jeremy Taylor, in
*Discourse of the Liberty of Prophesying* (1647), defends the right and
necessity of every man to interpret Scripture according to his own
light and reason: 'it is best every man should be left in that liberty from
which no man can justly take him, unlesse he could secure him from
errour: So that here also there is a necessity to conserve the liberty of
Prophesying, and Interpreting Scripture'.[20] Because there are no
failsafe human rules for interpretation, each man must rely on the
guidance of the spirit (which can be extinguished by the neglect of
one's understanding); hence true interpretation is synonymous with
prophecy. Taylor's position is unusually tolerationist, but a similar
identification of prophecy with interpretation can be found in the
writings of Charles Odingsells, who identifies four senses of prophecy
according to Scripture, the last of which is preaching or expounding
the doctrine of the prophets. 'The gift of Prophecying in this sense', he
writes, 'is perpetual in the Church, and must not faile.'[21] In prophecy
could lie the apostolic continuity of the true Catholic Church, which
is to say the Protestant Church. The centrality of prophecy is partly

consequent on the Protestant emphasis on the inner light, the priest-hood of all believers, and the need for a non-institutional apostolic succession (for which this *specific* sense of prophecy must not fail). Some, however, restricted this prophetic practice to the proper teachers of the Church.[22] This is a specific mode of prophecy, related to but distinct from the more general use of that term. It troubled the Church at times of heightened apocalypticism, but did not undermine the common understanding that prophecy had ceased.[23]

Putting this special sense to one side, how do Protestants understand prophecy and the prophetic office? Most agree that prophets speak of things far off in time or space: they speak of things done long ago, far away, or to come.[24] Vermigli, highly influential in early modern England, agrees that prophecy reveals past, present, and future, defin-ing it as 'a facultie given unto certeine men by the spirit of God, without teaching or learning, whereby they are able certeinlie to know things heavenlie, high, and secret, and open the same unto others'.[25] The gift of prophecy is independent of learning. However, prophets must understand the meaning of their words, or they are madmen. Vermigli distinguishes prophecy from dreams, oracles, and visions. Instead prophecy arrives through the light of inspiration:

And the heavenlie light, wherewith a mans mind is then lightened, is rather as a *sudden passion*, as that which may easily be remooved, than as a passible qualitie: and is as light in the aire, but not like the light of the celestial bodies: not as a palenesse comming of the natural temperature of the bodie; but as that which riseth of a *sudden frighting* of the mind.[26]

Without rushing ahead of my argument, recall Milton's invocation to *Paradise Lost* book 3:

> Hail holy light, offspring of heaven first-born,
> Or of the eternal co-eternal beam
> May I express thee unblamed?                                    (3. 1–3)

By 'unblamed' Milton seems to mean without misrepresentation or sin or error or blasphemy.

>                           ... Thee I revisit safe,
> And feel thy sovereign vital lamp; but thou
> Revisitst not these eyes, that roll in vain
> To find thy piercing ray
>                   .     .     .

> So much the rather thou celestial light
> Shine inward, and the mind through all her powers
> Irradiate, there plant eyes, all mist from thence
> Purge and disperse, that I may see and tell
> Of things invisible to mortal sight.                (3. 21–55)

This purging of 'mental sight' also happens to Adam when the angel Michael prepares him to receive a prophetic vision of future history (11. 411–22). This idea of visual enlightenment is integral to definitions of prophecy. True prophecy illuminates the mind.

John Smith, whose essay on prophecy is above all an attempt to understand prophecy by exploring rabbinical writings on the subject, describes a hierarchy of prophecy: from Mosaic through prophetic dreams and visions to prophecy with no visual content based on hearing the voice of God. All prophecy mixes reason and imagination, and the more elevated the mode, the greater the role of reason. Smith focuses on an issue that recurs throughout discussions of prophecy. With the exception of Moses and the lowest form of prophecy, all prophetic visions are mediated by angels: 'The Hebrew masters here tell us that in the beginning of Prophetical inspiration the Prophets use to have some *Apparition* or *Image* of a *Man* or *Angel* presenting itself to their *Imagination*.'[27] He quotes Moses Maimonides equating angelic conversations with prophetical visions, and approves Isaac Abarbanel's suggestion that the status or degree of the angel sent corresponded to the status of the receiving prophet.[28] Hence, an angel high in the hierarchy, a seraph or cherub, would bring a more significant message than a mere angel or archangel. Even those sceptical of contemporary prophecy—such as Harvey, who refers scornfully to 'seraphicall illuminations' and sensationalizing pamphlets—accept that angels are involved in prophecy.[29] The numerous prophets who appeared in Lutheran Germany and Scandinavia were frequently agitated by an encounter with an angel, sometimes disguised as an old man, usually dressed in white. The angel encourages the prophet to call his local community to repent.[30] Angels are a means by which inspiration is brought; they instigate visions; they authenticate the prophet; they also symbolize the moment of transition from ordinary man to visionary prophet.

How then could one distinguish between a true prophet and a false? Taylor writes that any sure distinction is impossible. Smith writes the false can be identified, that melancholy men cannot be prophets, for example, but he thinks that ultimately it requires inspiration to recognize the true prophet.[31] Others suggest more numerous external signs. For Vermigli, the only signs of the true prophet are that he does not lead his people into idolatry, and that his predictions are realized. False prophets use indecent gestures, and do not understand their own speech.[32] William Perkins asserts that false prophets are *personally* insufficient: they maintain heresies, they are rash and inconstant in judgement, they are inclined to vice, and have a strange complexion and body temperature. Young people, women, the talkative, and the unruly were also unlikely to be true. Other warning signs included ambiguous speeches (true prophecy was plainly spoken), and a tendency to provoke disquiet in church and commonwealth, or to touch upon private interests. Perkins also warned against prophets that seemed to go against the Word of God, including those who spoke in particulars about things about which God had chosen to be vague.[33] This implies the many predictions that circulated in early modern Britain under the name of Merlin, Nostradamus, Piers Plowman, and Mother Shipton, but it also seems to warn against visionary insights into heaven or the angelic orders.[34] Thomas Hobbes, to whom enthusiasm represented the greatest threat to social stability, thought a true prophet was simply defined. Visions, voices, and inspirations could not be persuasively communicated to another. Instead the true prophet was known by 'the doing of miracles' and 'not teaching any other Religion than that which is already established'. And as the age of miracles was over, so was the age of prophets.[35]

True prophecy is the gift of God. But this does not exclude all human effort. Maimonides had insisted that, though prophecy was a natural faculty of humankind, true prophets were prepared by education and training *and* prompted by the will of God. Fools and ignoramuses could no more be prophets than asses or frogs.[36] Most Protestants rejected the role of education, but did insist that prophets were honest and virtuous.[37] Honesty and virtuous conduct could therefore be a means of self-preparation for prophecy. Vermigli wrote that the gift of prophecy 'must be given freelie' and could not be obtained by industry or purgation; however, fasting and prayers could help prepare the prophet. Prophecy was not a habit, but 'a preparation' or 'disposition, being in a kind of qualitie'.[38] This does not imply collaboration with God, but that it is appropriate to cultivate prophecy by preparing for it. Hence, the spirit of prophecy is not the spirit of the buttery.

These theological descriptions for the most part keep modern prophecy at arm's length. However, prophecy was important to reformed communities, and early modern Protestant exegetes did find self-proclaimed prophets among their contemporaries. Calvin, Luther, and Vermigli had their prophets in Germany and Scandinavia and Italy; Perkins, Scott, and Harvey lived in the days of the enthusi-astic Elizabethan prophet 'Frantic Hackett'.[39] Milton lived during the apogee of English prophecy, the 1640s and 1650s, when radicals and antinomians challenged traditional theological decorums and claimed intimate relationships with God.[40] Lady Eleanor Davies, the most notorious prophet of the 1620s, was succeeded by Anna Trapnel, Elizabeth Poole, Mary Cary, Elinor Channel, and Esther Biddle, a generation of women prophets who were widely reported, and often abused in the pamphlet press.[41] The Philadelphians encouraged proph-esying among women (Poole visited John Pordage at Bradfield). Female prophecy was less controversial than female preaching, not least because it seemed to be authorized by Joel 2: 28: 'I will pour out my spirit upon all flesh; and your sons and your daughters shall prophesy.'[42] Prophecy was for women a means of negotiating a voice, in which agency could be deflected onto a higher power. Eleanor Davies's prophecies, though frequently political and critical of Laud and Charles I, were protected by their very obscurity (she nonetheless spent many months in prison). Trapnel fell into a trance and claimed not to recall her ecstatic outpourings.[43] Mary Cary was inspired by visions of angels.[44] Female prophets in the1640s and 1650s usually delivered their words in a semi-conscious state: they were merely conduits for God. However sincere such protestations were, these prophets present their own role as that of a passive channel not responsible for the form or content of their prophecies.

While such postures protect the prophetesses, act as a verification of the divine inspiration, and demonstrate that they do not consciously tinker with the inspired words—an important qualification—they do not fit the common Protestant requirement that the prophet under-stand his or her words. Such trances alienate the mind, whereas true prophecy, in Smith's words, 'doth not *ravish* the Mind, but *inform* and *enlighten* it'.[45] This can be contrasted with some of their male contem-poraries. Abiezer Coppe was one of the most eccentric of the period's prophets, but he presents himself as fully attuned to God's voice, and a co-author of his prophecies. He is called by God and speaks as a

Hebrew prophet, but he also fashions his words: 'And I expect prejudiciall hearts, eares, and eyes from some; But rejoyce exceedingly that I know *the Fathers voyce*, though I cannot yet speak plaine enough after him, or write that smoothly, which is written fairely in me, in this particular.'[46] John Reeve, another self-proclaimed messenger from God whose bearing and meaning was inimical to socially respectable forms of religion, claimed that on three consecutive mornings he heard the voice of Jesus, 'by voice of words', telling him that he had been given the gift of understanding Scripture. 'I being as perfectly awaked when he spoke to me ... as I was at the writing hereof'. His were not dream visions. The spirit of prophecy enables him to see things far off: 'I declare by Revelation from the Holy Spirit, what was from Eternity.' He proclaims: 'woe would have been unto us, if wee had come in our own name; but wee know that God sent us, as sure as he sent *Moses*, the Prophets, and the Apostles'.[47] Reeve was an antinomian, but he observes the rules of prophecy: his words are from God, they will come true, he has had revealed to him past, present, and future, he is conscious when he receives his insights, and he is convinced of his commission. This is neither like a Mother Shipton prophecy, not like an Anna Trapnel pamphlet. This is not to suggest that Reeve cynically fashions his prophecy according to Protestant textbooks; rather, his convictions fit the details of the Protestant theology of prophecy, and reveal the social force of that model.

## Wisdom's Sister, the Heavenly Muse

Which returns us to Milton. How does Milton relate to these pre-scriptions concerning true prophecy? Harvey warned, in the quotation with which I began this chapter, 'we must not in raging, or aspiring affection presume to mount above the cloudes in the highest region of the aire, or to pierce the unknowen deepes of the earthly Center'. The 'centre' referred to is hell. This soaring is what Milton does, and what he thinks poets *should* do. He writes in *Reason of Church Government* (1642) of 'a Poet singing in the high region of his fancies with his garland and singing robes about him', and imagines himself writing in the future the kind of poem not 'to be obtain'd by the invocation of Dame Memory and her Siren daughters, but by devout prayer to that eternall Spirit who can enrich with all utterance and knowledge, and

sends out his Seraphim with the hallow'd fire of his Altar to touch and
purify the lips of whom he pleases'.[48] The angel is a figure for divine
inspiration, purifying sins by touching the prophet's lips. It derives
from Isaiah, and informs many writings about prophecy.[49] Milton's
angel is a seraph, high in the Pseudo-Dionysian hierarchy. As we have
seen, the involvement of angels in the preparation for and experience
of prophecy is central to Protestant theological traditions, and it is
especially appropriate for Milton because of his understanding of the
Holy Spirit. In the same tract, Milton describes the prophetic vocation:
'when God commands to take the trumpet and blow a dolorous or a
jarring blast, it lies not in mans will what he shall say, or what he
shall conceal'. God writes the message, and man is the messenger.
Nevertheless, it is the duty of the would-be prophet and would-be
poet to prepare for this command, and to augment his talent by study,
prayer, and careful living.[50] The prophet is inspired by God, but
human labour and scholarship are necessary to the vocation. Milton's
allusions to prophecy in this passage—in contrast to those in the Latin
*Defensio*[51]—are not a merely decorative aggrandizing of his poetic
vocation: they engage deliberatively with discussions of what it
means to be a prophet. When referring to his experience of 'inward
prompting' he wants his readers to hear the motion of a divine spirit,
not a human impulse.[52]

In *Paradise Lost* the narrator describes the impulses of the spirit in
some detail. His muse is Urania, whom Guillaume du Bartas appro-
priated from astronomy to appoint as the muse for Christian poetry.[53]
But Milton's Urania is a figure for another, truer muse. His Urania, 'if
rightly thou art called', descends from heaven:

> The meaning, not the name I call: for thou
> Nor of the Muses nine, nor on the top
> Of old Olympus dwellst, but heav'nly born,
> Before the hills appeared, or fountain flowed,
> Thou with eternal wisdom didst converse,
> Wisdom thy sister, and with her didst play
> In presence of the almighty Father, pleased
> With thy celestial song.                                    (7. 5–12)

He tells her 'thou art heav'nly' while Orpheus' muse was 'an empty
dream' (7. 39). In writing an epic Milton observes epic conventions,
but assures the reader that his Christian version supersedes and flies
higher than its pagan predecessors. Du Bartas's Urania displaces the

classical version, but Milton's in turn displaces Du Bartas's. The muse is invoked earlier, in book 1, and it is the muse that inspired Moses and that witnessed Creation:

> Sing heavenly Muse, that on the secret top
> Of Oreb, or of Sinai, didst inspire
> That shepherd, who first taught the chosen seed,
> In the beginning how the heavens and earth
> Rose out of chaos . . .
>
> .      .      .
>
> thou from the first
> Wast present, and with mighty wings outspread
> Dovelike satst brooding on the vast abyss
> And mad'st it pregnant: what is dark in me
> Illumine . . .                                               (1. 6–23)

Though designated differently, this is the same muse (hence 'before the hills appeared') that inspires him throughout the poem; it is the spirit through which God moves prophets.[54] Juvencus, the earliest Christian epic poet, invoked the Holy Ghost as his muse; but this will not do for Milton.[55] Importantly for our understanding of his idea of prophecy, Milton does not believe in the Holy Spirit in this way. *De Doctrina Christiana* argues that it is not a being, but a series of offices: 'The name of Spirit is also frequently applied to God and to angels, and to the human mind.' Milton denies the Holy Spirit as understood in Trinitarian theology. The 'spirit' signifies different things. Sometimes it is the Son, the spirit that moves on the water. Sometimes it is an angel, such as the spirit that takes up Ezekiel. Elsewhere it is inspiration: 'Sometimes it means the light of truth, whether ordinary or extraordinary, wherewith God enlightens and leads his people.' And sometimes it is 'used to signify the spiritual gifts conferred by God on individuals, and the act of gift itself'.[56] This is the sense in which Milton's muse is the spirit, why he calls the meaning, not the name, and why the light that *shines inward* is invoked in book 3. The muse and the spirit and the light are not beings but human qualities, inspiration and creative power, direct from God, brought by an angel, or dwelling in the human. This is why blindness, *his* blindness, is like living in the shade of angels' wings ('cœlestium alarum umbra').[57]

If this is the spirit or muse that brings Milton his poetry, then he must mean that he is inspired, and that it is therefore in a sense true. However, I want to raise a possible objection at this point. What if Milton is simply engaged in playing the role of a Thamyris, Homer, or Tiresias?[58] What if the reality of prophecy makes a good archetype for fiction? What if he speaks metaphorically?

The possibility must be conceded. According to Ernst Robert Curtius, in an uncharacteristically torpid moment, the opening lines of *Paradise Lost* are an 'artistic yet artificial prologue', and Milton fails to give life to Urania (a classical figure whom the poet has dressed up as Christian).[59] If we read *Paradise Lost* as metaphor or uninterested fiction, Milton's interests are aesthetic, and detached from religious truths. His claim to superiority to pagan and Catholic poets can be understood as a secular claim, a purely egoistical pride in individual achievement. His interlocutors are not the 'fit audience . . . though few' (7. 31) of a godly remnant, but other poets: the tradition he supersedes, Hesiod, Lucretius, Ovid, Prudentius, Dante, and the poets that will follow him. As with all literary interpretation that disentangles the text from the inconveniences of history and ideology, a consistent case can be made for an uninspired literary Milton, a Milton who lives in a hall of textual mirrors.

This constitutes a strangely secular view of Milton, and one better fitting the modern literary academy than the world of early modern antinomianism, experimental theology, and political enquiry. Dante's *Commedia* describes a world that was, the poet believed, more or less like the real, invisible one. He did not think that each individual that Dante-the-narrator encounters on his voyage was located precisely where he put them. The narrative nonetheless exemplifies moral truths, and incorporates, often in non-narrative form, doctrinal truths based on Church teaching, such as the angelic hierarchies. In so far as it reaches beyond human understanding, it is through its imaginative plenitude, not because Dante had visited his other world. However, Milton's religious ambitions (and his account of faith) are different.[60] He writes with a startling literalism. In his religious beliefs, and his faith in prophetic visions, he is more like John Reeve and John Pordage than Dante. The grounds for thinking this are developed over the remainder of this book; the remainder of this chapter shows that Milton's account of inspiration reflects a Protestant blueprint, and that he takes care to authorize his own claims.

Milton not only writes about prophetic inspiration; he describes the experience. In profound contrast with Thomas Heywood and Lucy Hutchinson, Milton's prophecy is more than the light that guides scriptural interpretation and more than an event in scriptural history.[61] It is a poetic fury leading the poet to hidden truths. How does Milton experience inspiration? It is brought by the spirit, the spirit of God, an inner light, or an angel. After describing the dangers with which he is surrounded in the evil days of the Restoration, the poet remembers the muse's company:

> yet not alone, while thou
> Visitst my slumbers nightly, or when morn
> Purples the east . . .                    (7. 28–30)

Notice the 'or' that balances a nocturnal against a dawn visit from the spirit. Book 9's invocation charts Milton's decision to choose a divine theme, more heroic than the chivalric epics he had considered writing in his youth,

> If answerable style I can obtain
> Of my celestial patroness, who deigns
> Her nightly vision unimplored,
> And dictates to me slumbering, or inspires
> Easy my unpremeditated verse . . .        (9. 20–4)

He is concerned that if not inspired he may not finish his poem, that the climate or years may

> damp my intended wing
> Depressed, and much they may, if all be mine,
> Not hers who brings it nightly to my ear.  (9. 45–7)

The fact that the poem is finished is partial proof that it is inspired, that it has been brought to his ear and his muse is heavenly, more powerful than Orpheus'. The casualness of 'celestial patroness' almost conceals the careful repetition of that 'or': does the muse dictate when he is asleep, or inspire the lines after he wakes? Milton presents himself, twice, as uncertain over when he receives his inspiration. Milton's 'ors' are important.

Perhaps this gives a cue to his early biographers, who either repeat Milton's self-mythologization or offer independent observations. Milton's nephew Edward Phillips writes: 'And hee waking early (as is the use of temperate men) had commonly a good Stock of Verses ready against his Amanuensis came; which if it happend to bee later than ordinary, hee would complain, Saying *hee wanted to bee milkd.*' And Jonathan Richardson writes that Milton 'frequently Compos'd lying in Bed in a Morning ('twas Winter Sure Then) I have been Well inform'd, that when he could not Sleep, but lay Awake whole Nights, he Try'd; not One Verse could he make; at Other times flow'd *Easy his Unpremeditated Verse*, with a certain *Impetus* and *Æstro*, as Himself seem'd to Believe'.[62] The '*Æstro*' perhaps echoes the 'hallow'd fire' driving the poet in *Reason of Church Government*. The poem *and* the biographers describe a genius who receives his compositions at the boundary between sleep and waking, who discovers his words as much as he labours for them. This is a picture of prophetic inspiration.

Further, consider the line Richardson quotes: the verse is 'easy' because he has the assistance of the spirit and makes little effort himself; it is 'unpremeditated' because it is only partly conscious. If it were too purposefully studied, it would not be inspired. The true prophet's labour is to prepare himself, to furnish himself with virtue and learning, not to prepare the verse. Calvin would say that the words were either God's or the human's. The biblical prophets were 'forbidden to invent anything of their own'; they were merely the 'amanuenses' of the spirit, writes Calvin.[63] The instrument of God cannot also be an artist. If there is anything human in the prophecy, it cannot be divine. The voice of God cannot be tampered with. Vermigli writes that prophets 'above all things' must not add to or remove anything from their inspiration; to do so would be to corrupt it, and to deceive themselves and others.[64] For Perkins a prophecy that was false in the smallest detail signified a false prophet.

Smith proposes a more complex account of human agency in prophecy. He did so because of the influence of the Hebraic tradition: if Milton was unfamiliar with Smith's work, he certainly shared an interest in the same traditions, unusual at the time.[65] Prophets interpret their visions in the dialects familiar to them. Both Maimonides and Abarbanel agree in this, and it is why an element of human learning is necessary for a prophet. The spirit impressed his truth upon prophets so clearly that 'it became their own Sense'; and hence 'those *Words* and Phrases in which they were audibly express'd to the Hearers afterwards or penned down, should be *the Prophets own*'.[66] Smith allows an element of human agency not only in the interpretation but in the actual writing of prophecy. And in an unexpected turn of his argument, he suggests that if writing is too consistent or rational in its presentation, it is probably uninspired. Prophecy is naturally contradictory:

There is sometimes a seeming inconsistence in things spoken of, if we shall come to examine them by the strict Logical rules of Method: we must not therefore in the matter of any *Prophetical* Vision look for a constant Methodical contexture of things carried on in a perpetual coherence. The Prophetical Spirit doth not tie it self to these Rules of Art, or thus knit up its Dictates Systematically, fitly framing one piece or member into a combination with the rest, as it were with the joints and sinews of Method: For this indeed would rather argue an humane and artificial contrivance then any Inspiration, which as it must beget a Transportation in the Mind, so it must spend it self in such Abrupt kind of Revelations as may argue indeed the Prophet to have been inspired.[67]

Excessive artifice suggests human contrivance. Prophecy can contain inconsistencies and multiplicities precisely because it does not conform to the rules of art. Richardson reports that Milton 'would Dictate many, perhaps 40 Lines as it were in a Breath, and then reduce them to half that Number'.[68] Smith's Hebraic account of prophecy would permit room for revision. In this perspective, which I believe is Milton's, to call a poet a true prophet does not deny the imaginative power of his art; nor does it lessen engagement with literary traditions. Inspiration does not stop the prophet from using humanist learning, rhetoric, or the sinews of a vernacular tongue.

Protestants declare that the age of prophecy is over, but nonetheless outline in detail the circumstances in which prophecy takes place, the qualifications of the true prophet, the nature of the communication, and the means by which the true prophet can be distinguished from the impostor. In mid-seventeenth-century Britain a handful of religious enthusiasts declared that they were prophets in the tradition of biblical prophecy. Milton was among them.

*Paradise Lost* describes events from the beginning of time to its end, many in the words of angels: the narrator's voice frames a series of speeches and stories offered by angels to humans. Raphael's narrative of the war in heaven and Creation to Adam in books 5 to 8, and Michael's prophecy of future history in books 11 and 12, are true because they are spoken by angels. Unfallen angels do not need to present evidence or show their credentials: they are truth-speakers. The poet who repeats the things known only to God and angels in the voice of angels either presents a pure fiction, or something that has a special status, the status of a revealed truth. The centrality of angels to the narrative of *Paradise Lost*—a poem told by and about angels—constitutes part of a truth claim. The rest is disclosed in the representation of the inspired narrator in the poem, a narrator who is Milton himself, and confirmed in *De Doctrina Christiana*'s account of inspiration by the spirit. These are the truths revealed in Milton's dawn-waking vision, brought by a spirit of God, perhaps an angel. While these claims sit uncomfortably in the narratives of a secularized literary history, they are integral to the texture of early modern religious belief and practice.

# PART II

# Milton's Angels

# 8

# Can Angels Feign?

## Abdiel's Flight

At the beginning of book 6 of *Paradise Lost* the seraph Abdiel returns to
the throne of God, having deserted his superior officer, Satan. He
arrives at dawn and is surprised when light discloses the sight of an army:

> Chariots and flaming arms, and fiery steeds
> Reflecting blaze on blaze, first met his view:
> War he perceived, war in procinct, and found
> Already known what he for news had thought
> To have reported . . .                                  (6. 17–21)

Abdiel had expected to relate to his fellow angels and to God the news
of Satan's rebellion. The sight of the army reveals to him that this news
is already public. Milton's angels are in many ways strikingly human,
and here it appears they are subject to the vicissitudes of light and
optics. Why else would Abdiel not have seen the angelic army earlier?
But there is a more troubling anthropomorphism implicit here, one
which has not been formerly noted.

To see it we must cross the partition between books 5 and 6. The
relevant passages appeared on consecutive openings in the 1667
edition of *Paradise Lost* (see Fig. 6), and have seldom done so since.
In the 1674 edition an opening was introduced between the passages,
accommodating the prose 'argument' to book 6; the effect is to
interrupt the narrative, and it is the narrative continuity that matters
here. Book 5 ends with a magnificent stand-off between Satan and
Abdiel in which the zealous angel, surrounded by hostile forces,
presents in his fury a defence against the fallen angel's seductive
arguments that is both rhetorically accomplished and thoroughly

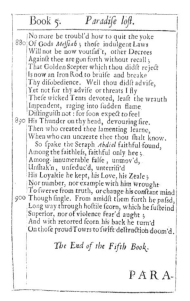
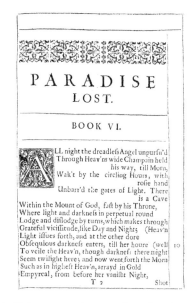

**Figure 6.** John Milton, Paradise Lost (1667), consecutive openings showing the end of book 5 and beginning of book 6

reasoned.[1] The 'Ambiguous words and jealousies' of Satan, his 'calumnious art | Of counterfeited truth' have turned a third part of the angels against their maker (5. 703, 771–2; 2. 692; 5. 710). Abdiel rises against Satan's falsehoods and defies him out of zeal for God's service. Yet in his zeal he may step beyond the bounds of his commission. Abdiel is alone:

> Among innumerable false, unmoved,
> Unshaken, unseduced, unterrified
> His loyalty he kept, his love, his zeal;
> Nor number, nor example with him wrought
> To swerve from truth, or change his constant mind
> Though single.                                    (5. 898–903)

He stands alone without help from God, who is characteristically reserved when he is needed. Milton's angels do not have perfect knowledge. Their knowledge, and their means of knowing things, are inferior to the penetrative, intuitive powers attributed to angels by Aquinas and others.[2] Abdiel has to rely on his own wits.

Book 6.     *Paradife loft.*

Shot through with orient Beams: when all the Plain
Coverd with thick embatteld Squadrons bright,
Chariots and flaming Armes, and fierie Steeds
Reflecting blaze on blaze, firft met his view:
Warr he perceav'd, warr in procinct, and found
20  Already known what he for news had thought
To have reported: gladly then he mixt
Among thofe friendly Powers had him receav'd
With joy and acclamations loud, that one
That of fo many Myriads fall'n, yet one
Returnd not loft: On to the facred hill
They led him high applauded, and prefent
Before the feat fupream; from whence a voice
From midft a Golden Cloud thus milde was heard.
   Servant of God, well done, well haft thou fought
30  The better fight, who fingle haft maintaind
Againft revolted multitudes the Caufe
Of Truth, in word mightier then they in Armes;
And for the teftimonie of Truth haft born
Univerfal reproach, far worfe to beare
Then violence: for this was all thy care
To ftand approv'd in fight of God, though Worlds
Judg'd thee perverfe: the eafier conqueft now
Remains thee, aided by this hoft of friends,
Back on thy foes more glorious to return
40  Then fcornd thou didft depart, and to fubdue
By force, who reafon for thir Law refufe,
Right reafon for thir Law, and for thir King
*Meffiah,* who by right of merit Reigns.
Goe *Michael* of Celeftial Armies Prince,
And thou in Military prowefs next
*Gabriel,* lead forth to Battel thefe my Sons
                     Invin-

*Paradife loft.*     Book 6.

Invincible, lead forth my armed Saints
By Thoufands and by Millions rang'd for fight;
Equal in number to that Godlefs crew
Rebellious, them with Fire and hoftile Arms   50
Fearlefs affault, and to the brow of Heav'n
Purfuing drive them out from God and blifs,
Into thir place of punifhment, the Gulf
Of *Tartarus,* which ready opens wide
His fiery *Chaos* to receave thir fall.
   So fpake the Sovran voice, and Clouds began
To darken all the Hill, and fmoak to rowl
In duskie wreathes, reluctant flames, the figne
Of wrauth awak't: nor with lefs dread the loud
Ethereal Trumpet from on high gan blow:   60
At which command the Powers Militant,
That ftood for Heav'n, in mighty Quadrate joyn'd
Of Union irrefiftible, mov'd on
In filence thir bright Legions, to the found
Of inftrumental Harmonie that breath'd
Heroic ardor to advent'rous deeds
Under thir God-like Leaders, in the Caufe
Of God and his *Meffiah.* On they move
Indiffolubly firm; nor obvious Hill,
Nor ftreit'ning Vale, nor Wood, nor Stream divides  70
Thir perfet ranks; for high above the ground
Thir march was, and the paffive Air upbore
Thir nimble tread; as when the total kind
Of Birds in orderly array on wing
Came fummond over *Eden* to receive
Thir names of thee; fo over many a tract
Of Heav'n they march'd, and many a Province wide
Tenfold the length of this terrene: at laft
                     Farr

Satan asserts that the angels were self-begot, and that God falsely claimed the credit for this (a well-known Gnostic heresy, and a particularly resonant one in a poem about Creation).[3] In response Abdiel counterblasts:

> I see thy fall
> Determined . . . henceforth
> No more be troubled how to quit the yoke
> Of God's Messiah; those indulgent laws
> Will not now be vouchsafed, other decrees
> Against thee are gone forth without recall;
>
>       .      .      .
>
>             soon expect to feel
> His thunder on thy head, devouring fire.      (5. 878–93)

This is for the most part a reasonable observation based on evident facts. Abdiel can see that Satan has fallen, and that punishment can soundly be predicted. But the declaration that 'decrees | . . . are gon forth' stretches beyond plausible inference.

In *Paradise Lost* 'decrees' specifically designate God's public proclamations. For example: the decree by which God begets and anoints his only Son. Milton is unusual among Christian exegetes in attributing Satan's fall to envy over the Son's promotion; one early attack on the unorthodox theology of Milton's epic singled out this 'Groundless Supposition', thinking it incompatible with orthodox Trinitarianism: 'This Scheme of the *Angels* revolt cannot Answer either to the *Eternal Generation* of the *Son*, which was before the *Angels* had a Being, or to His *Temporal Generation* of the B. *Virgin*, that being long after the *Fall* of the *Angels*.' Charles Leslie was probably right; Defoe also thought that the promotion of the Son laid a ground for Arianism, and another reader of a 1669 edition noted in the margin, 'this acco<unt> of X$^{ts}$ birth seems... prophan<e> & destroys coæternity'.[4] Milton's account of Satan's fall commences with a *decree*, so in *Paradise Lost* this word bears considerable weight. The force of a decree is amplified by Milton's God's intensely communicative nature. In *Paradise Lost* book 6, God converses aloud with the Son in heaven. When he pronounces his decree in book 5, the angels seemingly cannot see him, but they certainly hear the Word, and the decree is spoken aloud.[5] The audibility of speech and song in *Paradise Lost* follows from Milton's commitment to materialism and his sense of community. Throughout *De Doctrina Christiana* Milton uses the word 'decree' to designate both the general Decree by which God effects the world and all that will happen, and those special decrees by which he performs or proposes particular events; they are audible announcements. Decrees are communications, not private resolutions.[6]

When Abdiel tells Satan that decrees are gone forth, he means that God has told his court that Satan is to reap the consequences of his disobedience. Yet after a night's travelling he finds 'Already *known* what he for *news* had thought | To have *reported*'. Why does he not expect an army already to be mustered? If the decree has already been made, why does he expect to report news?

There are three possibilities. The first is that Milton overlooked this detail, obscured by the book division that separates the passages, and that it is an authorial inconsistency. If, however, an effective explanation can be found, then it should be preferred, not least on the grounds of charity. The second possibility is that Abdiel is confusingly referring to an earlier decree known to both himself and Satan. This could be the decree pronounced by God that elevates the Son to his right hand as the head of the angels; the angels must bow their knees to the Son, confess him Lord, and

>                                         abide
>                        United as one individual soul
>                        For ever happy.                                (5. 609–11)

This does not sound much like Abdiel's 'devouring fire'. Yet the omnipotent adds:

>                        Him who disobeys
>           Me disobeys, breaks union, and that day
>           Cast out from God and blessed vision, falls
>           Into utter darkness, deep engulfed, his place
>           Ordained without redemption, without end.         (5. 611–15)

If this is understood to be a corollary to the main decree, Abdiel could have just realized that Satan's rebellion is foreshadowed in this decree, and that his punishment is already certain.[7] In which case Abdiel is not fabricating, but articulating something that has just occurred to him.

Though this solution is neat, it is not persuasive. First, Abdiel does not explicitly invoke this earlier decree in order to strengthen his defence. Satan was not the only auditor of the anointing decree; the other rebel angels by whom Abdiel is surrounded and threatened were also present. At this compelling moment in the drama, Abdiel might hope to sway them by putting forward this interpretation, thereby undermining the rebellion against God. Persuading them would not only be brotherly, but would also diminish the physical threat he faces. Secondly, this interpretation does not explain why Abdiel thought he would *report news*; nor does it acknowledge the significance of the anticlimax when the army appears; it only explains his certainty that Satan is already doomed. The problem of why Abdiel thinks he is going to report news, and why Milton's narrator indicates this fact, remains. Thirdly, from a literary point of view, it undermines the dramatic tension of Abdiel's flight. His poise is heroic because of his felt isolation, and the nocturnal journey through the wide countryside bridges books 5 and 6 precisely to suspend Abdiel between flight and arrival. When at sunrise he sees 'all the plain | Covered with thick embattled squadrons bright', it is a powerful moment: he apprehends the full wonder of divine providence. If he has worked it all out in advance, the episode loses the 'blaze on blaze' of unanticipated fulfilment, and Abdiel ceases to be a heroic witness. If his rencounter with Satan and subsequent journey is coloured by mechanical certainty without doubt or hesitation, then God's applause to one who has 'fought | The better fight' and borne 'Universal reproach' (6. 29–30, 34) is complacently forensic. Abdiel has struggled; hence his meriting of praise; hence the significance 'of so many myriads fallen, yet one | Returned not lost' (6. 24–5). Finally, Abdiel states that '*other* decrees | Against thee are gone forth'. This firmly distinguishes them from the 'indulgent laws' of the anointment.[8] Abdiel means that these are decrees *other* than the decree anointing the Son heard by all, 'God's first and most excellent SPECIAL DECREE', as it is described in *De Doctrina*.[9] The plural of 'other decrees' emphasizes the distinction. These are something new and different, according to Abdiel; both Abdiel and Satan know what the earlier decree is, and they are not discussing it here.

This leaves a third, counter-intuitive interpretation. It is in accord with Milton's theology that Abdiel is surprised at this point, and this is not an oversight. There is a discrepancy between what Abdiel knows and what he affirms in the heat of argument. Abdiel, unswerving from a greater truth, is averring that which is merely speculative. In other words, while arguing with Satan, he risks telling an untruth.

Unfallen angels should not falsify. The distortion of facts is superficially harmless, but in the context of the poem is breathtaking. Abdiel, and through him Milton, is contending with the father of lies (John 8: 44). The preceding lines emphasize Satan's verbal evasion, his deception, his equivocation.[10] Raphael earlier told Adam that Satan 'with lies | Drew after him the third part of heaven's host' (5. 709–10). Commentators on Scripture commonly asserted that lies were essential to the Fall of humankind, as Satan could only tempt Eve by lying.[11] A fallen angel can lie without complication or compunction, but surely not an unfallen one? Abdiel is threatened by physical violence, a danger that echoes through Milton's imagination; yet lying is a more fearsome weapon than violence.[12] God predicts that Adam and Eve will not fall 'By violence, no, for that shall be withstood, | But by deceit and lies' (5. 242–3); and so it transpires, when God reports that man sins 'believing lies | Against his maker' (10. 42–3). Abdiel, moreover, is one who refuses to 'swerve from truth', and is usually held up as an example of virtuous conduct in the epic.[13] Received wisdom concerning Milton's angels tells us that he is unorthodox on two points: first, the matter of angelic digestion (angels not only eat real food when it is polite, they digest it); secondly, that angels embrace and penetrate each other for sexual pleasure.[14] Abdiel's rhetorical liberty here may be an even greater heterodoxy.

## Doctrine and Story

A good angel who deceives or misleads demands some consideration of the status of Milton's angels. What are their offices in the poem? How are they portrayed? What is their nature? Beginning with an overview of critical responses to Milton's angels, I will suggest that the tendency is to allegorize them, and that this is founded on a misapprehension of the nature of early modern angels. Milton's doctrine of angels—by which I mean beliefs, theological, political, and natural-philosophical, supported by learning and reason, and thus often distinguished from acts of faith and imaginative speculation—is interwoven with narrative. The basis for this, Milton's understanding of accommodation and inspiration, was outlined in the preceding two chapters. The question for this chapter is: how should we read *Paradise Lost* in the light of this? I will propose a reconsideration of the relationship between doctrine and narratives in Milton's poetry and in early modern imaginative writing.

Faced with interpretative difficulties, readers tend to separate Milton's angel-doctrine from his story. On the one hand, readers suggest, this is what he believes, and on the other, here is the story he tells in which angels play a fictional role. Patrick Hume, Milton's first annotator and a reader bent on establishing Milton's poem as a classic, was puzzled that immaterial beings, 'incapable of any Blow or Bruise', who could 'feel no destroying deadly Wounds', should wear armour.[15] A few years later Charles Leslie thought the narrative indecently fantastic: 'The Gravity and Seriousness with which this Subject ought to be treated, has not been Regarded in the Adventurous Flight of *Poets*, who have Dress'd *Angels* in *Armor*, and put *Swords* and *Guns* into their Hands, to Form *Romantick Battles* in the *Plains* of *Heaven*, a *Scene* of Licentious *fancy*.'[16] Samuel Johnson suggested that an 'inconvenience of Milton's design is, that it requires the description of what cannot be described, the agency of spirits. He saw that immateriality supplied no images, and that he could not show angels acting but by instruments of action; he therefore invested them with form and matter.' Johnson did not grasp the extent of Milton's materialism, and the philosophical underpinnings of angelic substance. For example, Milton was committed to the idea of angelic armour: Raphael describes it as 'panoply', referring to whole-body armour (see Eph. 6: 11, 13), and

thereby elegantly distinguishes angels' armour from the spiritual ar-
mour that was a commonplace of seventeenth-century divinity. The
'golden panoply' and 'celestial panoply' (6. 527, 760) is pointedly
material, and suggests that this is an aspect of angels' substantial
being, rather than a spiritual allegory.[17] The angels suffer as they
struggle to release themselves from it. Johnson thought that Milton
had made his angels material in order to tell a good story, which
seemed to him a poorly conceived poetic fancy, and he regretted
that Milton's angels 'unhappily perplexed his poetry with his philoso-
phy'.[18] More emphatically, T. S. Eliot asserted a division in Milton
between 'the philosopher, or theologian, and the poet', evidence of
the 'dissociation of sensibility' that broke the organic relationship
between a writer's thought and his language. Belief and poetry no
longer went hand in hand.[19] This view has cast a long shadow over
Milton and the interpretation of early modern imaginative writing.

The longest and most thoughtful account of Milton's angels appears
in Robert West's 1955 book *Milton and the Angels*, and it articulates
most clearly this critical paradigm. West distinguishes between
Milton's serious and casual angelology, separating those 'scientific'
and heterodox passages where Milton risks his poetry in order to
make a point about angels, from 'creative' passages involving angels,
in which their philosophical foundations—how they know things,
how they move, their physical composition—are merely incidental.[20]
In doing so he drives a wedge between imaginative storytelling and
deliberated accounts, intended to be taken literally, of things that are
believed to be true. West is followed by Alastair Fowler, whose
learned editorial annotations distinguish between 'story' and 'doc-
trine', as if the poetry is air *or* angels, but not both.[21]

It seems to me that we cannot do this if we want fully to read
*Paradise Lost* as a poem. Because to do so we must accept that its ideas,
learning, ethical imperatives, aesthetics, and its historical situation,
meet within its narratives and verse in ways that cannot be regarded
as incidental or always extricable. To formulate it crudely: what
Milton writes about angels in *Paradise Lost* does not conflict with his
deliberated beliefs; what he imagines, he imagines on the basis of a
sustained engagement with writing about angels; when he tells stories,
they elaborate upon knowledge, and this knowledge is articulated
through narration. Rabbinic Midrashim, one source for Milton's
thinking about and imagining of angels, tell stories around Scripture

to resolve its narrative discontinuities and contradictions, and in so doing indirectly elaborate theology or doctrine; just so Milton's poetry knots together story and doctrine, poetry and philosophy.[22]

The relationship between Milton's systematic theology and his epic suggests an intimacy between theology and the creative imagination. In *De Doctrina Christiana* Milton asserts, 'Anyone who asks what God did before the creation of the world is a fool; and anyone who answers him is not much wiser.'[23] By the 'creation' of 'this world', Milton means everything that is made by the Word and spirit of God, the visible and invisible world, not limited to that described in Scripture. Yet, despite his caveat, he is prepared to point out that God did not spend the period before Creation preordaining that which took place afterwards; and that he did make his own dwelling place in the highest heaven, and that he made angels before the creation of the world (indeed in all likelihood they fell before 'the first beginnings of this world'). He adds that angels have freewill, are assigned to oversee particular kingdoms or nations, that there are many things of which they are ignorant, and so on.[24] Likewise in *Paradise Lost*: heaven exists before the world, the angels are made and fall, of their own freewill, before visible Creation, and hell is not in the centre of the earth. The author exploits the grounds of his theology as the basis for narrative elaborations: certainly treatise and poem agree, but more importantly, belief is the premiss of imagination. The commonly held doctrine that angels maintained their position not so much by their own strength but by the grace of God might have made for a better poem, but it is not to be found in *Paradise Lost* because Milton did not hold it to be true.[25]

We can contrast Milton's imaginative latitude (and the word *imaginative* needs to be treated with some caution) with other Scripture-based poems that elaborate a version of accommodation. Thomas Hobbes and Sir William Davenant, in their mid-century exchange on literary theory, concurred that a presumptuous poetic familiarity with God was 'saucy', and a mark of dangerous inspiration.[26] Milton's boldness in representing the sacred is proportionate to the strength of his claim concerning accommodation and inspiration, but it is also evident in the relationship between his narrative and doctrine, and this can be seen in the very different narrative patterns on Heywood and Hutchinson. The angel-doctrine in the last four chapters of *Hierarchie of the Blessed Angells* is presented in ways that contrast with *Paradise*

*Lost*, and Heywood's account of the war in heaven is resoundingly allegorical:

> But shall I now tell
> The Weapons, Engines, and Artillerie
> Used in this great Angelomachy.
>     No Lances, Swords, nor Bombards they had then,
> Or other Weapons now in use with men;
> None of the least materiall substance made,
> Spirits by such give no offence or aid.
> Onely spirituall Armes to them were lent,
> And these were call'd *Affection* and *Consent*.[27]

Heywood invites us to read his war in heaven, as critics tend to read that in *Paradise Lost*, as an extended metaphor.[28] While Milton uses his imagination freely to describe the actions of angels in narrative form, Heywood reveals his hesitation about straying into heterodoxy by turning his elaboration into allegory, and by stressing that it is not meant literally. Like Milton, he goes beyond the testimony of Scripture: he contends, for example, that Lucifer had glory among the angels for six days, and that God revealed the Son's incarnation at the end of Creation, commanding that all angels should obey the Son and humankind, and that it was this that provoked the dissention between Lucifer and Michael. In this and other interpretations, Heywood engages with prose literature on the nature, office, and history of angels, borrowing and recasting exegesis. He does not allow his stories to stand by themselves, however, but supports (and constrains) each with extensive apparatus.[29] While Milton lets narrative do its work, Heywood's muse does not travel unfettered.

Lucy Hutchinson's *Order and Disorder*, written between 1660 and 1679, offers a revealing contrast with, and perhaps a conscious reaction against, Milton. Echoes suggest that Hutchinson had seen some or all of *Paradise Lost*, either in the 1667 edition or in manuscript, via a mutual acquaintance, Arthur Annesley, Earl of Anglesey. Anglesey's library was a refuge for literary Nonconformists; Milton had consulted him in connection with the publication of *History of Britain*; and to him Hutchinson dedicated her earlier translation of Lucretius.[30] Hutchinson's caution in *Order and Disorder*, which corresponds to her debt to du Bartas in Sylvester's translation, is also a reaction against Milton's lack of it. Hutchinson retreats from the scandal that writing fiction about Eden, heaven, and angels risks. 'Let's waive Platonic dreams', her narrator enjoins,

> Of worlds made in Idea, fitter themes
> For poets' fancies than the reverent view
> Of contemplation, fixed on what is true
> And only certain, kept upon record
> In the Creator's own revealèd Word,
> Which, when it taught us how the world was made,
> Wrapped up th'invisible in mystic shade.[31]

The story of the fall of angels is, according to Hutchinson's stern narrator, based on 'circumstances that we cannot know', and anything we invent or guess is probably inspired by reports that the same fallen angels themselves imparted to men gullible enough to believe 'their gross poetic fables'. She exhorts: 'look no further than the light doth show'.[32]

Hutchinson's censures suggest a dialogue with Milton's text. Whereas the exchange between God and the Son in book 3 of *Paradise Lost* represents their physical separateness, and suggests Milton's anti-trinitarianism, canto 3 of *Order and Disorder* begins with God's calling 'in himself a sacred council', stressing the triune nature of Hutchinson's God. Elsewhere Milton's Adam speaks with God 'concerning solitude and fit society' (8, argument) and convincingly maintains that he needs an equal mate, 'Collateral love, and dearest amity'; in response to which God admits that in resisting Adam's arguments he was only testing the man, and that the creation of Eve was 'Intended' all along (8. 426). This daring dramatization adroitly both notes and resolves the apparent discrepancy between the accounts of Eve's creation in Genesis 1 and 2.[33] It is hard not to hear Milton's creation being chastised in Hutchinson's single-line assertion: 'Whether he begged a mate it is not known' (3. 312; though a similar account of Eve's creation could be found in John White's 1656 *Commentary* on Genesis[34]). These and other passages intimate that Hutchinson had read *Paradise Lost* before writing the first five cantos of her epic.

It is possible to overstate the contrast between these authors and their attitude to elaboration on Scripture. Hutchinson's claims have the air of rhetorical ploy or modesty topos. In her brief passage on the creation and nature of angels, for example, despite her caveat against prying 'Too long on things wrapped up in mystery' (1. 292), she endorses the Pseudo-Dionysian orders of angels, and indicates that angels were made on the first or second days of Creation. There is some discrepancy between professed caution and practice. In later cantos Hutchinson is prepared to elaborate with impunity, most memorably in her account of the parting between Rebecca and Jacob, which is entirely extra-scriptural (18. 275 ff.). Hutchinson's warnings against the excessive elaboration upon scriptural narrative may reflect a dialogue with Milton, and anxiety over his influence. When Milton effectively retired after Genesis 3, Hutchinson felt relatively free to extemporize on the remaining chapters, though these are, of course, set in the fallen world. What Heywood and Hutchinson do not do, however, is develop doctrine through their narratives; they narrate and articulate doctrine in discrete modes.

The most remarkable comparison with *Paradise Lost* is Pordage's *Mundorum Explicatio* (1661). Pordage both explicates doctrine and explores it through narrative—as in the narrator's voyage through purgatory—and in this respect is as daring as Milton. Exploiting the trappings of epic, Samuel attempts to re-create in poetic narrative the spiritual revelations of his father, John.[35] The imaginative expansiveness of *Mundorum Explicatio* is founded on the authority of prophetic vision; Milton takes similar risks, and he does so because he feels possessed of a similar authority.

Milton himself articulates caution about speculation. On the mystery of the Incarnation, the deepest mystery remaining after disposing of the Trinity, *De Doctrina Christiana* warns, 'it is best for us to be ignorant of things which God wishes to remain secret', words that resonate with Raphael's reiterated counsel that the 'great architect' had wisely concealed the 'fabric of the heavens' and much of his creation.[36] Others' anxieties about the limits of knowledge draw attention both to the abundance of Milton's elaboration on Scripture, and to the intellectual consistency with which he sustains such elaboration. He does not insure himself by writing allegorically, except in a few distinctive passages. In his accommodated, prophetic mode, knowledge is central to the imagination, and the relationship between doctrine and narrative assumes profound importance. Milton binds together doctrine and narrative with an intensity that is unique, and to lose sight of the connection between his fictional imperatives and the divine truths he intended to impart through them is to diminish the force and ambition of his poetry.

## The Left Hand

Storytelling and doctrine were not antipathetic, and the powers of imagination and argument formed alliances in other kinds of writing. Another literary form, the pamphlet, can illuminate these connections, because of its close association with deception and manipulation, and because of what it reveals about the relationship between the literary imagination and the presentation of argument. Abdiel's looseness with the truth, his rhetorical opportunism, his feigning or deceiving (perhaps too strong a word), can be contextualized in the burgeoning culture of news and pamphlets in the seventeenth century. Abdiel expected to *report news*, and the rich meanings of these words developed in this context. Bringing news was an activity in which truth and lies competed, as the pamphleteer Milton well knew.

It is because of the reputation of pamphlets and newsbooks (whose patron was said to be another 'father of lies', the god Mercury) for manipulation, misrepresentation, temporizing, and lying, that it has represented something of a scandal that the poet and Puritan Milton in 1641 became so closely involved with them. After his youthful career Milton all but abandoned poetry for prose, returning to it in earnest only in the mid-1650s, after he had put some distance between himself and the compromised politics of Cromwell's Protectorate.[37] It is possible to impose upon Milton's life an opposition between his working in prose and in poetry, one Milton himself encouraged in 1642 in referring to pamphleteering as something undertaken with his left hand (with poetry, like the Son, seated on the right):

I should not choose this manner of writing [prose] wherein knowing myself inferior to myself, led by the genial power of nature to another task, I have the use, as I may account it, but of my left hand . . . a poet soaring in the high region of his fancies with his garland and singing robes about him might without apology speak more of himself than I mean to do . . . sitting here below in the cool element of prose.[38]

Some readers of the poetry have presented this pamphleteering career as a distraction from Milton's true vocation as a poet, an achievement merely of the left hand while waiting for a suitable opportunity to engage the right. Yet there are reasons beyond biography why, instead of seeing this reductive opposition, readings of *Paradise Lost* could be informed by pamphlets and non-canonical writings, reasons which speak to how we judge both Abdiel's and Milton's acts of poetic fabrication.

Between the mid-sixteenth century and the end of the seventeenth, pamphlets became part of everyday politics, a means of creating and influencing public opinion, a foundation of the influential moral and political communities that constitute a 'public sphere'. Printed words, and their exchanges with readers, moved to the centre of political life. At the same time the pamphlet became a model of public speech, a way of conceiving of the power of the word. Writers of poetry exploited the form or its generic elements, and engaged in traffic with this common and debased mode. Pamphlets were themselves a literary form, often highly artful and indirect, best understood and appreciated with reference not only to context, but also to the traditions and conventions of pamphleteering. Pamphlets can rarely be reduced to a simple argument, as they spoke through fictional and imaginative devices. They rely on intertextuality, on pamphlet genres, conventions, personae, and decorum, just as *Paradise Lost* acquires meaning through its relationship with Virgil and others.[39]

Pamphlets can teach us about seventeenth-century poetry. One adversary condemned the pamphleteer Milton as 'a fabulist and a mere poet, though his style is prosaic'.[40] That was in a sense true, and that was precisely why Milton was an accomplished propagandist. Despite his dismissal of his polemical prose as an accomplishment of the left hand, he knew that the work of the left and right hands was not clearly distinguished. The literary elements of pamphlets, their rhetorical tropes, eloquence, performances, persuasive fictions, were not mere dressing for argument, but integral to it. Pamphlets conducted arguments through imaginative discourse. The same is true of *Paradise Lost*. To accept this principle is to reject the narrowly literary approach that divorces figurative or allegorical writing from its historical contexts and literal referents, that feels comfortable, for example, in isolating *Paradise Lost* from technical writings on angels. This is the approach adopted when Milton is assumed to write about angels as angels infrequently, treating them more commonly as human figures. If this were the case, there would be no conundrum to be resolved in Abdiel's conduct. He is merely a fictional narrative device, modelled on humanity, and so deceit is no surprise. Poetry is thereby dissociated from ideas.

We need to integrate more fully our understanding of the relation-
ship between polemic and poetry, as the noise of the marketplace can
help us to appreciate the music of *Paradise Lost*. In listening to both, we
stand to refine our understanding of the nature of writing in the
seventeenth century.[41] At a more local and less ambitious level, this
integration of imagination and argument suggests another perspective
on Milton's deceiving angel: we should take both the narrative and the
doctrine seriously, as coexisting if not inseparably at least in a mutually
reinforcing framework.

The model for and condition of this approach mirrors Raphael's
description of accommodation:

> High matter thou enjoinst me, O prime of men,
> Sad task and hard, for how shall I relate
> To human sense the invisible exploits
> Of warring spirits; how without remorse
> The ruin of so many glorious once
> And perfect while they stood; how last unfold
> The secrets of another world, perhaps
> Not lawful to reveal? Yet for thy good
> This is dispensed, and what surmounts the reach
> Of human sense, I shall delineate so,
> By likening spiritual to corporal forms,
> As may express them best, though what if earth
> Be but the shadow of heav'n, and things therein
> Each to other like, more than on earth is thought?[42]

Humans are thereby able read about and discuss God in intelligible
terms without assuming that God is like us, and so the 'shadowy
types' accessible to limited human intelligence correspond to the
'truths' that are beyond human consciousness (12. 303). This associ-
ation between representation and truth, as I argued in Chapter 6,
underlies Milton's understanding of his poetry, and it provides a
model both for understanding the relationship between Milton's literal
narrative and its implicit doctrines, and for how he should be read.

Raphael's preamble has been used as the basis for historicist readings
that seek an allegory of recent history—of the civil wars, Common-
wealth, and Protectorate—in Milton's epic. In the early eighteenth
century, Francis Atterbury, reading *Paradise Lost*, commented alongside
the description of Moloch's portentous frown (2. 106), 'probably y^e
picture of some great man in Milton's time'.[43] This mode of reading

the epic, and particularly the war in heaven, has prevailed. If the imaginative narrative is understood to comprehend doctrinal truths, however, through a creative process that resembles accommodation, then any interpretative process that seeks encoded meanings will always fall short of grasping either the poetic intentions or the richness of the poetic outcomes. This is as true of interpretations that identify historical or political allegories as of those that discover numerological or alchemical subtexts. This is not to resist attempts to locate political or historical meanings in literary works, but to insist that our historicist hermeneutics need a fuller and more coherent account of signification, one that goes beyond the mainstays of allegory and metaphor.

It is possible to offer a reading of the Abdiel episode that is guided by just such a search for encoded history and politics, and this reading illuminates Milton's casuistry. To show this, I will erect my own straw man. It is not hard to identify in the heroic Abdiel, who does not change his mind under threat of violence, some degree of self-representation on Milton's part. It may be that Milton is using the occasion of the conflict with Satan to represent a particular biographical incident. Critics have suggested that Milton portrays himself in Abdiel and Cromwell in Satan; or that Abdiel's royalist rhetoric echoes Claudius Salmasius (the pro-monarchical polemicist with whom Milton exchanged tracts in 1649–54), while Milton puts himself in Satan, the good Puritan opposed to ceremony and prostration.[44] Neither analogy is persuasive.

There is a stronger case to be made for seeing Milton in Abdiel and in Satan those enemies of the Good Old Cause with whom Milton crossed quills. Milton's opponents laid against him charges of deceit, in resonant phrases. In the *Defensio Regia* (1649) Salmasius had suggested that the regicides were only academically accomplished in 'the arts of deceiving, dissembling, falsifying, and lying', in which arts none could overcome them.[45] Alexander More, attacking Milton in the dedication to *Regii Sanguinis Clamor* (1652), declared Charles II (so-called) 'chosen of God, guarded by angels, acknowledged and hailed king by all men (I do not name the executioners as exceptions, for they are not men, but devils)'.[46] Perhaps more damagingly for Milton, the anonymous author of the main text of *Clamor*, Peter du Moulin, warned of the dangers of pragmatism, of doing evil—telling lies perhaps—thinking that good may come out of it, as 'Satan has proved that there is no reward more powerful than this fallacy for driving good men to the side of evil; he has produced no artifice more certain to undermine the church.'[47] It was the printer Adrian Vlacq who, by reporting on his correspondence with Samuel Hartlib concerning the authorship of *Clamor*, drove home the charge that in *Defensio Secunda* (1654) Milton had knowingly misled his readers.

This obscure but significant episode in some ways supports the accusations of those who charged Milton with deceit. When *Regii Sanguinis Clamor* appeared in 1652, Milton suspected that Alexander More, who wrote the dedication, was in fact the author of the whole work. He proceeded to write a response on this basis. This assumption worked to Milton's advantage partly because rumours were circulating of More's sexual misconduct (he had fathered a child with Salmasius' maid, before abandoning her). Milton had apparently completed his rebuttal in *Defensio Secunda* when Samuel Hartlib informed him of grounds to doubt this attribution. Milton chose to ignore Hartlib, not least because he wished to exploit the rhetorical advantage that slander offered him. There were, then, real grounds for accusing Milton of deceit. In unhesitatingly identifying Alexander More as the author of that work, an identification that the printer Adrian Vlacq knew Milton had reason to question, Milton had lied with his 'black hand'. Vlacq asked: 'is that man in his right mind who writes something other than that which he knows and . . . is eager to impose upon the whole world and to defame a neighbor with calumnies and the blackest lies'.[48]

Milton's numerous antagonists thought that falsehood—misnaming, deception—was at the heart of his apologia, and of the regicides' cause. In his presentation of Abdiel's contest with Satan, Milton re-presented his isolation, and championed his own role as a zealous servant of the truth unmasking the duplicity of royalist rhetoric. The scenario inverts his various opponents' accusations of falsehood and diabolical complicity. Satan, like Salmasius, exploits the language of justice and liberty to uphold a self-interested monarchalism. The unfalling angel is an explicator of rhetorical deception and a guide to discriminating allegiance.[49] In *Mercurius Politicus*, the weekly newsbook that supported and chronicled the fortunes of the British Commonwealth, Marchamont Nedham condemned Salmasius for being a promoter of tyranny drunk with pride and ambition. In Abdiel's exchange with Satan, then, Milton interpreted and reappropriated the debates of the 1650s. The conclusion to book 5 reflects on his deliberately misleading attribution of *Clamor* to More, and his continuing support (with his left

hand, as a polemicist) of the Commonwealth after its republican ideals
had been tarnished by the establishment of the Protectorate. To reduce
this account to its boldest formulation: if it was legitimate for an angel to
tell half-truths for the greater good in the service of the state, then why
not Milton?

The deceiving Abdiel is using his left hand according to the occa-
sion. He lies for a greater good because he is Milton, required to
express, with his mastery of irony and fables, support of a government
for the good of the public, despite his uncertainties and the falsehoods
that make his work easier. Abdiel is Milton's self-representation, but
also his self-exculpation.

There is something persuasive about this as a reading, and it fits the
mould of much criticism on *Paradise Lost* over recent decades. As if we
should say that Satan raises his standard in the 'spacious north' (5. 726)
because he is in part Charles I, or that in Adam Milton relives his own
anxieties.[50] Yet there is also something unsatisfying in it, whether we
read this historicist interpretation as a forensic analysis of Milton's
encounter with Salmasius, or even as a more general reflection upon
the ethics of verbal exchange. Allegorical decoding—whether histori-
cist or aestheticist—belies the account of accommodation offered by
Raphael, and the role of the literary imagination in controversial
writing. Such readings translate, with greater or lesser confidence,
poetry into prose, finding in the allegorical or symbolic surface of
the poem coded references to or descriptions of other meanings and
events about which the poet could not or did not want to write
directly. This mode of allegorically inclined historical interpretation
supposes a fierce separation between representation and thing repre-
sented. It brings the left and right hands together only by finding the
left hand at work in a right-handed text. It finds continuity in Milton's
writings through the 1640s and 1660s, but at the expense of misrepre-
senting the nature of pamphleteering. It finds a single code where there
are many, and even the most left-handed of writers seek to persuade
through the interaction of multiple codes.

Moreover, this approach is not sympathetic to Milton's angels: it
treats them as figures or allegories for humans. Their dilemmas and
their emotions seem familiar to us because they are in fact humans
with wings. Hence critical judgements like: 'the good angels are
polemicists whose swords are symbolic of pens, printing presses,
pamphlets'. They encode political ideas or arguments. Their material

being is not relevant, as Milton's creation is a symbolic language in which a sword is a printing press and chaos political discord.[51] In this account (whether the refraction is considered 'flexibly symbolic' or rigid), a pamphlet is a prosy, stable, political proposition, and the poetry a dark glass through which we view the pamphlet. This is to misapprehend both. Even for a merely competent pamphleteer, political allegories are worked through narratives or performances that are independently coherent; the prima facie meaning has to work as well as any others it is intended to support. Pamphlets, at least imaginative, effective pamphlets, are inventive and singular, just as poetry is; singular both in their imaginative insight, and in their articulation of a historical occasion. And so in poetry, which verbally comprehends otherness: and, in Milton's case, one of the most powerful instances of otherness is the simultaneous familiarity and strangeness of angels. Abdiel only figures human values because in the first instance he stands tall as a representation of an angel.[52]

I have used a close reading of connected passages in *Paradise Lost* to reassess the nature of Milton's angels and to assert the value of associating imaginative angels with theology and natural philosophy. In contrast to Heywood's and Hutchinson's there is a peculiar intensity in Milton's representation of angels. This is in part because of his strong view of accommodation, and in part because of his inspiration. Writing in the seventeenth century, even in topical pamphlets and contentious prose, to which Milton committed his talents for two decades, suggests that a more sympathetic means of reading *Paradise Lost* might involve seeing the close relationship between doctrine and poetic narratives. Finally, I offered and rejected a species of historicist reading that used Milton's political life as a key for understanding Abdiel's actions, and read the poetry as figurative or allegorical. It is now time to resolve the main question.

## Truth and Lies

Can Milton represent an unfallen angel feigning? The answer resides in theology and in poetry, together. In the integration of story and doctrine we find both Milton's engagement with his communicative environment, and his ability to absorb these materials and tell a story self-sufficient enough to speak angelology and poetry at the same time.

Abdiel deceives because he is an angel. It is not really deceiving, but I will hold onto that word momentarily. Abdiel deceives not because he is really a human, but because he is an angel in a tight spot on a rhetorical roll. Milton's representation of Abdiel's circumstances is precise, and accords with the author's account of the nature of angels. Abdiel is confined by optics, he cannot see in the dark, cannot see across heaven, and therefore cannot see sympathetic faces; he is confined by topography, and finite in his speed, as he has to fly all night to find God; he is stranded with freewill, as just when he most needs a comforting word from God, he finds himself unsupported and utterly alone. But this does not make him human. If Milton's angels seem human, it is not because he wishes to use them imaginatively to reflect upon human situations, but he presents angels in ways that are sympathetic to human circumstances because his angels are also sentient and free material beings, confined by optics and subject to passion, love, and divine decrees, the creatures of God. Milton's angels act in accordance with his natural philosophy, and he takes as cues customary questions of theologians and natural philosophers, pressing the questions unusually far, and resolving them in characteristically trenchant ways.[53] Early readers from Hume and Leslie onwards were troubled with this uncompromising marriage of invention with learning. This is not just 'story', but story *and* a serious point about angels, and therefore a serious point about theology and natural philosophy.

Moreover, *De Doctrina Christiana* provides the ethical justification for Abdiel's actions. One chapter of the systematic theology attends to those special duties we owe a neighbour when we are mindful of his reputation or fortune. There, under the heading of veracity and its antithesis, falsehood, Milton cites Job 13: 7 ('should you speak wickedly for the sake of God?') as a proof text for the precept that 'We must not, then, tell a lie, even in the service of God.' It later emerges, however, that a characteristic Miltonic pragmatism governs this precept: 'In practice, however, it frequently happens that not only to disguise or conceal the truth, but actually to tell lies with deceitful intent makes for the safety or advantage of one's neighbor.'[54] Indeed, he goes on, the usual definition of falsehood—saying something untrue with the intention to deceive—is wholly inadequate, as falsehood involves both 'evil intent' and a duty of truthfulness to the auditor. In other words, you can lie to someone with a clean conscience if it is in his or her interest, and in any case falsehood only exists in relationships where truthfulness is specifically required. To say something that is not strictly true is not necessarily to lie. Exactly the same course appears in Milton's account of the works of the faithful, where he notes that, while these 'never run contrary to the love of God and of our neighbour', they may 'sometimes deviate from the letter even of the gospel precepts (particularly those which are special rather than general), in pursuance of their over-riding motive, which is charity'.[55] Hence, deceitfulness, even to a neighbour, can be a necessary course of action for the truly faithful.[56]

Perhaps Milton writes to exculpate himself here: he may well be supplying a retrospective defence of his own action in the 1650s, among them his wrongful accusation of More, and his failure to speak out against Cromwell during what he later called a 'short but scandalous night of interruption'.[57] But it also provides an explanation of why Abdiel can be creative with the truth: it is in the interest of Satan and the other falling angels that they are confronted with the inevitable consequences of their rebellion, and therefore Abdiel (who knows it, though he cannot prove it) is doing a service for Satan; and, moreover, Abdiel does not owe a duty of truthfulness to a rebel against God. Milton constrains himself here within a true, accommodated representation of an angel, and in a sense the angel really does feign something to Satan. According to Milton's own casuistry, Abdiel can therefore tell what may be the first untruth—it is wrong to call it a lie after Milton's careful casuistry—in history, and Satan can retain his title as father of lies, for it is Satan, and not Abdiel, who bears responsibility for Abdiel's fabrication.

In his elaboration on falsehood in *De Doctrina Christiana*, Milton explicitly reflects on the association between actual lies and modes of figurative speech: 'parables, hyperboles, fables and the various uses of irony are not falsehoods since they are calculated not to deceive but to instruct'.[58] Figures of speech are like lies, but are not lies because they are faithfully educative. Any reader of seventeenth-century pamphlets will find this proposition resonant. The figurative or fictional is an essential and recognized element in the explication of doctrine; pamphlets lie, but you knew that anyway and it is an instructive kind of lying, and therefore not really lying at all. In this respect, angels and pamphlets may be a little alike. *Paradise Lost* is as effective a gloss on *De Doctrina Christiana* as *De Doctrina Christiana* on *Paradise Lost*, because knowledge and imagination work together in the thought behind

both. This reminds us, moreover, that Milton's representation of a war
in heaven is no more feigned than, but just as feigned as, Abdiel's
speech: both are intended to instruct, to lead their auditor's attention
from a shadowy type to a truth. The parallel with angelic bodies is
exact, and this is because they are understood to be governed by
identical principles of truthful representation. Angels could not
deceive, and hence the virtual bodies they adopted were, though
angels had neither bodies nor shapes, nonetheless '*True and unfeyned
formes*'; angelic bodies, like scriptural figures of speech, were 'no slur
on the truthfulness of holy angels'.[59] Inspired poetry and angelic bodies
set truths before men's eyes.

   That an angel might justifiably mislead according to the standards of
human ethics is borne out by Raphael's own caution over the problem
of accommodation:

>             how shall I relate
>     To human sense the invisible exploits
>     Of warring spirits?

Raphael's shimmying here precisely resembles the structure of Milton's
argument about accommodation in *De Doctrina*: descriptions of God
are figurative, but the resemblance is real, and more semblable than
you can understand. Raphael's reservations are threefold: is narration
possible; is it lawful; is it too sad? He overcomes the last two reserva-
tions on the grounds of divine dispensation. The first he washes away
by likening the spiritual to the corporeal (Milton's monism means that
this is difference in degree and not kind, as both are substances), and
asking:

>             what if earth
>     Be but the shadow of heav'n, and things therein
>     Each to other like, more than on earth is thought?

What if we are more alike than you think? The premiss of Raphael's
speaking to Adam at all is that he can talk in 'parables, hyperboles,
fables and . . . irony' in order to instruct, because unfallen angels can
speak falsehoods. Abdiel invents God's decree both because Milton
needs to tell a good, coherent dramatic story, and because he is an
angel. And this, the poem tells us, is how we should read *Paradise Lost*.

# 9

# Look Homeward Angel
## Angelic Guardianship and Nationhood

### The Vision of the Guarded Mount

In November 1637 John Milton drafted an elegy for his friend and fellow student Edward King, in which the lyric voice instructs an angel to 'look homeward'. The poem, 'Lycidas', is a pastoral elegy for an anonymous drowned shepherd which observes a structure conventional to the genre: it is spoken by a nameless shepherd who, following an invocation, offers a history of their friendship in the pastoral mode, a series of recriminations, a digression, in which St Peter condemns the clergy for their failings, a laying on of flowers, and a consolation. It is towards the end of the poem, in the consolation, that the angel is invoked. That the shepherd might speak of an angel is understandable, conventional even, as angels look to human affairs as sympathetic witnesses. But where is an angel's home?

These are the lines as they appeared in Milton's notebook:

> Ay mee whilst thee ^the ~~floods~~ and sounding sea     *Shoars
> wash farre away, where ere thy bones are hurld
> whether beyond the stormie Hebrides
> where thou phapps under the humming tide
> visit'st the bottome of the monstrous world
> or whether thou to our moist vows deni'd
> sleep'st by the fable of ˣ~~Corineus~~ old     ˣBellerus
> where the great vision of the guarded mount
> looks toward Namanco- ^s, and Bayona's field
> looke homeward Angel now and melt wth ruth
> and O yee Dolphins waft the haplesse youth.[1]

Edward King drowned in the Irish Sea when travelling from Cambridge to his home in Ireland. In his poem Milton imagines a displaced mourning. Whereas the procession of mourners in Bion's *Lamentation for Adonis* pass by the youth's body on a 'glorious bed of State', Milton's mourners are deprived of a focus.[2] Edward King's body was lost, and, with its floating corpse, Milton's pastoral elegy threatens to turn away from Theocritus and Virgil and, perhaps inadvertently, towards Lucan's *Pharsalia*, another state-of-the-nation poem that exploits the pathos of unrecovered bodies. Cornelia laments there for her unburied husband, Pompey: 'Quid porro tumulis opus est aut ulla requiris | Instrumenta, dolor?' ('But what need is there of a grave, or why does grief require any trappings?'). She consoles herself that his image endures in her breast.[3] Perhaps one of the most extraordinary qualities of 'Lycidas' is that it can harbour such an intensity of both intertextual self-consciousness and sharp political criticism.

Not only is the body lost, the angel invoked for protection is not named. This renders more effective the unexpected change of subject in this sentence. When we read the verse 'looke homeward Angel now and melt wth ruth', we ask ourselves: has Lycidas/King been renamed an 'Angel', or is the unnamed angel addressed here 'the great vision' referred to earlier?[4] In retrospect, as soon as we have identified the 'guarded mount', it seems clear. The angel is the vision seen on the mount, but for a moment we might be consoled by the idea that Lycidas has become an angel, instructed to face his old home, from which he has been mercifully delivered. This theme—the transmigration of Edward King—is picked up again later when the poet addresses Lycidas: 'henceforth thou art the Genius of y^e shoare'.[5] Here Lycidas becomes a *genius loci*, a spirit associated with a particular feature of landscape, a pagan prefiguration of an angel.[6] The earlier passage is confusing because it does not yield meanings easily, and because the poet's voice, consistently unstable in 'Lycidas', shifts from addressing Lycidas to addressing the angel and the dolphins. Milton's conspicuous revision, replacing 'Corineus' with 'Bellerus', suggests that he wasn't inclined to give anything away too easily, almost, as some critics have suggested, as if the poem is coded.[7]

This emendation merits excavation. In Geoffrey of Monmouth's fantastical history of the settlement of Britain by Brutus, Aeneas' great-grandson, Corineus is one of Brutus' companions. Milton would later retell the story in his *History of Britain* (commenced in the late 1640s).

The land that Brutus arrived in was peopled by tyrannizing giants, which he proceeded to eliminate in the process of founding a civilized nation. Corineus was assigned to Cornwall, where he threw the greatest of the giants, Goëmagog, off a coastal cliff, giving its name to Langoëmagog.[8] The name Milton chose in the earlier draft suggests an imperial myth for the settlement of Britain. But he then crossed it out, in favour of another name inscribed in the landscape. Bellerus appears to be a coinage, but is clearly derived from 'Bellerium', the Latin name for Land's End.[9] Why is Bellerus a fable? The sense of 'fable of Corineus' is straightforward: it is the fabulous history of Geoffrey, and Lycidas could sleep near the place of this legend. The revised version is less direct. At first reading it seems to be a fable that the reader has forgotten—perhaps another of Brutus' companions, perhaps another giant[10]—and perhaps the fable is that of the vision of the guarded mount, which is quite close to Land's End. But Bellerus is at best the personification of Bellerium, no legend comes to the reader's aid, and 'quite close' has insufficient explanatory force in such a dense passage. The next reference intensifies the obscurity.

The 'guarded mount' is St Michael's Mount, located in the bay of the south side of Land's End, or Bellerium, and from this we can de-anonymize the angel as Michael, archangel, head of the created angels, antagonist of Satan in Revelation. Though one of the four angels named in Scripture, he is not named here. The pages on Cornwall in Camden's *Britannia* offer some clarification. There we find 'Belerium' identified as Land's End, the story of Corineus, and also an account of the vision of the mount:

In the very top heereof within the Fortresse, there was a Chappell consecrated to *S. Michael*, the Archangell, where William Earle of Cornwall and Moriton, who by the bounteous gift of King William the First had great lands, & large possessions in this tract, built a Cell for one or two monks; who avouched that *S. Michael* appeared in that mount: which apparition, or the like, the Italians challenge to their hill Carganus, and the Frenchmen likewise to their *Michaels* mount in Normandie.[11]

The 'great vision', then, was seen by monks, and there was reason for Protestants to suspect this vision as popish superstition, founded on spurious theology and a desire to manipulate the credulous. Camden notes how monks of various nations seem to want to claim Michael as their own, and implies that the multiplicity of visions suggest that all are spurious. Why would Milton seem to lay claim to this doubtful angel, asking it to 'looke homeward'?

Milton takes up the vision, though under suspicion of being a monkish fable, because it conforms to his theology and speaks to his idea of nationhood. The angel is a local guardian angel, assigned to watch over a particular place. This is the sense in which an angel has a home beyond or besides heaven. This doctrine appears elsewhere in Milton's writing, in *De Doctrina Christiana* and *Paradise Regained*, and it shapes the conclusion of 'Lycidas'.

## Angels Appointed as Governors

Belief in individual guardian angels marked a clear, though not absolute, difference between Protestants and Roman Catholics.[12] The question of angels assigned to a particular place or people, however, was less polarized. Andrew Willet ascribed two erroneous belief to papists: '*Michael* (say they) is the protector and keeper of the whole Church of Christ, *Dan.* 10. 21. And as earthly kingdoms have their speciall angels for their protectors, so also have particular Churches.' Protestants, he claimed, believed the opposite: 'The whole Church hath Christ himselfe, who is the true *Michael*, for her protector and defender: And so is that place in *Daniel* to be understood. . . . Secondly, It cannot be proved out of scripture, that kingdomes have their speciall Angels protectors.'[13] This overstates the dichotomy, as many Protestants, among them writers that Milton knew well, believed that the created angel Michael had a special role in protecting the Church, and that angels were assigned to particular places and communities.

The belief was founded on the reference to 'Michael your prince' in Daniel 10: 21, and also on Daniel 12: 1: 'at that time shall Michael stand up, the great prince which standeth for the children of thy people'. Pseudo-Dionysius elaborates the doctrine in *The Celestial Hierarchy*, where he writes that the lowest ternion, consisting of principalities, archangels, and angels, preside over human affairs, and among their purposes is to establish 'the boundaries of nations'. He adds:

the theologians also say that Michael presides over the government of the Jewish people and that this is in order to make clear that Israel, like the other nations, was assigned to one of the angels, to recognize through him the one universal ruling source. For there is only one Providence over all the world, a supra-being transcending all power visible and invisible; and over every nation there are presiding angels entrusted with the task of raising up toward that Providence, as their own source, everyone willing to follow, as far as possible.[14]

These presiders were sometimes specifically designated principalities or princes. Calvin accepted the doctrine: 'Surely when *Daniel* bringeth in the Angell of the *Persians*, & the Angell of the *Grecians*, he sheweth that he ment, that there are to kingdomes and provinces certaine Angels appointed as governours.'[15] Peter Martyr concurs that angels 'defend kingdoms and provinces (as it is written in *Daniel*)'.[16] William Lilly claimed that portents were 'framed by the *Guardian-Angels* or Intelligencees of that Kingdom where they appear'.[17] Later writers adduced the accepted notion of a local guardian in support of the more tendentious doctrine of individual guardians, perhaps following Origen in doing so. Hence, William Austin writes: 'Neither is it *strange*, that *one-Angel* should seeme *sufficient* to keepe *one Man*; since wee find in *Daniel*, that *one-Angel* is *Set* over a *Nation*. And, it may *well*-stand for *likelihood*; when we see *daily* before our Eies, that God sets *one Man* (a *Creature*, much *more-feeble*) to *rule and protect divers Kingdomes.*' And an anonymous pamphleteer in 1702 argued: 'It seems agreeable to Reason, that as each particular Kingdom hath it's Guardian Angel, so each Province, City, Town, Village, and Particular family should have theirs likewise; and then it will be easily inferred that every individual Person, in each Family should have a *Genius* alloted to him.'[18]

Other early modern British statements of the doctrine do not conflate individual and local angels in this way, but explore the scope of the body or community with which they are affiliated. These can be 'Bodies Politick', or, according to Lilly, kingdoms.[19] For the less monarchist Henry Lawrence, angels are assigned not only to 'Provinces & Countries' but also to Churches.[20] For Hardick Warren in 1651, '*Monarchies, Kingdoms* and *Cities*' had their '*presidential Angel*'.[21] And for Thomas Tryon in 1689: 'Communities, Nations and Countries have also particular Angels assigned to their government, or super-intendency.'[22] Robert Dingley expanded the list in 1654, making a politic nod to the Lord Protector under the new constitution: 'It is therefore most probable, that Cities, Shires, Provinces, Islands, Churches and Kingdoms have particular Angels to be presidential over them, and that each Republick hath an Angel to be its protector.'[23] Angels can protect natural bodies (islands, for example, or mounts), political bodies (countries and shires), and religious communities. In this doctrine of local guardianship, we can find an early modern means of understanding the significance of belonging to a place or nation.

This doctrine did not receive universal assent. Johannes Wollebius cautioned against looking too closely into it. The Westminster Assembly's *Annotations* evade the issue. It is a rabbinical fantasy according to the godly clergyman George Hughes. One Calvinist preacher condemned it as heathen and anti-Christian.[24] John Patrick, in his *Reflexions upon the Devotions of the Roman Church* (1671), suggests that Roman Catholic beliefs in guardian angels were formalized and made more elaborate in the early seventeenth century, introducing 'bold and presuming speculations' far beyond the legitimate interpretation of Scripture:

> howsoever some places may seem fairly to countenance this in the Scripture, and make it a probable opinion; that at some particular Seasons at least, there have been particular Angels deputed to preside over a Countrey or Province; and so also that they have had the charge of particular Persons; yet the evidence of it there, is not so cogent, as that it should be put as an Article of Faith into *Summs of Divinity*, or that *Praters* and *Offices* should be made to them, and they religiously courted and worshipped under that notion.[25]

Scandalously and absurdly, Patrick reports, papists go so far as to assign guardian angels to monasteries, colleges, even altars. The vision of Michael at the monastery on St Michael's Mount is, presumably, part of this popish fabulation.

Despite his anti-popish rhetoric, Milton subscribed to just such an account of angelic guardianship. Although the chapter on the 'Special Government of Angels' in Milton's *De Doctrina Christiana* generally follows Ames and Wollebius, he differs from them on this tenet. 'It is credible', he writes, 'that they also preside over peoples, kingdoms and fixed places' ('Præsidere etiam populis, regnis, et certis loci angelos credibile est'), citing Daniel 12: 1.[26] This is the sense intended by the Son in *Paradise Regained* when he refers to 'his angels president | In every province'.[27] Milton is more diffident about the idea of individual guardian angels, though he does not directly rule them out. In *The Doctrine and Discipline of Divorce* (1644) he refers to 'each ones alloted Genius', and in *De Doctrina* he quotes several of the common proof texts, and glosses: 'Tutelares nempe in cœtibus

fidelium, ut nonnulli putant'. 'To be sure, guardians at gatherings of
the faithful, as some suppose' implicitly dismisses stronger readings
of the same passages, but makes a concession to angelic representation
and protection of communities. He notes that there are many more
examples in Scripture.[28] In *Paradise Lost* the argument to book 9
describes how 'Mans transgression known, the Guardian Angels forsake
Paradise,' and the phrase clearly indicates the widespread doctrine,
though it might indicate that the office of guardianship ends with
original sin. When Milton appeals to 'the great vision of the guarded
mount' in 'Lycidas', he is not simply conjuring a poetic image, a
monkish fable, or another echo of his pagan intertexts. The vision of
Michael as a protecting angel, assigned to a particular place, people, or
nation, is one rooted in his personal theological beliefs. The speaker of
'Lycidas' summons the angel to 'look homeward', knowing that it is the
angel's responsibility to protect the people of country; this is the sense
in which an angel has a home.

At the end of the poem, following the consolation sequence in
which the angel appears, the poet–swain twitches his mantle and
heads for new woods and pastures. In 1638 Milton also departed his
country—where popular demonstrations and well-received covenant-
ing propaganda denounced the new Prayer Book in terms with which
Milton, judging by the anticlerical passages of 'Lycidas', would have
concurred—and travelled to Italy.[29] There he wrote his next extant
poem, a lyric addressed to the singer Leonora Baroni:

> Angelus unicuique suus (sic credite gentes)
> Obtigit æthereis ales ab ordinibus.

(Each individual has as his lot (believe thus, ye peoples) a winged angel from
the heavenly orders.[30])

Milton's phrase is terse, and allows of two possibilities: he could be
suggesting that the belief in tutelary angels is one held by Leonora's
audience at Rome, distancing himself from the belief; or the imperative
*credite* might encourage the belief ('believe me'). His doctrine on this
point is no clearer here than in *De Doctrina*. What the continuity between
'Lycidas' and 'Ad Leonoram' does indicate is Milton's grasp of the force
of this imagery: the intimate relations between humans and angels
suggests the enchantment of the world, the operation of providence,
hope emerging from a youth's death in a time of religious darkness.

## Christian Angel and Classical Genius

Milton's choice of angel is significant. As Pseudo-Dionysius writes,
Scripture identifies Michael as the principality responsible for protect-
ing the Jewish people. The Christian Church subsequently laid claim
to Michael as its own, understanding itself to have succeeded the Jews
as the true Church and to have inherited the protecting angel with
this status. Thereafter Michael could be associated with a Church or a
people.[31] Hence, John Prideaux in 1636: 'some of our later *writers*
reject the *particular deputations* of *severall Angels*, to *distinct Provinces*, or
*Persons*, and content themselves with that which is *certaine*, that the
*Angels* indefinitely have a *charge* over *Gods people*'. Transformations
in the fortunes of cities or peoples could be associated with their
losing their angel, who could migrate to favour another: 'so it is no
wonder if *Monarchies, Kingdoms* and *Cities* do change their manner of
*Government*, and as it were a thing forsaken of its *presidential Angel*,
flying to another nature of other power'. Prideaux, too, wondered if
angels always kept the same charge, or if they might be ambassadors
moving between negotiations while others succeeded to their
places.[32] At the end of the century John Dryden described it as a
commonplace:

'Tis a Doctrine almost Universally receiv'd by Christians, as well Protestants
as Catholicks, that there are Guardian Angels appointed by God Almighty,
as his Vicegerents, for the Protection and Government of Cities, Provinces,
Kingdoms, and Monarchies; and those as well of Heathens, as of true
Believers. . . . St. *Michael* is mention'd by his Name, as the Patron of the *Jews*,
and is now taken by the Christians, as the Protector General of our Religion.[33]

It was for this reason that competing visions of Michael were observed
in Italy and France, and off the Cornish coast. After the Reformation
these visions had a more specifically denominational appeal in the
opposition between Roman Catholic and reformed Churches. Such
a vision could appear to endorse the Church, but also to assert a right
to be seen as a (though not necessarily *the*) chosen people.[34]

To claim Michael as a protecting angel was to draw upon a tradition
that was rich with theological and ideological meanings. It was to
present England or Britain as Israel, and its people as the Jews. In this
account Michael indeed has a home, the place or people to which he is

assigned. When the shepherd–speaker of 'Lycidas' conjures this angel, leaving it unnamed, and tells it to 'look homeward', Milton not only draws upon the doctrine of local guardians, he also presses upon Michael the responsibility for protecting his home, protecting the true Church, and imagines this 'home' as a place coextensive with its people. As with the Jews, the people and the nation are one.

Milton's concern with a missing body gives way, especially in the digression in the voice of St Peter, to a broader theme, the sufferings of a political body. The poet who regrets the corruption of the Church hopes for a providential intervention by the angel responsible for protecting the people who make that Church. Though Milton's landscape seems enchanted in places with pagan myth and ancient history, it is also identified with a godly people, and a strictly Christian theology. 'Lycidas' is a politically charged poem, a prophetic, Spenserian attack on Laudianism and a call for reformation.[35]

There is also within this Christian story a pagan one. Samuel Johnson is one of many who have been troubled by the mixing of Christian and pagan imagery in the poem, attributing it to poor judgement and frivolousness, the display of a college education rather than grief or real invention.

With these trifling fictions are mingled the most awful and sacred truths, such as ought never to be polluted with such irreverent combinations. The shepherd likewise is now feeder of sheep, and afterwards an ecclesiastical pastor, a superintendent of a Christian flock. Such equivocations are always unskilful; but here they are indecent, and at least approach to impiety, of which, however, I believe the writer not to have been conscious.[36]

Johnson had a different notion of the funeral elegy from Milton, but repeatedly found Milton's angels irritating, mainly, I suspect, out of a lack of sympathy with and understanding of Milton's theology and natural philosophy.[37] Nonetheless, the unsettling relationship between the Christian and pagan imagery is intensified once the angel's role, and its theological foundations, have been elaborated. It is not, after all, a genial pagan god, a tree spirit, or an image borrowed from Virgil, but a precise part of Christian theology.

The nature of the relationship between classical and Christian ideas—and the opposed readings that it yields, some that see it as focused on poetic tradition, and others that stress its political critique[38]—cannot be lightly resolved. The archangel Michael and

St Peter rub shoulders with old Damoetas and Neptune, and they do so
with scandalous grace. However, we can see how one of the pagan
figures merges into a Christian, as an antetype is revealed as a type
under the Law of the Gospel. Lycidas is, as a final consolation towards
the end of the poem, transformed into 'the Genius of y$^e$ shoare', or a
*genius loci*, a classical spirit assigned to a place, much as Sabrina is in
*A Maske*. In this Lycidas bears an evident semblance to the local
guardian angel. If the syntactical ambiguity surrounding 'look home-
ward angel' invites a momentary misconception that Lycidas is that
angel, this line returns to that misconception and makes it true: he *is* a
sort of angel. Precedents for this have been identified in Virgil's
Eclogue V, where the dead shepherd Daphnis is imagined as a God:

> ipsi laetitia voces ad sidera iactant
> intonsi montes; ipsae iam carmina rupes,
> ipsa sonant arbusta: 'deus, deus ille, Menalca!'
> sis bonus o felixque tuis!

(The very mountains, with woods unshorn, joyously fling their voices star-
ward; the very rocks, the very groves ring out the song: 'A god is he,
Menalcas!' Be kind and gracious to thine own![39])

It has been claimed that Milton's 'genius of the shore' is 'more pagan
than Christian' because of Virgil's use of the same idea.[40] However,
though the landscape celebrates Daphnis' deification, Virgil's deity is
not assigned to the landscape. Virgil writes about not a *genius loci* but a
god, which is not the same thing as a spirit or an angel. A more likely
echo is Jacopo Sannazaro's first piscatory eclogue (1526), in which a
shepherd named Lycidas laments a drowned shepherdess:

> At tu, sive altum felix colis aethera, seu jam
> Elysius inter manes coetusque verendos
> Lethaeos, sequeris per stagna liquentia pisces,
> Seu legis aeternos formoso pollice flores . . .
>
>              .     .     .
>
> Aspice nos, mitisque veni; tu numen aquarum
> Semper eris, semper laetum piscantibus omen.

(But you, whether you in felicity dwell in the high Aether, or now among the
Elysian shades and venerable bands of Lethe pursue the fish through the crystal
streams, or whether you pluck unwithering flowers with your lovely hands . . .
look down on us and gently come to us; you shall ever be the godhead of
the waters, ever a happy sign to fishermen.[41])

After wondering where she rests, Sannazaro's Lycidas announces that his shepherdess is turned into a *genius loci*, a water deity, and beseeches her: 'behold us'. The similarity between Milton's angels and these pagan intertexts is as superficial as that between 'look homeward' and 'Aspice nos'. This semblance is limited as there is too much theology in Milton's genius. Milton's Lycidas returns from the company of saints in heaven to watch the shores and protect 'all that wander in that perilous flood' (line 185), the flood being, presumably, the Irish Sea. Though the notion of a 'genius' may be classical in origin, here it is thoroughly Christianized. While this does not hold for all of the classical elements in the poem, this one, at least, ought to have secured Dr Johnson's approval.

Milton's angel is not a literary device, adapting classical poetry to a Christian context; it is a concept grounded in Scholastic and Reformation theology. It is more sacred truth than trifling fiction. In choosing Michael, Milton lays claim to a providential, Protestant destiny for the country he protects. In the light of this, Lycidas becomes one of an army of subaltern spirits watching over the land under the wing of Michael, as well as a symbol of the failure of the Church. This angel too is looking homeward, to the sufferings of the political body, the people.

## The Boundaries of Nations

Where does an angel look when it looks home? Where did Milton think of as home in 1637, and how did he think of it?

Scholarship on the 'British problem', and especially on colonialism and orientalism, has placed Milton in a narrative of incipient nationalism, and accused 'Lycidas' of anti-Irish sentiment and an aggressive, imperialist sense of place.[42] Such a reading is typical of recent scholarship that identifies a strong nationalistic strain in Milton's writing, both poetry and prose.[43] Milton was concerned with issues of nationhood, the character of the English people, and especially with civility. However, to place him in a tradition of blood and soil nationalism is both to overstate the role of ethnicity in early modern identity formation, and anachronistically to assume a stable and coherent notion of the nation-state, something that did not develop until later.[44]

Milton's idea of Englishness did not assume a dichotomy between the English and the foreigner so much as between the civilized and the uncivilized. Hence, in *Tenure of Kings and Magistrates* (1649):

He therfore that keeps peace with me, neer or remote, of whatsoever Nation, is to mee as farr as all civil and human offices an Englishman and a neighbour: but if an Englishman forgetting all Laws, human, civil and religious, offend against life and liberty, to him offended and to the Law in his behalf, though born in the same womb, he is no better then a Turk, a Sarasin, a Heathen.[45]

In his *History of Britain* Milton sways between expressing pride in the resistance of the Britons (whom he associates with the Welsh) and subsequently of the Saxons to Roman rule, and lamentation of their shortcomings, describing lavishly the failures of these people. The origins of the English people lie as much in the Celtic Britons as in the Anglo-Saxons, and the continuities are as much cultural and civic as they are ethnic. When in the 1639 poem *Mansus* he offers to sing of the kings of his native land (*indigenas*), it is Arthur smashing Saxon phalanxes under the might of warring Britons that he mentions.[46] In the *History* Milton grudgingly reiterates the story of the Brutus, which he knows to be a fable, mainly in order to denigrate the Anglo-Saxons. His hero is not his people but civility itself, and his villain the barbarism that is spread widely among peoples and nations.[47] Milton's expressions of pride cannot be separated from his ambivalence, the same ambivalence that caused him to criticize the English and British for backsliding (often in advance of the offence), and to adopt the voice of a Jeremiah.[48] When he eventually wrote his earlier promised English epic, it neglected to mention the English people.[49]

Though Milton's rhetoric is sometimes marked by phobia and caricature, this does not originate in a stable, nationally focused identity. When he articulates a sense of pride in the English people, it is not with a simple sense of belonging; for his attention is simultaneously drawn towards civic-minded reflection on the state of the island, towards the fate of Protestantism in Europe, towards the spirit of liberty everywhere. In his most buoyant statements of national pride we find both qualifications, and a particularity of focus that takes us beyond England. In *Areopagitica* he asks: 'Why else was this Nation chos'n before any other, that out of her as out of *Sion* should be proclam'd and sounded forth the first tidings and trumpet of

Reformation to all *Europ.*'[50] He adds that the prelates suppressed the light of Wyclif, and so the reforming glory went to our neighbours. England was a chosen nation, but not *the* chosen nation, and he is in any case concerned with the light spread across Europe.[51]

Milton did define 'patriotism' in his later life, in his 1666 letter to Peter Heimbach. There he notes that he worked for the republican government in the 1650s not out of 'Politicam' ('policy', or 'politics') but out of 'Pietatem in Patriam' ('dutifulness towards one's country'). The civic-minded tone of this Ciceronian phrase is clear, and he playfully adds 'Patria est, ubicunque est bene' ('One's country is wherever it is good with one'). We might attribute this to the political and rhetorical invention of a disillusioned public servant cum epic poet, but it is a commonplace derived from Cicero, and one that, in its seventeenth-century appropriations, articulates a very tenebrous sense of belonging.[52] Milton's definition turns one's country into a matter of policy or politics; one's country is not a matter of ethnicity or culture, but wherever one can identify oneself as a citizen, wherever one can be and do good.

Interest in orientalism, imperialism, and empire, and in notions of 'otherness', has led critics to dwell on negative representations of the foreign, on caricatures and stereotypes, in pursuit of constructions of national identity. Boundaries and borders have eclipsed other considerations. Much less has been offered on the positive, insular construction of identity, on the sense of national spirit, on what lies within borders. This is in part because there is so much less to say about the latter in early modern Britain, because there was no fixed sense of national identity tied to the state. Milton's letter to Heimbach was written after his relationship with his country had suffered from revolutionary hopes being fulfilled and then dashed. The reality of events engaged two of his rhetorical tendencies: militant optimism and jeremiad. 'Dutifulness' towards his country had almost expatriated him ('expatriavit'), left him homeless. Writing from the perspective of 1666, however, Milton felt that he might still do some good for his country ('utinam ne inutilis, quicquid muneris in hac vita restat mihi peragendum').[53] Patriotism—perhaps the positive dimension of nationalism—was in early modern Britain a relativistic sentiment.[54] One looks homeward when looking towards what is good.

The doctrine of local guardian angels, in 'Lycidas' and elsewhere, alerts us to the possibility of another way of thinking about belonging to a place, the idea of home. The St Michael of 'Lycidas' expresses a sense of Protestant, providential destiny, its remit delineates a community by mapping shores around it, and, in assuming a role of tutelary authority and protection, it indicates a set of civic values that we associate with the nature of a good political community. In other words, the local guardian angel presents a substitute, or a metonym, for a missing notion of nationhood. The doctrine articulates a sense of what it means to be providentially attached to, to be identified with, to be rooted in a place.

In 'Lycidas' Milton reflects upon belonging. The poem sketches a landscape for the reader, first in a passage where the poet–speaker asks the nymphs where they were when Lycidas drowned, and answers that they were not at the place of the fatality, not

> on the steep,
> Where your old bards, the famous Druids, lie,
> Nor on the shaggy top of Mona high,
> Nor yet where Deva spreads her wizard stream . . .
>
> (lines 52–5)

Later the poet–speaker wonders where Lycidas' bones are, and introduces the sequence 'shores, and sounding seas . . . Hebrides . . . Bellerus' (lines 154–60). This emphasis on geography helps explain the substitution of Bellerus for Corineus: Milton chooses here place instead of legend. The imaginative landscape stretches from the Hebrides, Anglesey, the Welsh coastline, the Irish Sea, the Dee, Land's End, to St Michael's Mount. Pseudo-Dionysius wrote that local guardian angels established 'the boundaries of nations', and Michael's boundaries in 'Lycidas' include the shores of Britain, extending into the Irish Sea.

The status of Ireland, however, is unclear: it is present in the poem as King's home and intended destination, but it may be that a Roman Catholic country simply cannot be included as part of a chosen nation. In either case, Milton presents no contention for the inclusion or exclusion of Ireland in or from Michael's nation, from which it appears that Ireland is not a focus of his line of argument. It is easy to extrapolate anti-Irish sentiment backwards from his anti-prelatical polemics of 1641–2, his commonplace book notes probably made at the same time, and his *Observations* of 1649. Yet the poem itself does not suggest it. Nor does it seem right to infer that the geography of the poem is significantly shaped by anti-popery, nor by colonial ambitions.[55] The references to Spain do not construe it as a menace, but instruct the angel to look home, which is where the threat lies. The poem does not trouble itself with faith in Ireland, though it explicitly addresses the failed reformation in Britain. The poem constructs a landscape through a series of peripheral points, including those in Wales and Scotland, but also reaches into the Irish Sea. Ireland's relation to the imagined geography of these shores is left undetermined. Michael's protection is defined inclusively rather than exclusively.

What is the nature of that community, and how does one belong? As I have suggested, Michael's commission extends (at least) over Britain and effects protection rather than exclusion; the problem to which he is the solution concerns internal corruption rather than national boundaries. Secondly, it follows that it is unclear whether he is assigned to the people, Church, or nation. Seventeenth-century theological writings tended to isolate political or geographical units, stating that angels were assigned to nations and kingdoms or to major features of the landscape. Yet, as we have seen, Michael was specific-ally assigned to the Jewish people, and their history conflated nation and people, just as reformed theology identified the true Church with believers, rather than the institutional or architectural infrastructure. The nation is the community. So it is in 'Lycidas': Michael is associated with a feature of the landscape, but he protects the community that is his home, and his responsibility is to a chosen people, a people defined by civic values and neighbourliness, not race. His charge does not distinguish between people and land. This is more than prosopopoeia. It assumes a relationship between the nation and the people that is not based on political authority; the relationship between the nation and the people or land is not patrimonial. The most rigid or stable account of nationhood available to the early modern British was one that equated the nation with the king's jurisdiction, that treated the people as the king's subjects, and the nation as his personal territory. To remove the notion of kingship from the relationship between the land and the people, therefore, could be seen as an anti-monarchical gesture, a delineation of a notion of the people as citizens, or as having their identity through their tongue or their native landscape.[56] This belonging, an emphatically non-secular notion, is a pattern of identity formation that links landscape, community, neighbourliness, religion,

and, through the notion of protection, well-being. To have an angel
looking over one is to be well.

Thirdly, the widespread Protestant belief in guardian angels reminds
us that the land was still enchanted.[57] The landscape is full of invisible
meanings and spiritual beings.[58] Seeking the roots of modern national-
ism and national identity, looking for our reflection in the past, we
overlook this; and it is a fact of considerable importance for under-
standing nationhood and identity in the early modern period. I use the
word 'enchanted' for its defamiliarization effect, and because it stresses
that the water nymphs and deities of classical literature—which we,
for our own comfort, relegate to the past and transform into self-
consciously literary tropes—have their early modern Christian (and
therefore, in Milton's and his contemporaries eyes, *real*) correlatives.
Angels inhabit the landscape; they are witnesses to human actions, and
rejoice in or lament for them; they are the instruments of providence.
The landscape of pagan river gods, of Camus and Neptune, is not in
essence incompatible with one in which St Peter rises to denounce
ineffectual clergymen. Within the visible world there is an invisible,
consubstantial one, and the government of this world—by God, through
angels—asserts an association between the people and the land that is
above and beyond worldly politics. This providentialism leads not to
empire or race but to a sense of the history that is inscribed in the land,
and a concern for the country, its faith, and its future. This agrees with
what we have seen about Milton's patriotism. One's country is wherever
it is well with one: but that does not mean that it is just anywhere.

## Marvell's Protecting Angel

Andrew Marvell's poem *The First Anniversary of the Government under
His Highness the Lord Protector*, published in January 1655, celebrates the
constitution known as the 'Instrument of Government' introduced in
December 1653, under which Oliver Cromwell was made Lord Pro-
tector, and, within the framework of the constitution, the Protector
himself. Marvell concludes by likening Cromwell to an angel. It is a
puzzling comparison:

> While thou thy venerable head dost raise
> As far above their malice as my praise.

> And as the angel of our commonweal,
> Troubling the waters, yearly mak'st them heal.[59]

The lines allude to John 5: 4, which describes how a pool named Bethesda in Jerusalem was visited 'at a certain season', presumably annually, by an angel who 'troubled the water' and 'whosoever then first after the troubling of the water stepped in, was made whole of whatsoever disease he had'.[60] A man who had suffered an infirmity for thirty-eight years was unable to approach the water. Jesus saw and conversed with him, then healed him without recourse to the pool. Marvell's allusion presents Cromwell as 'the angel of our commonweal', a divine messenger who heals the English by bringing peace and political stability.[61]

The syntax of these lines, like Milton's in 'Lycidas', is resistant: 'them' designates the waters, and 'heal' is an intransitive verb attached to the waters, not, as it seems at first reading, the effect of Cromwell's troubling of the waters. It is the waters that do the healing, and not Cromwell, and the object of healing is not indicated, though the passage suggests that it is the commonwealth, or the troubled community that occupies it, that is healed. The lines also echo Robert Herrick's 'To the King, to Cure the Evill', a poem that praises King Charles by deliberately confusing the angel's healing power with that of Christ. Marvell may want to remind his readers that Cromwell is not to be confused with Christ, and that his abilities depend precisely upon his disturbing qualities: presumably his authoritarianism, his impatience, his bluff intellect.[62]

This concluding image adds yet another register to Marvell's complex admixture of panegyric and deliberation. Marvell's poem praises Cromwell with an eye upon the constitutional role and limits of the office of Lord Protector, while also admitting the imbalance between the man and the office.[63] The poem engages with the literature debating the strengths and weaknesses of the constitution published in the year following its introduction, deliberates its way through the political languages of 1654, and articulates active support of Cromwell specifically within the practical constraints imposed upon political and constitutional ideals by the immediate historical circumstances. This position, and the complex voice of the poem, were subsequently occluded: first, by Cromwell's dissolution of the first Protectorate Parliament in January 1655; secondly, by the increasing polarization

between principled republicanism and the pragmatism of the govern-
ment; and, thirdly, by the Restoration programme of rewriting the
history of the preceding decade. These conspired to dissipate
the political intricacies and evanescent constitutional discourse of
1653–4. In its aborted publication in Marvell's *Miscellaneous Poems* in
1681 (from which it was cancelled while the volume was in press) it
became a poem in praise of 'O.C.'

The concluding image is discomfiting in part because angels are
immortal and do not hold secular office. Cromwell is moved out of the
terms of the constitution; meanwhile, the annual process of healing
seems to concede, ever so tactfully, either that the Government was
itself unfinished, and that allegiance to it was therefore necessarily
provisional, or that the healing of the commonwealth will be ongoing.
These lines can be pressed a little further, however, through their
relationships with theology and with Milton's 'Lycidas'. We can ask:
where did angels fit in the political languages of 1654–5? Are concep-
tions of angelic offices a versatile simile, or do they bear upon the
argument of the poem? And what sense is conveyed by the preposition
'of' in 'angel of our commonweal'? Is Cromwell a representative or a
messenger?

Angels infrequently visit Marvell's poems. In 'On Mr. Milton's
Paradise Lost', published in the 1674 edition of the epic, they occupy
the 'vast Design' that initially troubles the reading poet:

> Messiah Crown'd, Gods Reconcil'd Decree,
> Rebelling Angels, the Forbidden Tree,
> Heav'n, Hell, Earth, Chaos, All.[64]

Angels are among the secret truths that the poet fears Milton will ruin.
Marvell is drawing on conventional reservations about penetrating the
mysteries of Scripture, reservations articulated in both theology and
poetry, by du Bartas for example, who interjects one of these passages
while narrating precisely the creation of angels.[65] Perhaps for this
reason Marvell seldom pries into invisible worlds. The dangers of
presumptuous knowledge appear in the nunnery episode of 'Upon
Appleton House'. There the subtle nun, seducing the virgin Thwaites
away from her destined public service, flatters her:

> I see the angels in a crown
> On you the lilies show'ring down:

> And round about you glory breaks,
> That something more than human speaks.
>
> (lines 141–4)

Angels are associated with popery and rhetorical deception, with wooden saints, beads, and holy water.

There is one other, more sympathetic apparition of an angel in Marvell's poetry, and that is earlier in *The First Anniversary*. Marvell anticipates a future epic, in 'graver accents', that will form the literary counterpart to the overthrow of monarchy, but:

> Till then my muse shall hollow far behind
> Angelic Cromwell who outwings the wind;
> And in dark nights, and in cold days alone
> Pursues the monster thorough every throne:
> Which shrinking to her Roman den impure,
> Gnashes her gory teeth; nor there secure.     (lines 125–30)

In contrast to the concluding couplet, there is no single, obvious scriptural allusion here. In what sense is Cromwell angelic? Does Marvell refer only to the speed of angels? One critic suggests that this is pure flattery, comparing Cromwell to a spiritual being that does not have to struggle with ponderous matter; another that Marvell here encourages Cromwell to chase the beast, so that in so doing he would become Christ and bring about the last days.[66] The comparison is not so direct, however. Just what kind of an angel Cromwell is here depends on the identification of the monster with the gory teeth—it is either the beast or Antichrist in Revelation 11: 7, commonly associated with the Church of Rome, or it is the Whore of Babylon, Revelation 17: 3–18—and the text is ambiguous.

Contemporary readings of Revelation contest the identity of the angels who fight Antichrist. The first, and the only angel assigned a personal name in Revelation, is Michael, who vanquishes the dragon Satan and casts him from heaven (Rev. 12: 7–8). Another angel, clearly identified as Christ mounted on a horse (Rev. 19: 11, 19–20), defeats 'the beast'; then a third angel locks the beast, now identified with Satan, in the bottomless pit (Rev. 20: 1–3). The majority of seventeenth-century commentators (among them Joseph Mede) identify the angel at 12: 7 as Christ; and the majority of these state that the angel at 20: 1 is also Christ. This is the reading of the Geneva Bible note.[67] Andrew Willet contended that this was a point of clear doctrinal difference between Protestants and Roman Catholics, the latter thinking that Michael was the head of the created angels, the former knowing him to be Christ.[68] Yet several Protestants offered alternative identifications, contending that Michael was either the angel Michael himself or that his name represents a force of angels. The same authors also dispute the reading of 20: 1.[69] John Napier, the influential interpreter of Revelation from the 1590s, states, somewhat anomalously, that Michael here represents the Holy Spirit. Thomas Brightman, among others, argues that the angel at 12: 7 was the emperor Constantine.[70] The Westminster *Annotations* state that Michael represents the emperor Constantine; though they dispute the identification of the angel at 20: 1 with Constantine on the grounds that there was not sufficient evidence.[71] John Mayer asks, 'why may not one Angell bee chiefe amongst the good Angels, as well as one Devill is chiefe amongst the evill Angels? . . . And therefore some hold Michael to be an Angell indeed.'[72] Mayer inclines to believe that Michael in Revelation was an angel, and this was the position of John Foxe, who is the sole commentator that Marvell recommends as a gloss on the apocalypse.[73]

We cannot know precisely how Marvell read these passages, but the range of commentators shows that there was no consensus within English Protestantism about the identification of Michael with Christ. To equate 'Angelic Cromwell' with an apocalyptic Christ is highly tendentious. The image is closer to Revelation 12 than to Revelation 19. The pursuit of the beast is an ongoing process; she shrinks to her Roman den, is not chained there. The last days are not upon us. Like the allusion to John 5: 4, which distinguished between the angel of Bethesda and the Christ figure who will follow, this passage, and the tenor of the allusion, differentiates between the Cromwell–angel figure, and Christ. If the allusion is primarily to Revelation 12, then angelic Cromwell is compared not to Christ but to Michael.

What did these details matter to Marvell? Why did angels creep into *The First Anniversary*, when they seem very remote from the language and sentiments of his two other poems on Cromwell, 'An Horatian Ode' and 'A Poem upon the Death of O.C.'? First, it reflects the widespread interest in angels in the 1640s and 1650s, their penetration into the language of soteriology and politics, and the intensification of speculative interest in their symbolic range. Some specific echoes, all chronologically proximate to the poem, help to gloss the final couplet, and to develop further the identification of 'Angelic Cromwell' with Michael. First, the newsbook *Certain Passages* in February 1655 included a set of astrological observations by William Lilly in which he eulogizes: 'the *Tutelary Angel of England* seems to direct the Noble *Protector*, who by wisdom prevents all mistakes'.[74] A guardian angel is guiding Cromwell and protecting the nation. A similar notion appears in Jacob Boehme's *Mysterium Magnum*, written in 1623, though published in English translation in 1654: 'Each Country hath its Princely *Angel-Protectour* with its *Legions*.'[75] The terminology of this otherwise conventional invocation of the doctrine of a local guardian angel is suggestive. A *protecting* angel echoes the title of Cromwell's office, moving away from the terms *guardian, tutelary,* or *custodian angel,* and consciously deploying the concept in a topical and political fashion.[76] A treatise by William Gurnall, published a few days before Marvell's poem, pressed angelology into the service of political debate about allegiance and the Protectorate, while an anonymous pamphlet of 1653 or 1654 dedicated to Cromwell promises that his record 'one day shall be revealed amongst Men and Angels'.[77] Most compellingly, Robert Dingley insisted in 1654 that it was probable that 'Cities, Shires, Provinces, Islands, Churches and Kingdoms have particular Angels to be presidential over them, and that each Republick hath an Angel to be its protector'.[78] Dingley's book, dedicated to Colonel William Sydenham, a member of the Protector's Council, here flatters Cromwell by implicitly comparing him to an angel whose responsibility is to protect the republic.

The angel Michael manifests itself in another way in these debates. Central to the story that *The First Anniversary* tells is the episode describing Cromwell's riding accident on 29 September 1654, the feast of St Michael, which Marvell uses to imagine a world without Cromwell. This incident had been seized upon in the hostile press as evidence of Cromwell's incompetence and as a providential warning against the Protectorate. The Welsh prophet Arise Evans interpreted it as a sign from the angel himself:

I beseech you again consider seriously what befell you on Saint *Michael* the *Archangels* day last past, and know what an Angel *Michael* is said to be in Scripture. . . . He is also the Prince of the people of God, and their angel to protect them, against which people you have appeared much, to destroy them hitherto, *Dan.* 10.21.

Michael himself has responded to the prayers of the Protestant Church, Evans says, and delivered a powerful omen.[79] Evans's *The Voice of Michael the Archangel* is among the texts that Marvell repudiates.

*The First Anniversary* displays an acute sensitivity to the linguistic registers of 1654. When Marvell describes Cromwell as 'the angel of our commonweal', he is using the same conceit as Dingley: Cromwell is neither a messenger nor a representative, though he is an angel, a protecting angel, assigned to the shores of Britain as the angel is assigned to the pool at Bethesda. This angel looks in two directions: first outwards to the political landscape of 1655, where the protecting angel is needed. Secondly, backwards, to a literary tradition and to another poem that meditates on the state the nation is in. Marvell's work was in an ongoing dialogue with Milton's, and *The First Anniversary* has a close relationship with 'Lycidas'. There are three echoes of the earlier poem: the 'kingdom blest of peace and love' (line 218) catches Milton's 'blest Kingdoms meek of joy and love' (line 177), the stops that Cromwell plays with his sweet touch (lines 58, 61) echo the shepherd poet's touching 'the tender stops of various quills' (line 188), and Marvell's 'beaked promontories' (line 358) reverberate with Milton's 'beaked promontory' (line 94).[80] Moreover, the dragon's swinging tail (lines 151–2) resembles the dragon in the 'Nativity Ode', and Amphion's building of the commonwealth (lines 87 ff.) echoes in diction and sense *Areopagitica*. Milton is a persistent presence throughout Marvell's writing.[81] The *First Anniversary*'s relationship with 'Lycidas' may lie behind Marvell's decision to place the protector angel so prominently and perplexingly. It is also possible that Marvell read the comparison of Cromwell to 'quasi tutelaris deus' in Milton's *Defensio Secunda* (a work the sublime eloquence of which he lauded) as implying a tutelary spirit or guardian angel.[82] We have seen how Milton invokes the doctrine of local guardian angels to tell the angel of St Michael's Mount to look homeward to his troubled country, and to imagine Edward King resurrected as 'the genius of the shore' responsible for protecting 'all that wander in that perilous flood'. He assumes that his readers will recognize the doctrinal basis for the imagery, as Marvell does in his concluding lines.

'Lycidas' is spoken by a poet within the poem, a shepherd who departs in the concluding lines, creating a frame (a broken frame: there is no corresponding voice in the opening). The poem spoken within the frame concludes with the image of the local guardian angel, offered in consolation, and the angel is Michael. Marvell's poem also ends with an angel, having invoked Michael as an analogue for Cromwell in the earlier passage praising 'Angelic Cromwell'. This buried allusion to 'Lycidas' *shapes* the poem; it is different in quality to the echoes of Dingley and others that establish the linguistic framework within which Marvell operates.[83] Marvell may well have believed in local guardians (his literary techniques do not permit us to make this kind of inference), but the purpose of the allusion is to create an additional layer of meanings that emerges from this double orientation.

First, there is a silent pun here on 'Protector'. The only reference to Cromwell's title is in the 'Roofs Protecting weight' (line 98) in the passage describing the construction of the commonwealth. The title was a puzzle in several respects. Milton addressed Cromwell in 1654: 'You suffered and allowed yourself, not indeed to be borne aloft, but to come down so many degrees from the heights and be forced into a definite rank, so to speak, for the public good.'[84] This acknowledges the odd political circumstance of late 1653, in which Cromwell's authority was unlimited by any constitutional restraints: in accepting the office of Lord Protector he placed significant boundaries on his prerogative.[85] Like Milton, Marvell praises Cromwell for 'Yielding to rule, because it made thee less' (line 228). Marvell's reticence about the title in a poem otherwise specific about the written constitution suggests his reservations about the effectiveness of the constitutional limits imposed on Cromwell; certainly the poem permits the reader to imagine him as an unprecedented kind of ruler, and a man greater than his position, whose restless and violent personal qualities threaten the very republic that he serves. There was, moreover, no significant political precedent for the role of Protector. Marvell's pun notes just such a precedent: the role of an angel whose duty it is to preserve the interests of a community.

It is a silent pun because this is part of the mode of *The First Anniversary*. Far from becoming a lesser poet as he entered the public realm of opinion, persuasion, and politics, Marvell, ever the ventriloquist and the intertextual magpie, found ways of articulating a vision of politics beyond the limits of extant political vocabulary, and he did so by subsuming this vocabulary within the languages and devices of poetry. The watery circles at the beginning and end of the poem recall the drowned and drifting body of Lycidas. In the earlier poem Michael protects the shores of Britain, and the waters, at first the source of grief,

the 'remorseless deep' (line 50) are miraculously transformed into a
source of comfort and healing, where the drowned shepherd protects
those who would otherwise be lost. Marvell's image relies on a
moment of self-conscious intertextuality which looks simultaneously
to two different kinds of intertexts. While he sublimates the language
of the dozens of pamphlets and newsbooks echoed throughout *The
First Anniversary*, he expects us to hear and to reflect upon this literary
echo, bearing argument and allusion together in mind. While the
other texts provide the evanescent language of politics (it is this that
matters rather than the texts themselves), 'Lycidas' is a palimpsest that
the poem will not release. An expression of support for the constitu-
tion and its Protector concludes by presenting the latter as an angelic
guardian of place, an image expressed in imitation of an earlier poem
that worries about the fate of the people, of true religion, and the role
of the civic-minded poet.

Finally, the role of the Protector is here imagined in terms other
than those spelled out in the constitution and the texts that debated it,
the language that Marvell has hitherto been using. It is not a crassly
flattering image; it moves Cromwell out of the constitutional frame-
work, but painstakingly. Marvell's angel is designated a role as well as a
limited place. The 'angel of our commonweal' signifies not a sublimely
good being but a divine instrument whose duty is to protect a place, to
comfort, to heal, to do his duty to those he serves. Angels, however
powerful, minister to humans. Cromwell's agelessness, signalled by the
watery circles in the opening lines, is a conventional trope of pan-
egyric, but the troubled waters at the end of the poem bind his angelic
agelessness to the hope of future anniversaries, and therefore to the
protecting duties he has been assigned and to which he is dutifully
limited.


## Prosopopoeia

Perhaps, of all angel-doctrine, the notion of guardianship, individual
and communitarian, is most easily understood in terms of psycho-
logical need. Angels populated the landscape, replacing fairies and
spirits and performing the tasks ascribed to them, leaving magic in
the land. They gave to acts of providence, signs, and strange events

an agency that looked human. Moreover, posting angels throughout the universe means that they are near when needed. An increasing awareness of the great distances of the universe, and of the time needed to traverse them at finite speeds, emptied space and made heaven remote. The logical consequence is that it must take an angel a considerable time to traverse the universe to come to a human's aid: consider Abdiel's nocturnal flight across heaven in *Paradise Lost*. Heywood's *Hierarchie of the Blessed Angells* notes in a passage discussing Satan's flight to earth the calculations of Persian mathematicians: if angels fly at a thousand miles an hour, it would take one at least six years and six months to descend from the eighth heaven.[86] For the purposes of human protection this does not strictly matter because God, unlike angels, is omnipresent, and can come to assist without restriction of time and space should all hell break loose on earth. Angels, however, cannot. If angels are to have a role intervening in human affairs, as all authors wish to maintain, they must be stationed proximately. The notion of angelic guardianship supports this, and so became more useful as theologians recognized natural-philosophical claims about space and velocity. The tenacity of the belief, then, could be seen to stem not from residuality as much as adaptability.[87]

However, this does not exhaust the imaginative potential of angels assigned to watch over a particular place. Milton and Marvell put the doctrine to subtle use. For other poets, local angels enable prosopo-poeia and a voice of moral authority. The land speaks within an eschatological drama. According to William Lilly, the angels president over nations sent portents and prophecies to their people.[88] George Wither's long pamphlet–poem *Prosopopoeia Britannica* (1648) uses this device to place a warning on the state of the kingdom in an angel's mouth. The poet–speaker describes how an angel arrives as he considers the kingdom's troubles and speaks a prophetic commentary on the civil war. The angel is 'brought into the room' by the poet–speaker's 'rambling *Fancie*' and his (his gender is explicit) physical appearance is an emblem (he wears a threefold broken crown): there is no pretence at verisimilitude in the poem. The angel's commentary articulates Wither's own perspective on what has gone wrong and what the people need to do to achieve peace. He is a literary angel, a device, and disengaged from angelology, except for the notion that he is the guardian angel of the three kingdoms (*not* Britain in the modern

sense). Towards the end the angel explains that what he has said should
be taken as true because 'I am that | Which is your GENIUS cal'd.' He
then explains the doctrine:

> A GENIUS, is an incorporeall creature,
> Consisting of an intellectuall nature;
> Which at the self-same time, a *being* had,
> With that, for whose *well-being* it was made.
> And, may be cal'd, that *Angell*, which designeth,
> Adviseth, moveth, draweth, and inclineth
> To happinesse; and, naturally restraineth
> From harme, that creature, whereto it pertaineth:
> And, this am I to you.[89]

It is hard to imagine that any of Wither's contemporary readers were
likely to believe that the visit represented an actual event, nor that
Wither intended them to. Nonetheless, the voice of the angel marks
understanding of and concern with the fate of the kingdoms, and this is
conveyed through the doctrine of guardianship that author and reader
know and share.

A final example of this vein: Abraham Cowley wrote during the
brief reign of Oliver's son Richard Cromwell *A Vision, Concerning his
Late Pretended Highnesse Cromwell, the Wicked; Containing a Discourse in
Vindication of him by a Pretended Angel, and the Confutation thereof by the
Author*, which was published in 1661 after the Restoration. It is a prose
pamphlet that occasionally rhapsodizes into verse. Cowley describes
how in a vision that was no dream he was transported to 'Mona'
(Anglesey), from which he sees the prospect of three kingdoms, and
there he breaks out into a lament on the chaos into which they have
descended. He is interrupted by a giant figure (his body also emblem-
atic), who proclaims: 'I am called The North-west Principality, His
Highnesse, the Protector of the Common-wealth of *England, Scotland*,
and *Ireland*, and the Dominions belonging thereunto, for I am that
Angel to whom the Almighty has committed the Government of those
three Kingdoms which thou seest from this place.'[90] Cowley doubts
that '*Cromwell* amongst all his forein Correspondences had ever held
any with Angels', but the angel insists that Cromwell was the greatest
Englishman ever, if not the greatest man ever, and that he now counts
himself 'a naturalized *English* Angel'. This collapses the careful distinc-
tion between the three kingdoms and England drawn earlier, which
distinction is also made in Wither's poem, but it carefully establishes a

sense in which this is the angel's home. Of course, Cowley soon realizes that this is a fallen angel, and they dispute perspectives on Cromwell, tyranny, and the 1650s. After seventy pages of this the evil angel is about to drag Cowley away when a good angel appears, 'The comeliest Youth of all the'Angelique race', who utters some unrecognizable words that drive the other off.[91]

The close connections between this and the poems by Milton, Marvell, and Wither are striking. All are state-of-the-nation poems that invoke the presence of national angels; Milton and Wither raise questions about the relationship between the islands and the kingdom (reading Milton in the backlight of Wither and Cowley sharpens the impression that Ireland is not simply excluded from Michael's protection); Cowley and, briefly, Milton both adopt the vantage point of Anglesey; Cowley's Cromwell driven by an evil angel retorts to Marvell's 'Angelic Cromwell'. Marvell may have known Wither's poem, and also Wither's later poem on Cromwell's riding accident, which, like *The First Anniversary*, construes a complex and qualified mode of praise.[92] Cowley claims in the preface that he had planned a sequel to his pamphlet, which 'was to be a Discourse with the Guardian-Angel of England, concerning all the late Confusions and Misfortunes of it'.[93] This savours of a response to Wither's poem, which fits precisely this description; it is possible that these two, and others, constitute a sub-genre that crosses the boundaries of poetry and prose. But all of these writings are rooted in an account of the nature and offices of angels that was common in early modern Britain. And all engage in a dialogue that is founded upon a sense of the imaginative possibilities of angels.

# 10

# Angels in *Paradise Lost*

## An Angel Sees Something Strange

Raphael describes to Adam his experience of the outbreak of war in heaven:

> strange to us it seemed
> At first, that angel should with angel war,
> And in fierce hosting meet, who wont to meet
> So oft in festivals of joy and love
> Unanimous, as sons of one great sire
> Hymning the eternal Father: but the shout
> Of battle now began, and rushing sound
> Of onset ended soon each milder thought.     (6. 91–8)

Raphael hedges his narrative with cautions about the difficulty of representing actions beyond human grasp. Here, however, he offers a glimpse of the inner life of angels. One of Milton's most distinctive skills as a narrative poet is to discover instants of astonishment, to step behind paradoxical acts of recognition, such as Adam and Eve's first moments of consciousness, and imaginatively to explore them. In this passage Raphael sounds naive, his diction simple, his language protestatory rather than rhetorically disciplined (contrasting with the preceding lines). Until this point in time angels had experienced little variety in heavenly life: suddenly they face the unknown. Instead of confining himself, as Aquinas had, to the moment of deciding to fall or stand, Milton imagines that decision developing in time. Moreover, and more challengingly, he describes an angel's response to these events, the angel's awareness of estrangement. The poetry imagines an angel's experience of being, his emotions, his sense of strangeness—paralleling Adam's self-alienation as he first experiences his body and realizes that it is his (8. 257–73)—as the nature of the universe is changed. The experience continues when the good angels first see military ordnance: 'to our eyes discovered new and strange' (6. 571).

What is strange to an angel? The question arises because of the decision to make angels creatures, not merely instruments of narrative but beings who live independently of the specific duties that God assigns them. *Paradise Lost* repeatedly focuses on the similarities and dissimilarities between human and angelic experience. It does so with an extraordinary tact. A discreet moment of such spiritual analysis, which is also a historical and theological analysis, takes place near the beginning of book 11. It is based on verses of Genesis (3: 22–3), following God's discovery of protoplasts' sin: 'And the Lord God said, Behold, the man is become as one of us, to know good and evil: and now, lest he put forth his hand, and take also of the tree of life, and eat, and Life for ever: Therefore the Lord God sent him forth from the garden of Eden'. To whom is God speaking? And what does he mean by 'become as one of us'? To the first question, some exegetes inferred the angels, others the remainder of the Trinity. Calvin demurred: 'Some refer to the plural number here used to the angels, as if God would make a distinction between man, who is an earthly and despised animal, and celestial beings; but this exposition seems far-fetched.' Nor did Calvin think the plural indicated the Trinity, the common alternative solution; instead he thought the 'us' indicated a fellowship between God and Adam. For Calvin, God's phrase was 'An ironical reproof', suggesting that Calvin and Milton shared a view of God's mordant and mocking sense of humour.[1] Milton, however, elaborated on the text considerably, and his reading is not Calvin's. After God explains to the Son that he intends to expel Adam and Eve from Eden, though with a promise of final redemption, he continues:

> But let us call to synod all the blest
> Through heaven's wide bounds; from them I will not hide
> My judgments, how with mankind I proceed,
> As how with peccant angels late they saw;
> And in their state, though firm, stood more confirmed.
>
> (11. 67–71)

It is a theologically distinctive action, and one that merits close attention. That angels can be 'more confirmed' in their unfallen state indicates that they have freewill. This is no surprise: while many

theologians deny freewill to angels, or seem to, it is essential to
Milton's Creation, and theory of angels, that beings are free to perform
good and evil. The problem that follows angelic freewill is that it seems
to imply that good angels might sin in the future (Origen argued that
all beings could backslide), or even that fallen angels might repent. Yet
the irreversible nature of the fall of angels was fundamental to Chris-
tianity since Satan was transformed from a testing angel, performing
God's will, to the metaphysical embodiment of evil. Thereafter there
were two kinds of angels: good and evil, and this antithesis was
reinforced by interpretations of Paul's words 'Satan himself is trans-
formed into an angel of light' (2 Cor. 11: 13–14). How, then, could
beings capable of acting freely at least once thereafter be fixed in their
moral status? And if the fallen angels did not act freely, how was God
not responsible for their evil actions?

Peter Lombard's deft handling of this dilemma was discussed earlier.
Those angels assisted by grace did not fall; by turning to God they
received more grace, confirming them in their goodness, and enabling
them to improve. Those who turned from God receive no grace, and
are thus confirmed in their fall; though free, they could not redeem
themselves without intervention by and support from God.[2] Though
both kinds of angels are free, they cannot change their state. Milton's
narrative is a variant of this: his 'blest' angels are confirmed in their
position by witnessing others' sins. A few lines earlier he has given his
readers a lesson in 'prevenient grace' (11. 3), showing how Adam and
Eve's free repentance is assisted—made possible—by the free offer of
grace by God, and Milton dramatizes the illusory dichotomy between
human agency and divine assistance by placing a book division
between them. Here, however, it is the experiential knowledge of
the consequences of sin that confirms them: God summons his angels
so they can see the humans judged. The possibility of the angels'
backsliding seems far more real than in Lombard's system, as is appro-
priate for a narrative poem, but also echoes Milton's greater concern
with individual responsibility. The angels are then summoned by a
trumpet—blown by an angel—take 'their seats' (11. 82) in the theatre,
and observe the judgement of humankind.

In these few lines a complex theological issue is explored and
quietly resolved. This tactful handling of doctrine is characteristic of
the poem. The poem is as indebted to scriptural annotation as it is to
hexameral poetry, yet it is easy to overlook its subtle doctrinal

statements.³ Raphael, Michael, and the narrator alike offer narrative as
a mode of exegetical commentary. In Chapter 5 I reconstructed the
angelology of Pordage and his circle, accepting his visionary integrity,
in contrast to materialist historiographical traditions that explain vi-
sions as symptoms of other historical phenomena, and Christian tra-
ditions that accept the principle of visions while discarding the
enthusiastic content. In this chapter I lay aside scepticism about Mil-
ton's inspiration, and reconstruct or redescribe his visions of angels
from the details of the poem. This chapter, as far as possible or useful,
detaches the imaginative narrative from the concerns with politics and
theology: if Milton witnessed heaven, then his testimony is worth
viewing from the inside.

## What Is Heaven Like?

*Paradise Lost* is an epic of space travel. The movement of angels is
followed from the empyreal heaven (beyond the fixed heaven of the
created world) through Creation to its centre, earth, down through
chaos to hell, the furthest extreme from God. Though angels are
remotely stationed in distant places, as local guardians, heaven is
their collective home. Milton's heaven has specific physical and men-
tal characteristics. Aquinas' heaven is featureless light; Dante's is
spheres of light.⁴ Milton's heaven embodies light with fields, 'happy
fields', 'vales', and hills (1. 249, 321; 6. 71; 5. 757; 6. 69). God's throne
is on a 'sacred hill' or 'holy mount' at the centre, higher than others (5.
619; 6. 743). When the angels move to war, they 'march' above the
ground and are thus undivided by the hills, vales, woods, and streams
below. Beneath the surface, 'Deep under ground', is the original matter
of the universe, 'sulphurous and nitrous foam', 'spirituous and fiery
spume'.⁵ This is covered by 'celestial soil', and on this 'bright surface'
grow 'plant, fruit, flower ambrosial, gems and gold' (6. 69–72, 478–9,
510–12, 472, 475), a profusion melding organic with inorganic.
Luther's idea of heaven similarly did not efface the material world,
but idealized earthly things, making rivers flow with pearls and pre-
cious streams.⁶ Flowerets grow in Eden and heaven (5. 379, 636; 6.
784). Except for the precious stones and metals and heaven's oft-
iterated spaciousness, the landscape looks much like England. Raphael
acknowledges this: '(For earth hath this variety from heav'n | Of

pleasure situate in hill and dale)' (6. 640–1). Heaven has a crystal wall, or
'battlements'; at the end of the war it recedes, leaving a verge, over
which the sinning angels throw themselves—their own agency is
important—in terror (1. 742; 6. 860–5). This, like the gems and gold,
suggests that heaven merges a natural landscape with architectural
features. All are manufactured by God, though on earth some are left
by nature and others introduced by man. There is a parallel, perhaps
entirely coincidental, with baroque ceiling paintings of the heavens,
which combine painted architecture, extending the real architecture of
the hall, with a visualization of the empyrean, breaking down the
barrier between reality and illusion, and the human and the divine.
Heaven also has 'high towers' and 'towered structures', some associated
with Satan's pride (2. 62; 1. 733; 5. 907). It has a gate which, at Raphael's
approach,

> self-opened wide
> On golden hinges turning, as by work
> Divine the sovereign architect had framed.          (5. 254–6)

The gate confounds any boundary between technology and provi-
dence. Angels sleep in 'pavilions numberless' interspersed among
'living streams' and 'the trees of life'. As they sleep, they are 'Fanned
with cool winds'. Angels sleep? They do, helped by soporific 'roseate
dews', heavenly medication (5. 652–3, 646–7). They sleep at night—
for there are days and nights in heaven, that measure the passage of
premundane time, which is a form of sequentiality (5. 580–2)—and
night in heaven is dark, but not very dark. Heaven is ordinarily
brightness itself, hence night is 'twilight (for night comes not there |  In
darker veil)'; and later, 'darkness there might well | Seem twilight
here' (5. 645–6; 6. 11–12).

    Given the widespread reluctance to represent heaven, and Calvinist
warnings about the danger of writing about it as if one had been there,
Milton's heaven is materially visualized. Heaven is not cloudy or delites-
cent, but is a landscape, as tangible as that of 'Lycidas'. It is also profoundly
musical. Music forms part of its internal logic as well as of its environ-
ment. The angels are sometimes organized as a choir, and their music is a
perpetual, rational pleasure, embodying joy, unity, love of God:

> Then crowned again their golden hearts they took,
> Harps ever tuned, that glittering by their side
> Like quivers hung, and with preamble sweet

> Of charming symphony they introduce
> Their sacred song, and waken raptures high;
> No voice exempt, no voice but well could join
> Melodious part, such concord is in heaven.          (3. 365–71)

This heavenly unanimity contrasts with the 'partial' song that is sung in hell; though hellish notes are still 'angelical' and ravishing, as the devils generate music to ease their suffering, consoling themselves for loss of heaven (2. 547–52). The angels commence with harps, a standard accessory in the visual arts and their instrument of choice in *Paradise Lost*, and then sing. The epic narrator then repeats their hymn. Over the next forty lines or so angelic voices sing words with complex, total harmony; though the song soon segues into the narrator's, and it ceases to be clear who is speaking:

> Hail, Son of God, saviour to men, thy name
> Shall be the copious matter of my song
> Henceforth, and never shall my harp thy praise
> Forget, nor from thy Father's praise disjoin.
>     Thus they in heaven . . .          (3. 412–16)

Their singing is 'as the sound of seas' (10. 642). In the scornful eyes of the devils, music characterizes heaven, and it is synonymous with praise of God. Mammon refers scornfully to heaven's 'warbled hymns' and 'Forced alleluias' (2. 242–3). In contrast, the Son looks forward to the end of time when God 'shalt be all in all' and the pure,

> circling thy holy mount,
> Unfeigned alleluias to thee sing,
> Hymns of high praise,

a compressed image synthesizing the geometry, topography, music, and praise essential to heaven (6. 732, 743–5; also 10. 641–2). When the angels move from peace to war, they silently march to 'instrumental harmony' in a more heroic mood (6. 62). This music, audible from heaven, forms a continuous part of Adam and Eve's experience of Eden, and angelic choirs sing when a 'genial angel' brings Eve to her nuptial bed (4. 712). While angels sleep, some keep watch and 'melodious hymns about the sovereign throne | Alternate all night long' (5. 656–7). Angelic music never stops in heaven.

Heaven and its angels are also defined by hierarchy. Milton adopts the
traditional, partly scripturally based nomenclature of the angelic orders,
descending from seraphim, cherubim, and thrones, through dominions,
virtues, and powers to principalities, archangels, and plain angels.[7] He
does not apply them as fixed markers of status, however, though differ-
entials of status are observed among the angels. Sin, speaking to Satan,
refers to 'all the seraphim with thee combined' (2. 750), which seems to
imply that a whole order fell with him; this was one theological tradition.
Raphael, moreover, narrating the war in heaven, repeatedly names the
fallen angels operating the ordnance as seraphim (6. 579, 604). However,
allusions to thrones and powers in hell, and especially to cherubim, and
the angelic hymn referring to 'The aspiring dominations' thrown down
by the Son, indicate that Satan did not lead a whole order to fall, nor were
all of his followers from a single order (1. 157, 324, 534; 2. 310; 3. 392).
Satan is repeatedly an archangel, the context implying elevation (1. 593,
600). Satan is 'the lost archangel' (1. 243), and Raphael tells Adam that
Satan was 'of the first, | If not the first archangel, great in power' (5. 659–
60, 694). Satan is matched against Michael (anticipating the final conflict
described in Revelation), and the narrator refers to Michael as an 'arch-
angelic power', and later an archangel (11. 126, 238, 884); Raphael calls
him 'The great archangel' (6. 257). However, Raphael, the 'affable
archangel' (7. 41), is also a seraph and an 'angelic virtue' (5. 277, 371)
and Satan scornfully mistitles Gabriel a 'Proud limitary cherub', a logical
insult only to a seraph, the sole rank above cherub in the conventional
Pseudo-Dionysian ordering (4. 971). The narrator describes Uriel as an
'archangel', though Satan addresses him as 'Brightest seraph' (ironically,
for Lucifer was among the brightest), and disguises himself as 'a stripling
cherub' in order to appear inconspicuous and deferential (3. 648, 667,
636). Either 'archangel' signifies an elevated rank, or the narrator uses it
to mean powerful or mighty angel, or, most likely, it means an angel
performing a distinctly important service, just as the word 'angel' might
refer to a specific rank or the species more generally.
      In the midst of the war, 'down they fell | By thousands, angel on
archangel rolled' (6. 594).[8] The juxtaposition of angel against archan-
gel, which disturbs the iambic rhythm, suggests distinction within
similarity (which 'cherub on throne' would not have); it represents
a cyclical inversion of proper hierarchy, without investing in the
specifics of that hierarchy (as 'dominion on principality' might). The
line, like all references to the orders of angels, is more committed to

the ideas of hierarchy and order than specific gradations. Milton's Creation is flexible and mobile: creatures are positioned according to their actions, and actions generate moral status rather than reflect it. Consequently, the notion of a fixed hierarchy of angels, through which enlightenment is channelled, developed by Pseudo-Dionysius and Aquinas, would be alien to Milton's understanding.[9] Milton's theory of matter, freewill, and evil depends on flexible hierarchies. Raphael tells Adam that 'great | Or bright infers not excellence' (8. 90–1), and looks forward to human bodies being 'Improved by tract of time' (5. 498).

This is not to say, however, that hierarchies do not matter. When he returns to hell having secured humankind's fall, Satan disguises himself as a 'plebeian angel militant | Of lowest order'. This is hell, where hierarchy is accorded greater social and symbolic presence, but the episode indicates that hierarchy is clear and visible (10. 442). The narrator describes Satan's farewell to Chaos:

> Satan bowing low,
> As to superior spirits is wont in heaven,
> Where honour due and reverence none neglects.     (3. 735–7)

Angels show due honour to Raphael as he heads towards earth, though the respect acknowledges his high message: there appears to be a correlation between the statuses of the messenger and of the message (as there is in prophecies brought by angels).[10] When God calls his angels before him, they appear

> Under their hierarchs in orders bright
> Ten thousand thousand ensigns high advanced,
> Standards, and gonfalons twixt van and rear
> Stream in the air, and for distinction serve
> Of hierarchies, of orders, and degrees...     (5. 587–91)

The organization folds in a military structure and multiplies the distinctions of the angelic orders. Satan is associated with the seraphim, and is a leader within the army (5. 684), and the military divisions correspond to the order; but the leader of the thrones is not, presumably, answerable to the leader of the cherubim. Ranking within the army works independently of the hierarchies. Offices and orders provide a sociological structure to the angels, but do not constitute a single, coherent hierarchy; they override it, and their plurality undermines a Pseudo-Dionysian account of heaven.

The names of the angelic orders do not reflect a fixed hierarchy. So what do they mean? On the eve of the war in heaven, Satan's forces travel north through heaven, through regions associated with particular ranks:

> Regions they passed, the mighty regencies
> Of seraphim and potentates and thrones
> In their triple degrees...                              (5. 748–50)

The hierarchies of the angels represent 'regions' and 'regencies', and areas of heaven are associated with particular ranks (Satan passes them to *his* seat). The different orders are like armies or encampments, and are mapped onto celestial topography. The ranks are treated as metaphors for orderliness. The names 'angel' and 'archangel' refer to offices that angels perform; the remaining terms describe not only ranks but properties.[11] There are particular qualities associated with the names of orders. Milton himself—assuming that he, and not the epic voice, is the author of the arguments—tells us that Abdiel is a seraph, a status reinforced in the poem (5. 804, 896). A seraph is the highest rank of angel, yet Abdiel is subordinate to Satan's command. Elevated status would undermine his appearance as a fearless, isolated, and physically threatened figure. Yet as a zealous angel it is fitting that he is a seraph, an angel *burning* with love of God. The name expresses a quality rather than status.

Raphael's reference to the fallen angel 'Nisroc, of principalities the prime', appears to indicate a clear hierarchy within an order, perhaps equivalent to Satan's primacy; this may refer exclusively to fallen angels, however. The desire to convert descriptive into definitional terms characterizes postlapsarian language. The fallen angels are concerned with titles. Hence, Satan in hell addresses the others:

> Thrones and imperial powers, offspring of heaven,
> Ethereal virtues, or these titles now
> Must we renounce, and changing style be called
> Princes of Hell?                                        (2. 310–13)

And to his followers as he falls:

> Thrones, dominations, princedoms, virtues, powers,
> If these magnific titles yet remain
> Not merely titular, since by decree
> Another now hath to himself engrossed
> All power...                                            (5. 772–6)

As Abdiel reminds Satan, all angels were made by God through the Son, and the names they were given are the gifts of God, describing their essences, not honorifics to which they are entitled:

> ... all the spirits of heaven
> By him created in their bright degrees,
> Crowned them with glory, and to their glory named
> Thrones, dominations, princedoms, virtues, powers
> Essential powers, not by [Christ's] reign obscured,
> But more illustrious made ...                          (5. 837–42)[12]

The same argument maintains that hierarchy does not degrade the lower ranks, but exalts them through association with the superior. Abdiel does not object to rank but to the appropriation of its terms for something other than a merited description of a property. The five names deployed in this debate are significant. Angel and archangel (literally, 'chief angel') describe duties (the bearing of messages); cherubim are the worldly angels who guard the gates of Eden (Gen. 3: 24); seraphim, meaning 'fiery', are six-winged figures in Isaiah 6.[13] The other five names, those used here, are found in Scripture, and are expressive of virtues, but are not clearly angels; their appropriation into clear ranks was the imaginative work of Pseudo-Dionysius. Hence their suitability as ambiguous, contested terms. Adam's tardy interest in the angelic ranks follows his fall. He addresses Michael:

> Celestial, whether among the thrones, or named
> Of them the highest, for such of shape may seem
> Prince above princes ...                                (11. 296–8)

Hierarchy shapes Milton's heaven, but it is not a chain of being.

Two models dominate the organization of heaven and its angels: armies and choirs. Angels sing, of course, but their organization into choirs emphasizes that music can involve social and spatial order. Milton uses 'quire' as a collective term for angels (punning on a gathering of paper). They sing in choirs, but they are also silent in a choir when God asks for volunteers to intercede for humankind, their collective silence underscoring the extraordinary sacrifice by the Son (3. 217). The 'angelic choirs' part in unison to give way to Raphael (5. 251). The organization of a choir is a spatial reflection of harmony: the individual identity is shaped by its position in a collective; their interaction indicates their joy and concord. The second model of social organization is the army. The angels are composed into camps and have a military command structure. The militancy of angels is not the consequence of the war: their creation is not described, but the earliest moment in the time scheme of the poem in which the angels are seen to have this military structure antedates their fall. The angels celebrate the elevation of the Son with dancing, but their 'camps' are then 'Dispersed in bands and files', and the disaffected Lucifer leads 'his legions'. They have banners and know how to march: the vocabulary is distinctly martial (5. 651, 687–8). There is no ontological transformation when they are assimilated into the army that unexpectedly meets Abdiel's eyes, 'thick embattled squadrons bright, | Chariots and flaming arms, and fiery steeds' (6. 16–17). Subsequently (in time, not narrative), Gabriel is 'chief of the angelic guards' in Eden protecting Adam and Eve, supervising angels that behave like idealized troops:

> About him exercised heroic games
> The unarmed youth of heaven, but nigh at hand
> Celestial armoury, shields, helms, and spears
> Hung high with diamond flaming, and with gold.
>
> (4. 551–4)

In narrative terms, this prepares us for the war in heaven in the following two books, and for the puzzling incident of the debilitating angelic armour. These are angels now at war. They have more in common with seventeenth-century English sermons than with Renaissance Italian art. These martial angels may also have been coloured by the presence in Milton's Britain of the idealized discipline and reputed theological devotion of the New Model Army.[14] Gabriel's troops show good discipline when faced with Satan:

>                the angelic squadron bright
> Turned fiery red, sharpening in mooned horns
> Their phalanx;                           (4. 977–9)

and Gabriel is sent on a military observation mission to the gates of hell (8. 29). Who is to say whether these images were rooted in the writings of Caesar or Thucydides, or in newsbook accounts of the recent wars in Britain? These twin modes of organization—the choir and the army—merge in book 12 at the birth of Christ, when the shepherds hear a carol sung by 'a choir | Of squadroned angels' (12. 366–7).

Michael's narrative announces the New Testament.[15] At the Incarnation the Church militant is also born, and the community of saints founded, hence the choir and the army become one.

A third, more abstract design governs the organization of heaven and angels, and it emerges from these two: this is geometry. The angels dance in circles; when they move to war, they shift into a 'quadrate' (squaring the circle?) and a 'cubic phalanx' (5. 163; 6. 62, 399, 743).[16] The circles are more complex than the squares, and are described as a geometrical pattern:

> That day, as other solemn days, they spent
> In song and dance about the sacred hill,
> Mystical dance, which yonder starry sphere
> Of planets and of fixed in all her wheels
> Resembles nearest, mazes intricate,
> Eccentric, intervolved, yet regular
> Then most, when most irregular they seem:
> And in their motions harmony divine
> So smooths her charming tones, that God's own ear
> Listens delighted.                              (5. 618–27)

The dancing is associated—by resemblance—with the movement of the spheres, traditionally understood to be rotated by angels, movement which generates music expressing complex and ideal harmonies ('their' in line 625 could refer to angels or the spheres). Like Hobbes, Milton imagines geometry to be a science with a special truth status: for him, however, it is created by God and not man, and the angels' dance expresses a perfection, the ideal behind man's clumsy attempts to 'model heaven' using arcs 'With centric and eccentric scribbled o'er' (8. 79–83). Movement, line, music, and truth are synthesized.

Perhaps heaven's most essential aspect is the hardest to describe: pleasure. Raphael's account includes brightness, fine dining, and sexual embraces. Satan scornfully identifies 'feast and song' as the slothful pleasures of heaven (6. 167). The pleasure implicit in heavenly life is best understood in contrast to the pain of the fallen. Hell is defined by pain. Nisroc, in the middle of the war in heaven, observes that 'Sense of pleasure' can be forgone in favour of a stoic contentment, 'But pain is perfect misery, the worst | Of evils,' and it is Satan who first sins, who 'first knew pain (6. 459–64, 327; cf. 2. 242–3, 278, 752; 6. 431). Heaven is painless. Angels are understood to be beings who live in a state of constant pleasure—though that pleasure can be solemn, disciplined, and arduous—and who do not know pain.

## What Are Angels Like?

*Paradise Lost* is unusual in combining both general and individualized portraits of angels. The portraits of named angels express character as well as the common properties of angels, in uncertain proportions. Angels, fallen and unfallen, have wings as part of their 'proper shape'. These wings are used to fly, they rustle in flight (1. 768), they symbolize speed. Raphael's are conspicuously 'gorgeous' and, as a seraph, he has six of them. His feathers shed 'heavenly fragrance' as he flies (5. 250, 277, 286). Wings punctuate the visual and metaphorical registers of the poem: the word and its derivations are used eighty-one times. Other features of attire are mentioned. Angels wear 'crowns inwove with amaranth and gold'; Uriel sports 'a golden tiar' (3. 352, 625). They have hair, and 'Bind their resplendent locks' with flowers (3. 361, 626). The false angel of Eve's dream has locks that 'distilled | Ambrosia' (5. 56–7). Michael wears a helm and a purple 'military vest', and carries a spear (11. 240–9). A particularly detailed description is offered of Satan's disguise as a 'stripling cherub' (evidently an exact disguise, but a securer subject for a poet than an unfallen angel, as it is a simulacrum):

> Not of the prime, yet such as in his face
> Youth smiled celestial, and to every limb
> Suitable grace diffused, so well he feigned:
> Under a coronet his flowing hair
> In curls on either cheek played, wings he wore
> Of many a coloured plume sprinkled with gold,
> His habit fit for speed succinct, and held
> Before his decent steps a silver wand.          (3. 637–44)

Angels wear appropriate clothes and head decorations, have locks of curly hair, and exude grace or spiritual substances. They are bright and colourful. Nothing in this would seem unfamiliar to a medieval or Renaissance artist.[17]

Traditional angels appear as young men, however (feminine men being conventionally beautiful, masculine women monstrous), while Milton's are differentiated according to age; Adam assumes they are all male (10. 893). The 'youth' in the above passage could be a universal characteristic of angels, but the 'stripling cherub' implies an appearance junior to Uriel's. Zephon is 'Severe in youthful beauty', in contrast to Satan, who is scarred (4. 845; 1. 601; 2. 401). This is a synecdoche, as angels are sempiternal and do not age. Yet the disguise is real enough, and there are other ways in which angels vary in their appearance or have distinguishing qualities, such as brightness and strength (7. 131; 5. 838; 10. 425; 4. 786). When Azazel is described as a 'cherub tall', the qualifier presumably refers to his activeness, elegance, or boldness rather than his height, but the visual texture of the poem benefits from this ambiguity (1. 534). While Milton relies heavily on traditional iconography, these qualifiers individualize the poem's angels: Zephon is severely beautiful, Abdiel zealous, Raphael 'the sociable spirit', Michael a 'gentle angel' yet solemn (5. 221; 11. 234–6, 421).

In addition to making love, Milton's angels eat. Their digestive process is significant to the theology and natural philosophy of the poem. Their food is also described with care:

> Tables are set, and on a sudden piled
> With angels' food, and rubied nectar flows:
> In pearl, in diamond, and massy gold,
> Fruit of delicious vines, the growth of heaven.
> On flowers reposed, and with fresh flowerets crowned,
> They eat, they drink, and in communion sweet
> Quaff immortality and joy . . .                    (5. 632–8)

These are not the nutritional properties of the food; it is in eating and drinking that immortality and joy are experienced. Hence, eating, commonly associated with transience and decay, is here associated with their opposites. Raphael emphasizes that angels have senses and emotions. In 1667 this last phrase had read 'with refection sweet | Are filled', which suggests a more literal-minded understanding of what goes on at those tables. The emendation further emphasizes the rejection of the metaphysics of the Church sacrament of Communion, by showing a truer communion which acknowledges the bounty of communion in everyday eating. Appetite and digestion are more angelic than submission and symbolic transcendence. While the passage invites a symbolic reading—surely this is spiritual nutrition?—it firmly declines to pursue that register, instead emphasizing the virtue of pure pleasure, and finding it in material food and drink. The symbolic and the literal appear as one.

The representation of angels at leisure, celebrating the promotion of the Son, provides opportunities for distinctive perspectives on angels as real creatures, such as the proposition that angels sleep, and that dews prompt them to do so (5. 646–7). The movement of angels is swift, though achieved with effort.[18] It is intriguing, then, to find their motion described as gliding:

> The cherubim descended; on the ground
> Gliding metéorous, as evening mist
> Ris'n from river o'er the marish glides . . .          (12. 628–30)

'Metéorous' suggests atmospheric movement, parried by 'on the ground', but it also intimates a portent. The cherubim come to keep humans in exile from Eden. The scene is viewed through Adam's eyes, and the obscurity of the movement, no longer the winged descent of Raphael spied from a distance, indicates Adam's impaired vision. However, Uriel glides on a sunbeam (4. 555), and Satan 'wrapped in mist | Of midnight vapour glide[s] obscure', and creeps 'like a black mist' (9. 158–9, 180): the repetition of the image suggests that something in angelic motion physically resembles the disembodied gliding of mist.

These depictions of angels meld the figurative and the literal, and Milton's heaven is a place where these two collapse into each other firmly and inexplicably. Individuation reaches its apogee in the proper noun, though for a poem awash with the names of classical figures there are few names given to unfallen angels: Gabriel, Michael, Raphael, Uriel, Abdiel, Ithuriel, Zephon, Uzziel, and Zophiel. Raphael gives a reason:

> I might relate of thousands, and their names
> Eternize here on earth; but those elect
> Angels contented with their fame in heaven
> Seek not the praise of men: the other sort
> In might though wondrous and in acts of war,
> Not of renown less eager, yet by doom
> Cancelled from heaven and sacred memory,
> Nameless in dark oblivion let them dwell.          (6. 373–80)

Angelic modesty informs Raphael's tact, and the poem resists the incantation of angelic names that is common in occult texts and ritual magic (especially that concerned with summoning angels). Elsewhere in the poem, the names of fallen angels are spoken more freely, because they are names invented by humans for the earthly manifestation of devils, and are used proleptically by Raphael and the epic narrator. Raphael speaks Lucifer's name to Adam, but indicates with a '(So call him ...)' that it is a translation that captures the angel's original brightness, rather than the actual name, a name mysteriously or politicly unspeakable (7. 132).[19] Raphael is here consciously adapting his speech for his auditor, and the angel explicitly indicates that he is doing so. Four unfallen angelic names are those most commonly used in writing on angels because of their scriptural status: Raphael and Michael appear in the Old Testament, Raphael in the apocryphal book of Tobit, Uriel in 4 Ezra and numerous pseudepigrapha. All four were developed in cabbalistic traditions; Uriel, for example, was associated with the sun in rabbinical writings on angels, and Milton makes him 'regent of the sun' (3. 690).[20] The other names are more unusual and complex. Abdiel, meaning 'servant of God', is a human in the Bible (1 Chr. 5); as an angel he appears in *Sefer Raziel Hamalach*, or *The Book of the Angel Raziel*, a cabbalistic work influential in occult writings though only available in Hebrew in seventeenth-century Britain, where the name appears in a treatise describing cosmic geography and the power of names.[21] Why Milton gave this name to such an important character in the poem is not known, though the *meaning* of the name is particularly resonant in context.

Ithuriel and Zephon are the 'two strong and subtle spirits' who discover Satan crouching at Eve's ear in book 4. They apparently fail to recognize Satan, though they may simply refuse to name him, as to do so would be to taint or misuse an unfallen name by association with evil. As the exchange concerns self-knowledge and recognition of another, naming is an important issue, and Milton's choice of names is provocative.[22] Ithuriel means 'discovery of God' and can be found in the *Key of Solomon*. 'Thuriel' can be found in Trithemius' *Steganography*, a source for occult angelology in seventeenth-century Britain, though doubtful as Milton's source.[23] Zephon, meaning 'a looking out' or 'searcher of secrets', is a human name in Numbers 26: 15. Milton probably used it mindful of the Baal-Zephon mentioned in Exodus 14: 2, and discussed in *De Diis Syris* (1617), where John Selden argues that Baal-Zephon was an idol sentinel. As Agrippa suggested, the names of good and bad angels might be paired. Milton therefore appropriates Zephon as the true, original sentinel, of which Baal-Zephon was a later, idolatrous corruption.[24] Uzziel is another human name (Exod. 6: 18), meaning 'strength of God', but was used as an angel-name in rabbinical writings including *The Book of the Angel Raziel*, where he is one of the seven angels that stand before the throne of God.[25] The non-scriptural Zophiel, or 'Spy of God', also figures in rabbinical traditions and the *Key of Solomon*. He is also mentioned as an archangel, whose name 'argueth pulchritude' in Robert Fludd's *Mosaical Philosophy*; and there is an Iophiel in Agrippa.[26] The name may derive from Iofiel or Jophiel; identifying sources for names is made more complicated by transliterating from the Hebrew.

Milton may not have been interested in angels' names: he chose to name few in a literary form that invited compendious lists. Perhaps his muse–angel did not speak of them. Dee searched for angel-names, believing that in the angelic tongue they held mystical power; yet in Milton's heaven they are seldom used. He avoided Metatron, Israel, Zadkiel, Samael, and Asriel, all names common in occult and rabbinical writing about angels. However, his nine do not simply reflect the canon of theologically inoffensive angel-names. In his reluctance to name, he partly avoided the unsafe territory of human inventions, and preserved the mysterious and poetic power of angels' names. Those he did use include scriptural names but also obscure names from occult traditions. His choices suggest that he was familiar with *The Book of the Angel Raziel*, or a manuscript copy of the *Key of Solomon*, or a manuscript of Solomonic magic.[27]

## What Do Angels Do?

Milton's angels sing, watch, play games and exercise, eat, sleep, make love, bear messages, interpret, bear witness, move the universe, and, above all, talk. They make mistakes: Raphael misunderstands Adam's account of his need of Eve; Uriel is deceived by Satan. They are agents with freewill, responsibility, and leisure time.

The four main activities of angels in Protestant doctrine are to praise God, bear messages, and act as ministering spirits and as witnesses. Milton's angels do these things, but his narrative mode requires that he asks what do they do the rest of the time, and whether their consciousness and freewill require other activities. Aquinas' angels would contentedly stand in choirs and sing praises, but Milton's need a more active, diverse life, expressing their freewill, without which their praise would be meaningless. The singing of Milton's angels colours the universe. It provides a backdrop for Adam and Eve's life, day and night.[28] When they praise God, they praise with hymns; Raphael reports one that follows Creation:

> Great are thy works, Jehovah, infinite
> Thy power; what thought can measure thee or tongue
> Relate thee . . . ?                                         (7. 602–4)

Their praise is endless (the fallen angels object to this), full of *copia* but always unable to reach the heights to which they must aspire. Milton's angels are, unlike any other angels, profoundly articulate beings. Angels are, as their name indicates, messengers, but messages are, as any narrative must discover, occasional. Angels who are primarily messengers must recede into the background when the story is being developed another way. These angels, however, talk all the time: to each other, to humans, and when free from other duties they make music that is verbal as well as tonal and rhythmic.

Milton's angels watch, and, though they sleep, vigilance is essential to their duties. This is not only a reflection on the state of war. Through the night, while others sleep, watches of angels take alternate duty in singing hymns around God's throne (5. 656–7), lest heaven fall silent. Watches protecting the human couple 'in warlike parade', led by Gabriel, change at 'the accustomed hour' of night (4. 779–80). Gabriel also guards the sole gate of Eden, overseeing 'The unarmed youth of heaven' who engage in 'heroic games', presumably training exercises (4. 542–54); this contrasts with the forbidding cherubim, who will guard the gates from human return. Raphael will later explain that he did not see Adam's creation because he was on an 'excursion toward the gates of hell', to ensure that none had escaped (8. 29–34). These are the actions of an army, but they also suggest the more extended duties of angels as part of the broader communications network of the universe. As part of these duties, angels not only interact directly with people, but witness human activity as an audience. This audience gives human actions meaning in a broader context, one more intelligible and familiar than the inexpressive and omniscient eyes of God. Adam inadvertently remarks on this when answering Eve's question about why the stars unseen shine at night. He tells her not to think,

> though men were none,
> That heaven would want spectators, God want praise;
> Millions of spiritual creatures walk the earth
> Unseen, both when we wake, and when we sleep:
> All these with ceaseless praise his works behold
> Both day and night . . .                                    (4. 675–80)

Among the works that these creatures behold are Adam and Eve.
Humans provide a kind of theatre for angels. Angels weep tears, and
though the only angelic tears the poem describes are dissembled, the
implication is that angels know pathos as well as joy (1. 620). In all four
outlines for a drama entitled 'Paradise Lost' or 'Adam Unparadiz'd'
drafted around 1640 (after the angels in 'Lycidas' and 'Ad Leonoram'),
Milton included a 'Chorus of Angels'.[29] In the epic, too, they are
spectators at the 'woody theatre' of Eden (4. 141), and sometimes
provide a chorus between Eden's couple and the human reader.

   Raphael and Michael act as messengers; though Raphael is also an
'angel guest' (9. 1), and is like an ambassador, greeting, dining, and
conversing politely.[30] These encounters are more extended than the
portentous scriptural visits of message-bearing angels; Milton recon-
ceives angelic–human sociability in order to imagine the prelapsarian
state. Raphael is likened to a 'friend' to humans (9. 2), suggesting
friendship is not possible between angels and humans, though some-
thing like it, perhaps fellowship, is. Adam calls Michael a 'heavenly
instructor', providing not a message but a Socratic lesson (11. 871). He
calls Raphael a 'divine *interpreter*', perhaps referring to Raphael's active
translation of the spiritual world and actions into human terms. This
much is suggested when Raphael qualifies an allusion to Lucifer's
palace with

> so call
> That structure in the dialect of men
> Interpreted,

another phrase in which Raphael indicates that he is consciously
adapting his speech (7. 72; 5. 760–2; also 3. 657). However, the label
'interpreter' also gestures to a broader role angels play: as beings that
stand between God and humans they present a step towards under-
standing the ineffable. As they provide an audience for human life, so,
by providing a mediating term between the finite and the infinite, they
ensure that space, literally and metaphorically, is not a vacuum.

Speaking is a duty for angels, who must praise God and bear his messages. Their hymns to the Son in book 3 and to Creation in book 7 are poems of praise, using epideictic rhetoric that is declarative and oddly passive. In the hymn to the Son their selfhood is erased in praising, and the syntax focused on the 'thou' being praised, so that the introduction of the first person singular ('the copious matter of *my* song' (3. 413), also embracing the narrator) is startling, and emphasizes that these are individuals, as well as voices in a choir. The hymn to Creation moves from the expulsion of the fallen angels, through a meditation on how providence brings forth good from evil, to praise of the world and men; there is no reflection on the singers' own place in this universe, and how it has been altered by this addition. As envy at man's creation is sometimes cited as the cause of the angelic fall, Milton expresses their selflessness. Their selflessness is remote from the rhetoric of rhetoricians, in profound contrast to the subtle manipulations in the diabolic synod in book 2. This pattern of selflessness can be contrasted, however, with the very different rhetoric Raphael uses to describe freewill and its dangers:

> freely we serve,
> Because we freely love, as in our will
> To love or not; in this we stand or fall:
> And some are fallen, to disobedience fallen,
> And so from heaven to deepest hell; oh fall
> From what high state of bliss into what woe!      (5. 538–43)

This passage begins with a seeming paradox, and works its way through a series of sonorous antitheses (free–serve, stand–fall, heaven–hell, bliss–woe) and emphatic syncrisis and homoioteleuton. The structured rhetoric is introduced because Raphael is talking theology, and he sounds not unlike God discussing freewill, grace, and salvation, using the schemes anaphora, anadiplosis, antithesis, and climax (3. 183–202). Angels are, naturally, rhetorical beings, and choose their styles, tropes, and figures to suit the occasion. Thus it is possible for a Miltonic angel—unlike a Thomist angel, who communicates by beams of pure intellectual thought—to flatter and deceive another through disguise and guileful words.

Angels protect, make love, eat, bring prophecies, blow trumpets; they also perform unique duties as required. Among these is guarding

paradise, assigned to cherubim with flaming swords (God invites
Michael to choose his best troops; 11. 101); and at the end of *Paradise
Regained* a 'fiery globe' of them lifts the Son from his 'uneasy station'
on the pinnacle (4. 581–4). Another is the catastrophic altering of the
cosmos that follows the fall, a task assigned to angels:

> While the creator calling forth by name
> His mighty angels gave them several charge,
> As sorted best with present things ...                (10. 649–51)

The sun is moved to create inhospitable seasons, and the moon and the
five planets are moved from their original, ideal trajectories so that
their convergences produce malignant influences and bad weather: the
earth's misalignment from the sun's axle results in discord among
animate things, antipathy, and death.[31] Angels were traditionally asso-
ciated with the planetary spheres, turning them and generating the
music of the spheres: in this passage Milton extends the astrological
framework, and envisions the destroying angels, the angels of terror,
creating discord within an erstwhile ideal creation. As with the cher-
ubim that bar access to Eden brandishing a fierce blazing sword
(12. 633–4), the reader is reminded that angels are terrible and sublime,
as well as protecting and sociable.

# II

# The Natural Philosophy
# of Angels

## Milton and Natural Philosophy

Milton's angels seemed strange to some early readers. Sir Samuel
Morland, who had worked with Milton during the 1650s, and as
an ambassador delivered at least one speech written by Milton,
thought the epic account of a war in heaven risible.[1] He presumes
his reader

> would be very little satisfied with my Endeavours, in case I should, in
> imitation of a late learned Author, try to squeeze a plausible Description of
> LOST PARADISE, out of St. *John's* Vision in the Isle of *Patmos*, and fancy to my
> self a formal and pitcht Battle, upon a vast and wide Plain, in the North part of
> Heaven, fought between two might Hosts of Blessed and Revolted Spirits,
> conducted and led up by mighty Arch-Angels, (for their Generals) riding in
> Brazen Chariots, drawn my foaming Steeds, and clad with *Adamantine* Coats,
> one of which was, by a massy Sword, cut down to the wast, and stain'd with
> Angelick blood: Where the one of these Armies dug up the Terrain of
> Heaven, and with the Materials they there found, made Powder, Bullets
> and great Guns (it is pity that Bombs were not in use when he wrote that
> Treatise) and with them did great Execution upon their Enemies, who in
> Revenge tore up great Mountains by the Roots, and hurl'd them at
> their Heads, with a great number of Romantick Stories, which is *Ludere
> cum Sacris* . . . [2]

Calling *Paradise Lost* a 'Treatise' reveals his doubt about Milton's
poetics, as well as his natural philosophy. Morland's satire looks
like a conventional attack on allegory, for its hostility to realism,
for rejecting the visible world.[3] It is not: Morland regrets that,
having made the invisible visible, Milton has made it absurd.

Spiritual truths should be less physical. His grounds are theological, because Milton uses his imagination where it is not appropriate, but also natural-philosophical, because questions about the invisible world and incorporeal beings were 'not to be fathom'd by the Line and Plummet of Human Understanding'.[4] Morland was not alone in his objections to the narrative of books 5 and 6. Patrick Hume, Milton's first annotator, wrote in 1695 that the representation of invulnerable angels wearing armour was a paradox; Charles Leslie in 1698 described these '*Romantick Battles*' as '*a Scene* of Licentious *fancy*'; Samuel Johnson thought that 'The confusion of spirit and matter which pervades the whole narration of the war in heaven fills it with incongruity.'[5] Such reservations have the merit of taking the creatureliness of Milton's angels seriously, while doubting their convincingness.

Milton used narrative to experiment with angels, and he was not alone in exploring their physical nature. Interest in angels was not outmoded or nostalgic in the 1660s. Early modern natural philosophers explored the nature of angels from both experimental and devotional perspectives; and early modern theologians asked questions about angels that were influenced by natural philosophy. Natural philosophy and theology enquired into angelic matter, movement, eyesight, and ingestion. *Paradise Lost* connects or overlaps with these concerns. The perplexity of Morland and his successors originated not only in Milton's conceits but also in his understanding of the natural world.

Milton did not directly engage with contemporary natural-philosophical debates, with arguments over experimentalism, or with the writings of the Royal Society, and there is no conclusive evidence for what he read or knew in this field. Critics have debated Milton's familiarity with seventeenth-century natural philosophy and astronomy, suggesting, for example, that *Paradise Lost* articulates sympathy for the 'old science', and that he assimilates 'scientific' interests only to subordinate them to aesthetic ends; that he is prescient of later science; and that he disliked the political and religious agendas of the Royal Society.[6] Milton's cosmology has been a focus of this debate. He alludes to five different models of the cosmos, while tending to geocentrism. Yet Michael censures those who seek the secrets of nature (12. 575–87), and Raphael warns Adam that God will hereafter laugh at those who

> come to model heaven
> And calculate the stars, how they will wield
> The mighty frame, how build, unbuild, contrive
> To save appearances, how gird the sphere
> With centric and eccentric scribbled o'er,
> Cycle and epicycle, orb in orb . . .                    (8. 79–84)

This might be a critique of scientific rationalism.[7] Some suggest that, through his inconsistencies, Milton cherrypicks, from various available paradigms, those notions that seem most useful or attractive.[8] Others still that Milton engaged attentively with natural philosophy, and sought to integrate it into his theological and poetic commitments: that his depiction of the natural world uses detailed knowledge of flora and fauna to create a poetry that subtends multiple and possibly contradictory meanings, poetry that is itself a reading of the Book of Nature;[9] that he engages with contemporary debates about mechanical philosophy and vitalism or animism (the belief in the existence of an active and organizing principle within all matter), and that his account of nature, especially in his narrative and his portrayal of angels, is rigorously systematic in its philosophical and political implications.[10]

The conflict originates in the inconclusive nature of the evidence, but also in the unsatisfactory dichotomy between the poet's being interested or not interested in natural philosophy, and a schematic division between 'old' and 'new' science. The cosmology of *Paradise Lost* cannot be pinned down to a heliocentric or a geocentric model, but this was something of a false dichotomy, as there were a range of available models, and the irrefutable demonstration of one was recognized as impossible. This was a matter of epistemology rather than ontology: the focus of contestation was the appropriate method and nature of analysis and demonstration.[11] Raphael does not dismiss enquiry into such matters, but rather suggests the multiplication of means of comprehending data, and particularly the complication of those means, will not lead to understanding. His is a point about how, rather than what, we know. While Milton may not have wished to engage with experimentalists or the Royal Society personally or polemically, he shared with them interests in matters concerning angels and the role of spiritual causes, where natural-philosophical issues converged with theology. He asked questions about the nature of matter, assumed a monist account of matter and motion (affirming the unity of matter and spirit), and believed that the liberty that was essential to human agency and salvation extended to the stuff humans were made of. There was a convergence of questioning, rather than intellectual alignment. Milton's position was not a conservative or anti-intellectual one: he was interested in natural philosophy as it assisted him in forming his narrative, and so offered a means of imagining and describing theological truths.

## Angelic Digestion and Lovemaking

'Orthodox' angelology represented a broad span of beliefs, covering much that was deemed *adiaphora*. There was a wide remit of speculation, and this speculation could be highly atypical and even controversial without being heterodox in the strict sense. Milton is conspicuously odd on two matters of angel-doctrine. First, digestion: angels eat food not only out of politeness, but enjoy and digest it. Secondly, lovemaking: they practise total interpenetration for pleasure. Both need to be understood in terms of the nature of matter as much as of theological doctrine.

Food, sustenance, and appetite were conventional markers of difference between humans and angels. Augustine described angels as beings that perceived and understood 'without needing to be sustained by food', but were instead 'sustained by a quickening Spirit'; 'it is not the power of eating and drinking, but the need to do so, which is removed from such spiritual bodies'.[12] Aquinas states that angels do not assimilate food into their assumed bodies, and that they present 'only an image of spiritual nutrition'.[13] The food of angels was therefore a metaphor for spiritual sustenance. As Robert Dingley wrote, 'Angels are Spirits, their nature, Communion, Food, Delights are Spiritual.' The logic of these commentators compasses both the physiological and the theological. In the next life, it was argued, man, freed from his mortal body, would become more like the angels and thus free not only from disease and deformity but also 'From want of meate, drinke, marriage'. In this life, however, plants and animals are given to humans, and human bodies depend upon consumption. By 1672 George Hughes, a Presbyterian-inclined clergyman who had been ejected under the Act of Uniformity in 1662, troubled by the deceptive implications of a virtual body that only seemed to eat, suggested that the angels that visited Abraham 'did truely eat, and the bodies were refreshed for the time that God made use of them'.[14] Here it is the words 'truely' and 'refreshed' that diverge from

Thomist traditions. Robert Fludd, who believed angels to be corporeal, interpreted the same text of Genesis: 'Surely a man so profound in divine mysteries, would not have beene so absurd, as to have offered them his food, if he had knowne that it would not naturally have nourished them.'[15] Both conflate real eating with nourishment, as does Milton's Raphael, who takes 'corporal nutriments' (5. 496). John White, whose imaginative exploration of Genesis 1–3 merits comparison with Milton's, asks why prelapsarian man needed such things:

> But why doth God abase Man so far, in this his happy condition, as to support, and as it were to prop him up, by the Creatures, whereas he might have preserved Man, as he doth the Angels, by immediate Influence from himself, without the help of any Creature at all, and have continued his life, as well without food as by food?[16]

He answers: because life on earth is a temporary abasement for mankind. Food indicates the humanity of humankind, both its corporeal being and its susceptibility to appetite; it designates the dichotomy between humans and angels.

This is a dichotomy that Milton deconstructs. He uses the food of angels to explore the fluid scales of Creation and the community between humans and angels. Milton's very unusual account of angelic digestion reflects a different vision of matter and of interspecies relations. When Raphael visits, Adam tentatively offers food, but the angel reassures him:

> what he gives
> (Whose praise be ever sung) to man in part
> Spiritual, may of purest spirits be found
> No ingrateful food.                    (5. 404–7)

Raphael proceeds to emphasize that not only can angels digest real food, turning 'corporeal to incorporeal' (5. 413), they actually require sustenance: 'whatever was created, needs | To be sustained and fed' (5. 414–15). So not only is the meal that Raphael takes with Adam a real one, the heavenly food of angels is described in sensual terms:

> in heaven the trees
> Of life ambrosial fruitage bear, and vines
> Yield nectar, though from off the boughs each morn
> We brush mellifluous dews, and find the ground
> Covered with pearly grain . . .          (5. 426–30)

This detail, lingering on the reality of heavenly food and nutrition, reappears later in Raphael's description of a four-Michelin-starred feast in Heaven:

> Tables are set, and on a sudden piled
> With angels' food, and rubied nectar flows:
> In pearl, in diamond, and massy gold,
> Fruit of delicious vines, the growth of heaven.          (5. 632–5)

Heaven is material and organic, and its physical properties are inter-laced with the mental.[17] Milton's unorthodoxy on the matter of angelic digestion, often understood to be an exceptionally literal-minded moment, is one aspect of a fuller theological picture of the creatureliness of angels, the spiritual congruity and legitimate sociability between humans and angels, and the continuity of matter across all of Creation.

Milton's second alleged heterodoxy, on angelic sex, is also more embedded in tradition than might at first appear. The penetrability of angels was a commonplace: though they could act with assumed bodies and upon material objects 'with external violence', according to Jan Amos Comenius, they themselves 'can be hindred or stayed by no body'.[18] 'They are creatures, that have not so much of a body as flesh is, as froth is, as a vapour is, as a sigh is,' preached Donne, 'and yet with a touch they shall moulder a rock into less atoms than the sand that it stands upon; and a millstone into smaller flour, than it grinds.'[19] The association between power and penetrability is a paradox. The fact of penetration was commonly iterated in both theological and natural-philosophical writings; it is the reimagining of this as a sexual and pleasurable act that distinguishes Milton. Moreover, he develops this by denying fallen angels the pleasure of sexual intercourse (as Satan laments; 4. 508–11), whereas in demono-logical and witchcraft writings it is the devils who have the active sex lives.[20] Sexual intercourse is intrinsically good. Angels interpenetrate 'union of pure with pure | Desiring' (8. 627–8); they feel desire, and what they desire is union with another pure being. The unstated antithesis here is the union of the sons of God with the daughters of men in Genesis 6: 1–4.[21] This interpretation is not endorsed in *Paradise Lost*, where Milton prefers the dominant alternative explan-ation in which the sons of God are descendants of the line of Seth, and the daughters of men are the descendants of Cain (11. 573–87,

621–2); it does find a place in *Paradise Regained*, however, where Satan reminds Belial:

> Before the flood thou with thy lusty crew,
> False titled Sons of God, roaming the earth
> Cast wanton eyes on the daughters of men,
> And coupled with them, and begot a race.[22]

Interspecies desire was associated with fallen angels, and sometimes with the fall of the angels itself.[23] *Paradise Lost* recovers this realm of creaturely experience for pure angels.

Matthew 22: 30 states: 'in the resurrection they neither marry, nor are given in marriage, but are as the angels of God in heaven'. Robert Bolton asserts that in heaven humans would be like angels and therefore free from 'want of marriage'. This implies not the satisfaction of all desires, nor a Neoplatonic pairing of souls, but an emancipation from longing and sexual difference, another distinction between angels and humans.[24] Interest in the gendering of angelic apparitions—in contrast to their natural sexlessness—might have derived from concern with this boundary.[25] Some commentators, however, explored the idea of angelic desire and procreation further. Richard Brathwaite describes the Albigensian heresy (*c.*1200), that Adam and Eve in innocence were unmarried and undifferentiated in sex, and that if they had continued so, 'mankind should have increased as Angells doe'.[26] Alessandro Piccolomini compares the desire for conjunction, penetration, and perfect union between lovers with the perfect union of celestial spirits.[27] Whereas sexual intercourse between humans and fallen angels was a form of metaphysical evidence—demonstrating the reality of the spiritual world—Milton's account of angelic lovemaking is at once an indicator of their material nature, but also proof that all rational beings, with the exception of God, experience community and desire as a principle of their being. Not only is lovemaking pure—as the narrator of *Paradise Lost* is at pains to declare in book 4's account of prelapsarian human intercourse—lovemaking can be driven by an appetite for union with another pure being. Purity, far from being based on abstention, separation, and order,[28] can be, at least in the angelic world, the basis for desire and intermingling and pleasure. Milton's implicit reading of Matthew 22: 30 finds heaven promising not the absence of desire and pleasure but pure promiscuity.

## Wind, Fire, and Light: The Bodies of Angels

Though these are the *loci classici* for discussions of Milton's angels, as if he was only earnest in his representations when being evidently unorthodox, there are other themes that suggest intense concern with the creatureliness of angels. One, closely related to sex, is the bodies and matter of angels. There was in early modern Britain a spectrum of beliefs about the corporeal and material nature of angels, and about the relationship between body and matter. As Henry More wrote in *An Explanation of the Grand Mystery of Godliness* (1660), 'Concerning *Angels*, some affirm them to be *Fiery* or *Aery Bodies*; some *pure* Spirits; some Spirits in Aery or Fiery Bodies; Others none of these, but that they are *momentaneous Emanations* from God; Others that they are *onely Divine Imaginations* in men.'[29]

The Thomist position is that angels are incorporeal and non-material. Angels do not have bodies, though they sometimes adopt bodies of air to appear before humans. These bodies are not manipulated by quasi-material mechanism but by divine power. Angels are not material. However, Aquinas' account of substances means that they are possessed of an unintelligible, purely intellectual substance: 'The angelic substances, on the other hand, are of a higher order than our minds; we cannot therefore apprehend them as they are in themselves, but only according to the way in which we apprehend realities composed of form and matter.'[30] This is also the understanding of Thomas Heywood and William Austin, though the latter also sketches another doctrine, popular in the early seventeenth century, that 'they have a most-*fine-thin-Substance* (like that, which the *Philosophers* call *Æthereum animæ vehiculum*; which *joynes* it to the *Body*). And, that they have a *forme* above *all Creatures*: but, *what* it is; *Ignoramus.*'[31] This fine, aetherial substance was devised to explain the material agency of spirits in the world—for those who were disinclined to appeal to the continuous action of divine power of the special providential intervention of God—and it received its fullest development in a British context by the Cambridge Platonists. It is an uneasy form of dualism, one that rejects a straightforward matter–spirit dichotomy in favour of a spiritualized form of matter. However, Henry More and Ralph Cudworth, the two authors who wrote most extensively on the subject of spirits, were opposed to the mechanism of Thomas Hobbes, and sometimes seem closer to Aquinas' dualist theory of material and immaterial substances than to monism or animism.[32] A similarly ambiguous corporealism, firmly grounded in dualism, is advocated by Henry Woolnor in a 1641 treatise attacking mortalism: 'though soules are of a simple spirituall substance, as are Angels in respect of elementary; yet even Angels themselves and much more mens soules, are not without a spirituall kinde of composition. For to be simply simple, is proper only to the nature of God.' He adds: 'all created spirits, being compounded of act and potency, have a kinde of similitude with corporall natures, both in regard of matter and forme; yea, even Angels themselves'.[33] John Trapp's account of the corporeality of heaven, impenetrable even by angels (except by miracle), suggests a similar, tenuous corporeality.[34]

Others suggest that angels are corporeal and substantial, a position that seems less complex and ambiguous. This is Hobbes's position, grounded in materialist and mechanist philosophy. In *Leviathan* (1651) Hobbes seeks to elaborate, on the basis of reason, a comprehensive and inclusive description and justification of absolutist sovereignty. His system relies on the exclusion of alternative authorities, such as religious inspiration and prophecy, which he associates with both fairies and linguistic nonsense, so the notion of angels as spiritual beings that appear to humans represents a challenge both to his politics and to his theory of matter. He dismisses spirits as 'Idols of the brain', and argues that even 'real, and substantial' apparitions were 'subtile Bodies' formed supernaturally by God and described as 'angels' because they were in a sense messengers. They were not spiritual beings. In the Old Testament 'Angels were nothing but supernaturall apparitions of the Fancy, raised by the speciall and extraordinary operation of God.' He concedes that in the New Testament there is evidence 'that there be also Angels substantiall, and permanent'.[35] His language indicates extreme reluctance, as if this is a weakness in God's design, and he is emphatic that such spirits must also be corporeal.

This puts Hobbes in some odd company. Robert Fludd writes that angels have fully corporeal, albeit aerial bodies.[36] Jacob Boehme's mysticism blurs categories like (in)corporeal, but he writes about angels as visible and substantial, as if material: 'Paradise consisteth in the power [and vertue] of God: it is not corporeall, nor comprehensible; but its corporeity or comprehensibility is like the Angels, which yet is a bright, cleere, visible substance, as if it were materiall; but it is figured meerely from the vertue [or power] where all is transparent and shining.' In their first creation angels were hidden, but in their second creation they 'were bodified'.[37] Boehme girds his system by speaking of similitudes and analogies, but his angels are certainly corporeal and probably substantial; as the writings of his disciple Pordage show, the cautious use of language conflicts with the material, sensuous reality of the experiences described.

A third conceivable position is that angels are corporeal and insubstantial, though no early modern writer seems to have advocated this, unless one considers the tenuous corporeality of the Cambridge Platonists, Woolnor, and Trapp a sufficient approximation. Boehme gestures in this direction, as does Robert Gell with significant qualification: he writes that angels 'hath a subsistence without the grosse elements', and that, like man, who consists of three parts (spirit, soul, and body), angels 'have something analogical to a body, and that's wind . . . Somewhat proportionable to the soul, and that's fire . . . Somewhat answerable to the to the spirit, and that's light'.[38] Gell is a traditionalist dualist metaphorically attributing corporeality as a way of enhancing the metaphoric range of angels, and because even a figurative body makes the actions of spirits easier to comprehend.

Finally, there is a strange position that is distinct from the Cambridge Platonists and Aquinas in its thoroughgoing monism, and distinct from Hobbes in rejecting any simple notion of corporeality. This is Milton's position: angels are substantial and material, but, unlike humans, their matter is highly spiritual and therefore they are not corporeal. Milton uses angels to explore the nature of matter. His position can briefly be summarized as follows. Milton was, like Hobbes, a materialist; in contrast to Hobbes, he rejected mechanism in favour of the view that matter is animate and therefore free. Creation was *ex deo*, and therefore all matter is in origin good; evil is a perversion of matter, and is thus a privation of being. Matter and spirit exist on a continuous scale, from the incorporeal to the merely corporeal. This scale permits movement, and beings can ascend and descend it through continuing obedience to God, refining the very corporeality of their being.[39] The most penetrating imagining of this in *Paradise Lost* is in Raphael's explanation to Adam of why angels can eat with men:

> O Adam, one almighty is, from whom
> All things proceed, and up to him return,
> If not depraved from good, created all

Such to perfection, one first matter all,
Indued with various forms, various degrees
Of substance, and in things that live, of life;
But more refined, more spirituous, and pure,
As nearer to him placed or nearer tending
Each in their several active spheres assigned,
Till body up to spirit work, in bounds
Proportioned to each kind.                              (5. 469–79)

Though in heaven he eats the food of angels, Raphael can digest
human nourishment, converting it, he says, 'To proper substance',
discreetly leaving ambiguous whether 'proper' means 'suitable
for angels' or 'superior in substance to paradisal vegetation'. He
continues:

time may come when men
With angels may participate, and find
No inconvenient diet, nor too light fare:
And from these corporal nutriments perhaps
Your bodies may at last turn all to spirit,
Improved by tract of time, and winged ascend
Ethereal, as we, or may at choice
Here or in heavenly paradises dwell;
If ye be found obedient, and retain
Unalterably firm his love entire
Whose progeny you are.                                  (5. 493–503)

Milton's metaphor for understanding the gradual transitions of matter
and the move to and from gross and tenuous corporeality is digestion.[40]
The angel explains the relative places of angel and man on this scale in
order to justify his own eating, but it is, elegantly, also a governing
trope in the poem, meaningfully framing the human act of illicit
consumption that violates order and human freedom. This, the most
striking statement of Milton's monist natural philosophy in the epic, is
also one of the most informative and poetically memorable passages
about angels, and one in which the communicative nature of Milton's
universe is symbolized. They are eating together in order to talk.
Matter, the Fall, and conversation are all linked through digestion.
This is testimony to the importance of natural philosophy in the poem.
Angels explore matter by explaining and embodying its properties.
Their agency, their speech and hearing, their movement, are 'proof'
for Milton's metaphysics. What Raphael tells Adam about Creation

must be in some sense true, and is a means of engaging with natural philosophy. It is why angels fight a war, why they eat, why they make love. However, it is not only natural philosophy, it is self-evidently theology, and also politics (as the politics of angels, sex, and the Fall were inescapable in the 1650s).[41]

According to Milton, corporeality and incorporeality are extremes of a hierarchy, one that permits movement through a process analogous to digestion, and so a material being need not be corporeal.[42] This is an unusual notion, though Descartes similarly accepted the existence of incorporeal substances.[43] It is a difficult position to sustain: if corporeality and incorporeality are extremes on a spectrum, then there must be forms between that possess elements of both and thus hold properties that we do not have language adequate to describe. Moreover, as theologians since John of Damascus commonly observed, the most extreme form of incorporeality must be God, not an angel. 'They hang between the nature of God, and the nature of man, and are of a middle condition,' wrote Donne; 'to be simply simple, is proper only to the nature of God', wrote Henry Woolnor. Hence, angels must possess some degree of what God is not.[44] It is also a difficult position to adumbrate in a narrative poem (a poem less static and didactic than Heywood's *Hierarchie*) for some of the reasons that Johnson and Eliot identified. The angels of *Paradise Lost* can be seen as 'tenuously corporeal'.[45] Though Milton imagines them as 'pure | Intelligential substances' (5. 407–8), there are passages where they seem to have an essential, if infinitely malleable, physical shape. Even describing the voluntary assumption of shapes by spirits, the narrator suggests some anterior form:

> spirits when they please
> Can either sex assume, or both; so soft
> And uncompounded is their essence pure . . .          (1. 423–5)

The 'when' implies limitations: at rest they have a shape, and when imprisoned by the will of God, as when the fallen angels are turned into serpents:

> supplanted down he fell
> A monstrous serpent on his belly prone,
> Reluctant, but in vain, a greater power
> Now ruled him, punished in the shape he sinned . . .

(10. 513–16)

God pronounces Satan 'vitiated in nature', and his being is thus impaired (10. 169; cf. 6. 691). Henry More agreed with the effect upon the substance of the fallen angels ('*this Rebellion . . . changed their pure Æthereal Bodies into more Feculent and Terrestrial*'), but Milton extends this effect to the malleability of substance.[46] As serpents they remain until they are permitted to resume 'their lost shape' (10. 574). When the fallen angels shrink themselves to enter Pandaemonium at the end of book 1, it is a sign of their debasement:

> they who now seemed
> In bigness to surpass Earth's giant sons
> Now less than smallest dwarfs, in narrow room
> Throng numberless . . .
>                  .         .         .
> Thus incorporeal spirits to smallest forms
> Reduced their shapes immense . . .                    (1. 777–90)

The devils retain their 'shapes' while diminishing their proportions. Ironically their sense of rank is intensified at this point, as the 'great seraphic lords and cherubim' are distinguished from the lesser devils by sitting deeper within the building and 'in their own dimensions like themselves' (1. 793–4). As the commoners diminish themselves in an evil cause, their natural leaders (nature having been perverted and inverted) assert usurped authority by retaining their full size. This assertion of an unjust hierarchy through physical domination—and the visual effect is comic—is a greater transgression against nature than self-compression.

   Travelling to earth, Satan is a shape-shifter. His cherubic appearance is distinguished from 'his proper shape' (3. 634), and in Eden he assumes the shape of a cormorant, a lion, and a tiger (4. 196, 402–3) before he is discovered by an angel guard 'Squat like a toad, close at the ear of Eve' (4. 800). The disguise is transformed when Ithuriel touches the toad with a spear, provoking a reaction that is both symbolic and chemical:

> no falsehood can endure
> Touch of celestial temper, but returns
> Of force to its own likeness: up he starts . . .       (4. 811–13)

And finds himself 'in his own shape' (4. 819). The nature of an angel's shape is not a question most theologians address. To espouse a dualist philosophy, and therefore to believe that angels are purely spiritual

beings, is to believe that angels only adopt bodies or shapes, and
therefore that the limitations and symbolic significance of these bodies
is a matter of volition.[47] Bodies and shapes are more significant for
occult writers like Boehme, Fludd, Pordage, for whom an angel's shape
is not only a matter of symbolism. Milton joins with them in this. Even
his unfallen angels have shapes. After identifying Eden with his tele-
scopic eyesight, Raphael flies there, apparently in the shape of a bird:

> He lights, and to his proper shape returns
> A seraph winged; six wings he wore, to shade
> His lineaments divine . . .                                    (5. 276–8)

A description of the wings follows, as sensuous as it is symbolic; these
are real wings, which shed fragrance when shaken. He 'wears' the
wings, in the sense that he is free to choose other limbs, but this is his
'proper shape', drawing on Isaiah 6: 2. One difference is striking. In
Isaiah the first pair of wings covers the seraphim's face; here the first
pair 'clad | Each shoulder broad' and 'came mantling o'er his breast |
With regal ornament' (5. 278–80). Raphael's face is exposed, and the
'lineaments divine' that his wings conceal are the rest of his being. This
makes conversation easier, but it also emphasizes the divinity of the
form, the 'proper shape' of an angel.

Milton's angels do not have bodies, but they do have proper shapes.
Their incorporeality is tenuous or tentative; they do, after all, wear
armour, and must choose a shape for that armour, and this ultimately
impedes as well as protects them. The good angels struck by Satan's
gunpowder fall trapped in their armour:

> unarmed they might
> Have easily as spirits evaded swift
> By quick contraction or remove.                               (6. 595–7)

The unfallen angels respond by throwing heaven's hills at the rebels:

> Their armour helped their harm, crushed in and bruised
> Into their substance pent, which wrought them pain
>
>                    .        .        .
>
>                              ere they could wind
> Out of such prison, though spirits of purest light,
> Purest at first, now gross by sinning grown.                  (6. 656–61)

The purest, intelligential substances are equally trapped in their
armour, though they have not begun to slide from incorporeality to

corporeality (unlike the fallen angels they feel no pain but only shame). To have a shape—which pure, intelligential substances do—is to possess some of the properties associated with having a body. To have a shape is glorious and divine, yet it is also a potential weakness, especially when incorporeality begins to decline into corporeality (downward movement on the sliding scales in Milton's universe is always more troubling, more damaging and corrupt, than stasis on a lower part of the scale). It is an essential part of being a creature, as even the most spiritual substances are made of prime matter. *De Doctrina*, discussing the nature of angelic senses, similarly intimates angelic shapes: spirit contains inferior substance as the spiritual and rational faculty contains the corporeal.[48] Bodies emanate from spirit, and the shape that a spiritual being has is not only a manifestation of its identity: it is the potential it has to turn corporeal. As corporeal beings can be sublimated into intelligential by a process of digestion, so incorporeal beings can decline into corporeality through corruption and impairment by sin. The body will be implicit in the shape, and suffer a loss of beauty through the diminution of brightness and loss of lustre, as Satan unhappily discovers when Ithuriel fails to recognize him even when he returns to his 'own likeness' (4. 836, 850).

## 'As Far as Angels' Ken': Angelic Optics

When Satan awakes lying prone on the burning lake at the beginning of book 1, his eyes emit light and feeling perceptible to his companion Beelzebub, despite the visible darkness: the narrator refers to his 'eye | That sparkling blazed' (1. 193–4). The description is based on an extromissive theory of vision in which eyes emit rays that are reflected by objects and return to the eye.[49] The dominant alternative model in the early modern period was intromissive, arguing that the eye saw by apprehending light that was reflected from objects. In either case light could be understood as particles or as waves, alternatives advocated by Pierre Gassendi and Robert Hooke, respectively, in books published in the 1660s. Questions of optics appear tangentially and repeatedly in book 1, in which a series of extended similes that play with proportion and perspectives are attached to the fallen angels. One alludes to Galileo viewing the moon through a telescope, the only living person, other than Milton, identified in *Paradise Lost* (1. 287–91). These figures of scale and optics warn the reader of the profoundly visual properties of the epic, the role of perspective, and the dangers involved in interpreting Satan.

Satan's very first action in the poem, the first active verb that marks the transition from the past experience of falling from heaven, and the passive experience of being tormented by thoughts, is to look around:

> round he throws his baleful eyes
> That witnessed huge affliction and dismay
> Mixed with obdurate pride and steadfast hate:
> At once as far as angels' ken he views
> The dismal situation waste and wild . . . [50]

The reference to angelic optics performs a number of tasks: it indicates that the fallen angel's faculties have not (yet) deteriorated; it indicates that angels have a finite field of vision; and it raises interpretative questions, including how far and by what means angels see. These are issues that the narrative poet encounters out of necessity, but they also arise for theologians and philosophers. For the former, angelic optics is a conventional motif in considerations of the nature and offices of angels; for the latter, angelic optics is a useful simile for describing the efficacy of lenses.

For Aquinas, senses are a property of bodies, unlike the 'faculties' of spirits. Though his account of angels is profoundly concerned with their creaturely properties, he therefore does not dwell on angelic eyesight.[51] Some later commentators say that angels both see and know from God. God is a kind of lens or mirror—lenses and mirrors were commonly conflated in discussions and rumours of instrumentation at this time[52]—through which angels see all of nature. Dante describes this in the *Paradiso*:

> Queste sustanze, poi che fur gioconde
>     della faccia di Dio, non volser viso
>     da essa, da cui nulla si nasconde:
> però non hanno vedere interciso
>     da novo obietto, e però non bisogna
>     rememorar per concetto diviso . . . [53]

(These beings, since they were made glad with God's face from which nothing is hid, have never turned their eyes from it, so that their sight is never intercepted by a new object and they have no need to recall the past by an abstract concept . . . )

John Dee's angels see by similar means.[54] God limits angelic eyesight by concealing the interior life of humans, and certain mysteries of nature. Joseph Hall described this eloquently:

so perfectly knowing are they, as that the very heathen Philosophers have styled them by the name of *Intelligences*, as if their very being were made up of understanding; Indeed what is there in this whole compass of the large universe, that is hid from their eyes? Only the closet of mans heart is lockt up from them, as reserved solely to their maker.

He develops this further, suggesting that angels do not 'look through the dim and horny spectacles of senses, or understand by the mediation of phantasms: but rather, as clear mirrours, they receive at once the full representations of all intelligible things; having besides that connaturall light, which is universally in them all, certain speciall illuminations from the Father of lights'.[55] Hall opposes the mirror to the lens, perhaps juxtaposing an extromissive against an intromissive theory of vision, though also stressing the superiority of angelic cognition to human sensory perception (even with the best of lenses, human insight would be inferior). The imagery is indebted to Pseudo-Dionysius, who describes angels as 'clear and spotless mirrors'.[56] This view is adopted by Robert Gell and perhaps also by Milton's friend Henry Vane, who describes angels as 'flames of fire, consuming and dissolving all objects of outward sense', who receive light from Christ and are therefore 'high and vast' in their 'natural capacities'.[57]

Some dismiss this first account, associating it with Scholasticism and Jesuitism, and provide a second explanation of their optics, in which angels have powerful sight through their own faculties, though the mechanics of this perception is different from human eyesight.[58] Comenius writes that angelic knowledge is more sublime than human because nothing obscures angels' understanding and they can 'penetrate any whither, and see things plainly'. He adds that they are 'not omniscious', but are 'a thousand times more quick sighted upon us' and thus can infer the thoughts of men even while they cannot see them.[59] This penetrative capacity of angelic perception implies a difference not only in degree but in kind. Nevertheless, we can understand this perception as being something like human perception, and Comenius' project is to reform natural philosophy through sacred knowledge, and to understand man's nature better by comparison with an understanding of the nature of angels: 'Although ... they perceive without Organs, yet we must needs hold that they are not unlike to our spirit which perceiveth by organs.'[60] John White, the Dorchester clergyman, similarly restricts angelic perception and repudiates the divine lens or mirror theory: he writes that when angels accept an earthly ministry and leave heaven, it is a form of condescension that deprives them of 'the Vision of God'.[61] Angelic eyesight is imperfect, though less imperfect than in *Paradise Lost*, in which Abdiel cannot see across heaven. This account of vision supposes that angels' sight is, like humans', finite, but that it does not depend on conventional optics. Angels can see through objects if not into human thoughts.[62] Their perception depends upon their own faculties, and is immeasurably more powerful than human sight.

A third account of suprahuman vision suggests that it conforms to conventional optics, as an enhanced version of human perception. This is found in the writings of natural philosophers promoting experimental knowledge. Robert Hooke's *Micrographia* (1665) stresses the limitations of human knowledge based on narrow senses, and it seeks to establish a more solid knowledge based on observation supported by 'the adding of *artificial Organs* to the natural'. Optical lenses, among those who understood clearly the differences between lenses and mirrors, are imagined as the means to a new 'Science of Nature' grounded on sound observation:

By the means of *Telescopes*, there is nothing so *far distant* but may be represented to our view; and by the help of *Microscopes*, there is nothing so *small*, as to escape our inquiry; hence there is a new visible World discovered to the understanding. By this means the Heavens are open'd, and a vast number of new Stars, and new Motions, and new productions appear in them, to which all the antient Astronomers were utterly Strangers.

Hooke also imagines that other devices will improve other senses, but it is enhanced eyesight that will revolutionize knowledge. Prosthesis will bring man closer to perfection: 'And who knows but the Industry of man, following this method, may find out wayes of improving this sense to as great a degree of perfection as it is in any Animal, and perhaps yet higher.'[63] The comparison to a sense more powerful than any animal's may imply an angel, just as the tongue of angels suggests ideal speech, and angelic knowledge, superior understanding.[64] Sight, moreover, has a special status among the senses: it is the telescope that provides the basis for modelling the universe and conceiving of space, the place where angels travel and which they shape with their interventions.

In Roman Catholic Europe natural philosophers similarly deployed angels in their writings, initially within explanations of agency and causation, and later as rhetorical flourish. This demotion can be seen in the career of Galileo, where it must be understood as belonging to communicative strategy rather than disenchantment. Athanasius Kircher writes that 'A perfect observation, free from all error and falsehood could only be carried out by an angel,' which confers authority on instruments as much as it recognizes human inferiority. Angels authorized telescopes and certified their capacity for perfection, and thus their ability to extend the human. In Britain, perhaps because of suspicion of Jesuit interest in angels, this role was performed by both angels and Adam.[65] Hooke's acquaintance Joseph Glanvill, another early member of the Royal Society, uses the power of the telescope to imagine ideal human senses. In *The Vanity of Dogmatizing* (1661) he considers the power of prelapsarian Adam's eyes, regarding his deductions as a form of experimental knowledge. Adam would have received 'better information from the most distant objects, than we by the most helpful *Telescopes*'. The prosthetic enhancement of the senses provides the most useful and vivid point of comparison. Because of the natural sensitivity of his eyes, '*Adam* needed no Spectacles. The acuteness of his natural Opticks (if conjecture may have credit) shew'd him much of the Cœlestial magnificence and bravery without a *Galilæo*'s tube: And 'tis most probable that his naked eyes could reach as much of the upper World, as we with all the advantages of art.'[66] Glanvill's account of the protoplasts aligns him with Hooke on two points: first, that inferences about the idealized faculties of spirits can be considered as a form of experimental knowledge (Henry More says this in 1681, and elsewhere writes of angels' 'terrestrial Omnipercipiency'[67]); secondly, that ideal senses can be imagined and described most effectively not through spiritual metaphors but through analogies with instruments. By implication, even the most powerful senses operate through conventional optics. Distance, which does not affect the first two accounts of angelic perception, is a consideration in this third model.

How far do Milton's angels see, and by what means? Milton's angels have superior eyesight, though it follows some of the same restrictions of human vision. Waking on the burning lake, Satan sees 'as far as angels' ken' (1. 59), and travelling through Limbo 'far distant he

descries' the allegorical Jacob's Ladder (3. 501), reminding us of the
limits of his vision. Seeking earth, he lands on the sun, and the poet
describes perspective through the geometry of light:

> Here matter new to gaze the devil met
> Undazzled, far and wide his eye commands,
> For sight no obstacle found here, nor shade,
> But all sunshine, as when his beams at noon
> Culminate from the equator, as they now
> Shoot upward still direct, whence no way round
> Shadow from body opaque can fall, and the air,
> Nowhere so clear, sharpened his visual ray
> To objects distant far, whereby he soon
> Saw within ken a glorious angel stand . . .            (3. 613–22)

Again the emphasis is on the limits of angelic eyesight, and again the
poet refers to angels' ken; but Milton carefully imbricates this descrip-
tion with an explanation of the movement of light and the making of
shadows. Satan's 'visual ray' also suggests the extromission of rays from
the eye to the perceived object, recalling his 'sparkling' eyes in book 1.
   Eyesight and optics are not peripheral issues in this passage. The
angel that Satan sees is Uriel, 'regent of the sun' (3. 690), one of
the seven angels of God's presence, the first unfallen angel presented
in the poem, who, because of his association with light, is 'held | The
sharpest sighted spirit of all in heaven' (3. 690–1). Satan approaches
him disguised as a cherub, and his deception is

> unperceived;
> For neither man nor angel can discern
> Hypocrisy, the only evil that walks
> Invisible, except to God alone . . .            (3. 681–4)

Uriel cannot see through the disguise because he sees by conventional
optical means. Their conversation emphasizes earth's obscure remote-
ness from heaven. Uriel praises the cherub for making the effort 'To
witness with thine eyes what some perhaps | Contented with report
hear only in heaven' (3. 700–1). Some angels know earth only through
the inferior sense of hearing, and, indirectly, the inferior medium of
news. This is a more material universe than others imagined: it is hard
to see the earth. Standing at the gates of heaven, Raphael can see the
earth only because the weather is good. After Uriel has sent Satan
earthwards (locating it with a description that combines perspective

with the mechanics of the solar system; 3. 722–33), he sees that he has been deceived when Satan's emotions 'marred his borrowed visage' (4. 116). Uriel does not penetrate the disguise; the disguise is ruptured, and Uriel, at an enormous distance, interprets the visual evidence. His vision is at once powerful and limited, and its failure is central to the poem's narrative: it enables Satan's invasion of Eden, his corrupting of Eve's dream, and Gabriel's interruption of Satan, and it is why Raphael descends to Eden to warn Adam and Eve, and to describe the war in heaven.

Angelic optics are integral to the adumbration of Milton's plot. Perhaps as important is the way the emphasis on light and perspectives shapes the aesthetic architecture of the poem. We follow characters' movement and points of view, and the effect is cinematographic. The organization of Milton's universe is conceptual, symbolic, and hierarchical, but the primary mode in which his narrative is organized is visual, and this visual dimension is organized along perspectival lines. Sometimes the narrator draws attention to a perspectival device ('he then surveyed'[68]), but the device permeates the narrative and imagery of the poem more generally. Angelic sight is, in this account, a matter of experience. Whereas Aquinas' angels know purely intuitively (God creates all knowledge in them), Milton's have a full range of senses (senses that are part of their whole being rather than particular organs). Their knowledge increases through the use of these senses, and hence is both experimental and finite. In this respect Milton is aligned with Hooke, Glanvill, and More.

Milton prevaricates between heliocentric and geocentric models of the universe, models that did not at his time seem straightforwardly antithetical.[69] Evoking the dislocation of the stable and orderly orbit of the sun at the Fall, a catastrophic vision of the effect of the Fall that suggests why prelapsarian cosmology cannot be comprehended by postlapsarian humans, Milton imagines two possible explanations that preserve the geocentric model while elucidating the seasons and other imperfections of the postlapsarian universe. One of them involves the action of angels:

> Some say he bid his angels turn askance
> The poles of earth twice ten degrees and more
> From the sun's axle; they with labour pushed
> Oblique the centric globe: some say the sun
> Was bid turn reins from the equinoctial road . . .          (10. 668–72)

The intervention of angels is only a fancy, albeit one consonant with the belief that angels govern the spheres and their harmonies (the model magnificently detailed in Dante's *Paradiso*, canto 28), though the poet is careful to note the 'labour' that this involves, in contrast to the effortlessness of Creation. Others had, of course, doubted that humans could understand without direct revelation whether the spheres were moved with angels, and whether heavenly bodies moved 'by Excentricks and Epicycles: or onely by Concentricks: or the Earths motion: or the motion of the Starres in the heavens'.[70] The structures of Milton's universe are irresolvable, and that is Raphael's point: elaborate geometry ('centric and eccentric scribbled o'er') is invoked in order 'To save appearances' because the means by which we know are imperfect (8. 79–84). The weakness of human calculations is that increasingly complex qualifications are required to assimilate new observations to existing models of explanation, in order to preserve both the apparent universe and formerly understood truths.[71] The poet does not scorn the efforts of astronomers to understand the universe. When Satan lands on the sun, Milton imagines that this creates a sunspot, a symbol of moral corruption but one with a material cause:

> There lands the fiend, a spot like which perhaps
> Astronomer in the sun's lucent orb
> Through his glazed optic tube yet never saw.          (3. 588–90)

This '*in* the sun' is powerful. The narrator's speculations make a different claim upon truth than an astrological treatise would, but Milton found the explanation of a sunspot as a surface imperfection on the sun stimulating. This was Galileo's explanation, and it showed that the sun was rotating, and was thus an important proof of the heliocentric universe. Jesuits, by contrast, proposed that sunspots were caused by moons or other impediments at a distance from the surface. This Satanic sunspot is presumably unlike those yet seen by the astronomer on account of its size (though perhaps Milton was aware that sunspots had become rare in recent years—since 1645—in which case Galileo's observations may have had a special status, despite improvements in telescope technology).[72]

Astronomy also furnishes a powerful simile to comprehend the vertiginous description of Raphael's perspective of earth from heaven:

> From hence, no cloud, or, to obstruct his sight,
> Star interposed, however small he sees,
> Not unconform to other shining globes.
> Earth and the garden of God, with cedars crowned
> Above all hills. As when by night the glass
> Of Galileo, less assured, observes
> Imagined lands and regions in the moon . . .          (5. 257–63)[73]

Raphael sees his destination because there are no obstacles. He sees the cedars on the hills because he sees by natural means. This is the combination of enormous distances and minute detail that Hooke and Glanvill dream of in their account of the enhanced human senses that will bring sound experimental knowledge. Galileo's perception of the moon, and his inferences about its geography, are less reliable, perhaps because he is human and hence more fallible, perhaps because his sense is artificially enhanced by prosthesis, perhaps because God is the better lens-maker. The telescope is Milton's comparison for the superiority of angelic eyesight, and it follows from the essential similarity in mode between angelic and human optics. This way of seeing accords with Milton's unusual account of dawn and twilight in heaven (5. 628, 645–6, 667); and it explains why Abdiel, stranded with his enemies in the northern parts of heaven, cannot see his friends or God until he flies through 'heaven's wide champaign' towards them, and morning brings light to illuminate the unfallen legions.

## Sensing without Organs

Angels have other senses, at least according to Milton. Aquinas did not think so. Whereas humans knew through both the senses and the intellect, according to Aquinas, angels were wholly intellectual. While the senses were employed to apprehend only the outward properties of an object, the intelligence apprehends the essence of the object:

If an angel had to derive his knowledge of material things from these things themselves, he would have first to render them actually intelligible by a process of abstraction. But it is not thus that he knows such things; he knows them by possessing, as part of his nature, intellectual representations of things—representations actually intelligible from the start; as our mind knows them by the representations which it renders intelligible by a process of abstraction.[74]

Angelic knowledge is complete: angels cannot learn by experience, and the angelic intellect is a repository for the essences of almost all Creation (constituting a second Creation).[75] Less Scholastic accounts of angels attribute to them other forms of knowledge. The *Institutions* of William Bucanus, for example, distinguished between three sources of angelic knowledge: natural, instilled in them by God; supernatural, whereby they see and know God and are moved to virtue by this knowledge; and, thirdly, 'experimentall knowledge, which is obtained by experience, and by observation of those things which we do here'.[76] Fallen and unfallen angels were assumed, in the sixteenth and seventeenth centuries, to be able to learn; Satan was attributed skill as a natural philosopher on account of his 'experimentall knowledge'.[77] Accounts of angelic learning firmly emphasized sight, the least bodily of the senses. An exception is Comenius, who insists upon a mode of sensory perception independent of corporeality:

There is in Angels a sense of things, as well as in our spirits. (For they see, hear, touch, &c. though they themselves be invisible, and intangible.[)] Also they have a sense of pleasure and griefe: for as much as joyes are said to be prepared for the Angels, and fire for the divells, (into which wicked men are also to be cast.) Although therefore they perceive without Organs, yet we must needs hold that they are not unlike to our spirit which perceiveth by organs.[78]

The coy '&c.' implies without stating both smelling and tasting, which are more closely linked to particular organs (touch can imply movement without specifically indicating the tactility of skin). Comenius glosses over the complex relations among organs and therefore bodies and senses, though he acknowledges a connection between organs and emotions. This association troubled Thomas Heywood, who contends that if angels have bodies and organs then they must have senses and therefore passions and thus alteration: this is not possible in a perfect, immutable being, and therefore angels cannot have any of these.[79]

Milton attributes organs, senses, and emotions to angels. Satan's passions reflect his corrupted state. The unfallen angels feel joy, and this is another commonplace, deriving from Job 38: 7 ('When the morning stars sang together, and all the Sons of God shouted for joy?'). Some commentators interpret this strongly. Duppa makes an angel's capacity for joy depend on its ability to perceive a sinner's conversion 'not onely by outward signes, but sometimes by discovery of our hearts too'. The proof is: 'There is knowledge, or else there would be *no joy*

in the presence of the Angels.'[80] Milton goes beyond joy: Raphael
seems to blush with pleasure when he describes angelic intercourse to
Adam (8. 618–19); he frowns at Adam's perceived misconceptions
(8. 560) as Michael frowns with an 'inflamed' face at Satan (6. 260–1).
Gabriel expresses disdain for Satan (4. 903); God and his Son laugh
with scorn and derision at their enemies. The narrator also mentions
the organs of angels, eyes, knees, ears, tongues, wings, and scars.
Because his angels are substantial without being corporeal, they assume
organs suited to their actions, though they also possess a natural,
normative shape to which they return as a matter of habit. Among
the purposes to which organs and body parts are suited is sensory
perception, hence, as Raphael explains to Adam, 'All heart they live,
all head, all eye, all ear' (6. 350). Angels sing, they converse with each
other and with humans, they taste ambrosial nectar, and interpenetrate
with pleasure. Although Uriel does not see through Satan's disguise,
he hears his approach with his back turned, 'admonished by his ear'
(3. 647). Raphael explains to Adam that 'Intelligential substances',
meaning angels, as distinct from the rational substance of humans,

> contain
> Within them every lower faculty
> Of sense, whereby they hear, see, smell, touch, taste.
>
> (5. 408–11)

Explaining 'Spirit' in *De Doctrina Christiana*, where spirit is the uni-
versal substance, expelled from God, out of which body is created,
Milton writes: 'spirit, being the more excellent substance, virtually, as
they say, and eminently contains within itself what is clearly the
inferior substance; in the same way as the spiritual and rational faculty
contains the corporeal, that is, the sentient and vegetative faculty'.[81]
Milton makes the same point here as in Raphael's speech in *Paradise
Lost*, and the passage explicates the material nature of Milton's angels.[82]
Angels sense with their whole being.

## 'Knowne to be of Strange Velocitie': The Speed of Angels

When Satan disguises himself, he chooses a 'habit fit for speed succinct'
(3. 643). He is concerned about aerodynamics. Having a body, or

being composed of matter, brings limitations upon movement and
speed. In 1672 George Hughes, in his *Analytic Exposition of . . . Genesis*,
warned that conjectures about how Abraham's angels travelled so fast
were vain.[83] Yet this was a tardy intervention which more closely
resembled the reservations of late seventeenth-century natural philo-
sophers than generations of theologians. Aquinas argued that although
angels had no bodies, they moved through space, and that movement
was not instantaneous. Angels moved in time, though that time and
their movement could be discontinuous. 'But notice that this angelic
time—whether continuous or not—is not the same as the time which
measures the motions of the heavens and of all the corporeal things
whose changes depend on that motion. For the angel's movement is
independent of the heavens.'[84] This means that the speed of an angel
does not depend on physical force so much as 'a decision of his will',
and that an angel is able to will to move through discontinuous time
and therefore 'he can be now here and now there, with no time-
interval between'.[85] This distinction is a technicality, then: to humans
an angel's speed seems fantastically swift because the angel passes
between two points without any time lapse, but this is only because
the angel has moved from being in one place at one moment, to
another at the next moment, without actually passing through the
space between. It is not instantaneous only because instantaneousness
is a property of continuous time. With these complications, Aquinas
maintains that angels move at a finite speed, though they are very fast.[86]

   Most sixteenth- and seventeenth-century writers follow Aquinas.
John Salkeld writes that 'Angels may in some sort be sayd to be in
[a specific] place,' and when Origen and Tertullian say that angels are
everywhere (*'Angelum esse ubique'*) they mean 'that Angels have such
swift motion, that they can be in almost an unimaginable short space of
time in any place'.[87] Bucanus writes that angels are 'finite spirits,
though not circumscribed, because they are not measured by their
place, but limited, because they are so in one place, as they cannot be
in another'. They are 'so nimble and so swift, that they are moved in an
unconceivable time'. Hence, they are said to have wings.[88] Wollebius
similarly distinguishes between being in a definite place and being
circumscribed.[89] Perhaps Milton uses this distinctive word with similar
signification, while making the opposite point, when Abdiel observes
that God 'formed the powers of heaven' including angels, 'Such as he
pleased, and circumscribed their being'.[90] This emphasis on location,

and the finite speed of movement, arises out of the need to distinguish between angels and God, who is uniquely infinite. As Richard Sibbes writes, angels move 'Suddenly, in an unperceivable time, yet in time because there is no motion in a moment, no creature moves from place to place in a moment, God is every where.'[91] Jeremy Taylor's claim that angels 'move in an instant' probably means the same as Sibbes' or Aquinas', though the phrase invites a stronger construction.[92] Comenius, as interested in the 'Physicks' of the question as in the theology, writes that angels are stronger and more agile than corporeal creatures, moving, unlike wind or lightning, without resistance, so 'though an Angell be not in many places at once, (*Dan.* 10. 13. 20.) yet they can in a moment passe themselves whither they will'.[93] More enthusiastic authors, including Fludd and John Everard, concur with these interpretations.[94] It is because of their speed that angels figure in ideal messaging systems, as a point of comparison in John Wilkins's *Mercury, or, The Secret and Swift Messenger* (1641), and as the bearers of messages in Trithemius' *Steganographia*. Heywood notes that it is through spirits 'that Magitions have such speedy intelligence (almost in an instant) of things done in the farthest and remotest places of the world'.[95] One seventeenth-century alchemical text claimed that, through natural magic, 'all that Spirits can do (except velocity) may be performed'.[96]

The speed of angels was a theological topic that was associated with astrological calculations of the size of the universe. Robert Bolton insisted, in a posthumous work of 1632, that no human knowledge of 'Geometry, Arithmetike, Opticks, Hypotheses, Philosophy. &c.' could 'illighten us' about the nature of the third, celestial heaven; he nonetheless acknowledged 'the severall computations of Astronomers' concerning the 'incredible distance from the earth to the Starry Firmament' as praise of Creation.[97] Later writers were more inclined to calculate, though inexactly, the speed of angels. The 1649 commentary on Ezekiel by the independent minister William Greenhill merits quoting at length:

Astronomers observe, that from the center of the earth (which is 3000. to the surface) up to the Sun is above foure millions of miles[;] to the Firmament, where the fixed stars are, above fourescore millions of miles, and from thence to the place of the blessed, where Saints and Angels are, more millions then from the earth to the Firmament. So that according to their account, it must be above 160. millions from heaven to earth; and this space the Angel came flying in a little time: we think a bullet out of a Musket flyes swiftly, and it doth, for it hits the bird or mark ere the report is heard, and will flye 180. miles in an houre, according to its motion. The Sunne moves swifter 1160000. miles in one hour; the fixed stars about the æquinoctiall move 42 millions of miles each houre; and yet the motion of an Angel is swifter, being a Spirit, and passing through the air without opposition; no creature in heaven or earth, moves faster then an Angel.[98]

Robert Dingley, who accepted Aquinas' doctrine that angels were not circumscribed by place, borrowed from this passage in an elaboration on Luke 23: 43. Christ says that he will see the thief beside him that same day in heaven, and such swift motion 'was done by the conduct and celerity of Angels that conveyed it'. Dingley specifies the speeds of a bullet and the sun, and concludes that 'the Seat of Angels and blessed Souls is at an huge distance from us'.[99] Greenhill's figures suggest that an angel must take less than three hours forty-eight minutes to fly from heaven to earth; I suspect he intends considerably less, without wishing to be imprudently specific. Heaven is profoundly distant, however, and even at their superlative speed, angels can take some time to reach earth; a consideration that has implications, as the previous chapter indicates, for the remote stationing of guardian angels. The often reserved Thomas Heywood, made bold by the Arabic astronomers Thābit ibn Qurra and al-Farghānī, whose calculations (developed in their commentaries on Ptolemy) he probably read in Roger Bacon's *Opus Maius* (1266) while at university, expands:

> 'T must likewise follow, That such as are sent
> Downe to the Earth, cannot incontinent,
> But with much difficultie or'ecome the way;
> Have time to penetrate (as needs it is)
> Now that Cœlestiall Body, and then this.
> When as (if *Alphraganius* we may trust,
> Or *Thebit*, Arabs both) of force it must
> Be a great distance. For these Authors write,
> If that an Angell in his swiftest flight,
> Should from the eighth Heaven, to the Earth descend,
> A thousand miles in threescore minutes to spend,
> (So far remote they are, if truly told)
> Six yeares six months his journey would him hold.[100]

At a thousand miles an hour an angel would take six and a half years to travel the (approximately) 56,979,000 miles from the earth to heaven (i.e. the fixed stars), beyond which lies the celestial heaven and God's throne. Elsewhere, however, Heywood describes Thomist discontinuous movement, and the complex relationship between angelic being and location:

> Know then, He
> Is not contain'd in place, as Brutes and we;
> But Place it selfe he in Himselfe containes,
> Bee'ng said to be still where his Pow'r remaines.
> And though it passe our weake ingeniositie,
> Yet He is knowne to be of strange velocitie;
> And without passing places, can with ease
> Or go or come at all times when he please . . .
> It is agreed upon, the Good and Evill,
> The blessed Angell, as the cursed Divell,
> Have all those faculties, and without [p]aine
> Or passing intermediat things, can gaine
> To what they purpose, in one instand round
> The spatious world, and where they please be found.[101]

Angelic flight is limited, but angels have swifter modes of transport. The words echo Bucanus: an angel is not circumscribed, but is limited because it operates in a single place. Heywood reconciles the theological and the natural-philosophical and the poetic; like later natural philosophers, however, his emphasis is more on diabolical speed and transvection than on the abstract question of angelic motion.[102]

Milton does not aspire to measure speed and distance in this way. Adam suggests that the movement of the stars is in 'spaces incomprehensible' (8. 20), and Raphael affirms this:

> me thou thinkst not slow,
> Who since the morning hour set out from heaven
> Where God resides, and ere mid-day arrived
> In Eden, distance inexpressible
> By numbers that have name.           (8. 110–14)[103]

Raphael undertakes in a continuous time of approaching six hours (assuming the morning hour is a modest six; Milton would rise at four) what Heywood suggests by ordinary motion should take six and a half years (though the distance that Heywood suggests, travelled at the speed that Greenhill suggests, would take less than eighty minutes). The scope and nature of space is beyond human understanding; though Milton is interested in the notion of multiple worlds which may imply infinite space.

The Copernican universe was larger and harder to measure than Ptolemy's, and, like Galileo, Milton found the idea of infinity intriguing. Speed and movement shape Milton's narrative, and seep into the language of the poem despite his insistence that questions about 'celestial motions' are at best 'doubtfully answered' (8, argument). Adam refers to the 'incorporeal speed' of light, 'Speed, to describe whose swiftness number fails' (8. 37–8). Raphael confirms the 'Speed almost spiritual' of the 'corporeal substances' of the heavenly spheres, which are themselves moved by angels (8. 109–10). The incorporeal is faster than the corporeal. Do angels travel at the same incorporeal speed of light? Precisely this speed is suggested when Uriel descends to earth to warn Gabriel of the suspicious spirit he met in the sun:

> Thither came Uriel, gliding through the even
> On a sunbeam, swift as a shooting star
> In autumn thwarts the air . . .                    (4. 555)

Imagine this is meant literally: Uriel travels at the same speed as the beam of light on which he surfs. He is in a hurry, and the speed of light must be at least equal to his own unassisted speed. If the comparison to a shooting star, an effect of light, is meant literally, then the analogy is exact. The movement may be mechanically precise too: as Milton thought light substantial, and its rays physically moved between the object and the eye, then a spirit equally material might be supported by it.[104] Yet, according to Milton, there are faster things than angels. The Son refers to Grace as 'the speediest of [God's] winged messengers', implying that grace is a messenger, like an angel, and that it is faster: perhaps because it is the gift of God its speed is infinite.[105] When the Son himself descends to Eden to declare God's judgement to the transgressing Adam and Eve, he travels in a manner entirely different from messengers: 'Down he descended straight; the speed of gods | Time counts not, though with swiftest minutes winged' (10. 90–1). The divine—the speed of Christ, the architecture of the universe—is uncountable, beyond numbers and reckoning. Angels are creatures and are therefore subject to numbers. *De Doctrina* suggests that the wings of angels indicate their great velocity.[106] However, the 'winged' minutes are a reminder that wings also represent finite speeds, the fastest speed a creature can attain to, *almost* immeasurable.

The concepts of numbers and numberlessness are threaded through the poem. The distance from heaven to earth is inexpressible in numbers with names, and numbers fail to describe the speed of light. The fallen angels are repeatedly 'innumerable' and 'numberless' (1. 338, 344, 780). During Creation 'numberless' angels surround the chariot of the Son, and when the angels shout for joy after the prophecy of the apocalypse and the promotion of the Son, the cry is 'Loud as from numbers without number' (7. 197; 3. 346). More suspiciously, Satan promises 'angels numberless' to Eve (9. 548). Angels seem numberless, but are not so. When Satan summons his fallen legions into a kind of order and inspects them, 'Their number last he sums' (1. 571). At first, Raphael describes the heavenly forces as 'Army against army numberless' (6. 224; also 5. 653); then tempers this, revealing that God 'limited their might' though they were

> numbered such
> As each divided legion might have seemed
> A numerous host.                                    (6. 229)

To describe the numbers of angels Milton suggests numberlessness before retreating from the idea. They are almost infinite in number, according to *De Doctrina*, 'so numerous that they are almost innumerable'.[107] And in *Paradise Lost*, they are only almost numberless, in contrast to the uncountable nature of God and the extent of the universe.

The poem vividly delineates the limitations of angels' speed. Abdiel takes a whole night to fly across heaven. Raphael takes a morning to fly to earth. Uriel surfs the sunbeam. Wings are an encumbrance, subject to obstruction by the medium through which they impel. On his 'flight precipitant' from the sun to the earth, Satan 'winds with ease | Through the pure marble air his oblique way' (3. 563–4). This downward ('precipitant' suggests both speed and geometry) voyage through the 'calm firmament' (3. 574) is easier than his vertiginous (and upward) flight through Chaos, where he plummets through a vacuum, a fashionable natural-philosophical subject when the poem was published, and is buffeted by winds. The narrator stresses the physical effort of flight and the resistance of the environment:

> with expanded wings he steers his flight
> Aloft, incumbent on the dusky air
> That felt unusual weight, till on dry land
> He lights . . .                                    (1. 222–8)

These are inclement conditions, but flying involves effort for unfallen angels. Raphael's flight to earth, which symbolically and physically parallels Satan's, is limited in speed and tasking:

> Down thither prone in flight
> He speeds, and through the vast ethereal sky
> Sails between worlds and worlds, with steady wing
> Now on the polar winds, then with quick fan
> Winnows the buxom air . . .                    (5. 266–70)

The 'steady wing' suggests both control and sustained exertion. Most theologians dwell only on the theoretical limitations of angelic speed, its symbolic properties, its implications for diabolic agency; Milton lingers on the impeded experience of flight, the implications of limited speed for the messengers. The near-infinite is much more open to exploration, and more poetically evocative, than the infinite. Milton's angels are creatures, and their speed reflects this.


## Conclusions

Milton's angels are objects of natural-philosophical knowledge. This was not, c.1667, a nostalgic enterprise. Angels were not killed off by a scientific revolution, nor did they constitute an embarrassment to mechanist philosophers.[108] As the assumptions of saving appearances were discarded in favour of the more systematic practice of experimentalism in the late 1660s, angels shifted as objects of knowledge. Angels do not appear in the pages of the *Philosophical Transactions*. Angels cannot be dissected, grafted, excavated, weighed or measured, or asphyxiated in an air pump. However, mechanist philosophers, experimentalists, and members of the early Royal Society—men such as Robert Hooke, Joseph Glanvill, and Henry More—did write about angels, and used them for thought experiments. John Locke's *Essay* (1690) repeatedly touches upon angels, reluctantly conceding that they cannot contribute to actual knowledge, but in his manuscripts he willingly reflects on them in considering the distinction between space and extension.[109] More was still writing about angelic invocation, the 'terrestrial Omnipercipiency' of angels, and their relationship with saints, in 1672. Boyle collected manuscripts about angel magic and the philosophers' stone.[110] There was no divorce between mechanical and occult or spiritual philosophy; rather, it was the opponents of the Society, such as Hobbes, who doubted that spiritual beings were reliable evidence. For other Restoration natural philosophers, a doctrine of the existence and actions of spirits was entirely necessary. Religious convictions urged them towards pneumatics, and they developed doctrines of immateriality to attack perceived Sadducism and purely mechanical explanations. They formulated accounts of the actions of spirits in the material world, finding various means of explaining spiritual agency and occult causation that could complement empirical accounts. The experimentalist or mechanist spirit of enquiry did not vanquish the investigation of spirits. Rather, angels were naturalized.

Increasingly the 'proof' of the spirit world lay in descriptions and explanations of apparitions, such as those compiled by Robert Boyle, Glanvill, and More. The spirits concerned were predominantly demons because the age of miracles and angels was over; otherwise unfallen angels would have been as useful as fallen. These compendiums were a contested area in which the status of fact could be explored. Catalogues of actions of spirits were a necessary corollary to mechanist philosophies. The language used to write about angels in natural-philosophical contexts *dilated*, became detached from precise theological connotations, and became part of the language of *spiritual* action and causation. This was fundamental to the language of mechanical explanation, but at the same time it shifted angels to, and fixed them in, a distant area of knowledge, just as the Reformation had marginalized them from the everyday experience of worship.[111]

Early modern theologians and natural philosophers discussed angelic materiality, bodies, reflection, eyesight, communication, and speed. These discussions often have different terms, different directions, and different purposes, though the overlap is extensive. Milton's interest is in telling a story. Through storytelling he asks questions and finds answers.[112] He makes narratives that are informed by an understanding of nature and theology that turn his narrative into something truer and more solid, more given to grace and redemption. While he was doing this, inserting angels within, or inserting within angels an understanding of natural philosophy, natural philosophers were taking up questions that had previously belonged to theologians, and theologians were responding to or drawing upon natural philosophy. These were importantly permeable boundaries.

This intellectual exchange had a finite lifespan, but it was a productive one for Milton and for others. It would go too far to claim that Milton had a positive relationship with the new science, but his significant field of interests included space, telescopes, sunspots, the nature of infinity, subjects not indifferent to the agendas of the Royal Society. His narrative discloses perspectives on angelic optics, physics, speed, numbers, and bodies that are as remarkable and as considered as his explicit discussions of the more provocative issues such as angelic digestion and lovemaking. This engagement gives the lie to the image of a purely literary Milton, a poet whose angels converse solely with those of other poets, and whose ambition is predominantly to surpass his predecessors. The invention of this secular figure, both disinterested and uninterested in the spheres of politics and religion and the natural world, is not only anachronistic, but misrepresents the poet's God, his monism, and his desires to unify spirit and matter and to reconcile poetic with spiritual concerns. The representation of Satan is influenced by Homer's Achilles and Beaumont's *Psyche*, but this is but one element in a compound the purpose of which extends beyond poetic allusion. *Paradise Lost* is a Lucretian epic and a hexameron that absorbs poetic knowledge as well as theological and natural-philosophical knowledge, and works with these materials to fashion an intended truth that can only be apprehended through literary means.[113]

We should not reduce the truth to these means. There is no real division between the philosopher, theologian, and poet, because the story is 'a complex narrative organism', and the part and whole must be understood together.[114] Milton's account of bodies is consubstantial with his account of the senses and of perception, of freewill and reason. All are elaborated through narrative, and whether he formulated them before writing the narrative or as the narrative developed, we cannot say: the narrative and the doctrine are inseparable. Accordingly, the theology and the physics are also inseparable. Milton's theology, his physics of angels, and his poetic narrative are cut from the same cloth, and his fabrication of narrative through the various kinds of knowledge in which angels could figure was in some ways symptomatic of his age.

# 12

# 'With the Tongues of Angels'

## Angelic Communication

### Spiritual and Audible Sounds

For seventeenth-century Protestants angels were unlike people, and
their interaction with humans could be fraught. Conversation between
angels and humans—understood not only as verbal communication,
but as the experience of being with and around angels as part of the
normal human environment—was essential to humankind's place in
Creation. Yet the most immediate form of conversation, verbal com-
munication and the relay of information that happens in Scripture, was
made difficult by angels' disembodiment and incorporeality. The
theme by which theologians explored this nexus of issues was widely
discussed in seventeenth-century Britain: the speech of angels. Milton
saw this, and human–angelic conversations are complicated in *Paradise
Lost* in a way that further develops his natural philosophy.

Milton frequently interrogates interspecies communication. For
example, when Raphael is describing to Adam the war in heaven, he
several times pauses to comment on the difficulty of description, the
condition of narrating this 'fight | Unspeakable'. He asks:

> who, though with the tongue
> Of angels, can relate, or to what things
> Liken on earth conspicuous, that may lift
> Human imagination to such height
> Of godlike power.[1]

Raphael draws attention to two problems here. The first is, as discussed
in Chapter 6, the doctrine of accommodation: representing God and
heaven presents a problem to Raphael, so too describing the actions of

warring spirits, and his preface warns the reader that what she reads may
be neither novelistic realism nor simple allegory.[2]

But there is another problem here, one that has been overlooked,
perhaps because we too hastily assume that Milton's angels are like his
humans, in which case the problem disappears. This is the practical
basis of the exchange between angel and human.[3] Raphael speaks with
the 'tongue | Of angels': how does Adam hear him? Does an angel
make noise? Do angels have tongues? This is a recurrent point of
exegesis in medieval and early modern discussions of angels, and one
that Milton reflects on in *Paradise Lost*.

For mainstream theology from Pseudo-Dionysius through Aquinas to
Calvin, angelic speech is a metaphor. It is used as a 'human' or accom-
modated figure for the mediation between the hierarchy of God, angels,
and man, and serves a large purpose: in Aquinas' *Summa Theologiae*, for
example, *conversio* (referring to a communication in either direction, but
also a turning to God) explains or describes how the angelic hierarchy, an
intellectual foundation for his entire theology, is bound together with
relationships of subordination and exaltation. For Milton, however,
angelic speech is not a metaphor, or not just a metaphor. First, because
he offers a dramatization, a narrative account of the communications not
just between God and his angels, but between God and man and between
man and angels, among all of Creation, in which it is a literary necessity
that characters speak to each other. Secondly, because his angels are
material beings, with imperfect senses, limited knowledge, subject to
the laws of motion, optics, to freewill. Like humans, they are the
creatures of God. So they speak to man, and to each other, and when
they do, their converse is not simply a turning towards illumination, but
material sociability. Later Raphael will echo himself:

> to recount almighty works
> What words or tongue of seraph can suffice,
> Or heart of man suffice to comprehend?          (7. 112–14)

Raphael's warnings are the formula of a storyteller, a modesty topos that
reminds the listener that she is listening. But the epic also impresses
upon us that Adam really hears the words, and admires the voice. When
Raphael finishes telling the story of Creation, the narrator tells us:

> The angel ended, and in Adam's ear
> So charming left his voice, that he awhile
> Thought him still speaking, still stood fixed to hear.     (8. 1–3)

These three lines were interpolated in the revised, twelve-book version of 1674, appearing at the beginning of the new book 8; they are a transitional frame, of course, but they tell us that Raphael's is a real voice, that real music sounds in Adam's ear. Following Raphael's account of angelic digestion (pp. 279–80, above) and of the nature of human and angelic freewill, Adam exclaims:

> Thy words
> Attentive, and with more delighted ear,
> Divine instructor, I have heard, than when
> Cherubic songs by night from neighbouring hills
> Aërial music send. (5. 544–8)

Adam's pleasure is in part a pleasure in the music of the voice. Angels characteristically, in Milton and elsewhere, sing hymns of praise to God. This music forms part of Adam's sense experience, his universe. He comments to Eve:

> How oft from the steep
> Of echoing hill or thicket have we heard
> Celestial voices to the midnight air,
> Sole, or responsive each to other's note
> Singing their great creator. (4. 680–4)

He sounds like no one more than Caliban, musing that

> the isle is full of noises . . .
> Sometimes a thousand twangling instruments
> Will hum about mine ears.[4]

Milton's angels, like Prospero's enchantments, are noisy. When God anoints the Son, 'The multitude of angels' issue

> a shout
> Loud as from numbers without number, sweet
> As from blest voices. (3. 345–7)

We are told of the 'Angelic harmonies' with which the heavens resound when God completes Creation, harmonies 'intermixed with voice | Choral or unison'.[5] Milton's angels sing and speak in a manner audible to humans. Even when they are not speaking directly to humans, their voices can be heard.

There is a close association between angels and music. Their song is a pattern for human praise and for human prayers, more perfect and therefore an ideal to be striven for.[6] All prayers in Mass imitated the prayers of angels, and antiphonal singing was understood to derive from angelic worship. In medieval churches the Annunciation was sometimes staged as a musical costume drama, in which the angel sang antiphons. Angelic speech can be represented *through* music. Music articulated theology.[7] Hildegard of Bingen, the twelfth-century Benedictine nun, believed herself directly inspired and authorized by the Spirit; she wrote music, which she believed to be based on the prophetically revealed principles of heavenly music, in which angels themselves sing. Human music was an imperfect reflection of celestial.[8] The liturgy was modelled on suppositions, tenuous though rooted in sophisticated Scholastic thought, about the nature of angelic praise of God. Milton follows a similar logic when his angelic hymn modulates into the narrator's own voice, without an apparent seam (3. 372–412; pp. 258–9, above). Milton suggest that the protoplasts can hear angelic song; a few other writers, including Pordage, suggest that postlapsarian humans can also hear it if they reach a state of spiritual purity.[9] For many this singing is not an audible phenomenon, however, not the creaturely practice of Milton and Pordage. Hence, John Wall writes of the tongues of angels, but he means a divine symbol; he writes: 'The walls of Jerusalem are the companies of Angels . . . Therefore do they rejoice and sing'.[10]

The singing of angels is often associated—and conceptually enriched—with the music of the spheres. Renaissance Neoplatonism adopted the ancient cosmology that described Creation as a hierarchical series of concentric spheres ascending from earth to heaven. The rotation of each sphere generated a note that combined to make a heavenly harmony, based on Pythagorean proportions, inaudible to humans because of the impurities of the body, and each of the nine orders of angels was assigned a corresponding sphere; the seraphim, for example, the highest of the angelic orders, associated with divine love, governed the outermost sphere, the *Primum mobile*, from which the other, inferior spheres derived their motion. Lorenzo's bittersweet speech in the final act of Shakespeare's *Merchant of Venice* draws on the idea:

> There's not the smallest orb which thou behold'st
> But in his motion like an angel sings,
> Still quiring to the young-eyed cherubins;
> Such harmony is in immortal souls.

It is also something that Thomas Heywood outlines in his *Hierarchie of the Blessed Angels*.[11] Angelic hierarchies and the music of the spheres are closely related. We need to recognize, however, that angelic hymns are rooted in theological traditions, and the music of the spheres in Renaissance Neoplatonic philosophy that was generally understood as a weaker description of reality, sometimes as no more than metaphor. This was especially the case among Protestants.

For Milton the doctrine of the nine angelic orders was popish, and such hierarchy as did exist in Creation was flexible and permeable.[12] His facetious second prolusion discusses the music of the spheres (suggesting that human ears are not able or worthy enough to hear it) and makes no mention of angels.[13] Angelic music in *Paradise Lost* does not resemble the music of the spheres in two ways: first, it is profoundly verbal; these are words that are being sung. Secondly, it is far more creaturely than any account of the celestial harmonies. These are words sung by beings that have independent intellectual faculties, freewill, and a purpose to their singing.

## Angelic Bodies and Organs

This merits some contemplation, not least because it suggests Milton's deliberation over conventional accounts of angelic speech, and his conscious move away from contemporary commonplaces. The account of angelic speech most influential upon early modern angelology was Aquinas' *Summa*. Augustine scarcely touched upon the subject, though he was clear that angels, fallen and unfallen, had spiritual bodies rather than material.[14] He does observe that 'God does not speak to the angels in the way that we speak to each other, or to God, or to the angels, or as the angels speak to us, or as God speaks to us through them.' He speaks without sound, and when we hear him 'with our inward ears, we ourselves come close to the angels'. Beyond this Augustine will not resolve.[15] Aquinas is far more specific. He argues that angels communicate between each other by directing thought with their will. Human communication is obstructed by the body, and thus 'We have to make use of an outward, vocalized communication.' As angels have no bodies, 'there is no place for outward, but only for inward speech; this includes not only a conversing with itself in an inner thought, but also the thought's being directed by the will towards communicating with another. Accordingly the *tongues of angels* is a metaphor for the power they have to make their thoughts known.' Such communication is unaffected by distance. Though the medium of Aquinas' angelic communication is immensely powerful, the messages are very restricted: the strict hierarchy means that enlightenment is exclusively passed down from greater to lesser; when a lesser angel speaks to a greater, it is only to express a wish to know or receive, though he adds that angels are also always speaking in praise of God.[16] When speaking to us, the arrangement is different, as he shows in a discussion of angelic bodies that attends to the question of speech. Angels sometimes need bodies for their actions in our world, for which purpose they adopt bodies of air (the view famously exploited in Donne's 'Air and Angels'). This is in fact a form of accommodation; it is a sensible analogy to give us an idea of their actual being. The body is not a functioning one, however: it is merely a representation, and is not used for speech. So Aquinas writes: 'An angel does not really speak through his assumed body; he only imitates speech, forming sounds in the air corresponding to human words.'[17] This argument, that spirits impelled the air to make audible sounds, was endorsed in sixteenth-century commentaries on Genesis by David Pareus, Johannes Mercerus, Benedictus Perereius, Andreas Rivetus, and Martin Luther, for example in their accounts of the vocal powers of Abraham's visitors, Balaam's ass, and the serpent of Genesis.[18] Leonardo doubted the persuasiveness of this account, insisting that it was speculative, and that a body of air would instantly dissolve.[19]

This problem was widely discussed in seventeenth-century England. John Salkeld was sympathetic to Jerome's opinion that 'the Angels have their manner of tongue, though different from all humane, without all corporall motion, or sound'; even when they adopt bodies and present the appearance of speaking, 'they can have no true vitall locution or vocall speech'; though he finally prevaricates that 'it cannot be declared, neyther how the Angels doe outwardly speake into us in our eare; neither how inwardly in our hearts'.[20] The enterprising public lecturer Balthasar Gerbier, in a manual on well-speaking published in 1650, contrasts 'sensible vocall action' with the 'intellectual speech' of angels, who speak 'not as men doe, with a moving tongue, with a shrill throat, their speech is wholly Spirituall'.[21] The minister, poet, and translator of Boehme into Welsh, Morgan Llwyd, wrote that God and the angels had a single language, in which the angels 'glorify God, and converse with one another, and with the Saints, without the Noise of Tongues or Sounds of Words'.[22]

The Westminster Assembly's *Annotations*, the distillation of patristic, Scholastic, and Reformation commentary published in 1645 and 1651 that had a special status as a statement of establishment orthodoxy, stated:

As God gave them bodies for a time, so he gave them the faculties thereof to walk, to speak, to eat, and drink, and such like; yet what was let into the body in an extraordinary manner, might afterwards be resolved into ayr; and what they did might not be so much by any natural faculties of those bodies they assumed, as by a supernaturall application of those parts they had to what they did . . . [23]

At Numbers 22: 28, however, the Assembly articulates a marginally different position, glossing the powers of speech of Balaam's ass: 'the Angel of the Lord formed his own words by the mouth of the Ass, as the Devil did by the mouth of the Serpent, Gen. 3'. This is a distinction Milton would have noticed. Do spirits produce the sounds themselves while simultaneously moving the body, or do they use material bodies to generate sounds? The first comment from the *Annotations* suggests the former, the second the latter. Committees often fail to secure perfect coherence in their publications; here it seems they prevaricate on two sides of a complex but nonetheless relatively inconsequential question.

Gervase Babington, in his not entirely accurately entitled *Certaine Plaine, Briefe, and Comfortable Notes upon Everie Chapter of Genesis*, presents a simpler, mechanical explanation of the instrumental use of an assumed body:

But how could the Serpent speake, since this power is not geven to beasts, but only to man? No question it was not the Serpent by his owne power, but Satan in and by the Serpent, which is not impossible. . . . When God permitteth, Satan is able to shrowde himselfe under the creatures, as may best fit his purpose. Many wicked Southsayers Satan casteth into pangs and fits of furie, and then speake they by him, or he rather by them what he will.[24]

Andrew Willet, whose *Hexapla in Genesin* of 1605 is one of the weightiest commentaries produced in English, preferred a similar explanation: 'the devill used the serpent a subtile beast as his instrument, and spake out of him'. Eve was deceived 'by the craft of the devill speaking and working by the serpent'.[25] This intimates that the

serpent is the bodily cause of the sound, manipulated by the Devil.
Willet seems to be following Calvin here, who annotates Genesis 3: 4:
'the serpent was not eloquent by nature: but when Sathan by the
Sufferance of God, had gotten him a meete instrument, he caused
his tongue to speake, whiche God also permitted'.[26] Glossing the visit
of the angels to Abraham at Genesis 18 (where they consume a meal,
which gave rise to extended reflections on angels in many commen-
taries and treatises), Calvin writes:

> I doubt not, but that God which made al the world of nothing, and which is a
> wonderfull workmaister in fashioning his creatures, gave unto them bodies for
> a time, wherin they might do that office whiche was committed unto them.
> And as they did truely walke, speake, and doe other duties, so I judge that they
> did as truely eate.[27]

Willet on the same chapter surveys the possibility that the angels
adopted counterfeit bodies or real bodies that undertook counterfeit
eating, and resolves: 'it is the sounder opinion, that these angels, as they
were endued with true bodies for the time, so they did verily eate, as
they did walke and speake and doe other actions of the bodie truly'.[28]
On the same text the Devon minister George Hughes, in his learned
*Analytical Exposition* of Genesis (1672), writes that the angels assumed
'True humane bodies', as discovered by the fact that they ate and spoke
and so on.[29]

   Finally, for John Gumbleden, the distinction between implicit and
audible could practically and clearly be made. In a sermon on the
apparition of an angel to the soldier Cornelius in Acts 10 (published in
1657 though preached some years earlier), Gumbleden navigates some
of the standard issues of angelology, considering angelic communica-
tion at unusual length. He writes: 'The *Angel* said unto him; but, can
*Angels* speak? it seems they can: and that, either unto God; or, unto
themselves; or, unto men'. For the former, he follows Aquinas; for the
speech of angels to men he elaborates:

> to men also do *Angels* speak; and that, either *without*, or, *with assumed Bodies*:
> when the *good Angels* (as they are in themselves, *Spirits*, and *without material
> Bodies*) speak unto the hearts, and soules of faithfull men (as no doubt,
> oftentimes they do) then, after a *spiritual*, and *heavenly Manner*, without
> words, without any *vocall* noise, or *audible* speech (but to him only, to
> whom they speak, if to him) they *secretly instill, insinuate, conveigh*, and *commu-
> nicate* their meaning to the minds, and understandings of men; in a manner,

like as they do their own minds, one unto another . . . but, when they *appeared* in the forme of men (as in *ages past* they did,) then they *assumed* such Bodies as we ourselves have, with all their *integral* parts, together with all *instruments* of *Speech*, and therefore *Tongues*: wherewith, they so *appeared*, they *spake vocally*, and *audibly* to the eares of men.[30]

When angels speak to humans without assuming bodies, they speak inwardly, imposing their thoughts upon the mind. This was commonly described as 'impressing', which, while deriving from Aquinas' 'impressa', compares virtual sense impressions to printing on the human senses; in the words of Milton's friend Henry Lawrence, 'Angells . . . speake to the internall, first of all, making such compositions there, as the understanding presently takes of, and reades what is written.'[31] The term suggests the spiritual, communicative power attributed to printing. When, however, angels assume a body, they use the instruments of speech wherewith the body is furnished in order to speak vocally and audibly to the ear. There are, then, contrasting accounts of how angels speak to humans that contest whether their speech is audible, and, if so, how it is generated. Not a great deal seems to be at stake here, as either account proves the reality of the spiritual world. For all of these writers, however, the notion of angelic song would be a metaphor, a form of perfect, idealized speech, praise directed by the will to God. Adam would not hear it in paradise. Only those radicals whose angels were material and corporeal—Laurence Claxton and the Pordages among them—would contend that angels made real noise, and that audible speech was integral to angelic faculties.[32]

Several poets concerned themselves with the matter of angelic song and speech, and some specifically affirmed that angels did not have tongues. The sixteenth-century Huguenot Guillaume du Bartas describes Satan's vocalization through the serpent in his creation poem *La Semaine* (1578, translated into English by Joshua Sylvester in 1605):

> Sith such pure bodies have nor teeth, nor tongues,
> Lips, artires, nose, palate, nor panting lungs,
> Which rightly plac'd are properly created
> True instruments of sounds articulated.[33]

Ethereal natures want language, states du Bartas, because they have no tongues or other organs of speech. Influenced by du Bartas, Lucy Hutchinson describes Abraham and Sarah feeding their angelic visitors a calf, milk, and butter:

> Not knowing that they, from heaven's high courts employed,
> In human shapes did angels' natures hide
> Till, after the conclusion of the meal,
> Th'ambassadors their message did reveal . . . [34]

She reveals nothing about the digestive process. She is similarly reticent on the matter of angelic conversation. In contrast to Milton's prelapsarian man, who speaks with angels as with equals, Hutchinson's Adam stands below celestial beings just as he stands above brute creatures. His nature is not 'sublime | Enough' to delight 'in angelic converse':

> No, though man partake intelligence,
> Yet that, being joined to an inferior sense,
> Dulled by corporeal vapours, cannot be
> Refined enough for angels' company . . . [35]

She does not explain how angels convey their messages, or unpick the other angelological controversies that necessarily underpin any narrative of angelic–human relations. She is more concerned with morality and symbolic meanings, the matter of practical divinity, than in the abstract, systematic theology of the annotator.

In *Hierarchie of the Blessed Angells*, Thomas Heywood develops a discussion of Augustine and Aquinas on angels into an argument that angels cannot have bodies:

> If they have bodies? They must needs be linkt
> Of members, as Mans is; Organs distinct,
> And like composure; else they must be fram'd
> Confus'd, and without those which we have nam'd.[36]

If angels had bodies, then they must have organs such as tongues; and if organs then senses, and if senses then passions, then perturbation and alteration. For Heywood, materiality, senses, passions, and speech are logically connected, and none are properly attributed to angels. Milton sees similar connections, and finds them all in angels.

These poets are writing imaginatively, but nonetheless make strenuous efforts to conform to their rigorously developed theological position; all subordinate their poetics to a pre-formulated doctrine yet seek space for the inventive exposition and exploration of that doctrine. Angelic tongues are a theme in which theology and imaginative representations necessarily interact.

## Noise in Paradise

Do Milton's angels have tongues? Milton's angels are substantial, physical beings; they are spirits, but nonetheless material. They are, however, not corporeal.[37] They have no bodies, and therefore they have no tongues and no ears. Except, as we have seen, their matter has a 'proper' shape, the angel's 'own' shape, and they assume form according to their purposes and will. This is seen in the war in heaven, which shows, as Raphael explains, that angels live 'Vital in every part' (6. 345), though they bleed real blood, blood such as angels bleed. Yet Raphael continues in a way that radically qualifies any simple notion of disembodiment, lest we should think Milton's substantial angels similar to Aquinas', or to Pseudo-Dionysius', for whom angel's limbs are purely symbolic:[38]

> All heart they live, all head, all eye, all ear,
> All intellect, all sense, and as they please,
> They limb themselves, and colour, shape or size
> Assume, as like them best, condense or rare.          (6. 350–3)

Angels may not have corporeal forms with ears; they are *all* ear.[39] They have limbs according to their wills, as necessary to fulfil their works of love or enmity. In this specific sense they do have bodies, spiritual bodies, that contain all the virtue of corporeal bodies without the corporeality. This explains, moreover, what Raphael means when he tells Adam that 'pure | Intelligential substances' contain within them 'every lower faculty | Of sense'; that is, all the human senses are contained within the angelic senses, a claim that I think we need to take literally (5. 408–11). Angels can hear and they do have substantial senses. This is Milton's God's assurance of downward software compatibility.

Angels do, then, have tongues after a fashion. They are all tongue, which is why their singing is audible from earth. It is not mere allegory when Milton refers to angelic limbs and organs.[40] As his angels are really vocal and audible, so they have limbs and organs and senses without mundane corporeality. Hence the many references to the knees of angels, to the ears of angels, to the tongues of angels; perhaps even to Satan's scars; certainly the tears that Satan sheds prior to his first address to the fallen angels in hell, 'Tears such as angels weep', false, dissembling tears, but they must be real, wet tears otherwise they would not be persuasive oratory.[41] Angel body parts, not only tongues, are all over Milton's Creation.

Because his angels are substantial, Milton circumnavigates Scholastic arguments about angelic noise production. He does not have to debate assumed bodies, strange acts of ventriloquism, or the impressing of angelic thought upon the human mind. His angels speak and hear, participate in the production and reception of sound waves in a world that seems to be fully audible. When Satan, disguised as a cherub, approaches Uriel—'the sharpest sighted spirit of all in Heaven' (3. 691), who cannot penetrate the disguise—he admonishes him 'by his ear' (3. 647). While Aquinas' angels are transparent, enabling their perfect, silent communication, Milton's are substantial and opaque.[42] Milton's narratives should not be understood to be 'imaginative' in any simple or post-Romantic sense; he also believes them to carry the burden of the truth. Hence, Milton's account of angelic conversation, the noise in heaven and the substantiality of angelic tongues, should be understood as both imaginative narrative and natural philosophy.

There is an impediment to this reading, however, a problem Milton might have drawn from reading Calvin, Luther, Willet, the Westminster *Annotations*, or one of any number of commentaries. He introduces it in the temptation. The serpent approaches Eve, attracts her eye with a 'gentle dumb expression', and,

> glad
> Of her attention gained, with serpent tongue
> Organic, or impulse of vocal air,
> His fraudulent temptation thus began.          (9. 528–31)

The narrator leaves undetermined whether Satan speaks as spirits speak, or uses the serpent's tongue as an instrument.[43] Undetermined, that is, after raising the alternative possibilities that were commonly proposed in writings about angels. Alternatives, moreover, that seem irrelevant to Milton's narrative, as Satan has no need of the serpent's tongue to issue audible speech. The 'or' here does little other than raise the disputes of angelology, the same 'common gloss | Of theologians' that Milton earlier dismisses. Why raise the issue at this stage in the poem if there is nothing to be resolved, if it is a non-question?

The solution has three parts. First, there is nothing to stop Satan from using the serpent's tongue for the purposes of audible speech. It adds a virtuoso shine to his fraudulence. In many discussion of angelic speech, from Aquinas onwards, authors are concerned about the ethical implications of assumed bodies and bodies of condensed air. For an angel to present the illusion of bodily existence or the illusion of speech or of a speaking body, they knew, might constitute a form of deception, deluding the human senses with a simulacrum of a reality that was not. Devils were understood to do this, working false wonders and exploiting their superior natural-philosophical knowledge to create illusions to deceive and delude human senses; but illusions were more morally complicated in the case of unfallen angels. Lawrence argues that Abraham's angels must have really eaten, 'for they never deceived your senses'; Peter Le Loier, that when angels appear in the form of men they do not intend to be mistaken for men, and that there is no cause for saying 'that there is fiction and feyning in the angels'; Gumbleden says that the soldier and the angel really encountered each other and 'spake, mouth to mouth', that there was 'no *painting*, no *counterfeiting*, no *deluding* here'.[44] The solutions are various, but many authors raise counterfeiting, feigning, the making of fictions, as a concern. This is not a problem for Milton's Satan, the father of lies: if he uses the serpent as an instrument of speech when he could speak for himself, then the deception has an additional twist (he is practising not just diabolical possession, but strangely unnecessary ventriloquism).[45] Secondly, Milton thereby hints that those angelologists who claim that unfallen angels cannot really speak, but can create the illusion of speaking without feigning, are themselves guilty of fictions. Thirdly, Satan's illusion of a serpent that really speaks is essential to Milton's story. Demonologists acknowledged the difficulty of distinguishing between the Devil's illusions and reality, but also the difficulty of separating illusions from those preternatural effects that the Devil was able to work within nature using his skills as a natural philosopher.[46] Milton's Eve's immediate response to the speaking serpent is to ask, in syntax that discloses her puzzlement, 'What may this mean? Language of man pronounced | By tongue of brute, and human sense expressed?' (9. 553–4). The fact that the serpent has a tongue that can produce meaningful speech becomes part of Satan's confidence trick, the pseudo-evidence that deceives her.[47] Before taking the fruit, Eve muses on the virtue that 'taught | The Tongue not made for speech to speak thy praise' (9. 748–9).

The alternatives offered in this passage, then, reflect the exchange between natural philosophy and theology in Milton's imaginative narrative. Poetry and knowledge are not meant to be opposites. Hence, many authors shift freely between accommodated representation, angelic bodies and apparitions, and speech; the tongues of angels and sacred poetry have a deep association that speaks to the preoccupations and the logical and intellectual foundations of the culture. The angels of *Paradise Lost* are genuinely and emphatically noisy. Speech and vocal communication constitute relationships, those mutual relationships that reject the strict hierarchies that Pseudo-Dionysius, Aquinas, Thomas Heywood, and others attributed to the angelic orders. In conversing, a reciprocity is achieved that benefits both parties, that exalts both as the differences of a hierarchy are traversed and narrowed.[48] Sociability and conversation are good things. When God sends his messenger Raphael—the 'sociable spirit' (5. 221)—to bring a warning to Adam, he orders him to converse 'half this day as friend with friend' (5. 229). He arrives, in his 'proper shape' as a seraph with six wings (5. 277), while Eve is preparing dinner, and leaves when the day is spent and Adam retires to his bower. Raphael's message is not a pithy interdiction, but a warning that depends upon a lengthy narrative, questions and answers and counter-questions. Its force is acquired not through the unyielding concrete direction of a commandment, but through conversation. Both man and angel express the pleasure they take in this conversation. To speak with the tongue of angels is to speak eloquently without feigning, to speak aloud, and to listen with pleasure; this is both the story that Milton tells, and his doctrine of angels.

# PART III

# Literature and Representation

# 13

# Dryden's Fall

## Dreams, Angels, Freewill

### Dryden versus Milton

Picture yourself at the theatre in London, watching a play about the Fall of Mankind. Adam and Eve are sleeping in paradise. Enter Lucifer, who tells you about dreams and the susceptibility of women to vain shows. So he crouches at Eve's ear, whereupon a vision arises: deformed shapes dance around a tree; an angel enters, with a woman 'habited like Eve' (the script does not elaborate on this), sings praises of the tree; the woman objects. The angel gives the fruit to the shapes who transform into angels. The woman concedes this empirical proof, and the angel moralizes that forbidden pleasures are more rewarding. You might be forgiven for thinking you are seeing an exchange between the Earl of Rochester and Margery Pinchwife, until the Eve-figure flies to the sky with the angels.

It is Milton, but strangely transformed. It is *The State of Innocence and the Fall of Man*, *Paradise Lost* transposed into opera by John Dryden. Written in 1674, it was never performed, and was not printed until 1677. It was nonetheless a popular success.

Dryden's first question in adapting *Paradise Lost* must have been: what can I cut? There were other issues: the use of heroic verse, the limitations of stage machinery, the dilemma of costume, the aesthetic demands of representing an idea of paradise. How could one visually represent the invisible? But the first and, from the perspective of practicality, the most necessary question was: what could be dispensed with? Creation? Hell? The war in heaven? How could Milton's epic— which extends from the creation of time through human history and

the apocalypse to the end of time, from the marital bower through all
the visible universe and beyond, and takes twelve hours and upwards
to read aloud—be compressed into two and a half hours of traffic for
the commercial stage?[1] One of Dryden's many criticisms of Milton's
epic was that 'he runs into a flat of Thought, sometimes for a Hundred
Lines together . . . 'tis when he is got into a Track of Scripture'.[2] He
himself intended to be—needed to be—economical.

Yet there are a handful of places where *The State of Innocence* amplifies
on its original, and they are significant. They indicate Dryden's creative
and intellectual interests, interests which made him engage sympathet-
ically with his source but also carried him away from it. One is Eve's
dream. In *Paradise Lost* the dream is inspired in Eve's imagination when
Satan, 'Squat like a toad', whispers in her ear (4. 800). When Eve
awakens, troubled by her dream, she narrates it to Adam, who in
turn explains the physiology of dream-work:

> know that in the soul
> Are many lesser faculties that serve
> Reason as chief; among these fancy next
> Her office holds; of all external things,
> Which the five watchful senses represent,
> She forms imaginations, airy shapes,
> Which reason joining or disjoining, frames
> All what we affirm or what deny, and call
> Our knowledge or opinion; then retires
> Into her private cell when nature rests.
> Oft in her absence mimic fancy wakes
> To imitate her; but misjoining shapes,
> Wild work produces oft, and most in dreams,
> Ill matching words and deeds long past or late.
> Some such resemblances methinks I find
> Of our last evening's talk, in this thy dream,
> But with addition strange; yet be not sad.          (5. 100–16)[3]

The senses receive data which they then represent to the fancy, fancy
supplies conjectures based on these data, reason affirms or denies these
conjectures, and thus is formed what we think or know. When we
sleep, reason sleeps with us, but fancy ('mimic' suggests an attribute of
fancy rather than a substitute for true fancy, though the ambiguity is
there to be dwelt on) can continue to act upon old sense data to
generate the uncensored simulacra of reality that are dreams. The
passage is characteristically Miltonic: it supplies a physical basis for

ERE 

mental processes, explained using a dynamic metaphor, one that risks turning into romance. Moreover, by putting the metaphor into Adam's prelapsarian mouth it becomes knowledge or perfect science. Milton thereby uses fictional premises to articulate knowledge that is keener and truer than that in non-fictional writing.[4]

In Dryden's *State of Innocence*, Lucifer himself articulates the physiology of dreams. As in Milton's original he crouches at Eve's ear and whispers, but in this version the dream is performed: in the dream deformed shapes dance, and an angel persuades a figure representing Eve, in a similar state of undress, to eat the fruit, before praising interdicted joys.[5] It is possible to read this episode as an attempt to vulgarize or even systematically to efface the radical political implications of Milton's poem. Dryden introduces singing and dancing and stage machinery—effectively a masque interlude—into the work of a resolutely and consciously untheatrical author. We see the dream itself. We do not hear Eve's own, unnerved relation of it, and Adam's response is merely to hope that heaven will avert what the dream seems to portend (4. 1. 1–2). Though the performance is a transposition of Eve's thoughts received through diabolical suggestion, Lucifer's plan is to 'set' dreams 'before the Woman's eyes' (3.3.10). This suggests something more than mental drama; and the intended audience see a real drama, the elaborate stage management that Lucifer imposes upon Eve. Dryden inverts much of Milton's design, and the result is almost burlesque.

Dryden famously visited Milton and asked his permission to adapt *Paradise Lost*. The main authority for this event is John Aubrey, whose notes on Milton report: 'Jo Dreyden Esq Poet Laureate, who very much admires him: & went to him to have leave to putt his Paradise-lost into a Drama in Rhyme: M^r Milton recieved him civilly, & told him he would give him leave to tagge his Verses.' The two poets had worked in physical proximity at Whitehall for the Council of State during the later 1650s, but by the occasion of this visit, between 1669 and 1674, Dryden was Poet Laureate, Historiographer Royal, and a successful playwright, while the blind Milton was living in relative isolation. Aubrey's narrative invites us to read the meeting as a clash between an old world and a new, between two cultures. The temptation is to read subtexts into the alleged exchange, as if Dryden said, 'John, let me subject your dried-out and washed-up 1650s politics to the final humiliation by converting your life's work into that slavish and fashionable form that you so roundly dismissed in the note that you added to the fourth issue of the first edition in 1668 as "the troublesome and modern bondage of rhyming", and turning it into a stage play, the form you sneeringly eschewed in *Samson Agonistes* (1671), and, what's worse turning a fair profit out of it while you have nothing to look forward to but the grave'; and Milton said, 'Sure John, go ahead, because, first, you're going to look stupid, and, secondly, both of us know that this is the epigone of the English epic form and your long-standing ambitions to write an epic are now dead and buried, and by the way I heard that when you read my book you said to the Earl of Dorset, "this man cuts us all out, and the ancients too".' This may be reading too much into Aubrey's story.

Andrew Marvell, who had worked alongside Milton and Dryden for the Council of State during the late 1650s, added a note of adversarialism in his commendatory poem to the 1674 edition of *Paradise Lost*, which reflects on the difficulty early readers had with Milton's blank verse:

> Well mightst thou scorn thy readers to allure
> With tinkling rhyme, of thine own sense secure;
> While the town-Bayes writes all the while and spells,
> And like a pack-horse tires without his bells:
> Their fancies like our bushy points appear,
> The poets tag them, we for fashion wear.[6]

Marvell's diction, and swipe at Dryden under the nickname Mr Bayes, suggests that he knew of the visit that Aubrey relates, and saw the excellence of Milton's poem, and he pins its distinction from the fashionable sphere of Restoration literature on Dryden's tags, or rhymes. Marvell suggests a struggle over the politics of form. These perspectives suggest that it was form that most concerned Dryden: the epic form and heroic verse.

Milton in his youth had planned a biblical tragedy, sketching outlines entitled 'Paradise Lost' and 'Adam Unparadized', which included a chorus of angels alongside the paradisal couple and the personification of vices and virtues. In his later years he left these aside in favour of epic. There is reason to suspect that there was a literary–political dimension to this decision: Milton chose to abandon the dramatic form because the public stage was closed during the 1650s, because epic more comfortably suited his reflective, ambitious design, and because drama was a mode of representation he no longer felt comfortable with. By the Restoration Milton was well versed in the world of print, and used it to his own advantage. The absence of any dedication, the starkness of the frontmatter of *Paradise Lost*, suggests his self-perception as a print author, freed from the constraints of patronage, and this also is in stark contrast to Dryden's fulsomely dedicated drama.[7] When Milton did compose a tragedy, *Samson Agonistes*, probably written in the mid-1660s and published in 1671, he was careful to distinguish himself from the fashionable drama of the day, including Dryden's, returning to a more ancient manner and specifying that he never intended it for the stage.[8] Dryden's adaptation reverses this deliberated rejection of theatre. His script, moreover, purports to be an opera, a mixed form even more distant from Milton's aesthetic of the sublime. *The State of Innocence* includes songs, dances, and elaborate stage effects: it begins with the heavens opening and angels wheeling in the air, and later, a 'Cloud descends with six Angels in it; and when it's near the ground, breaks; and on each side, discovers six more.'[9]

Despite this interest in performance and theatricality, Dryden's opera never reached the stage. Though it was probably written in the spring of 1674 (it was entered in the Stationers' Register on 17 April, licensed by Milton's old detractor Roger L'Estrange), it was not printed until 1677, and Dryden then declared that he allowed it to go to the press only because of the number of imperfect manuscript copies of the texts then circulating. The most probable reason why the opera was never performed is that it was unfinished. It carries several marks of a text awaiting further revision: the songs and music are unevenly distributed, and one scene (2. 2) is in blank verse, and jars with the couplets of the remainder. Dryden may have been experimenting with mixed forms, or he may have intended to revise it, and add rhyme, at a future stage. This may seem like an improbably mechanical procedure, but in Dryden's *Essay of Dramatic Poesie* (1668), Neander comments:

When a poet has found the repartee, the last perfection he can add to it, is to put it into verse. However good the thought may be; however apt the words in which 'tis couch'd, yet he finds himself at a little unrest while Rhyme is wanting: he cannot leave it till that comes naturally, and then is at ease, and sits down contented.[10]

This is not Dryden's own voice, but that of a character in a dialogue; nonetheless, Dryden defended rhyme in a analogous manner frequently enough, and what is interesting here is the implication that rhyme is a decoration that may arise from the thought but can nonetheless be applied towards the end of the process of composition (Milton implies the same in *Eikonoklastes*).[11] Dryden's blank-verse scene may have been awaiting further work.

Whether or not Dryden was satisfied with the work, whether or not he found it derivative, inadequate, or incomplete, it was nonetheless a popular success of a sort he had not intended. Under the title 'The Fall of Angels and Man in Innocence' (matching the Stationers' Register entry), it became his most popular dramatic work in manuscript, was printed in nine editions between 1677 and 1701, and was second in reproducibility only to his *Absalom and Achitophel*. As a text, particularly as a manuscript text, it took on a different guise in adapting to the new medium, circulating alongside libertine poetry and satire. In manuscript, Eve's account of her sexual experience, and the prurient hints of nakedness, had a quite different quality.[12] Charles Leslie, who complained about the licence and impiety of Milton's armoured angels, thought Dryden's adaptation worse: 'the *Truth* has been Greatly *Hurt* thereby, and Degraded at last, even into a *Play*, which was Design'd to have been *Acted* upon the *Stage*: And tho' once Happily Prevented, yet has Pass'd the *Press*, and become the Entertainment of *Prophane Raillery*'.[13]

In contrast, and despite early recognition that it was a work of the imagination that rivalled the classics, Milton's book sold fairly slowly. *The State of Innocence* may have been the version of *Paradise Lost* known to the widest Restoration public, a crib for a demanding text. The adaptation appropriated the lustre of an imaginative narrative based on the Genesis story, translating the unyielding anti-heroism and theological earnestness of an anti-theatrical author into zestful savouries for the Restoration palate. 'Let them please their appetites in eating what they like,' Dryden writes in his preface, 'but let them not force their dish on all the Table.'[14]

Readers have concurred with Marvell that *Paradise Lost* and Dryden's adaptation are antipathetic. An early and insightful response to Dryden's drama appeared in a pamphlet entitled *The Reasons of Mr. Bays Changing his Religion* (1688), by the presumably pseudonymous Dudley Tomkinson. The pamphlet presents a dialogue between Crites, Eugenius (two of the three interlocutors in Dryden's *Essay of Dramatic Poesy*), and Bays, the persona by which the Duke of Buckingham satirized Dryden in *The Rehearsal* (1672). In the dialogue Bays—that is Dryden—confesses that he 'affronted the whole Celestial

Hierarchy' when he was seized by the 'Spirit of Contradiction' and 'undertook to clear *Miltons* Paradice of Weeds, and garnish that noble Poem with the additional beauty and softness of Rhyme'. Bays proceeds to incriminate himself: in Milton's epic Adam speaks so ungracefully, so unlike a gentleman, that 'you'd pitty his condition. And then for *Eve*, as he has drawn her Character, she talks so like an insipid Country House-keeper, whose knowledge goes no farther than the Still or the Dairy, who is as little acquainted with the tenderness of passion, as the management of an Intreague, that one cannot choose but wonder at it.'[15] In his improved version, Bays continues, Eve speaks feelingly of love, and Adam, having benefited from a university education, has learned all about supralapsarianism. For Tomkinson, Dryden has turned the sublime lines of *Paradise Lost* into a polite drama of court intrigue that is artistically grotesque and theologically confused.

For the most part critics have concurred on the question of artistry. Walter Scott thought Dryden's task 'may be safely condemned as presumptuous' and that in places it 'strangely degraded' Milton's verse. Others have suggested that Dryden's drama 'merited obscurity' despite its early popularity; that his characters are crude parodies, and the whole an 'offensive vulgarisation of *Paradise Lost*'.[16] A few dissenters have contended that Dryden's version of the Fall story is in some ways stronger—more natural, more admitting of the transformative power of love—than Milton's; that Dryden brings out the comedy implicit in the theological problem of God's foresight; that its compression is masterful.[17] One eccentrically suggests that Dryden presents a more complex account of gender; another that Dryden's Eve is 'decidedly less suppressed' than Milton's, a page before he notes that discretion is not one of womankind's strengths.[18] For most readers, however, Dryden's *State of Innocence* can be read as *Paradise Lost* thrown in a blender.[19]

There is deeper sense in the adaptation. There was a nuanced and mutual influence between Milton and Dryden, and *The State of Innocence* shows a complex attitude to, and sophisticated transformations of, its source.[20] Some of the aesthetic decisions are politically motivated. Dryden was undertaking a hostile political coup, seeking to contain the dangerous enthusiasm and inspiration of the old republican in a rational and polite form. *The State of Innocence* set bounds around the enthusiastic licence of the epic, wrapping its harsh language and unruly

structures in rhyme and decorous narrative.[21] Dryden took Milton to
task for his politics, though with punctilious and perhaps generous
specificity. In the debate in hell in the first act, the fallen angels
appropriate the constitutional language of the 1650s, conferring 'in
frequent Senate' (not a word *Paradise Lost* uses in this context); they
have become the 'States-General of Hell', a term that clearly indicates
the Dutch republic; they hate 'Universal Monarchy', a phrase that
echoes Whig anti-French rhetoric of the 1670s.[22] Dryden seems to
criticize the popular pro-Dutch sentiment that swelled during the third
Anglo-Dutch war (which some blamed on France), and associates
Whig rhetoric with republicanism.[23] While Milton shows Satan
using the language of liberty cynically and improperly, Dryden's
Lucifer is at ease with it. Moreover, the images of the devils sitting
'as in Council' in their palace is an allusion to popular engravings in
broadsides around 1660 that represented Cromwell and his Council of
State as Lucifer and his peers sitting around a table.[24] Dryden also
rendered the narrative and the language of *Paradise Lost* banal by
translating it into the terms of Restoration comedy, transforming
Milton's radical vision of sexual politics into a courtship. When
Adam suggests to Eve that they lock themselves in close embrace,
she responds that something that is not shame forbids her, 'some
restraining thought, I know not why, | Tells me, you long should
beg, I long deny' (2. 3. 54–5). He praises Eve's beauty, and she agrees
to be his delight even while worrying that some other new-made
beauty might creep into his heart. After the Fall their desire is articu-
lated through libertine commonplaces, Adam sounding like Dorimant
when he asks 'Where appetites are giv'n, what sin to tast?' (5. 2. 78).
Small wonder that Tomkinson mocks Dryden's implicit criticism of
Milton's Eve:

she talks of love as feelingly as a Thrice-married Widdow, yet rails at marriage
with the same concern as if she had seen the misfortunes of half her Daughters;
tells her Gallant that it was the Practice of all his *Sex* to decoy poor Innocent
Maids with sham stories of their Passion; and that he'd be as apt to forget her
after the enjoyment was over, as a Sharper of the Town forgets the last friend
he borrowed money of.[25]

There is none of the breathless eroticism of Milton's postlapsarian
lovemaking, and Dryden has accommodated Edenic love-relations
within the patterns and mores conventional upon the Restoration stage.

Yet the relationship between these texts is not exclusively one of political opposition, and Dryden's account of Milton, deeply ingrained with ambivalence, is not a thoroughly hostile or an ignorant one. Dryden's adaptation *is* an adaptation, emerging from Dryden's close and conflicted relationship with Milton; it is a dialogue, an imitation, a translation that discloses the shift in Restoration literary modes. An exploration of the matrix of this adaptation can show how Dryden's angelology and his extended account of freewill disclose a seriousness of purpose and a degree of coherence in his adaptation. Angels, dreams, and freewill, it will be seen, were intimately related.

## Angels

Though Dryden was certainly concerned with the form and politics of *Paradise Lost*, what he does with angels suggests that he was also occupied with content: he takes Milton to task over his angelology. Dryden believed in guardian angels. Milton, too, believed in angels assigned to a particular place or kingdom, though perhaps more diffidently. In *De Doctrina Christiana*, Milton writes, 'It is probable, too, that angels are put in charge of nations, kingdoms, and particular districts.' St Michael appears in this capacity at the end of 'Lycidas', and *Paradise Lost* suggests such a connection between Uriel and the sun, and between Raphael and Michael and earth.[26] To Dryden the doctrine was intellectually and aesthetically significant. In his 'Discourse Concerning the Original and Progress of Satire' (1693) Dryden reflects at length on the possibility of modern epic. The aspiring author of a Christian epic, he writes, faced a problem with the machinery, which is so much less rich than in heathen epic. Moreover, there is another dilemma in the conflict between omnipotent good and the over-matched forces of the Devil, which is little conducive to dramatic tension. The solution to these problems lies in the same Christian doctrine, he writes:

'Tis a Doctrine almost Universally receiv'd by Christians, as well Protestants as Catholicks, that there are Guardian Angels appointed by God Almighty, as his Vicegerents, for the Protection and Government of Cities, Provinces, King-doms, and Monarchies; and those as well of Heathens, as of true Believers. All this is so plainly prov'd from those Texts of *Daniel*, that it admits of no father Controversie. . . . St. *Michael* is mention'd by his Name, as the Patron of the

*Jews*, and is now taken by the Christians, as the Protector General of our Religion. These Tutelar *Genij*, who presided over the several People and Regions committed to their Charge, were watchful over them for good, as far as their Commissions cou'd possibly extend. The General Purpose, and Design of all, was certainly the Service of their Great Creatour.

These guardian angels are not in possession of God's power nor sight of his whole plan. They are 'Finite Beings, not admitted into the Secrets of Government, the last resorts of Providence'.[27] This means that they can oppose each other, and be deceived by the wicked, and this creates uncertainty and therefore drama. Dryden both believes in the existence of guardian angels, and thinks that they solve the problems of Christian epic. They may even be its enabling condition. Poets might have found in the Old Testament 'the Machines which are proper for their Work'. Reading Daniel,

and Accommodating what there they find, with the Principles of *Platonique* Philosophy, as it is now Christianis'd, wou'd have made the Ministry of Angels as strong an Engine, for the Working up of Heroique Poetry, in our Religion, as that of the Ancients had been to raise theirs by all the Fables of their Gods, which were only receiv'd for Truths by the most ignorant, and weakest of the People.[28]

Guardian angels have a symbolic role in the 1677 dedication of *The State of Innocence*; there Dryden plays with angels, associating them with the Roman Catholic baroque in a dedication that is intended to chafe the sensibilities of many Protestants. The dedicatee was Maria Beatrice of Modena, who in November 1673 became Duchess of York and wife to the heir to the throne: Dryden wryly praises the celestial beauty of this most prominent Catholic in imagery drawn from the opera: 'your Person is a Paradice, and your Soul a Cherubin within to guard it'. She has 'subverted . . . even our Fundamental Laws' and reigns 'absolute' over the English, despite their stubborn assertions of liberty. Meanwhile, it is the poet's duty to celebrate such beauty: 'Beauty is their Deity to which they Sacrifice, and Greatness is their Guardian-Angel which protects them.'[29] The doctrine of guardianship is also exploited in the dramatic text, where, however, a significant variation is introduced. Gabriel and Ithuriel refer to themselves as 'the Guardians of this new-made pair' (3. 2. 2), suggesting that they are individual guardian angels rather than guardians of place. In *Paradise Lost* it is Gabriel who assigns Ithuriel and Zephon to protect Adam and Eve, and the angels assume a collective responsibility for the humans.[30] The distinction may well be intended to pass unnoticed. It is, however, theologically significant, particularly in the light of Dryden's stressing, in the 'Discourse Concerning Satire', that both Protestants and Catholics adhere to certain beliefs about angels. While the existence of local guardian angels was relatively uncontroversial, credence in individual guardian angels was used by some to distinguish Roman Catholic doctrine from Protestant.[31] Dryden's two phrases about guardian angels do not indicate that he held such beliefs; he had not yet converted to Catholicism; and in any case Protestants who rejected the doctrine of custodian angels after the Fall might hold that angels were assigned to Adam and Eve in paradise, at least until they were debarred by the fiery cherubim.[32] Dryden's language nonetheless articulates a doctrine that marks confessional difference, and we know from his 'Discourse' that it was a confessional difference he understood in 1693. If he does not believe it, then his choice of terminology foregrounds the imaginative uses that can be made of the elaborate dogma of angelologists. Theological arguments about the nature and status of angels provide an apparatus for the poet, who can elaborate doctrine through narrative and complex imagery, who can articulate subtle distinctions or create scandal by the lightest of touches upon issues that are deeply rooted in doctrinal or confessional differences. It is, in part, the complexity of their theological basis that makes angels a useful register for the poet.

All Dryden's angels are male. In 'The Authors Apology for Heroique Poetry and Poetique Licence', which appears as a preface to the printed *State of Innocence*, he justifies this decision: 'how are Poetical Fictions, how are Hippocentaures and Chymæras, or how are Angels and immaterial Substances to be Imag'd? ... For Immaterial Substances we are authoriz'd by Scripture in their description: and herein the Text accommodates itself to vulgar apprehension, in giving Angels the likeness of beautiful young men.'[33] What is remarkable here is not Dryden's uncharacteristic conformity to erroneous 'vulgar apprehension', but his concern with the nature of matter (the pseudo-paradox of 'Immaterial Substances'), his association of this with poetical creation, and his use of the hard word 'accommodates', which is doing more work than at first appears. We have already seen his reference to readers 'accommodating' their reading of Daniel with the principles of (Neo-) Platonic philosophy. He invokes the doctrine

of accommodation (see Chapter 6, above), and humorously responds
to the several passages in *Paradise Lost* in which the angel Raphael
puzzles over how to relate the 'invisible exploits | Of warring Spirits'
and 'lift | Human imagination' to apprehend the divine. His own text,
Dryden says, has to lower itself to the apprehension of the vulgar
audience, and in doing this he will represent all angels as beautiful
young men. This is doubtless convenient for the Restoration stage. It
also enables Adam to vent his misogyny following the Fall: 'Our wise
Creator, for his Quires divine, | Peopled his Heav'n with Souls all
masculine' (5. 4. 66–7). Yet there is more at stake here, because
Dryden is correcting Milton's angelology, with its startling, sexually
active angels:

> To whom the angel with a smile that glowed
> Celestial rosy red, love's proper hue,
> Answered. Let it suffice thee that thou knowst
> Us happy, and without love no happiness.
> Whatever pure thou in the body enjoyst
> (And pure thou wert created) we enjoy
> In eminence, and obstacle find none
> Of membrane, joint, or limb, exclusive bars:
> Easier that air with air, if spirits embrace,
> Total they mix, union of pure with pure
> Desiring; nor restrained conveyance need
> As flesh to mix with flesh, or soul with soul.          (8. 618–29)

As Dryden makes the sexual encounter between Adam and Eve
conform to the norms of Restoration comedy (when he offers a close
embrace, she protests, 'Somewhat forbids me, which I cannot name';
2. 3. 52), he cancels the sexuality of unfallen angels in a silent correc-
tion of Milton's heterodoxy.

Dryden's angels are not free of sexual longing, however, and there is
a sting in the tail. While in hell, Lucifer remarks how odd the
rumoured mankind is:

> Of form Divine; but less in excellence
> Than we; indu'd with Reason lodg'd in Sence:
> The Soul pure Fire, like ours, of equal force;
> But, pent in Flesh, must issue by discourse:
> We see what is; to Man Truth must be brought
> By Sence, and drawn by a long Chain of thought:
> By that faint light, to will and understand;
> For made less knowing, he's at more command.          (1. 1. 146–53)

This is far from Raphael's distinction between intuitive and discursive reason (5. 486–90); for Dryden angelic cognition is different in nature. For Milton there was a fundamental continuity between human and angelic comprehension that followed from the material nature of both creatures; Dryden was a dualist. Not only does Lucifer not have a body; unlike Milton's Satan he is immaterial, insubstantial. He looks upon Adam and Eve and thinks that they are odd. Strikingly, we learn the characteristics of angels from their mouths while they are reflecting on what a peculiar creature man is. Later Lucifer spies on Adam and Eve and discovers lust; and Dryden exploits the dramatic potential of angelic disembodiment. Eve, having given in to Adam's expectations, describes her experience of orgasm (ecstasy, immortal pleasures, breathlessness, loss of selfhood; 3. 1. 39–46), and Lucifer expresses envy:

> Why have not I like these, a body too,
> Form'd for the same delights which they pursue?
> I could (so variously my passions move)
> Enjoy and blast her, in the act of love.          (3. 1. 92–5)

It is a clever defamiliarizing device, reflecting on human difference from a non-human perspective: Lucifer initially thinks that Eve is odd because she has a body; later he wishes he had one, so he could rape her and experience orgasm himself.

The conjunction between sexual desire and malicious and destructive violence appears plentifully on the Restoration stage, but Lucifer's fantasy has a basis in Christian exegesis. This is the story of the sons of God who take to wife the daughters of men in Genesis 6, and who, according to one reading, were fallen angels.[34] Milton rejects this reading of Genesis; Dryden dramatizes the diabolical temptation, while making it plain that it was mechanically impossible: angels, to Lucifer's chagrin, don't have the right equipment. In doing so he follows Milton, and thus differs from most seventeenth-century narrative poems about angels, in presenting an angel reflecting upon its experience of being, upon what it feels like to be an angel.

None of this is as difficult as Milton's dense angel-learning, but it does show Dryden consciously responding to and reworking his original in terms of its angelology. It is not only in the detail that their uses of angels differ, however, but in their very mode of representation. For Milton accommodation is what makes his poem possible, which is to say, is what makes it true. Everything Milton writes about angels develops from his beliefs about their nature and fits with and follows from what he knows about them. He articulates knowledge through his narratives, and his poetry posits that doctrine and story, inspired feigning and fact, are inseparable. For Dryden the case is quite different. His account of accommodation permits the misrepresentation of angels as young men, in order to fit a common misperception. Spiritual reality matters less than the beauty of the images. 'You are not oblig'd, as in a History, to a literal belief of what the Poet says,' he writes; 'but you are pleas'd with the Image, without being couzen'd by the Fiction.' Milton's enthusiastic faith and aesthetics did not allow of this distinction. Dryden again: 'And Poets may be allow'd the like liberty, for describing things which really exist not, if they are founded on popular belief: of this nature are Fairies, Pigmies, and the extraordinary effects of Magick: for 'tis still an imitation, though of other mens fancies.'[35] He does not here name angels, though these words appear in a discussion of the legitimacy of representing angels. In the near-contemporary essay 'Of Heroique Playes' (prefatory to *The Conquest of Granada*, 1672) he makes the same point: 'an Heroick Poet is not ty'd to a bare representation of what is true, or exceeding probable: but that he may let himself loose to visionary objects, and to the representation of such things, as depending not on sence, and therefore not to be comprehended by knowledge, may give him a freer scope for the imagination'. This judgement may be understood as a direct response to reading *Paradise Lost*. Milton freely imagines such visionary objects, but ties himself to theology. Dryden's visionary objects are governed by the proper conventions of heroic poetry, only through which could ideal beauty be wrought.[36] It is both acknowledgement and criticism of Milton.

Dryden then raises the question of representing 'spirits', and continues:

This I say is foundation enough for Poetry: and I dare farther affirm that the whole doctrine of separated beings, whether those Spirits are incorporeal substances, (which Mr. *Hobbs*, with some reason thinks to imply a contradiction,) or that they are a thinner and more Aerial sort of bodies (as some of the Fathers have conjectur'd) may better be explicated by Poets, than by Philosophers or Divines.[37]

'Spirits' here slips straight into angels, and the value of angels is that we cannot know about them; they are machinery for literature; a matter for feigned representations, visionary objects. This is what makes them beautiful and therefore useful.

## Freewill

Dryden had just been reading Hobbes. Curiously (and perhaps it is no more than a curiosity), in his notes of Milton, following the mention of Dryden, Aubrey adds: 'His [Milton's] widow assures me that Mr. Hobbs was not one of his acquaintance,' as if familiarity with Hobbes and with Dryden were connected. To see how Dryden is responding to Milton, it is necessary to shed more light on his reading of Hobbes, and the importance to Dryden's writings of debates about freewill. Some evidence for this lies in another passage of *The State of Innocence* in which Dryden deviated from and expanded upon *Paradise Lost*.

Between the dream and the separation scenes Raphael and Gabriel enter paradise to warn Adam that an 'Apostate Angel' seeks their downfall and has whispered 'Delusive dreams' into Eve's ear. Adam must protect Eve's frailty, and, though the warning assists with the outward threat, responsibility is ultimately his: 'Ills, from within, thy reason must prevent' (4. 1. 13–18). To which Adam responds with a question: 'what praises can I pay | Defended in obedience; taught t'obey' (21–2). Adam asks in what sense his praise can be meaningful if he is protected and instructed in obedience, which makes his expression of prayer subservient rather than voluntary. His question provokes a long and unresolved debate. The scene is the most powerful in the opera, and it is where Dryden's adaptation of Milton is most complex.

The debate between Adam and the angels in *The State of Innocence* parallels the exchange over the nature of freewill between Hobbes and John Bramhall, Bishop of Derry, which found its way into print in the 1650s. The texts were first juxtaposed, perhaps without his realizing the nature of their association, by John Dowell in 1681.[38] The exact nature of the parallel is confusing: Adam and the angels cannot be straightforwardly aligned with one or other position, and Dryden's own relationship with Adam and the angels is not clear.[39] To interrogate which of Hobbes's and Bramhall's arguments Dryden is echoing, the nature of those echoes, and where Dryden's allegiances in the dichotomies he presents lie, it is necessary to summarize the debate. It is inspired by God's instructions to Raphael, the angel's words on freewill to Adam in book 5 of *Paradise Lost*, and Satan's complaint about the praise owed to God and 'The debt immense of endless gratitude' (5. 235–45; 4. 46, 52). In response to Adam's question, Dryden's Raphael states that man possesses freewill as he was given reason; Adam doubts that 'finite man' can possess freewill, as that would make his state equal his Creator's. Adam's increasingly sophisticated arguments, here, closely keyed to the terms of Hobbes's and Bramhall's debate, are what spurred the scorn of Tomkinson; his philosophical inclinations seem absurd, perhaps intentionally so, from his waking moments, when his first words recapitulate the proof of the existence of God from Descartes's *Meditations* (2. 1. 1–12). Raphael suggests that God does not give his power away, but can give away liberty of choice, just as—and the mechanical analogy is interestingly unfortunate—he can set an orb in motion then leave it to revolve of its own accord. But, Adam asks, how does this square with preordination? Either freewill or preordination must be in vain. Gabriel responds (a little lamely; the purpose must be to introduce a discussion of various kinds of causality) that the rest of Creation is governed by necessity, and Adam asks: 'Yet causes their effects necessitate | In willing agents: where is freedom then?' (4. 1. 51–2). In other words, even if man wills something, this does not make him free unless his will is a cause; otherwise he may will that which is ordained by other causes, and not be free in any sense that Adam can understand. Raphael then posits the distinction between God's inference of what must be and the bringing about of events, thus 'Causes which work th'effect, force not the will' (4. 1. 64). The sense is not entirely clear, but the angel's point seems to be that there are first and second causes, and freewill exists within the realm of second causes, the realm which Adam understands; God's foreknowledge pertains to the realm of first causes, which is beyond Adam's apprehension and does not interfere with freewill. Adam responds, perhaps with some justification, 'the long chain makes not the bondage less' (4. 1. 66). He may feel free, but is in fact not; he can choose, but in so doing wills the inevitable. At this point the weary Gabriel—their limitations are another respect in which Dryden's angels resemble Milton's—states that these 'impious fancies . . . Make Heav'n, all pure, thy crimes to preordain' (4. 1. 75–6).

Who said anything about crimes? Dryden is less meticulous about
the condition of innocence than Milton, though his mode of repre-
sentation has in any case abandoned all notions of plausibility. Adam is
duly chastised, but he might well have asked how Gabriel has inside
information about the crimes he will freely commit. Gabriel's point is
that Adam's scepticism about freewill risks the scandal of imputing
the origins of evil to God. Here Adam's Scholastic training breaks
down. He apologizes and asks perhaps his most important question: if
freedom is founded on the necessity of first causes, and first causes are
sufficient to produce effects, how is man free? And Raphael responds:

> Sufficient causes, only work th'effect
> When necessary agents they respect.
> Such is not man; who, though the cause suffice,
> Yet often he his free assent denies.           (4. 1. 85–8)

In other words: causes may be sufficient but nonetheless not take effect
because the human will, not subject to necessity, denies them. We are
witnessing a confusion about the meaning of sufficiency, and I will
look at these lines more closely below. Adam asks in what sense these
causes are then 'sufficient', and Raphael points out that Adam's
account of causality only works with the benefit of hindsight, from
which perspective anything can be proved necessary.

The exchange approaches its climax as Adam changes direction and
asks the central question about the origins of evil: why does not God
prevent man from sinning, because by not preventing ill he seems to
will it? Gabriel's Miltonic response is that such intervention would
take away freewill. And Adam answers, of course, wouldn't that be
better for man than to be allowed freely to sin? What then would
be the point of reward and punishment? responds Raphael. We have
returned to the starting point: how can rote praise be meaningful?
Crimes are necessary to allow just punishment and reward. Then, with
a dramatic panache only angels could get away with, Gabriel and
Raphael announce that they have completed their task and leave.
They have not: Adam is left to reflect on how hard his condition is,
wishing that he were 'ty'd up from doing ill' (4. 1. 114), just as Milton's
Adam would do after the Fall. The angels have failed to explain the
problem of freewill to Adam, and he is left helpless on stage, a character
in a drama, faced with choices, riven with doubts, and waiting for the
next scene. Enter Eve, wanting to spend some time on her own.

Hobbes's argument with Bramhall about liberty and necessity began at the Marquess of Newcastle's Paris residence in 1645, when they were all in exile. Bramhall's 'A Discourse of Liberty and Necessity' circulated in manuscript, articulating his position and provoking Hobbes's response. The fruits of this debate then appeared in print, increasingly hostile in tone, between 1654 and 1658. Dryden could have read everything he needed to read to write his scene in a single volume, *The Questions Concerning Liberty, Necessity, and Chance. Clearly Stated and Debated between Dr. Bramhall Bishop of Derry, and Thomas Hobbes of Malmesbury* (1656). Though the volume was Hobbes's, as the title page suggests it presents animadversions between both parties, printing lengthy extracts from Bramhall's anterior texts. The typography requires patience. Hobbes begins by quoting a passage of Bramhall's 'Discourse' under the initials J.D. (John, Bishop of Derry), then quotes, under T.H., his own *Of Libertie and Necessitie* (1654) in response, then J.D.'s *A Defence of True Liberty* (1655). Then he incorporates a section of new argument, headed 'Animadversions', which consists mainly of compressed quotations from the previous sections threaded towards a conclusion. Hobbes does not explain what he is doing, how he is doing it, or even identify the texts that he is quoting:

Animadversions upon the Bishops Reply Number, XI.

This argument was sent forth only as an espie, to make a more full discovery, what were the true grounds of *T.H.* his supposed Necessity.

*The Argument which he sendeth forth as an Espie, is this,* If either the decree of God, or the Fore-knowledge of God, or the Influence of the Stars, or the Concatenation (*which he sayes falsly I call a Concourse)* of causes, or the Physical or Moral Efficacy of objects, or the last Dictate of the Understanding, do take away true liberty, then *Adam* before his fall had no true liberty. *In answer whereunto I said, that all the things now existent, were necessary to the production of the effect to come*; that the Fore-knowledge *of God causeth nothing though the* Will *do*; *that the influence of the Stars is but a small part of that cause which maketh the Necessity; and that this consequence* If the concourse of all the causes necessitate the effect, then *Adam* had no true liberty, *was false. But in his words, if those do take away true liberty, then* Adam *before his fall had no true liberty, the consequence is good; but then I deny that Necessity takes away Liberty; the reason whereof which is this*, Liberty is to choose what we will, not to choose our Will, *no inculcation is sufficient to make the* Bishop *take notice of, notwithstanding he be otherwhere so witty, and here so crafty, as to send out Arguments for spies. The cause why I denied the consequence was, that I thought the force thereof consisted in this, that Necessity in the* Bishops *opinion destroyed Liberty*.[40]

For the most part the roman text repeats Bramhall's words, the italic type Hobbes's voice; he begins with *A Defence*, works backwards to 'A Discourse', then justifies his former response in *Of Libertie*. It is a cumbersome procedure, though it is marked by professional honesty: a reader sympathetic to Bramhall could find his argument at length here, and in his own words, albeit fragmented by Hobbes's contradictions.

   This paragraph, despite its oblique formulation, reveals both how Hobbes's arguments could inform Dryden's reading and rewriting of *Paradise Lost*, and the proximity between Hobbes's words and Dryden's angels' position on necessary causes and the human will. Hobbes is a compatibilist: he contends that freewill exists, and that there is no conflict between this and God's prescience. Liberty consists in the absence of external impediments, so that one can do as one wills, and divine prescience is not an impediment to this. It is compulsion that obstructs liberty, and not necessity, which is the realm in which God's foreknowledge and first causes operate. Hobbes's conception of what it meant to possess freewill was more restricted than that assumed by many contemporaries. Man is free because he experiences himself as free (Dryden's Gabriel points out that man is the best judge of whether or not he is free), because he deliberates upon an action and then wills it.[41] Man's will is nonetheless subject to causes. This is most clearly stated in a passage of *Leviathan* which uses the same chain metaphor against which Dryden's Adam remonstrates. Hobbes writes:

because every act of mans will, and every desire, and inclination, proceedeth from some cause, and that from another cause, in a continual chaine, (whose first link is in the hand of God the first of all causes,) they proceed from *necessity*. So that to him that could see the connexion of those causes, the *necessity* of all mens voluntary actions, would appeare manifest.[42]

In these terms foreknowledge is an effect, not a cause: knowledge, even foreknowledge, depends on events, not vice versa.[43] Raphael says just this in a crisp triplet:

> Heav'n by fore-knowing what will surely be,
> Does only, first, effects in causes see;
> And finds, but does not make necessity.          (4. 1. 56–8)

Hobbes's position looks like Raphael's, not like Adam's position, and Adam inverts Hobbes's argument about the chain. For Hobbes, the chain does not preclude liberty; for Adam it does.

Bramhall's defence of liberty does not rule out a notion of preordination; he maintains that freedom and necessity are irreconcilable, but nonetheless does not deny that human freewill and preordination exist. His resolution of the problem is different, however, from Hobbes's insistence that they are compatible. He is critical of attempts to separate causes: consider, he writes, 'a man imprisoned and fettered, is he therefore free to walk where he will because he has feet and a locomotive faculty?'[44] This is Adam's chain once again, and Hobbes may have had in mind this passage when writing about freewill in *Leviathan*. Man must be free, Bramhall insists, or punishment could not be just (here he resembles the angels' position), hell could not exist, and society would fall apart. This is certain, even if we cannot comprehend how it is so. We must simply accept that we cannot understand. Dryden's Adam resists passivity and refuses to concede the limits of reason. Bramhall accepts ineffability and places the harmony between prescience, causes, and freedom in a realm of temporality beyond human experience or comprehension, introducing a note of mystical obscurity:

the readiest way to reconcile contingence and liberty with the decrees and prescience of God, and most remote from the altercations of these times, is to subject future contingents to the aspect of God, according to that presentiality which they have in eternity. Not that things future, which are not yet existent, are co-existent with God; but because the infinite knowledge of God, incircling all times in the point of eternity, does attain to their future being, from whence proceeds their objective and intelligible being.[45]

This is a form of compatibilism, which places the resolution of the apparent tensions between prescience, causes, and freedom in a realm of temporality beyond human experience or comprehension. Bramhall's terminological imprecision was sure to irritate Hobbes, who responded that he shared this opinion, and it seemed to go against the rest of Bramhall's argument. Hobbes also noted that, while they both seemed to believe that good angels were free, Bramhall's claim that they were 'more free than we' was nonsensical.[46]

On the question of the chain, and the separation between first and second causes, Dryden's Adam seems to side not with Hobbes but with Bramhall. Adam thinks he cannot be free if only within a realm of secondary causes, whereas for Hobbes that is just how far freedom extends. Adam's comments on causes necessitating effects iterates Bramhall's answer to Hobbes. The angels use compatibilist arguments, and while Bramhall himself defended a kind of compatibilism, the angels do so by distinguishing between first and second causes. This is Hobbes's distinction, and the angelic notion of freewill looks more like Hobbes's, which for many (including Bramhall and Adam, and subsequent philosophers) was not freewill at all.

However, at one stage at least in the argument the resemblances between Adam and Bramhall and between the angels and Hobbes falter. This is in the lines quoted above, when Raphael says that 'sufficient causes' are only effective when they function through 'necessary agents', and not through man, who can freely deny his assent. Hobbes had argued that a sufficient cause was one in which nothing was lacking to produce an effect; which was the same as a necessary cause. The notion that a free agent is something that might not produce an effect when all the necessary causes were present 'is non-sence, being as much to say, The cause may be *sufficient*, that is to say, *necessarie*, and yet the *effect* shall not follow'.[47] For Bramhall there was no contradiction: 'a cause is said to be sufficient in respect of the ability of it to act, not in respect of its will to act. The concurrence of the will is needful to the production of a free effect. But the cause may be sufficient, though the will do not concur.' For Bramhall, Hobbes was wilfully confusing two sorts of sufficiency, one defined inclusively of the will, the other exclusively, and was guilty of 'a meer Logomachy, or contention about words'.[48] The distinctions are also played out in the opera:

> ADAM.   What causes not, is not sufficient still.
> GABRIEL.  Sufficient in it self; not in thy will.          (4. 1. 89–90)

Gabriel's position here is clearly that of Bramhall; and Adam articulates Hobbes's position, that if causes do not produce effects, then they are not sufficient. The terminological match is precise: Dryden had these texts in mind when writing this scene.

There is no one-to-one correspondence between the positions of the disputants. Adam and the angels both articulate arguments and assumptions drawn from both Hobbes and Bramhall. The debate is the same, but the skirmish-lines are drawn differently, and there is no single, simple alteration that explains the transformations. Dryden is using the arguments, not offering us a *roman-à-clef*. His appropriations

reflect the presentation of Hobbes's *Questions*: animadversions which
exhibit both sides of the case and both voices, before digesting the
voices into a new argument, a third, hybrid, though partial, voice.[49]
Dryden's reworking of the Hobbes–Bramhall debate is self-consciously
unresolved, and it impinges directly upon his understanding of
dramatic form. It is, therefore, not an anomalous intrusion into a
disunified text but his considered response to the form of Milton's
epic. This can be seen in what ensues: Adam is abandoned on stage, the
angels having flown off after their glib 'Our task is done' (4. 1. 111),
and faced with a decision. He feels helpless under the burden of a
freewill he cannot understand and which the angels cannot explain to
him. He is not a proposition in a debate but a character in a drama. The
debate concerns freewill specifically inflected in a dramatic context.
This is not about Hobbes and Bramhall: it is about theatre.

Dryden had puzzled over freewill before he read *Paradise Lost*, and
his interest caused him to pick out this theme in reading and subse-
quently adapting the epic. One of the reasons the Hobbes–Bramhall
debate mattered to Dryden was because it addressed his conception of
theatre. Just as angels presented a perspective on literary representation
and the machinery of epic, so freewill was a means of understanding
the two grandest literary genres, tragedy and epic, not least because it
necessarily illuminated heroism. I will unpick some of the connections
between these themes before returning to the matter of dreams.

Dryden proposed one link between freedom and heroism in his
1664 dedication of *The Rival Ladies* to Roger, Earl of Orrery. There he
writes that Orrery governs men in his role as a statesman as he also
governs them on the stage in his plays:

Here is no chance which you have not fore-seen; all your Heroes are more
than your Subjects; they are your Creatures. And though they seem to move
freely, in all the Sallies of their Passions, yet you make Destinies for them
which they cannot shun. They are mov'd (if I may dare to say so) like the
Rational Creatures of the Almighty Poet, who walk at Liberty, in their own
Opinion, because their Fetters are Invisible; when indeed the Prison of their
Will, is the more sure for being large: and instead of an absolute power over
their Actions, they have only a wretched Desire of doing that, which they
cannot choose but do.[50]

The relationship between freedom and necessity is one that is played
out on the stage. It is the same relationship that Dryden seeks to resolve
in his proposals concerning guardian angels: what is the role of

uncertainty and therefore drama when the omnipotent fights against
the finite, or when the outcome of the conflict dramatized is already
universally known?[51] It is the playwright's art to make his creatures
seem to walk and choose at liberty, when in fact he has already sealed
their future. If all the world's a stage, then the playwright is God, and
vice versa. Freewill is a dramatic problem. The stage is also, therefore,
a place where the relationship between freewill and divine preordina-
tion can be represented and explored. The apparent freewill of the
characters coexists with the aesthetic design of the author. Humans
and characters are both 'Rational Creatures' (which is to say, things
created); the poet is also the 'Almighty'. And both humans and
characters walk—or might walk—in invisible fetters, the chains of
which Adam complains. According to the 'Discourse Concerning
Satire', God furnished his angels with insight into only part of the
story, not the 'Main design'. According to the *Essay of Dramatic Poesie*,
the 'Unity of Action' of a play depends on whether the lesser,
'imperfect actions of the Play are conducing to the main design'.[52]
The playwright's plot is described with the same phrase as divine
providence: both plan a 'main design', which is beyond the cogni-
zance of their creatures. An agent's ignorance of the main design is
what enables both the perception of freedom to act and drama itself.
Freewill is for Dryden a concept inscribed within dramatic and
aesthetic theory. Dryden's critical theory, the first sustained body
of criticism in English, is recognizably prompted by theology and
political and natural philosophy.

Freewill, angels, and their dramatic and aesthetic consequences are
what is at stake in the pivotal scene in *The Conquest of Granada, Part II*,
performed in January 1671 (three years before *The State of Innocence*,
and, I propose, after Dryden had read *Paradise Lost*). Almanzor, the
charismatic and faintly ridiculous hero of the burlesque heroic drama,
is approached by the ghost of his mother, sent, she relates, by an angel
from the battlements of heaven to warn him that he is in danger of
committing a terrible crime in battle (killing his father, though she
does not disclose this). The visit echoes *Hamlet*, though the ghost is
specifically not a purgatorial visitor; after death she flew, she says, to
the middle sky, but could go no further until she had completed the
assigned task. Immediately after the ghost disappears, Almanzor reflects
upon the nature of freewill, just as Dryden's Adam asks the angels

about freewill when they convey to him a warning message. Almanzor exclaims:

> Oh Heav'n, how dark a Riddle's thy Decree,
> Which bounds our Wills, yet seems to leave 'em free!
> Since thy fore-knowledge cannot be in vain,
> Our choice must be what thou didst first ordain:
> Thus, like a Captive in an Isle confin'd,
> Man walks at large, a Pris'ner of the Mind:
> Wills all his Crimes, (while Heav'n th'Indictment draws;)
> And, pleading guilty, justifies the Laws.——— (4. 3. 143–50)

How can punishment be just in such circumstances? The analysis is fundamentally Hobbesian, though Almanzor colours it with Bramhall's criticism of Hobbes: this account of freedom might actually be a form of bondage. Our wills appear to be free, we experience our selves as free, though we are in fact prisoners invisibly confined. In an extraordinary turn a few lines later Almanzor meets his love Almahide, who compares true love to angelic digestion:

> For it, like Angels, needs no Nourishment.
> To eat and drink can no perfection be;
> All Appetite implies Necessity. (4. 3. 170–2)

The associations are striking and revealing. Dryden later noted that 'Thoughts, according to Mr. *Hobbs*, have always some Connexion,' and the thematic connection here, between angels and freewill, appetite and necessity, seems to be via Milton, whose angels eat with real appetite and discuss freewill.[53] Milton places angelic meals at the centre of a heroic poem, and Dryden alludes to these topics, seemingly without other motivation or association, in a play that explores heroic form, a recurring preoccupation of his criticism. In invoking these themes, Dryden is pursuing an analysis of heroic drama and poetry.

The essay 'Of Heroique Playes' prefaced to *The Conquest of Granada*, with its reflections on the representation of 'visionary objects' and 'incorporeal substances', is also, in part, a response to *Paradise Lost*. In his dedication of the same play to the Duke of York (in which he raptures that 'the Guardian Angel of our Nation' takes a particular interest in the duke), Dryden suggests that Almanzor is himself an experimental character of 'excentrique vertue', whose 'excessive and overboyling courage' and transgressions and imperfections cause him to shine more brightly in an epic context.[54] Almanzor is governed only by pride and appetite, yet defies the impositions of the chains of necessity. His reflection upon freewill is a unique moment in the drama, prompted by the ghost's intervention, which itself announces the imminence of the dramatic resolution, and it is a foil by which his defining heroism is illuminated. Almahide tells Almanzor: 'Great Souls discern not when the leap's too wide' (4. 2. 451). His heroism is one that will defy society and the divine 'main design', and thus plays a role in defining just what constitutes a heroic play. It is as if a dramatic character can challenge the necessity that the great playwright imposes upon his freewill. The hero defies the chains of inevitability. No wonder Dryden thought Satan the hero of *Paradise Lost*.[55]

Dryden's long-standing concern with the nature of heroism and how it could be represented was inseparable from his concern with literary form, and implicitly conceived an account of freewill; and, conversely, an understanding of the nature of freewill was fundamental to a coherent account of dramatic action and of the formal properties of heroic poetry and drama. Dryden's reading and subsequent adaptation of *Paradise Lost* had at its centre his enduring concern with freewill and dramatic form, and the virtue of angels in the machinery of representation.

## Dreams

Dryden's engagement with Milton on the terms of contemporary debates about the nature and office of angels, and his extended, discursive treatment of freewill, reveal that *The State of Innocence*, for all its many aesthetic shortcomings, was more than an offensive vulgarization or assault on the politics of *Paradise Lost*. The adaptation provided for Dryden an occasion not only to respond publicly to the poet whose greatness he had cautiously acknowledged, and who may have scotched his own plans to write a British epic, but also to deal with a series of themes that recurred throughout his work: freewill, immaterial substances and their representation, angels, and literary form. Seventeenth-century authors moved fluidly between these themes because one implied another and because the notions associated with each substantially overlapped.

Dryden's purpose in adapting *Paradise Lost* was a serious one, and we can see its coherence in terms of its author's interests, though the adaptation may sometimes seem tendentious and incoherent in relation to the epic. In conclusion, let us return to the dream scene in both Milton's and Dryden's versions and see what is to be learned about both texts from Dryden's reworking. Eve's dream does not appear in traditional Christian exegesis, though in the pseudepigraphal *Apocalypsis Moses* she has a premonitory dream of Abel's murder by Cain.[56] An implicit influence upon Milton's poem may be the corpus of works on witchcraft that testify to the diabolical use of dreams to tempt unsuspecting women.[57] Some authors suggested that unfallen angels, especially guardian angels, had a power to influence dreams.[58] Dreams and angels are intimately related in both poetry and theology. The dream as a literary motif, a stage in a progress towards a fall, such as Redcrosse's dream in *The Faerie Queene*, is also behind Milton's passage. Less well known, but which may have had a greater impression on Milton, was the discussion of dreams in Heywood's *Hierarchie of the Blessed Angells*, in which dreams are stated as proof of the existence of angels. While Hobbes dismissed the idea of efficacious witchcraft on the grounds of the absurdity of the notion of an 'incorporeal' substance, Heywood took more or less the opposite tack, arguing that there must be a creature 'intermediate' between God and man, and that, as there are bodies without spirits and bodies with spirits, so must there be spirits without bodies:

> Unbodied things that have both life and sence,
> And these the *Spirits*, Dreames will teach us plaine,
> By their events, that such about us raine,
> To warne us of the future.[59]

Heywood then lists a number of prophetic dreams, from the Bible and classical literature, that prove the existence of immaterial beings and therefore of angels. Hence, dreams prove the existence of angels. Others believed that dreams were dangerous because they were false. Lucy Hutchinson expressed reservations about Milton's poem, suggesting that he pushed too far into what could not be known, the mysteries that God concealed from man's knowledge. Instead the religious poet should stick to what is true and certain, that is, in the Creator's Word as recorded in Scripture, 'Which, when it taught us how the world was made, | Wrapped up th'invisible in mystic shade'.[60] This was something of a commonplace: Hobbes and Sir William Davenant had suggested as much, Marvell expressed his concerns over Milton's invasion of the

'sacred truths', and Milton's Raphael warns Adam not to conjecture on
the secrets of the heavens or to dream on other worlds.[61] For Dryden
this was of no concern. He concurs with Hutchinson that dreams are by
definition untrue, but for him it is this that gives them their peculiar
literary force: they are feigning, like art itself, and therefore a suitable
medium for reflecting upon art and for drawing attention to the
artfulness of art.

For all its literary allusiveness, Milton's Eve's dream is unassailably
real. This is one of the distinctive qualities of Milton's aesthetic against
which Dryden reacts. The reader is given, in Adam's voice, a physio-
logical explanation of how dreams are produced. When Satan crouches
at Eve's ear in book 4, he assays her in order to 'forge | Illusions as he
list, phantasms and dreams' (4. 802–3). We do not know whether Eve
dreams a story that Satan whispers to her, or whether she constructs her
own dream-story in response to his whispered seductions. In either
case, the dream is figured as a real dream in Milton's narrative, so real
that it has provoked critical debates about whether the dream itself
imparts sinful notions to Eve. Dryden's dream scene, by way of con-
trast, is a play within a play, or a masque within an opera, in which
Lucifer is the playwright and director. The condition of its possibility is
not human psychology or physiology, but the theatre itself. Dryden's
Adam comments that women are 'With shows delighted' (5. 4. 64);
Lucifer, that 'Vain shows, and Pomp, the softer sex betray' (3. 3. 12);
and it is a show that Eve gets. Whereas Milton's Eve is tempted by a
serpent that speaks and offers eloquent, reasoned arguments, Dryden's
Eve watches a serpent take the fruit from the tree and then reappear in
human shape (4. 2, stage directions). She is deceived by show. In
Dryden's adaptation what tempts Eve is theatricality, the dramatization
of her temptation which takes place not in her head but in front of her
sleeping eyes. Lucifer has invented theatre.[62] In the separation scene
Adam warns Eve of the fallen archangel: 'Full of Art is he' (4. 1. 162).

Dryden's Eve's dream is not a real dream, but a metatheatrical
reflection upon the nature of the show that the King's Company
would be putting on at Drury Lane: it plays with the idea of show-
as-temptation and transgression because it is a fiction. We are not
obliged literally to believe the playwright, writes Dryden in his pref-
ace, 'but you are pleas'd with the Image, without being couzen'd by
the Fiction'. Milton writes his account of the invisible and immaterial
bolstered by his self-assurance that he writes nothing contrary to what

he knows is or could be true, and relying on the theological principle of accommodation to collapse the distance between human understanding and impenetrable celestial truths. In Dryden's criticism the figuration or imaging of nature is primary, but the art takes on its own life, and can transcend questions of verisimilitude by displacing or becoming identical with nature itself. Accommodation is for theologians, not dramatists. Art must imitate nature, but when it is successful it goes beyond imitation and is judged on the terms of art, on whether its images are, he writes, 'strongly and beautifully set before the eye of the Reader'.[63] Lucifer stages Eve's dream, for Eve and Dryden's audience, as a piece of theatre which is to be valued according to the beauty of its singing, dancing, machinery, and text. In adapting *Paradise Lost* for the theatre, Dryden is demolishing the political underpinnings of its aesthetics and its enthusiastic religion, and translating it—painstakingly and thoughtfully, if unsatisfactorily and incompletely—into a new literary mode. We are tempted, with Eve, by the theatre itself.

# 14

# Conclusion

## Angels and Literary Representation

### Angels in Protestant Culture

Wherefore, if we will be rightly wise, we must leave those vanities that idle men have taught without warrant of the word of God, concerning the nature, degree, and multitude of Angels. I know that such matters as this, are by many more greedily taken hold of, & are more pleasant unto them than such things as lie in their daily use. But if it greeve us not to be the schollers of Christ, let it not greeve us to follow that order of learning that he hath appointed. So shall it so come to passe, that being contended with his schooling, we shall not onely forbeare, but also abhorre superfluous speculations, from which he calleth us away. No man can deny, that the same *Denyse*, whatsoever man he was, hath disputed many things both subtlely and wittilie in his Hierarchie of Heaven: but if a man examine it more neerely, he shall finde that for the most part it is but meere babling. But the dutifull purpose of a Divine is, not to delite eares with prating, but to stablish consciences with teaching things true, certaine, and profitable. If one should read that booke, he would thinke that the man were slipped downe from heaven, and did tell of things not that he had learned by hearesay, but that he had seene with his eyes. But *Paul* which was ravished above the third heaven, hath uttered no such thing, but also protesteth, that it is not lawfull for man to speake the secrets that he had seene. Therefore bidding farewell to that trifling wisedome, let us consider by the simple doctrine of the Scripture, what the Lord would have us know concerning his Angels.[1]

Calvin's words were echoed and reiterated more than they were heeded. In this book I have shown that Protestants did not shy away from writing or thinking about angels out of embarrassment, but that they rather used them imaginatively, often drawing upon pre-Reformation traditions but also exploiting them in innovative ways, grounded less in anti-popish reaction than in the recognition of new opportunities. The emphasis on *sola scriptura* opened up interpretation of the Bible to new and inventive hermeneutics, invited readers to explore territory that was only imperfectly and half-knowingly mapped. Revitalized biblical exegesis, Scripture reading in new social and intellectual contexts, the impact of apocalypticism and of natural philosophy, these and other trends opened up the study of angels to new and diverse uses.

Protestantism in Britain did result in a decline in interest in, and articulated opposition to, visual representations of angels. It also resulted in diminished daily experience of angels in the context of worship and prayer (and to a lesser extent in liturgical music): angels were no longer invoked as intercessors, which role was reserved for Christ alone. However, angels were invoked in ritual magic, which remained a substantial, if clandestine, presence in Tudor and Stuart Britain. And, more significantly, thinking and writing about angels flourished, occupying many forms and social spaces. Protestants related to angels through words and ideas, not pictures and gestures. The Protestant imagination was perhaps more susceptible to images than traditional accounts allowed,[2] but concerning angels its engagements were intensively verbal. Britain produced no Lucas Cranach, able to adapt the visual to new theology and replace unacceptable with acceptable images (and in any case, Cranach was able to express little of the Protestant view of angels).[3] In Britain especially, the visual iconography of angels did not develop, but the written word intensified to replace it. Words enabled Protestants to embrace angels, but also to keep them at a respectful distance, allowed them to represent angels in powerful and detailed ways without risking the idolatry and doctrinal confusion associated with visualization.

This was a reciprocal relationship: angels presented a language through which Protestants examined the nature of representation. Following medieval traditions, Protestant discussions of accommodation, and of the affinity between remote truths and their human representations, turned to angelic figuration of bodies as an explanatory analogy. Protestant epic—by Guillaume de Salluste du Bartas, Phineas Fletcher, Thomas Heywood, Samuel Pordage, and Lucy Hutchinson—used angels in central ways as topics or narrative devices. The Protestant imagination embraced angels, and angels facilitated and justified the Protestant imagination.

The theological impetus of the Reformation in Britain was not hostile to poetry, and poets did not find theology an impediment to their making. Many critics have suggested an antipathy between poetry and theology. C. A. Patrides writes that theology provides a gloomy airless room for poets, that *Paradise Lost* offers a 'window to the sun' only in so far as it can distance itself from theological discourse.[4] The roots of this view lie as far back as the seventeenth century: as we have seen, Dryden complained that Milton sometimes 'runs into a flat of Thought, sometimes for a Hundred Lines together . . . 'tis when he is got into a Track of Scripture'.[5] For Dryden the usefulness of angels lay in the fact that they were unknown, and therefore ideal substance for the feigning that was integral to literature; Milton deadened the imagination by sticking to theology.[6] The reaction was strong enough for John Dennis to need to defend 'the use of Religion in Poetry' and vice versa as early as 1704, though his instrumental language suggests an awkward, static relationship.[7] Yet this was at a time when Milton's reputation was waxing as a national poet who transcended political differences.[8] Some who have championed Milton have done so by insisting that his sources are literary rather than theological and that the epic does not present or reveal a coherent system of ideas.[9] This presents an unnecessarily narrow and homogeneous view of tradition and influence that reinforces the assumption that poetry and doctrine are not friends. This view has influenced or been echoed by those who are sympathetic to Christianity as well as those who are hostile to it.[10] It is evident in Daniel Featley's smart quip about uneducated preachers presenting themselves as true ministers: 'a Metamorphosis after Ovid, not made by Poeticall license, but Propheticall Liberty'.[11] It also presumes that fiction and truth are irreconcilable opposites.

Yet there was a considerable overlap between poetry and theology, and ways in which they were profoundly cross-fertilizing.[12] Looking at writing about angels brings this creative intersection into focus. Angels were discussed in many and diverse modes of theological writing— scriptural commentary and annotation, systematic theology, sermons and practical divinity, ritual magic—and the kinds of questions asked, and the answers given, were often the same. Are there hierarchies of angels? How did angels eat with Abraham? How fast do angels fly? The means by which these answers are presented, however, vary between modes of writing, and in poetry especially the manner of asking and resolving questions tended to differ sharply from other modes. Angels continued to be a means of poetically answering questions about the nature of the universe and man's place in it into the eighteenth century and beyond, in admittedly inferior epics such as Samuel Catherall's *Essay on the Conflagration* (1720) and Thomas Newcomb's *The Last Judgment of Men and Angels . . . After the Manner of Milton* (1723).[13] I cannot agree with Robert West's judgement, expressed in 1955:

As the seventeenth century moved on towards Deism angels and devils became increasingly inconvenient. . . . In the eighteenth century the usual attitude towards angelology was that it was an exploded study which might well be dropped from sight. . . . The nineteenth century . . . was likely to think of angelologists as absurd and amusing, sometimes engagingly human, more often horrifyingly inhuman, and as always the purest type of man-in-error-before-the-establishment-of-science. Much of this view has persisted into the twentieth century, even in an age of global conflict and nuclear weapons.[14]

Newcomb and Catherall seem to live in a different world from Milton and Pordage, though this need not imply a thesis of modernization, such as secularization, the disenchantment of the world, the scientific revolution, or a 'dissociation of sensibility'.

In this chapter I consider what broader changes might have taken place in writing and thinking about angels during the two centuries and more following the Reformation. This concerns not only the relationship between angels and natural-philosophical enquiry, but *knowledge* more broadly understood. I will also make some proposals concerning the relationship between theology and literature, the demise of allegory, the secularization of writing, and the idea, persistent if diffidently handled, of a dissociation of sensibility. These themes are interconnected, and therefore this chapter offers not only an account of literary representation in the early modern period, but also proposals about the relationship between poetry and theology, and an alternative to some narratives of transition and transformation in seventeenth-century thought and culture.

## Fiction, Allegory, and Iconoclasm

Allegory, an exegetical procedure and a mode of writing about abstract principles or higher ideas through a material narrative, lost prestige in early modern Britain. The attack on allegory in the late seventeenth century focused in its complaints on the fact that allegorical writing abandoned the world of observable phenomena. Thus Richard Blackmore in 1695:

*Ariosto* and *Spencer*...are so hurried on with a *boundless, impetuous* Fancy over Hill and Dale, till they are both lost in a Wood of Allegories,—Allegories so *wild, unnatural*, and *extravagant*, as greatly displease the Reader. This way of writing mightily offends in this Age; and 'tis a wonder how it came to please in any.[15]

Allegory seemed absurd as it was construed in opposition to history and realism and the world of 'fact'.[16] This opposition was exaggerated, however, and continues to be. Allegorical writing borrowed from other modes to complicate its surface; allegory was preserved undamaged as a reading strategy, and can be seen as a dominant hermeneutic mode in modern scholarship.[17] Blackmore's complaint parallels Samuel Morland's mockery, made the same year, of Milton's war in heaven, 'fought between two might Hosts of Blessed and Revolted Spirits...clad with *Adamantine* Coats, one of which was, by a massy Sword, cut down to the wast, and stain'd with Angelick blood'.[18] Whereas Blackmore's complaint is that allegory is insufficiently real, Morland's is that Milton's angels are too real.

Milton represented his angels with a discomforting literalness. Milton shies, as many modern scholars have suggested, from allegory as it did not offer a sufficiently *truthful* medium. Allegory has no substance. It foregrounds its fictionality, tells the reader to find something else in there. This can be seen in the three main allegorical passages in *Paradise Lost* that are clearly demarked as such. First, Satan's encounter with Sin and Death and Chaos, which occupies 400 lines in book 2, and which is then reprised in book 3 with Satan's flight through limbo, or the 'Paradise of Fools', perhaps the most sharply anti-Catholic passage in the poem (3. 444–97); and thirdly, the bridge that Sin and Death build between earth and hell in book 10 (229–418). Sin, Death, Chaos, and the bridge are not real things, but negations within a positive reality. These allegories are associated with evil, and allegory, something that by its very nature is not, may be a distinctively appropriate mode with which to represent the perversion of matter and the privation of being.[19] Allegory separates representation and thing represented, which creates, for Milton, a kind of ontological paradox or deficiency. The allegories can be read as tests for the reader that illustrate the dangers of reification.[20] But when writing about true things, Milton's aesthetic seeks to rise above a mere 'lie' that points to the truth, and instead to present the truth as directly as possible.[21] This possibility is guaranteed by prophetic inspiration and by the spirit that facilitates accommodation.

*Paradise Lost* is nonetheless a fiction. It is a fiction in the sense that it uses a non-literal narrative to explore a truth that is *in some way* close but not identical to the narrative. But the way in which it is close is not the way of allegory, which foregrounds its alterity and posits a real, onto-logical separation; it is rather the way of accommodation, which posits as close a proximity as possible within the limits of human language and comprehension, and one that even pushes beyond these limits.[22] Literal and figurative collapse together. *Paradise Lost* is not a fiction in the sense that it is made up and untrue. It is a fiction in the sense that Milton uses literary modes and structures in his representation. The underlying critical anxiety about the relationship between literature and theology obscures the sense in which this is a natural and inevitable association. Tony Nuttall, considering the risks that Milton took in representing God, concludes that Milton avoided the risk of being accused of presumption by being literary. Milton's poem is an epic, and could not be mistaken for anything other than fiction. Milton did not think he was inspired.[23] Angels were only 'somewhat as he described them', and Raphael has to offer defensive preliminaries to Adam (7. 115–20), which would be unnecessary if Milton were truly inspired. Nuttall adds that accommodation is performed by God and not man, and that Milton uses extra-scriptural language. Accommodation could not occur to a mind living entirely within the accommodated world.[24] We have seen that stronger versions of accommodation were available to Milton and were implied by him in his representations of inspiration in the poem; they were sufficiently strong to make his description more than 'somewhat' like real angels. But Nuttall's subtext is that the truth has to sound like truth, and that literary manoeuvres indicate a commitment to worldli-ness, to literary value, that is at odds with or divorced from commit-ments to justifying God. We find the same in frequently iterated and generally unexceptionable statements that 'The ultimate goal' of *Paradise Lost* was to create a 'national or Christian heroic' work to rival the classics in its power and universality, despite the explicit statement of the invocation to book 1.[25]

For Milton, however, any poetic superiority he achieved would have afforded the appearance of truth to the truths he believed to be conveying (and might also have proved that his was the one true God, and that he was truly inspired). Narrative is one means to poetry, but also a means to truth, not, as Blackmore would have it, mere wild stories. To Milton narrative offered explanatory structures. It can be used to expound doctrine, and links in the chain of narrative used to infer doctrine. Sometimes narratives collapse or implode, and this can present problems for those seeking doctrinal consistency, as well as those seeking to read doctrinal consistency into a narrative.[26] This is particularly evident in a text as consequential and closely scrutinized as Genesis, a text which, moreover, generally prompted strongly literalist interpretation (in contrast to Revelation, which was always read as a mixture of literal and allegorical modes).[27] These exegetical practices recognize that even sacred texts are literary. Exegesis is a literary procedure, and represents the roots of the tradition that lies behind the critical appreciation of literature.[28] Andrew Willet, whose interventions on angels have been discussed earlier in this book, offers the following intervention on the story of the planting of vines and the invention of wine in Genesis 9: 20:

And mention is made rather of Noahs planting of vines, then sowing of corne, wherein he no doubt was occupied also: not because the invention of things necessarie he would leave unto God, and of things for pleasure unto man, as *Ambrose* supposeth (for there is no doubt, but that wheat was in use before the flood) but for that it ministreth occasion to the storie following.[29]

Such exegetical manoeuvres, explaining and exploiting narrative structures, also shape *Paradise Lost*, such as the separation scene between Adam and Eve, motivated by the fact that they are not together in a later verse in Genesis. It is Milton's narrative method to show the story, rather than to explain it. His narrative is, however, bound to notions of truth.

A similar relationship between narrative and doctrine shapes the first panel on the east doors of the Baptistery in Florence, designed by Lorenzo Ghiberti between 1424 and 1452. Milton would almost certainly have seen this during his trip to Florence in 1638, but its value here is not as an influence but as an analogous way of developing doctrine through narrative. The panel shows Genesis 1–3, representing the creation of Adam (bottom left), the creation of Eve from Adam's rib (centre right), the temptation (upper left, receding into background), and the expulsion. On the right Adam and Eve have been driven though the gates of Eden, and appear in relief, closer to the postlapsarian viewer. Ghiberti abandoned the quatrefoil frames of earlier panels, and used the open square to create

**Figure 7.** Panel on east doors of the Baptistery in Florence, designed by Lorenzo Ghiberti, 1424–52

dramatic effects with ruptured planes and frames: the bottom ledge, and with it Adam's right hand, breaks out of the picture; a choir of angels form a canopy sheltering the scene of sin from God and Eve, who occupy the centre of the image, though one of them appears to be watching the sin; and an angel bursts through the door through which the humans are expelled, pushing them towards the viewer and away from the paradisal scenes to the left. In this panel several images form a narrative, and they are visually linked by angels. Angels witness Adam's creation, and separate that scene from the centre of the picture; they appear to be having a conversation except for one that peers behind the others at the temptation, creating a temporal paradox. Angels clutch the newly created Eve as she emerges from Adam's side; another choir forms a canopy over this second creative act. The angle of these figures directs the eye to the left, where sin takes place furtively in the background. In creating a canopy that separates this scene, Ghiberti isolates sin from Creation, indicating the purity of the unfallen couple (they were not made flawed and thus susceptible to sin). The trees guide the eyes upward, to a swirl of angels around God, rippling across the less dense top third of the picture. Their movement points downwards and to the right, where it converges in the angel that breaks through the plane of the picture in expelling Adam and Eve, only here with their nakedness covered. Angels are witnesses and God's assistants, but also narrative devices: as in *Paradise Lost*, a narrative structured around angels tells the story of the Fall. Time and space are imperfectly distinguished, as successive images are interspersed within the same frame, much as in the complex time scheme of *Paradise Lost* and other Renaissance narratives that imperfectly distinguish, or make interdependent, space and time.[30] It is a virtuoso creation that shows how the imagination explicates doctrine through narrative. Milton's poetry works like this, but it also discovers doctrine in the necessary logic of storytelling. As the argument to book 1 informs its reader: 'hell, described here, not in the centre (for heaven and earth may be supposed as yet not made, certainly not yet accursed) but in a place of utter darkness, fitliest called chaos'.

Milton came from a culture that viewed with suspicion the representation of the sacred, on the basis of the commandment against making graven images or likenesses of anything in heaven, earth, or the waters. However, distinctions were drawn, implicitly and explicitly, between different kinds of representation. The visualization of the sacred was the focus of the strongest objections. Words were different, and Protestants turned to words for imagining angels. Raphael warns Adam about the difficulties of representing spirits to human senses, and promises that he will when necessary compare 'spiritual to corporal forms | As may express them best'; Michael Murrin argues that consequently the reader can never know when she is being presented a simile and when a literal description, 'so that we cannot distinguish tenor and vehicle in the narrative'.[31] Such an interpretation suggests a sequential deployment of metaphor. If the likening is understood to describe the process of accommodation, however, Raphael's metaphors and literalisms may be concurrent. He does not switch between a non-literal mode and a literal mode, leaving the reader confused as to when this happens. His words are simultaneously literal and non-literal. A similar possibility is suggested in

Murrin's insightful reading of Milton's description of heaven, in which the compiling of multiple similes ultimately thwarts visualization (3. 344–71: angelic shouts loud as from an infinite number; sweet as from blessed voices; pavement like a sea of jasper; and harps hung at sides like quivers). This method is, Murrin suggests, drawn from the example of Scripture, and suited to Protestantism: 'The iconoclast could either multiply images or dispense with them altogether, opposite verbal techniques which have the same function.'[32] Words are used to challenge the tendency to reify and to idolize. Milton's representations of heaven are both material and literal *and* fraught with meanings.

Murrin does not suggest that Milton is inspired; rather, he links the death of allegory to the end of claims to prophetic inspiration, which occurs because of a shift from a metaphysical to a craftsman's conception of poetic creativity. Poetry became associated with human skills and pleasures, and this in part because of the dawn of the 'age of reason' and Baconian experimental science.[33] (Once again natural philosophy appears to determine literary transformation.) Thus, Murrin understands Milton's rejection of allegory to follow from his iconoclasm and conscious commitment to biblical language. However, it is also possible to describe it as characteristic of the Protestant imagination: it is iconoclasm performed through excessive visualization, a visualization so rich that it pushes the reader to resolve its challenges conceptually. For Catherine Gimelli Martin, Milton does not reject allegory but straddles its transformation. A traditional mode of allegory, held together by mysticism, correspondences, and signatures, is displaced by the new science, which turns allegory into a relativistic meta-critique that critiques the new empirical world. The transitory synthesis during this period of transformation was a mode of baroque allegory that realistically reflects the uncertainty and indeterminacy that the Cartesian–Newtonian world view sought to efface, and in doing so anticipates the postmodern critique of certainty. For Martin, Milton embodies this approach: he is an allegorical poet, as well as a realistic one.[34] Her conclusions are not so far from Murrin's: they both describe a literary transformation that corresponds to a shift in modernity, driven by science and empiricism, and though Martin insists that allegory survives, it does so by absorbing a great deal that allegory was understood not to be. 'Accommodation' is a better way to understand that doubleness (as early modern theology and rhetoric are better tools for reading Milton than Nietzsche and Foucault), and it recognizes that the literal and metaphoric meanings were understood to be simultaneous. Moreover, *Paradise*

*Lost* would resemble baroque aesthetics,[35] as would Ghiberti's Renaissance doors, were it not so theologically driven, and if the relationship between narrative and doctrine were not so intensive. And if Milton *is* inspired—which is to say, if he believes himself to be inspired and founds his literary mode on this belief—then this rejection of allegory as a literary mode goes hand in hand with a belief that a higher truth is being represented in this more literalistic mode; and his conception of creativity is not that of a craftsman but that of a prophet.

Milton's rejection of allegory is not typical of seventeenth-century writing, however. First, allegory does survive into modernity, adapting to empiricism, historicism, and realism, and negotiating hostility to its more baroque elements.[36] It even persists in scientific writing and in religious writing, denuded of the scholarly apparatus of fourfold exegesis. Hence, a number of epic poems in the early eighteenth century use heavenly machinery to expound natural-philosophical principles (and in them angels appear as representations of principles and as voices of authority).[37] Secondly, the disappearance of allegory has more to do with the decline, through collective forgetting, of the medieval intellectual apparatus within which it made sense. Thirdly, the grounds supplied by those who reject allegories tend to be its excesses, its distraction from the real, increasingly understood in material terms. Milton had mastered the apparatus of allegory, and understood the arguments against it, but he moved away from allegory on theological grounds, and not in favour of a natural-philosophical literalism but in order to espouse a superior form of fiction, an inspired truth-telling fiction. He occasionally uses allegory in order to reject it, and, however repellent he makes its associations, his allegories form part of the dynamic contrasts within the poem.

Where does *Paradise Lost* stand in relation to the literary currents of the seventeenth century? If it does not follow the pattern of the rejection of allegory, can the theological commitments that made allegory inappropriate to Milton's purposes be said to place him on one side of a divide that led to modernity?

## A Dissociation of Sensibilities?

In a brave essay E. M. W. Tillyard once tried sympathetically to sketch the emotional foundations of the theological content of Milton's poetry, not to attribute the poet's religion to personal psychology so much as to show how the theological might be associated with intellectual conflict and creative powers. Tillyard rightly contends that Milton's theology was connected to every department of his thought. Following Arthur Barker, he asserts that this refusal to separate theology from poetry and science made Milton old-fashioned. The future lay with those who would divide the natural from the theological, whereas Milton's allegiances lay with a hierarchical and 'traditional conception' of the world which 'was pretty well exempt from theological controversy before it was undermined by the new science'. Milton's belief in this is 'emotionally the most powerful theological element in his poetry'. Hence, for Tillyard, Milton's poetry is *imaginatively* committed to an *interconnectedness* that science destroys.[38] There are many valuable insights in Tillyard's essay, but germane here is his association of a narrative of secularization, the scientific revolution, and a dissociation of sensibility in which Milton stands on the pre-dissociation side of the chasm. Tillyard focuses on a powerful series of correlations and common assumptions that need to be challenged.

The theory that a 'dissociation of sensibility' took place in the middle of the seventeenth century was forwarded by T. S. Eliot, though certainly rooted in previous literary history and grounded in his reading of George Saintsbury and Herbert Grierson. Eliot's historical-critical thesis was part of a prehistory of his own poetics, one in which a fragmented language accurately reflected a broken sensibility, one that longed for reintegration through the deep structures of myth and religion while rejecting a romantic view of a world unified and made meaningful by the perceiving self (with different values it corresponds closely to Martin's analysis). In his essay on the so-called metaphysical poets he writes:

The difference is not a simple difference of degree between poets. It is something which had happened to the mind of England between the time of Donne or Lord Herbert of Cherbury and the time of Tennyson and Browning; it is the difference between the intellectual poet and the reflective poet. . . . A thought to Donne was an experience; it modified his sensibility. . . . The poets of the seventeenth century, the successors of the dramatists of the sixteenth, possessed a mechanism of sensibility which could devour any kind of experience. . . . In the seventeenth century a dissociation of sensibility set in, from which we have never recovered; and this dissociation, as is natural, was aggravated by the influence of the two most powerful poets of the century, Milton and Dryden.[39]

The nostalgic tone underscores the parallel with the Fall. Donne lived in a prelapsarian age of passionate and rational apprehension; Milton, in an intellectual age when these unities were broken. Eliot's essay on Marvell indicates one culprit: the civil war.[40] Unity was broken when Parliament (read innovation and enthusiasm) and king (tradition, hierarchy, and spiritual unity) fell out in 1642. Though it is hard to find external support for the thesis—justified as it is only through gestures: to an Elizabethan world-view, to the rise of Puritanism, to an allegorical civil war—it found many supporters.[41] Frank Kermode described its tenaciousness, though being untenable as a way of describing the seventeenth century, as early as 1957.[42]

Gordon Teskey, a more sympathetic and gifted reader of Milton than Eliot, has recently offered a more persuasive, yet similarly shaped narrative, a transition from a theological world to a humanist world in which Milton straddles the boundary. 'Milton is the last major poet in the European literary tradition for whom the act of creation is centered in God and the first in whom the act of creation begins to find its center in the human.' Teskey inverts some of Eliot's categories. In the condition of modernity, the artist does not represent understood things about the world using technical expertise so much as communicate lived experiences, mediating them to us with a shamanistic power.[43] Milton is not a divinely inspired poet, but one who exploits the modern condition of delirium, a mode of poetic inspiration that oscillates between heavenly flight and rational composition.[44] This 'delirium' looks very much like a translation into literary poetics of the theology of prophetic inspiration, and Teskey denudes Milton's poetics (if not his poetry) of its religion.[45] What makes Milton unique in the story Teskey tells is that he embodies the paradox in the shift: in order to praise his Creator, he must assume his power; in becoming the apotheosis of a tradition he looks to the future. For Teskey, the true subject of *Paradise Lost* is *making*, and the epic is haunted by a self-consciousness about art that enriches the dialogues it has beyond its moment, and makes it reach beyond history, religion, and metaphysics to the power of imaginative structures despite the author's metaphysical and theological commitments.[46]

Two other narratives inhabit this glorification of the poet-as-maker, this 'immense cultural change'. The first is secularization, cast as the disappearance of God, the decay of the coherent system of Christianity, the ascent of poets as creators with a power not only equivalent to

but also distinct from God's. It is 'the change from the imaginary
perception that we live in a world created by God to the equally
imaginary perception that we live in a world, an environment, created
by Man'. The syncrisis emphasized with the repetition of 'imaginary'
conceals the disappearance of a foundation of absolute truth in this
movement. In Teskey's account, making the knowledge of the world
appears equivalent to making the world itself (which is to take the side
of modernity). Embedded in this modernization thesis is a second
narrative, that of the scientific revolution. 'Cosmic disarray' is brought
on by 'the new science', which complements terrifying change with
the promise of a 'new world', a 'technological and scientific civiliza-
tion', for which Bacon's *Novum Organum* is the 'prophetic text'.[47]
Teskey's account of Milton as a poet of modernity, even a poet of
the future, presupposes a narrative of transition that resembles Eliot's
on several points: a decay of traditional hierarchies and loss of a
coherent universe, the rise of science, secularization, the poet as
creator of his own authority; where they differ most significantly is
in their accounts of the poet's relationship with language. Teskey also
rejects the idea that modernity disenchanted the world, but he does so
by claiming that it is the poet, the poet's mind and her creativity, that is
the place of modern enchantment, not the land, rivers, or sky.[48] Like
Eliot he suggests that philosophy and theology enter into conflict with
art during the seventeenth century, though it is Milton's ability to
inhabit both sides of this conflict that for Teskey makes him great.

   Tillyard and Teskey exemplify how a story of literary transform-
ation—whether disenchantment and dissociation or the shamanization
of the poet—can dovetail with a traditional view of the scientific
revolution, in which experimentalism shattered a coherent world-
picture that had survived for centuries through 'saving knowledge'.[49]
Instead of adapting an existing paradigm to accommodate new obser-
vation, the new science of the later seventeenth century razed the
ground of knowledge and built it anew on Baconian principles. Such
an account of later seventeenth-century natural philosophy, and the
empirical principles of the scientific revolution, has been extensively
and intensively challenged in recent decades. Without rehearsing those
well-established arguments here, this book has already shown that
angels were *not* killed off by natural philosophers. Natural philosophers
complemented experimental knowledge with other forms of knowledge:
they conducted thought experiments, they devised pneumatologies,

they imported the language of spiritual causation to describe mechanical causation, and they compiled compendiums of the actions of spirits. Angels had to be spoken of to construe a necessary corollary to mechanical philosophy. Hence, natural philosophers dilated the vocabularies in which angels were written of, while detaching them from experimental means of describing the world.[50]

This book has also brought into doubt elements of the third narrative of emergent modernity, the disenchantment of the world. The development of a secular model of enlightenment rationality, as sketched by Max Weber, should have erased angels from the immediate world-view. Yet, as I have argued, many Protestants saw the landscape as inhabited not only by symbolic meanings but by guardian angels who were connected to particular places and topographical features.[51] Angels stayed in the landscape, though they may have remained invisible. This testifies to a *multiplicity* of perspectives, an angelic world within, or imposed as upon a palimpsest, the visible world of the ordinary senses.

The air pump and microscope did not rout angels, which should lead us to ask whether a deeper significance inhabits the connection between these narratives of a scientific revolution, an intellectual rupture or dissociation, and of the disenchantment of the world. Significant shifts in the understanding and practice of natural philosophy, in perceptions of the spirit world, and in the place and generation of literature took place in the two centuries following the Reformation. Perhaps Eliot, Tillyard, and others were partly correct in their account of interconnectedness, and the enrichment of discourses and perspectives that took place in natural philosophy had its parallel in the sphere *of the imagination.*

A broader literary picture is valuable here, including the role of angels on the medieval and Renaissance stage. Whereas Shakespeare used the supernatural world of ghosts and fairies more extensively and imaginatively than his contemporaries, his angels are word-pictures. This presents a significant shift away from the place of angels in medieval drama, and it is worth identifying some of the changes and continuities here. Medieval drama is traditionally seen as didactic and allegorical;[52] yet it was a mixed mode, one that combined narrative and dramatic visual elements both to entertain and to explicate Scripture. The performances were instigated and implicitly approved by the Church, but, like Elizabethan plays, they were the product of collaboration with and between trade companies, carpenters, actors, and the writers (probably usually clergymen); hence, the instruction they gave could be playful and complicated.[53] Yet they were representing sacred truths, and the souls of humans and the good of the Church were at stake. Angels on the medieval stage embody coherent thought about doctrine: about music, with which they are closely associated, and the heavens, for example.[54] They represent the nine Pseudo-Dionysian hierarchies, either through references in the spoken word, as characters (each order played by a single actor), or through stage machinery: the records of the Mercers' Company equipment include nine figures of angels that moved by mechanical operation.[55]

The main purpose of angels in the cycle plays is to represent the greatness of God; they do, however, go beyond mere iteration of recognized doctrine. In the Towneley Creation play Lucifer declares, 'I am so seemly, blode and bone' (line 102). He has not yet seduced any fellow angels (though they are, presumably to clarify the script, designated as 'Angelus Malus' and 'Angelus Bonus'), nor fled heaven, though he is expressing his envy of the Son and planning his rebellion. He is an angel in mid-fall if not already fallen, and his bodily metaphors are thus less incongruous than they would be in the mouth of a good angel. He is still in heaven, however, and this sense of the material embodiment of blood and bone are located in the spiritual world. After their Fall the materiality associated with corrupted spirits is further developed, as their degradation is described in physical terms: 'Now ar we waxen blak as any coyll | And ugly, tatyrd as a foyll' (lines 136–7). In the Chester Tanners' play at precisely the same moment—as Lucifer offers to sit in God's throne and exalt himself in pride—he imagines himself in bodily terms: 'Behoulde my bodye, handes and head— | the mighte of God is marked in mee' (lines 188–9). Lucifer's words parody the Mass, and his recognition of body parts corresponds to his shifting status. Once fallen, demons are the subject of material, scatological humour, as in the N-Town play, where, as soon as he falls, Lucifer exclaims: 'For fere of fyre a fart I crake!' (line 81). By associating not only physical torment but embodiment with spiritual corruption, the plays define angels as incorporeal, spiritual beings.

Some cycle plays, then, are inventive and exploratory, and their storytelling pushes beyond doctrinal explication. The Chester Tanners' play devises a partner to Lucifer, an angel named Lightborne, who encourages Lucifer in his attempt on God's throne and praises the brightness of his body. He plays a role similar to Beelzebub in *Paradise Lost*, a second-in-command who supports Lucifer's arguments against the orders of unfallen angels, and falls with him. Lightborne becomes 'secundus demon' on his fall, and he and the newly named 'primus demon' engage in mutual recrimination. Though the good angels speak as distinct orders, and though they sound human in their sensible advice, they are not personalized to the extent that this testy exchange between the two demons enables. A similar imaginative effect is achieved in primus demon's final, self-pitying exclamation:

> Out, alas! For woo and wickednesse
> I ame so fast bounde in this cheare
> and never awaye hense shall passe,
> but lye in hell allwaye heare.          (lines 270–3)

The dramatic effect is not the corporeal binding of the demon in a chair that parodies the throne to which he aspired so much as realization of the mental chains that fix his spirit to hell. This notion can be found in Aquinas ('the devils, while abroad in this dark atmosphere, are not actually imprisoned in the fire of hell, yet their punishment is not the less for that, since they know that the imprisonment awaits them'); in Christopher Marlowe's *Faustus*, where Mephistopheles explains,

> Hell hath no limits, nor is circumscribed,
> In one self place. But where we are is hell,
> And where hell is there must we ever be;

and in *Paradise Lost*, where Milton transforms it into a matter of the psyche:

>                              within him hell
> He brings, and round about him, nor from hell
> One step no more than from himself can fly
> By change of place.[56]

The reiteration of the word 'hell' in paradise, and at line-endings, performs this sense of containment and recurrence. The Tanners' play shows the demon experiencing something that is similarly both internal and external. The theological exposition here is part of a dramatic realization that is based in part on, if not sympathy, at least the attribution to the demon of human characteristics.

The exploratory and narrative-based approach to angel-doctrine in the cycle plays is in some ways closer to Milton than to Shakespeare, for whom angels are figures for virtue and outward beauty: 'O, what may man within him hide, | Though angel on the outward side!' exclaims the Duke in *Measure for Measure*. In *Richard III* and in *Richard II* angels are one among numerous markers of moral good and emblems of military might.[57] There are elements of more specific angel-doctrine. In *The Merchant of Venice* Lorenzo alludes to the angels and cherubim that inhabit the celestial spheres that generate music inaudible to human ears.[58] In *The Tempest*, a play rich with the occult and with spiritual beings, angels are an ideal of visible beauty; Gonzalo, unnerved by mysterious noise, invokes them (he is a Catholic); and Ferdinand speaks of 'Our worser genius'.[59] This refers to the doctrine that each human has a pair of guardian angels, one good, one evil. The same doctrine appears in *Henry IV, Part II*, in *Othello*, and in Sonnet 144.[60] It was perhaps a doctrine to which Shakespeare was theologically drawn, though his use of it is not dramatic, and we do not see the struggle of human conscience externalized in this form. This contrasts with Marlowe's *Faustus*, where the paired good and evil angels, visible to the audience, speak to Faustus' conscience, their interaction becoming increasingly evident to his senses as he falls. In *Antony and Cleopatra*, however, the idea of a guardian angel theatrically enters Shakespeare's imagination, when the soothsayer cautions Antony:

> Thy daemon, that thy spirit which keeps thee, is
> Noble courageous, high, unmatchable,
> Where Caesar's is not. But near him thy angel
> Becomes afeard, as being o'erpowered.[61]

An angel-doctrine more than decorative appears in the first scene of *Henry V*, too, when the Archbishop of Canterbury reports the transformation in the prince upon his father's death:

> at that very moment
> Consideration, like an angel came
> And whipped th'offending Adam out of him,
> Leaving his body as a paradise
> T'envelop and contain celestial spirits.[62]

Hal's moral regeneration is imagined as a purifying process conducted by an angel, not a guardian angel but an intervening providential angel, an agent of God's judgement.

And in *Hamlet*, where the confessional differences between Lutheran Wittenberg (where both Hamlet and Faustus studied) and Counter-Reformation Paris (Laertes' university) may be at stake, angels linger invisibly behind the action. Accosting the priest who denies full burial rites to Ophelia, Laertes exclaims: 'A minist'ring angel shall my sister be | When thou liest howling.' The suggestion that blessed human souls become angels, or become like angels, is a common theme in Catholic writing, though it may be merely figurative here. Not so Hamlet's response to the ghost of his father, a ghost that claims to have returned from purgatory. On his first sighting Hamlet exclaims: 'Angels and ministers of grace defend us!' When he sees the ghost for a second time, in Gertrude's closet, he entreats, 'Save me and hover o'er me with your wings, | You heavenly guards!' Luther implicitly accepted belief in individual guardian angels, and suggested that it was appropriate to call upon their support *in extremis*, though not to pray to or invoke angels.[63] If his words are understood as calls and not prayers, Hamlet's angel-doctrine precisely fits Luther's (and not Calvin's). When Claudius is seeking forgiveness, kneeling in his chapel, he asks, 'Help, angels!', invoking angels in a manner contrary to Luther. Appropriately a false prayer follows. The contrasting invocations of angels by Claudius and the prince may reflect competing attitudes to prayers to angels, a fault line of confessional differences over angels in the Reformation, in which case Shakespeare represents the theology with some care.[64]

Shakespeare's angels are images and ideas. He uses doctrine when it is imaginatively powerful. Something similar can be said of Donne. Several of the songs and sonnets assume the notion of tutelary angels. He suggests that human spirits replace fallen angels in heaven; that angel-worship is idolatrous; he notes that angels assume bodies of condensed air to communicate with humans. He imagines angels looking down on us from heaven. These doctrines are voiced in poetry and sermons alike. In one of the Holy Sonnets, the narrator asks:

> If faithful souls be alike glorified
> As angels, then my father's soul doth see,
> And adds this even to full felicity,
> That valiantly I hell's wide mouth o'erstride:
> But if our minds to these souls be descried
> By circumstances, and by signs that be
> Apparent in us, not immediately,
> How then shall my mind's white truth by them be tried?[65]

The doubt is expressed whether humans in heaven (he knows that his father is there) see like angels. If they do, then his father will be able to see directly into Donne-the-speaker-of-the-poem's soul, and see that he is indeed in a state of grace. If they do not, then his father will have to judge him by the external evidence of his behaviour. The speaker knows that humans are transparent to angels' eyes (a view more closely associated with Catholic than Protestant theology). The sonnet turns to consider the disparity between outward conduct and inner existence, especially 'Dissemblers [who] feign devotion', before concluding:

> Then turn
> O pensive soul, to God, for he know best
> Thy true grief, for he put it in my breast.

The grief could be Donne-the-speaker's father's grief at his son's apparently perilous condition, in which case the soul is the father's in heaven, and the son instructs the father to ask God for enlightenment concerning his son's spiritual condition; though it is possible that God also gave the father's grief (spiritual doubt?) to the son. Alternatively, the soul could be the speaker's and the dichotomy between 'thy . . . grief' and 'my breast' indicates that human souls are not even transparent to themselves. We cannot know, and so the irresolvable ambiguity reminds the reader that we are bound by our senses, and cannot know another's state of grace, in contrast to angels. However, in an Easter sermon of 1622 he quotes Luke 20: 36 ('There we shall be as the angels'), and infers, 'our curiosity shall have this noble satisfaction, we shall know how the angels know by knowing as they know'.[66] This runs against the doubt of the sonnet. The difference may be explained by genre, as the certainty of the prose sermon contrasts with the ambiguity of the sonnet. However, a later sermon cautions that 'even in heaven our faculties shall be finite'.[67] The sermon carefully distinguishes angelic knowledge from human, identifying in Thomist terms their three kinds of knowledge (through nature, confirmation in grace, and revelation); whereas the earlier sermon insists that humans know God better than angels, for he has revealed himself to us in his actions more than angels have.[68] For Donne, angels are above all a means of gauging and understanding human knowledge. What he actually believes—or knows—about them is limited.

In 'The Dream' similar doctrine is handled differently. The lyric speaker describes being woken from a happy and rational dream by a visitor both true and associated with fantasy, capable of turning dreams into reality: so he suggests that they enact his dream. This is complicated in the second stanza:

> As lightning, or a taper's light,
> Thine eyes, and not thy noise waked me;
>     Yet I thought thee
> (For thou lov'st truth) an angel, at first sight,
> But when I saw thou saw'st my heart,
> And knew'st my thoughts beyond an angel's art,
> When thou knew'st what I dreamed, when thou knew'st when
> Excess of joy would wake me, and cam'st then,
> I must confess, it could not choose but be
> Profane, to think thee any thing but thee.[69]

Her appearance suggests the visitor is an angel, but a human can see into a human heart better than an angel, which proves her to be human. Doubtless the speaker's thoughts are *too* human for an angel's grasping. By the next stanza their love has been consummated, and the angel–woman rises, causing him to doubt: if she is leaving, perhaps her love is impure, which is to say not 'all spirit'. He resolves that she is leaving only to return: 'Thou cam'st to kindle, goest to come' (there must be a pun here on orgasm, though a very early usage in this sense), so he resolves to dream again. Donne's poetry relies on the temporality of its experiences and revelations: he describes here a compulsive erotic cycle of sleep, half-waking, seduction, satisfaction, doubt, consolation, and sleep. The speaker never really wakes, and the opening and closing lines leave ambiguous whether the visitor wakes the dreamer and controls the cycle, or the dreamer ultimately holds sway over the boundary between the two states. The poem imagines a dream vision, ambiguously interrupted by an angel and then renewed; but it also describes a compulsive sexual relationship between two lovers who share a space and are not yet perfectly familiar with each other. The hook of the poem is this near-substitutability: by comparing the visitor to an angel, an identification from which she never emerges, Donne is imagining sex with an angel.

The conceit appears elsewhere. An epistolary poem to a fellow clergyman ('To Mr. Tilman') draws upon the conventional iconography of angels; 'Elegy 2: To his Mistress Going to Bed' does so in a less orthodox fashion:

> In such white robes heaven's angels used to be
> Received by men; thou, angel, bring'st with thee
> A heaven like Mahomet's paradise; and though
> Ill spirits walk in white, we easily know
> By this these angels from an evil sprite;
> Those set our hairs, but these our flesh upright.[70]

Evil angels inspire fear; good angels give men an erection. Instructions on how to distinguish good and bad angels identify haloes or beards, or insist that humans are unable reliably to make such distinctions. Donne's criterion is unusual (Tony Kushner echoes it in *Angels in America*, in which the arrival of an angel is presaged by involuntary sexual arousal[71]). Again the outcome is sexual consummation. 'Air and Angels' has a related imaginative premiss: the common doctrine that angels adopt bodies of air in order to appear to humans. The poem's speaker begins by noting that angels appear as voices or 'a shapeless flame' (and are 'worshipped': a distinctively Roman Catholic word choice), then argues that the speaker's love must adopt a body ('else could nothing *do*', a pun on sexual activity), just as his own soul does, and that body must not be 'More subtle' than its parent, which is to say the speaker. In the second stanza the speaker realizes that he has loaded his love with *too much* body, that his love is overwhelmed with matter:

> For, nor in nothing, nor in things
> Extreme, and scatt'ring bright, can love inhere;
>    Then as an angel, face and wings
> Of air, not pure as it, yet pure doth wear,
>    So thy love may be my love's sphere;
>       Just such disparity
>    As is 'twixt air and angels' purity,
> 'Twixt women's love, and men's will ever be.[72]

His love will wear *her love* (rather than her body) as a body in order to live in this world, just as an angel adopts a body of less pure air in order to communicate with a lesser being. The sweetness of tone disguises the disparagement. Here the speaker is the angel, the love object the less pure air, and here the speaker implicitly posits the possibility that angels experience themselves as sexual beings.

Two lovers are also angels in 'The Ecstasy', in which 'we are | The intelligences, they [our bodies] the sphere'.[73] And in 'The Relic' the speaker imagines himself and his lover as both angels: 'Difference of sex no more we knew, | Than our guardian angels do' (using Matt. 22: 30, on which he would later preach a sermon).[74] The theological context of this poem is playfully peculiar. The poem imagines itself to be a 'paper' left in a tomb accompanying a 'bracelet of bright hair about the bone'. The speaker speculates that the tomb may be broken in an age and place 'Where mis-devotion doth command', which is to say under Roman Catholicism, in which case it might be treated as a holy relic; and the poem concludes with the miracles wrought by the lovers. These play with some familiar Renaissance paradoxes: the two lovers are one, they love something unknowable, and they find unity without touching. The resolution, the miracle that is the loved object, the speaker implies, is inexpressible. It is these paradoxes that make their love more perfect, and their angelic lack of sexual difference is listed among them. The comparison is paradoxical because angels are not sexual beings; but there is a sense in which their gender-sameness makes them more perfectly sexual, because they love as equals. Milton pushed this a stage further with his angelic sexual intercourse, yet is anticipated by Donne's imagining of angels as beings who might experience intercourse, or whose experience might serve as a model for human intercourse.

These are not fleeting references but ideas that occasion imaginative exploration and play. They do not directly reveal what Donne believes. In a 1627 marriage sermon he does outline legitimate knowledge of angels, and he emphasizes its limits: 'Onely the Angels themselves know one another.' They are spirits, but we do not know what spirits are. They have offices, but we do not know how they perform them. We know they are creatures, but do not know when they were created, whether before or with the world. There may be one angel for every man, but we do not know it. They know and see, but we do not know how. They exist in distinct orders, but the details are not revealed. More affirmatively: they do not have bodies, but have great physical power; they were formed in time, but do not age; they are God's eldest sons; 'they hang between the nature of God, and the nature of man, and are of middle Condition'. They are divine enigmas, and the rest is speculation. This is prose: there is no angelic sex here. Despite this negative approach, Donne does speculate. He follows his angelology with logical questioning: 'If by being *like* the Angels, we shall *know* the Angels, we are more then *like* ourselves, we are our selves, why doe we not know our selves?' Why did Adam, knowing himself immortal, relinquish his body to death? Why do we not know ourselves immortal, and resist the temptations of sin? Logic moves—like his lyrics, Donne's sermons exist in narrative time—into something else.

To know this immortality, is to make this immortality, which otherwise is the heaviest part of our Curse, a Blessing unto us, by providing to live in *Immortall happinesse*: whereas now, we doe so little know our selves, as that if my soule could aske one of those *Wormes* which my dead body shall produce, Will you change with me? that worme would say, No; for you are like to live eternally in torment; for my part, I can live no longer, then the putrid moisture of your body will give me leave, and therefore I will not change; nay, would the *Devill* himselfe change with a damned soule? I cannot tell...[75]

Donne's delivery might have clarified whether that last question was spoken by the worm or the preacher, but probably not. Within a few lines of his sober angelology the preacher is engaged in an imaginary conversation with a worm, the worm destined to feed upon his corpse, about human immortality. Sermons occupy different social spaces from poems, and observe distinct generic conventions, but they are, of course, literary performances, and imaginatively speculate in order to express ideas. Donne's sermons only imperfectly offer a doctrinal key with which to interpret poems, and if we do not find angelic sex in his preaching then that may have been a matter of social propriety more than literary decorum. Theology mattered to Donne, and angels constituted a narrow and necessary area of that theology. But his religion did not tell him what to say, and what he thought about angels was less important to his writing than how he used them to think. Angels furnished him with a voice, a set of concepts, and a language that was both affirmative and imaginative.

Many other writers during this century of alleged transformation used angels as literary devices, underpinned by doctrine in a minimal way, but appearing only to support an argument or story without much interest in the nature of angels, the problems of doctrine, or even of the imagination. Perhaps the most interesting dramatic deployment of angels, alongside Marlowe's *Faustus*, is in William Percy's *Mahomet in his Heaven*, written in 1601 probably for private performance.

Taking its cue from a story in the Qur'ān, and risking the representa-
tion of Muhammad on stage, the play is partly set in heaven, where
angels dance and sing and observe the hierarchies, as in medieval cycle
plays. Two hapless angels descending to earth are caught in sexual
intrigue, and are tricked by humans. The play takes place in a Muslim
cosmos—Mahomet *is* in heaven—and its fictional world is in a sense
inverted and demonized. Within the context of the play the Muslim
heaven is none the less real: it is not satirizing a Muslim concept of
heaven but using this concept as a setting for comedy. Moreover, this
Muslim universe is partly fused with the Christian: Islam is both the
inversion of Christianity, and also partly identified with Protestant
values and beliefs. When a human succeeds in transporting herself to
heaven through trickery, Mahomet (who later falls in love with her)
exclaims:

> By Cherubin, by Seraphin, by the
> Virtues, Potestates, and Dominions,
> By the Thrones, the Angells and Archangells,
> Zaniel, Chamnel, Zaphiel,
> By Haniel, Gabriel, Jurobates,
> I do adjure thee, tell mee whence thou beest.

Perhaps Mahomet's heaven is a kind of pure fiction, where no religious
values can be threatened.[76]

Spenser's 'An Hymne of Heavenly Love' (1596) tells the story of
divine love from the beginning of time and the begetting of the Son
(within time, which seems heterodox), through the creation and fall of
angels, to the Passion. It compresses a good deal of doctrine, especially
angel-doctrine, into a superficially transparent narrative, but declines
to explore; it is love of God that inspires the poet to transcend the
'feeble reach of earthly sight', not inspiration.[77] Henry Burkhead's *A
Tragedy of Cola's Fury* (1645–6), a play about the Irish Rebellion of
1641, is one of the few early modern English dramas featuring an
unfallen angel; Milton's unfulfilled drafts for a tragedy promised
another; like Grotius, in his influential *Adamus Exul* (1601), his angels
are real and unfallen. Burkhead's angel unexpectedly materializes to
provide succour to, and perhaps release from captivity, the hero,
Caspilona. It is a *deus ex machina*, providing a providential turning
point in the plot. Later the angel sings the epilogue, fulfilling a merely
decorative function.[78] Charles Fitz-Geffrey's *The Blessed Birth-Day*

(1634), a poem that takes off from the angels' hymn on the Incarnation, professes itself uninspired and makes no claims to accommodation ('Sing we high myst'ries in an humble straine, | And lofty matters in a lowly vaine'). It comments didactically on the properties of angels, but the tone never rises above scholarly distance:

> He who the glorious Angels did create,
> Becomes a Worme yet keeps his owne estate.
> God had his lowlinesse enough commended,
> Had he but to an Angels state descended.
> For twixt an Angel and a Worme, more ods
> Is not, then twixt an Angels state and Gods.[79]

Abraham Cowley's angels in *Davideis* (1656), speedy, hymning, and prophetic, are similar. These works, and many others, show little more than a rhetorical deployment of angels, or literal commentary on angels occupying digressions or asides in a narrative. This kind of use precedes and postdates the early modern period, and shows the dissemination of angel-doctrine and little angelological verve.

Shakespeare and Donne can be contrasted with Dryden, whose theory and practice were explored in the previous chapter. Dryden writes freely about angels precisely because they are unknowable. Whereas Milton is at pains to stick to truth (relying on the theological principle of accommodation), for Dryden theology should be left to the theologians. We cannot know about angels, and that is why they are so useful. They are ideal matter for feigned representations. In Dryden's criticism perhaps lies one origin of the modern sense of an antipathy between theology and imaginative poetry. It is not *typical* of his age, however; rather it is one of several, competing contemporary positions.

John Dennis, writing a letter on the problem of angelic bodies in 1722, hampered by ignorance of angel-doctrine and discomfited by Milton's confounding of spirit and matter, nonetheless offers insights into contrasts between Milton and his contemporary Cowley and his non-contemporary Torquato Tasso (1544–95): it is because Milton expressly declares that his angels are spirits that he creates problems for himself, whereas the other poets leave it to the reader's imagination, and thereby avoid inconsistency.[80] The problem, then, is where narrative and doctrine collide, and the sensible route is to separate them, leaving one to reason and the other to the imagination. But these were, as Dennis saw, contemporary positions, and the contrast is in modes of representation. Shakespeare and Donne use angel-doctrines because they provide a language with which to think and write; what they believe matters less than how they think through these beliefs. Milton works through doctrine, so that the imaginative and the doctrinal develop together. What Dryden believes is entirely irrelevant, which is not to say that he was irreligious: angels are mysterious images that can be exploited. Whereas for Shakespeare and Donne the content of the ideas supplies imaginative potency, for Dryden it is the mere form of the idea that triggers the labours of the imagination. In the eight-eenth century angels were used to demonstrate Newtonian physics, though their value was consistently rhetorical—as narrators and symbols—rather than empirical or experimental.

I am not tracing a transformation of literary representation on the basis of these authors; nor am I importing natural philosophy or theology to explain poems that perform or open up very well without them. Rather, I am suggesting that some of the dichotomies conven-tionally discovered in the seventeenth century—Renaissance–modernity, enchantment–secularization, God–man, theory–history, apprehension–comprehension—those dichotomies beloved of those critics who hold most fervently the autonomy of literature as a patri-monial inheritance—are not supported by an analysis of the fortunes of angels in early modern imaginative writing, and that if these dichoto-mies cannot be supported by an analysis of these beings that subtend across such broad areas of knowledge, belief, and practice, then they did not operate in the way that is presently believed.

For both Eliot and Teskey, Milton sits on the cusp of transform-ations, though he faces in different directions. Eliot sees philosophy or theology and poetry becoming divided in Milton; his view in large part derived from his lack of sympathy with the enthusiasm that gave Milton the confidence to explore theological issues in stories of the sacred and invisible world, and the politics that persuaded him to put his literary abilities into public service. It is this imaginative antipathy that separates doctrine and story. Teskey positions Milton as a 'theor-etical poet', yet the natural philosophy of his angels, and much else besides, marks him out as a material poet as much as an abstract one.[81] His writing challenges this dichotomy. He develops his angels both theoretically and practically. His narrative discloses perspectives on the properties of angels that are as remarkable and as considered as his self-conscious representations of angelic digestion and lovemaking. Narrative can do this. Milton does not himself represent a turning point; Dryden is his contemporary, and an account of the 1660s that places Milton as the past and Dryden as the future is undertaking too much ideological work at the expense of history.[82] It is an irony of chronology that the two are placed on either side of a shift, and yet shared a government office in the later 1650s. Milton's is one of a plurality of perspectives, discourses, techniques, or beliefs that developed and coexisted in the same period. It is, of course, enlightening to ask how typical Milton is of his times, and the process of sifting out the ways in which he is typical from those in which he is extraordinary, heterodox, and original may lead to a more intimate understanding of his writings. But the idea of typicality itself may presuppose too much, for personal and for social reasons. A writer holds a 'typical' belief in conjunction with other beliefs that may have been atypical and which shape and give meaning to the 'typical' belief; in this context the apparent typicality may dissipate. Social reasons also make typicality doubtful: Milton's sensibility, his understanding of the relationship between words and the world, his doctrine of angels and sense of what it means to live alongside them and why it is legitimate to write about them, developed alongside those of Dryden, Locke, and Glanvill. Their positions are interconnected and in an important sense simultaneous. What takes place in early modern imaginative writing, which we find fragmentarily reflected in the several narratives of transformation, may be the same that takes place in non-imaginative writing. Writing about angels suggests that there is a multiplication of languages or discourses that assume different modes of referentiality, languages that are simultaneous and interdependent, though divergent if not contradictory.

In the course of the late sixteenth and seventeenth centuries there is a profound confluence of concerns about representation, faith, spiritual practice, and knowledge, in which areas of knowledge *proliferate* and are *rearranged* without being, in any simple sense, *superseded*. Not until Blake would another great poet earnestly claim the authority of angels themselves for his imaginative representation of them (as opposed to using angels to represent authority). However, poets continued to exploit the permeable intersections between theology and natural philosophy, and one way to do this was to figure conversations with, protection by, or the flight of angels. Though it became easier to separate fiction and truth, and to keep the imagination free from inspiration, one paradigm did not displace another. The fortunes of angels show no dissociation or profound rupture.


## Last Things

In this book I have sketched the landscape of angel-learning and angel-writing in early modern Britain. *Paradise Lost* has been at the centre of this map, because of its intrinsic interest as the greatest poem of the period, and one that relies on angels for its aesthetics and theology, and because it provides a persuasive point of entry to the vast body of writing that concerns or touches upon angels. I have presented a reading of the poem and its representational modes, and suggested some of the implications of this reading of Milton and his solid angels for our understanding of the way poetry intervenes in political and intellectual culture.

Over the past two decades the range of interpretative devices for reading poems politically and historically has been extended and enriched. The best historicist interpretations do not make poetry seem any less guileful; indeed, more precise local contextualization has disclosed the ingenuity of poetic performances. But the tenor of such interpretations is to emphasize allegorical encodings, political allusions, and verbal echoes. In this interpretative decoding, the role of imaginative discourse in political language—both in poetry and in prose exposition and argument—has been underexplored. The literary elements of political discourse, its fictional devices, tropes, eloquence, performances, persuasive fictions, were not mere dressing for argument, but integral to it. Poetry shared its imaginative devices with other kinds of writing, and the exchange between modes was multilateral and mutual. When a scriptural commentary employs an extended metaphor, it can be to avoid an uneasy point through studious ambiguity, sustained with rhetorical conviction. Drama, dialogue, a scene in hell, could be useful to sophisticated and sober political debate. Scriptural commentary could be exploratory as well as analytic. Even at its most imaginative and indirect—a war in heaven, with armour and uprooted mountains—poetry can be engaging with the force of argument. Poetry was not 'safe' because it was disengaged from knowledge and truth.

Early modern writings of all modes used imaginative narrative to explore and to explicate theological and political positions; and these positions correspondingly formed the basis for diverse imaginative exercises. This was especially so for epic, a form more associated with knowledge than empire or romance. This cross-fertilization was not a universal characteristic of writing—indeed, these connections can be shown to be shifting during the course of the seventeenth century—but it was a powerful potential that was exploited not only by Milton but also by other poets and polemicists.

The period also witnessed, as the literary culture of Protestant Britain developed and was consolidated, a multiplication of modes of writing about angels. Some of these were attached to the idea that angels were remote from human understanding—as they were from godly worship—that the separation between the visible and the invisible world necessarily drove a wedge between beliefs and literary performances. In the eighteenth century this would result in much writing about angels that presented them didactically, or proselytizingly, but not harmoniously. What is unique about Milton, and what makes *Paradise Lost* so distinctively great, is not his relationship to rupture, but the conjunction he effects between a story about humans and angels and a sustained doctrine of the being and action of angels. The force of his poem lies in a narrative taut enough to knit together story and doctrine and a language capacious enough to speak angelology and poetry at the same time. Savouring this, we can feel the pathos of Milton's first two humans moving in the shadows of angels with all the more weight.

# *Notes*

CHAPTER I

1. BL, Sloane MS 3188, 1–3 (note by Ashmole); the other books are bound in Sloane MS 3191.
2. Pp. 112–15 below.
3. For Shippen, see BL, 719.m.12. Also pp. 112–15, 306–8, below; Michael Hunter, 'Alchemy, Magic and Moralism in the Thought of Robert Boyle', *British Journal for the History of Science*, 23 (1990), 387–410: 409.
4. Margaret Aston, *England's Iconoclasts*, i: *Laws Against Images* (Oxford, 1988); Julie Spraggon, *Puritan Iconoclasm during the English Civil War* (Woodbridge, 2003).
5. Trevor Cooper (ed.), *The Journal of William Dowsing: Iconoclasm in East Anglia during the English Civil War* (Woodbridge, 2001), 155–6; see also John Morrill, 'William Dowsing and the Administration of Iconoclasm in the Puritan Revolution', ibid.
6. Eamon Duffy, *The Stripping of the Altars: Traditional Religion in England, c.1400–c.1580* (New Haven, 1992), 269–71; Richard Marks, *Image and Devotion in Late Medieval England* (Thrupp, 2004), 65; Peter Burton and Harland Walshaw (eds), *The English Angel* (Moreton in the Marsh, 2000).
7. But see esp. Keck, *Angels*; West, *Angels*; Marshall and Walsham (eds), *Angels*; Raymond (ed.), *Conversations*.
8. *PL* I, argument.
9. *Philosophical Transactions*, 3/38 (1668), 742; pp. 292–3 below.
10. Margaret Cavendish, *Political Writings*, ed. Susan James (Cambridge, 2003), 51, 96, 97.
11. John Locke, *An Essay Concerning Humane Understanding* (1690), 97; see also pp. 141, 185, 209, 279, 351.
12. *Athenian Mercury*, 10/3 (1691), 30; *Athenian Oracle*, 4 vols (1728), i. 4–5.
13. Once to a Roman Catholic priest. During this conversation he said to me: 'the problem with Protestants is that they cannot say where their church was before the Reformation', an objection that most ten-year-olds could have responded to in 17th-century Britain.
14. Rilke, *Ahead of All Parting: The Selected Poetry and Prose of Rainer Maria Rilke*, ed. and trans. Stephen Mitchell (New York, 1995), 331.

15. On anachronism, see Nick Jardine, 'Uses and Abuses of Anachronism in the History of the Sciences', *History of Science*, 38 (2000), 251–70, and 'Whigs and Stories: Herbert Butterfield and the Historiography of Science', *History of Science*, 41 (2003), 125–40; Quentin Skinner, *Visions of Politics*, i: *Regarding Method* (Cambridge, 2002), chs 3 and 4; and Joad Raymond, 'Describing Publicity in Early Modern England', *Huntington Library Quarterly*, 67 (2004), 101–29.

CHAPTER 2

1. John Prideaux, 'The Patronage of Angels', 16, in *Certaine Sermons* (1637); Antoine Le Grand, *An Entire Body of Philosophy*, trans. Richard Blome (1694), 18; also John Scott, *The Christian Life* (1687), 317; Heywood, *Hierarchie*, 341; and works mentioned in text.

2. Gideon Harvey, *Archelogia Philosophica Nova* (1663), first part, fourth book, p. 1. *OED* first use is 1753.

3. S. G. F. Brandon, 'Angels: The History of an Idea', *History Today*, 13 (Oct. 1963), 655–65; Allison Coudert, 'Angels', in Mircea Eliade (ed.), *The Encyclopedia of Religion*, i (New York, 1987), 282–6; Peter R. Carrell, *Jesus and the Angels: Angelology and the Christology of the Apocalypse of John* (Cambridge, 1997); Charles A. Gieschen, *Angelomorphic Christology: Antecedents and Early Evidence* (Leiden, 1998); and works in next note.

4. Edward Leigh, *Annotations upon all the New Testament* (1650), 243; Williams, *Ideas of the Fall*, 20–8; John Skinner, *A Critical and Exegetical Commentary on Genesis*, 2nd edn (1930; Edinburgh, 1994), 139–47; Williams, *Expositor*, 151–3; Neil Forsyth, *The Satanic Epic* (Princeton, 2003) and *The Old Enemy: Satan and the Combat Myth* (Princeton, 1987); Michael E. Stone, *A History of the Literature of Adam and Eve* (Atlanta, Ga., 1992); Elaine Pagels, *The Origin of Satan* (New York, 1995), ch. 2; West, *Angels*, 129–30; Kathryn Powell and Donald Scragg (eds), *Apocryphal Texts and Traditions in Anglo-Saxon England* (Cambridge, 2003); Ariel Hessayon, *'Gold Tried in the Fire': The Prophet Theauraujohn Tany and the English Revolution* (Aldershot, 2007), 244–59; Philo-Judaeus (or Philo of Alexandria), *Philo*, trans. F. H. Coulson and G. H. Whitaker, Loeb Classical Library, 10 vols (1929–62), ii. 449–75, esp. 453–5; John Leonard, *Naming in Paradise: Milton and the Language of Adam and Eve* (Oxford, 1990), 52; Mindele Treip, *Allegorical Poetics and the Epic: The Renaissance Tradition to 'Paradise Lost'* (Lexington, Ky., 1994), 211; Fowler's notes to *PL* 11. 621–2, 642; 3. 463–5; R. H. Charles, *The Apocrypha and Pseudepigrapha of the Old Testament* (Oxford, 1913); and James H. Charlesworth (ed.), *The Old Testament Pseudepigrapha*, 2 vols (Garden City, NY, 1983–5).

5. Henry Ansgar Kelly, *Satan: A Biography* (Cambridge, 2006), 36–41, 175–82.

6. Ibid. 182–3, 191–9.

7. Pseudo-Dionysius, *Works*, 26–9.
8. Karlfried Froehlich, ibid. 33–46; also 69 n. 128, 57 n. 89, 72, 117, 166.
9. Ibid. 161–73; quotation at p. 167.
10. Keck, *Angels*, 55–8.
11. Dante Alighieri, *The Divine Comedy*, iii: *Paradiso*, trans. John D. Sinclair (1939; New York, 1979), 406–9.
12. Pseudo-Dionysius, *Works*, 168; Ch. 6 below; Aquinas, *Summa*, xiv. 183, 99–105, 111–13.
13. Keck, *Angels*, 53–68.
14. My paraphrases are based on the English–Latin text (trans. Alexis Bugnolo) at <http://www.franciscan-archive.org/lombardus/>, accessed 17 Oct. 2007; see also Marcia Colish, *Peter Lombard*, 2 vols (Leiden, 1994), i. 303–97; Keck, *Angels*, 73, 89–91.
15. Keck, *Angels*, 75–6; the texts are available at <http://www.franciscan-archive.org/index2.html>, accessed 17 Oct. 2007.
16. Kelly, *Satan*, 253–5.
17. Bonaventure, *Commentaries on the Four Books of Sentences*, trans. Alexis Bugnolo et al., bk 2, distinction 2, pt 2, art. 2, qu. 4, <http://www.franciscan-archive.org/index2.html>.
18. Divine government at Aquinas, *Summa*, xiv. 89–167; angels in vol. ix; qu. 54 at ix. 73–91; quotations at pp. 81, 85.
19. Henry Mayr-Harting, *Perceptions of Angels in History* (Oxford, 1998), 15–19.
20. James McEvoy, *Robert Grosseteste* (New York, 2000), 106–10, and Robertus Grossetesta Lincolniensis, 'An Essay in Historiography, Medieval and Modern', in Maura O'Carroll (ed.), *Robert Grosseteste and the Beginnings of a British Theological Tradition* (Rome, 2003); Deborah E. Harkness, *John Dee's Conversations with Angels: Cabala, Alchemy, and the End of Nature* (Cambridge, 1999), 117–18; Nicholas H. Clulee, *John Dee's Natural Philosophy: Between Science and Religion* (1988), 52, 54; Richard Day (ed.), *The Testament of the Twelve Patriarchs* (1658); Grosseteste, *On the Six Days of Creation*, trans. C. F. J. Martin (Oxford, 1997); Edward Brown (ed.), *Fasciculus Rerum*, 2 vols (1690), i. 305–7. I am indebted to John Flood for correspondence on Grosseteste.
21. D. P. Walker, *Spiritual and Demonic Magic: From Ficino to Campanella* (1958; Stroud, 2000).
22. West, *Angels*, 12; Robert Elrodt, *Neoplatonism in the Poetry of Spenser* (Geneva, 1960), 9; Clay Daniel, 'Milton's Neo-Platonic Angel', *Studies in English Literature*, 44 (2004), 173–88; Michael B. Allen, 'The Absent Angel in Ficino's Philosophy', *Journal of the History of Ideas*, 36 (1975), 219–40. Also Bruce Gordon, 'The Renaissance Angel', in Marshall and Walsham (eds), *Angels*. On conjuration, see pp. 107–9, 132–2, below.
23. Calvin, *Institution*, 69.
24. John Biddle, *Twelve Arguments Drawn out of Scripture* (1647), 4, and *A Twofold Catechism* (1654), sig. a1[r], identifying Henry More among others.

25. Edward Knott, *A Direction to be Observed by N.N.* ([London or St Omer], 1636), 19–20; William Chillingworth, preface to *Religion of Protestants* (1638), sig. §§§2ᵛ; James Long, 'Of Angels and Pinheads: The Contributions of the Early Oxford Masters to the Doctrine of Spiritual Matter', *Franciscan Studies*, 56 (1999), 239–54 (esp. n. 23); Marshall and Walsham in eid. (eds), *Angels*, 1; James Steven Byrne's essay in Raymond (ed.), *Conversations*.
26. Henry More, *The Immortality of the Soul* (1659), 190–1.
27. Calvin, *Institution*, 64–5.
28. [Thomas Lamplugh, Archbishop of York?], Folger Shakespeare Library, MS V.a.63 (MS sermons, 1653–8), 1658 sermon on Mark 10: 17, no foliation.
29. John Bayly, *Two Sermons: The Angel Guardian* (Oxford, 1630), 5–6.
30. William Jenkyn, *An Exposition of the Epistle of Jude . . . Second Part* (1654), 47–9; quotation at p. 48.
31. John Patrick, *Reflexions upon the Devotions of the Roman Church* (1674), 418, 425.
32. Martin Luther, *A Commentarie upon the Fiftene Psalmes*, trans. Henry Bull (1577), 91–2; Philip M. Soergel, 'Luther on the Angels', in Marshall and Walsham (eds), *Angels*, 69.
33. Quoted in Soergel, 'Luther on the Angels', 69.
34. See esp. *A Sermon on Preparing to Die* (1519), in *Luther's Works*, 55 vols, ed. Jaroslav Pelikan et al. (St Louis, Mo., 1955–86), xlii. 113, also vi. 88, xx. 170; see also Soergel, 'Luther on the Angels', 72–3; Peter Marshall, 'The Guardian Angel in Protestant England', in Raymond (ed.), *Conversations*; Kelly, *Satan*, 310 (referring to Luther's *Little Catechism*); also pp. 230–7, 333–4, below.
35. Luther, *Works*, iii. 271–5, xx. 74, ii. 355; p. 371 below.
36. Williams, *Expositor*, 116–17; also p. 320 below; Soergel, 'Luther on the Angels', 78–9.
37. Augustine, *City*, 533; Luther, *Works*, i. 111.
38. Samuel Ward, *The Life of Faith* (1621), 2; also C. A. Patrides, 'Hierarchy and Order', in Philip P. Weiner (ed.), *Dictionary of the History of Ideas* (1973–4), ii. 436, <http://etext.virginia.edu/DicHist/dict.html>, accessed May 2007.
39. Calvin, *Institution*, 64–8, and *Commentarie*, *passim*, esp. 381–2, 413, 663–4; *Institution* is ambivalent about guardians, while *Commentarie* states that the belief is wicked.
40. Calvin, *Institution*, 6, and book 1 *passim*; William A. Dyrness, *Reformed Theology and Visual Culture: The Protestant Imagination from Calvin to Edwards* (Cambridge, 2004), 49–89.
41. Joseph Wright, *A Testimony for the Son of Man* (1661), 139.
42. Graham Parry, *The Arts of the Anglican Counter-Reformation: Glory, Laud and Honour* (Woodbridge, 2006).

43. Kate Harvey, 'The Role of Angels in English Protestant Thought 1580 to 1660', Ph.D. thesis (Cambridge University, 2005).

44. Alexandra Walsham, 'Angels and Idols in England's Long Reformation', in Marshall and Walsham (eds), *Angels*; also Raymond Gillespie, 'Imagining Angels in Early Modern Ireland', ibid. 24–5.

45. Elizabeth Reis, 'Otherworldly Visions: Angels, Devils and Gender in Puritan New England', and Owen Davies, 'Angels in Elite and Popular Magic, 1650–1790', both in Marshall and Walsham (eds), *Angels*.

46. *Good Angel of Stamford* (1659); BL, Add. MS 43410, fos 144$^v$–146$^v$.

47. *Certaine Sermons Appoynted by the Quenes Maiesty* (1563), sig. Riiii$^r$; *An Homelie against Disobedience and Wylfull Rebellion* (1570), sig. Ai$^{r-v}$.

48. E-text available at <http://www.piar.hu/councils/ecum12.htm>, accessed Oct. 2007; see also Kelly, *Satan*, 316.

49. [Westminster Assembly], *The Protestation of the Two and Twenty Divines* (1643), sig. A2$^v$.

50. *The Booke of the Common Praier* (1549), sig. Niv$^v$. Also the editions in London (1586), Edinburgh (1637), Cambridge (1638), London (1639, 1642).

51. John Boughton, *God and Man, or, A Treatise Catechetical* (1623), 35.

52. On scriptural literalism, see Peter Harrison, *The Bible, Protestantism, and the Rise of Natural Science* (Cambridge, 1998), 107–14, and Ch. 6 below.

53. Gervase Babington, *Certaine Plaine, Briefe, and Comfortable Notes* (1592), fo. 65$^v$.

54. Andrew Willet, *Hexapla in Genesin* (Cambridge, 1605), 203.

55. George Hughes, *Annotations upon all the Books of the Old and New Testament* (1651), at Gen. 18: 8; George Hughes, *An Analytical Exposition of the Whole First Book of Moses* (1672), 217.

56. Babington, *Certaine Plaine, Briefe, and Comfortable Notes*, fo. 7$^v$. Franciscus Junius was a 16th-century Huguenot theologian, and editor, with Emmanuel Tremellius, of a Latin Bible that Milton used.

57. Willet, *Hexapla*, 17; Williams, *Expositor*, 61; cf. Columbia, xv. 30–1.

58. *Annotations upon all the Books of the Old and New Testament*, following Gen. 1: 31; also Alexander Ross, *An Exposition on . . . Genesis* (1626), 31–2.

59. Columbia, xv. 32–5; p. 11 above.

60. Williams, *Ideas of the Fall*; James Grantham Turner, *One Flesh: Paradisal Marriage and Sexual Relation in the Age of Milton* (Oxford, 1987); William Poole, *Milton and the Idea of the Fall* (Cambridge, 2005).

61. Gordon Campbell, Thomas N. Corns, John K. Hale, and Fiona J. Tweedie, *Milton and the Manuscript of 'De Doctrina Christiana'* (Oxford, 2007), 92–8.

62. Samuel Rutherford, *Lex, Rex* (1644), 372, 419, and *The Due Right of Presbyteries* (1644), 3, 4, and *passim*; Richard Baxter, *Christian Directory* (1673), 927; Richard Montagu, *Appello Caesarem* (1625), 11–12.

63. Cf. Henry Hibbert, 'Gloria in Altissimis', 18, in *Syntagma Theologicum* (1662).
64. Ann Moss, *Printed Commonplace Books and the Structuring of Renaissance Thought* (Oxford, 1996); Peter Beale, ' "Notions in Garrison": The Seventeenth-Century Commonplace Book', RETS/Newberry Lecture, 2 Apr. 1987, TS in Bodl.; William Sherman, *John Dee: The Politics of Reading and Writing in the English Renaissance* (Amherst, Mass., 1995), 61–5; Kevin Sharpe, *Reading Revolutions: The Politics of Reading in Early Modern England* (New Haven, 2000), 76–120, 277–307.
65. Folger Shakespeare Library, MS V.b.108; Andrew J. Hopper, 'Henry Fairfax', in *ODNB*.
66. Folger Shakespeare Library, MS V.a.356.
67. Cornelius Burgess, 'The Grounds of Divinity handled according to the Method of the Vulgar Catechisme', CUL, Add. MS 6164; Campbell et al., *Manuscript of 'De Doctrina'*.
68. Mary Morrissey, 'Sermons, Prayer Books and Primers', in Joad Raymond (ed.), *The Oxford History of Popular Print Culture*, i (forthcoming).
69. John Hume, *Bios Epoyranios, or, The Character of an Heavenly Conversation* (1670); John Everard, *Some Gospel-Truths Opened* (1653), 381; Thomas Lamplugh's sermons in Folger Shakespeare Library, MS V.a.63, e.g. sermon dated 25 July 1658; Thomas Hill, *The Militant Church Triumphant over the Dragon and His Angels* (1643), 5; *The Works of John Owen, D.D.*, ed. William H. Goold, 16 vols (New York, 1851–3), ix. 610; John Wall, *Alae Seraphicae* (1627), *passim*; pp. 371–2, 375–6 below.
70. Nathaniel Cannon, *Three Sermons* (1616): see the third item, 'The Court of Guard'; cf. Brian Duppa, *Angels Rejoicing for Sinners Repenting* (1648).
71. John Gumbleden, *Two Sermons*, pub. with *Christ Tempted: The Devil Conquered* (1657).
72. Bayly, *Two Sermons*, 4; Prideaux, 'Patronage of Angels'.
73. Christopher Love, *The Dejected Soules Cure . . . To which is added I. The Ministry of Angels* (1657), sig. A4ᵛ.
74. William Austin, *Devotionis Augustinianae Flamma* (1635), 243–57. See also Richard Holsworth, *The Valley of Vision* (1651), 489–538.
75. Increase Mather, *Angelographia* (Boston, 1696) and *Coelestinus: A Conversation in Heaven* (Boston, 1713); Cotton Mather, *The Angel of Bethesda* (1722); Elizabeth Reis, 'Otherworldly Visions: Angels, Devils and Gender in Puritan New England', in Marshall and Walsham (eds), *Angels*.
76. Pp. 367–71, 376–7 below; Richard Sibbes, *Light from Heaven* (1638), 111–12; John White, *A Commentary upon . . . Genesis* (1656), III. 240 (cited by book and page); CUL, Add. MS 6164; Ross, *Exposition*, 73.
77. Henry More, *An Explanation of the Grand Mystery of Godliness* (1660), 37.
78. J. A. Comenius, *Naturall Philosophie Reformed by Divine Light* (1651), 232. Contrast Holsworth, *Valley of Vision*, 508–9.

CHAPTER 3

1. Edward Leigh, *A Treatise of Divinity* (1646), 40.
2. Andrew Willet, *Synopsis Papismi, That is, A Generall Viewe of Papisty* (1592), 291–3.
3. William Bucanus, *Institutions of Christian Religion*, trans. Robert Hill (1606), 69.
4. William Perkins, *A Golden Chaine* (Cambridge, 1600), 12.
5. Kate Harvey, 'The Role of Angels in English Protestant Thought 1580 to 1660', Ph.D. thesis (Cambridge University, 2005), 92–6; Henry Hibbert, *Syntagma Theologicum* (1662), 33; Myles Davies, *Athenae Britannicae*, 3 vols (1715–16), iii. 7; John Bayly, *Two Sermons: The Angel Guardian* (1630), 4.
6. C. A. Patrides, 'Renaissance Thought on the Celestial Hierarchy: The Decline of a Tradition', *Journal of the History of Ideas*, 20 (1959), 155–66, and 'Renaissance Views on the "Unconfused Orders Angellick"', *Journal of the History of Ideas*, 23 (1962), 265–7.
7. Joseph Hall, *The Great Mysterie of Godliness . . . Also, The Invisible World* (1652), 144–5; referring to 2 Cor. 12: 2 and Col. 1: 16.
8. Hall, *Great Mysterie*, 146–53.
9. John Blenkow, *Michaels Combat with the Devil* (1640), 7.
10. Richard Sibbes, *Light from Heaven* (1638), 206; William Jenkyn, *An Exposition of the Epistle of Jude* (1652), pt 1, p. 465, pt 2, pp. 47–8.
11. John Salkeld, *Treatise of Angels* (1613), 125–6, 291–322.
12. [Joseph Glanvill], *A Blow at Modern Sadducism* (1668), 52.
13. This is the tenor of Jenkyn, *Exposition of Jude*, pt 1, p. 465; Cornelius Burgess, 'The Grounds of Divinity' (begun 1619), CUL, Add. MS 6164, p. 54; Isaac Ambrose, 'War with Devils', in *The Compleat Works* (1682), 104–5.
14. Brian Duppa, *Angels Rejoicing for Sinners Repenting* (1648), 8–9.
15. Heywood, *Hierarchie*, 194–5; for Sadducism, see pp. 194–6; cf. Dante, pp. 24–6 above.
16. See also John Heydon, who explicitly supported the nine orders and individual guardian angels: *Harmony of the World* (1662), 2, 92; *Theomagia, or, The Temple of Wisdome* (1663–4), vol. iii, sig. Aaa2ʳ, pp. 126, 148–9. See also Robert Boyle, *Some Motives and Incentives to the Love of God* (1663 edn), 9.
17. See pp. 90–2 below.
18. E.g. Nathanael Hardy, *The Hierarchy Exalted* (1661), 22.
19. John Taylor, *Peace, Peace, and We Shall Be Quiet* (1647), 8–9.
20. George Lawson, *Theo-Politica* (1659), 49–51.
21. John Swan, *Redde Debitum* (1640), 16–17; Heywood, *Hierarchie*, 282–3.
22. *CPW* i. 752–3.
23. Henry More, *A Plain and Continued Exposition of . . . Daniel* (1681), 25–6.

24. *Contra* Harris Francis Fletcher, *Milton's Rabbinical Readings* (Hamden, Conn., 1967), 217, 220–1; West, *Angels*, 131–6 ('His achievement with the hierarchical terms in *Paradise Lost* is a sort of general allusiveness that does not seriously exceed what Protestants would accept not yet fall wholly short of what Catholics claimed'); Feisal G. Mohamed, 'Renaissance Thoughts on the Celestial Hierarchy: The Decline of a Tradition?', *Journal of the History of Ideas*, 65 (2004), 559–82, and '*Paradise Lost* and the Inversion of Catholic Angelology', *Milton Quarterly*, 26 (2002), 240–52. See also John Leonard, *Naming in Paradise: Milton and the Language of Adam and Eve* (Oxford, 1990), 57–68; and Howard Schultz, *Milton and Forbidden Knowledge* (New York, 1955), 123.

25. Witness Aquinas on angelic communication proceeding purely downward (*Summa*, xiv. 112–15, and below, pp. 70, 313–14), and John Colet's summary of Dionysius in *Two Treatises on the Hierarchies of Dionysius*, ed. and trans. J. H. Lupton (1869), 16–18.

26. See pp. 245–6 below. Also Johannes Wollebius, *The Abridgment of Christian Divinitie*, trans. Alexander Ross (1650), 51.

27. Westminster Assembly, *Annotations upon all the Books of the Old and New Testament* (1651), at Rev. 12: 7; Heywood, *Hierarchie*, 336; Jenkyn, *Exposition of Jude*, pt 2, p. 45; Columbia, xv. 104–7.

28. Willet, *Synopsis Papismi*, 293–5.

29. Calvin, *Institution*, 66; Peter Martyr, *Common Places*, 357; see pp. 230–7, 333–5, below.

30. John Pringle (trans.), *The Three Books of Hermas* (1661), 58–9.

31. Philip M. Soergel, 'Luther on the Angels', in Marshall and Walsham (eds), *Angels*; Urbanus Rhegius, *An Homely or Sermon of Good and Evill Angels*, trans. Ri[chard] Robinson (1583; 1593), 30ᵛ; Bayly, *Two Sermons*, 9–10, citing Zanchius. See, idiosyncratically, Thomas Tryon, *Pythagoras His Mystick Philosophy* (1691), 157, 181, 188.

32. Calvin, *Institution*, 66; Calvin, *Commentarie*, 663–4; cf. the very Calvinist Bodl. MS Sloane 1233, fo. 78ᵛ.

33. Gervase Babington, *Certaine Plaine, Briefe, and Comfortable Notes upon Everie Chapter of Genesis* (1592), fo. 127ᵛ; Westminster, *Annotations*, at Gen. 32: 2. The identical phrase appears in John Richardson, *Choice Observations and Explanation upon the Old Testament* (1655), at Gen. 32: 2.

34. See Peter Marshall, 'The Guardian Angel in Protestant England', in Raymond (ed.), *Conversations*; Love, *Dejected Soules Cure*, 4 and *passim*; cf. John White, *A Commentary upon . . . Genesis* (1656), i. 44; BL, Add. MS 1233, fo. 78ʳ⁻ᵛ.

35. Salkeld, *Treatise*, 251–80; cf. Benjamin Camfield, who reserves judgement in *A Theological Discourse of Angels and their Ministries* (1678), 70–5.

36. Thomas Browne, *Religio Medici* (1642), 44–5, 60–1.

37. Lawrence, *Angells*, 19–22; Robert Dingley, *The Deputation of Angels* (1654), see esp. his list of predecessors at pp. 69–76; Edward Hyde,

*Christian Vindication* (1659), 351–6; Thomas Tryon, *Treatise of Dreams and Visions* (1689), 143–76; BL, Add. MS 4454, fo. 6; Pordage, at p. 131 below.

38. Dingley, *Deputation*, 149.
39. Bucanus, *Insitutions*, 73–4.
40. Marshall, 'Guardian Angel'; also Harvey, 'Role of Angels', 79–87.
41. [George Wither], 'Terrae-Filius', in *Prosopopoeia Britannica* (1648), 105.
42. See pp. 90, 189–93, 307.
43. Quoted in Anthony Grafton, *Cardano's Cosmos: The Worlds and Works of a Renaissance Astrologer* (Cambridge, Mass., 1999), 171. See also Robin Briggs, 'Dubious Messengers: Bodin's Demon, the Spirit World and the Sadducees', in Marshall and Walsham (eds), *Angels*; Walter Stephens, 'Strategies of Interspecies Communication, 1100–2000', in Raymond (ed.), *Conversations*.
44. Henry More, *An Antidote Against Atheisme* (1653), 257–7, 258; Girolamo Cardano, *The Book of my Life*, trans. Jean Stone, introd. Anthony Grafton (New York, 2002), 209–15; Grafton, *Cardano's Cosmos*, 166–8.
45. BL, Sloane MS 3188; Meric Casaubon, *A True and Faithful Relation of What Passed for Many Yeers between Sr. John Dee... and Some Spirits* (1659); Deborah E. Harkness, *John Dee's Conversations with Angels: Cabala, Alchemy, and the End of Nature* (Cambridge, 1999); Lauren Kassell, *Medicine and Magic in Elizabethan London: Simon Forman, Astrologer, Alchemist, and Physician* (Oxford, 2005), 33, 215–21; Bodl., MS Ashmole 235, fos 186ᵛ–193ʳ; Bodl., MS Rawlinson D. 864, fo. 233; Sophie Page, 'Speaking with Spirits in Medieval Magic Texts', in Raymond (ed.), *Conversations*; pp. 106–9 below.
46. Briggs, 'Dubious Messengers', 182–3; Trevor Johnson, 'Guardian Angels and the Society of Jesus', in Marshall and Walsham (eds), *Angels*, 191; Owen Davies, 'Angels in Elite and Popular Magic, 1650–1790', in Marshall and Walsham (eds), *Angels*, 306–7; D. P. Walker, *Spiritual and Demonic Magic: From Ficino to Campanella* (1958; Stroud, 2000), 224–9; Ingrid D. Rowland, 'Athanasius Kircher's Guardian Angel', in Raymond (ed.), *Conversations*.
47. Durand Hotham, *Life of Jacob Boehme* (1653), sig. Dᵛ; Peter Marshall, 'Angels around the Deathbed: Variations on a Theme in the English Art of Dying', in Marshall and Walsham (eds), *Angels*.
48. Pp. 111, 120, 123 below; Heydon, *Theomagia*, iii. 126.
49. Reginald Scott, *The Discoverie of Witchcraft* (1665), 223–4; West, *Angels*, 61–6.
50. Willet, *Synopsis Papismi*, 295–6.
51. On Pordage and his disciples, Ch. 5 below.
52. Willet, *Synopsis Papismi*, 297–9. Cf. Richard Montagu's rejection of the notion that angels see through God-as-mirror; *Immediate Addresse unto God Alone* (1624), 139–41. For more on angelic eyesight and knowledge, see pp. 67–9 and 289–97 below.

53. Keck, *Angels*, 172–3; Margaret Aston, *England's Iconoclasts*, i: *Laws Against Images* (Oxford, 1988), 47–8.

54. Willet, *Synopsis Papismi*, 299–300.

55. Willet makes a more elaborate case in relationship to Gen. 17, where 'Abraham fell on his face, and God talked with him.' He argues that if this were an angel, then Abraham's falling on his face was not a gesture of adoration (because of Rev. 22: 9); if it is such a gesture, then God must have appeared directly; *Hexapla*, 198. Cf. George Hughes, *An Analytical Exposition of the Whole First Book of Moses* (1672), 239.

56. Edward Leigh, *Annotations upon all the New Testament* (1650), 612.

57. Wollebius, *Abridgment*, 272.

58. Hall, *Great Mysterie*, 175–81.

59. Lawrence, *Angells*, 51.

60. Arise Evans, *The Voice of Michael the Archangel* (1654), 18–19.

61. Willet, *Synopsis Papismi*, 300–1.

62. Dingley, *Deputation*, 147–50.

63. *Luther's Works*, 55 vols, ed. Jaroslav Pelikan et al. (St Louis, Mo. 1955–86), xlii. 113, iii. 271–5; Calvin, *Commentarie*, 875–6; Calvin, *Institution*, 426–32.

64. Montagu, *Immediate Addresse*, ¶4$^v$, 95, 91, 98–9. Alexandra Walsham, 'Angels and Idols in England's Long Reformation', in Marshall and Walsham (eds), *Angels*, 154–5, describes this as a shift in emphasis rather than a departure from Calvinist tradition. I think Montagu manipulates Calvin's *Institution*, 427–8, to conceal how radical his departure is.

65. Graham Parry, *The Arts of the Anglican Counter-Reformation: Glory, Laud and Honour* (Woodbridge, 2006), 51, 77–8, 94, 97–8, 103, 125–6; Austin, *Devotionis Augustinianae Flamma*; R[obert] B[aillie] K., *A Parallel or Brief Comparison* (1641), 15–16; p. 94 below.

66. See pp. 106–9, 131–2 below.

67. Richard Baxter, *The Certainty of the World of Spirits* (1691), 176, 222–3.

68. Reginald Scott, *The Discoverie of Witchcraft* (1584), 156; King James I (*sic*), *Daemonologie (1597)*, ed. G. B. Harrison (1922; Edinburgh, 1966), 65–6. On prophecy, see pp. 189–202 below.

69. Alexandra Walsham, 'Miracles in Post-Reformation England', in Kate Cooper and Jeremy Gregory (eds), *Signs, Wonders, Miracles: Representations of Divine Power in the Life of the Church*, Studies in Church History, 41 (Woodbridge, 2005); D. P. Walker, 'The Cessation of Miracles', in Ingrid Merkel and Allen G. Debus (eds), *Hermeticism and the Renaissance: Intellectual History and the Occult in Early Modern Europe* (Washington, DC, 1988); West, *Angels*, 56.

70. John Trapp, *A Commentary or Exposition upon all the Epistles, and the Revelation of John the Divine* (1647), 659.

71. Williams, *Expositor*, 48, 62; Calvin, *Institution*, 64. Examples include: John Trapp, *A Clavis to the Bible* (1650), 3, 5; Babington, *Comfortable*

*Notes*, 7ᵛ; Henry Ainsworth, *Annotations upon the Five Bookes of Moses* (1627), 8; Wollebius, *Abridgment*, 40; Alexander Ross, *An Exposition on the Fourteene First Chapters of Genesis* (1626), 31–2; William Ames, *The Marrow of Sacred Divinity* (1642), 53; John Richardson, *Choice Observations and Explanations upon the Old Testament* (1655), at Gen. 1: 8; Love, *Dejected Soules Cure*, 21, 31–2; Lawrence, *Angells*, 7; among those who suggest the fourth day are Willet, *Hexapla*, 17, and John Lightfoot, *The Harmony, Chronicle and Order, of the Old Testament* (1647), 2. The pseud-epigraphal book of Jubilees states that angels were the fourth of seven creations on the first day; Henry Ansgar Kelly, *Satan: A Biography* (Cambridge, 2006), 35–6.

72. Salkeld, *Treatise*, 8–21; Columbia, xv. 32–5.

73. Westminster, *Annotations*, at the various places indicated in the text. See also Love, *Dejected Soules Cure*, 31; Ross, *Exposition*, 32.

74. Williams, *Expositor*, 61–2.

75. Christopher Love, *Treatise of Angels*, 31–3, in *The Dejected Soules Cure* (1657).

76. John Lightfoot, *Erubhin, or, Miscellanies* (1629), 150–1.

77. R.B., *A Muster Roll of the Evill Angels* (1655), 3, 12; Samuel Clarke, *A Mirrour or Looking Glasse*, 2nd edn (1654), 216; White, *Commentary*, II. 104; Wollebius, *Abridgment*, 39.

78. White, *Commentary*, I. 5.

79. Salkeld, *Treatise*, 116–42; Aquinas, *Summa*, ix. 33, 73–165; Kelly, *Satan*, 245.

80. John Colet, *Two Treatises on the Hierarchies of Dionysius*, ed. and trans. J. H. Lupton (1869), 21.

81. Lawrence, *Angells*, 28–32.

82. Wollebius, *Abridgment*, 53.

83. Richard Hooker, *Of the Lawes of Ecclesiastical Politie Eight Bookes* (1611), 12; Jenkyn, *Exposition of Jude*, pt 1, p. 455; Richard Bovet, *Pandaemonium, or, The Devil's Cloister* (1684), 22; Hall, *Great Mysterie*, 126.

84. J. A. Comenius, *Naturall Philosophie Reformed by Divine Light* (1651), 237, 238; John Everard, *Some Gospel-Truths Opened* (1653), 381; Austen's notebook, BL, Add. MS 4454, fo. 8.

85. Sibbes, *Light from Heaven*, 95; Gumbleden, *Christ Tempted*, 23.

86. Gumbleden, *Christ Tempted*, 9; Richard Sibbes, *A Glance of Heaven* (1638), 139–40; Matthew Poole, *Blasphemoktonia: The Blasphemer Slaine*, 2nd edn (1654), 25–6.

87. Columbia, xv. 106–7.

88. Dingley, *Deputation*, 118, 123.

89. CUL, Add. MS 6164, p. 55.

90. Aquinas, *Summa*, ix. 37, 13; Thomas Aquinas, *Treatise on Separate Substances*, trans. Revd Francis J. Lescoe (West Hartford, Conn., 1963), 146–7.

91. Calvin, *Commentarie*, 381; Peter Martyr, *Common Places*, 341.

92. White, *Commentary*, I. 116.

93. Lauren Kassell, ' "The Food of Angels": Simon Forman's Alchemical Medicine', in William R. Newman and Anthony Grafton (eds), *Secrets of Nature: Astrology and Alchemy in Early Modern Europe* (Cambridge, Mass., 2001), and ead., *Medicine and Magic*, 199–206; pp. 130, 282–9 below.

94. Ross, *Exposition*, 2nd pagination, 129.

95. White, *Commentary*, I. 32; Ross, *Exposition*, 2nd pagination, 100; Light-foot, *Erubhin*, 97; David S. Katz, 'The Language of Adam in Seven-teenth-Century England', in Hugh Lloyd-Jones, Valerie Pearl, and Blair Worden (eds), *History and Imagination: Essays in Honour of H. R. Trevor-Roper* (1981); pp. 309–18 below.

96. Aquinas, *Summa*, xiv. 111; ix. 4, 81, 125. Cf. Hall, *Great Mysterie*, 127; Heywood, *Hierarchie*, 39–40.

97. Wollebius, *Abridgment*, 53.

98. Pp. 282–99 below, p. 69 above; Comenius, *Naturall Philosophie Reformed*, 232.

99. Marcia L. Colish, *Peter Lombard*, 2 vols (Leiden, 1994), i. 343–6, 348–9.

100. Aquinas, *Summa*, xi. 177–9, 227–39, 259–77.

101. Willet, *Hexapla*, 34. This complex problem was developed most extensively in relation to human freewill and the problem of original sin. See Williams, *Ideas of the Fall*; Neil Forsyth, *The Satanic Epic* (Princeton, 2003) and *The Old Enemy: Satan and the Combat Myth* (Princeton, 1987).

102. Salkeld, *Treatise*, 182–209, esp. 189–90. Hooker also says the elect angels cannot fall; *Ecclesiastical Politie*, 10–11.

103. Hall, *Great Mysterie*, 257–62; quotation at p. 261.

104. Henry More, *An Explanation of the Grand Mystery of Godliness* (1660), 359–60.

105. Wollebius, *Abridgment*, 32–3.

106. Boyle, *Some Motives*, 110; Lawrence, *Angells*, 57; BL, Sloane MS 1233, fo. 75$^{r-v}$.

107. Columbia, xv. 96–9.

108. Williams, *Expositor*, 117–18.

109. Keck, *Angels*, 24.

110. Kelly, *Satan*, 205–6, 175–6.

111. Aquinas, *Summa*, ix. 251–7.

112. Heywood, *Hierarchie*, 340.

113. Salkeld, *Treatise*, 335–44; quotation at p. 342.

114. Wollebius, *Abridgment*, 32.

115. Hooker, *Ecclesiastical Politie*, 10–11.

116. William Ames, *Medulla Theologiae* (1629), 53; Willet, *Hexapla*, 37; also Jenkyn, *Exposition of Jude*, pt 2, pp. 480–1.

117. *Vita*, 13: 1–16: 4, in R. H. Charles (ed.), *The Apocrypha and Pseudepig-rapha of the Old Testament in English*, 2 vols. (Oxford, 1913); <http://www.ccel.org/c/charles/otpseudepig/adamnev.htm>, accessed Nov. 2007.

118. Lightfoot, *Harmony*, 3.
119. Thomas Peyton, *The Glasse of Time in the First Age* (1620), 29.
120. Williams, *Ideas of the Fall*, 20–8, 112–18, 161–2; John Skinner, *A Critical and Exegetical Commentary on Genesis*, 2nd edn (1930; Edinburgh, 1994), 139–47; Williams, *Expositor*, 117–18, 151–3; Forsyth, *Old Enemy*, 147–81, and *Satanic Epic*, 38, 128, 145, 181; Kelly, *Satan*, 13, 34–5, 131–4; Michael E. Stone, *A History of the Literature of Adam and Eve* (Atlanta, Ga., 1992); Elaine Pagels, *The Origin of Satan* (New York, 1995), ch. 2; Kathryn Powell and Donald Scragg (eds), *Apocryphal Texts and Traditions in Anglo-Saxon England* (Cambridge, 2003). Ruben had been translated into Latin by Robert Grosseteste, and appeared in English in Richard Day (ed.), *The Testament of the Twelve Patriarchs* (1658).
121. Williams, *Expositor*, 152; Elaine Pagels, *Adam, Eve and the Serpent* (New York, 1998), 42.
122. Annotations in Geneva Bibles; Westminster, *Annotations*, at Gen 6: 2 and Job 1: 6, 38: 7; Richardson, *Choice Observations*, at Gen. 6: 2 and p. 156; Salkeld, *Treatise*, 324–4; CUL, Add. MS 7338 (Philip Henry's Genesis commentary, on Gen. 6, 27 June 1658); Lightfoot, *Erubhin*, 13–15, and *Harmony*, 8; Ross, *Exposition*, 93–5; Babington, *Comfortable Notes*, fo. 28$^r$. Trapp, *Clavis*, 62–3, is unusual in not mentioning the reading.
123. *PL* 11. 573–87, 621–2; *PR* 2. 178–81; see also James Grantham Turner, *One Flesh: Paradisal Marriage and Sexual Relation in the Age of Milton* (Oxford, 1987), 268–9.
124. Willet, *Hexapla*, 73.
125. Williams, *Expositor*, 118.
126. Bayly, *Two Sermons*, 2.
127. Lawrence, *Angells*, 54.
128. Hall, *Great Mysterie*, 264; also Love, *Dejected Soules Cure*, 44.
129. Folger Shakespeare Library, MS V.a.127.
130. Ross, *Exposition*, 96.
131. Henry Mayr-Harting, *Perceptions of Angels in History* (Oxford, 1998), 17–18.
132. White, *Commentary*, III. 240.
133. Walter Stephens, *Demon Lovers: Witchcraft, Sex, and the Crisis of Belief* (Chicago, 2002), 58–86.
134. Heywood, *Hierarchie*, 230.
135. *Masekhet Avot de-Rabi Natan*, trans. Francis Tayler (1654); Golda Werman, *Milton and Midrash* (Washington, DC, 1995), 42.
136. Henry Cornelius Agrippa, *Three Books of Occult Philosophy*, trans. J. F. (1651), 453–4.
137. Bucanus, *Institutions*, 67; also R. Saunders, *Angelographia* (1701), 6–12; Robert Gell, *Aggelokratia Theon, or, A Sermon Touching Gods Government of the World by Angels* (1650), 12.

138. Calvin, *Institution*, 65.

139. Amy Boesky, 'Milton's Heaven and the Model of the English Utopia', *Studies in English Literature*, 36 (1996), 91–110; pp. 263–5 below.

140. Casaubon, *True and Faithful Relation*, sig. E$^r$.

141. Lawson, *Theo-Politica*, 52; Bayly, *Two Sermons*, 15–16; *Bartas: His Devine Weekes and Workes*, trans. Joshua Sylvester (1605), 204; Edward Leigh, *A Treatise of the Divine Promises* (1641), 171.

142. Colet, *Two Treatises*, 17–18.

143. Heywood, *Hierarchie*, 373, 209; Leonard, *Naming in Paradise*, 61–3.

144. Gumbleden, *Christ Tempted*, 9.

145. Fletcher, *Milton's Rabbinical Readings*, 223–45; Uriel also appears in the pseudepigraphical *Vitae Adae et Evae* and *Prayer of Joseph* and the apocryphal 2 Macc. 15; pp. 82–3, 149–57, below.

146. Lewis Sperry Chafer, *Systematic Theology*, ii (Dallas, 1947), 19–20; though see Kelly, *Satan*, 191–214 and *passim*.

147. Gell, *Aggelokratia*, 12.

148. Gustav Davidson, *A Dictionary of Angels including the Fallen Angels* (New York, 1971), 339–56.

149. Ronald H. Isaacs, *Ascending Jacob's Ladder: Jewish Views of Angels, Demons, and Evil Spirits* (Northvale, NJ, 1998); West, *Angels*, 77; Davidson, *Dictionary of Angels*; Rosemary Ellen Guiley, *Encyclopedia of Angels* (New York, 1996); Agrippa, *Three Books*, 414–37; Heydon, *Theomagia*, iii. 148–51; on the power of names in *PL*, see Leonard, *Naming in Paradise*.

150. *Mr. William Lilly's History of his Life and Times* (1715), 49–50, 54.

151. Heywood, *Hierarchie*, 215–16.

152. Westminster, *Annotations*, at Gen. 32: 29.

153. See also Bayly, *Two Sermons*, 5.

154. Thomas Hobbes, *Leviathan*, ed. Richard Tuck (Cambridge, 1991), 270, 274, 278, and 269–89 *passim*.

155. Aquinas, *Summa*, ix. 13.

156. Matthew Kellison, *A Treatise of the Hierarchie* (Douai, 1629), 1–2.

157. Blenkow, *Michaels Combat*, 5.

158. Charles A. Gieschen, *Angelomorphic Christology: Antecedents and Early Evidence* (Leiden, 1998), 124–51 and esp. 124–5 n. 3; Kelly, *Satan*, 36–9, 62, 146; Isaacs, *Ascending Jacob's Ladder*, 66; Davidson, *Dictionary of Angels*, pp. ix–xi, 40; Peter R. Carrell, *Jesus and the Angels: Angelology and the Christology of the Apocalypse of John* (Cambridge, 1997), 69–70.

159. Evans, *Voice of Michael the Archangel*, 19.

160. Columbia, xv. 102–3. The Latin is dense: 'Et septem praecipue orben terrae perlustrant.'

161. Fletcher, *Milton's Rabbinical Readings*, 245–8, 255. On the names of Milton's angels, see also Larry R. Isitt, *All the Names in Heaven: A Reference Guide to Milton's Supernatural Names and Epic Similes* (Lanham,

Md., 2002); Jason P. Rosenblatt, *Renaissance England's Chief Rabbi: John Selden* (Oxford, 2006), 74–92.

162. Gell, *Aggelokratia*, 12.
163. Augustine, *City*, 353.
164. Quoted by María Tausiet, ' "Patronage of Angels and Combat of Demons": Good versus Evil in Seventeenth-Century Spain', in Marshall and Walsham (eds), *Angels*, 255.
165. Aquinas, *Summa*, xiv. 154–5.
166. Harvey, 'Role of Angels', 3–4.
167. Jacob Behme (*sic*), *Forty Questions of the Soul*, trans. John Sparrow (1665), 134.
168. Ross, *Exposition*, 23, 31.
169. Sibbes, *Light from Heaven*, 106.
170. Trapp, *Clavis*, 252–3.
171. More, *Explanation*, bk 5, ch. 6.
172. George Lawson, *An Exposition of the Epistle to the Hebrewes* (1662), 29–30, 325.
173. BL, Add. MS 4454, p. 8.
174. Calvin, *Institution*, 65.
175. Babington, *Certaine Plaine, Briefe, and Comfortable Notes*, 10ʳ.
176. Hall, *Great Mysterie*, 130–3.
177. Mayr-Harting, *Perceptions of Angels*, 13–15.
178. Rhegius, *Homely or Sermon*, 26ʳ.
179. Boyle, *Some Motives*, 168; John Wall, *Alæ Seraphicæ* (1627), 121–43, at 122; Erik Peterson, *The Angels and the Liturgy: The Status and Significance of the Holy Angels in Worship*, trans. Ronald Walls (1964).
180. Rhegius, *Homely or Sermon*, 26ᵛ; Leonard, *Naming in Paradise*, 61–3.
181. Willet, *Hexapla*, 304.
182. Calvin, *Institution*, 67.
183. Rhegius, *Homely or Sermon*, 26ᵛ.
184. Patrick Hume discussed the ministerial functions of Milton's angels; *Annotations on Milton's 'Paradise Lost'* (1695), 120, 195.
185. Love, *Dejected Soules Cure*, 15–17.
186. Peter Marshall, 'Angels around the Deathbed: Variations on a Theme in the English Art of Dying', in Marshall and Walsham (eds), *Angels*; Bruce Gordon, 'Malevolent Ghosts and Ministering Angels: Apparitions and Pastoral Care in the Swiss Reformation', in Bruce Gordon and Peter Marshall (eds), *The Place of the Death: Death and Remembrance in Late Medieval and Early Modern Europe* (Cambridge, 2000).
187. Trapp, *Clavis*, 147; Calvin, *Commentarie*, 413.
188. Keck, *Angels*, 108–9.
189. More, *Antidote*, 255; they are watchers in the book of Enoch, Job 7: 20 ('preserver' in King James translation), and in Dan. 4: 13; Kelly, *Satan*, 23, 34; Williams, *Ideas of the Fall*, 24.
190. H[enry] A[insworth], *The Communion of Saints* (Amsterdam, 1640), 200.

191. See p. 243 below; Marshall and Walsham (eds), *Angels*, p. 33 and chs 12, 13; Robert Fludd, *Doctor Fludds Answer unto M. Foster* (1631), 64 and *passim*; William Foster, *Hoplocrisma-Spongus* (1631), 4 and *passim*; Ainsworth, *Communion of Saints*, 198.

192. John Patrick, *Reflexions upon the Devotions of the Roman Church* (1674), 405–7; Eamon Duffy, *The Stripping of the Altars: Traditional Religion in England c.1400–c.1500* (New Haven, 1992), 73, 269–71; Keith Thomas, *Religion and the Decline of Magic: Studies in Popular Beliefs in Sixteenth and Seventeenth Century England* (1971).

193. Hall, *Great Mysterie*, 174 (paraphrasing an unidentified author).

194. Ainsworth, *Communion of Saints*, 196.

195. For this language of fellowship, see John Gaule, *Practique Theories, or, Votive Speculations* (1630), 31; Harvey, 'Role of Angels', 159, 301.

196. CUL, Add. MS 6164, p. 58.

197. *Pace* West, *Angels*, ch. 2.


CHAPTER 4

1. Christopher Love, *The Dejected Soules Cure* (1657), sigs A4ᵛ–Bʳ.

2. [William Spenser?], 'The Apocalypse Revelation of St John', CUL, MS Dd. 1. 24.

3. By 'radical' I mean imagining the transformation of the present by pursuing an idea to its roots, a usage this chapter justifies. See Conal Condren, *The Language of Politics in Seventeenth-Century England* (Basingstoke, 1994), 140–68; 'Rethinking the English Revolution', *History Workshop Journal*, 61 (2006), 153–204; Glenn Burgess and Matthew Festenstein (eds), *English Radicalism 1550–1850* (Cambridge, 2007).

4. [Joseph Hall], *Humble Remonstrance* (1640 [1641]), 23–4; Peloni Almoni, *A Compendious Discourse* (1641), sig. A4ᵛ.

5. Smectymnuus, *An Answer to a Booke Entituled, An Humble Remonstrance* (1641), 53.

6. Ibid. 56–8.

7. *CPW* i. 711–14; quotation at p. 721.

8. Ibid. 850. Cf. Constantine Jessop, *The Angel of the Church of Ephesus* (1644), 3.

9. *CPW* i. 820–1; also Ch. 7 below.

10. *CPW* vi. 310–15, 343–50; Maurice Kelley, *This Great Argument: A Study of Milton's 'De Doctrina Christiana' as a Gloss upon 'Paradise Lost'* (Princeton, 1941), 110–18.

11. John White, *Speeches and Passages* (1641), 421.

12. *Dr. Reignolds His Letter to that Worthy Councellor... As Also a Question Resolved* (1641), also published as *The Judgement of Doctor Reignolds* (1641); first pub. posthumously in *Informations, or, A Protestation* (1608).

13. Also William Prynne, *The Antipathie of the English Lordly Prelacie* (1641); Henry Ainsworth, *Counterpoyson Considerations* (1641); Paul Baynes, *The Dioceans Tryall* (1641); Robert Greville, Baron Brooke, *A Discourse Opening the Nature of that Episcopacie* (1641).

14. *Peace Againe in Sion, or, Heaven Appeased* (1641).

15. Kevin Sharpe, 'Reading Revelations: Prophecy, Hermeneutics and Politics in Early Modern Britain', in Kevin Sharpe and Steven N. Zwicker (eds), *Reading, Society and Politics in Early Modern England* (Cambridge, 2003).

16. See Joseph Mede, *The Key of the Revelation*, trans. Richard More (1643).

17. Joseph Mede, *The Apostasy of the Latter Times* (1641), 9, 24, 43, 66. See also John Archer, *The Personal Reign of Christ upon Earth* (1642).

18. Thomas Brightman, *A Revelation of the Apocalyps* (1611) and *A Revelation of the Revelation* (Amsterdam, 1615), 109, 124–5.

19. *A Revelation of Mr. Brightmans Revelation* (1641), 27–8.

20. Ibid. 34–5; Raymond, *Pamphleteering*, 27–52, 179–81, 204–5, 229–33, and sources cited there; David Como, 'Secret Printing, the Crisis of 1640, and the Origins of Civil War Radicalism', *Past and Present*, 196 (2007), 37–82.

21. On 1640s millenarianism, see Christopher Hill, *Antichrist in Seventeenth-Century England* (1971), 78–115, and *The English Bible and the Seventeenth-Century Revolution* (1993), 196–250, 314–23; William M. Lamont, *Godly Rule: Politics and Religion, 1603–1660* (1969); H. R. Trevor-Roper, 'The Fast Sermons of the Long Parliament', in *Religion, the Reformation and Social Change and Other Essays* (1967); Paul Christianson, 'From Expectation to Militance: Reformers and Babylon in the First Two Years of the Long Parliament', *Journal of Ecclesiastical History*, 24 (1973), 225–44; Katharine R. Firth, *The Apocalyptic Tradition in Reformation Britain 1530–1645* (Oxford, 1979), 204–41; Norman T. Burns, *Christian Mortalism from Tyndale to Milton* (Cambridge, Mass., 1972); Bernard Capp, 'The Political Dimension of Apocalyptic Thought', in C. A. Patrides and Joseph Wittreich (eds), *The Apocalypse in English Renaissance Thought and Literature: Patterns, Antecedents and Repercussion* (Ithaca, NY, 1984); Sharpe, 'Reading Revelations', 138–43.

22. R[obert] B[aillie] K., *A Parallel or Brief Comparison* (1641), 15–16.

23. *The Protestation of the Two and Twenty Divines* (1643), sig. A2ᵛ.

24. *The Petition and Articles Exhibited in Parliament Against Doctor Heywood* (1641), 4; the work was François de Sales, *An Introduction to a Devoute Life*, probably the 1637 edition, though I have not located Heywood's licence. For the offending passage, see *Introduction*, trans. John Yakesley (Paris, 1637), 667 [691].

25. *A New Discovery of the Prelates Tyranny* (1641), 1.

26. *Seven Arguments Plainly Proving that Papists Are Trayterous Subjects to all True Christian Princes* (1641), 13.

27. *Sions Charity towards her Foes in Misery* (1641), 2–3.

28. Ibid. 3.

29. John Geree, *The Down-Fall of Anti-Christ* (1641), sig. B$^r$.

30. John Taylor, *The Brownists Conventicle* (1641), 6–7.

31. *Three Propositions of the Angels of Light* (1642), 5.

32. Donne, *Major Works*, 308.

33. *Three Propositions*, 15, 10.

34. Ibid. 9, 11. See Kate Harvey, 'The Role of Angels in English Protestant Thought 1580 to 1660', Ph.D. thesis (Cambridge University, 2005), chs 5 and 6, for theological contexts.

35. *Three Propositions*, 18, 10.

36. Ibid. 15 (printed '17').

37. Jacob Bauthumley, *The Light and Dark Sides of God* (1650).

38. See Sharpe, 'Reading Revelations', 138–9 and *passim*.

39. *A Suddaine Answer to a Suddain Moderatour* (1642 [1643]), 7; Brian Duppa, *Angels Rejoicing for Sinners Repenting* (1648), 10–11.

40. *Malignants Trecherous and Bloody Plot* (1643), TT 669 f.8 (22).

41. Theophilus Philanax Gerusiphilus Philalethes Decius, *An Answer to the Lord George Digbies Apology* (1642 [1643]), 27; Robert Bacon, *The Labyrinth the Kingdom's In* (1649), 34.

42. *A Discovery of the Juglings and Deceitfull Impostures* (1643), 4.

43. *The Necessity of Christian Subjection* (Oxford, 1643), 4.

44. J. V., *A Discovery of the Rebels* (1643), 9.

45. J. T., Gent., *Peace, Peace, and We Shall Be Quiet* (1647), 8–9.

46. Edward Symmons, *A Vindication of King Charles* (1648), 27, 204; *Mercurius Pragmaticus*, 51 (17–24 Apr. 1649), TT E551(19), sig. Ppp$^v$; *Mercurius Elencticus*, quoted in Jason McElligott, *Royalism, Print and Censorship in Revolutionary England* (Woodbridge, 2007), 70.

47. *Maximes Unfolded* (1643), 40; see also John Pordage, *Innocencie Appearing through the Dark Mists of Pretended Guilt* (1655), 106–7; Robert Austine, *Allegiance not Impeached* (1644), 31–2, in which angels represent impartial judgement.

48. *An Elegie Sacred to the Immortal Memory* (1643), TT 669 f.8 (42).

49. Richard Arnway, *The Tablet or Moderation of Charles the First Martyr* ([The Hague], 1649), 22–3.

50. Raymond, *Pamphleteering*, 218–19; e.g. T. B., *Newes from Rome* (1641); J. M., *Newes from Hell* (1641); *Archy's Dream* (1641). For the purposes of Lucianic allusion, and perhaps to seem less inflammatory, the Devil is sometimes displaced by Pluto.

51. Sharon Achinstein, *Milton and the Revolutionary Reader* (Princeton, 1994), 182–93; *The Devil in his Dumps* (1647); *The Devill and the Parliament* (1648).

52. *Mercurius Pragmaticus*, [51] (17–24 Apr. 1649), TT E551(12), sig. A$^v$. Cf. Richard Overton, *The Araignement of Mr. Persecution* (1645), 1.

53. *Mercurius Fidelicus*, 1 (17–24 Aug. 1648), 5.

54. Love, *Dejected Soules Cure*, 27; Robert Bacon, *The Labyrinth the King-dom's In* (1649), 33; Edward Hyde, *A Christian Vindication of Truth Against Errour* (1659), 351; *Three Propositions*, 10.

55. See pp. 245–6 below.

56. *Theologica Germanica* could be mentioned here. John Everard translated this into English as 'Theologica Deutsch' in 1628–36. A Latin edition (originally Antwerp, 1558) was published in London in 1632. It circulated in manuscript in English translated by John Everard (CUL, MS Dd. 12. 68), and was printed in an English translation by Giles Randall, *Theologia Germanica, or, Mysticall Divinitie* (1648). It is not a systematic theology, but a mystical account of God and human morality; it reflects growing interest in mysticism in the 1640s, and probably influenced Coppe and Bauthumley's thought about angels.

57. On Milton, Wollebius, and Ames, see William B. Hunter, 'The Millennial Moment: Milton vs. "Milton" ', in Juliet Cummins (ed.), *Milton and the Ends of Time* (Cambridge, 2003); Maurice Kelley, 'Milton's Debt to Wolleb's *Compendium Theologiae Christianiae*', *PMLA*, 50 (1935), 156–65; *CPW* vi. 17–21 and index.

58. Folger Shakespeare Library, MS V.a.356.

59. John Trapp, *A Commentary or Exposition* (1647), title page, 559.

60. Henry Ainsworth, *The Communion of Saints* (1640), 19–22, 194–201.

61. William Jenkyn, *An Exposition of the Epistle of Jude . . . Delivered in XL Lectures* (1652), 447–52 and *passim*; see also *An Exposition of the Epistle of Jude . . . The Second Part* (1654). Jenkyn retains much Aristotelian philosophy, and returns repeatedly to angelic hierarchies, dismissing them, then diffidently restating the schema of 'popish Schoolmen' (*Exposition*, pt 2, pp. 47–50). This troubled and interested him more than any other topic.

62. Love, *Dejected Soules Cure*, angels treatise, separate pagination, 1–46; see pp. 106–11 below.

63. Calvert entered both this and Lawrence's *Of Basptisme* (1646) in the Stationers' Register on 7 July 1646.

64. TT E509(2); Thomason also noted that *Of Basptisme* (1646) was published in Rotterdam.

65. D. F. McKenzie, 'Milton's Printers: Matthew, Mary and Samuel Simmons', *Milton Quarterly*, 14 (1980), 87–91; Peter Lindenbaum, 'The Poet in the Marketplace: Milton and Samuel Simmons', in Paul G. Stanwood (ed.), *Of Poetry and Politics: New Essays on Milton and his World* (Binghamton, NY, 1995); Peter Lindenbaum, 'Rematerializing Milton', *Publishing History*, 41 (1997), 5–22; Joad Raymond, 'Milton and the Book Trade', in John Barnard and D. F. McKenzie (eds), *A History of the Book in Britain*, iv: *1557–1695* (Cambridge, 2002).

66. See Barbara K. Lewalski, *The Life of John Milton* (Oxford, 2000), 349; Milton, *Poems*, 343–4. David Masson tentatively suggests the men

may been acquaintances; *The Life of John Milton*, 7 vols (1859–94), vii. 658.

67. Pordage, *Innocencie Appearing*, 25; Christopher Fowler, *Daemonium Meridianum: Satan at Noon* (1655), 80, 84; Pordage, *Mundorum*, 50. See also Richard Baxter, *The Certainty of the Worlds of Spirits* (1691), 159, and *The Saints Everlasting Rest* (1650), 242; West, *Angels*, 23; Robert Dingley, *The Deputation of Angels* (1654), 159–65.

68. Ann Blair, 'Mosaic Physics and the Search for a Pious Natural Philosophy in the Late Renaissance', *Isis*, 91 (2000), 32–58; Brian Harrison, *The Bible, Protestantism, and the Rise of Natural Science* (Cambridge, 1998), 104–5; Charles Webster, *The Great Instauration: Science, Medicine and Reform 1626–1660* (1975), 113–14 and *passim*; Howard Hotson, *Johann Heinrich Alsted 1588–1638: Between Renaissance, Reformation, and Universal Reform* (Oxford, 2000), 56, 138–9, 158, 182–201.

69. J. A. Comenius, *Naturall Philosophie Reformed by Divine Light* (1651), 228.

70. Ibid. 232.

71. Lawrence, *Angells*, 16–17; pp. 94–5 above and 189–93 below.

72. *A Great Wonder in Heaven* (1642 [1643]), 3, 4, 7. Cf. B. G., *The Relation of a Strange Apparition in the Air* (1654); William Radmore, *Wonderful News, from the North* (1651).

73. L. P. and P. M., *Strange Predictions Related at Catericke* (1648), 2–5. Cf. *Most Fearefull and Strange Newes from the Bishoppricke of Durham* (1641).

74. Joseph Hall, *The Great Mysterie of Godliness* (1652), 159; Alexandra Walsham, *Providence in Early Modern England* (Oxford, 1999), 182.

75. *The Marine Mercury* (1642), A3$^r$.

76. Anna Trapnel, *A Legacy for Saints* (1654), 14.

77. Mary Cary, *The Little Horns Doom* (1651), 32; also Walsham, *Providence*, 213.

78. Fowler, *Daemonium Meridianum*, 61.

79. *Mercurius Politicus*, 32 (9–16 Jan. 1651); Joad Raymond (ed.), *Making the News: An Anthology of the Newsbooks of Revolutionary England, 1641–1660* (Moreton in the Marsh, 1993), 182–4; *A Declaration at Oxford* (1651), 4; Raymond, *Pamphleteering*, 113–15.

80. William Lilly, *Merlinus Anglicus Junior: The English Merlin Revived* (1644), 6.

81. Arise Evans, *The Voice of Michael the Archangel* (1654), 16; also pp. 252–3 below.

82. *Mr. W. Lilly's History of his Life and Times* (1715), 101; C. H. Josten (ed.), *Elias Ashmole (1617–1692)*, 5 vols (Oxford, 1966), v. 542; Ch. 5 below.

83. Lilly, *History*, 14. On Forman's astrology, see Lauren Kassell, *Medicine and Magic in Elizabethan London: Simon Forman, Astrologer, Alchemist, and Physician* (Oxford, 2005).

84. *Ars Notoria: The Notory Art of Solomon*, trans. Robert Turner (1657) (for voices, see e.g. p. 35); BL, MS Sloane 1712; Peter Forshaw, ' "Behold, the

dreamer cometh": Hyperphysical Magic and Deific Visions in an Early-Modern Theosophical Lab-Oratory', and Stephen Clucas, 'False Illuding Spirits & Cownterfeiting Deuills: John Dee's Angelic Conversations and Religious Anxiety', in Raymond (ed.), *Conversations*; Lynn Thorndike, *A History of Magic and Experimental Science*, 8 vols (New York, 1923–58), ii. 279–89.

85. Lilly, *History*, 24–5.
86. Ibid. 49–50.
87. John Aubrey, *Miscellanies* (1696), 128–32. Uriel is probably here appointed as one of the four or seven Angels of the Presence; pp. 82–3 above. He is a significant figure in occult writings.
88. Lilly, *History*, 101–2.
89. Ibid. 88.
90. Ibid. 54; Michael Macdonald, *Mystical Bedlam: Madness, Anxiety and Healing in Seventeenth Century England* (Cambridge, 1981), 16–19, 210, 212–14.
91. Bodl., MS Ashmole 235, fos 186$^v$–193$^r$.
92. Aubrey, *Miscellanies*, 133–6.
93. Lilly, *History*, 59–60.
94. Lilly, *The World's Catastrophe, or, Europe Many Mutations Untill, 1666* (1647); Ann Geneva, *Astrology and the Seventeenth-Century Mind: William Lilly and the Language of the Stars* (Manchester, 1995), 31. On Trithemius' intentions, however, see Anthony Grafton's essay in Raymond (ed.), *Conversations*.
95. Lilly, *Merlini Anglici Ephemeris 1648* (1648), sig. C$^r$; see also sigs C3$^r$, E8$^{r-v}$, F6$^r$.
96. See pp. 56–7 above and 230–7 below.
97. Meric Casaubon, *A True and Faithful Relation of What Passed for Many Yeers between Sr. John Dee ... and Some Spirits* (1659), 394.
98. William Lilly, *The Starry Messenger* (1645), 11; also Lilly, *An Astrologicall Prediction of the Occurrences in England, Part of the Yeers 1648, 1649, 1650* (1650), 6.
99. Stuart Clark, *Thinking with Demons: The Idea of Witchcraft in Early Modern Europe* (Oxford, 1997), chs 14–15.
100. *Merlini Anglici Ephemeris 1648*, sig. A3$^v$.
101. H. Johnsen, *Anti-Merlinus, or, A Confutation of Mr. William Lillies Predictions* (1648), title page (quotation), sig. A3$^r$, pp. 4, 21.
102. Malcolm Gaskill, *Witchfinders: A Seventeenth-Century English Tragedy* (Cambridge, Mass., 2005); Alan Macfarlane, *Witchcraft in Tudor and Stuart England: A Regional and Comparative Study* (1970), 135–44.
103. Westminster, *Annotations*, at Gen. 15: 5; Henry More, *An Explanation of the Grand Mystery of Godliness* (1660), 339; though contrast Gervase Babington, *Certaine Plaine, Briefe, and Comfortable Notes upon Everie Chapter of Genesis* (1592), fos 6$^v$–7$^r$; Andrew Willett, *Hexapla in Genesin*

(Cambridge, 1605), 11; George Hughes, *An Analytical Exposition of . . . Genesis* (1672), 6; Francis Bampfield, *All in One* (1677), 114–24. See also Reginald Scott, *The Discoverie of Witchcraft* (1584), 169–71.

104. Calvin, *Commentarie*, 37; Johannes Wollebius, *The Abridgement of Christian Divinity*, trans. Alexander Ross (1650), 53; Folger Shakespeare Library, MS V.a.356, fo. 72$^v$.

105. Harry Rusche, '*Merlini Anglici*: Astrology and Propaganda from 1644 to 1651', *English Historical Review*, 80 (1965), 322–33; Geneva, *Astrology and the Seventeenth-Century Mind*; Bernard Capp, *Astrology and the Popular Press: English Almanacs 1500–1800* (1979), ch. 3.

106. Nathanael Homes, *Daemonologie and Theologie* (1650); *A Collection Out of the Best Approved Authors, Containing Histories of Visions, Apparitions, Prophesies* (1657).

107. Homes, *Daemonologie and Theologie*, 106–40; Samuel Clarke, *A Mirrour or Looking Glasse*, 2nd edn (1654), 453–8; *A Collection Out of the Best Approved Authors*, sigs Mm2$^r$, Pp1$^v$; John Vicars, *Against William Li-Lie (alias) Lillie* (1652); John Raunce, *A Brief D[e]claration Against Judicial Astrologie* (1650).

108. On Cotton's library, see Kevin Sharpe, *Sir Robert Cotton 1586–1631: History and Politics in Early Modern England* (Oxford, 1979). For Dee's books, see Deborah E. Harkness, *John Dee's Conversations with Angels: Cabala, Alchemy, and the End of Nature* (Cambridge, 1999), 218–20; Lilly, *History*, 100–1. On Ashmole's and Dee's manuscripts, see Josten (ed.), *Elias Ashmole*, iii. 1264–74; BL, Sloane MS 3188, fos 2–3.

109. West, *Angels*, 193 n. 10; Casaubon, *True and Faithful Relation*, sig. A$^{r-v}$; for William Shippen's perceptions of Casaubon's partiality, see his copy, BL, 719.m.12.

110. Casaubon, *True and Faithful Relation*, 92.

111. Peter J. French, *John Dee: The World of an Elizabethan Magus* (1972), 89–125; Nicholas H. Clulee, *John Dee's Natural Philosophy: Between Science and Religion* (1988); W. A. Sherman, *John Dee: The Politics of Reading and Writing in the English Renaissance* (Amherst, Mass., 1995); Deborah E. Harkness, 'Shows in the Showstone: A Theater of Alchemy and Apocalypse in the Angel Conversations of John Dee', *Renaissance Quarterly*, 49 (1996), 707–37, and *John Dee's Conversations*; Michael Wilding, *Raising Spirits, Making Gold and Swapping Wives: The True Adventures of Dr John Dee and Sir Edward Kelly* (Nottingham, 1999); Julian Roberts and Andrew G. Watson, *John Dee's Library Catalogue* (1990).

112. Meric Casaubon, *A Treatise Concerning Enthusiasme* (1655) and *Of Credulity and Incredulity* (1668), 47.

113. Casaubon, *True and Faithful Relation*, sig. A$^v$.

114. Ibid., sig. D2$^v$.

115. Ibid., Actio Tertia, 10; the episode is discussed on pp. 9–23.

116. Ibid., sigs E3$^{r-v}$.

117. *PL* 1. 358 ff.; John Selden, *De Diis Syris* (1617); Jason Rosenblatt, *Renaissance England's Chief Rabbi: John Selden* (Oxford, 2006), 74–92.

118. Casaubon, *True and Faithful Relation*, sigs E3$^v$–E4$^r$.

119. McKenzie and Bell, i. 411; French, *John Dee*, 12; *A Transcript of the Registers of the Worshipful Company of Stationers; From 1640–1708 A.D.*, 3 vols (1913), ii. 167.

120. BL, 719.m.12, p. 6 and *passim*.

121. Norman T. Burns, *Christian Mortalism from Tyndale to Milton* (Cambridge, Mass., 1972).

122. Thomas Hicks, *A Discourse of the Souls* (1657), 4–5.

123. Ibid. 4.

124. Henry Woolnor, *The True Originall of the Soule* (1641), 16–21, 91–3, 290, 297. Woolnor's book provoked defences of mortalism by Richard Overton, *Mans Mortalitie* (1643) and *Man Wholly Mortal* (1655).

125. McKenzie and Bell, i. 307, 308, 310–11; W. R. Parker, *Milton: A Biography*, 2 vols, vol. ii rev. Gordon Campbell (1968; Oxford, 1996), i. 395, ii. 994 n. 153, and sources cited there.

126. John Biddle, *Twelve Arguments Drawn Out of Scripture* (1647), 1; McKenzie and Bell, i. 209–10; Biddle, *A Confession of Faith Touching the Holy Trinity* (1648), 3.

127. Biddle, *Confession of Faith*, 9–10, 15–16, 57.

128. McKenzie and Bell, i. 354–5, 363–4.

129. *The Faithful Scout*, 205 (8–15 Dec. 1654), TT E237(4), 1680; *Certain Passages*, '76' (8–15 Dec. 1654), TT E237(5); *Perfect Diurnall of Some Passages*, 262 (11–18 Dec. 1654), TT E237(6), 4024; *Mercurius Politicus*, 235 (7–14 Dec. 1654), 4086; 236 (14–21 Dec. 1654), 5002; *Weekly Post*, 205 (12–19 Dec. 1654), TT E237(7), 1675, 1678; *Severall Proceedings in Parliament*, 274 (21–8 Dec. 1654), 4335–6; McKenzie and Bell, i. 363–6.

130. *Mercurius Politicus*, 238 (28 Dec.–4 Jan. 1654 [1655]); Raymond (ed.), *Making the News*, 405; Ariel Hessayon, *'Gold Tried in the Fire': The Prophet Theauraujohn Tany and the English Revolution* (Aldershot, 2007) and 'Thomas Totney [Theaurau John Tany]', in *ODNB*.

131. On the political and publishing contexts of these weeks, see Joad Raymond, 'Framing Liberty: Marvell's *First Anniversary* and the Instrument of Government', *Huntington Library Quarterly*, 62 (2001), 313–50; Sarah Mortimer, 'Refuting Satan: Owen, Socinianism and the Interpretation of Scripture', M.Phil. thesis (University of Oxford, 2003).

132. John Owen, *Vindiciae Evangelicae* (Oxford, 1655); Owen and Biddle's exchange is discussed below, pp. 171–3.

133. *The Racovian Catechisme* ('Amsterdam', 1652), 14–25; Biddle, *A Two-Fold Catechism* (1654) and *The Apostolical and True Opinion Concerning the Holy Trinity* (1653); John Owen, *Christologia, or, A Declaration of the Glorious*

*Mystery of the Person of Christ* (1679), in *The Works of John Owen, D.D.*, ed. William H. Goold, 16 vols (New York, 1851–3), i; John Brayne, *The Divinity of the Trinity Cleared* (1654); Nicholas Estwick, *Mr Bidle's Confession of Faith* (1656).

134. Agrippa, *Three Books of Occult Philosophy*, trans. J. F. (1651); Jacob Boehme, *The Tree of Christian Faith* (1644), *The Way to Christ Discovered* (1647), *XL. Questions Concerning the Soule* (1647), *The Second Booke. Concerning the Three Principles* (1648), *The Third Booke of the Authour, Being the High and Deepe* (1650), *Of Christs Testaments* (1652), *Mysterium Magnum, or, An Exposition of the First Book of Moses* (1654), all trans. John Sparrow.

135. Abiezer Coppe, *A Fiery Flying Roll* (1649), 8–9.

136. Abiezer Coppe, *A Second Fiery Flying Roule* (1649 [1650]), 11–12, 13.

137. Richard Coppin, *Michael Opposing the Dragon* ([1659]), 39; Coppe, *Second Fiery Flying Roule*, 3.

138. Richard Coppin, *The Exaltation of All Things in Christ*, pt 3 of *Divine Teachings* (1649), 42; though Satan exercises Coppin's imagination as if an independent being.

139. Gerrard Winstanley, William Everard, et al., *The True Levellers Standard Advanced* (1649), 6. On antinomianism and perfectionism, see esp. Nigel Smith, *Perfection Proclaimed: Language and English Radical Religion 1640–1660* (Oxford, 1989), and David Como, *Blown by the Spirit: Puritanism and the Emergence of an Antinomian Underground in Pre-Civil-War England* (Stanford, Calif., 2004).

140. Hessayon, *Gold Tried*, 197–8.

141. Jacob Bauthumley, *The Light and Dark Sides of God* (1650), 27, 28.

142. Ibid. 25, 24, 27.

143. Thomas Tany, *Theauraujohn His Theou Ori Apokolipikal* (1651), 32, 22, 25; *Theauraujohn Tany His Second Part* (1653), 'To the Reader', 75; see Hessayon, 'Gold Tried', 332–3, 353–6.

144. Paracelsus, *Selected Writings*, ed. Jolande Jacobi, trans. Norbert Guterman (Princeton, 1979), 164.

145. Casaubon, *True and Faithful Relation*, 237, 394; Pordage, *Innocencie Appearing*, 14, and below pp. 129, 132; Bodl., MS Rawlinson D. 864, fo. 233ᵛ; Hessayon, 'Gold Tried', 330–1.

146. Robert Norwood, *The Form of an Excommunication* (1651), 26.

147. Laurence Claxton [Clarkson], *The Lost Sheep Found* (1660), 32, also 24–5; *Journal of the House of Commons*, vi. 474–5 (the report of the Committee for Suppressing Licentious and Impious Practices; the committee was ordered to investigate Coppe on the same day); on Pordage and Everard, see pp. 129, 130, 133 below.

148. Laurence Claxton [Clarkson], *A Paradisal Dialogue betwixt Faith and Reason* (1660), 13, 26–9, 23, 30, and *Lost Sheep Found*, 55.

149. Claxton, *Paradisal Dialogue*, 29, 26–7; John Reeve and Lodowick Muggleton, *Joyful News from Heaven* (1658), 21.

150. Claxton, *Paradisal Dialogue*, 28, 38.

151. Stephen M. Fallon, *Milton among the Philosophers: Poetry and Materialism in Seventeenth-Century England* (Ithaca, NY, 1991), 102–5; pp. 278–80, 284–5 below.

152. Claxton, *Paradisal Dialogue*, 13, 33, and *Lost Sheep Found*, 55. Christopher Hill suggests Milton's close proximity to the Muggletonians, *Milton and the English Revolution* (1977), 111–12; on Milton's materialism's hermetic dimension, pp. 324–33.

153. *PL* 2. 150, 911; 10. 477. On Claxton's mortalism and materialism (understood partly through Reeve and Muggleton's theology), see Claxton, *Paradisal Dialogue*, 14–21, 33, 58, 63; Reeve and Muggleton, *Joyful News from Heaven*, 28–32, 47 (cf. *PL* 3. 340–1; 5. 496–7); pp. 282–9 below; B. J. Gibbons, *Gender in Mystical and Occult Thought: Behmenism and its Development in England* (Cambridge, 1996), 131.

154. Claxton, *Paradisal Dialogue*, 61, 45.

155. Ibid. 44; pp. 22–3 above.

156. Claxton, *Paradisal Dialogue*, 44.

157. Though he affirms truths 'Against Angels and all thy Seed', and declares 'against Angel and man', because angels are pure reason and it is Faith and not Reason that speaks true; Claxton, *Paradisal Dialogue*, 37, 64, 13, 33, 89–90.

158. Claxton, *Paradisal Dialogue*, 75, and *Lost Sheep Found*, 43, sig. H3$^v$.


CHAPTER 5

1. Manfred Brod, 'A Radical Network in the English Revolution: John Pordage and his Circle, 1646–54', *English Historical Review*, 119 (2004), 1230–53, 1238–9 on date.

2. Richard Baxter, *Reliquiae Baxterianae* (1696), 74, 77, 78; on the Pordages, see also Ariel Hessayon on John and Nigel Smith on Samuel, in *ODNB*.

3. Richard Baxter, *The Certainty of the Worlds of Spirits* (1691), 176–7.

4. Agrippa, *Three Books of Occult Philosophy*, trans. J. F. (1651); Jacob Boehme, *The Tree of Christian Faith* (1644), *The Way to Christ Discovered* (1647), *XL. Questions Concerning the Soule* (1647), *The Second Booke. Concerning the Three Principles of the Divine Essence* (1648), *The Third Booke . . . the Threefold Life of Man* (1650), *Of Christs Testaments* (1652), *Mysterium Magnum, or, An Exposition of . . . Genesis* (1654), *Aurora* (1656), all trans. John Sparrow; Hendrik Niclaes, *An Introduction to the Holy Understanding* (1649), *Revelatio Dei* (1649), *A Figure of the True and Spiritual Tabernacle* (1655), *An Apology for the Service of Love* (1656). Agrippa, Paracelsus, Pictorius, and the *Ars Notoria* were all translated by Robert Turner in the 1650s.

5. John Pordage, *Innocencie Appearing through the Dark Mists of Pretended Guilt* (1655), 70, 91. Margaret Lewis Bailey, *Milton and Jakob Boehme:*

*A Study of German Mysticism in Seventeenth-Century England* (New York, 1914), 106, suggests that Mrs Pordage introduced John to his own visions; see also Bodl., MS Rawlinson D. 833, fos 64–82. On Pordage's Behmenism, see esp. Nigel Smith, *Perfection Proclaimed: Language and English Radical Religion 1640–1660* (Oxford, 1989), 205–10.

6. William Lilly, *Mr. William Lilly's History of his Life and Times* (1715), 14, 24–5, 49–50, 54, 88, 100–2; see also Deborah E. Harkness, *John Dee's Conversations with Angels: Cabala, Alchemy, and the End of Nature* (Cambridge, 1999), 218–20; and C. H. Josten (ed.), *Elias Ashmole (1617–1692)*, 5 vols (Oxford, 1966), iii. 1264–74.

7. Anthony Wood, *Athenae Oxonienses*, 3rd edn, ed. Phillip Bliss, 4 vols (1813–20), iii. 110; Bodl., MS Aubrey 7, fo. 9ᵛ; John Aubrey, *Brief Lives*, ed. A. Clark, 2 vols (1898), ii. 160–1.

8. Sheffield University Library, HP 29/2/40B, quoted in Ariel Hessayon, 'John Pordage', in *ODNB*, and in David Como, *Blown by the Spirit: Puritanism and the Emergence of an Antinomian Underground in Pre-Civil-War England* (Stanford, Calif., 2004), 71 and n. 95. Como notes that this may have happened in the Low Countries.

9. John Etherington, *A Brief Discovery of the Blasphemous Doctrine of Familisme* (1645), 10; Como, *Blown by the Spirit*, 43–6, 445; Peter Lake, *The Boxmaker's Revenge: 'Orthodoxy', 'Heterodoxy' and the Politics of the Parish in Early Stuart London* (Manchester, 2001), *passim* and 183.

10. Hessayon, 'John Pordage'; Josten (ed.), *Ashmole*, i. 109; Wood, *Athenae Oxonienses*, iii. 110; Bodl., MS Rawlinson D. 833, fo. 63ᵛ; Désirée Hirst, *Hidden Riches: Traditional Symbolism from the Renaissance to Blake* (1964), 103–9, 168–71.

11. 'An Acct. of yᵉ Rise & Progress of the Philadelphian Society', Bodl., MS Rawlinson D. 833, fos 63ᵛ–64ʳ; 'gale' perhaps echoes Samuel's 'Gale | Of Love', Pordage, *Mundorum*, sig. b7ᵛ.

12. M.P., *The Mystery of the Deity in the Humanity* (1649), 40, 20, 14.

13. Pordage, *Innocencie Appearing*, 37, 50–83. Nigel Smith proposes Mary Pocock; *Perfection Proclaimed*, 190 n. 28 and 210–12. Phyllis Mack, *Visionary Women: Ecstatic Prophecy in Seventeenth-Century England* (Berkeley, 1992), and Brod, 'Radical Network', 1238, follow him. Mary Pordage is proposed by B. J. Gibbons, *Gender in Mystical and Occult Thought: Behmenism and its Development in England* (Cambridge, 1996), 114; Hessayon is uncommitted, *'Gold Tried in the Fire': The Prophet Theauraujohn Tany and the English Revolution* (Aldershot, 2007), 195–6. A late MS note in Bodl. copy, Vet. A3 f.306(4), attributes it to Mary Pennington.

14. Nigel Smith, '"And if God was one of us": Paul Best, John Biddle, and Anti-Trinitarian Heresy in Seventeenth-Century England', in David Loewenstein and John Marshall (eds), *Heresy Literature and Politics in Early Modern English Culture* (Cambridge, 2007); Sarah Mortimer,

'Refuting Satan: Owen, Socinianism and the Interpretation of Scripture', M.Phil. thesis (University of Oxford, 2003).

15. Brod, 'Radical Network'.

16. Pordage, *Innocencie Appearing*, 22; Christopher Hill, *The World Turned Upside Down: Radical Ideas during the English Revolution* (1972; Harmondsworth, 1975), 154–8; William Erbery, *The Great Earthquake* (1654), sig. A2$^v$, and *The Great Mystery of Godlinesse* (1649). John Tickell, *The Bottomless Pit Smoaking in Familisme* (1651), 49, 81, associates Coppe and Pordage with familism, accurately identifying the influence of Hendrik Niclaes.

17. Christopher Fowler, *Daemonium Meridianum: Satan at Noon* (1655), 60–1; Pordage, *Innocencie Appearing*, 62. Smith, *Perfection Proclaimed*, 320, describes Coppin as a 'near Ranter'; his *Divine Teachings* (1649) contained an epistle by Coppe. See pp. 117–18 above.

18. A less likely candidate is John Everard, a divine accused of familism, Anabaptism, and antinomianism, who preached on angels, and produced the first English translation of *The Divine Pymander of Hermes Mercurius Trismegistus* (1649) and Pseudo-Dionysius' *Mystical Divinity* (1653), which he believed to be authentic. Everard was deprived of his benefice under Laud on charges of heresy. He died in obscurity around 1650, and his sermons were posthumously published in 1653. Everard mixed learned angelology with mysticism. See *Some Gospel-Truths Opened* (1653).

19. Pordage, *Innocencie Appearing*, 11–13, 68. On Everard's identity, and on Pordage and Tany, see Hill, *World Turned Upside Down*, 284–6, 180–2; on Tany's Behmenism, see Smith, *Perfection Proclaimed*, 214–17. A news pamphlet reporting Pordage's visions, *A Most Faithful Relation of Two Wonderfull Passages Which Happened Very Lately* (1650), judges that he is mad, and blames Everard; it is probably derived from Pordage's account.

20. Fowler, *Daemonium Meridianum*, 61.

21. Laurence Claxton [Clarkson], *The Lost Sheep Found* (1660), 24–5; Gerrard Winstanley, *Saints Paradise* (1648), 64–71, 77–8; Brod, 'Radical Network', 1241; pp. 120–2 above.

22. Stuart Clark, *Thinking with Demons: The Idea of Witchcraft in Early Modern Europe* (Oxford, 1997), 384, 544.

23. See esp. Laurence Claxton [Clarkson], *A Paradisal Dialogue* (1660), 6–7; also John Reeve and Lodowick Muggleton, *Joyful News from Heaven* (1658), 15; for later Pordage on anthropomorphism, see J[ohn] P [ordage] M.D., *Theologia Mystica, or, The Mystic Divinitie of the Eternal Invisibles* (1683), 36.

24. Pordage, *Innocencie Appearing*, 29, 84.

25. Ibid. 76.

26. Lauren Kassell, *Medicine and Magic in Elizabethan London: Simon Forman, Astrologer, Alchemist, and Physician* (Oxford, 2005), 206 n., 227–30.

27. Pordage, *Innocencie Appearing*, 14–15, 16, 19.

28. Ibid. 15.
29. Ibid. 25; cf. Fowler, *Daemonium Meridianum*, 80, 84.
30. Pordage, *Innocencie Appearing*, 26.
31. Ibid. 68.
32. *The Life and Death of Vavasor Powell* (1671), 8.
33. Pordage, *Mundorum*, 41, and *Innocencie Appearing*, 66–7, 74.
34. Richard Baxter, *The Certainty of the Worlds of Spirits* (1691), 221–2. Baxter thought that good and bad angels could only be distinguished by their effects: anything that promoted uncharitableness, revenge, or division was clearly bad (p. 236). Aubrey thought, however, that good and bad spirits could indeed be differentiated by smell; John Aubrey, *Miscellanies* (1696), 136.
35. Baxter, *Certainty of the Worlds of Spirits*, 222–3. While not endorsing angel-worship, he rejects the suggestion that it turned the Roman Church into Antichrist (p. 234).
36. A digest of the trial was published in 1693 as an example of (Everard's) witchcraft: *A Collection of Modern Relations of Matters of Fact Concerning Witches* (1693), 9–20.
37. Pordage, *Innocencie Appearing*, 72.
38. Ibid. 73.
39. Ibid. 73–4.
40. Ibid. 74–5.
41. Ibid. 75; for *Mahanaim*, a marginal note refers to Gen. 32: 1, 2 (cf. *PL* 11. 214); for colours, Dan. 10: 6. The vision resembles Augustine's second revelation; see Colleen McDannell and Bernhard Lang, *Heaven: A History*, 2nd edn (1988; New Haven, 2001), 55.
42. Pordage, *Innocencie Appearing*, 76, 67.
43. On antinomianism, see J. C. Davis, *Fear, Myth and History: The Ranters and the Historians* (Cambridge, 1986); Como, *Blown by the Spirit*, *passim* and 387–8. Pordage was associated with Ranterism in one pamphlet, *The Ranters Declaration* (1650), 3.
44. Pordage, *Innocencie Appearing*, 78–9.
45. Brod, 'Radical Network', proposes alchemy, 1239–40, 1250. Pordage wrote a traditional alchemical tract; see Gibbons, *Gender in Mystical and Occult Thought*, 75.
46. Fowler, *Daemonium Meridianum*, 100–1, 157–8; Pordage, *Innocencie Appearing*, 66–7.
47. Brod, 'Radical Network', 1249–50.
48. Folger Shakespeare Library, MS V.a.95, unfoliated.
49. Pordage, *Innocencie Appearing*, 52, 72.
50. Around this time Samuel may also have published anonymously *Eliana: A New Romance* (1661), with a preface dismissing those who condemn romance as a genre. If it is his, this long work must have been written at least partly concurrently with *Mundorum Explicatio*. The 1663 edition

of *Mundorum* is a reissue of the same sheets with a different title page, and a slightly different title: *Mundorum Explicatio; Wherein are couched the Mysteries of the External, Internal, and Eternal Worlds; Showing the true progress of a Soul, from the Court of Babylon to the City of Jerusalem; from the Adamical fallen state, to the Regenerate and Angelical. Also the Explanation of an Hieroglyphical Figure. A Sacred Poem* (1663). The manuscript in BL (Sloane MS 1401A) is a part transcription from a printed edition, though with some variations. Wellcome Library MS 3592 is a later part copy of *Theologia Mystica* with some changes.

51. Though see Christopher Hill, *The Experience of Defeat: Milton and Some Contemporaries* (New York, 1984), 220–42; and *Pordage's Mundorum Explicatio*, ed. Harriet Spanierman Blumenthal (New York, 1991).

52. Pordage, *Mundorum*, 'Proaemium', sig. b8$^r$.

53. For Sadducism, Pordage, *Mundorum*, 37, 41; poets' fancies, p. 8; four worlds, see the hieroglyph and below; the encomium, sigs a4$^r$–a5$^v$; the spirit world, pp. 32–40; angelical corporeality, pp. 40, 41, 43.

54. John White, *A Commentary upon . . . Genesis* (1656), III. 8–29.

55. Pordage, *Mundorum*, 99; see Bodl., Malone 463.

56. See pp. 230–7, below.

57. Michael Murrin, *History and Warfare in Renaissance Epic* (Chicago, 1994), ch. 12 and *passim*; Robert T. Fallon, 'Michael Murrin's Milton and the "Epic without War": A Review Essay', and Murrin, 'A Reply to Robert Fallon', *Milton Quarterly*, 31 (1997), 119–23, 123–4.

58. Bodl., MS Rawlinson D. 865, fo. 230.

59. Pordage, *Innocencie Appearing*, 75–6.

60. Hill notes the theological similarity to Henry Stubbe; *Experience of Defeat*, 242 n. 3.

61. Tongues, Ch. 12; accommodation, Ch. 6 below.

62. John Heydon, *Theomagia, or, The Temple of Wisdome*, 3 vols (1664), i. 1, *The Idea of the Law* (1660), and *The Harmony of the World* (1662). The Firestone Library Copy of this last (shelfmark 6487.456) bears a 17th-century inscription dismissing it as 'all Rosy-Crucian'. The Pordages sought to avoid such a reception; for Heydon it would have been a badge of learning.

63. Jane Lead, *A Fountain of Gardens* (1696 [1697]), sig. *D4$^{r-v}$. See also *Notes and Materials for an Adequate Biography of . . . William Law* (privately printed, 1854), 148.

64. John Pordage, *Theologia Mystica, oder, Geheime und verborgene gottliche Lehre von den ewigen unsichtbarlichfeiten* (Amsterdam, 1698); *Vier Tractätlein des seeligen Johannes Pordädschens, M.D., in manuschriptis hinterlassen: und nun . . . übergesetzt* (Amsterdam, 1704). See also *Göttliche und wahre Metaphysica* (Frankfurt, 1715); *Ein gründlich Philosophisch Sendschreiben vom rechten und wahren Steine der Weissheit* (1727).

65. Bodl., MS Rawlinson A. 405, p. 230; also MS Rawlinson A. 404.

66. Bodl., MS Rawlinson A. 405, p. 232.

67. Bodl., MS Rawlinson A. 354, fos 27$^{r-v}$, 57$^v$, 61$^v$. As this is a fair copy it is possible that this reader–rewriter is Dr Keith.

68. The reader or copyist of Pordage's tract on the Incarnation identifies an apparent contradiction in whether human faculties can penetrate into the divine, or, as Pordage suggests elsewhere, 'only y$^e$ Superior can penetrate into y$^e$ Inferior'; fo. 13$^v$. The opposite view is stated in Bodl. MS Rawlinson A. 404, p. 14; the treatise to which this is prefatory may be the one to which the first reader is referring, in which case the contradiction could be Pordage's or one of his copiers'. See also the manuscript notes, inscribed in a copy of *Theologia Mystica*, on the state of Pordage's printed and manuscript works, reproduced in Hirst, *Hidden Riches*, 325–6.

69. Roach's miscellaneous papers are Bodl., MSS Rawlinson D. 832–833; see also B. J. Gibbons, 'Richard Roach', in *ODNB*, and *Gender in Mystical and Occult Thought*, 152–7. Roach discusses angels in *The Great Crisis* (1725), *passim*. For other evidence of influence, see John Case, *The Angelical Guide* (1697).

70. Pordage, *Theologia Mystica*, 16.

71. Bodl., MS Rawlinson A. 404, pp. 144–7.

72. Bodl., MS Rawlinson A. 405, p. 195; MS Rawlinson A. 404, pp. 164–5; MS Rawlinson A. 354, fo. 27$^r$.

73. Bodl., MS Rawlinson A. 404, pp. 152.

74. Pordage, *Theologia Mystica*, 74–5.

75. Ibid. 71–3; see also Bodl., MS Rawlinson A. 354, fos 59$^r$, 64$^r$; MS Rawlinson A. 404, p. 145; cf. Boehme, *XL. Questions*, 252, and *Second Booke Concerning Three Principles*, 90; on seven spirits, pp. 82–3 above.

76. Bodl., MS Rawlinson A. 354, fo. 37$^r$.

77. Ibid., fos 66–7.

78. Pordage, *Theologia Mystica*, 87, 89, 92, 129–30.

79. Bodl., MS Rawlinson A. 404, p. 13.

80. Ibid., p. 11; Pordage, *Theologia Mystica*, 36.

81. Bodl., MS Rawlinson A. 404, p. 118.

82. West, *Angels*, 144–8; Agrippa, *Three Books*, 453; Thomas Stanley, *The History of the Chaldaick Philosophy* (1662), 51–5; p. 78 above.

83. Bodl., MS Rawlinson A. 405, pp. 225, 228.

84. Ibid., pp. 201 ff.

85. Jane Lead, *The Enochian Walks with God* (1694), 16–18.

86. Bodl., MS Rawlinson A. 404, p. 145.

87. Hirst, *Hidden Riches*, 168. Rufus M. Jones argues, unsympathetically, for Lee's superior intellectual powers over Pordage and Lead; *Spiritual Reformers in the 16th and 17th Centuries* (1914), 229–30.

88. *The Threefold World*, in *The Works of Jacob Behmen, the Teutonic Philosopher*, 4 vols (London, 1764–81), ii. *A Compendious View of the Grounds of*

*Teutonic Philosophy* (1770) includes Boehme's writings and Pordage's. Boehme, *Mysterium Magnum*, 26 ff., *XL. Questions*, 31 ff., and anon., *The Life of one Jacob Boehmen* (London, 1644), sig. A4$^v$.

89. Gibbons, *Gender in Mystical and Occult Thought*, 143–4; Sylvia Bowerbank, 'Jane Lead', in *ODNB*; Lead, in Pordage, *Theologia Mystica*, 2; Paula McDowell, *The Women of Grub Street: Press, Politics, and Gender in the London Literary Marketplace* (Oxford, 1998), 167–79, 196–201; Julie Hirst, *Jane Leade: Biography of a Seventeenth-Century Mystic* (Aldershot, 2005), 27, 92.

90. Richard Roach, 'An Acct. of y$^e$ Rise & Progress of the Philadelphian Society', Bodl., MS Rawlinson D. 833, fo. 64$^r$.

91. Ibid., fos 82–8; Jane Lead, *A Message to the Philadelphian Society* (1696), internally dated 1 Jan. 1696 [1697?].

92. Lead, *Enochian Walks*, 37.

93. Lead, *A Fountain of Gardens*, [i.] 17, 299; ii (1697), 313, 470.

94. Ibid. ii. 73.

95. Ibid. i. 58, 495.

96. Ann Bathurst, 'Transportations', Bodl., MS Rawlinson D. 1262, p. 9; 'a Dream or Vision', p. 7; 'Visionall Dreams', MS Rawlinson D. 833, fos 89$^r$, 92$^r$.

97. Bodl., MS Rawlinson D. 833, fo. 65$^r$. Three non-holograph manuscripts of Bathurst's spiritual diary are extant, two overlapping (without being identical): Bodl., MSS Rawlinson D. 1262, 1263, and 1338. The first two are consecutive, and the first contains the ownership inscription 'This Book belongs to Dr Keath's Library at M$^{rs}$ Brackley's in Tufton Street Westminster.'

98. Bodl., MS Rawlinson D. 1262, pp. 9–13.

99. Ibid., pp. 69, 79, 81, 83.

100. Ibid., pp. 85–6.

101. Bodl., MS Rawlinson A. 404, p. 14.

102. Bodl., MS Rawlinson D. 1262, pp. 118–19, 170.

103. Ibid., p. 90.

104. Ibid., pp. 143, 280, 386; see also the spirits (not angels) at p. 358.

105. Ibid., irregular pages e and f, which follow p. 96.

106. Ibid., pp. 154–6, 177.

107. Ibid., p. 157.

108. Ibid., p. 174. Describing a vision of 1676, Lead mentions 'the outward Astrum of this World's Principle'; *Fountain of Gardens*, i. 245.

109. Bodl., MS Rawlinson D. 1262, pp. 174, chart between pp. 170 and 171, 180.

110. Ibid., pp. 185, 197, 228, 233, 235–6, 245, 348.

111. Simon Schaffer, 'The Consuming Flame: Electrical Showmen and Tory Mystics in the World of Goods', in John Brewer and Roy Porter (eds), *Consumption and the World of Goods* (1993), 489–526 (quotation at p. 494)

and fig. 24.8. The figures appear in *The Works of Jacob Behmen, the Teutonic Philosopher*; the figures were 'left' by William Law, but were drawn by his disciples from Andreas Freher's designs.

CHAPTER 6

1. Aquinas, *Summa*, i. 15–17; Keck, *Angels*, 47–52.
2. Peter Harrison, *The Bible, Protestantism, and the Rise of Natural Science* (Cambridge, 1998), 107–14; David Lawton, *Faith, Text and History: The Bible in English* (Charlottesville, Va., 1990), 16–47; Debora Kuller Shuger, *The Renaissance Bible: Scholarship, Sacrifice, and Subjectivity* (Berkeley, 1998), 11–53; William A. Dyrness, *Reformed Theology and Visual Culture: The Protestant Imagination from Calvin to Edwards* (Cambridge, 2004).
3. Quoted in Tessa Watt, *Cheap Print and Popular Piety, 1550–1640* (Cambridge, 1991), 136.
4. *O&D* 4. 43–9, pp. 57–60; on Lucy's prying, cf. the theological contexts outlined in C. A. Patrides, *Milton and the Christian Tradition* (Oxford, 1966), 7–14.
5. Joseph Leo Koerner, *The Reformation of the Image* (2003), 157–61 and *passim*.
6. On narrative and interpretation, see pp. 73–4 above, Chs 8 and 14 below; A. D. Nuttall, *Overheard by God: Fiction and Prayer in Herbert, Milton, Dante and St John* (1980), 101–8, and *The Alternative Trinity: Gnostic Heresy in Marlowe, Milton, and Blake* (Oxford, 1998), 115.
7. Shuger, *Renaissance Bible*, 18–19; Lawton, *Faith, Text and History*, 38–9.
8. Nuttall, *Alternative Trinity*, 10; C. S. Lewis, *The Discarded Image: An Introduction to Medieval and Renaissance Literature* (Cambridge, 1964), 14–15; G. E. R. Lloyd, 'Saving the Appearances', *Classical Quarterly*, 28 (1978), 202–22; pp. 277, 296 below.
9. The key passages include Exod. 31: 17; 1 Cor. 2: 4; 2 Cor. 3: 4–6; and Heb. 9: 23–4.
10. Alexander Ross, *An Exposition on the Fourteene First Chapters of Genesis* (1626), 32.
11. *Philo*, trans. F. H. Coulson and G. H. Whitaker, 10 vols (1929– ), i. 125.
12. Ibid. ii. 166–7.
13. Ibid. iii. 39, 41.
14. *The Works of Lactantius*, ii, trans. William Fletcher, Ante-Nicene Christian Library, xx (Edinburgh, 1871), 1, 12, 32. See also Kathleen Ellen Hartwell, *Lactantius and Milton* (Cambridge, Mass., 1929).
15. In Theophilus of Alexandria's annual paschal epistle, which Milton knew from Theodoret's Church history: *CPW* vi. 136–7 n. 16; i. 377, 498.
16. *A Select Library of Nicene and Post-Nicene Fathers of the Christian Church*, 2nd ser., 9: *St. Hilary of Poitiers: John of Damascus*, ed. W. Sanday, trans. E. W. Watson and L. Pullan (Oxford, 1899), 45, 71.

17. H. R. MacCallum, 'Milton and Figurative Interpretation of the Bible', *University of Toronto Quarterly*, 31 (1961–2), 397–415.

18. Augustine, *City*, 411, 686. Cf. Milton, *CPW* vi. 136.

19. Pseudo-Dionysius, *Works*, 49.

20. Ibid. 49, 50.

21. Ibid. 150 (quotation), 152, 81 (quotation), 83.

22. Thomas Aquinas, *Treatise on Separate Substances*, trans. Francis J. Lescoe (West Hartford, Conn., 1963), sect. 101.

23. Aquinas, *Summa*, ix. 41.

24. MacCallum, 'Milton and Figurative Interpretation', 411–12; Kevin Killeen, '"A Nice and Philosophical Account of the Origin of All Things": Accommodation in Burnet's *Sacred Theory* (1681) and *Paradise Lost*', *Milton Studies*, 46 (2006 [2007]), 106–22. More generally, see James Holly Hanford, *A Milton Handbook*, 4th edn (New York, 1954), 205; Roland Mushat Frye, *God, Man, and Satan: Patterns of Christian Thought and Life in 'Paradise Lost', 'Pilgrim's Progress', and the Great Theologians* (Princeton, 1960), 9–15; James H. Sims, *The Bible in Milton's Epics* (Gainesville, Fla., 1962), 27–35; Patrides, *Milton and the Christian Tradition*; William G. Madsen, *From Shadowy Types to Truth: Studies in Milton's Symbolism* (New Haven, 1968); W. B. Hunter, C. A. Patrides, and J. H. Adamson, *Bright Essence: Studies in Milton's Theology* (Salt Lake City, 1971); Lee A. Jacobus, *Sudden Apprehension: Aspects of Knowledge in 'Paradise Lost'* (The Hague, 1976); John Guillory, *Poetic Authority: Spenser, Milton, and Literary History* (New York, 1983), ch. 6; Robert L. Entzminger, *Divine Word: Milton and the Redemption of Language* (Pittsburgh, 1985), 29; Kathleen M. Swain, *Before and After the Fall: Contrasting Modes in 'Paradise Lost'* (Amherst, Mass., 1986); Mindele Treip, *Allegorical Poetics and the Epic: The Renaissance Tradition to 'Paradise Lost'* (Lexington, Mass., 1994), chs 15–16 and app. E; Jeffrey Shoulson, *Milton and the Rabbis* (Columbia, NY, 2001), ch. 3; John C. Ulreich, 'Making the Word Flesh: Incarnation as Accommodation', in Charles W. Durham and Kristin A. Pruitt (eds), *Reassembling Truth: Twenty-First-Century Milton* (Selinsgrove, Pa., 2003); Neil D. Graves, 'Milton and the Theory of Accommodation', *Studies in Philology*, 98 (2001), 251–72.

25. Calvin, *Institution*, 35, 37; quotation at p. 33.

26. Calvin, *Commentarie*, 176, 178.

27. Calvin, *Institution*, 34.

28. Ibid. 67; cf. Calvin, *Commentarie*, 122, where he attributes agency to Moses.

29. 'To Mr. Tilman', lines 19–20, in Donne, *Major Works*, 287; cf. *CW* xv. 34–5; *CPW* vi. 315.

30. Peter Martyr, *Common Places*, 29, 30.

31. Ibid. 358, 341.

32. Terms from Harrison, *Bible, Protestantism, and the Rise of Natural Science*, 111.

33. Thomas Wilson, *Theologicall Rules* (1615), 22–3, citing St Hilary.

34. John Gaule, *Practique Theories, or, Votive Speculations* (1630), 30–1.

35. John White, *A Commentary upon . . . Genesis* (1656), I. 98–9. White died in 1648, and this was posthumously published under the supervision of his eponymous son, with Stephen Marshall and Thomas Manton.

36. William Riley Parker, *Milton: A Biography*, 2 vols, vol. ii rev. Gordon Campbell (1968; Oxford, 1996), i. 395, ii. 994 n. 153; David Norbrook, 'Lucy Hutchinson', in *ODNB*.

37. John Biddle, *A Two-Fold Catechism* (1654), a2$^{r-v}$.

38. John Biddle, *Twelve Arguments Drawn out of Scripture* (1647), 4. John Owen attributed his heresies to 'brainsick men'; *Vindiciae Evangelicae* (Oxford, 1655), 71.

39. Owen, *Vindiciae Evangelicae*; John Brayne, *The Divinity of the Trinity Cleared* (1654); Nicholas Estwick, *Mr Bidle's Confession of Faith* (1656); Biddle, *A Two-Fold Catechism*, sig. a1$^{r-v}$ (naming Henry More's *Conjectura Caballistica*, 1653).

40. Harrison, *Bible, Protestantism, and the Rise of Natural Science*, 108–14.

41. Biddle, *Two-Fold Catechism*, sig. A5$^{v}$.

42. Thomas Hobbes, *Leviathan*, ed. Richard Tuck (Cambridge, 1991), 24–31.

43. Biddle, *Two-Fold Catechism*, sigs A7$^{r}$–A8$^{r}$.

44. Owen, *Vindiciae Evangelicae*, 14.

45. Ibid. 13.

46. John Owen, *A Brief Declaration and Vindication* (1669), sigs A6$^{v}$–A7$^{r}$.

47. John Owen, *Of the Divine Originall* (1658), 22.

48. He does not mean the use of the language of Scripture in such a way as to preserve some of its special qualities (a common position, shared by Milton); Owen, *Brief Declaration*, 30, 31.

49. Francis Bampfield, *All in One: All Useful Sciences and Profitable Arts* (1677), 50.

50. Wilson, *Theologicall Rules*, 28; cf. White, *Commentary*, I. 5.

51. Aquinas, *Summa*, ix. 41.

52. Peter Le Loier, *A Treatise of Specters or Straunge Sights* (1605), fo. 45$^{v}$.

53. Lawrence, *Angells*, 15–16.

54. John Gumbleden, *Christ Tempted: The Devil Conquered* (1657), 13.

55. Nuttall, *Alternative Trinity*, 149.

56. Peter Martyr, *Common Places*, 550; Pseudo-Dionysius, *Works*, 148, 152, 153.

57. George Puttenham, *The Arte of English Poesie* (1589), 22–3; Dryden, 'Discourse Concerning the Original and Progress of Satire' (1693), in *The Works of John Dryden*, iv, ed. A. B. Chambers and William Frost (Berkeley, 1974), 18; Pt III below.

58. Barbara Kiefer Lewalski, *Protestant Poetics and the Seventeenth-Century Religious Lyric* (Princeton, 1979).

59. Heywood, *Hierarchie*, 68.
60. Ibid. 69.
61. Ibid. 69–70.
62. Ibid. 334, 339–42.
63. See also *Bartas: His Devine Weekes and Workes*, trans. Joshua Sylvester (1605); Thomas Peyton, *The Glasse of Time* (1620); J. A. Rivers, *Devout Rhapsodies* (1647).
64. Heywood, *Hierarchie*, 31.
65. *O&D* 4. 43, 3. 295–8.
66. Lucy Hutchinson, *On the Principles of the Christian Religion . . . and On Theology* (1817), 33–4, 11; cf. 15.
67. David Norbrook, 'Lucy Hutchinson's "Elegies" and the Situation of the Republican Woman Writer', *English Literary Renaissance*, 27 (1997), 468–521: 471–2.
68. Lucy Hutchinson, *Memoirs of the Life of Colonel Hutchinson*, ed. N. H. Keeble (1995), 16, 19, 28, 49.
69. *O&D*, p. 5.
70. Lewalski, *Protestant Poetics*, 3–27.
71. *O&D*, p. 3.
72. E.g. *O&D* 8. 87 ff., 15. 95 ff., 19. 126 ff.
73. Pordage, *Mundorum*, 93.
74. Ibid. 331.
75. See pp. 313–18 below.
76. Pordage, *Mundorum*, 43; 'self-Taylors' at p. 42.
77. Ibid. 39, 41.
78. Arnold Stein, 'Milton's War in Heaven—An Extended Metaphor', *ELH*, 18 (1951), 201–20; Catherine Gimelli Martin, *The Ruins of Allegory: 'Paradise Lost' and the Metamorphosis of Epic Convention* (Durham, NC, 1998), ch. 5.
79. Gordon Teskey, *Allegory and Violence* (Ithaca, NY, 1996), 1–30.
80. For accounts of Milton's theory of accommodation that associate it with literalism, see Michael Bauman, *Milton's Arianism* (Frankfurt-am-Main, 1987), 115–17; Treip, *Allegorical Poetics*, chs 12–21.
81. On the authorship of this work, see Gordon Campbell, Thomas N. Corns, John K. Hale, and Fiona J. Tweedie, *Milton and the Manuscript of 'De Doctrina Christiana'* (Oxford, 2007), and the literature therein cited.
82. Columbia, xiv. 30–3. John Carey translates these phrases as 'described or outlined' and 'in bringing himself within the limits of our understanding'; *CPW* vi. 133–4.
83. Columbia, xiv. 32–3. Cf. Carey's 'the nonsense poets write about Jove'; *CPW* vi. 134.
84. See Maurice Kelley's useful note, *CPW* vi. 136–7 n. 16.
85. Columbia, xiv. 35.
86. Ibid. 36.

87. Ibid. 37–9.
88. *PL*, p. 54.


CHAPTER 7

1. John Harvey, *A Discoursive Problem Concerning Prophesies* (1588), 38–9.
2. William Kerrigan, *The Prophetic Milton* (Charlottesville, Va., 1974), 83–124.
3. David Norbrook, *Poetry and Politics in the English Renaissance* (1984; Oxford, 2002); also Michelle O'Callaghan, *The Shepherd's Nation: Jacobean Spenserians and Early Stuart Political Culture 1612–1625* (Oxford, 2000).
4. This is not to deny the valuable insights of these works: see Joseph Anthony Wittreich, ' "A Poet amongst Poets": Milton and the Tradition of Prophecy', in Wittreich (ed.), *Milton and the Line of Vision* (Madison, 1975); Kerrigan, *Prophetic Milton*, 159, 168–9 (though he is ambivalent on the point); A. D. Nuttall, *Overheard by God: Fiction and Prayer in Herbert, Milton, Dante and St John* (1980), 93, 97.
5. Norbrook, *Poetry and Politics*, 12–13, 14 (quotation), 28–52, 224–69.
6. Phillip Sidney, *An Apologie for Poetrie* (1595), sig. B4$^r$.
7. Ibid., sig. H$^r$.
8. Norbrook, *Poetry and Politics*, 93; Debora Shuger, *Censorship and Cultural Sensibility: The Regulation of Language in Tudor–Stuart England* (Philadelphia, 2006), 191.
9. *The Critical Works of John Dennis*, i: *1692–1711*, ed. Edward Niles Hooker (Baltimore, 1939), 370.
10. Barbara Kiefer Lewalski, *Protestant Poetics and the Seventeenth-Century Religious Lyric* (Princeton, 1979).
11. The claim appears in the headnote to 'Lycidas' in Milton, *Poems* (1645), but not in *Iusta Eduardo King* (1638). Norbrook, *Poetry and Politics*, 252–69; pp. 227, 235 below.
12. Alexandra Walsham, 'Miracles in Post-Reformation England', in Kate Cooper and Jeremy Gregory (eds), *Signs, Wonders, Miracles: Representations of Divine Power in the Life of the Church*, Studies in Church History, 41 (Woodbridge, 2005); D. P. Walker, 'The Cessation of Miracles', in Ingrid Merkel and Allen G. Debus (eds), *Hermeticism and the Renaissance: Intellectual History and the Occult in Early Modern Europe* (Washington, DC, 1988).
13. King James I (*sic*), *Daemonologie (1597)*, ed. G. B. Harrison (1922; Edinburgh, 1966), 65–6; William Bucanus, *Institutions of Christian Religion*, trans. Robert Hill (1606), 76; cf. BL, Sloane MS 1233, fo. 80$^r$.
14. Reginald Scott, *The Discoverie of Witchcraft* (1584), 156, 158–9; quotation at p. 160.
15. John Smith, *Select Discourses* (1660), 270–2.

16. Alexandra Walsham, *Providence in Early Modern England* (Oxford, 1999), 205–7, 226–32. The occult philosopher Thomas Tryon disagreed entirely; *Pythagoras* (1691), 202–18.

17. Peter Martyr, *Common Places*, 18, 24.

18. William Perkins, *A Fruitfull Dialogue Concerning the End of the World*, iii (1631), 468; also Smith, *Discourses*, 190–209; Thomas Hobbes, *Leviathan*, ed. Richard Tuck (Cambridge, 1991), 257–8.

19. Calvin, *Institution*, fo. 15$^r$.

20. Jeremy Taylor, *Theologia 'Eklektike: A Discourse of the Liberty of Prophesying* (1647), 82–3. Also Peter Harrison, *The Bible, Protestantism, and the Rise of Natural Science* (Cambridge, 1998), 133.

21. Charles Odingsells, *Two Sermons Lately Preached* (1620), 6–9; quotation at p. 9.

22. Harvey, *Discoursive Problem*, 35–7; Peter Martyr, *Common Places*, 23.

23. Kevin Sharpe, 'Reading Revelations: Prophecy, Hermeneutics and Politics in Early Modern Britain', in Kevin Sharpe and Steven N. Zwicker (eds), *Reading, Society and Politics in Early Modern England* (Cambridge, 2003).

24. Harvey, *Discoursive Problem*, 36–7; Odingsells, *Two Sermons*, 6–7.

25. Peter Martyr, *Common Places*, 19.

26. Ibid. 23. Charles Dempsey notes the iconographical distinctions of prophetic and allegorical dreams; *Inventing the Renaissance Putto* (Chapel Hill, NC, 2001), 129, 135.

27. Smith, *Discourses*, 176–83, 261, 203.

28. Ibid. 211, 212, 218.

29. Harvey, *Discoursive Problem*, 88; *The Good Angel of Stamford* (1659); *Strange Predictions Related at Catericke in the North of England* (1648).

30. Jürgen Beyer, 'A Lübeck Prophet in Local and Lutheran Context', in Bob Scribner and Trevor Johnson (eds), *Popular Religion in Germany and Central Europe, 1400–1800* (Basingstoke, 1996).

31. Smith, *Discourses*, 266.

32. Peter Martyr, *Common Places*, 20, 21.

33. Perkins, *Fruitfull Dialogue*, 468.

34. Harvey, *Discoursive Problem*, passim.

35. Hobbes, *Leviathan*, 257, 259.

36. Moses Maimonides, *Guide for the Perplexed*, trans. M. Friedländer (1942), 219–21.

37. Smith, *Discourses*, 241, 244.

38. Peter Martyr, *Common Places*, 22, 23.

39. Ottavia Niccoli, *Prophecy and People in Renaissance Italy*, trans. Lydia G. Cochrane (Princeton, 1990); Beyer, 'Lübeck Prophet'; Walsham, *Providence*, 203–18; Alexandra Walsham, ' "Frantic Hackett": Prophecy, Sorcery, Insanity, and the Elizabethan Puritan Movement', *Historical Journal*, 41 (1998), 26–66.

422          NOTES TO CHAPTER 7: INSPIRATION & PROPHECY

40. Humphrey Ellis, *Pseudochristus* (1650); Nigel Smith, *Perfection Proclaimed: Language and English Radical Religion 1640–1660* (Oxford, 1989).

41. Raymond, *Pamphleteering*, 295–7, 307–12; Nicholas McDowell, *The English Radical Imagination: Culture, Religion, and Revolution, 1630–1660* (Oxford, 2003); Phyllis Mack, *Visionary Women: Ecstatic Prophecy in Seventeenth-Century England* (Berkeley, 1992); Hilary Hinds, *God's Englishwomen: Seventeenth-Century Radical Sectarian Writing and Feminist Criticism* (Manchester, 1996); Stevie Davies, *Unbridled Spirits: Women of the English Revolution: 1640–1660* (1998); Marcus Nevitt, *Women and the Pamphlet Culture of Revolutionary England, 1640–1660* (Aldershot, 2006); Smith, *Perfection Proclaimed*, 45–53, 86–90.

42. See 1 Cor. 14: 34–5; 1 Tim. 2: 11–12. Also Peter Martyr, *Common Places*, 20.

43. See e.g. *Strange and Wonderful Newes from White-Hall* (1654); *Anna Trapnel's Report and Plea* (1654).

44. Mary Cary, *The Little Horns Doom* (1651), 32.

45. Smith, *Discourses*, 197.

46. Coppe, *Some Sweet Sips, of Some Spirituall Wine* (1649), 57; also Nicholas McDowell, 'A Ranter Reconsidered: Abiezer Coppe and Civil War Stereotypes', *Seventeenth Century*, 12 (1997), 173–205.

47. John Reeve and Lodowick Muggleton, *Joyful News from Heaven* (1658), 5, 12, (2nd pagination) 4.

48. *CPW* i. 808, 820–1.

49. Kerrigan, *Prophetic Milton*, 84.

50. *CPW* i. 803, 816–17, 821.

51. Milton, *Political Writings*, ed. Martin Dzelzainis, trans. Claire Gruzelier (Cambridge, 1991), 183, 82.

52. *CPW* i. 810; Columbia, viii. 67–9; Kerrigan, *Prophetic Milton*, 175–6.

53. Guillaume du Bartas, *L'Uranie, ou, Muse Celeste* (1589); Lewalski, *Protestant Poetics*, 8–10, 231–2; Lily B. Campbell, *Divine Poetry and Drama in Sixteenth-Century England* (Berkeley, 1959), 74–92.

54. See David Daiches' superb 'The Opening of *Paradise Lost*', in Frank Kermode (ed.), *The Living Milton* (1960).

55. Ernst Robert Curtius, *European Literature and the Latin Middle Ages*, trans. Willard R. Trask (1953; Princeton, 1990), 235.

56. Columbia, vi. 359–63.

57. *CPW* iv. 590; Columbia, viii. 72.

58. *Paradise Lost*, 3. 35; also *CPW* i. 803.

59. Curtius, *European Literature*, 243–4.

60. I am indebted to, but disagree with, Nuttall, *Overheard by God*; see esp. pp. 357–9 below.

61. E.g. *O&D* 4. 57–60; also pp. 185, 189, 192, 199, 210.

62. Helen Darbishire (ed.), *The Early Lives of Milton* (1932; New York, 1965), 33, 291.

63. Kerrigan, *Prophetic Milton*, 95; also pp. 137–8, where the stimulating discussion of agency follows Calvin.
64. Peter Martyr, *Common Places*, 20.
65. Jason P. Rosenblatt, *Torah and Law in 'Paradise Lost'* (Princeton, 1994) and *Renaissance England's Chief Rabbi: John Selden* (Oxford, 2006).
66. Smith, *Discourses*, 272–4; my emphasis.
67. Ibid. 277.
68. Darbishire (ed.), *Early Lives*, 291.

## CHAPTER 8

1. Emotions resound through Milton's heaven; it is an important and difficult theme in scriptural exegesis as it risks anthropopathy. On heavenly anger and laughter, see John N. King, *Milton and Religious Controversy: Satire and Polemic in 'Paradise Lost'* (Cambridge, 2000), 109–32; Catherine Bates, 'No Sin but Irony: Kierkegaard and Milton's Satan', *Literature and Theology*, 11 (1997), 1–26; Paul Rovang, 'Milton's War in Heaven as Apocalyptic Drama: "Thy Foes Justly Hast in Derision"', *Milton Quarterly*, 28 (1994), 28–35; John Kerrigan, *Revenge Tragedy: Aeschylus to Armageddon* (Oxford, 1996), 121–31; Golda Werman, *Milton and Midrash* (Washington, DC, 1995), 50.
2. Pp. 67–9 above. Feisal G. Mohamed's discussion of this passage is flawed by the assumption, contrary to contemporary writing about angels, that this reflects Abdiel's inferior rank; '*Paradise Lost* and the Inversion of Catholic Angelology', *Milton Quarterly*, 36 (2002), 240–52: 242.
3. William Empson found support for Satan's confusion on this point; *Milton's God* (1961; Cambridge, 1981), 59–62. Regina Schwartz, *Remembering and Repeating: Biblical Creation in 'Paradise Lost'* (1988; Cambridge, 1993), 21–2, argues that the epic is a repudiation of this claim of self-creation. See also Neil Forsyth, *The Old Enemy: Satan and the Combat Myth* (Princeton, 1987); Evans, *Genesis Tradition*, 113. Philip Pullman's *His Dark Materials* trilogy develops this heresy.
4. [Charles Leslie], *The History of Sin and Heresie* (1698), sig. A2ᵛ. Cf. Zanchius in Williams, *Expositor*, 118; Defoe in Henry Ansgar Kelly, *Satan: A Biography* (Cambridge, 2006), 276; CUL, SSS.32.40, sig. S. The ownership inscription is 'Chas: Blount', perhaps the author of *A Just Vindication of Learning* (1679), derivative of *Areopagitica*.
5. According to *De Doctrina Christiana*, the Word is audible, while God is not; *CPW* vi. 239. Milton's theologically peculiar stance on the Word merits further study. Pseudo-Dionysius' extended discussion of the Word is nowhere concerned with audibility; *Works*, 58–67. St Augustine

states that while God's speech is explained to us in our fashion, 'it has no audible and transient sound'; *City*, 705. Also pp. 309–11 below.

6. Here (and elsewhere) Milton agrees with J. A. Comenius, who writes that angels 'know not the decrees of God, before they be revealed'; *Naturall Philosophie Reformed* (1651), 238. Leslie, *History of Sin and Heresie*, A2ᵛ–A3ʳ, objected to the angel's ignorance of this point in Milton's poem. Cf. also Aquinas, *Summa*, ix. 143.

7. Thanks to John Leonard, Barbara Lewalski, and Tom Luxon for disputing this with me.

8. *De Doctrina Christiana* affirms this indulgence; *CPW* vi. 163.

9. *CPW* vi. 166. *De Doctrina Christiana* does not mention a special degree concerning the angels; *CPW* vi. 167.

10. David Loewenstein, *Representing Revolution in Milton and his Contemporaries: Religion, Politics, and Polemics in Radical Puritanism* (Cambridge, 2001), 202–41; though note pp. 178–9, 183, where Loewenstein disagrees with my argument here.

11. A detailed account of Satan's deceptive strategies is offered by John White, *A Commentary upon . . . Genesis* (1656), III. 45, 160; other commentators include Urbanus Rhegius, *An Homely or Sermon of Good and Evill Angels*, trans. Richard Robinson (1583; 3rd edn, 1593), fos 9ʳ⁻ᵛ, 10ʳ; Gervase Babington, *Certaine Plaine, Briefe, and Comfortable Notes* (1592), fo. 15ʳ. Satan's invention of deception interested occult writers: John Heydon, *Theomagia, or, The Temple of Wisdome*, 3 vols (1664), ii. 212; Jacob Boehme, *Mysterium Magnum, or, An Exposition of . . . Genesis*, trans. J. Ellistone and J. Sparrow (1654), 34. See also Evans, *Genesis Tradition*, 91; Philip C. Almond, *Adam and Eve in Seventeenth-Century Thought* (Cambridge, 1999); Arnold, *Expositor*, 112–38.

12. Michael Lieb, *Milton and the Culture of Violence* (Ithaca, NY, 1994); Rachel Falconer, *Orpheus Dis(re)membered: Milton and the Myth of the Poet–Hero* (Sheffield, 1996).

13. Loewenstein, *Representing Revolution*, 226–31; Thomas N. Corns, *Regaining Paradise Lost* (1994), 48–50.

14. Pp. 309–11, 319–22 below.

15. Patrick Hume, *Annotations on Milton's 'Paradise Lost'* (1695), 199. Cf. Voltaire's comments in John T. Shawcross (ed.), *John Milton: The Critical Heritage*, 2 vols (1970–2; 1995), i. 255–6. For Voltaire this was symptomatic of the problems of imaginative literature.

16. Leslie, *History of Sin and Heresie*, sig. A2ʳ.

17. See *OED*. Cf. Lawrence, *Angells*, 122 ff.; and William Gurnall, *The Christian in Compleat Armour* (1655), 245; also pp. 288–9 below.

18. Shawcross (ed.), *Milton*, ii. 305. On the substantiality of Milton's angels, see Fallon, *Philosophers*; John Rogers, *The Matter of Revolution: Science, Poetry and Politics in the Age of Milton* (Ithaca, NY, 1996); William Kolbrener, *Milton's Warring Angels: A Study of Critical Engagements*

(Cambridge, 1997); John P. Rumrich, *Milton Unbound: Controversy and Reinterpretation* (Cambridge, 1996); pp. 284–9 below.

19. T. S. Eliot, *On Poetry and Poets* (1957), 144, and *Selected Essays, 1917–1932* (1932), 274; C. S. Lewis, *A Preface to 'Paradise Lost'* (1942), 108–15; Ch. 14 below.

20. West, *Angels*, 104–6. Cf. Harris Francis Fletcher, who writes that when *PL* is difficult to understand on nature, 'Always the difficulty arises... because Milton is much more concerned with a poetic solution to a problem than he was interested in its doctrinal solution'; *Milton's Rabbinical Readings* (Urbana, Ill., 1930), 121; and contrast Fallon, *Philosophers*, ch. 5. John A. Himes found himself struggling with this dichotomy in 'Milton's Angels', *New Englander*, 43 (1884), 527–43.

21. *PL*, p. 320; also Fowler's note at p. 171; Corns, *Regaining Paradise Lost*, 14–19; Fletcher, *Milton's Rabbinical Readings*, 121–2; Howard Schultz, *Milton and Forbidden Knowledge* (New York, 1955). The choice is not between novelistic realism and allegory: Milton's theology of accommodation instead suggests that he chooses a form of realism that is not novelistic. Fowler suggests a more persuasive account of Milton's mixed narrative and representational modes in *Renaissance Realism: Narrative Images in Literature and Art* (Oxford, 2003).

22. On Milton's indebtedness to Hebraic scholarship, see Evans, *Genesis Tradition*; Jason P. Rosenblatt, *Torah and Law in 'Paradise Lost'* (Princeton, 1994); Werman, *Milton and Midrash*; Shoulson, *Milton and the Rabbis*; Fletcher, *Milton's Rabbinical Readings*. See also Harris Francis Fletcher, *The Intellectual Development of John Milton*, 2 vols (Urbana, Ill., 1956–61), i. 264–92, ii. 289–99, and *The Use of the Bible in Milton's Prose* (Urbana, Ill., 1929); Jason P. Rosenblatt, *Renaissance England's Chief Rabbi: John Selden* (Oxford, 2006), 74–92. Milton's debt to Selden's *De Diis Syris* (1617) merits further study.

23. *CPW* vi. 299.

24. Ibid. 346, also 299, 311, 313, 343, 347–8. Cf. *PR* 1. 444; see pp. 71–3 above and pp. 230–7 below.

25. This argument is developed in Maurice Kelley, *This Great Argument: A Study of Milton's 'De Doctrina Christiana' as a Gloss upon 'Paradise Lost'* (Princeton, 1941).

26. *Sir William Davenant's 'Gondibert'*, ed. David F. Gladish (Oxford, 1971), 22, 49.

27. Heywood, *Hierarchie*, 341.

28. Cf. e.g. Arnold Stein, 'Milton's War in Heaven: An Extended Metaphor', *ELH*, 18 (1951), 201–20; Catherine Gimelli Martin, *The Ruins of Allegory: 'Paradise Lost' and the Metamorphosis of Epic Convention* (Durham, NC, 1998), ch. 5.

29. Pp. 176–8 above.

30. David Norbrook suggests composition in 1660–4 and/or 1673 onwards: *O&D*, pp. x–xi, xix–xx; Annabel Patterson and Martin Dzelzainis,

'Marvell and the Earl of Anglesey: A Chapter in the History of Reading', *Historical Journal*, 44 (2001), 703–26; *Lucy Hutchinson's Translation of Lucretius: 'De Rerum Natura'*, ed. Hugh de Quehen (1996).

31. *O&D* 1. 173–80. The dismissal of 'Worlds made in Idea' alludes to, and ostensibly chastises, du Bartas' *Semaine*, 1. 1. 202. Cf. also *Bartas* (1605), 4, 6, 33–4, and 21, in a passage describing the creation of angels: 'Whether *This Day* God made you (Angels bright) | Under the name of Heav'n, or of the Light: | Whether you were, after, in th'instant borne | With those bright Spangles that the Heav'ns adorne: | Whether you doo derive your high Descent | Long time before the World and Firmament | (For I will stifly argue to and fro | In nice Opinions, whether so, or so; | Especially, where curious search (perchance) | Is not so safe as humble Ignorance).'

32. Cf. Meric Casaubon, *The Originall Cause of Temporall Evils* (1645), though this argument was frequently directed at Sadducism during and after the 1650s; *O&D* 4. 43, 49, 60.

33. Possibly inspired by White, *Commentary*, I. 79, 89.

34. Ibid. II. 89: White writes that God saw that Adam needed a fit companion, 'but this was not yet so manifest to *Adam*'. So he showed Adam the animals, and Adam figured it out for himself. 'Withall, this Circumstance seems to be of special use, to clear God, of thrusting in the woman upon *Adam*, unnecessarily, as a snare to entrap him; when it appeared so evidently, that it was meer Necessity that moved God to create, and, in compassion unto man, to provide him such an help and companion for him as he could neither be without, nor find amongst all the Creatures.'

35. Pp. 137–45, 180–1, above.

36. *CPW* vi. 424; *PL* 8. 72–6. On these dangers, cf. Robert Dingley, *The Deputation of Angels* (1654), 37; Lawrence, *Angells*, sig. *3$^r$, p. 6; Joseph Hall, *The Great Mysterie of Godliness* (1652), 144–53; Reginald Scott, *The Discoverie of Witchcraft* (1665), 10; Isaac Barrow, *Several Sermons* (1678), 67; Richard Sibbes, *Light from Heaven* (1638), 206.

37. Don M. Wolfe, *Milton in the Puritan Revolution* (1941; 1963), 287–9; Christopher Hill, *Milton and the English Revolution* (1977), 189–97; Nigel Smith, *Literature and Revolution in England, 1640–1660* (New Haven, 1994), 189–96; Martin Dzelzainis, 'Milton and the Protectorate in 1658', and David Armitage, 'John Milton: Poet Against Empire', both in David Armitage, Quentin Skinner, and Armand Himy (eds), *Milton and Republicanism* (Cambridge, 1995); Austin Woolrych, 'Milton and Cromwell: "A Short but Scandalous Night of Interruption?" ', in Michael Lieb and John T. Shawcross (eds), *Achievements of the Left Hand: Essays on Milton's Prose* (Amherst, Mass., 1974); Blair Worden, 'John Milton and Oliver Cromwell', in Ian Gentles, John Morrill, and Blair Worden (eds), *Soldiers, Writers and Statesmen of the English Revolution* (Cambridge, 1998); David Norbrook,

*Writing the English Republic: Poetry, Rhetoric, and Politics, 1627–1660* (Cambridge, 1999), 395–6, 453–4; Joad Raymond, 'Framing Liberty: Marvell's *First Anniversary* and the Instrument of Government', *Huntington Library Quarterly*, 62 (2001), 313–50. For counter-arguments, see Robert T. Fallon, *Milton in Government* (University Park, Pa., 1993), and '*A Second Defence*: Milton's Critique of Cromwell?', *Milton Studies*, 39 (2000), 167–83; and Paul Stevens, 'Milton's "Renunciation" of Cromwell: The Problem of Raleigh's *Cabinet-Council*', *Modern Philology*, 98 (2001), 363–92. On the extent of Milton's literary labours for the government, see Leo Miller, *John Milton's Writings in the Anglo-Dutch Negotiations, 1651–1654* (Pittsburgh, 1992) and *John Milton and the Oldenburg Safeguard* (New York, 1985).

38. *CPW* i. 808.

39. Raymond, *Pamphleteering*; Sharon Achinstein, *Milton and the Revolutionary Reader* (Princeton, 1994); Jason Peacey, *Politicians and Pamphleteers: Propaganda during the English Civil Wars and Interregnum* (Aldershot, 2004).

40. *CPW* iv. 1087.

41. *Paradise Lost* has been illuminated through comparison with particular pamphlets and pamphlet genres: Norbrook, *Writing the English Republic*; Achinstein, *Milton and the Revolutionary Reader*; Loewenstein, *Representing Revolution*; Smith, *Literature and Revolution*; King, *Milton and Religious Controversy*.

42. *PL* 5. 563–76; cf. pp. 181–6 above. Perhaps the oddest aspect of this passage is that it imitates Virgil (himself echoing Homer): 'Infandum, regina, iubes renovare dolorem . . .' (*Aeneid* 2. 3). While in *Paradise Lost* the echoes of du Bartas come from the mouth of Raphael, in *Order and Disorder* it is the narrator who echoes the *Devine Weekes*. See also George Coffin Taylor, *Milton's Use of du Bartas* (Cambridge, Mass., 1934).

43. Quoted in Steven N. Zwicker, *Lines of Authority: Politics and Literary Culture, 1649–1689* (Ithaca, NY, 1993), 5.

44. Lucy Newlyn, *'Paradise Lost' and the Romantic Reader* (Oxford, 1993), 35–6. Roger Lejosne, 'Milton, Satan, Salmasius and Abdiel', in Armitage et al. (eds), *Milton and Republicanism*, 107–9. Lieb finds a refraction of Milton's debates with Salmasius and Morus in the exchange between Samson and Harapha in *Samson*; Michael Lieb, *Milton and the Culture of Violence* (Ithaca, NY, 1994), 237–44. Hill suggests a similarity between Abdiel and Milton pondering whether to publish *The Readie and Easie Way* in 1660; *Milton and the English Revolution*, 370–1.

45. *CPW* iv. 1034.

46. Ibid. 1044.

47. Ibid. 1054.

48. Ibid. 1093; Paul R. Sellin, 'Alexander Morus before the Hof van Holland: Some Insight into Seventeenth Century Polemics with John Milton', in Martinus A. Bakker and Beverly H. Morrison (eds), *Studies in Netherlandic Culture and Literature* (Lanham, Md., 1994), 'Alexander

Morus and John Milton (II): Milton, Morus, and Infanticide', in William Z. Shetter and Inge Van der Cruysse (eds), *Contemporary Explorations in the Culture of the Low Countries* (Lanham, Md., 1996), and 'Alexander Morus before the Synod of Utrecht', *Huntington Library Quarterly*, 58 (1996), 239–48. See also Gordon Campbell, *A Milton Chronology* (Basingstoke, 1997), 142–58.

49. Loewenstein, *Representing Revolution*, 226–31.

50. Hill, *Milton and the English Revolution*, 371, a book both partial and inspiring. Satan also raises his standard in the northern borders of heaven in the Anglo-Saxon Genesis poem; see Bodl., Codex Junius 11, liber 1, lines 28–46. The source of the notion is probably Isa. 14: 12–14. See also Loewenstein, *Representing Revolution*, 224. On Milton's anxieties, see Tom Paulin, *Crusoe's Secret: The Aesthetics of Dissent* (2005), 22–40. This tendency affects even Neil Forsyth's *The Satanic Epic* (Princeton, 2003), 42–3, 169, 344, a book focused on ancient religion.

51. Paulin, *Crusoe's Secret*, 23.

52. On the nature of literature, creativity, and interpretation, I have found instructive Derek Attridge, *The Singularity of Literature* (2004); Peter de Bolla, *Art Matters* (Cambridge, Mass., 2001); and Edward W. Said, *Humanism and Democratic Criticism* (Basingstoke, 2004).

53. On the natural philosophy of angels, see Ch. 11.

54. *CPW* vi. 759, 760.

55. Ibid. 640.

56. That the same standards apply to angels and men is suggested by the chapter on oath-taking, where Milton claims that it is not a sin to defraud a fraudulent man by an oath, and that both angels and men take oaths; *CPW* vi. 684–6.

57. *CPW* vii. 274, 85–7.; Neighbourliness was the relationship that Vlacq claimed Milton had violated; see above, p. 221. Paul Phelps Morand, *The Effects of his Political Life upon John Milton* (Paris, 1939), 69, wondered whether Milton's defence of lying was in part a piece of 'self-justification' following his period of public office; though it is equally likely that these beliefs preceded the actions they might justify; cf. *CPW* vi. 674 n. 19. Similarly, Milton the moneylender defended usury in his systematic theology, in contrast to most contemporary authors; *CPW* vi. 775–8.

58. *CPW* vi. 761. They nonetheless come under the same heading.

59. Aquinas, *Summa*, ix. 41; Peter Le Loier, *A Treatise of Specters or Straunge Sights* (1605), fo. 45$^v$; pp. 174–5 above.

## CHAPTER 9

1. 'Lycidas', quoted from *Facsimile of the Manuscript of Milton's Minor Poems*, ed. William Aldis Wright (Cambridge, 1899), pl. 31.

2. 'Lamentation for Adonis', imitated by John Oldham, *Some New Pieces Never Before Publisht* (1681), 96.
3. Lucan, *The Civil War*, trans. J. D. Duff, Loeb edn (1928; Cambridge, Mass., 1988), 508–9.
4. G. W. Pigman III unpersuasively argues that Lycidas is the angel; *Grief and English Renaissance Elegy* (Cambridge, 1985), 117.
5. *Milton's Minor Poems*, pl. 32.
6. For the relationship between angels and classical genii loci in 17th-century Britain, see *Scala Naturae: A Treatise . . . the Existence of Good Genii, or Guardian-Angels* (1695), 24; Terrae-Filius [George Wither], *Prosopopoeia Britannica* (1648), 105 and *passim*; *A Modest Enquiry into the Opinion Concerning a Guardian Angel* (1702), 3–4; Pordage, *Mundorum*, 52; Bodl., MS Rawlinson A. 404, p. 152; John Heydon, *The Harmony of the World* (1662), 89–92; Tomasso Campanella, *A Discourse Touching the Spanish Monarchy*, trans. Edmund Chilmead (1654), 7. I owe this last reference to Nicole Greenspan.
7. David Norbrook, *Poetry and Politics in the English Renaissance* (1984; Oxford, 2002), 262–3; Michael Wilding, *Dragon's Teeth: Literature in the English Revolution* (Oxford, 1987), 10–12; John N. King, *Milton and Religious Controversy: Satire and Polemic in 'Paradise Lost'* (Cambridge, 2000), 23–43; Annabel Patterson, ' "Forc'd Fingers": Milton's Early Poems and Ideological Constraint', in Claude Summers and Ted-Larry Pebworth (eds), *'The Muses Common-Weale': Poetry and Politics in the Seventeenth Century* (Columbia, Mo., 1988).
8. Columbia, x. 14.
9. Milton, *Poems*, 254.
10. Pigman says that 'Bellerus' might be 'the giant', but I cannot discern which; *Grief and English Renaissance Elegy*, 117.
11. William Camden, *Britain, or, A Chorographicall Description*, trans. Philemon Holland (1637), 187–8; quotation at p. 188. Carganus is Monte Gargano in northern Apulia, the oldest shrine of Michael; the angel's apparition there is described in the Roman Breviary for 8 May.
12. West, *Angels*, 49; Marshall and Walsham (eds), *Angels*, 15–16. However, support for individual guardians can be found among English Protestants: Joseph Glanvill, *A Philosophical Endeavour* (1666), 39; Sir Thomas Browne, *Religio Medici* (1642), 60; Robert Burton, *Anatomy of Melancholy*, ed. T. C. Faulkner et al. (Oxford, 1989), pt 1, sect. 2, member 1, subsect. 2; also Fred van Lieburg, 'Sanctifying Pillars of Pietism and Methodism: Guardian Angels or Heavenly Helpers in International Story-Telling', in Jürgen Beyer, Albrecht Bukardt, Fred van Lieburg, and Marc Wingens (eds), *Confessional Sanctity (c.1500–c.1800)* (Mainz, 2003); and pp. 56–61 above.
13. Andrew Willett, *Synopsis Papismi* (1592), 293–4; pp. 48–9, 56 above.
14. Pseudo-Dionysius, *Works*, 172–3.

15. Calvin, *Institution*, 66.
16. Peter Martyr, *Common Places*, 357.
17. William Lilly, *An Astrologicall Prediction . . . 1648, 1649, 1650* (1648), 6.
18. Robert Gell, *Aggelokratia Theon* (1650), 17; William Austin, *Devotionis Augustinianae Flamma* (1635), 250; *A Modest Enquiry*, 11, 16, 21–2. See also *Scala Naturae*, 38.
19. Ibid.; Lilly, *Astrologicall Prediction*, 6.
20. Lawrence, *Angells*, 22–3.
21. Hardick Warren, *Magick and Astrology Vindicated* (1651), 21.
22. Philotheos Physiologus [Thomas Tryon], *A Treatise of Dreams and Visions* ([1689]), 151–2.
23. Robert Dingley, *The Deputation of Angels* (1654), 159–60.
24. Johannes Wollebius, *The Abridgment of Christian Divinitie*, trans. Alexander Ross (1650), 63; Westminster Assembly, *Annotations upon all the Books of the Old and New Testament* (1651), at Dan. 10: 13; George Hughes, *An Analytical Exposition of . . . Genesis* (1672), 407; also Christopher Love, *The Dejected Soules Cure* (1657); BL, Sloane MS 1233, fo. 77$^r$.
25. John Patrick, *Reflexions upon the Devotions of the Roman Church* (1674), 417–18. See also Trevor Johnson, 'Guardian Angels and the Society of Jesus', in Marshall and Walsham (eds), *Angels*.
26. Columbia, xv. 102.
27. *PR* i. 446–7; Milton, *Poems*, 441.
28. *CPW* ii. 271; Columbia, xv. 102.
29. Raymond, *Pamphleteering*, ch. 5; Gordon Campbell, *A Milton Chronology* (Basingstoke, 1997), 56–68. For the possible influence of these events on 'Lycidas', see Christopher Hill, *Milton and the English Revolution* (1977), 49–53; Norbrook, *Poetry and Politics*, 265–9.
30. Lines 1–2. Carey (Milton, *Poems*, 257–8) infers an elided reflexive pronoun in the parenthetical clause, translating it 'believe me, you peoples', implying the poet's own avowed commitment to the doctrine of tutelary angels. Charles Knapp, Columbia, i. 228–9, renders it 'such be your belief, ye people', which distances the poet from the doctrine.
31. Campanella, *Spanish Monarchy*, 7; John Blenkow, *Michaels Combat with the Devil* (1640), 7; William Camden, *The Historie of the Life and Reigne of that Famous Princesse Elizabeth* (1634), Kkk4$^v$–Lll$^r$; François Eudes de Mézeray, *A General Chronological History of France*, trans. John Bulteel (1683), 491–2; C. S. Lewis, *The Discarded Image: An Introduction to Medieval and Renaissance Literature* (Cambridge, 1964), 72; Keck, *Angels*, 38, 202.
32. John Prideaux, *The Patronage of Angels* (1636), 19; Warren, *Magick and Astrology*, 21.
33. John Dryden, 'Discourse Concerning the Original and Progress of Satire' (1693), in *The Works of John Dryden*, iv, ed. A. B. Chambers and William Frost (Berkeley, 1974), 19–20.

34. Christopher Hill, *The English Bible and the Seventeenth-Century Revolution* (1993), 264–70; John K. Hale, 'England as Israel in Milton's Writings', *Early Modern Literary Studies*, 2/2 (1996), 3.1–54, < http://extra.shu.ac. uk/emls/02-2/halemil2.html>, accessed 23 Feb. 1997; Colin Kidd, *British Identities before Nationalism: Ethnicity and Nationhood in the Atlantic World, 1600–1800* (Cambridge, 1999), 211–14. See Clay Hunt, *'Lycidas' and the Italian Critics* (New Haven, 1979), 141–4, which manages by sleight of hand to link Michael to Arthur and thence to 'the manifest destiny of the English nation'.

35. See n. 7 above.

36. John T. Shawcross (ed.), *John Milton: The Critical Heritage*, 2 vols (1970–2; 1995), ii. 293–4.

37. Ibid. 305.

38. The former camp is a catholic one. See e.g. Hunt, *'Lycidas' and the Italian Critics*; J. M. Evans, *The Road from Horton: Looking Backward in 'Lycidas'* (Victoria, BC, 1983); Christopher Kendrick, 'Anachronism in "Lycidas" ', *ELH*, 64 (1997), 1–40; Lloyd Edward Kermode, 'To the Shores of Life: Textual Recovery in *Lycidas*', *Milton Quarterly*, 31 (1997), 11–25; for the latter approach, see n. 7 above.

39. Eclogue V, lines 62–5; Virgil, *Eclogues, Georgics, Aeneid I–VI*, trans. H. Rushton Fairclough, Loeb edn (1916; Cambridge, Mass., 1998), 38–9; Milton, *Poems*, 256 n.

40. James H. Hanford, 'The Pastoral Elegy and Milton's *Lycidas*', in C. A. Patrides (ed.), *Milton's 'Lycidas': The Tradition and the Poem* (New York, 1961), 39–40.

41. Jacopo Sannazaro, *Arcadia and Piscatorial Eclogues*, trans. Ralph Nash (Detroit, 1966), 162–3, lines 91–8; Hanford, 'Pastoral Elegy', 46–7. The passage itself echoes Virgil's fifth eclogue; see William J. Kennedy, *Jacopo Sannazaro and the Uses of Pastoral* (Hanover, Nebr., 1983), 160–1.

42. Lawrence Lipking, 'The Genius of the Shore: "Lycidas", Adamastor, and the Poetics of Nationalism', *PMLA*, 111 (1996), 205–21: 207–8; quotation at p. 210.

43. For a fuller treatment of these matters, see my 'Look Homeward Angel: Guardian Angels and Nationhood in Seventeenth-Century Britain', in David Loewenstein and Paul Stevens (eds), *Early Modern Nationalism and Milton's England* (Toronto, 2008). I have benefited from dialogue with and writings by Paul Stevens; see e.g. 'Milton's Nationalism and the Rights of Memory', in Elizabeth Jane Bellamy, Patrick Cheney, and Michael Schoenfeldt (eds), *Imagining Death in Spenser and Milton* (Basingstoke, 2003); 'Spenser and Milton on Ireland: Civility, Exclusion, and the Politics of Wisdom', *Ariel*, 26 (1995), 151–67; 'Milton's Janus Faced Nationalism: Soliloquy, Subject, and the Modern Nation State', *Journal of English and Germanic Philology*, 100 (2001), 247–68; ' "Leviticus

Thinking" and the Rhetoric of Early-Modern Colonialism', *Criticism*, 35 (1993), 441–61; '*Paradise Lost* and the Colonial Imperative', *Milton Studies*, 34 (1997),
33–21; and 'How Milton's Nationalism Works', in Loewenstein and Stevens (eds), *Early Modern Nationalism*.

44. Krishnan Kumar, *The Making of English National Identity* (Cambridge, 2003), ch. 6; David Armitage, *The Ideological Origins of the British Empire* (Cambridge, 2000), ch. 2; Kidd, *British Identities before Nationalism*; Benjamin Braude, 'The Sons of Noah and the Construction of Ethnic and Geographical Identities in the Medieval and Early Modern Periods', *William and Mary Quarterly*, 3rd ser., 54 (1997), 101–42.

45. *CPW* iii. 215. See also Joad Raymond, 'Complications of Interest: Milton, Scotland, Ireland, and National Identity in 1649', *Review of English Studies*, 55 (2004), 315–45.

46. 'Mansus', lines 80–4; Columbia, i. 292–3; Milton, *Poems*, 267; John K. Hale, *Milton's Languages: The Impact of Multilingualism on Style* (Cambridge, 1997), 57, 62.

47. *CPW* v; Raymond, 'Complications of Interest'; Linda Gregerson, 'A Colonial Writes the Commonwealth: Milton's *History of Britain*', *Prose Studies*, 19 (1996), 247–54; Nicholas von Maltzahn, *Milton's 'History of Britain': Republican Historiography in the English Revolution* (Oxford, 1991); Graham Parry, 'Milton's *History of Britain* and the Seventeenth Century Antiquarian Scene', *Prose Studies*, 19 (1996), 238–46.

48. Raymond, 'Complications of Interest', 328; Raymond, 'The Cracking of the Republican Spokes', *Prose Studies*, 19 (1996), 255–74; Laura Lunger Knoppers, 'Milton's *The Readie and Easie Way* and the English Jeremiad', in David Loewenstein and James Grantham Turner (eds), *Politics, Poetics, and Hermeneutics in Milton's Prose* (Cambridge, 1990).

49. In *PL*, that is. However, in *Defensio Secunda* he implies that this Latin prose work was his promised epic, a heroic celebration of his countrymen's exploit ('ita mihi quoque vel ad officium, vel ad excusationem satis fuerit, unam saltem popularium meorum heroicè rem gestam exornasse'); Milton, *Pro Populo Anglicano Defensio Secunda* (1654), 172. This patriotic account of deliverance from monarchy is situated within a European context.

50. *CPW* ii. 552.

51. Ibid. 553; Milton makes the same point, with a similar interest in Europe, in the divorce tracts; ibid. 231–2, 707.

52. Columbia, xii. 114–15; Cicero, *Tusculan Disputations*, trans. J. E. King, Loeb edn (1927; 1945), 532–3.

53. Columbia, xii. 114–15.

54. Maurizio Viroli, *For Love of Country: An Essay on Patriotism and Nationalism* (Oxford, 1995).

55. See e.g. Willy Maley, 'How Milton and Some Contemporaries Read Spenser's *View*', in Brendan Bradshaw, Andrew Hadfield, and Willy

Maley (eds), *Representing Ireland: Literature and the Origins of Conflict, 1534–1660* (Cambridge, 1993); Lipking, 'Genius of the Shore', 209–13; and Raymond, 'Complications of Interest'. For the date of Milton's reading of Spenser, see the location of the entries in the commonplace book; *CPW* i. 465, 496.

56. Kumar, *English National Identity*, 98–103; Richard Helgerson, *Forms of Nationhood: The Elizabethan Writing of England* (Chicago, 1992), ch. 3, though the afterword suggests the existence of a nation-state in 17th-century England; Michelle O'Callaghan, *The 'Shepheards Nation': Jacobean Spenserians and Early Stuart Political Culture* (Oxford, 2000).

57. Cf. Robert W. Scribner, 'The Reformation, Popular Magic, and the "Disenchantment of the World" ', *Journal of Interdisciplinary History*, 23 (1993), 475–94, esp. 483–7.

58. As it is in *A Masque Presented at Ludlow Castle*, 1634; in this, however, less effort is made to unify the classical and the Christian: instead its world of nymphs and spirits is an allegory for Christian values. 'Lycidas' is all the more disturbing for not simply being allegorical. Dr Johnson—who praised the *Masque*'s poetical language and condemned its 'tediously instructive' form (Shawcross (ed.), *Critical Heritage*, ii. 297)—might have found more to criticize here, were it not for the fact that so much less theology is at stake.

59. *The First Anniversary*, lines 399–402, in *The Poems of Andrew Marvell*, ed. Nigel Smith (2003), 298; further references to Marvell's poems in this edition appear parenthetically in the text.

60. For contemporary uses of this text in relation to angels, see, in addition to scriptural commentaries, especially John Mayer's *Commentarie upon the New Testament* (1631) and Edward Leigh's *Annotations* (1650); William Foster, *Hoplocrisma-Spongus* (1631), 4; Robert Fludd, *Doctor Fludds Answer unto M. Foster* (1631), 39; Benjamin Camfield, *A Theological Discourse of Angels* (1678), 96; (doubtfully) John Patrick, *Reflexions upon the Devotions of the Roman Church* (1674), 374.

61. On 'heal' as understood in public discourse, see Wilbur Cortez Abbott, *The Writings and Speeches of Oliver Cromwell*, 4 vols (1937–47; Oxford, 1988), iii. 439, 435; Henry Vane, *A Healing Question* (1656) and *The Proceeds of the Protector (so called) and his Councell against Sir Henry Vane* (1658), 3.

62. Annabel Patterson, *Marvell: The Writer in Public Life* (2000), 43–4.

63. For the argument of this paragraph, see Joad Raymond, 'Framing Liberty: Marvell's *First Anniversary* and the Instrument of Government', *Huntington Library Quarterly*, 62 (2001), 313–50; also Derek Hirst, ' "That Sober Liberty": Marvell's Cromwell in 1654', in John M. Wallace (ed.), *The Golden and the Brazen World: Papers in Literature and History, 1650–1800* (Berkeley, 1985).

64. Lines 2–5.

65. *Bartas: His Devine Weekes and Workes*, trans. Joshua Sylvester (1605), 6, 21, 292. Du Bartas was highly influential on Marvell, and the extent of his influence and the number of allusions have yet to be traced. Marvell's poem can be seen to steer the interpretation of Milton's epic towards classical precedents, a literary move that disarms theological objections. See also Philip Hardie, 'The Presence of Lucretius in *Paradise Lost*', *Milton Quarterly*, 29 (1995), 13–24; Andrew Shifflett, *Stoicism, Politics, and Literature in the Age of Milton: War and Peace Reconciled* (Cambridge, 1998), 110–18; see also Stephen M. Fallon, 'Intention and its Limits in *Paradise Lost*: The Case of Bellerophon', in Diana Treviño Benet and Michael Lieb (eds), *Literary Milton: Text, Pretext, Context* (Duquesne, Pa., 1994), 177–9; Diana Treviño Benet, 'The Genius of the Wood and the Prelate of the Grove: Milton and Marvell', in Margo Swiss and David A. Kent (eds), *Heirs of Fame: Milton and Writers of the English Renaissance* (1995), 230–46.

66. John Klause, *The Unfortunate Fall: The Moral Imagination of Andrew Marvell* (Hamden, Conn., 1983), 66–7; Margarita Stocker, *Apocalyptic Marvell: The Second Coming in Seventeenth Century Poetry* (Brighton, 1986), 13, 20.

67. See Edward Leigh, *Annotations upon all the New Testament* (1650), 597; Arthur Dent, *Ruine of Rome* (1603), 158, 270; James Durham, *A Commentary upon the Book of Revelation* (Edinburgh, 1680), 345–6, 470; Joseph Mede, *The Key of the Revelation*, trans. Richard More (1643), pt 2, p. 32. David Pareus, *A Commentary upon the Divine Revelation*, trans. Elias Arnold (Amsterdam, 1644), 265–6.

68. Willet, *Synopsis Papismi*, 291–3.

69. Richard Bernard, *Key of Knowledge* (1617), 213; Patrick Forbes, *An Exquisite Commentarie on the Revelation of Saint John* (1613), 105–6, 221; Henry More, *Apocalypsis Apocalypseos* (1680), 117, 205.

70. Thomas Brightman, *A Revelation of the Revelation* (Amsterdam, 1615), 409: 'Constantine therefore that faithfull Souldier of Christ, who was right nowe called the man-childe of manly Sonne, is here called Michael, by a name that is communicable from God to the Creature.' Brightman also thought the angel at Rev. 20: 1 was Constantine; p. 839.

71. John Napier, *A Plaine Discovery of the Whole Revelation of Saint John* (1593), 159, 163–4; John Downame et al., *Annotations upon all the Books of the Old and New Testament* (1645), *ad locos*. One ground for resistance to the Michael-as-Christ reading was repeated warnings against the worship of angels in Revelation (19: 10; 22: 9), important for the distinctive Protestant case against angel-worship: if the angel was Christ, why would he reject the offer of worship on the grounds of being a 'fellow servant'?

72. John Mayer, *A Commentarie upon the New Testament*, iii (1631), 394. Mayer did think that the angel at Rev. 20: 1 represented Constantine,

however: 'whom God did singularly use in this service of binding Satan'; p. 502.

73. Andrew Marvell, *The Rehearsal Transpros'd*, ed. D. I. B. Smith (Oxford, 1971), 89. On 17th-century interpretation of Revelation, see Kevin Sharpe, 'Reading Revelations: Prophecy, Hermeneutics and Politics in Early Modern Britain', in Sharpe and Steven N. Zwicker, *Reading, Society and Politics in Early Modern England* (Cambridge, 2003); Christopher Hill, *Antichrist in Seventeenth-Century England* (1971); Anthony Milton, 'The Church of England, Rome, and the True Church: The Demise of a Jacobean Consensus', in Kenneth Fincham (ed.), *The Early Stuart Church, 1603–1642* (Basingstoke, 1999); C. A. Patrides and Joseph Wittreich (eds), *The Apocalypse in English Renaissance Thought and Literature* (Manchester, 1984).

74. Quoted in Marvell, *Poems*, ed. Smith, 298; see also Edmund Waller, *Panegyrick* (1655).

75. Jacob Boehme, *Mysterium Magnum, or, An Exposition of . . . Genesis*, trans. J. Ellistone and J. Sparrow (1654), 27.

76. For precedents, see Willet, *Hexapla*, 338, though Willet did not believe in guardian angels and is describing an action; Downame et al., *Annotations, ad locum* Gen. 32, though these *Annotations* also use other verbs, including 'guard'.

77. William Gurnall, *The Christian in Compleat Armour* (1655), 104 ff.; *Stereoma: The Establishment* (1654 [George Thomason dated it Nov. 1653]), a$^v$.

78. Dingley, *Deputation of Angels*, 159–60.

79. Arise Evans, *The Voice of Michael the Archangel* (1654), 16, 17, 18, 19. Cf. Lilly on guardian angels and parahelii, p. 110 and n. 98, above.

80. See H. C. Beeching, in the *National Review* in 1901, in Elizabeth Story Donno (ed.), *Andrew Marvell: The Critical Heritage* (1978), 289–90; editorial annotations in *Poems and Letters of Andrew Marvell*, ed. H. M. Margoliouth, rev. Pierre Legouis and E. E. Duncan Jones, 2 vols (Oxford, 1971), i. 319–28; and Marvell, *Poems*, 281–98.

81. Marvell, *Poems, passim*; Patterson, *Marvell*, 46.

82. Columbia, viii. 226–7; *CPW* iv. 673; Marvell, *Poems and Letters*, ii. 306.

83. See Thomas M. Greene's distinction between allusion and repetition in *The Light in Troy: Imitation and Discovery in Renaissance Poetry* (New Haven, 1982), 49. I would argue, however, that there is more to the echoes of non-literary sources in *First Anniversary* than mere repetition: they establish the meaning and context of Marvell's language, and so are integral to the argument of the poem, whereas the *imitatio*—not uncommonly—seems justified without reference to argument.

84. *CPW* iv. 672; Columbia, viii. 224–5.

85. Raymond, 'Framing Liberty', 340.

86. Heywood, *Hierarchie*, 212.

87. Ann Blair, 'Mosaic Physics and the Search for a Pious Natural Philosophy in the Late Renaissance', *Isis*, 91 (2000), 32–58; Brian Harrison, *The Bible, Protestantism, and the Rise of Natural Science* (Cambridge, 1998); pp. 299–306 below.

88. Lilly, *Astrologicall Prediction*, 6, and *Merlini Anglici Ephemeris 1648* (1648), sigs A3$^v$, C$^r$, C3$^v$.

89. Wither, *Prosopopoeia Britannica*, 2, 105.

90. Abraham Cowley, *A Vision* (1661), 3, 4, 9.

91. Ibid. 11, 14, 26 ff., 80, 81; good and evil angels also witness the battle of Edgehill in Cowley's *A Poem on the Late Civil War* (1679), 11, 13.

92. George Wither, *Vaticinium Casuale* (1655); Joad Raymond, 'The Daily Muse; or, Seventeenth-Century Poets Read the News', *Seventeenth Century*, 11 (1995), 198–203, and 'Framing Liberty', 342.

93. Cowley, *Vision*, sig. A2$^r$.

## CHAPTER 10

1. John Calvin, *A Commentary on Genesis*, ed. and trans. John N. King, 2 vols (1847; 1965), i. 182–3; John N. King, *Milton and Religious Controversy: Satire and Polemic in 'Paradise Lost'* (Cambridge, 2000), 109–32; Paul Rovang, 'Milton's War in Heaven as Apocalyptic Drama: "Thy Foes Justly Hast in Derision"', *Milton Quarterly*, 28 (1994), 28–35.

2. P. 71 above; Marcia L. Colish, *Peter Lombard*, 2 vols (Leiden, 1994), i. 343–6, 348–9.

3. Jason P. Rosenblatt, *Torah and Law in 'Paradise Lost'* (Princeton, 1994), 156–63.

4. Colleen McDannell and Bernhard Lang, *Heaven: A History* (1988; New Haven, 2001), 84–5.

5. Edgar Hill Duncan, 'The Natural History of Metals and Minerals in the Universe of Milton's *Paradise Lost*', *Osiris*, 11 (1954), 386–421.

6. McDannell and Lang, *Heaven*, 152–3.

7. Pp. 49–56 above.

8. West, *Angels*, 133–4, interprets this to indicate the Pseudo-Dionysian order of archangels.

9. See pp. 23–6, above; Aquinas, *Summa*, ix. 227–31, 245; xiv. 89–105, 121–57.

10. 5. 289–90; p. 192 above.

11. CPW vi. 315; John Leonard, *Naming in Paradise: Milton and the Language of Adam and Eve* (Oxford, 1990), 61.

12. See also Leonard, *Naming in Paradise*, 57–68.

13. *CPW* i. 808, 820–1; pp. 91–2 above.

14. Amy Boesky, 'Milton's Heaven and the Model of the English Utopia', *Studies in English Literature*, 36 (1996), 91–110; Ian Gentles, *The New Model Army in England, Ireland and Scotland, 1645–1653* (Oxford, 1992), ch. 4.

15. Rosenblatt, *Torah and Law*, 43, 1–70, and *passim*; but cf. Jeffrey S. Shoulson, *Milton and the Rabbis: Hebraism, Hellenism, and Christianity* (New York, 2001), 228.

16. Dance is another pattern of heavenly organization, precedented in Renaissance art; Françoise Carter, *John Milton and the Image of Dance*, Renaissance Monographs, 22 (Tokyo, 1996).

17. Roland Mushat Frye, *Milton's Imagery and the Visual Arts: Iconographic Tradition in the Epic Poems* (Princeton, 1978), 169–88.

18. Pp. 299–306 below.

19. Leonard, *Naming in Paradise*, 86–146.

20. In Trithemius' *Steganographia*, however, it is Michael who is angel of the sun; Raphael is the angel of Mercury; and Gabriel the angel of the moon; Usiel (Uzziel?) also appears there, but without significance for Milton. Milton seems not to have used Trithemius for names. Lilly, *The Worlds Catastrophe* (1647), 42–56.

21. On *Raziel*, see Sophie Page, 'Speaking with Spirits in Medieval Magic Texts', and Walter Stephens, 'Strategies of Interspecies Communication, 1100–2000', in Raymond (ed.), *Conversations*; West, *Angels*, 154–5; Robert H. West, 'The Names of Milton's Angels', *Studies in Philology*, 47 (1950), 211–23: 219; Steve Savedow (ed.), *Sepher Reziel Hemelach: The Book of the Angel Raziel* (San Francisco, 2000), 207.

22. Leonard, *Naming in Paradise*, 125–32.

23. West, 'Names of Milton's Angels', 213 n. 6, 219 n. 22, and *Angels*, 155.

24. West, 'Names of Milton's Angels', 221; Jason P. Rosenblatt, *Renaissance England's Chief Rabbi: John Selden* (Oxford, 2006), 76–81.

25. Harris Francis Fletcher, *Milton's Rabbinical Readings* (Urbana, Ill., 1930), 252–4; pp. 82–3 above.

26. West, 'Names of Milton's Angels', 222.

27. On sources for the names more generally, see Fletcher, *Milton's Rabbinical Readings*, chs 6– 7; West, 'Names of Milton's Angels' and *Angels*, 151–6.

28. *PL* 4. 681; see pp. 310–11 below.

29. *Facsimile of the Manuscript of Milton's Minor Poems* (Cambridge, 1899), 3, 38.

30. J. Martin Evans, *Milton's Imperial Epic: 'Paradise Lost' and the Discourses of Colonialism* (Ithaca, NY, 1996), explores the narrative in terms of embassies.

31. *PL* 10. 668–72, 707–9; pp. 295–6 below.


## CHAPTER 11

1. Columbia, xiii. 481–5; H. W. Dickenson, *Sir Samuel Morland: Diplomat and Inventor, 1625–1695* (Cambridge, 1970), 6–13; Robert Thomas Fallon, *Milton in Government* (University Park, Pa., 1993), 143–51.

2. Samuel Morland, *The Urim of Conscience* (1695), 13–14 ('to play with the sacred').

3. Cf. Richard Blackmore on Spenser and Ariosto, in Theresa M. Kelley, *Reinventing Allegory* (Cambridge, 1997), 1 and *passim*; pp. 356–7 below.

4. Morland, *Urim of Conscience*, 15.

5. Pp. 211–12 above; Patrick Hume, *Annotations on Milton's 'Paradise Lost'* (1695), 192–210; [Charles Leslie], *The History of Sin and Heresie* (1698), sig. A2ʳ; John T. Shawcross (ed.), *John Milton: The Critical Heritage*, 2 vols (1970–2; 1995), i. 306.

6. Kester Svensden, *Milton and Science* (Cambridge, Mass., 1956), *passim*, 77–8, 241; Catherine Gimelli Martin, ' "Boundless the Deep": Milton, Pascal, and the Theology of Relative Space', *ELH*, 63 (1996), 45–78; William Kolbrener, ' "In a Narrow and to Him a Dark Chamber": Milton Un-abridged', *Common Knowledge*, 4 (1995), 72–96, and *Milton's Warring Angels: A Study of Critical Engagements* (Cambridge, 1997), 102–32; William Poole, 'Milton and Science: A Caveat', *Milton Quarterly*, 38 (2004), 18–34.

7. Svensden, *Milton and Science*, 47–8; Grant McColley, 'Milton's Dialogue on Astronomy', *PMLA*, 52 (1937), 728–62, and 'The Astronomy of *Paradise Lost*', *Studies in Philology*, 34 (1937), 209–47.

8. Harinder S. Marjara, *Contemplation of Created Things: Science in 'Paradise Lost'* (Toronto, 1992).

9. Karen Edwards, *Milton and the Natural World: Science and Poetry in 'Paradise Lost'* (Cambridge, 1999).

10. John Rogers, *The Matter of Revolution: Science, Poetry, and Politics in the Age of Milton* (Ithaca, NY, 1996), 1–38, 103–43; Fallon, *Philosophers*, 98–107, 116–17, 137–8. Fallon states that Milton believes in an Aristotelian version of hylomorphism, in which an object is defined by form and matter: spirit is a form of matter that is inseparable from it (though Milton, like Aristotle, alternates between this and the view that spiritual matter is tenuously corporeal). Hylomorphism does not appear in the index, however; hylozoism does, but Fallon associates it exclusively with Gassendi. Hylozoism is perhaps closer to the view that Fallon (brilliantly) describes in ch. 5, which is about angels. The view that matter is free is associated with hylozoism, and this is the belief assigned to Milton in the central thesis of the book.

11. Nicholas Jardine, *The Birth of History and Philosophy of Science: Kepler's 'A Defence of Tycho against Ursus' with Essays on its Provenance and Significance* (Cambridge, 1984); Eileen Reeves, *Painting the Heavens: Art and Science in the Age of Galileo* (Princeton, 1999); Albert van Helden, *Measuring the Universe: Cosmic Dimensions from Aristarchus to Halley* (Chicago, 1985).

12. Augustine, *City*, 321, 569.

13. Aquinas, *Summa*, ix. 43; cf. Augustine, *City*, 321, 569.

14. Robert Dingley, *The Deputation of Angels* (1654), 210; Robert Bolton, *Mr. Boltons Last and Learned Worke of the Foure Last Things*, 4th edn

(1649), 129–30; John White, *A Commentary upon . . . Genesis* (1656), I. 115; George Hughes, *An Analytical Exposition of . . . Genesis* (1672), 217.

15. Robert Fludd, *Doctor Fludds Answer unto M. Foster* (1631), 44.
16. White, *Commentary*, I. 115.
17. Fallon, *Philosophers*, 198; A. D. Nuttall, *Overheard by God: Fiction and Prayer in Herbert, Milton, Dante and St John* (1980), 87–93.
18. J. A. Comenius, *Naturall Philosophie Reformed by Divine Light* (1651), 236; cf. West, *Angels*, 172.
19. Donne, *Major Works*, 383.
20. Walter Stephens, *Demon Lovers: Witchcraft, Sex, and the Crisis of Belief* (Chicago, 2002).
21. Pp. 76–7 above.
22. *PR* 2. 178–81; at 4. 518 both humans and angels are acknowledged sons of God.
23. Williams, *Expositor*, 117–18; id., *Ideas of the Fall*, 20–9, 161.
24. Bolton, *Mr. Boltons Last and Learned Worke*, 129–30; above, p. 78.
25. Keck, *Angels*, 187; Henry Mayr-Harting, *Perceptions of Angels in History* (Oxford, 1998), 17–18; Thomas Tryon, *Pythagoras His Mystick Philosophy Reviv'd* (1691), 123–4; Deborah E. Harkness, *John Dee's Conversations with Angels: Cabala, Alchemy, and the End of Nature* (Cambridge, 1999), 115–16; Meric Casaubon, *A True and Faithful Relation of What Passed for Many Yeers between Sr. John Dee . . . and Some Spirits* (1659), 10–11.
26. R[ichard] B[rathwaite], *A Mustur Roll of the Evill Angels* (1655), 74.
27. Quoted in D. C. Allen, 'Milton and the Love of Angels', *Modern Language Notes*, 76 (1961), 489–90; the passage in *PL* 8 develops *PL* I. 423–31, which, as West shows, echoes Michael Psellus (West, *Angels*, 144–6, 170). See also Jason P. Rosenblatt, *Renaissance England's Chief Rabbi: John Selden* (Oxford, 2006), 72–3.
28. Mary Douglas, *Purity and Danger: An Analysis of Concepts of Pollution and Taboo* (1966).
29. Henry More, *An Explanation of the Grand Mystery of Godliness* (1660), 6.
30. Aquinas, *Summa*, ix. 37, 13; Thomas Aquinas, *Treatise on Separate Substances*, trans. Revd Francis J. Lescoe (West Hartford, Conn., 1963), sects 98–102; also Keck, *Angels*, 31.
31. William Austin, *Devotionis Augustinianae Flamma* (1635), 246.
32. Fallon, *Philosophers*, 71–4; West, *Angels*, ch. 5.
33. Henry Woolnor, *The True Originall of the Soule* (1641), 91, 93.
34. John Trapp, *A Clavis to the Bible* (1650), 8.
35. Thomas Hobbes, *Leviathan*, ed. Richard Tuck (Cambridge, 1991), 270, 274, 278, and 269–89 *passim*; mocked by Alexander Ross, in *Leviathan Drawn Out* (1653), 38–40.
36. Fludd, *Doctor Fludds Answer*, 44, 50, 51–2.

37. Jacob Boehme, *The Second Booke: Concerning the Three Principles*, trans. J.S. (1648), 69–70, 39 (square brackets original).

38. Robert Gell, *Aggelokratia Theon* (1650), 13, 14.

39. See Fallon, *Philosophers*; John P. Rumrich, *Milton Unbound: Controversy and Reinterpretation* (Cambridge, 1996), 94–116; Rogers, *Matter of Revolution, passim*; Joad Raymond, 'Milton', in Andrew Pyle (ed.), *Dictionary of Seventeenth Century British Philosophers* (Bristol, 2000).

40. Fallon, *Philosophers*, 103–6, 143–4; Michael C. Schoenfeldt, *Bodies and Selves in Early Modern England: Physiology and Inwardness in Spenser, Shakespeare, Herbert and Milton* (Cambridge, 1999), ch. 5.

41. Christopher Hill, *The World Turned Upside Down: Radical Ideas during the English Revolution* (1972; Harmondsworth, 1975), 151–83, 306–23, and *Milton and the English Revolution* (1977), 341–53; William Poole, *Milton and the Idea of the Fall* (Cambridge, 2005); James Grantham Turner, *One Flesh: Paradisal Marriage and Sexual Relations in the Age of Milton* (Oxford, 1987).

42. *CPW* vi. 307–10; *PL* 5. 407–13.

43. Fallon, *Philosophers*, 66; More, *Explanation*, 34.

44. Donne, *Major Works*, 384; Woolnor, *True Originall*, 91; Heywood develops this nicely in *Hierarchie*, 211. See also John of Damascus in *A Select Library of Nicene and Post-Nicene Fathers of the Christian Church*, 2nd ser., 9: *St. Hilary of Poitiers: John of Damascus*, ed. W. Sanday, trans. E. W. Watson and L. Pullan (Oxford, 1899), 19.

45. Fallon, *Philosophers*, 142.

46. More, *Explanation*, 35–6.

47. Thus, Tryon argues that angels never appear as women (contrast Casaubon, *True and Faithful Relation*, 10–11), and that, the beard being a symbol of lechery, good angels can never appear bearded; Tryon, *Pythagoras His Mystick Philosophy*, 123–4; Harkness, *John Dee's Conversations*, 46. This contrasts with an older iconographic tradition. See also John Guillory, *Poetic Authority: Spenser, Milton, and Literary History* (New York, 1983), 146–51.

48. 'Spiritus enim, ut substantia excellentior, substantiam utique inferiorem virtualiter, quod aiunt, et eminenter in se continet; ut facultas facultatem spiritualis, et rationalis corpoream, sentientem nempe et vegetativam'; Columbia, xv. 24; *CPW* vi. 309.

49. A. D. C. Simpson, 'Robert Hooke and Practical Optics: Technical Support at a Scientific Frontier', in Michael Hunter and Simon Schaffer (eds), *Robert Hooke: New Studies* (Woodbridge, 1989); Adrian Johns, 'The Physiology of Reading in Restoration England', in James Raven, Helen Small, and Naomi Tadmor (eds), *The Practice and Representation of Reading in England* (Cambridge, 1996).

50. *PL* 1. 56–60; the manuscript of book 1 and early editions read 'angels ken'; Fowler revises this to 'angels' ken', converting ken from verb to noun.

51. Aquinas, *Summa*, ix. 41.

52. Eileen Reeves, *Galileo's Glassworks: The Telescope and the Mirror* (Cambridge, Mass., 2008).

53. Canto 29, lines 76–81; Dante Alighieri, *The Divine Comedy*, iii: *Paradiso*, trans. John D. Sinclair (1939; New York, 1979), 420–1.

54. Harkness, *John Dee's Conversations*, 114.

55. Joseph Hall, *The Great Mysterie of Godliness* (1652), 126, 127.

56. Pseudo-Dionysius, *Works*, 154.

57. Gell, *Aggelokratia Theon*, 13; Henry Vane, *The Retired Mans Meditations* (1655), 46. See also Jean Baptiste van Helmont, *A Ternary of Paradoxes*, trans. Walter Charleton, 2nd edn (1650), 126.

58. Brian Duppa, *Angels Rejoicing for Sinners Repenting* (1648), 10.

59. Comenius, *Naturall Philosophie Reformed*, 237, 238.

60. Ibid. 232.

61. White, *Commentary*, i. 44.

62. Michael Baxandall, *Painting and Experience in Fifteenth-Century Italy* (1972; Oxford, 1988), 103–4.

63. Robert Hooke, *Micrographia* (1665), sigs A2$^r$, b$^r$, A2$^v$, b2$^v$, c2$^r$.

64. Joad Raymond, 'Perfect Speech: The Public Sphere and Communication in Seventeenth-Century England', in Willy Maley and Alex Benchimol (eds), *Spheres of Influence: Intellectual and Cultural Publics from Shakespeare to Habermas* (Frankfurt, 2006).

65. Nick Wilding, 'Galilean Angels', in Raymond (ed.), *Conversations*; Kircher, quoted in Michael Gorman, 'The Angel and the Compass', in Paula Findlen (ed.), *Athanasius Kircher: The Last Man Who Knew Everything* (New York, 2004), 248; Simon Schaffer, 'Regeneration: The Body of Natural Philosophers in Restoration England', in Christopher Lawrence and Steven Shapin (eds), *Science Incarnate: Historical Embodiments of Natural Knowledge* (Chicago, 1998); see also Charles Dempsey, *Inventing the Renaissance Putto* (Chapel Hill, NC, 2001).

66. Joseph Glanvill, *The Vanity of Dogmatizing* (1661), sig. B2$^r$, p. 5.

67. Glanvill, *Saducismus Triumphatus . . . With a Letter of Dr. Henry More* (1681), 12, 43. The letter is dated 1678; Henry More, *Antidote Against Idolatry* (1672), 91–4; I owe this reference to Simon Schaffer.

68. *PL* 3. 69; Alastair Fowler, *Renaissance Realism: Narrative Images in Literature and Art* (Oxford, 2003), 75.

69. See pp. 276–7 and nn. 6–11, above.

70. Thomas N. Corns, *Regaining Paradise Lost* (1994), 105. Dante, however, follows al-Farghānī; see van Helden, *Measuring the Universe*, 39; Bolton, *Mr. Boltons Last and Learned Worke*, 143.

71. E. M. W. Tillyard, *The Elizabethan World Picture* (1963); C. S. Lewis, *The Discarded Image: An Introduction to Medieval and Renaissance Literature* (Cambridge, 1964); G. E. R. Lloyd, 'Saving the Appearances', *Classical Quarterly*, 28 (1978), 202–22.

72. Alastair Fowler, *Time's Purpled Masquers* (1996); Reeves, *Painting the Heavens*; van Helden, *Measuring the Universe*, ch. 7.

73. During the temptation Eve deceives herself that heaven is too far for earth to be distinctly seen from there, even by God; *PL* 9. 811–13.

74. Aquinas, *Summa*, ix. 125.

75. Ibid. 81, 129; also pp. 67–9 above.

76. William Bucanus, *Institutions of Christian Religion*, trans. Robert Hill (1606), 70.

77. Stuart Clark, *Thinking with Demons: The Idea of Witchcraft in Early Modern Europe* (Oxford, 1997), 161–2, quoting R[ichard] G[ilpin], *Daemonologia Sacra, or, A Treatise* (1677); Brian Duppa, *Angels Rejoicing for Sinners Repenting* (1648), 10–11.

78. Comenius, *Naturall Philosophie Reformed*, 232.

79. Also pp. 313–18 below.

80. Duppa, *Angels Rejoicing*, 11.

81. *CPW* vi. 309. Cf . Robert Fludd: 'Dæmones ex subtilissimorum cœli spiritualis elementorum materia componi . . . quorum compositio, si cum creaturis cœlorum inferiorum comparetur incorporea dicitur, sed respectu simplicitatis substantiæ lucidæ cœli Empyrei in quo, um quo et ex cujus elementis primo die creati sunt, non aliter equam plantæ, herbæ, carumque semina die tertio cum terra facta fuerunt'; Denis Saurat, *Milton: Man and Thinker* ([*c*.1924]), 308.

82. Fallon, *Philosophers*, 137–67; Rosenblatt, *Renaissance England's Chief Rabbi*, 98–9; John Rogers, 'The Secret of *Samson Agonistes*', *Milton Studies*, 33 (1996), 111–32: 118, 120.

83. Hughes, *Analytical Exposition of Genesis*, 228.

84. Aquinas, *Summa*, ix. 69.

85. Ibid. 71.

86. Cf. John of Damascus, *Select Library of Nicene and Post-Nicene Fathers*, 19.

87. John Salkeld, *A Treatise of Angels* (1613), 60, 66–9.

88. Bucanus, *Institutions*, 68–9.

89. Johannes Wollebius, *The Abridgement of Christian Divinity*, trans. Alexander Ross (1650), 42.

90. *PL* 5. 824–5. And perhaps the doctrine also underpins the words of Marlowe's Faust: 'Hell hath no limits, nor is circumscribed, | In one self place. But where we are is hell, | And where hell is there must we ever be'; *Faustus*, 1. 5. 124–6, *Christopher Marlowe: The Complete Plays*, ed. J. B. Stearne (1969).

91. Richard Sibbes, *Light from Heaven* (1638), second treatise, p. 209.

92. Jeremy Taylor, 'Episcopacy Asserted', in *Treatises* (1648), 173.

93. Comenius, *Naturall Philosophie Reformed*, 237.

94. Fludd, *Doctor Fludds Answer*, 38; John Everard, *Some Gospel-Truths Opened* (1653), 414.

95. John Wilkins, *Mercury, or, The Secret and Swift Messenger* (1641), 2; Johannes Trithemius, *Steganographia* ([*c*.1500]; Frankfurt, 1606); Heywood, *Hierarchie*, 261; see also William Lilly, *The World's Catastrophe* (1647); and p. 109 above.

96. John Frederick Houpreght, *Aurifontina Chymica* (1680), 115.

97. Bolton, *Mr. Boltons Last and Learned Worke*, 119, 121.

98. William Greenhill, *An Exposition of the First Five Chapters of the Prophet Ezekiel* (1649), 104. Greenhill uses a pattern of doubling, calculating that from the earth to the fixed stars is *c*.80 million miles. Ptolemy calculated this figure as 50 million miles; al-Farghānī and Roger Bacon as over 65 million miles; (approximately 26,666 earth radii); Kepler's universe was much larger; van Helden, *Measuring the Universe*, 24, 35, 88.

99. Dingley, *Deputation*, 142–3. He offers a marginal note to Greenhill in the preceding paragraph, but does not indicate where he quotes verbatim; it is a scholarly act of plagiarism.

100. Heywood, *Hierarchie*, 212; see also pp. 252–3, 261. See van Helden, *Measuring the Universe*, 29–37. Bacon, however, gives the distance to the fixed stars as 65,357,500 miles; quoted ibid. 35.

101. Heywood, *Hierarchie*, 438–9.

102. Cf. also *Bartas: His Devine Weekes and Workes*, trans. Joshua Sylvester (1605), 24: 'much more these Spirits can | Worke strange effects, exceeding sense of Man? . . . | And free from bodies clogge, with lighter speed | And with less let, they doo what they decreed.'

103. *PL* 2. 915–16; 7. 225–7.

104. Cf. Corns, *Regaining Paradise Lost*, 32–3.

105. *PL* 3. 229; cf. 7. 572–3.

106. 'sunt velocitate summa quasi alis induti'; Columbia, xv. 34–5; *CPW* vi. 315. The proof text is Ezek. 1: 6.

107. 'sunt numero pene innumerabili'; Columbia, xv. 34–5; *CPW* vi. 315.

108. *Pace* West, *Angels*, 15–16.

109. P. 12 above; Bodl., MS Locke f.3, entry dated 20 Jan. 1678; I am indebted to Olivia Smith for this reference.

110. Boyle writes repeatedly about angels in *Excellency of Theology* (1674), e.g. pp. 15–18, where he states that reason cannot prove their existence; and in *Some Motives and Incentives to the Love of God* (1660). He avoids them in his other writings; though see Lawrence M. Principe, *The Aspiring Adept: Robert Boyle and his Alchemical Quest* (Princeton, 1998), 190–201 and *passim*; Michael Hunter, 'Alchemy, Magic and Moralism in the Thought of Robert Boyle', *British Journal for the History of Science*, 23 (1990), 387–410; More, *Antidote against Idolatry*, 91–4.

111. Clark, *Thinking with Demons*, 294–310; Simon Schaffer, 'Making Certain', *Social Studies of Science*, 14 (1984), 137–52: 147–8, 'Occultism and Reason in the Seventeenth Century', in A. J. Holland (ed.), *Philosophy: Its History and Historiography* (Dordrecht: Reidel, 1985), and 'Godly Men

and Mechanical Philosophers: Souls and Spirits in Restoration Natural Philosophy', *Science in Context*, 1 (1987), 55–85; Shapin, *A Social History of Truth: Civility and Science in Seventeenth-Century England* (Chicago, 1994).

112. A. D. Nuttall, *The Alternative Trinity: Gnostic Heresy in Marlowe, Milton, and Blake* (Oxford, 1998), ch. 3; for Nuttall this understanding points in a very different direction.

113. As Svensden suggests; *Milton and Science*, 245–6.

114. Evans, *Genesis Tradition*, 4.

CHAPTER 12

1. *PL* 6. 297–301. Milton echoes 1 Cor. 13: 1: 'Though I speake with the tongues of men and of Angels, and have not charitie, I am become as sounding brasse or a tinkling cymbal.' Paul refers to the power of angelic speech, not to its mechanics. The passage is frequently cited in early modern discussions not only of angelic speech but also of ideal human speech.

2. Fowler suggests that we have a choice between allegory and novelistic realism: *PL*, p. 171. Mindele Treip suggests that Milton moved between allegory and realism in his accommodated poetics; *Allegorical Poetics and the Epic: The Renaissance Tradition to 'Paradise Lost'* (Lexington, Mass., 1994), chs 15–16.

3. Tongue also means 'language', i.e. the perfect prelapsarian Hebrew (cf. Meric Casaubon on the imperfect Latin of Dee's angels, in *A True and Faithful Relation*, 1659, sig. E3ᵛ) in which the angels communicate to Adam and Eve. Ideas are not impressed onto the minds of the humans; they are actually speaking in a language. Interpretations of this text from 1 Corinthians which imply that angels spoke Hebrew include: John White, *A Commentary upon . . . Genesis* (1656), 1. 32; John Lightfoot, *Erubhin, or, Miscellanies* (1629), 103; Henry Cornelius Agrippa, *Three Books of Occult Philosophy*, trans. J. F. (1651), 412.

4. *The Tempest*, 3. 2. 130–2, *Norton Shakespeare*, 3087.

5. *PL* 7. 558–64, 598–9; see also 7. 633, 3. 371.

6. Alexander Ross, *An Exposition on the Fourteene First Chapters of Genesis* (1626), 109; Richard Sibbes, *Light from Heaven* (1638), second treatise; Joad Raymond, 'Perfect Speech: The Public Sphere and Communication in Seventeenth-Century England', in Willy Maley and Alex Benchimol (eds), *Spheres of Influence: Intellectual and Cultural Publics from Shakespeare to Habermas* (Frankfurt, 2006), 43–69.

7. See Jessie Ann Owens, '"And the angel said . . .": Conversations with Angels in Early Modern Music', and Walter Stephens, 'Strategies of Interspecies Communication, 1100–2000', in Raymond (ed.), *Conversations*; Henry Mayr-Harting, *Perceptions of Angels in History* (Oxford, 1998), 14–15.

8. See William T. Flynn, 'Singing with the Angels: Hildegard of Bingen's Representations of Celestial Music', and Stephens, 'Strategies of Inter-species Communication', in Raymond (ed.), *Conversations*.

9. Richard Rastall, *The Heavens Singing: Music in Early English Religious Drama*, i (Cambridge, 1996), 187–9; Pordage, *Mundorum*, 40.

10. John Wall, *Alae Seraphicae* (1627), 131.

11. Pseudo-Dionysius, *Works*, 161–2; C. S. Lewis, *The Discarded Image: An Introduction to Medieval and Renaissance Literature* (Cambridge, 1964), 92–121; John Hollander, *The Untuning of the Sky: Ideas of Music in English Poetry, 1500–1700* (Princeton, 1961); D. P. Walker, *Studies in Musical Science in the Late Renaissance* (1978); Shakespeare, *The Merchant of Venice*, 5. 1. 59–62, *Norton Shakespeare*, 1139; Heywood, *Hierarchie*, 272, 292.

12. West, *Angels*, 132–6; Diane McColley, 'Beneficent Hierarchies: Reading Milton Greenly', in Charles W. Durham and Kristin Pruitt McColgan (eds), *Spokesperson Milton: Voices in Contemporary Criticism* (1994).

13. Columbia, xii. 148–57. See also pp. 260–2 above.

14. Augustine, *City*, 680–5, 1066–8, 1152–3.

15. Ibid. 705–6; John Gumbleden, *Christ Tempted: The Devil Conquered* (1657), 22.

16. Aquinas, *Summa*, xiv. 107–9, 117, 111–15. Seventeenth-century meta-phoric uses of 1 Cor. 13: 1 include Richard Allestree, *The Government of the Tongue*, 2nd edn (Oxford, 1674), 211; John Heydon, *Theomagia, or, The Temple of Wisdome*, 3 vols (1664), iii. 196.

17. Aquinas, *Summa*, ix. 31–43; quotation at p. 43.

18. David Pareus, *In Genesin Mosis Commentarius* (1609; Geneva, 1614); Johannes Mercerus, *In Genesin Commentarius* (Geneva, 1598); Benedic-tus Pererius, *Commentariorum et Disputationum in Genesin* (Cologne, 1601); Andreas Rivetus, *Theologicae et Scholasticae Exercitationes Centum Nonaginta in Genesin* (Leyden, 1633); Williams, *Expositor*, 116–17.

19. Jean Paul Richter (ed.), *The Notebooks of Leonardo da Vinci*, 2 vols (1883; New York, 1970), ii. 303–8. I am grateful to Norah Carlin for this reference.

20. John Salkeld, *A Treatise of Angels* (1613), 172, 176.

21. Balthasar Gerbier, *Art of Well Speaking* (1650), 13, 26. Similarly, *A Satyr, Occasioned by the Author's Survey of a Scandalous Pamphlet* (Oxford, 1645), 2: 'When *Angels* talke, all their *Conceipts* are brought | From *Mind* to *Mind*, and they discourse by *Thought*.'

22. Morgan Llwyd, *A Discourse of the Word of God*, trans. Griffith Rudd (1739), quoted in Nigel Smith, *Perfection Proclaimed: Language and English Radical Religion 1640–1660* (Oxford, 1989), 221.

23. *Annotations upon all the Books of the Old and New Testament* (1651), at Gen. 18: 8. Among contemporaries who support this position are Edward

Hyde, *A Christian Vindication of Truth Against Errour* (1659), 351;
Agrippa, *Three Books of Occult Philosophy*, 413.

24. Gervase Babington, *Certaine Plaine, Briefe, and Comfortable Notes upon Everie Chapter of Genesis* (1592), fo. 15ᵛ.

25. Andrew Willet, *Hexapla in Genesin* (Cambridge, 1605), 44.

26. Calvin, *Commentarie*, 86. See also Thomas Bromhall, *A Treatise of Specters* (1658).

27. Calvin, *Commentarie*, 381.

28. Willet, *Hexapla*, 203.

29. George Hughes, *An Analytical Exposition of . . . Genesis* (1672), 214.

30. Gumbleden, *Christ Tempted*, 21–2; Gumbleden notes Augustine's opinion that this question of how angels speak to men cannot be answered, but resolves it by choosing both answers, according to the occasion.

31. Lawrence, *Angells*, 46.

32. Pp. 283–4 above; Laurence Caxton [Clarkson], *Paradisal Dialogue* (1660), 61.

33. *Bartas: His Devine Weekes and Workes*, trans. Joshua Sylvester (1605), 304.

34. *O&D* 12. 243–6, p. 167.

35. *O&D* 3. 295–8, p. 41; contrast the anonymous *Scala Naturae* (1695), 31: '*Adam* and *Eve* were by their Original Innocence and Integrity fitted in Paradice for the Conversation of Angels.'

36. Heywood, *Hierarchie*, 211–12.

37. See pp. 284–9 above; Stephen M. Fallon, *Milton among the Philosophers: Poetry and Materialism in Seventeenth-Century England* (Ithaca, NY, 1991), 137–67.

38. Pseudo-Dionysius, *Works*, 185.

39. Heywood, *Hierarchie*, 68, mentions God's ears in a discussion of accommodation: 'As, when we attribute unto him Wings, | It straight unto our apprehension brings, | How he protects and shadowes us. If Eares? | With what facilitie and grace he heares | Our devout Prayers.' God does not have ears, so it must be a metaphor. Milton too repeatedly refers to God's ears in this metaphoric vein; *PL* 3. 193; 5. 626; 11. 30, 152.

40. Contrast with Pseudo-Dionysius, *Works*, 185–6, where heavenly body parts and senses symbolize spiritual agency and qualities: 'The powers of hearing signify the ability to have a knowing share of divine inspiration. . . . Shoulders, arms, and also the hands signify acting, achieving.'

41. Knees: 6. 194; 8. 608, 782, 817, etc. Ears: 2. 117, 920, 953; 3. 647; 5. 771, 810. Tongues: 2. 112; 6. 135, 154, 297, 360; 7. 113, 603. Scars: 1. 601; 2. 401. Tears: 1. 620. Note also Zephon's assertion that Satan's appearance is diminished; 4. 835.

42. Aquinas, *Summa*, xiv. 109: 'The second barrier closing the mind of one person off from another is the opaqueness of the body . . . In an angel, however, no such obstacle exists.'

43. Fallon (interestingly if tenuously) suggests that the narrator's indecision points to the problem of dualism and makes an anti-Cartesian point: 'The uncertainty as to the manner of the operation of an artificial Satan/snake dualism might reflect the mystery of the operation of metaphysical spirit/body dualism'; *Milton among the Philosophers*, 205.

44. Lawrence, *Angells*, 15; Peter Le Loier, *A Treatise of Specters or Straunge Sights, Visions and Apparitions* (1605), fo. 45ᵛ; Gumbleden, *Christ Tempted*, 13.

45. Philip C. Almond, *Demonic Possession and Exorcism in Early Modern England: Contemporary Texts and their Cultural Contexts* (Cambridge, 2004); D. P. Walker, *Unclean Spirits: Possession and Exorcism in France and England in the Late Sixteenth and Early Seventeenth Centuries* (1981); Walter Stephens, *Demon Lovers: Witchcraft, Sex, and the Crisis of Belief* (Chicago, 2002); Stuart Clark, *Thinking with Demons: The Idea of Witchcraft in Early Modern Europe* (Oxford, 1997), 389–422.

46. Clark, *Thinking with Demons*, 161–78; 'Demons, Natural Magic, and the Virtually Real: Visual Paradox in Early Modern Europe', in Gerhild Scholz Williams and Charles D. Gunnoe, Jr, *Paracelsian Moments: Science, Medicine and Astrology in Early Modern Europe* (Kirksville, Mo., 2002).

47. On the role of evidence, and thus of scientific argument, in the temptation, see Karen Edwards, *Milton and the Natural World: Science and Poetry in 'Paradise Lost'* (Cambridge, 2000).

48. McColley, 'Beneficent Hierarchies'; Kristin Pruitt McColgan, 'Abundant Gifts: Hierarchy and Reciprocity in *Paradise Lost*', *South Central Review*, 11 (1994), 75–86.

## CHAPTER 13

1. Duration in *An Essay of Dramatic Poesie* (1668), in *The Works of John Dryden*, 20 vols, gen. ed. Edward Niles Hooker et al. (Berkeley and Los Angeles, 1956–2000), xvii. 35, 36. Cf. Benjamin Stillingfleet's compression for an oratorio libretto: Kay Gilliland Stevenson and Margaret Seares, *'Paradise Lost' in Short: Smith, Stillingfleet, and the Transformation of Epic* (Madison, Wis., 1998).

2. Dryden, 'Discourse Concerning the Original and Progress of Satire' (1693), in Dryden, *Works*, iv. 15.

3. Paul Stevens argues that in this passage Milton remembers Puck's misjoining of an ass head to Bottom's body, and that Milton is at his most Shakespearean when he describes fancy because he associates it with Shakespeare; *Imagination and the Presence of Shakespeare in 'Paradise Lost'* (Madison, Wis., 1985), 15, 94–6.

4. This is also Margaret Cavendish's device in *The Blazing World* (1667). When the Empress and the Duchess play at imagining a world, they

create a form of knowledge that is true because it is created by the knower. This meta-fiction then reflects back upon the Empress's natural-philosophical pronouncements to and on behalf of the various societies of virtuosi (the bird- and beast-men that represent the Royal Society); the natural-philosophical knowledge that is articulated here in a fictional form is therefore, precisely because it is feigned, in a sense truer than that generated by the Royal Society. *Margaret Cavendish: Political Writings*, ed. Susan James (Cambridge, 2003), 17–45, 69, 72–3.

5. Dryden, *The State of Innocence*, ed. Vinton A. Dearing, in Dryden, *Works*, xii. 118–20. Further references, to act, scene, and lines, appear in the text.

6. J. M. French, *The Life Records of John Milton*, 5 vols (New Brunswick, NJ, 1949–58), iv. 439–40, 446–7; v. 46–8, 467; Aubrey, *'Brief Lives,' Chiefly of Contemporaries, Set Down by John Aubrey, between the Years 1669 and 1696*, ed. Andrew Clark (Oxford, 1898), ii. 72; Helen Darbishire (ed.), *The Early Lives of Milton* (1932), 7, 295–6; Marvell, 'On Mr Milton's *Paradise Lost*' (1674), lines 45–50, in *The Poems of Andrew Marvell*, ed. Nigel Smith (2003). In addition to the sources cited above, see Morris Freedman, 'Dryden's "Memorable Visit" to Milton', *Huntington Library Quarterly*, 18 (1955), 99–108; Earl Miner, 'Dryden's Admired Acquaintance, Mr. Milton', *Milton Studies*, 11 (1978), 3–27.

7. For the early plans, *PL*, pp. 1–3. On Milton and print: Stephen B. Dobranski, *Milton, Authorship, and the Book Trade* (Cambridge, 1999); Joad Raymond, 'Milton and the Book Trade', in John Barnard and D. F. McKenzie (eds), *A History of the Book in Britain*, iv: *1557–1695* (Cambridge, 2002); Dustin Griffin, 'The Beginnings of Modern Authorship: Milton to Dryden', *Milton Quarterly*, 24 (1990), 1–7; and the following articles by Peter Lindenbaum: 'John Milton and the Republican Mode of Literary Production', in Cedric C. Brown (ed.), *Patronage, Politics, and Literary Traditions in England, 1558–1658* (Detroit, 1993); 'Milton's Contract', in Martha Woodmansee and Peter Jaszi (eds), *The Construction of Authorship: Textual Appropriation in Law and Literature* (Durham, NC, 1994); 'The Poet in the Marketplace: Milton and Samuel Simmons', in Peter G. Stanwood (ed.), *Of Poetry and Politics: New Essays on Milton and his World* (Binghamton, NY, 1995); 'Authors and Publishers in the Late Seventeenth Century: New Evidence on their Relations', *The Library*, 6th ser., 17 (1995), 250–69; 'Rematerializing Milton', *Publishing History*, 41 (1997), 5–22.

8. Milton, *Poems*, 355–7. For *Samson* as a response to Dryden's heroic drama, Steven N. Zwicker, 'Milton, Dryden, and the Politics of Literary Controversy', in Gerald MacLean (ed.), *Culture and Society in the Stuart Restoration* (1995). For the date, Christopher Hill, *Milton and the English Revolution* (1977), and Blair Worden, 'Milton, *Samson Agonistes*, and the Restoration', in MacLean (ed.), *Culture and Society*. For Milton's reaction

against Restoration culture: Laura Knoppers, *Historicizing Milton: Spectacle, Power, and Poetry in Restoration England* (Athens, Ga., 1994); David Norbrook, *Writing the English Republic: Poetry, Rhetoric, and Politics, 1627–1660* (Cambridge, 1999).

9. Dryden, *Works*, xii. 123.

10. Ibid. xvii. 77.

11. *CPW* iii. 406; 'I begun to think that the whole Book might perhaps be intended a peece of Poetrie. The words are good, the fiction smooth and cleanly; there wanted only Rime, and that, they say, is bestow'd upon it lately.'

12. See Dearing in Dryden, *Works*, xii. 320–44; Nicholas von Maltzahn, 'Dryden's Milton and the Theatre of Imagination', in Paul Hammond and David Hopkins (eds), *John Dryden: Tercentenary Essays* (Oxford, 2000), 33–6, 39–42.

13. Pp. 211, 276 above; [Charles Leslie], *A History of Sin and Heresie* (1698), sig. A2$^{r-v}$.

14. Dryden, *Works*, xii. 89.

15. Dudley Tomkinson, *The Reasons of Mr. Bayes Changing his Religion* (1688), 18–19.

16. James Kinsley and Helen Kinsley (eds), *Dryden: The Critical Heritage* (1971), 342–3, 4; Anne Ferry, *Milton and the Miltonic Dryden* (Cambridge, Mass., 1968), 21.

17. A. W. Verrall, *Lectures on Dryden* (Cambridge, 1914), 220–36; Bernard Harris, ' "That Soft Seducer, Love": Dryden's *The State of Innocence and the Fall of Man*', in C. A. Patrides (ed.), *Approaches to 'Paradise Lost': The York Tercentenary Lectures* (1968); K. W. Gransden, 'Milton, Dryden, and the Comedy of the Fall', *Essays in Criticism*, 26 (1976), 116–33; James Anderson Winn, *John Dryden and his World* (New Haven, 1987), 261–72, 294–7.

18. Jean Gagen, 'Anomalies in Eden: Adam and Eve in Dryden's *State of Innocence*', in Albert C. Labriola and Edward Sichi, Jr (eds), *Milton's Legacy in the Arts* (University Park, Pa., 1988); Verrall, *Lectures on Dryden*, 228, 229.

19. See also Derek Hughes, *English Drama 1660–1700* (Oxford, 1996), 179–83; D. W. Jefferson, 'Dryden's Style in *The State of Innocence*', *Essays in Criticism*, 32 (1982), 361–8; Neil Forsyth, *The Satanic Epic* (Princeton, 2003), 139; James Grantham Turner, *One Flesh: Paradisal Marriage and Sexual Relations in the Age of Milton* (Oxford, 1987), 264.

20. Zwicker, 'Milton, Dryden, and the Politics of Literary Controversy'; von Maltzahn, 'Dryden's Milton'; P. S. Havens, 'Dryden's "Tagged" Version of *Paradise Lost*', in Hardin Craig (ed.), *Essays in Dramatic Literature: The Parrott Presentation Volume* (1935; New York, 1967). See also Hugh MacCallum, '*The State of Innocence*: Epic to Opera', *Milton Studies*, 31 (1994), 109–31, and Bruce King, 'The Significance of Dryden's *State of*

Innocence', *Studies in English Literature*, 4 (1964), 371–91, which also appears in his *Dryden's Major Plays* (Edinburgh, 1966).

21. Sharon Achinstein, 'Milton's Spectre in the Restoration: Marvell, Dryden, and Literary Enthusiasm', *Huntington Library Quarterly*, 59 (1997), 1–29, and *Literature and Dissent in Milton's England* (Cambridge, 2003), 168, 171–2, quotation at p. 171; Norbrook, *Writing the English Republic*, 492. See also William Poole, *Milton and the Idea of the Fall* (Cambridge, 2005), 113–21.

22. *The State of Innocence*, I. i. 68, 86, 90, in Dryden, *Works*, xii. 100–1; 'frequent Senate' may catch the 'senate free' of Marvell's *First Anniversary*, line 97, in Marvell, *Poems*, 290. Certainly it echoes constitutional debate from the later 1650s, among them those inspired in and by Harrington's Rota Club. On popular sentiment in the 1670s, see Gary S. De Krey, *London and the Restoration, 1659–1683* (Cambridge, 2005); Steven C. A. Pincus, 'From Butterboxes to Wooden Shoes: The Shift in English Popular Sentiment from Anti-Dutch to Anti-French in the 1670s', *Historical Journal*, 38 (1995), 333–61; on the idea of Universal Monarchy, see Pincus, 'Popery, Trade and Universal Monarchy: The Ideological Context of the Outbreak of the Second Anglo-Dutch War', *English Historical Review*, 107 (1992), 1–29, and *Protestantism and Patriotism: Ideologies and the Making of English Foreign Policy, 1650–1668* (Cambridge, 1995).

23. The last scene seems to comment on the third Anglo-Dutch war, which had ended on 9 Feb. 1674. The opera substitutes for Milton's compressed future human history Raphael's desolate vision of a land battle and a naval fight. Dryden is probably expressing anti-war sentiment.

24. Laura Knoppers, *Constructing Cromwell: Ceremony, Portrait, and Print, 1645–1661* (Cambridge, 2000), 178–9.

25. Tomkinson, *Reasons of Mr. Bayes*, 19.

26. *CPW* vi. 346; pp. 239–40 above.

27. Dryden, *Works*, iv. 19–20; see also the reference to guardian angels in *Conquest of Granada* (1672), Part One, III. i. 77, ibid. xi. 137.

28. Dryden, *Works*, iv. 19; see also *Absalom and Achitophel* (1681), line 853.

29. Dryden, *Works*, xii. 84, 83, 81.

30. *PL* 4. 786–7; and book 4, argument. The argument to book 10 notes that 'the guardian angels forsake Paradise', and at 10. 18, 'The angelic guards ascended': they are an anonymous troupe, of whom Gabriel is the chief (4. 550).

31. Pp. 56–61, 230–7, above.

32. John Salkeld, *A Treatise of Angels* (1613), 251–69, 280–91.

33. Dryden, *Works*, xii. 94–5. Dryden is taking liberties with accommodation here. In the same year that *The State of Innocence* was printed, Francis Bampfield wrote: 'The Scriptures are not accommodated to vulgar received Errours, or mere imaginary conceits, or vain false appearances,

but they speak of things, as the things themselves really are, Is not the LORD Christ Truth it self?'; *All in One* (1677), 50.

34. Pp. 76–7 above.

35. Dryden, *Works*, xii. 92, 95.

36. Dryden returns to this throughout his criticism: see also *Essay of Dramatic Poesy* (1668), the 'Discourse Concerning . . . Satire' (1693) and the Dedication of the *Aeneis* (1697).

37. Dryden, *Works*, xi. 12.

38. John Dowell, *Clergies Honour* (1681), sigs A2$^v$–A4$^r$.

39. Louis I. Bredvold, *The Intellectual Milieu of John Dryden: Studies in Some Aspects of Seventeenth-Century Thought* (Ann Arbor, 1934), ch. 3, erroneously presents it as a debate between materialist determinism and Anglican (and Royal Society) libertarianism; see also King, 'Significance of Dryden's *State of Innocence*', 381–8. Von Maltzahn, 'Dryden's Milton', 48, argues that Adam adopts a Hobbesian position, and the angels represent Bramhall's, though he complicates this: 'The difficulty is that Dryden's sympathies are sufficiently Hobbesian that these angels propose not Bramhall's defence of human freedom but a more dubious compatibilism.' He implies that Dryden sides with the angels.

40. Thomas Hobbes, *The Questions Concerning Liberty, Necessity, and Chance* (1656), 85–6.

41. Thomas Hobbes, *Of Libertie and Necessitie* (1654), 67–72; Vere Chappell (ed.), *Hobbes and Bramhall on Liberty and Necessity* (Cambridge, 1999), 37–8; Tom Sorrell, *Hobbes* (1986), 92–5; Quentin Skinner, *Hobbes and Republican Liberty* (Cambridge, 2008), 129–31, 157–8, 170–3.

42. Thomas Hobbes, *Leviathan*, ed. Richard Tuck (Cambridge, 1991), 146–7, 34. To be free is to be free from opposition, not free from causes.

43. Hobbes, *Of Libertie and Necessitie*, 15–16; Chappell (ed.), *Hobbes and Bramhall*, 20.

44. Chappell (ed.), *Hobbes and Bramhall*, 8; Chappell's text of the 'Discourse' is extracted from subsequent publications.

45. Chappell (ed.), *Hobbes and Bramhall*, 13.

46. Ibid. 8–9, 30–1; Hobbes, *Of Libertie and Necessitie*, 47–9. Hobbes added that church doctrine did not set down the sense in which angels were free, or how necessity governed them.

47. Hobbes, *Of Libertie and Necessitie*, 72, 73; Chappell (ed.), *Hobbes and Bramhall*, 38–9.

48. Bramhall, quoted in Hobbes, *Questions Concerning Liberty, Necessity*, 295; Bramhall, *Castigations of Mr. Hobbes* (1657), 365–6.

49. On animadversion, see Raymond, *Pamphleteering*, 210–14, 376–8; Dryden used animadversion in *His Majesties Declaration Defended* (1681).

50. Dryden, *Works*, viii. 97.

51. Pp. 333–4 above.

52. Dryden, *Works*, xvii. 47.

53. Preface to *Fables* (1697), in Dryden, *Works*, vii. 25.

54. Dryden, *Works*, xi. 5–6.

55. Ibid. v. 275.

56. Golda Werman, *Milton and Midrash* (Washington, DC, 1995), 184.

57. The Devil's influence over dreams was a frequently used example of how he operated within the limits God placed upon him, allowing him no real power; Forsyth, *Satanic Epic*, 160–6; John M. Steadman, *Milton's Biblical and Classical Imagery* (Pittsburgh, Pa., 1984), 160–6; cf. William B. Hunter, 'Eve's Demonic Dream', *ELH*, 13 (1946), 255–65.

58. Thomas Bromhall, *A Treatise of Specters* (1658), pt 1; Isaac Ambrose, 'War with Devils' (1661), in *The Compleat Works* (1682), 128; Robert Dingley, *The Deputation of Angels* (1654), 123; Philotheos Physiologus [Thomas Tryon], *A Treatise of Dreams and Visions* [1689]; Stephens, *Demon Lovers*, 129–34.

59. Heywood, *Hierarchie*, 197; Hobbes, *Leviathan*, 18–19.

60. *O&D* 1. 173–80.

61. Thomas Hobbes and Sir William Davenant in *Sir William Davenant's 'Gondibert'*, ed. David F. Gladish (Oxford, 1971), 22, 49; Marvell, *Poems*, 180–4; *PL* 8. 70–84, 175.

62. Raphael's prophecy of human history in Dryden's final scene is another piece of stagecraft, but he has been beaten to it by the father of lies.

63. 'Authors Apology for Heroique Poetry and Poetique Licence', in Dryden, *Works*, xii. 91, 93, 96.

CHAPTER 14

1. Calvin, *Institution*, 65.

2. Tessa Watt, *Cheap Print and Popular Piety, 1550–1640* (Cambridge, 1991), 134–9.

3. Bodo Brinkmann (ed.), *Cranach* (2008), and accompanying exhibition at the Royal Academy of Arts, London; Joseph Koerner, *The Reformation of the Image* (2004).

4. W. B. Hunter, C. A. Patrides, and J. H. Adamson, *Bright Essence: Studies in Milton's Theology* (Salt Lake City, Ut., 1971), 165–78 and *passim*; for an implicit corrective, see Brian Cummings, *The Literary Culture of the Reformation: Grammar and Grace* (Oxford, 2002).

5. Dryden, 'Discourse Concerning the Original and Progress of Satire' (1693), in *The Works of John Dryden*, iv, ed. A. B. Chambers and William Frost (Berkeley and Los Angeles, 1974), 15; see p. 326 above.

6. Pp. 338, 351–2 above.

7. Dennis, *The Grounds of Criticism in Poetry* (1704), in *The Critical Works of John Dennis*, ed. Edward Niles Hooker, 2 vols (Baltimore, 1939–43), i. 325.

8. Nicholas von Maltzahn, 'The Whig Milton, 1667–1700', in David Armitage, Armand Himy, and Quentin Skinner (eds), *Milton and*

*Republicanism* (Cambridge, 1995), and von Maltzahn's forthcoming study of Milton's reception.

9. Kester Svensden, *Milton and Science* (Cambridge, Mass., 1956), 239–40; Watson Kirkconnell, *The Celestial Cycle: The Theme of 'Paradise Lost' in World Literature with Translations of the Major Analogues* (Toronto, 1952), p. xii.

10. Lewis Sperry Chafer, *Systematic Theology*, ii (Dallas, 1947), 8.

11. Quoted in Nicholas McDowell, *The English Radical Imagination: Culture, Religion, and Revolution, 1630–1660* (Oxford, 2003), 43.

12. Michael Lieb, *Theological Milton: Deity, Discourse and Heresy in the Miltonic Canon* (Pittsburgh, Pa., 2006), 1–11 and *passim*.

13. See Joanna Poppleton, 'Truth Cannot Be an Enemy to Truth: Natural Philosophy, Poetry and Politics, 1680–1730', Ph.D. thesis (University of East Anglia, 2006).

14. West, *Angels*, 16–19.

15. Quoted in Theresa M. Kelley, *Reinventing Allegory* (Cambridge, 1997), 1.

16. Ian Hacking, *The Emergence of Probability* (Cambridge, 1975); Barbara Shapiro, *A Culture of Fact: England, 1550–1720* (Ithaca, NY, 2000); J. Paul Hunter, *Before Novels: The Cultural Contexts of Eighteenth-Century British Fiction* (New York, 1990); Michael McKeon, *The Origins of the English Novel, 1600–1740* (1988).

17. Kelley, *Reinventing Allegory*, 1–14.

18. Samuel Morland, *The Urim of Conscience* (1695), 13–14; see pp. 275–6 above.

19. Anne Ferry, *Milton's Epic Voice: The Narrator in 'Paradise Lost'* (Cambridge, Mass., 1963), 116–46; Fallon, *Philosophers*, 182–5.

20. Victoria Kahn, *Machiavellian Rhetoric: From the Counter-Reformation to Milton* (Princeton, 1994), 215–24.

21. Fallon, *Philosophers*, 160.

22. Pp. 181–6 above.

23. A. D. Nuttall, *Overheard by God: Fiction and Prayer in Herbert, Milton, Dante and St John* (1980), pp. ix, 84–5, 96–7.

24. Ibid. 93, 97, 98–100; A. D. Nuttall, *The Alternative Trinity: Gnostic Heresy in Marlowe, Milton, and Blake* (Oxford, 1998), 149–55.

25. John G. Demaray, *Milton's Theatrical Epic: The Invention and Design of 'Paradise Lost'* (Cambridge, Mass., 1980), p. xiii, which does not seek to downplay the significance of Milton's religious interests.

26. William Empson, *Milton's God* (1961; Cambridge, 1981), *passim*; Nuttall, *Overheard by God*, 101–8; William Poole, *Milton and the Idea of the Fall* (Cambridge, 2005), 19, 30, 57, 64, 96.

27. Henry Ansgar Kelly, *Satan: A Biography* (Cambridge, 2006), 159; Poole, *Milton and the Idea of the Fall*, 68.

28. David Lawton, *Faith, Text and History: The Bible in English* (Charlottesville, Va., 1990), 1.

29. Andrew Willet, *Hexapla in Genesin* (Cambridge, 1605), 109.

30. Alastair Fowler, *Renaissance Realism: Narrative Images in Literature and Art* (Oxford, 2003), 5–8 and *passim*.
31. Michael Murrin, *The Allegorical Epic: Essays in its Rise and Decline* (Chicago, 1980), 161.
32. Ibid. 158–9, 164–6, 167.
33. Ibid. 251 n. 26; Michael Murrin, *The Veil of Allegory: Some Notes Towards a Theory of Allegorical Rhetoric in the English Renaissance* (Chicago, 1969), 176 and *passim*.
34. Catherine Gimelli Martin, *The Ruins of Allegory: 'Paradise Lost' and the Metamorphosis of Epic Convention* (Durham, NC, 1998).
35. See Roland Mushat Frye, *Milton's Imagery and the Visual Arts: Iconographic Tradition in the Epic Poems* (Princeton, 1978), pt 3.
36. Kelley, *Reinventing Allegory*.
37. Poppleton, 'Truth Cannot Be an Enemy'.
38. E. M. W. Tillyard, 'Theology and Emotion in Milton's Poetry', in *Studies in Milton* (New York, 1951), 141.
39. T. S. Eliot, *Selected Essays, 1917–1932* (1932), 273–4.
40. Ibid. 280.
41. Not least because the rise of Puritanism would become tied to the rise of the novel; Ian Watt, *The Rise of the Novel: Studies in Defoe, Richardson and Fielding* (1957). For analyses of Eliot's thesis and its impact, see Evans, *Genesis Tradition*, 1–4 and *passim*; William Kolbrener, *Milton's Warring Angels: A Study of Critical Engagements* (Cambridge, 1997), 59–61; Kester Svensden suggests that Milton would have seemed 'old-fashioned' to scientifically knowledgeable contemporaries, and distinguishes between Milton's knowledge as a poet and his knowledge as a man; *Milton and Science*, 4, 43.
42. Frank Kermode, 'Dissociation of Sensibility', in John R. Roberts (ed.), *Essential Articles for the Study of John Donne's Poetry* (Hamden, Conn., 1975).
43. Gordon Teskey, *Delirious Milton: The Fate of the Poet in Modernity* (Cambridge Mass., 2006), 1–9; quotation at pp. 5–6 (and 29).
44. Ibid. 24, 40–4.
45. Ibid. 45–64, esp. 49, 61. Knowingly so: on p. 172 he writes, 'I think Miltonists evince far too much faith in theological concepts and theological language.' I have no faith in them, but I believe that Milton did. Teskey complains that Miltonists think that 'theology may be used to grasp what is more subtle, mobile, and living: poetry'. The problem here is surely Teskey's assumption that 17th-century theology was obvious, rigid, and deceased.
46. Ibid. 29, 143, 48, 75, and *passim*.
47. Ibid. 24–9, quotations at pp. 29, 25.
48. Ibid. 21–4.
49. Pp. 162, 295–6 above.

50. Pp. 306–8 above.
51. P. 242 above; Robert W. Scribner, 'The Reformation, Popular Magic, and the "Disenchantment of the World"', *Journal of Interdisciplinary History*, 23 (1993), 475–94; Alex Walsham, 'Invisible Helpers: Apparitions of Angels in Post-Reformation England', *Past and Present*, forthcoming.
52. Murray Roston, *Biblical Drama in England: From the Middle Ages to the Present Day* (1968), 15–20.
53. Rosemary Woolf, *The English Religious Lyric in the Middle Ages* (Oxford, 1968); Eleanor Prosser, *Drama and Religion in the English Mystery Plays* (Stanford, Calif., 1961); James Simpson, *The Oxford English Literary History*, ii: *1350–1547: Reform and Cultural Revolution* (Oxford, 2002), 502–57; John D. Cox, *The Devil and the Sacred in English Drama, 1350–1642* (Cambridge, 2000), 29–34.
54. Richard Rastall, *The Heavens Singing: Music in Early English Religious Drama*, i (Cambridge, 1996), 175–93, 328–44, esp. 179–80, 183–6, 328, 332–6.
55. Peter Happé (ed.), *English Mystery Plays* (Harmondsworth, 1975), 291; R. M. Lumiansky and David Mills (eds), *The Chester Mystery Cycle*, i: *Text*, Early English Text Society, suppl. ser., 3 (1974), 3; Stephen Spector (ed.), *The N-Town Play: Cotton MS Vespasian D.8*, 2 vols, Early English Text Society, suppl. ser., 11–12 (1991), i. 22; Martin Stevens and A. C. Cawley (eds), *The Towneley Plays*, i: *Introduction and Text*, Early English Text Society, suppl. ser., 12 (1994), 7, 11 (lines 142, 254–6); Richard Beadle and Pamela M. King (eds), *York Mystery Plays: A Selection in Modern Spelling* (1984; Oxford, 1995), pp. 2, 279, xx.
56. Aquinas, *Summa*, ix. 297; *Faustus*, 1. 5. 124–6, in Christopher Marlowe, *The Complete Plays*, ed. J. B. Stearne (1969); *PL* 4. 20–3.
57. *Measure for Measure*, 3. 1. 492, 2. 4. 16; *Richard III*, 1. 4. 53, 4. 2. 68, 5. 5. 129; *Richard II*, 3. 2. 57; *Norton Shakespeare*, 2063, 2049; 534, 568, 590; 982.
58. *The Merchant of Venice*, 5. 1. 60–1, *Norton Shakespeare*, 1139.
59. *The Tempest*, 1. 2. 484, 2. 1. 392, 4. 1. 27, *Norton Shakespeare*, 3069, 3077, 3091.
60. *Henry IV, Part II*, 1. 2. 150–2; *Othello*, 5. 2. 215; *Norton Shakespeare*, 1314, 2168.
61. *Antony and Cleopatra*, 2. 3. 17–20, *Norton Shakespeare*, 2649.
62. *Henry V*, 1. 1. 28–32, *Norton Shakespeare*, 1456.
63. *Hamlet*, 5. 1. 224–5, 1. 4. 20, 3. 4. 94–5, *Norton Shakespeare*, 1745, 1682, 1722; pp. 62–3 above.
64. *Hamlet*, 3. 3. 69, *Norton Shakespeare*, 1718. Greenblatt overstates the doctrinal differences between Protestants and Catholics on angels: they appear in Protestant iconography as well as in Catholic. *Hamlet in Purgatory* (Princeton, 2001), *passim*, but esp. 50–5, 62–4, 118, 145–6,

182, 223 (here he interprets Hamlet's words as a prayer). Christopher Devlin finds an allusion to the Office of St Michael in the Roman Catholic Breviary; see *Hamlet's Divinity* (1963), 31–2.

65. Donne, *Major Works*, 180.
66. Ibid. 312.
67. Ibid. 387.
68. Ibid. 311.
69. Ibid. 111–12.
70. Ibid. 287, 13. The allusion to 'Mahomet's paradise' is odd; perhaps he refers, intelligibly to his coterie audience, to William Percy's play; see Matthew Dimmock (ed.), *William Percy's Mahomet and his Heaven: A Critical Edition* (Aldershot, 2006).
71. Tony Kushner, *Angels in America* (London, 1992–4); performed variously 1990–2; HBO mini-series 2003.
72. Donne, *Major Works*, 101.
73. Ibid. 123.
74. Ibid. 130; p. 376 below.
75. *The Sermons of John Donne*, viii (Berkeley, 1956), 107–8.
76. Dimmock (ed.), *William Percy's Mahomet*, 121 (4. 5. 16–21); Heywood, *Hierarchie*, 215–16, echoes or overlaps with this passage. Like Shakespeare, Percy adapts some of his demonology from Reginald Scott, *The Discoverie of Witchcraft* (1584).
77. Edmund Spenser, *Fowre Hymnes* (1596), 24.
78. Henry Burkhead, *A Tragedy of Cola's Fury* (Kilkenny, 1646; written 1645), 49–50, 61.
79. Charles Fitz-Geffrey, *The Blessed Birth-Day* (1634), 19 (also 2, 5, 16).
80. Dennis, *Critical Works*, ii. 228–9.
81. Teskey, *Delirious Milton*, 1.
82. Steven N. Zwicker, 'Milton, Dryden, and the Politics of Literary Controversy', in Gerald MacLean (ed.), *Culture and Society in the Stuart Restoration* (1995).

# Index

Abarbanel, Isaac 194, 202
Abdiel 207–28 *passim*, 264–5, 271, 294, 299
accommodation 7, 81, 114, 119, 122, 139, 145, 162–88, 218, 221–2, 311–14, 360, 364
adiaphora 4, 36, 65, 163
Agrippa 78, 80, 114, 117, 136, 145, 271
Ainsworth, Henry 86, 87, 101
Albigenses 283
alchemy 130, 135, 303
al-Farghānī 304, 443 n. 98
allegory 7, 99, 120, 136–44 *passim*, 153, 157–60 *passim*, 162, 165, 169, 173–4, 175, 185, 213–16 *passim*, 220–5, 277, 312, 358–65, 433 n. 58
almanacs 109–10
Alsted, Johann Heinrich 93, 103
Ambrose, Isaac 46
Ambrose, Saint 65, 361
Ames, William 42, 43, 44, 75, 100
angels
    Angels of the Presence 22, 62, 79, 82–3, 154
    of Bethesda 86, 245, 248, 250
    bodies 69, 118, 122, 139, 150, 168, 169–87 *passim*, 228, 284–90, 321–2
    communication or conversation with 104–15, 125–61, 311–24
    creation of 42, 65–7
    deception by 176, 212, 221–8, 247, 323, 424 n. 11
    eating 41, 69, 172, 176, 280, 318, 323

fall of 71, 73–7, 120, 122, 149, 154, 163, 209–10, 256–9, 283
food of 69, 118, 130, 143, 150, 269–70, 280–2, 286–7, 350
freewill 71–3, 257–8, 341–51
guardians of place 111, 141, 230, 232–9, 242–4, 249–51, 252–5, 335–7
guardianship 45, 56–61, 63, 101, 120, 129, 132, 143–4, 145, 154, 155–6, 336–7, 372, 430 n. 30
hierarchies 22–6, 34, 49–56, 60, 64, 67, 71, 101, 135, 136, 179–80, 198, 262–5, 315, 370
knowledge 30, 67–9, 374
matter 32–3
military nature 79, 263, 265–7
names 78–83, 270–2
offices 84–7
physical appearance 57, 134, 155, 157–8, 159, 160, 168, 183, 194, 268–9, 290, 440 n. 47
prayers to and invocation of 62–4
pre-Christian 20, 79–80
providential apparitions 105–6, 110, 132, 194
senses 68, 70–1, 140, 143, 150–1, 269, 299–301
of the Seven Asian churches 53, 91
sex, gender and reproduction 78, 152, 269, 282–3, 337, 338–9, 375–6
sight and optics 66, 68, 226, 291–9
singing and music 85, 134, 141, 260–1, 265, 313–15, 370

angels (*cont.*)
  Sons of God 76–7, 282–3, 339
  speech 69–70, 275
  speed 253, 301–308
  subjectivity 67–9, 104, 256–7,
    339
  words pertaining to 19–20
  worship of 39, 61–2
angelology (as genre) 19–20, 45–6,
  100
Anglesey 242, 254, 255
Anglo-Dutch War, third 334,
  450 n. 23
Annesley, Arthur, Earl of
  Anglesey 216
Anselm of Canterbury 31
anthropomorphism 165–6, 170,
  172, 174–5, 186, 207, 446 n. 39
anthropopathy 165–6, 169–70, 172,
  174–5, 177, 179, 185–6,
  423 n. 1
antitrinitarianism 116–17, 173–5,
  199, 209–10, 217
*Apocalypsis Moses*, see *Vitae Adae et*
  *Evae*
apocalypticism, *see* millenarianism
Aquinas, Thomas 26, 29–31, 36, 38,
  65, 67, 69, 70, 71–2, 81, 83, 162,
  168, 173, 259, 263, 272–3, 280,
  284, 292, 297, 299–300, 302,
  312, 315–16
Arianism 77, 208
Aristotle and Aristotelianism 21,
  28–9, 48, 68
Arnway, Richard 98
*Ars Notoria* 107, 117
Ashmole, Elias 1–2, 106, 126, 127,
  130
astrology 45, 68, 80, 106–12, 120–1,
  126–7, 130, 145, 249, 276,
  303–5
astronomy 72, 198, 298–9, 303–5
*Athenian Mercury* 12
Atterbury, Francis 221
Aubrey, John 80, 107, 109, 329–30,
  341, 412 n. 34

Augustine 28, 36, 60, 64, 65, 71,
  73–4, 78–9, 83, 119, 162,
  166–7, 168, 280, 315
Austen, Katherine 84
Austin, William 45, 63–4, 233, 284

Babington, Gervase 40, 41, 42, 58,
  85, 317
Bacon, Francis 103, 368
Bacon, Roger 31, 304, 443 n. 98
Baillie, Robert 94
Bampfield, Francis 176, 450 n. 33
Bartas, Guillaume de Salluste de 46,
  144, 198–9, 216, 246, 319,
  426 n. 31, 427 n. 42, 443 n. 102
Bathurst, Ann 147, 153–60
Bauthumley, Jacob 97, 119, 120, 123
Baxter, Richard 43, 64, 100, 126,
  132–3, 412 n. 34
Bayly, John 34, 45, 77
Beaumont, Joseph 310
Behmenism, *see* Boehme
Bernard, St 24
Biddle, John 116–17, 173–5
Bion, Greek poet 230
Blackmore, Richard 359, 438 n. 3
Blenkow, John 51, 81, 101
Blome, Richard 19
Bodin, Jean 59–60
Boehme, Jacob and Behmenism 83,
  117, 120, 121, 125, 126–7, 129,
  135, 136, 140, 150, 153, 161,
  183, 249, 285–6, 290
Bolton, Robert 283, 303
Bonaventure 26, 28–9, 83, 162
Book of Common Prayer 40, 94,
  235
Boughton, John 40
Boyle, Robert 73, 308, 309,
  443 n. 110
Bradfield, Berks. 117, 131, 137, 142,
  147
Bramhall, John 340–8
Brathwaite, Richard 283
Brightman, Thomas 93
Bromley, Thomas 127

Browne, Edward 31
Browne, Robert 60
Browne, Thomas 58
Brownism 95
Bucanus, William 42, 43, 49, 58–9, 300, 302, 305
Bunyan, John 137
Burgess, Cornelius 44, 69, 87
Burkhead, Henry 379

Cabbala 32, 60, 80, 271
cacodemology 111, 113, 131–2
Calamy, Edmund 89
Calvert, Giles 102, 129
Calvin, John 33–4, 36, 42, 45, 56, 58, 59, 63, 65, 67, 69, 79, 85, 169–70, 189, 192, 202, 233, 257, 312, 318, 355
Cambridge Platonists 191, 284, 286
Camden, William 230–2
Camfield, Benjamin 38, 46
Campanella, Tomasso 32, 60
Cannon, Nathaniel 44
Cardano, Girolamo 60
Cartwright, Thomas 58
Cary, Mary 105, 196
Caryl, Joseph 45
Casaubon, Meric 3, 112–15
Casman, Otto 19
Catherall, Samuel 358
Catholicism 4–6, 48–64, 87–8, 174, 232, 234, 236, 242, 248, 337, 373, 376–7
Cavendish, Margaret 12, 447–8 n. 4
Charles I 53, 194, 224
Charles II 222
Chillingworth, William 32–3
Christ 30, 39, 56, 61, 62, 77, 81, 100, 116–17, 149, 247–8, 266
Chrysostom 65
Cicero 241
Clarke, Samuel 112
Claxton, or Clarkson, Laurence 120–2, 129–30, 319

Colet, John 67, 79
Comenius, Jan Amos 47, 68, 70–1, 103–4, 282, 293–4, 300, 424 n. 6
Coppe, Abiezer 117–18, 122, 123, 127, 129, 196–7
Coppin, Richard 118, 127, 129
cosmology 276, 278–9, 297–9, 303–6
Cotton, Robert 3, 112
Cowley, Abraham 46, 106, 254–5, 380
Cranach, Lucas 356
Cromwell, Oliver 3, 106, 115, 136, 219, 222, 227, 233, 244–52 *passim*, 334
Cromwell, Richard 254
Cudworth, Ralph 284–5
Curtius, Ernst Robert 200
Cyprian 22

Damascus, John of 288
dancing 32, 266, 267, 327, 329, 379
Dante 24–6, 53, 61, 137, 200, 259, 292
Davenant, Sir William 215, 352
Davenport, John 127
Davies, Lady Eleanor 196
Dee, John 2–4, 31, 60, 106, 107, 110, 111, 112–15, 120, 126, 272, 293
Defoe, Daniel 210
demons 3, 8, 99, 110, 111, 113, 114, 130–2, 133–4, 282–3, 289–91, 309, 323, 370–1
Dennis, John 190, 357, 380–1
Dent, Arthur 56, 100
Descartes, Rene 288, 342
Dingley, Robert 45, 58, 62, 101, 233, 249, 250, 280, 304
Dionysius 4, 5, 23–4, 28, 31, 34, 50, 67, 80, 135, 162, 163, 167–8, 175, 177, 179, 198, 218, 232–3, 263, 265, 293, 312, 321, 446 n. 40
*see also* angels—hierarchies

*Discovery of the Juglings and Deceitfull*
    *Impostures* (1643) 98
*Discovery of the Rebels* (1643) 98
Donne, John 46, 96, 282, 288, 316,
    373–8
Dowell, John 341
Dowsing, William 5
drama 47, 314, 525–54 *passim*,
    369–73
  Medieval cycle plays 370–1
dreams 193, 194, 328–9, 351–3
Dryden, John 10, 13, 137, 177, 236,
    357, 380–1, 382
  *State of Innocence* 327–54
  *Essay of Dramatic Poesie* 331, 349
  'Discourse Concerning
    Satire' 335–7
  'Of Heroique Playes' 340, 350
  *The Rival Ladies* 348
  *Conquest of Granada* 349–50
Duppa, Brian 51–2, 300–1
Dury, John 127

Eaton, Samuel 95
*Elegie Sacred to the Immortal Memory*
    (1643) 98
Eliot, T. S. 214, 366–7, 381
England 242, 243, 254 and *passim*
Enoch 22, 76–7, 80, 110
episcopacy 90–8
Erasmus 35
Erbery, William 127, 129
Eriugena, John Scotus 23, 31
Etherington, John 127
Evans, Arise 45, 62, 82, 106, 111,
    249–50
Evans, John, astrologer 107, 126
Everard, John 45, 303, 403 n. 56,
    411 n. 18
Everard, William 118, 121, 127,
    129–30, 133

Fairfax, Henry 44
Fall of humankind 9, 73, 122,
    140–1, 276, 297
Fallon, Stephen 438, 447 n. 43
Familism, Family of Love 127, 129

Featley, Daniel 357
Ficino, Marsilio 32
Fifth Monarchists 62, 117, 141
Fitz-Geffrey, Charles 379–80
Flavel, Mrs 130
Fludd, Robert 80, 272, 281, 285,
    290, 303, 442 n. 81
Foxe, John 248
Forman, Simon 60, 107, 109, 111,
    126
Fowler, Alastair 214, 425 n. 21
Fowler, Christopher 129, 136
Freke, John 161
Fulke, William 58

Gabriel 27, 79–82, 85, 107, 109,
    112, 122, 159
  in *Paradise Lost* 262, 266, 273, 301,
    336
  in *State of Innocence* 341–47
Galileo Galilei 291, 295, 298,
    299
Gaule, John 170
Gell, Robert, *Aggelokratia Theon* 19,
    45, 80, 286, 293
Geneva Bible 56, 247
genius loci, *see* angels—guardians of
    place
geocentrism, *see* cosmology
Geoffrey of Monmouth 230–1
Gerbier, Balthasar 316
Geree, John 95
Ghiberti, Lorenzo 361–2
Giorgi, Francesco 32
Glanvill, Joseph 51, 295, 299, 308,
    309
Gnostics and Gnosticism 21, 32, 80,
    81, 209
*Great Wonder from Heaven* (1642
    [3]) 104–5
Greene, Anne 105–6
Greenhill, William 303–4
Gregory the Great 5, 24, 65, 80
Grosseteste, Robert 31
Gumbleden, John 44, 68, 79, 176–7,
    318–19
Gurnall, William 249

Habila, Helon 14
Hall, Joseph 50–1, 62, 72, 77, 85, 87, 91, 101, 105, 293
Hammond, Henry 100
Hart, Alexander 107, 126
Hartlib, Samuel 223
Harvey, Gideon 20
Harvey, John, physician 187, 194, 197
Heimbach, Peter 102, 241
heliocentrism, *see* cosmology
Herbert, Philip, Earl of Pembroke 127
Hermas, *The Shepherd* 57
Herrick, Robert 245
Heydon, John 60, 145, 413 n. 62
Heywood, Thomas 6, 19, 38, 46, 50, 52–3, 54, 56, 74, 78, 79, 80, 146, 178–80, 200, 215–16, 253, 284, 300, 304–5, 315, 320, 352, 446 n. 39
Heywood, William 94
Hibbert, Henry 42–3
Hicks, Thomas 116
Hilary of Poitiers 166
Hildegard of Bingen 314
Hobbes, Thomas 81, 174, 195, 215, 267, 284, 285, 340
on freewill 341–51
Hodges, William 107
Holy Spirit, *see* Spirit
Homer 137, 200, 310
homilies 39
Hooke, Robert 3, 12, 291, 294, 295, 299, 308
Hooker, Edward 147
Hooker, Richard 75
Hughes George 40, 41, 234, 280, 302, 318
Hume, Patrick 10, 213, 226, 278
Hutchinson, John 180
Hutchinson, Lucy 6, 46, 146, 163, 180–82, 200, 216–18, 319–20
hylozoism 438

iconoclasm 5, 38, 92, 364
imagination 6–8, 13, 30, 67, 113, 163–4, 177–88, 213–18, 220, 227–8, 256–9, 309–10, 353–4, 355–84
Ireland 110, 230, 239, 242–3, 254
Irenaeus 22
Ithuriel 271, 289, 291, 336

James VI and I 53, 191
Jenkyn, William 34, 56, 101, 403 n. 61
Jerome 65, 74, 316
Jesuits and Jesuitism 46, 94, 293, 295, 298
Johnsen, H. 111
Johnson, Samuel 213–14, 237, 239, 278
Jubilees 22, 76, 82
Justin Martyr 22, 74
Juvencus 199

Keith, Dr, Philadelphian 149, 154
Kelley, Edward 107, 112–13
Kellison, Matthew 81
Kermode, Frank 367
King, Edward 230, 250
Kircher, Athansius 60, 295
Knott, Edward 32
Knox, Elizabeth 14
Kushner, Tony 14, 376

L'Estrange, Roger 331
Lactantius 166, 186
Laudianism 37, 52, 63, 237
Law, William 161
Lawrence, Edward 102
Lawrence, Henry 38, 46, 58, 59, 62, 68, 73, 77, 99, 101, 102–3, 104, 115, 131, 136, 176, 233, 319, 323
Lawson, George 53, 84
Lead, Jane 147, 152, 153–4, 161
Lee, Francis 153, 161
Leigh, Edward 62, 99
Leonardo da Vinci 316
Leslie, Charles 210, 213, 226, 332

Lightfoot, John 67, 76, 100
Lilly, William 60, 106–11, 112,
    126–7, 233, 239, 253
Llwyd, Morgan 122, 316–17
Locke, John 12, 308
Loier, Pierre Le 60, 176
Lombard, Peter 26–9, 65, 71, 258
Love, Christopher 45, 58, 86, 101,
    234
Lucan, Marcus Anneus 230
Lucifer 27, 49, 73–7, 79, 98, 105,
    141–4, 150, 179, 216, 262, 266,
    271, 327, 329, 334, 338–9,
    353–4, 370–1
Lucretius 200, 216
Luther, Martin 35–6, 45, 57, 63,
    259, 316, 373

Madimi 113–14
magic 2–3, 107–9, 121, 126, 130,
    131–2, 142, 145, 151, 270–1,
    357
Maimonides, Moses 193, 195, 202
Malignants Trecherous and Bloody Plot
    (1643) 98
Maltzahn, Nicholas von 451 n. 39
manuscripts, magical 2, 60, 107, 109,
    112–13, 121, 272, 308
Maria Beatrice of Modena 336
Marine Mercury (1642) 105
Marlowe, Christopher 371, 372,
    442 n. 90
Marprelate 93
Marsh, Mr., of Dunstable 109
Martin, Catherine Gimelli 364
Martyr, Peter, Vermigli 42, 56, 69,
    170–1, 190, 193, 195, 202, 233
Marvell, Andrew 188, 244–52, 255,
    330, 352, 434 n. 65
Mather, Cotton 46
Mather, Increase 19, 46
Maximes Unfolded (1643) 98
Mayer, John 248
Mede, Joseph 56, 92–3
Mercerus, Johannes 316
Mercurius Politicus 223
Mercurius Pragmaticus 98

Michael 5, 27, 35, 40, 45, 49, 51,
    56–7, 64, 75, 79–82, 94–5, 98,
    100, 106, 107, 109, 110, 112,
    114, 118, 141, 161, 179, 231–9,
    243, 247–8, 335–6
  in Paradise Lost 184, 194, 203,
    262, 268–71 passim, 274, 301,
    335
millenarianism 31, 90, 92
Milton, John 8–10, 15, 42, 44, 47,
    56, 65, 68, 73, 79, 102, 104, 116,
    121–2, 126, 140, 167, 173,
    190–1, 197–204, 207–384
    passim
  Nativity Ode 250
  A Masque 238, 433 n. 58
  'Lycidas' 92, 190, 229–55
  'Ad Mansus' 240
  'Ad Leonoram' 235
  Animadversions 91
  Reason of Church Government 55,
    91–2, 197–8, 202, 219
  Doctrine and Discipline of
    Divorce 234
  Areopagitica 240–1, 250
  Tenure of Kings and Magistrates 240
  History of Britain 216, 230–1, 240
  Observations 242
  Defensio 198
  Defensio Secunda 223, 250,
    432 n. 49
  Paradise Lost 6, 8–9, 11, 13, 46, 55,
    74, 77, 78, 79, 82, 86, 102, 121,
    137, 138–40, 141, 144, 146, 164,
    183–5, 190–1, 193–4, 207–384
    passim; arguments 11, 179, 207,
    235
  Samson Agonistes 330, 331
  Paradise Regained 77, 232, 234, 283
  De Doctrina 9, 11, 43, 44, 82, 92,
    100, 185–7, 199, 204, 210, 212,
    215, 218, 226–8, 232, 234–5,
    291, 301, 306, 307, 335
  Letter to Heimbach 102, 241
miracles 52–3, 59, 64, 90, 191, 195
Modest Enquiry . . . Guardian Angel
    (1702) 45, 233

Mohamed, Feisal 423 n. 2
monism 228, 279, 286, 438 n. 10
Montagu, Richard 43, 63, 394 n. 64
More, Alexander 222–4, 227
More, Henry 33, 47, 55, 60, 72, 84,
    284–5, 295, 308, 309
Morland, Sir Samuel 277–8, 359
mortalism 116, 121, 285
Moulin, Peter du 222–3
Muggleton, Lodowick 121
Muggletonianism 121, 123
Muhammad, prophet 23, 378–9
Murrin, Michael 363–4

Napier, John 92, 93, 238
Napier, Richard 60, 109, 111
narrative 7, 11, 163–4, 213–18,
    256–9, 309–10, 361–5, 380–2,
    384
nationalism, see patriotism
natural philosophy 277–310, 368–9,
    381–2
Necessity of Christian Subjection
    (1643) 98
Nedham, Marchamont 223
Neoplatonism 32, 150, 168–9, 174,
    181, 217, 314–15, 336
nephilim 76–7, 78
    see also angels—Sons of God
New Discovery of the Prelates Tyranny
    (1641) 94
New Model Army 266
Newcomb, Thomas 358
Niclaes, Hendrik 125, 127
    see also Familism
Norwood, Robert 120
numbers 306–7
Nuttall, Tony 360

Odingsells, Charles 192
Old Newes Newly Revived (1641) 95
Origen 65, 71, 73, 165, 258,
    302
Overton, Richard 116
Ovid 180, 200, 357
Owen, John 117, 173–5
Oxenbridge, Joanna 154

pamphlets 93–9, 219–21, 224–5,
    252
Paracelsus 114, 117, 125, 140, 145
Pareus, David 56, 316
Paris 28, 344, 373
Parkes, Christopher 136
Patrick, John 34–5, 86–7, 234
Patrides, C. A. 357
patriotism 236, 239–44, 432 n. 49
Paul, St 34, 37, 57, 162
Paulin, Tom 224
Peace, Peace, and We Shall Be Quiet
    (1647) 98
Pendar, Margaret 131
Pennington, Mary 128
Percy, William 378–9
Perereius, Benedictus 316
perfectionism 118, 127
Perkins, William 49, 100, 163,
    191–2, 195, 202
Perrot, John 122
Peyton, Thomas 76
Philadelphians 125, 128, 147–61,
    196
Phillips, Edward 201
Philo 162, 165–6, 172
Philosophical Transactions 12, 308
Piccolomini, Alessandro 283
Pietism 161
Plato 32, 58, 168, 190
Pocock, Mary 128
Poole, Elizabeth 105, 129, 196
Pordage, John 15, 64, 105, 106, 117,
    118, 120, 121, 123, 125–61,
    196, 200, 286, 290, 319,
    414 n. 68
Pordage, Mary 127–8, 153
Pordage, Samuel 125, 127, 136–46,
    187, 412 n. 50
    Mundorum Explicatio (1661) 6, 46,
    137–46, 150, 182–3, 218
Powell, Vavasor 132
predestination 59, 72–3, 143
    see also freewill
Presbyterians 45, 89, 91, 99, 101
Prideaux, John 19, 45, 236
Pringle, John 57

prophecy 7, 64, 90, 107–8, 122,
    145–6, 178–9, 189–204 *passim*,
    218
Protestantism 4–6, 11–14, 32–8,
    48–64, 87–8, 162–4, 169–83,
    189–203 *passim*, 232, 236, 239,
    244, 247–8, 337, 355–7
Prynne, William 43, 94
Psellus, Michael 77, 78, 152
pseudepigrapha 22–4, 73, 75, 76, 80,
    82, 271, 352
Pseudo-Dionysius, *see* Dionysius
Pullman, Philip 14, 423 n. 3
Puttenham, George 177, 178, 179, 185
Pythagoras 58
    *see also* Tryon, Thomas

Qu'rān 57, 378
Quakers 37, 116, 117, 122, 126, 141

rabbinical scholarship 23, 67, 78, 82,
    194, 202, 213–15, 271–2
Racovian catechism 116, 173
Rainold, John 92
Ranters 120, 123, 126, 129, 141
Raphael 27, 79–82, 87, 107, 109
    in *Paradise Lost* 121, 144, 187, 203,
    212, 213, 218, 228, 256, 259–75
    *passim*, 278–9, 281, 286–7, 290,
    298–9, 301, 307–8, 311–13,
    321, 324, 335, 338, 353, 360–3
    in *State of Innocence* 341–47
*Raziel, Book of the Angel* 80, 82, 271,
    272
Reeve, John 121, 122, 197, 200
Rhegius, Urbanus 45, 57, 85–6
Richardson, John 40, 100
Richardson, Jonathan 201–2, 203
Rilke, Rainer Maria 14
Rivetus, Andreas 316
Rivius, Johannes 57–8
Roach, Richard 128, 150, 153
Ross, Alexander 43–4, 78, 83, 100,
    165
Royal Society 3, 278–9, 295, 308–9
Rutherford, Samuel 43

Sadducism 46, 55, 89, 113, 115,
    128–9, 140, 171, 309
Salkeld, John 38, 46, 51, 58, 67, 72,
    74, 136, 302, 316
Salmasius, Claudius 222, 223, 224
Sannazaro, Jacopo 238–9
Satan, history of 22–3, 49, 73–7,
    118, 132
Saunders, Richard 19
Scotland 242, 243, 254
Scott, John 19–20
Scott, Reginald 60, 191
Scott, Sir Walter 333
scripture 21–3, 33, 41–7 *passim*, 57,
    73–4, 78, 81, 87, 100, 103, 131,
    136, 162–88 *passim*, 190,
    214–15, 217, 271, 356, 361
    *see also* pseudepigrapha
scriptural annotations 40–2, 99–100
    *see also* Westminster Assembly—
        *Annotations*
Selden, John 271
sermons 44–5, 374, 377–8
*Seven Arguments Plainly Proving*
    (1641) 94
Shakespeare, William 105, 314, 369,
    372–3
Shippen, William 3, 115
Sibbes, Richard 51, 83, 303
Sidney, Sir Philip 141, 190
Simmons, Matthew 102
Simmons, Samuel 11
Simon Magus 67
Simon, Richard 163
*Sions Charity* (1641) 94
Skelhorn, Sarah 107
Smectymnuus 89, 91
Smith, John 189, 194–5, 196,
    202–3
Socinianism 116–17, 128–9, 173–5
Socrates 60
Solomon, *Key of Solomon* 107, 271–2
Son 154, 155–6, 209–11
    *see also* Christ
Sparrow, John 140
Spenser, Edmund 46, 144, 352, 379

spheres 32, 68, 80, 267, 276, 279,
   287, 298, 306, 314–15, 372
Spirit 116–17, 151, 164, 167, 173,
   177, 199, 238
Stationers' Register 95, 115, 331,
   332
Stockwel, Richard 129
Stortford, Herts. 44, 100–1, 111
*Strange Predictions Related at Catericke*
   (1648) 105
*Suddaine Answer to a Suddain
   Moderatour* (1642[3]) 97–8
Sydenham, William 249
Sylvester, Joshua 144, 216, 319
systematic theology 42–4, 100

Tany, Thomas 120, 123, 127, 129
Taylor, Jeremy 19, 192, 194, 303
Taylor, John 53, 95
Tertullian 22, 302
Teskey, Gordon 367–8, 381,
   454 n. 45
Thābit ibn Qurra 304
Theocritus 230
Thomason, George 102
*Three Propositions of the Angels of Light*
   (1642) 95–7
Tillyard, E. M. W. 365–6, 364
Tobit 22, 79, 82
Tomkinson, Dudley (pseud.) 332–3,
   334, 342
Trapnel, Anna 105, 196
Trapp, John 40, 64–5, 83–4, 100,
   101, 285
Trinity 29, 43, 66, 117, 151, 156,
   159, 173, 175, 217, 218, 257
   *see also* antitrinitarianism
Trithemius, Johannes 109, 114, 117,
   145, 271, 303, 437 n. 20
Tryon, Thomas 233
Turner, Robert 117
tutelary angels, *see* angels, guardianship

universe, *see* cosmology
Urania 140, 198–9, 200
Uriel 79–82, 107, 109, 112, 161

in *Paradise Lost* 82, 262, 268–72
   *passim*, 296–7, 306, 322, 335
Ussher, William 3, 112
Uzziel 272

Valla, Lorenzo 24, 163
Vane, Sir Henry 126, 293
Vere, Mary, Lady 127
Vermigli, *see* Martyr, Peter
Verney, Sir Edmund 105
Vicars, John 112
Virgil 220, 230, 237, 238, 427 n. 42
*Vitae Adae et Evae* 23, 75–6, 77
Vlacq, Adrian 223

Wale, Thomas and mistress 1–2
Wales 240, 242, 243, 254
Wall, John 85, 314
Ward, Samuel 35
Weber, Max 369
Wenders, Wim 14
West, Robert 214, 358, 392 n. 24
Westminster Assembly 40, 94, 99
   *Annotations* 40, 41, 42, 56, 58,
      65–6, 80–1, 99, 102, 233, 248,
      317
White, John, divine 67, 78, 100,
   141, 172–3, 217, 294, 426 n. 34
White, John, MP 92
Wilkins, John 109, 303
Willet, Andrew 40, 41, 42, 43,
   48–64, 66–7, 72, 75, 85, 232,
   247–8, 317–18, 361, 394 n. 55
Wilson, Thomas 172, 176
Winstanley, Gerard 118, 129
witchcraft 20, 78, 111, 112, 131, 133,
   352
Wither, George 59, 253–4
Wollebius, Johannes 42, 43, 56, 62,
   68, 72–3, 74–5, 100, 111, 234,
   302
Woolnor, Henry 116, 285, 288
Wright, Joseph 37

Zanchius, Jerome 77
Zephon 269–72 *passim*, 336